The Routledge Handbook of Second Home Tourism and Mobilities

Second homes have become an increasingly important component of both tourism and housing studies. They can directly and indirectly contribute a significant number of domestic and international visitors to destinations and may be part of longer-term retirement, lifestyle and amenity migration that can have significant economic and social effects on communities and destination development.

This volume offers an overview of different disciplinary and methodological approaches to second homes while simultaneously providing a broad geographical reach. Divided into four parts exploring governance, development, community and mobile second homes, the book provides a contemporary account of the major issues in an area of growing international interest.

This timely handbook covers a wide range of dimensions – from planning to the role of second homes in development and the management of their impact. The international and cross-disciplinary nature of the contributions will be of interest to numerous academic fields in the social sciences, as well as urban and regional planners.

C. Michael Hall is Professor of Marketing, University of Canterbury, New Zealand; Docent in Geography, Oulu University, Finland; and Visiting Professor, Linnaeus University, Sweden. He has published widely on – tourism, sustainability, regional development, governance and environmental change.

Dieter K. Müller is Professor of Social and Economic Geography and currently Deputy Vice-Chancellor, Umeå University. He has research interests in tourism and regional development, mobility and tourism in peripheral areas. He has previously co-edited *Tourism, Mobility and Second Homes* and several books on polar tourism.

THE ROUTLEDGE HANDBOOK OF SECOND HOME TOURISM AND MOBILITIES

Edited by C. Michael Hall and Dieter K. Müller

Routledge
Taylor & Francis Group

LONDON AND NEW YORK

First published 2018 by Routledge

2 Park Square, Milton Park, Abingdon, Oxon OX14 4RN
605 Third Avenue, New York, NY 10017

Routledge is an imprint of the Taylor & Francis Group, an informa business

First issued in paperback 2022

Publisher's Note
The publisher has gone to great lengths to ensure the quality of this reprint but points out that some imperfections in the original copies may be apparent.

British Library Cataloguing-in-Publication Data
A catalogue record for this book is available from the British Library

Library of Congress Cataloging-in-Publication Data
A catalog record has been requested for this book

ISBN: 978-1-138-67831-6 (hbk)
ISBN: 978-1-03-233915-3 (pbk)
DOI: 10.4324/9781315559056

Typeset in Bembo
by Deanta Global Publishing Services, Chennai, India

CONTENTS

FIGURES

TABLES

CONTRIBUTORS

Czesław Adamiak, Department of Spatial Management and Tourism, Faculty of Earth Sciences, Nicolaus Copernicus University, ul. Lwowska 1, 87-100 Toruń, POLAND

Ulrika Åkerlund, Department of Geography and Economic History, Umeå University, Umeå, SWEDEN

Helene Balslev Clausen, Tourism Research Unit, Department of Culture and Global Studies, Aalborg University, Copenhagen, DENMARK

Lisa Barnes, Avondale Business School, Faculty of Education, Business and Science, PO Box 19, Cooranbong, NSW 2265, AUSTRALIA

Caroline Blondy, UMR 7266 CNRS Littoral, Environnement et Sociétés (LIENSs), Université de la Rochelle - Institut du Littoral et de l'Environnement, 2, rue Olympe de Gouges, 17000 La Rochelle FRANCE

Caroline Bontet, Comité Départemental du Tourisme de Charente-Maritime, Maison de la Charente-Maritime, 85, boulevard de la République, 17076 La Rochelle, FRANCE

Paul Brunt, University of Plymouth, Hepworth House, Plymouth, Devon PL4 8AA, UK

Rod Caldicott, School of Business and Tourism, Southern Cross University, Military Road, PO Box 157, Lismore 2480 AUSTRALIA

Salvador Anton Clavé, Parc Científic i Tecnològic de Turisme i Oci, Carrer de Joanot Martorell, 15, 43480 Vila-seca, Tarragona, SPAIN

Adam Czarnecki, Department of Rural Economy, Institute of Rural and Agricultural Development, Polish Academy of Sciences, 00-330 Warsaw, POLAND

Joana Afonso Dias, Department of Management and Marketing, Instituto Superior Dom Afonso III – INUAF, 8100 Loulé, PORTUGAL

Alexandre Domingues, Division of Regional Studies, Directorate of Regional Development Services, CCDR Algarve, 8000-164 Faro, PORTUGAL

Maja Farstad, Centre for Rural Research, University Centre Dragvoll, 7491 Trondheim, NORWAY

Dana Fialová, Charles University, Faculty of Science, Department of Social Geography and Regional Development, Albertov 6, 128 43 Praha 2, CZECHIA

Mario Alberto Velázquez García, Colegio del Estado de Hidalgo, 42000 Pachuca de Soto, Hidalgo, MEXICO

C. Michael Hall, University of Canterbury, Christchurch, NEW ZEALAND 8140; Linnaeus University, Kalmar, SWEDEN; & Department of Geography, University of Oulu, FINLAND

Greg Halseth, Geography Program, University of Northern British Columbia, 3333 University Way, Prince George, BC, V2N 4Z9, CANADA

Olga Hannonen, Karelian Institute, University of Eastern Finland, P.O. Box 111, Joensuu 80101, FINLAND

Gijsbert Hoogendoorn, Department of Geography, Environmental Management and Energy Studies, University of Johannesburg, P.O. Box 525, Auckland Park, Johannesburg, 2006, SOUTH AFRICA

John M. Jenkins, School of Business and Tourism, Southern Cross University, Military Road, PO Box 157, Lismore 2480 AUSTRALIA

Clare Keogh, Newcastle Business School, University of Newcastle, Central Coast Campus, Ourimbah 2258 NSW AUSTRALIA

Miha Koderman, Department of Geography, Faculty of Humanities, University of Primorska, Titov trg 5, 6000 Koper, SLOVENIA

Anton Kriz, Newcastle Business School, University of Newcastle, Central Coast Campus, Ourimbah 2258 NSW AUSTRALIA

Tereza Kůsová, Charles University, Faculty of Science, Department of Social Geography and Regional Development, Albertov 6, 128 43 Praha 2, CZECHIA

Maja Lagerqvist, Department of Human Geography, Stockholm University, 106 91 Stockholm, SWEDEN

Hege Høyer Leivestad, Department of Social Anthropology, Stockholm University, 10691 Stockholm, SWEDEN

Contributors

Roger Marjavaara, Department of Geography and Economic History, Umeå University, 901 87 Umeå, SWEDEN

Dieter K. Müller, Department of Geography and Economic History, Umeå University, 901 87 Umeå, SWEDEN

Urban Nordin, Department of Human Geography, Stockholm University, 106 91 Stockholm, SWEDEN

Vuk Tvrtko Opačić, Department of Geography, Faculty of Science, University of Zagreb, Marulićev trg 19/II, 10000 Zagreb, CROATIA

Ingrid Persson, Blekinge Institute of Technology, Department of Spatial Planning, SE-371 79 Karlskrona, SWEDEN

Chris Paris, Emeritus Professor Housing Studies, University of Ulster, NORTHERN IRELAND

Felicity Picken, School of Social Sciences and Psychology, University of Western Sydney, Locked Bag 1797, Penrith, NSW 2750 AUSTRALIA

Kati Pitkänen, Environmental Policy Centre, Finnish Environment Institute, P. O. Box 111, 80101 Joensuu, FINLAND

Christine Plumejeaud, UMR 7266 CNRS Littoral, Environnement et Sociétés (LIENSs), Université de la Rochelle - Institut du Littoral et de l'Environnement, 2, rue Olympe de Gouges 17000 La Rochelle FRANCE

Maria Trinitat Rovira Soto, Facultat de Turisme i Geografia, Universitat Rovira i Virgili, Carrer de Joanot Martorell, 15, 43480 Vila-seca, Tarragona, SPAIN

Pascal Scherrer, School of Business and Tourism, Southern Cross University, Military Road, PO Box 157, Lismore 2480 AUSTRALIA

Richard Sharpley, School of Management, University of Central Lancashire, Preston PR1 2HE, UK

Martyn Steer-Fowler, former researcher, University of Plymouth, Plymouth, UK

Annika Strandin Pers, Department of Human Geography, Stockholm University, 106 91 Stockholm, SWEDEN

Kristina Svels, Rural Studies, Åbo Akademi University, Strandgatan 2, 65100 Vasa, FINLAND

Luc Vacher, UMR 7266 CNRS Littoral, Environnement et Sociétés (LIENSs), Université de la Rochelle - Institut du Littoral et de l'Environnement, 2, rue Olympe de Gouges 17000 La Rochelle FRANCE

Jiří Vágner, Charles University in Prague, Faculty of Science, Department of Social Geography and Regional Development, Albertov 6, 128 43 Praha 2, CZECHIA

Mia Vepsäläinen, Centre for Tourism Studies, University of Eastern Finland, Kuninkaankartanonkatu 7, P.O.Box 86 FI-57101 Savonlinna, FINLAND

Serena Volo, Faculty of Economics and Management, Competence Centre in Tourism Management and Tourism Economics, Free University of Bozen-Bolzano Piazza dell'Università 1, Brunico (BZ) 39031, ITALY

Didier Vye, UMR 7266 CNRS Littoral, Environnement et Sociétés (LIENSs), Université de la Rochelle - Institut du Littoral et de l'Environnement, 2, rue Olympe de Gouges 17000 La Rochelle FRANCE

Imren Uysal Waller, School of Management, University of Central Lancashire, Preston PR1 2HE, UK

Yuefang Wu, Department of Financial Management, Foshan Polytechnic College, Foshan, Guangdong, P.R. CHINA

Honggang Xu, The Center of Tourism Planning and Research, Sun Yat-sen University, 510275, Guangzhou, P.R. CHINA

ACKNOWLEDGEMENTS

Although being a migrant contributes to having multiple homes, the rhythms of regularly researching and teaching in different parts of the world also contribute to a set of multiple place attachments. I'm not sure about multiple dwelling, as I am not sure I dwell long enough when travelling away from my core home, but I certainly have been to places long enough to have a favourite coffee shop. I do not have a permanent second home, not yet anyway, but eventually one will happen and maybe then it will be time to go fishing.

Initially, of course, I must thank Dieter for being able to continue our interests in second homes, even if I am not able to visit Umeå as often as I would like these days. I would especially like to acknowledge a number of colleagues who specifically research second homes, who I have worked with in various ways over the years. In terms of the researchers at the University of Umeå, I would like to note Roger Marjavaara and Ulrika Åkerlund and at the University of East Finland, Kati Pitkänen, Czesław Adamiak and Olga Hannonen; special mention must also be made of Anna Strandell and Riikka Paloniemi, who also contributed greatly to the Finland Academy-funded project (SA 255424) on second homes. Special thanks must also be given to Gustav Visser and Gijsbert Hoogendoorn in South Africa, and my old comrades, now retired, Thor Flognfeldt and John Selwood.

There are also a number of other colleagues who have contributed to my understandings of home, circulation and mobility. In particular, thanks go to Dorothee Bohn, Tim Coles, David Duval, Alexandra Gillespie, Martin Gren, Stefan Gössling, Johan Hultman, Girish Prayag, Yael Ram, Jarkko Saarinen, Dan Scott, Anna Dóra Sæþórsdóttir and Allan Williams for their thoughts (and sometimes homes), as well as for the stimulation of Agnes Obel, A Long Walk, Ann Brun, Beirut, Paul Buchanan, Nick Cave, Bruce Cockburn, Elvis Costello, Stephen Cummings, Chris Difford and Glenn Tilbrook, David Bowie, Ebba Fosberg, Aldous Harding, Father John Misty, Mark Hollis, Hoodoo Gurus, Margaret Glaspy, Aimee Mann, Larkin Poe, Vinnie Reilly, Susanne Sundfør, Matthew Sweet, David Sylvian, and *The Guardian*, BBC6 and KCRW – without whom the four walls of a hotel room or an office would be much more confining. Special mention must also be given to Koppi in Helsingborg, Balck and Postgarten in Kalmar, and Nicole Aignier and the Hotel Grüner Baum in Merzhausen. Finally, and most importantly, Michael would like to thank the Js and the Cs who stay at home and mind the farm.

Laylands

Time is really running quickly nowadays. It is more than 14 years ago that our previous book on second homes was published. It is great to see that many researchers have picked up the topic since then and contributed with new perspectives, ideas and empirical evidence for a metamorphic phenomenon that seems to grow and change all the time. Without any doubt, in my eyes it is still one of the most exciting topics available, and indeed I already have some new ideas on where to go from here in second home tourism research.

When we did our previous book on second homes it certainly altered my career path substantially. I was then a young and rather inexperienced scholar and Michael showed me how to do a book and taught me one and the other thing about academia. This enabled me to contribute something relevant, hopefully to academic knowledge not only in the field of second home research. It therefore feels particularly good to do another book on second homes and the fact that it is once again done with Michael is a great pleasure. Hence my greatest thankfulness to him, also for accepting that my ability to contribute texts on time nowadays is somewhat constrained by administrative assignments for the management of Umeå University. And of course, your room in our apartment in Umeå is always waiting for you.

Besides Michael, I would also like to acknowledge all my other second home research friends that contributed to enrich the research topic. In Umeå these have been Roger Marjavaara, Ulrika Åkerlund and Andreas Back. Even Linda Lundmark, Marco Eimermann, Lars Larsson and Louise Robertsson made excursions into the wonderful world of second home research and contributed to making the geography department in Umeå probably the place with the largest amount of second home researchers in the world. Kati Pitkänen and Czesław Adamiak contributed to this environment temporarily too, which was great fun and highly treasured. Elsewhere in Sweden Urban Nordin has been a highly appreciated colleague to work with. Big thanks also to Kjell Overvåg, Mervi Hiltunen and Olga Hannonen. Furthermore, Team South Africa with Gustav Visser and Gijsbert Hoogendoorn are always highly esteemed visitors to Umeå. Finally, I would like to thank all contributors to the book and of course the people at Routledge for accepting the volume for the Handbook series.

Twenty-five years after starting to work on second homes, I still have no cottage of my own. At least I consider it as an option nowadays (though Åsa does not think it will ever happen), but that is maybe something to write about in the next book on second homes.

Umeå

PART I

Introduction

1

SECOND HOME TOURISM

An introduction

Dieter K. Müller and C. Michael Hall

Introduction

Second homes have been a focus of tourism research for many years, though the number of publications on the topic has risen considerably over the years and particularly since 2004 (Müller & Hoogendoorn 2013; Hall 2014; Müller 2014). A bibliometric review of the quantitative development of second home research based on Scopus (search terms in title, abstract and keywords: "second homes" AND tourism) identified 288 entries since 1978. Although this measure is crude and does not cover older materials such as Coppock's (1977) book, it is obvious that a quantitative increase has taken place. Indeed, although Coppock's 1977 volume was the seminal academic contribution, its role has been taken over by Hall and Müller's *Tourism, Mobility and Second Homes: Between Elite Landscape and Common Ground* since its publication in 2004. The exceptional position of these two books is also mirrored in the numbers of citations as measured in Google Scholar, where Hall and Müller's book has 429 citations and Coppock's book 318 (as of 1 August 2017). These volumes also indicate that the literature on second homes is now mature and increasingly specialised, which also implies that overviews of the research field are increasingly difficult to accomplish. However, this chapter aims at providing a short review of research on second home tourism. This is done by presenting some aspects of the history of second home research, before moving forward to conceptual and definitional issues.

A short history of second home research

Second home research has its origins not least in the Nordic countries (e.g. Ljungdahl 1938; Aldskogius 1968, 1969; Hansson & Medin 1954; Svenson 1954; Linkoaho 1962; Finnveden 1960) and in Canada, where the first cohesive body of literature was produced by Roy Wolfe (1951, 1952, 1962, 1965, 1977, 1978; see also Lundgren 1974) (Hall & Smith 2015). Elsewhere, early examples of second home research can be found in Australia (e.g. Marsden 1969; Mercer 1970), France (e.g. Clout 1969, 1971), the United Kingdom (e.g. Bielckus et al. 1972; Martin 1972; Downing & Dower 1974), and the United States (e.g. Ragatz 1970).

Increasing personal mobility owing to car ownership entailed a growth in second homes in the Western world and triggered a rising academic interest as well. Coppock's *Second Homes: Curse or Blessing?* (1977) marked a peak in the growing concern regarding the impact of second homes on rural communities and the environment, as well as significant community opposition in some locations. The book presented studies from Europe, North America and Australia on various aspects of second homes and formed an influential product of early scholarship that mirrored the increasing importance and geographical spread of the phenomenon (Müller & Hoogendoorn 2013).

Globalisation and the growing number of households purchasing property abroad, not least within Europe, caused renewed interest in second homes from the mid-1990s on, which otherwise had more or less disappeared from the international research agenda during the 1980s (Buller & Hoggart 1994; Müller 1999). Several reviews have addressed the topics covered since then, but a dominant feature in the first period has been to map current patterns of second homes and second home tourism in various states (Müller 2004, 2014; Casado-Diaz 1999, 2012; Hall 2014). Hall and Müller's *Tourism, Mobility and Second Homes: Between Elite Landscape and Common Ground* (2004) marked the peak of this period providing a set of national benchmark chapters. However, it seems that the book also contributed to re-animate a rather sleepy field of research by setting the phenomenon in the relevant context of globalisation, changing mobilities, ageing societies and rural restructuring. Other volumes describing various aspects of second home tourism were also published and provided important contributions to the understanding of second home tourism (e.g. Gallent et al. 2005; McIntyre et al. 2006; Mazón et al. 2009; Paris 2011; Roca 2013; Janoschka & Haas 2014; Walters & Duncan 2016).

Second home research has changed since the topic was first addressed. Rural geographers, regional scientists and planners led the debate on second homes during the 1970s (Pacione 1984), while tourism geographers and other tourism researchers have engaged more intensively from 2000 onward. Müller (2011) argued that this developed separate discourses with limited interaction, where particularly tourism perspectives tended to be neglected.

Today's situation is even more complex, since tourism researchers are not the only ones to present relevant literature on the topic. Instead, the fields of housing studies (Paris 2010), rural research (Rye & Gunnerud Berg 2011; Halfacree 2012), ageing research (King et al. 2000; Breuer 2005), and population studies (Benson & O'Reilly 2009; Janoschka & Haas 2014) have recently recognised second homes as a pertinent issue for research. This also entailed variations in the used terminology referring to the phenomenon of second home tourism: "lifestyle mobility" (Benson & O'Reilly 2009; Casado-Diaz 2012), "lifestyle migration" (Janoschka & Haas 2014), "heterolocal lifestyles" (Halfacree 2012), "multi-local living" (Schier et al. 2015), "multiple dwelling" (McIntyre et al. 2006), and "residential tourism" (Mazón 2006; McWatters 2009) refer to roughly the same phenomenon. Residential tourism is often used in southern locations and refers to the seasonal "snowbird" mobility (McHugh & Mings 1996), bringing retired North Europeans and North Americans to destinations with more pleasant climatic conditions. In contrast to much of other second home research, residential tourism addresses urban apartments and mobile homes rather than rural cottages, which dominate in many other parts of the world.

Another change in second home research is the remarkable expansion of second home research beyond its origins in Europe and North America. Today the scientific literature contains case studies from all inhabited continents. This change includes a shift in that it rejects the assumption that second home tourism would only be a phenomenon among the rich and in developed Western countries (Halfacree 2012). Instead, as Hoogendoorn (2011) points out, second home use is also a phenomenon among less well-off groups of society. This reminds researchers that second home tourism probably never was a phenomenon of the Western world alone. For example, Huang and Yi (2011) and Hui and Yu (2009) deliver pioneering work from China, Hajimirrahimi et al. (2017) discuss second homes in Iran, and Barrantes-Reynolds (2011) and Hidalgo et al. (2017) report on the residential tourism in Latin America. Wong and

Musa have also highlighted campaigns to stimulate second home tourism in Malaysia (Wong & Musa 2017; Wong et al. 2017). Similarly, Visser and Hoogendoorn have produced a substantial body of knowledge regarding second home tourism in South Africa (e.g. Visser 2004, 2006; Hoogendoorn & Visser 2004, 2011, 2015; Hoogendoorn et al. 2009; Visser & Hoogendoorn 2015; Hay & Hay 2017), highlighting among other aspects the challenges of research on second homes in a context where accessible data is lacking.

A bibliometric perspective

The growing interest in second home research discussed above is also manifested in bibliometric databases (Figure 1.1). One should keep in mind that the figures derived from the Scopus database discriminate against many scientific sources and not least a wide array of contributions in languages other than English. The overall amount of publications is thus even higher. Still the Scopus figures show a significant increase in publishing activities since the early 2000s. The relatively low numbers of publication prior to 2004 does not only mirror a limited interest, but also that literature has not always been published in English or in scientific journals and books (see also Hall 2014). Hence, the dramatic increase shows a change in publication practice as well.

Figure 1.2 presents a bibliometric account of the international dimension of second home research based on data from the Scopus database. The figure displays the countries of origin of the authors of the entries on second home tourism and residential tourism and furthermore shows the bibliometric similarities in terms of referenced literature between the national bodies of literature. The figure shows that the largest body of literature is Spanish, but it is rather isolated and has only limited similarity with other national bodies of literature. A core position is taken by literature coming out of Sweden. This body of literature is closely related to literature from Finland, New Zealand and South Africa.

This situation is also mirrored when looking at the authors of second home research. Here the analysis of Scopus puts Nordic second home research in the centre, but also detects national

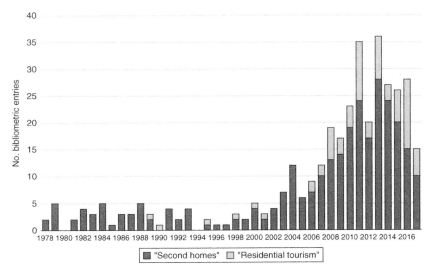

Figure 1.1 Annual numbers of bibliometric entries (published articles, books, book chapters, reviews).

Source: In Scopus for search terms "'second home' AND tourism" and "residential tourism" (date for retrieval 1 August 2017).

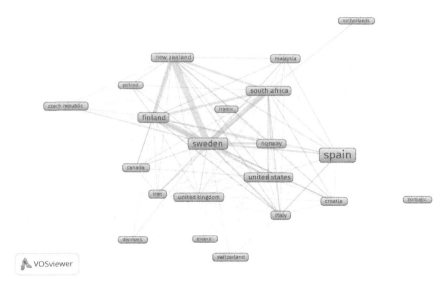

Figure 1.2 Bibliometric network of second home literature according to the countries of origins.

Source: Based on Scopus database and analysed with VOS Viewer August 2017.

clusters with respect to bibliometric similarities (Figure 1.3). Hence, Pitkänen, Vepsäläinen and Hiltunen form a Finnish cluster previously related to the research unit of University of Eastern Finland in Savonlinna. Bibliometrically they are strongly related to Müller and Marjavaara, Umeå University, Sweden, who shape another cluster with Hall. Even Visser and Hoogendoorn in South Africa, like Müller and Marjavaara, previously supervisor and PhD student, are related to the Nordic cluster, but share otherwise more bibliometric similarities with the Mediterranean cluster containing Roca and Oliveira (Portugal), Opacic (Croatia) and Volo and Brida (Italy). Wong and Musa (Malaysia) and some Spanish researchers from Mantecón focusing on residential tourism make up two more remote clusters.

Some of the names mentioned above can also be detected when scrutinising a list of the most cited articles on second homes in Scopus (Table 1.1). Even here the Nordic community dominates but it is accompanied by the South African researchers and other Europeans. The list also demonstrates how second home research has travelled away from North America, where early publications originate. Furthermore, the list shows the popularity of second home research related to environmental challenges, which has been pointed out elsewhere as a rather neglected area (Müller 2004, 2014).

However, it should be noted that second home research changes quickly. Only one of the contributions of the list originates from after 2010, which is the peak period for second home research so far. Moreover, the inclusion of book chapters would add three chapters in the top twenty list as well (Hall et al. 2004; Williams et al. 2004; Müller 2005). This makes every attempt to summarise second home tourism research a snapshot only, but also an important documentation of the current state of the art, as the books by Coppock (1977) and Hall and Müller (2004b) indicate.

Second homes in mobile societies

As Müller (2004) noted, early second home research has been engaged with mapping patterns of mobility within different national and international settings. However, research has

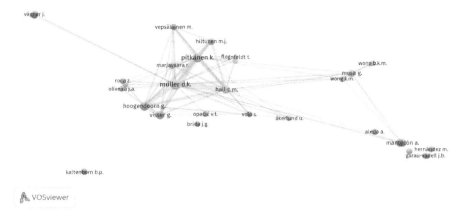

Figure 1.3   Bibliometric network and clusters of second home literature according to the authors.
Source: Based on Scopus database and analysed with VOS Viewer August 2017.

also increasingly addressed the theoretical consequences of the detected patterns. Therefore, an important notion has been that second homes have to be seen in the context of current mobilities (Williams & Hall 2000; Hall & Williams 2002; Williams et al. 2004). In accordance, the notion of second home tourism challenges so far very persistent conceptualisations of "home" and "away". As a statistical category, "second homes" does not necessarily make sense since boundaries between "permanent" and "temporary" homes are increasingly blurred. And, even theoretically, Gallent (2007) argues that an imagined hierarchy of dwelling is obsolete as from a Heideggerian perspective dwelling implies homemaking, which always requires engagement with place and local community. Similarly, Haldrup (2004) demonstrates empirically that even second home renters indeed engage in homemaking practices in their rented cottage.

Hence, second home tourism research also comprises debate about terminology and despite the current growth in literature, as already mentioned, there are competing terms used, not least aimed at an acknowledgement of non-hierarchical, multiple place attachments. For example, Kaltenborn uses the term "alternate home" (1998) and sometimes "recreational home" (1997; see also Gartner 1987; Sievänen et al. 2007). The recreational aspect is also mirrored in "holiday homes" (Marsden 1969; Mottiar & Quinn 2003) and "vacation homes" (Ragatz 1970; Burby III et al. 1972; Fritz 1982). Similarly, the term "summer home" or "summer house" refers to use during a certain season (cf. Leetma et al. 2012). Other terms used refer to the form of the second home – hence "cottage" has been a popular term (Wolfe 1951, 1965, 1977), but it delimits of course the phenomenon to detached house types and neglects other forms of buildings or mobile homes. Hence, departing from Newig's (2000) classification, Hall and Müller (2004a) argue that the term second home is used as an umbrella for different terms that all refer to different but often related ideas of usage, including both stationary and mobile second homes.

The need for an umbrella term arises partly because of national differences in available data, sometimes including apartments and sometimes not, and partly because of the diverging characteristics of the phenomenon in different countries and locations. While early studies often referred to cottage-type accommodation and rural second homes, more recent studies, including those referring to the idea of residential tourism, address urbanised forms of second home tourism (e.g. Visser 2004; Mazón 200; Paris 2013). In many countries, multiple and different

Table 1.1 Twenty most cited articles on second home tourism and residential tourism in Scopus (Article titles and keywords, September 2017)

Authors	Year	Title	Journal	Citations Sept. 2017
Williams, A. M., Hall, C. M.	2000	Tourism and migration: New relationships between production and consumption	*Tourism Geographies*, 2 (1): 5–27	240
Jaakson, R.	1986	Second-home domestic tourism	*Annals of Tourism Research*, 13 (3): 367–391	104
Haldrup, M.	2004	Laid-back mobilities: Second-home holidays in time and space	*Tourism Geographies*, 6 (4): 434–454	74
Girard, T. C., Gartner, W. C.	1993	Second home second view: Host community perceptions	*Annals of Tourism Research*, 20 (4): 685–700	58
Hof, A., Schmitt, T.	2011	Urban and tourist land use patterns and water consumption: Evidence from Mallorca, Balearic Islands	*Land Use Policy*, 28 (4): 792–804	44
Kaltenborn, B. P., Andersen, O., Nellemann, C., Bjerke, T., Thrane, C.	2008	Resident attitudes towards mountain second-home tourism development in Norway: The effects of environmental attitudes	*Journal of Sustainable Tourism*, 16 (6): 664–680	44
Marjavaara, R.	2007	The displacement myth: Second home tourism in the Stockholm archipelago	*Tourism Geographies*, 9 (3): 296–317	44
Rodriguez, V.	2001	Tourism as a recruiting post for retirement migration	*Tourism Geographies*, 3 (1): 52–63	42
Pitkänen, K.	2008	Second-home landscape: The meaning(s) of landscape for second-home tourism in Finnish Lakeland	*Tourism Geographies*, 10 (2): 169–192	40
Müller, D. K.	2006	The attractiveness of second home areas in Sweden: A quantitative analysis	*Current Issues in Tourism*, 9 (4–5): 335–350	39
Hiltunen, M. J.	2007	Environmental impacts of rural second home tourism – Case Lake District in Finland	*Scandinavian Journal of Hospitality and Tourism*, 7 (3): 243–265	36
Mazón, T.	2006	Inquiring into residential tourism: The Costa Blanca case	*Tourism and Hospitality, Planning and Development*, 3 (2): 89–97	32
Tress, G.	2002	Development of second-home tourism in Denmark	*Scandinavian Journal of Hospitality and Tourism*, 2 (2): 109–122	32
Hoogendoorn, G., Visser, G.	2010	The role of second homes in local economic development in five small South African towns	*Development Southern Africa*, 27 (4): 547–562	31

(Continued)

Table 1.1 (Continued)

Authors	Year	Title	Journal	Citations Sept. 2017
Hoogendoorn, G., Visser, G., Marais, L.	2009	Changing coutrysides, changing villages: Second homes in Rhodes, South Africa	*South African Geographical Journal*, 91 (2): 75–83	28
Müller, D. K., Hall, C. M.	2003	Second homes and regional population distribution: On administrative practices and failures in Sweden	*Espace-Populations-Societes*, 2003–2: 251–261	28
Breuer, T.	2005	Retirement migration or rather second-home tourism? German senior citizens on the Canary Islands	*Erde*, 136 (3): 313–333	27
Barke, M.	1991	The growth and changing pattern of second homes in Spain in the 1970s	*Scottish Geographical Magazine*, 107 (1): 12–21	27
Visser, G.	2006	South Africa has second homes too! An exploration of the unexplored	*Current Issues in Tourism*, 9 (4–5): 351–383	25
Pitkänen, K., Vepsäläinen, M.	2008	Foreseeing the future of second home tourism. The case of Finnish media and policy discourse	*Scandinavian Journal of Hospitality and Tourism*, 8 (1): 1–24	23

forms of second home tourism can be found, all featuring distinct sets of opportunities and challenges (Müller et al. 2004; Back & Marjavaara 2017). Therefore, differences occur not least with regard to location in relation to major urban demand markets and to the composition of the second home stock, including both converted and purpose-built second homes. This implies that it becomes increasingly difficult to generalise for various aspects of second home tourism, such as motivations and impacts. A common denominator remains however: second home mobility continues to make homes nodes in the scapes and flows of tourism and migration (Williams & Hall 2002; Williams et al. 2004).

A further complication is that the increasing confluence of leisure and work now challenges dichotomies between homes, as well as between previously stable categories such as "home" and "away"; particularly within the white-collar sector, work can be conducted in a recreational setting as well. Distinctions between primary and secondary homes can, thus, be increasingly challenged not only with respect to use, but also in regard to the phenomenological and emotional meaning of home (Kaltenborn 1998; Gallent 2007; Hui 2008). As a result, a main argument is that second homes are alternate homes rather than secondary homes when it comes to aspects such as identity and belonging. Arnesen et al. (2012) launched the idea that home indeed can comprise several houses and suggest the term "multi-house homes", further challenging traditional ideas of a hierarchy of dwellings. Even the term "residential tourism" aims at highlighting the blurring of boundaries between primary and secondary homes and home and away. Acknowledging the existence of mobile second homes such as RV vehicles, caravans, motorhomes and boats further complicates the situation and illustrates the justification for acknowledging the significance of mobility in the social sciences.

With this notion in mind, the administrative treatment of second home owners as non-locals has to be seen as a failure (Müller & Hall 2003; McKenzie et al. 2008). Increasingly, mobile societies with second homes as important nodes within mobility networks collide with administrative routines rooted in times before individual car ownership and other motorised transportation became common (Hall 2015). This has consequences for statistics of second homes as well. Second homes are not classified in all countries as a distinct category in census or property databases. Instead, they may be distinguished from other residential properties by the fact that they are considered "unoccupied" dwelling on census night, qualifying for certain tax regulations, or are simply registered and hence owner-defined second homes (Hall and Müller 2004a). However, it is obvious that all these ways of distinguishing second homes are somewhat arbitrary. Moreover, few administrative practices manage to capture the entire phenomenon and hence, second home apartments, boats, caravans and other kinds of mobile homes are left aside. As a consequence, for example, the Swedish government decided to discontinue all classifications of second homes in the property register. Instead, second homes are defined as dwellings lacking registered population.

In summarising the debate on second homes it can be noted that second homes have multiple dimensions all carrying a variety of loadings (Table 1.2). Originally, research focused on geographical locations and second home functions. Increasingly however, second home tourism is understood as a phenomenon with many shades resulting from the almost endless possible combinations of variations and loadings occurring in specific places.

Outline of the handbook

This handbook offers a snapshot of current second home research and summarises the state of the art after a period of rapid expansion of second home research. This is done in 4 parts and 30 chapters addressing a variety of aspects of second homes. Each part is introduced by a chapter briefly reviewing the literature on the current topic, followed by a number of case studies, introducing empirical results and theoretical discussions from various parts of the world.

The first part of the book focuses on governance issues, planning and the role of environmental quality for second home tourism. This is followed by a part on development and commercialism, understanding second home tourism mainly as an economic phenomenon. Here, not least, the nexus of second homes and rural development is addressed. Thereafter, in a part on community, culture and identity, second homes are seen in relation to community development and social change. Finally, the last part addresses second homes in the context of mobility and focuses on the so far least researched aspect of second home tourism, i.e. RVs and caravans. The book ends with an outlook to the future.

Table 1.2 Dimensions of variations among second homes and their loadings

Variations	*Loadings*				
Functional	work	mixed		leisure	recreation
Physical	RV	caravan	boat	cottage	apartment
Temporal	days	weekend	vacations	seasons	most of the year
Geographical	urban	periurban	resort	rural	remote
Political	local	regional	national		international
Psychological	commodity for speculation				emotional bonds
Evolutionary	converted				purpose-built

References

Aldskogius, H. (1968) *Studier i Siljansområdets fritidshusbebyggelse*. Uppsala, Sweden: Geografiska Institutionen.

Aldskogius, H. (1969) *Modelling the Evolution of Settlement Patterns: Two Studies of Vacation House Settlement*. Uppsala, Sweden: Department of Geography.

Arnesen, T., Overvåg, K., Skjeggedal, T. and Ericsson, B. (2012) 'Transcending orthodoxy: The multi-house home, leisure and the transformation of core periphery relations'. In M. Danson and P. de Souza (eds) *Regional Development in Northern Europe. Peripherality, Marginality and Border Issues*. London: Routledge, 182–195.

Back, A. and Marjavaara, R. (2017) 'Mapping an invisible population: The uneven geography of second-home tourism', *Tourism Geographies*, 17 (4): 595–611.

Barke, M. (1991) 'The growth and changing pattern of second homes in Spain in the 1970s'. *The Scottish Geographical Magazine*, 107 (1): 12–21.

Barrantes-Reynolds, M. P. (2011) 'The expansion of "real estate tourism" in coastal areas: Its behaviour and implications'. *Recreation and Society in Africa, Asia and Latin America*, 2 (1).

Bielckus, C. L., Rogers, A. W. and Wibberley, G. P. (1972) *Second Homes in England and Wales: A Study of the Distribution and Use of Rural Properties Taken over as Second Residences*. Wye, UK: Wye College, Countryside Planning Unit, School of Rural Economics and Related Studies.

Breuer, T. (2005) 'Retirement migration or rather second-home tourism? German senior citizens on the Canary Islands', *Die Erde*, 136 (3): 313–333.

Buller, H. and Hoggart, K. (1994) *International Counterurbanization: British Migrants in Rural France*. Avebury, UK: Ashgate.

Burby III, R. J., Donnelly, T. G. and Weiss, S. F. (1972) 'Vacation home location: A model for simulating the residential development of rural recreation areas', *Regional Studies*, 6 (4): 421–439.

Casado-Diaz, M. A. (1999) 'Socio-demographic impacts of residential tourism: A case study of Torrevieja, Spain', *International Journal of Tourism Research*, 1 (4): 223–237.

Casado-Diaz, M. (2012) 'Exploring the geographies of lifestyle mobility: Current and future fields of enquiry'. In J. Wilson (ed.) *The Routledge Handbook of Tourism Geographies*. London: Routledge, 120–125.

Clout, H. D. (1969) 'Second homes in France', *Journal of the Town Planning Institute*, 55, 440–443.

Clout, H. D. (1971) 'Second homes in the Auvergne', *Geographical Review*, 61 (4): 530–553.

Coppock, J. T. (ed.) (1977) *Second Homes: Curse or Blessing?* Oxford: Pergamon.

Downing, P. and Dower, M. (1974) *Second Homes in England and Wales: An Appraisal*. Cheltenham, UK: Countryside Commission.

Finnveden, B. (1960) 'Den dubbla bosättningen och sommarmigrationen: Exempel från Hallandskustens fritidsbebyggelse', *Svensk Geografisk Årsbok*, 36: 58–84.

Fritz, R. G. (1982) 'Tourism, vacation home development and residential tax burden', *American Journal of Economics and Sociology*, 41 (4): 375–385.

Gallent, N. (2007) 'Second homes, community and a hierarchy of dwelling', *Area*, 39 (1): 97–106.

Gallent, N., Mace, A. and Tewdwr-Jones, M. (2005) *Second Homes: European Perspectives and UK Policies*. Avebury, UK: Ashgate.

Gartner, W. C. (1987) 'Environmental impacts of recreational home developments', *Annals of Tourism Research*, 14 (1): 38–57.

Girard, T. C. and Gartner, W. C. (1993) 'Second home second view: Host community perceptions'. *Annals of Tourism Research*, 20 (4): 685–700.

Hajimirrahimi, S. D., Esfahani, E., Van Acker, V. and Witlox, F. (2017) 'Rural second homes and their impacts on rural development: A case study in East Iran', *Sustainability*, 9 (4): 531.

Haldrup, M. (2004) 'Laid-back mobilities: Second-home holidays in time and space', *Tourism Geographies*, 6 (4): 434–454.

Halfacree, K. (2012) 'Heterolocal identities? Counter-urbanisation, second homes, and rural consumption in the era of mobilities', *Population, Space and Place*, 18 (2): 209–224.

Hall, C. M. (2014) 'Second home tourism: An international review', *Tourism Review International*, 18 (3): 115–135.

Hall, C. M. (2015) 'Second homes: Planning, policy and governance', *Journal of Policy Research in Tourism, Leisure & Events*, 7 (1): 1–14.

Hall, C. M. and Williams, A. M. (eds) (2002) *Tourism and Migration: New Relationships between Production and Consumption*, Dordrecht, Netherlands: Kluwer Academic Publishers.

Hall, C. M. and Müller, D. K. (2004a) 'Introduction: Second homes: Curse or blessing? Revisited'. In C. M. Hall and D. K. Müller (eds) *Tourism, Mobility and Second Homes: Between Elite Landscape and Common Ground*, Clevedon, UK: Channel View, 3–14.

Hall, C. M. and Müller, D. K. (2004b) (eds) *Tourism, Mobility and Second Homes: Between Elite Landscape and Common Ground*. Clevedon, UK: Channel View.

Hall, C. M. and Smith, S. L. J. (2015) 'The contribution of Roy Wolfe (1917–2014) to Tourism Geography', *Tourism Geographies*, 17 (2): 300–305.

Hall, C. M., Müller, D. K. and Keen, D. (2004) 'Second home tourism impact, planning and management'. In C. M. Hall and D. K. Müller (eds) *Tourism, Mobility and Second Homes: Between Elite Landscape and Common Ground*, Clevedon, UK: Channel View, 15–33.

Hansson, U. and Medin, S. (1954) 'Halmstads, Jönköpings, Kalmars och Växjös sommarortsfält', *Svensk Geografisk Årsbok*, 30: 179–185.

Hay, A. and Hay, J. (2017) 'Indicators of post-productivism in South Africa's platteland: A second home case study of Rosendal, Eastern Free State', *Bulletin of Geography. Socio-Economic Series*, 37: 35–49.

Hidalgo, R., Rivas, L. D. S., Haller, A. and Borsdorf, A. (2017) 'Utopia or dystopia? Results and perception of second-home production in the central coastal area of Chile 1992–2012', *Die Erde*, 148 (1): 27–38.

Hiltunen, M. J. (2007) 'Environmental impacts of rural second home tourism: Case Lake District in Finland', *Scandinavian Journal of Hospitality and Tourism*, 7 (3): 243–265.

Hof, A. and Schmitt, T. (2011) 'Urban and tourist land use patterns and water consumption: Evidence from Mallorca, Balearic Islands', *Land Use Policy*, 28 (4): 792–804.

Hoogendoorn, G. (2011) 'Low-income earners as second home tourists in South Africa?', *Tourism Review International*, 15 (1–2): 37–50.

Hoogendoom, G. and Visser, G. (2004) 'Second homes and small-town (re)development: The case of Clarens', *Journal of Consumer Sciences*, 32 (1): 105–115.

Hoogendoorn, G. and Visser, G. (2010) 'The economic impact of second home development in small-town South Africa', *Tourism Recreation Research*, 35 (1): 55–66.

Hoogendoorn, G. and Visser, G. (2011) 'Tourism, second homes, and an emerging South African postproductivist countryside', *Tourism Review International*, 15 (1–2): 183–197.

Hoogendoorn, G. and Visser, G. (2015) 'Focusing on the "blessing" and not the "curse" of second homes: Notes from South Africa', *Area*, 47 (2): 179–184.

Hoogendoorn, G., Visser, G. and Marais, L. (2009) 'Changing countrysides, changing villages: Second homes in Rhodes, South Africa', *South African Geographical Journal*, 91 (2): 75–83.

Huang, Y. and Yi, C. (2011) 'Second home ownership in transitional urban China', *Housing Studies*, 26 (3): 423–447.

Hui, A. (2008) 'Many homes for tourism: Re-considering spatializations of home and away in tourism mobilities', *Tourist Studies*, 8 (3): 291–311.

Hui, E. C. M. and Yu, K. H. (2008) 'Second homes in the Chinese mainland under "one country, two systems": A cross-border perspective', *Habitat International*, 33 (1): 106–113.

Jaakson, R. (1986) 'Second-home domestic tourism', *Annals of Tourism Research*, 13 (3): 367–391.

Janoschka, M. and Haas, H. (eds) (2014) *Contested Spatialities, Lifestyle Migration and Residential Tourism*. London: Routledge.

Kaltenborn, B. P. (1997) 'Recreation homes in natural settings: Factors affecting place attachment', *Norsk Geografisk Tidsskrift*, 51 (4): 187–198.

Kaltenborn, B. P. (1998) 'The alternate home-motives of recreation home use', *Norsk Geografisk Tidsskrift*, 52 (3): 121–134.

Kaltenborn, B. P., Andersen, O., Nellemann, C., Bjerke, T. and Thrane, C. (2008). 'Resident attitudes towards mountain second-home tourism development in Norway: The effects of environmental attitudes', *Journal of Sustainable Tourism*, 16 (6): 664–680.

King, R., Warnes, T. and Williams, A. (2000) *Sunset Lives: British Retirement Migration to the Mediterranean*. Oxford: Berg.

Leetmaa, K., Brade, I., Anniste, K. and Nuga, M. (2012) 'Socialist summer-home settlements in post-socialist suburbanisation', *Urban Studies*, 49 (1): 3–21.

Linkoaho, R. (1962) 'Sommarhaussiedlung und Sommeraufenthalt der Stadtbevölkerung von Tampere', *Fennia*, 87 (4).

Ljungdahl, S. (1938) 'Sommar-Stockholm', *Ymer*, 58: 218–242.

Lundgren, J. O. J. (1974) 'On access to recreational lands in dynamic metropolitan hinterlands', *Tourist Review*, 29 (4): 124–131.

McHugh, K. E. and Mings, R. C. (1996) 'The circle of migration: Attachment to place in aging', *Annals of the Association of American Geographers*, 86 (3): 530–550.

McIntyre, N., Williams, D. and McHugh, K. (eds) (2006) *Multiple Dwelling and Tourism: Negotiating Place, Home and Identity*. Wallingford, UK: CAB International.

McKenzie, F., Martin, J. and Paris, C. (2008) 'Fiscal policy and mobility: The impact of multiple residences on the provision of place-based service funding', *Australasian Journal of Regional Studies*, 14 (1): 53–71.

McWatters, M. R. (2009) *Residential Tourism: (De)Constructing Paradise*. Bristol: Channel View.

Marjavaara, R. (2007) 'The displacement myth: Second home tourism in the Stockholm Archipelago', *Tourism Geographies*, 9 (3): 296–317.

Marsden, B. S. (1969) 'Holiday homescapes of Queensland', *Australian Geographical Studies*, 7 (1): 57–73.

Martin, I. (1972) 'The second home dream', *New Society*, 18 May, 349–352.

Mazón, T. (2006) 'Inquiring into residential tourism: The Costa Blanca case', *Tourism and Hospitality Planning and Development*, 3 (2): 89–97.

Mazón, T., Huete, R. and Mantecón A. (eds) (2009) *Turismo, Urbanización y Estilos de Vida: Las Nuevas Formas de Movilidad Residencial*. Barcelona: Icaria.

Mercer, D. C. (1970) 'Urban recreational hinterlands: A review and example', *Professional Geographer*, 22 (2): 74–78.

Mottiar, Z. and Quinn, B. (2003) 'Shaping leisure/tourism places – The role of holiday home owners: A case study of Courtown, Co. Wexford, Ireland', *Leisure Studies*, 22 (2): 109–127.

Müller D. K. (1999) *German Second Home Owners in the Swedish Countryside: On the Internationalization of the Leisure Space*. Umeå, Sweden: Department of Human Geography.

Müller D. K. (2004) 'Mobility, tourism, and second homes'. In A. A. Lew, C. M. Hall and A. M. Williams (eds) *A Companion to Tourism*. Oxford: Blackwell, 387–398.

Müller, D. K. (2005) 'Second home tourism in the Swedish mountain range'. In C. M. Hall and S. Boyd (eds) *Nature-Based Tourism in Peripheral Areas: Development or Disaster?* Clevedon, UK: Channel View, 133–148.

Müller, D. K. (2006) 'The attractiveness of second home areas in Sweden: A quantitative analysis', *Current Issues in Tourism*, 9 (4–5): 335–350.

Müller, D. K. (2011) 'Second homes in rural areas: Reflections on a troubled history', *Norsk Geografisk Tidsskrift*, 65 (3): 137–143.

Müller, D. K. (2014) 'Progress in second-home tourism research'. In A. A. Lew, C. M. Hall and A. M. Williams (eds) *The Wiley Blackwell Companion to Tourism*. 2nd ed., Chichester, UK: Wiley-Blackwell, 389–400.

Müller, D. K. and Hall, C. M. (2003) 'Second homes and regional population distribution: On administrative practices and failures in Sweden', *Espace, Populations, Sociétés* 21 (2): 251–261.

Müller, D. K. and Hoogendoorn, G. (2013) 'Second homes: Curse or blessing? A review 36 years later', *Scandinavian Journal of Hospitality and Tourism*, 13 (4): 353–369.

Newig, J. (2000) 'Freizeitwohnen: Mobil und stationär', In *Nationalatlas Bundesrepublik Deutschland: Freizeit und Tourismus* (CD-ROM). Heidelberg, Germany: Spektrum.

O'Reilly, K. and Benson, M. (2009) *Lifestyle Migration: Escaping to the Good Life?* Avebury, UK: Ashgate.

Pacione, M. (1984) *Rural Geography*. London: Harper & Row.

Paris, C. (2010) *Affluence, Mobility and Second Home Ownership*. London: Routledge.

Paris, C. (2013) 'The homes of the super-rich: Multiple residences, hyper-mobility and decoupling of prime residential housing in global cities'. In I. Hay (ed.) *Geographies of the Super-Rich*. Cheltenham, UK: Edward Elgar, 94–109.

Pitkänen, K. (2008) 'Second-home landscape: The meaning(s) of landscape for second-home tourism in Finnish Lakeland'. *Tourism Geographies*, 10 (2): 169–192.

Pitkänen, K. and Vepsäläinen, M. (2008) 'Foreseeing the future of second home tourism. The case of Finnish media and policy discourse', *Scandinavian Journal of Hospitality and Tourism*, 8 (1): 1–24.

Ragatz, R. L. (1970) 'Vacation homes in the northeastern United States: Seasonality in population distribution', *Annals of the Association of American Geographers*, 60 (3): 447–455.

Roca, Z. (ed.) (2013) *Second Homes Tourism in Europe: Lifestyle Issues and Policy Responses*. Farnham, UK: Ashgate.

Rodriguez, V. (2001). 'Tourism as a recruiting post for retirement migration'. *Tourism Geographies*, 3 (1): 52–63.

Rye, J. F. and Gunnerud Berg, N. (2011) 'The second home phenomenon and Norwegian rurality', *Norsk Geografisk Tidsskrift*, 56 (3): 126–136.

Schier, M., Hilti, N., Schad, H., Tippel, C., Dittrich-Wesbuer, A. and Monz, A. (2015) 'Residential multi-locality studies: The added value for research on families and second homes', *Tijdschrift voor Economische en Sociale Geografie*, 106 (4): 439–452.

Sievänen, T., Pouta, E. and Neuvonen, M. (2007) 'Recreational home users–potential clients for countryside tourism?', *Scandinavian Journal of Hospitality and Tourism*, 7 (3): 223–242.

Svensson, H. (1954) 'En studie över sommarortsfältet för Malmö stad', *Svensk Geografisk Årsbok*, 30: 168–178.

Tress, G. (2002). 'Development of second-home tourism in Denmark', *Scandinavian Journal of Hospitality and Tourism*, 2 (2): 109–122.

Visser, G. (2004) 'Second homes and local development: Issues arising from Cape Town's De Waterkant', *GeoJournal*, 60 (3): 259–271.

Visser, G. (2006) 'South Africa has second homes too! An exploration of the unexplored', *Current Issues in Tourism*, 9 (4–5): 351–383.

Visser, G. and Hoogendoorn, G. (2015) 'A decade of second home tourism research in South Africa: Research prospects for the developing world?', *South African Geographical Journal*, 97 (2): 111–122.

Walters, T. and Duncan T. (eds) (2016) *Second Homes and Leisure: New Perspectives on a Forgotten Relationship*. London: Routledge.

Williams, A. M. and Hall, C. M. (2000) 'Tourism and migration: New relationships between production and consumption', *Tourism Geographies*, 2 (1): 5–27.

Williams, A. M. and Hall, C. M. (2002) 'Tourism, migration, circulation and mobility: The contingencies of time and place'. In C. M. Hall and A. M. Williams (eds) *Tourism and Migration: New Relationships between Production and Consumption*. Dordrecht, Netherlands: Kluwer, 1–52.

Williams, A. M., King, R. and Warnes, T. (2004) 'British second homes in Southern Europe: Shifting nodes in the scapes and flows of migration and tourism'. In C. M. Hall and D. K. Müller (eds) *Tourism, Mobility and Second Homes: Between Elite Landscape and Common Ground*. Clevedon, UK: Channel View, 97–112.

Wolfe, R. I. (1951) 'Summer cottagers in Ontario', *Economic Geography*, 27 (1): 10–32.

Wolfe, R. I. (1952) 'Wasaga Beach: The divorce from the geographic environment', *Canadian Geographer*, 1 (2): 57–66.

Wolfe, R. I. (1962) 'The summer resorts of Ontario in the nineteenth century', *Ontario History*, 54: 149–161.

Wolfe, R. I. (1965) 'About cottages and cottagers', *Landscape*, 15 (1): 6–8.

Wolfe, R. I. (1977) 'Summer cottages in Ontario: Purpose-built for an inessential purpose'. In J. T. Coppock (ed.) *Second Homes: Curse or Blessing?* Oxford: Pergamon, 17–34.

Wolfe, R. I. (1978) 'Vacation homes as social indicators: Observations from Canadian census data', *Leisure Sciences*, 1 (4): 327–343.

Wong, B. K. M. and Musa, G. (2017) 'Malaysia My Second Home (MM2H): Retirees' demographic profile and spending dynamics', *Tourism Management*, 60 (1): 42–46.

Wong, B. K. M., Musa, G. and Taha, A. Z. (2017) 'Malaysia my second home: The influence of push and pull motivations on satisfaction', *Tourism Management*, 61: 394–410.

PART II

Governance, planning and environmental quality

2

GOVERNING AND PLANNING FOR SECOND HOMES

C. Michael Hall and Dieter K. Müller

Introduction

Although the spatial and land-use planning of second homes has long been a significant element of second home related regional planning (Nystrom 1989; Müller et al. 2004; Müller & Hoogendoorn 2013), it is only post-2000 that second home policy and planning has come to be framed within the concept of governance. Although there is no single accepted definition of governance, it can be best understood as being the act of governing. In respect to tourism public policy, the term has often referred to an increased diversity of power in decision making and a shift from hierarchies to networks: 'from coordinated, hierarchical structures and processes of societal steering to a network-based process of exchange and negotiation' (Salskov-Iversen et al. 2000: 183). Nevertheless, there are a range of different forms of governance by which the state seeks to steer policy of which networks are only one example.

Approaches to governance

Hall (2011, 2013) distinguished between four governance structures derived from governance literature: hierarchies, markets, networks and communities (Table 2.1). These categories are derived from the relationship between state or public authority on the one hand, and stake-holder autonomy on the other (Figure 2.1). Hierarchical governance shows the highest degree of state or public intervention, market governance the least. Network and community govern-ance structures signal different modes of public–private partnerships and community participa-tion in destinations. Significantly, different types of governance approaches and structures occur in tourism and second homes, especially given the multiple ways in which their policy meaning can be framed, leading to different governance approaches that operate simultaneously within a destination economy, or between different municipalities or governments within the same country, even though they may be tackling the same policy "problem", such as second homes.

Despite governance having emerged, in part, as a response to the implications of globalisation, including the increased international movement of people, and for the state (Salskov-Iversen et al. 2000), the governance of mobility presents enormous challenges for the state whether under the rubric of migration or tourism. 'Governance, policies and regulatory structures are much better geared to the stationery and the immobile than they are to the movement of

Table 2.1 Frameworks of governance and their characteristics

	Hierarchies	Communities	Networks	Markets
Classificatory type characteristics	• Idealised model of democratic government and public administration • Distinguishes between public and private policy space • Focus on public good • Command and control (i.e. "top-down" decision making) • Hierarchical relations between different levels of the state	• Notion that communities should resolve problems with minimum of state involvement • Builds on a consensual image of community and positive involvement of its members • Governance without government • Fostering of civic spirit	• Facilitate coordination of public and private interests and resource allocation, often through public–private partnerships and therefore improve policy implementation • Can take different forms ranging from policy communities to single issue coalitions • Regulate and coordinate policy areas according to the preferences of network actors	• Belief in the market as the most efficient resource allocative mechanism • Equates citizens with consumers • Employment of monetary criteria to measure efficiency • Policy arena for economic actors where they cooperate to resolve common problems
Governance/policy themes	Hierarchy (multi-level governance), control, compliance	Complexity, local autonomy, devolved power, decentralised problem-solving	Networks, steering, bargaining, exchange and negotiation	Markets, bargaining, exchange and negotiation
Policy standpoint	"Top": policymakers; legislators; central government	"Bottom": implementers, "street level bureaucrats" and local officials	Where negotiation and bargaining take place	Where bargaining takes place between consumers and producers
Underlying model of democracy	Elitist/representative	Participatory	Hybrid/stakeholder, significant role given to interest groups	Consumer determined
Primary focus	Effectiveness: extent to which policy and planning goals are met	What influences action in an issue area?	Bargained interplay between goals set centrally and actors	Efficiency: markets will provide the most efficient outcome

(Continued)

Table 2.1 (Continued)

	Hierarchies	Communities	Networks	Markets
View of non-central (initiating) actors	Passive agents or potential impediments	Potentially policy innovators or problem shooters	Tries to include all actors who interact in the development and implementation of policy	Market participants are best suited to "solve" policy and planning problems
Distinction between policy formulation and implementation	Actually and conceptually distinct; policy is made by the top and implemented by the bottom	Blurred distinction: policy is often made and then re-made by individual and institutional policy actors	Policy-action continuum: policy-making and implementation seen as a series of intentions around which bargaining takes place	Policy-action continuum
Criterion of success	When outputs/outcomes are consistent with a priori objectives	Achievement of actor (often community/local) goals	Success depends on actor perspectives	Market/economic efficiency
Implementation gaps/deficits	Occur when outputs/outcomes fall short of a priori objectives	"Deficits" are a sign of policy change, not failure. They are inevitable	All policies are modified as a result of negotiation (there is no benchmark)	Occur when markets are not able to function
Reason for implementation gaps/deficits	Good ideas poorly executed	Bad ideas faithfully executed	"Deficits" are inevitable as abstract policy ideas are made more concrete	Market failure; inappropriate indicator selection
Solution to implementation gaps/deficits	Simplify the implementation structure; apply inducements and sanctions	"Deficits" are inevitable	"Deficits" are inevitable	Increase the capacity of the market

(Continued)

Table 2.1 (Continued)

	Hierarchies	Communities	Networks	Markets
Primary policy instruments	• Law • Regulation • Clear allocation and transfers of power between different levels of the state • Development of clear set of institutional arrangements • Licensing, permits, consents and standards • Removal of property rights • Development guidelines and strategies that reinforce planning law	• Self-regulation • Public meetings/town hall meetings • Public participation • Non-intervention • Voluntary instruments • Information and education • Volunteer associations • Direct democracy (citizens initiated referenda) • Community opinion polling • Capacity building of social capital	• Self-regulation and coordination • Accreditation schemes • Codes of practice • Industry associations • Non-government organisations	• Corporatisation and/or privatisation of state bodies • Use of pricing, subsidies and tax incentives to encourage desired behaviours • Use of regulatory and legal instruments to encourage market efficiencies • Voluntary instruments • Non-intervention • Education and training to influence behaviour

Source: After Hall 2011.

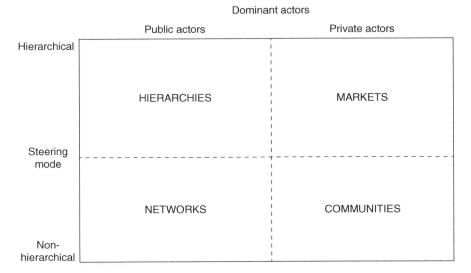

Figure 2.1 Frameworks of governance typology.

people (and capital) between jurisdictions, as well as to mobile homes themselves' (Hall 2015:4). This issue arises because for the purposes of governance everybody has to be "somewhere", and governance systems find it difficult to cope with people that are in multiple locations, e.g. have both a "permanent" and a "second" home, or are mobile, e.g. have a caravan or mobile home as a residence. Most countries' taxation and personal identification systems are geared to the notion of a single permanent residence and do not usually account for the contemporary spatial mobility of many individuals, e.g. multiple work places as well as domiciles, while not only is tourism and leisure marked by growing mobility but also health, education and the mainte-nance of family and friendship relations (Coles et al. 2004; Coles & Hall 2006, 2008, 2011). It is therefore unsurprising that the boundaries between tourism, migration and second home use have become ever more fluid as the distinctions between types of movement have become increasingly blurred (Åkerlund et al. 2015), often leading to difficulties for locations to "trap" the capital that they often sought to attract from mobile populations on an ongoing basis (Müller & Hall 2003; Hjalager et al. 2011; Rinne et al. 2014). As Hall (2015: 4) observed, 'while many jurisdictions seek to attract mobility they often appear poorly equipped to govern the implica-tions of mobility', a situation which appears to well describe the governance of second homes.

The governance of second homes

The governance of second homes occurs at different regulatory scales, including the supra-national and international, national, regional and local. The capacity to regulate is a reflection of territorial jurisdictional and legal norms. The subject of regulation is usually either people, property or land use, with a fourth subject, that of capital, closely tied to all three categories (Table 2.2). One of the most significant governance and policy issues for second homes is that as a policy category they fall into multiple policy arenas, such as housing, regional planning and development, environmental protection, tourism, and migration, meaning that there can be con-flicting policy goals coexisting within the same jurisdiction, and differences in policy emphasis being a norm between jurisdictions both within and between different scales of governance.

Table 2.2 Different dimensions for the assessment of second homes governance

Dimension	Elements
Governance of the individual	• citizenship • locale/place of permanent residence (relationship to how tax is paid and used for undertaking public services) • political & legal rights
Governance of the land/ property title	• land use/environmental regulations and requirements; significance of environmental codes and their enforcement • ownership/occupancy category: freehold or leasehold/rental • investment property (intended life course of the property) • non-commercial vs commercial use (is it rented out? Airbnb? Other uses)
Governance of the structure	• the structures' building requirements/composition, design; importance of building codes and regulations • permanent or mobile structures, tiny portable house movement

For example, in Sweden, in coastal areas of national interest, because of their natural and cultural assets the Swedish Parliament has codified particular conservation regulations in the Swedish Environmental Code. Development is not illegal in such areas, since they are not intended to be nature reserves in general, although municipalities have the responsibility to ensure they are developed sustainably. Persson (2014) reviewed almost 70 comprehensive plans in coastal areas protected by the Code and found that planning practice varies substantially between municipalities with respect to current and future vacation home development, in spite of the same applicable legal framework.

The regulation of second homes can often be the same as any other form of housing development, i.e. planning regulation does not distinguish between a primary or secondary residence but is instead more interested in the structure as well as land use (Chipeniuk 2005; Clivaz 2006). Nevertheless, in other jurisdictions, second home properties can have additional layers of regulatory requirements because of their impacts on amenity landscapes and the housing stock available to permanent residents (Collins & Kearns 2010; Hidle et al. 2010). In the case of international second homes there are often substantial issues of rights and citizenship (Stapa et al. 2013), as well as potential concerns over foreign land ownership by local interests (Pitkänen & Vepsäläinen 2008; Pitkänen 2011) although the relationship between second homes and international amenity and retirement migration means that concerns over second home development are strongly interconnected to broader migration debates. For example, Malta has an Individual Investor Programme that grants full citizenship to successful applicants. The programme costs a minimum of 880,000 euros (£800,000; $1m), rising for each additional family member. It also requires applicants to either buy a property worth at least 350,000 euros, or rent one for at least 16,000 euros a year for five years. The programme is attractive to applicants because Malta is a member of the European Union and part of its Schengen Area, therefore enabling passport-free movement across most of the EU, while the programme is also estimated to be worth about 2.5% of Malta's GDP (220 million euros). Tulett (2017) reports that more than 80% of applicants for passports take the rental option. However, some people in Malta question the programme, particularly as it is regarded as one of the factors pushing up house prices in Malta by some 7% each year, and rents by about 10% (Tulett 2017). Indeed, the post-Brexit situation is leading to reassessments of amenity migration and second home ownership by many British people who have purchased properties in the European Union, given changes in rights and responsibilities as British citizens cease to also have EU citizenship.

Concerns over mobility and citizenship are not restricted to international second home ownership and can also apply in a domestic context as well. Issues associated with domestic second home ownership often relate to the primacy given to the declared permanent or primary residence with respect to its status for tax purposes and formal political representation. For example, in countries such as Sweden, the selection of place of permanent residence can provide for monetary flows from central to local government as well as inform government investment decisions, such as those related to health care, public infrastructure and public transport, that are often based on population estimates (Müller & Hall 2003). Multiple dwelling also provides fundamental challenges to understandings of democratic representation because of the relationship between political standing and property ownership and rights (Ostrow 2002). In political systems where voting is not based on property, there remain significant issues in enabling meaningful political representation for "non-permanent" dwellers at the local scale (Rinne et al. 2014).

Issues of individual political representation aside, second home development and promotion remain an important part of many regional and local development plans (Müller et al. 2004; Brida et al. 2011; Paris 2011; Oliveira, Roca & Roca 2013). Nevertheless, new political and regulatory issues are emerging in light of unintended policy consequences and technological change. One of the most significant of these is the commercialisation of second homes so that owners can use rental platforms to offer their second home for short-term accommodation. The growth of Airbnb, for example, not only places pressure on housing markets but also provides usually unregulated competition for commercial accommodation. The potential size of such accommodation offerings may be substantial. Rovira Soto and Clavé (Chapter 3, this volume) report that in Spain there are 5.3 million beds available in second home accommodation versus 1.7 million beds in regulated accommodation (hotels, apartments and campsites) in coastal municipalities.

In many jurisdictions it can be extremely difficult, if not impossible, to differentiate between second homes for leisure and recreation and those purchased as an investment mechanism (Hui & Yu 2009; Norris & Winston 2009; Norris et al. 2010; Huang & Yi 2011). Where retirement, superannuation and taxation policies are favourable to investors, as in Australia, there may even be positive incentives to develop second homes as short-term rental properties (Paris 2011). Such policies also potentially feed into long-term debates over the impacts of second homes on housing availability and affordability (Allen et al. 1999; Bianco 2006; Marjavaara 2007; Gkartzios & Scott 2009; Hadsell & Colarusso 2009; Bhattacharya & Kim 2011; Paris 2011). Such issues have led to questioning as to whether second homes are contributing to the development of elite landscapes (Hall & Müller 2004). Undoubtedly, in some jurisdictions, this has been the case as a result of broader issues with respect to housing stock provision and planning approaches. Yet the influence of British perspectives on second homes, which present a limited case globally with respect to competition for rural housing stock and only give limited recognition to broader issues of planning restrictions on housing development for lower socio-economic groups in rural areas, has meant a distortion of the wider positive contribution of second homes in many cases (Hall 2015).

Conclusions

The governance of second homes is an important dimension of the overall problem of governing mobility and multiple dwelling (Hall 2015) (Figure 2.2). Issues which clearly need further attention are the ways in which the multi-layered governance of second home related policy areas change over time vertically as well as horizontally. For example, there is relatively little knowledge of the way which policies at the national level (or supranational in the case of the EU), in a wide

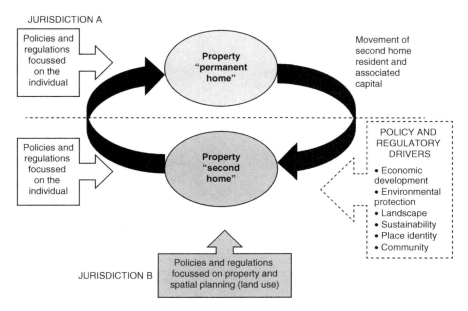

Figure 2.2 The governance of property, mobility and structure.

variety of fields including housing and migration, frame the policy and planning initiatives at lower scales. Indeed, one of the interesting long-term effects of Brexit will be its impact on the international second home activities of British citizens and the consequent flow-on effects for a number of European locations in which British second homes are concentrated.

With respect to "horizontal" policy analysis, the uniformity of approach to second homes is regarded as a significant governance issue. However, given the differences in housing stock pressures between regions, as well as different economic, environmental and social conditions, the opportunity for individual municipalities/local government jurisdictions to undertake their own initiatives with respect to second homes can be a good thing as it demonstrates innovation and responsiveness to local circumstances. Nevertheless, much depends on the overall requirements of policy and regulation as there is a possibility of a "lowest common denominator" approach to development in which some requirements are bypassed for second home developments. In addition, there is a clear national need, regardless of the local context for second homes, for better data collection with respect to second homes, which in the case of some countries will actually mean the basic requirement of defining and identifying the second home housing market and its implications.

References

Åkerlund, U., Lipkina, O. and Hall, C. M. (2015) 'Second home governance in a European context: In and out of Finland and Malta', *Journal of Policy Research in Tourism, Leisure & Events*, 7 (1): 77–97.

Allen, C., Gallent, N. and Tewdwr-Jones, M. (1999) 'The limits of policy diffusion: Comparative experiences of second-home ownership in Britain and Sweden', *Environment and Planning C: Government and Policy*, 17 (2): 227–244.

Bhattacharya, R. and Kim, S.-W. (2011) 'Economic fundamentals, subprime lending and housing prices: Evidence from MSA-level panel data', *Housing Studies*, 26 (6): 897–910.

Bianco, L. (2006) 'Malta: Housing and real estate, 1980–2005', *Architectural Design*, 76 (3): 76–81, 98.

Brida, J. G., Osti, L. and Santifaller, E. (2011) 'Second homes and the need for policy planning', *Tourismos: An International Multidisciplinary Journal of Tourism*, 6 (1), 141–163.

Chipeniuk, R. (2005) 'Planning for the advent of large resorts: Current capacities of interior British Columbian mountain communities', *Environments*, 33 (2): 57–69.

Clivaz, C. (2006) 'Crans-Montana-Aminona (Switzerland): Is there anyone in charge of the resort?', *Revue de géographie alpine*, 94 (1): 84–94.

Coles, T. and Hall, C. M. (2006) 'Editorial: The geography of tourism is dead. Long live geographies of tourism and mobility', *Current Issues in Tourism*, 9 (4–5): 289–292.

Coles, T. and Hall, C. M. (2011) 'Rights and regulation of travel and tourism mobility', *Journal of Policy Research in Tourism, Leisure and Events*, 3 (3): 209–223.

Coles, T., Duval, D. and Hall, C. M. (2004) 'Tourism, mobility and global communities: New approaches to theorising tourism and tourist spaces'. In W. Theobold (ed.), *Global tourism*, 3rd ed., Oxford: Heinemann, 463–481.

Coles, T. E. and Hall, C. M. (eds) (2008) *International Business and Tourism: Global Issues, Contemporary Interactions*. London: Routledge.

Collins, D. and Kearns, R. (2010) 'It's a gestalt experience: Landscape values and development pressure in Hawke's Bay, New Zealand', *Geoforum*, 41: 435–446.

Gkartzios, M. and Scott, M. (2009) 'Planning for rural housing in the Republic of Ireland: From national spatial strategies to development plans', *European Planning Studies*, 17: 1751–1780.

Hadsell, L. and Colarusso, C. (2009) 'Seasonal homes and the local property tax: Evidence from New York State', *American Journal of Economics and Sociology*, 68: 581–602.

Hall, C. M. (2011) 'A typology of governance and its implications for tourism policy analysis', *Journal of Sustainable Tourism*, 19 (4–5): 437–457.

Hall, C. M. (2013) 'Framing behavioural approaches to understanding and governing sustainable tourism consumption: Beyond neoliberalism, "nudging" and "green growth"?', *Journal of Sustainable Tourism*, 21 (7): 1091–1109.

Hall, C. M. (2015) 'Second homes: Planning, policy and governance', *Journal of Policy Research in Tourism, Leisure & Events*, 7 (1): 1–14.

Hall, C. M. and Müller, D. (eds) (2004) *Tourism, Mobility and Second Homes: Between Elite Landscape and Common Ground*. Clevedon, UK: Channel View.

Hidle, K., Ellingsen, W. and Cruickshank, J. (2010) 'Political conceptions of second home mobility', *Sociologia Ruralis*, 50: 139–155.

Hjalager, A. M., Staunstrup, J. K. and Ibsen, R. (2011) 'Trade and value developments in the Danish second-home sector: Implications for tourism policies', *Tourism Economics*, 17 (3): 677–691.

Huang, Y. and Yi, C. (2011) 'Second home ownership in transitional urban China', *Housing Studies*, 26 (3): 423–447.

Hui, E. C. M. and Yu, K. H. (2009) 'Second homes in the Chinese Mainland under one country, two systems: A cross-border perspective', *Habitat International*, 33 (1): 106–113.

Lipkina, O. and Hall, C. M. (2014) 'Russian second home owners in Eastern Finland: Involvement in the local community'. In M. Janoschka and H. Haas (eds), *Contested Spatialities of Lifestyle Migration*. London: Routledge, 158–173.

Marjavaara, R. (2007) 'The displacement myth: Second home tourism in the Stockholm Archipelago', *Tourism Geographies*, 9 (3): 296–317.

Müller, D. K. and Hall, C. M. (2003) 'Second homes and regional population distribution: On administrative practices and failures in Sweden', *Espace Population Societes*, 2003 (2): 251–61.

Müller, D. K., Hall, C. M. and Keen, D. (2004) 'Second home tourism: Impact, management and planning issues'. In C. M. Hall and D. Müller (eds), *Tourism, Mobility and Second Homes: Between Elite Landscape and Common Ground*. Clevedon, UK: Channel View, 15–32.

Müller, D. K. and Hoogendoorn, G. (2013) 'Second homes: Curse or blessing? A review 36 years later', *Scandinavian Journal of Hospitality and Tourism*, 13 (4): 353–369.

Norris, M. and Winston, N. (2009) 'Rising second home numbers in rural Ireland: Distribution, drivers and implications', *European Planning Studies*, 17: 1303–1322.

Norris, M., Paris, C. and Winston, N. (2010) 'Second homes within Irish housing booms and busts: North-south comparisons, contrasts, and debates', *Environment and Planning C: Government and Policy*, 28: 666–680.

Nystrom, J. (1989) 'From the city to the city's countryside', *Geografiska Annaler*, Series B 71 (3): 183–200.

Oliveira, J. A., Roca, M. N. O. and Roca, Z. (2013) 'Second homes and residential tourism: New forms of housing, new real estate market', *Revista Portuguesa de Estudos Regionais*, 32 (1), 57–72.

Ostrow, A .P. (2002) 'Dual resident voting: Traditional disenfranchisement and prospects for change', *Columbia Law Review*, 102 (7): 1954–1991.

Paris, C. (2011) *Affluence, Mobility and Second Home Ownership*. London: Routledge.

Persson, I. (2014) 'Second homes, legal framework and planning practice according to environmental sustainability in coastal areas: The Swedish setting', *Journal of Policy Research in Tourism, Leisure & Events*, 7 (1): 48–61.

Pitkänen, K. (2011) 'Contested cottage landscapes: Host perspective to the increase of foreign second home ownership in Finland 1990–2008', *Fennia*, 189 (1): 43–59.

Pitkänen, K. and Vepsäläinen, M. (2008) 'Foreseeing the future of second home tourism. The case of Finnish media and policy discourse', *Scandinavian Journal of Hospitality and Tourism*, 8 (1): 1–24.

Rinne, J., Kietäväinen, A., Tuulentie, S. and Paloniemi, R. (2014) 'Governing second homes: A study of policy coherence of four policy areas in Finland', *Tourism Review International*, 18 (3): 223–236.

Salskov-Iversen, D., Krause Hansen, H. and Bislev, S. (2000) 'Governmentality, globalization, and local practice: Transformations of a hegemonic discourse', *Alternatives*, 25 (2): 183–223.

Stapa, S. H., Musaev, T., Hieda, N. and Amzah, N. (2013) 'Issues of language choice, ethics and equity: Japanese retirees living in Malaysia as their second home', *Language and Intercultural Communication*, 13 (1): 60–77.

Tulett, S. (2017) What price would you put on a passport? BBC, 23 August. Retrieved from: http://www.bbc.com/news/business-41013873 (accessed 24 August 2017)

3

THE ROLE OF SECOND HOMES IN A MEDITERRANEAN COASTAL MASS TOURISM DESTINATION

An evolutionary perspective

Maria Trinitat Rovira Soto and Salvador Anton Clavé

Introduction

Second homes, housing used temporarily for recreational purposes (Hall & Müller 2004), have been one of the driving forces of change in the landscape of the Mediterranean coast over the past sixty years (Karayiannis et al. 2013; Romano & Zullo 2014; Prévost & Robert 2016). In the case of Spain, their expansion can be interpreted as a clear result of the implementation of a holiday model that has been dominated by development with a rather more residential than strictly tourism-related purpose (Anton Clavé et al. 2011).

The process of developing second homes has led to urban structures with unique features that have often been characterised by their rapid rate of growth (Pié 2005), their predatory, uncontrolled, improvised, unplanned, scattered and discontinuous nature (Quero 2004), their aterritorial, meaningless or banal character (Nogué 2007) and the heterogeneity and fragmentation of the resulting landscape (Muñoz 2007). In addition to this vision, it has also been observed that second homes have created singular urban landscapes that are permanently evolving and have transformed the local identity of places (Coëffé & Violier 2008). The process cannot obviate the attraction of the permanent resident population to second home areas in a context of transformation of population mobility (Hall 2005) and, more generally, to tourist destinations (Williams & Hall 2000, 2002), especially those in metropolitan regions (González Reverté 2008).

Given this background, this chapter seeks to analyse the evolution of the role of areas of second homes as components of tourism destinations in the Spanish Mediterranean coast, using as a case of study the second home developments of the central part of the Costa Daurada in Catalonia between 1960 and 2010. The basic information sources used for the analysis are quantitative indicators derived from urban planning documents that include areas of second homes. In Spain, modifications to urban planning statements (referred to as "partial plans") regulate the land use of new developments. The results show the extent to which the urban planning of second home areas has been used recently as a tool for the redevelopment of the whole destination and how second home spaces have become multifunctional.

The first section highlights the extent of second homes on the Spanish Mediterranean coast and the role they play in the creation of an urban structure with a unique landscape. The second section discusses the utility of partial plans as a source of information for studying the evolution of areas of second homes. Thirdly, the results of quantitative and qualitative analysis are discussed and the evolution of the role of areas of second homes in central Costa Daurada is explained. Finally, the conclusions are presented.

Theoretical background

In 2011, more than 3.6 million dwellings in Spain were second homes. In 1950 they accounted for approximately 2.8% of all homes built, while in 2011 they accounted for 14% of the total (Serrano 2003). The last period of intense growth pertaining to this evolution took place between 1990 and 2007. This period ends with the global economic crisis that began at the end of the first decade of the new millennium, the immediate consequence of which was the practical paralysis of building works for both second homes and primary residences. Between 1990 and 2007 there was a housing boom characterised by some authors as a "tsunami" of urban development (Gaja 2008) that drastically increased the pool of housing in Spain, including second homes, and accentuated their concentration on the coast.

In Spain, almost 50% of second homes are located on the Mediterranean coast (del Pino Artacho 2015). This is a consequence of the implementation of a "sun, sea and sand" tourism model that came into being in the 1960s and was characterised by the formation of large holiday spaces set on the coast with an intense production of temporary residential dwellings (Cortés-Jiménez & Anton Clavé 2015). It gave rise to another outcome, from the perspective of the structure of the supply: the predominance of second home accommodation (5.3 million beds) over regulated accommodation (1.7 million beds in hotels, apartments and campsites) in Spanish coastal municipalities.

Parallel to their consolidation, since the 1980s a process of transformation of some mature tourist destinations has taken place where areas of permanent residence have been developed. This occurs especially at destinations located in areas close to the major coastal metropolitan regions. This process is also described in other contexts (Équipe MIT 2002; Mullins 1992; Butler 2014) and some classic theoretical models are even attributed to it (e.g. Lundgren 1974). In the case analysed below, these dynamics result in the integration of areas of second homes in both processes of tourism restructuring and the urban transformation of the actual destination.

The incorporation of spaces of second residences in the dynamics of tourism and urban restructuring has, in many cases, ensured their gradual functional integration in the urban fabric of towns and cities. This transformation has taken place in two ways: (1) fully consciously and proactively in cases in which the public administration has provided existing second home areas with new functions and facilities with the aim of turning them into areas of permanent residence, or, (2) reactively in cases in which the growing concentration of the permanent resident population in the areas that were initially of temporary residences has led the generally local administration to react to meet the basic needs of the permanent population which has different requirements from the temporary population. In either case, there has been a process of transformation that has been documented in urban planning instruments specific to local administrations. As Pié (2005: 25) states, when it has come about proactively, this has also meant a "qualitative leap" that has enabled dealing with the problems of the different spaces of second homes from a perspective of 'pursuing the transformation of the present agglomerate into an urban system that facilitates the arrival of new activities, the transformation of much of the residential stock into permanent residence and improved tourism'. How this proactive transformation has been implemented by planning is the focus of this chapter. Moreover, the results also provide for debate on the evolution of urban dynamics in coastal tourist destinations

(Smith 1991; Papatheodorou 2004; Andriotis 2006) and the role of territorial planning in their (re)development (Clivaz et al. 2014).

Material and methods

The following case study is of central Costa Daurada in Catalonia, a specialised mass tourism destination located in the urban area of Tarragona, near Barcelona. The area is well connected with France and with other Spanish Mediterranean regions via the AP-7 motorway and to northwestern Spanish inland regions and Madrid via the AP-2 motorway. These are the most important terrestrial routes for the arrival of domestic and international tourist flows in addition to Barcelona-El Prat and Reus airports.

Central Costa Daurada in Catalonia comprises three different resorts: Salou, Cambrils and La Pineda (municipality of Vila-seca) (Figure 3.1), and was home to more than 60,000 permanent inhabitants in 2014. It receives about 4.5 million tourists each year. The main attractions of the destinations are their beaches and the Port Aventura theme park, which welcomes more than 3.5 million visitors annually. This 20 km strip of coast offers a concentration of hotels, campsites, registered tourist apartments (all of them supplying more than 11 million overnight stays per year) and second homes (Sanz-Ibáñez et al. 2017). Between 2006 and 2011, 40% of tourists coming to the Costa Daurada stayed in one of 45,285 second homes that are found in this sector. In fact, second homes dominate the tourism landscape. Interestingly, in terms of the focus of this chapter, according to the census, the number of houses used as second homes decreased in the study area by 5% between 2001 and 2011.

As is customary in Spain, urban areas (including those with existing second home uses, which are usually known as second home urbanisations), were planned via a planning instrument

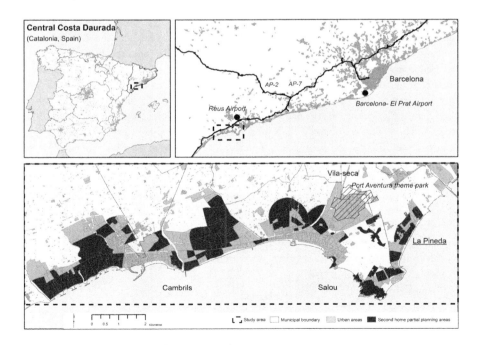

Figure 3.1 The central part of Costa Daurada.

Source: Authors.

known as a partial plan. The partial plan is the planning instrument 'aimed at ordering in detail a usually homogeneous area, of small size to be urbanised and built on in a relatively short time to join the city' (López de Lucio 1999: 160). Partial plans actually guide and reflect the local authority's desire to organise, on the basis of the city's social needs. It is, therefore, a document that effectively builds 'the physical space of the city and its tangible form' (Esteban 1984: 160), and it marks the urban fabric, defines its structure, and determines functions and uses in detail.

The study of these documents in the case of second home urbanisations allows for exploration of how the planning of spaces has evolved in form and function, how new urban developments have adapted to the requirements of the prevalent visitor markets, and how the desires and imagination of planners and, more generally, of the end users of the urban space have transfered to urban planning. In this sense, for example, Ursic, Misetic and Misetic (2016) highlight the importance of their regulatory role but also the fact that they reflect different visions of society and affect quality of life and sustainable development.

For the analysis, a total of 94 partial plans with second home uses were taken into account representing a total surface area of 10.27 km^2 in central Costa Daurada. Twenty-four of them were adopted in the early 1960s and represent 19.71% of the total developed surface area arranged by partial plans analysed in the area of study. They are plans located closer to the coastline. In the 1970s, another 21 partial plans developed 17.94% of the total developed land based on the partial plans analysed, while in the 1980s, 15 partial plans developed 14.99%. In the 1990s, 19 plans developed 22.2% of the area arranged. The first decade of the new millennium had only 14 partial plans approved. However, these 14 plans developed the highest contingent of potential building land of the entire study period, accounting for 25.13% of the total area designated for building based on the partial plans under study in central Costa Daurada.

Partial plans allow identifying the basic elements that compose and configure newly created residential units such as the area dedicated to open green areas, the area dedicated to the local road communications network, the area for accommodation facilities, the area given over to public and collective facilities, and the area dedicated to private space. They also require the forms from which this private space is built (e.g. single family home, semi-detached home and multifamily housing), intensity in the use made of private space and the occupancy of urban space.

Based on this basic information, two variables have been used to distinguish the different types of plans that exist in the study area and to study their evolution: (1) the area given over to private building, and (2) the area occupied or built on, whether public or private property. The occupied area incorporates not only private housing, whether permanent or temporary, but also all necessary urban facilities for the running of the city.

In addition to the quantitative information, partial plans also include qualitative information such as the objectives or needs each urban area aspires to satisfy, the justification of new developments or issues related with the design, and construction processes of residential areas for temporary use. This other information allows for understanding the changes that are proposed in terms of the physical arrangement of space. Finally, thanks to the cartographic information taken from plans it is also possible to find out the proposed spatial configuration for urban areas used for second homes, and specifically the way in which their constituents are arranged.

Results

By combining the variables set out, nine types of partial plans with secondary residential uses in central Costa Daurada have been identified (see Table 3.1). By taking into account their year of approval, it is observed that the analysis results in a chronological cadence for the set typologies (see Figure 3.2).

Table 3.1 Partial urban plans with second home uses in central Costa Daurada

Type	Decade	Description
A	**1960**	Urban areas with second home uses with a low average of building space, and with a medium average of private use surface
B	**1960**	Urban areas with second home uses with a low average of building space, and with a high average of private use surface
C	**1970**	Urban areas with second home uses with a medium–low average of building space, and with a medium average of private use surface
D	**1970**	Urban areas with second home uses with a high–medium average of building space, and with a medium average of private use surface
E	**1970**	Urban areas with second home uses with a medium–low average of building space, and with a high average of private use surface
F	**1980**	Urban areas with second home uses with a high–medium average of building space, and with a low average of private use surface
G	**1980**	Urban areas with second home uses with a medium–low average of building space, and with a low average of private use surface
H	**1980**	Urban areas with second home uses with a low average of building space, and with a low average of private use surface
I	**1990**	Urban areas with second home uses with a high average of building space, and with a low average of private use surface

Source: Authors.

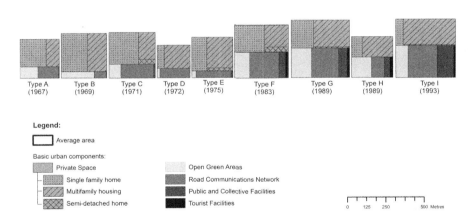

Figure 3.2   Characteristics of partial plans with second home uses.

Two types of plans were characteristic of the 1960s. Partial plans belonging to type A were generally approved in 1967, while type B plans were generally passed in 1969. Types A and B are characterised by presenting large spaces without any constructed elements, between 30% and 40% on average respectively of the total surface of the partial plan, but at the same time, with built-on areas that are mostly dedicated to private space, between 70% and 80% of the total surface of the partial plan.

Types C, D and E reflect the tourist landscape of the areas of second residence of the 1970s. Type C partial plans were more likely to be approved in 1971. Types D and E were generally

Table 3.2 Characterisation of the three stages of development of areas of second homes in central Costa Daurada

Stage	Functional characteristics	Formal characteristics	Characteristics of configuration
1	**Monofunctionality** Predominance of the residential function. Between 67% and 87% of the surface of the partial plans is given over to private space.	**Simplicity** The dominant types of construction are single family homes in the inner part of the partial plans and multifamily housing close to the coastline. Both types include open green areas for private use.	**Reiteration** Urban configuration in response to the expectations of temporary users. Urban components that allow identification of the landscape as typical of a space used by temporary residents.
2	**Complexity** Increase in the surface dedicated to the public components of the urban space that represent more than 50% of the surface area of partial plans.	**Diversity** Increase in the types of construction with a presence of semi-detached housing.	**Dedifferentiation** Configuration that includes a greater diversity of urban components and that responds to expectations not only associated with temporary residence and recreational uses.
3	**Multifunctionality** Predominance and diversification of public components. Planning of permanent residences in spaces traditionally for second homes.	**Heterogeneity** A great variety of building. For single family housing there is a low-density model, scattered housing near the coast, and a second, denser, more uniform model heading inland. For multifamily housing there is: a higher density model, without facilities for private use, and a second model of lower density and with facilities for private use in residential complexes enclosed in themselves.	**Diversification** Sustainability criteria are introduced in the planning of spaces with second home uses and are integrated in the urban structure.

approved in 1972 and 1975, respectively. The land of these types of developments is occupied with elements built on 40–55% of the total area. However, types C and D had between 65% and 75% of their total surface area dedicated to private construction, while for type E, private space accounts for over 80% of the total area of the partial plan.

The areas of second homes developed during the 1980s are defined by type F, which includes the partial plans more likely to be approved in 1983, and for types G and H, that include partial plans generally approved in 1989. These plans are characterised by devoting between 45% and 65% of the surface area to private space. For urban development types F and G, between 45% and 55% of the total surface area is occupied by some constructed element while in type H urbanisation this development occurs on less than 40% of its total surface area. The plans of the 1990s, and by extension of the first decade of the 2000s, make up type I. They are characterised by their dedication of a lower percentage of the total surface area to private space, less than 40%, but have more than 60% of the total area occupied by a constructed element.

Suitably grouped, the nine types of partial plans make it possible to differentiate three evolutionary stages in the development of areas of second homes in central Costa Daurada. The definitions of these three stages are summarised in Table 3.2. As can be seen, the resulting characterisation explains the different role of second home urbanisations in the development of central Costa Daurada as a tourist destination.

The first evolutionary stage is characterised by the simplicity of the landscape and is reflected in types of urbanisations A, B, C, D and E. The result is spaces whose goal is simply the production of second homes and was a main factor of the initial plans that were focused on meeting the demand for housing in the area during the peak tourist season. In addition, the construction of housing was also justified by the creation of employment opportunities, and the increased capital gains arising as a result of the change in land designation.

The landscape resulting from this first stage is characterised by its monofunctionality, since more than half of the land designated for building is devoted to the construction of second homes. Open green areas were poorly defined and appreciated in the planning process. For example, in the 1960s the planning process even envisaged the incorporation of public spaces into the private domain, and consideration was given to defining as open green areas locations that were not accessible to the population, such as cliffs, for example. In the 1970s, open green areas were directly considered in the *1975 Land Law* (Land Law 19/1975), requiring a minimum percentage for each area in each partial planning action. The uncertainty of the first stage also affected public and collective facilities. Some plans indicate that public facilities, such as schools and cultural buildings, were not regarded as an "indispensable" requirement because of the temporary presence of the user population of the planned spaces. Some attention was given to the recreational use of urban space, as in the case of Carolina Mar in 1961, although roads were often only considered in terms of giving accessibility to the newly constructed units rather than in terms of developing an efficient transport network. Inland road connections, situated between the coastline and the urbanised areas, also represented a space of transition between different planning regimes.

The formal simplicity of the constructed space also characterises this first stage. Despite this, there is a predominance of isolated single family homes in types A, B and C, and a predominance of multifamily housing in types D and E. The multifamily housing, that reaches a considerable height, is situated along the coastline, creating a screen effect that affects the low-density constructions that are located further inland. These are enclosed residential complexes with beach views and are concentrated in the parcel earmarked for private building, leaving the rest for recreational facilities and private leisure areas. The rest of the urbanised area is occupied by private single family homes, visually heterogeneous low-density constructions.

The second stage in the evolution of partial plans with second home uses includes residential areas F and G that are characteristic of the 1980s. This stage represents a change in the way of arranging the basic urban components and generates a new way of configuring and understanding the landscape of second homes. Not only does the process of growth continue, but areas that were developed in earlier decades start to be regenerated. The 1980s saw the emergence of minimum legal standards governing public spaces in land designated for building and greater awareness of their role in built-up areas. This period continued the focus on the construction of second homes. The combination of these elements led to an increase in the structural and functional complexity of the landscape and a reduction in the land dedicated to private space in favour of public spaces. In addition, a different urban landscape from the one developed in the 1960s and 70s is planned. A more diverse range of public and collective facilities is considered, some related to the needs of the resident population, such as schools, for example, although, in general, they do not occupy a central role in the configuration of the plans. The road communications network is also more regular, supported by elements that optimise traffic and seek to facilitate access. However, road planning continues without taking connectivity with other urban pieces into account. Finally, the role of open green areas becomes established, as they start to occupy large areas in the inner part of the sectors for development. Parks begin to occupy central areas and are located adjacent to public and collective facilities thereby increasing the quality of life of the inhabitants whether temporary or permanent. There is also a marked increase in multifamily housing, thus diversifying the forms of the urban landscape. Single family homes are located on the coastline where, for the first time, the landscape is no longer dominated by multifamily housing. Apartment blocks also start to incorporate private spaces with private facilities such as swimming pools. However, overall, the plans envisage denser construction due to a greater use of urban space.

The last evolutionary stage includes types H and I urbanisations. This stage is characterised by a more complex configuration of the landscape from both formal and functional points of view. It is worthwhile noting that in some cases, the partial plans of this period respond to the paradigm of sustainability design criteria. Under them, the 1990s reflect a new model of growth that erased the boundary between tourist areas and the "conventional" city. This intention is reflected in strategies aimed at providing continuity to the urban fabric (so far the growth process of residential tourist areas had been discontinuous along the coast, with unconnected residential units popping up), urbanising open spaces between urbanised units and providing facilities to already established residential areas. In the 2000s there was a clear commitment to creating a "more compact and complex" model of town that 'reconciles its tourist orientation with its emerging role as a medium-sized coastal city … [There are] new processes of urban development [and] the reconversion of existing urban areas – densities, open green areas, roadways and mobility, etc. – to the extent possible' (Municipality of Cambrils 2005: 25). For this, partial planning seeks to ensure the consolidation of initially temporary residential spaces as components of some coastal towns that have ended up becoming a part of a genuine metropolitan area.

The resulting landscapes, which are multifunctional in nature, are characterised by their dedication of a high percentage of land to public space. As for open green areas, planning strategies tend to create continuous, integrated and balanced spaces. Thus, in addition to their role of "cushioning" the process of urbanisation, and as elements that facilitate traffic, a new role is added to them as connectors of established urban areas. Open green spaces also emerge as social meeting places and provide additional landscape quality. With respect to road communication networks, some impermeable urban areas remain around single family homes with the aim of preserving private space. However, in general, the road communication networks are now more regular and more extensive and ultimately more efficient. In the most recent planning strategies, public and collective facilities also play an important role and their location becomes essential from the perspective of turning them into places of permanent residence and is reflected in the explicit construction of permanent residences in areas traditionally used for second homes. However, areas continue to be reserved for establishing tourist facilities, such as hotels, that begin to occupy areas near the coastline. There is, lastly, a huge variety in the forms of constructions in these residential areas, given their diversity, especially when it comes to multifamily housing. The multifamily model coexists with other constructions whose occupation of the area designated for building is lower and is spread out within their private space.

Conclusions

Since the works of Wolfe (1952), Lundgren (1974) and Coppock (1977), academic interest in second homes has included such topics as housing, planning, leisure and tourism (Müller 2004). Currently, this interest takes the economic, social and environmental dimensions into account (Hall & Müller 2004), relates to a variety of geographical environments (Roca 2013), and has been developed by different academic disciplines ranging from tourism studies to housing studies (Hall 2014; Müller 2014). The planning of secondary residences has also been a topic of growing interest (Müller 2014; Hall 2015). This is a relevant issue for the case of the Spanish Mediterranean, where second homes are directly associated with the processes of urbanisation generated by tourism in coastal areas (García-Ayllón 2015). This, as Roca (2013: 15) explains, has led to the 'convergence between social science research, spatial planning and public policy concerns regarding second homes and the evolving functional and morphological features of tourism as a steady driving force behind increased geographical mobility, on the one hand, and the various motives for establishing second homes, on the other'.

The focus of this chapter has been on the analysis of the changing role of second homes in the urban dynamics of a tourism destination in the Mediterranean Coast. It becomes clear that, in this case, the planning of areas of second homes has become a deliberate tool for the transformation of both the destination and the urban space. Their analysis has allowed us to better understand the impact and prevalence of second home developments within a metropolitan context in the sense put forward by Visser (2004).

The results obtained for central Costa Daurada confirm that the role of areas with second home uses and their relationship to mass tourist destinations located in metropolitan contexts of the Spanish Mediterranean coast has evolved from the 1960s to the present. They have gone from being urban spaces fundamentally geared towards use by temporary residents to becoming much more structurally and functionally complex areas (Rovira Soto & Anton Clavé 2014). This evolution has gone through the 'de-recreation of the secondary residence [that] means their defunctionalization and reduced regional specialization, resulting in their direct insertion into broader demographic and regional processes' (del Pino Artacho 2015: 18), and by the dissolution of differences between second home development areas and the conventional city, as a result of the harmonisation of the urban landscape and the creation of new public facilities and services (even primary schools and basic health services). These processes are reflected in the previously noted 5% decrease in the number of secondary residences in the region between 2001 and 2011. Interestingly, such changes have also been identified in the South Tyrol (Brida et al. 2011), suggesting a shared process of evolutionary change with respect to second homes and the transformation of the urban landscape.

As observed in this chapter, in all these processes, planning has been the key factor for the destination and urban change (Brouder et al. 2017). In the case studied, the transformation has been observed proactively on the basis of urban planning with sustainability criteria as of the last stage. On the other hand it has provided for their continued ability to attract both visitors and residents to an established urban area. Specifically, the evolution of the processes of planning areas of second homes in central Costa Daurada has led to: balancing the low levels of public urban components (open green areas, local road communication networks and public and collective facilities) inherited from the 1960s to 1980s, connecting areas of second homes with other permanent residential areas already built (linking them to a sustainable urban form), holding back the geographic expansion of urban growth, covering the needs of tourists and residents in terms of public services, and homogenising the typology of developments and the urban landscape.

This functional and morphological transformation highlights the importance of planning for areas of second residences (inherited or new) on the Mediterranean coast of Spain both from an urban perspective and from the perspective of destination regeneration strategies, particularly taking into account the conversion of some of the temporary housing areas into permanent residence neighbourhoods and, at the end, into good places to live. In addition, the results highlight the need to keep the issue of the continuous urban and landscape change and transformation in coastal mass tourism destinations on the research agenda (Brey et al. 2007)

Acknowledgements

The research on which this paper is based was financed by the Spanish Ministry of Science and Innovation (CSO2011-23004/GEOG and CSO2014-51785-R).

References

Andriotis, K. (2006) 'Hosts, guests and politics: Coastal resorts morphological change', *Annals of Tourism Research*, 33 (4): 1079–1098.

Anton Clavé, S., Rullán, S. and Vera Rebollo, J. F. (2011) 'Research into mass tourism development on the Mediterranean coast', *Tourism Geographies*, 13 (3): 495–501.

Brey, E. T., Morrison, A. M. and Mills, J. M. (2007) 'An examination of destination resort research', *Current Issues in Tourism*, 10 (5): 415–442.

Brida, J. G., Osti, L. and Santifaller, E. (2011) 'Second homes and the need for policy planning', *Tourismos*, 6 (1): 141–163.

Brouder, P., Anton Clavé, S., Gill, A. and Ioannides, D. (2017) 'Why is tourism not an evolutionary science? Understanding the past, present, and future of tourism destination evolution'. In P. Brouder, S. Anton Clavé, A. M. Gill and D. Ioannides (eds) *Tourism Destination Evolution*. London: Routledge, 1–18.

Butler, R. W. (2014) 'Coastal tourist resorts: History, development and models', *Architecture, City and Environment*, 9 (25): 203–228.

Clivaz, C., Crevoisier, O., Kebir, L., Nahrath, S. and Stock, M. (2014) *Resort Development and Touristic Capital of Place*, Neuchâtel: University of Neuchâtel, Maison d'Analyse des Processus Sociaux.

Coëffé, V. and Violier, P. (2008) 'Les lieux du tourisme: De quel(s) paradis parle-t-on? Variations sur le thème de l'urbanité touristique', *Journal of Urban Research*, 4. [online] Available at: http://articulo.revues.org/158#text

Coppock, J. T. (ed.) (1977) *Second Homes: Curse or Blessing?* New York: Pergamon Press.

Cortés-Jiménez, I. and Anton Clavé, S. (2015) 'Tourism in Spain: Southern European perspectives'. In J. C. Dissart, J. Dehez and J. B. Marsat (eds) *Tourism, Recreation and Regional Development: Perspectives from France and Abroad*. New York: Ashgate, 241–258.

del Pino Artacho, J. A. (2015) *Estructuras residenciales y movilidad: más allá de la segunda residencia*. Madrid: CIS.

Équipe MIT. (2002) *Tourismes 1. Lieux Communs*. Paris: Belin.

Esteban, J. (1984) *Elementos de ordenación urbana*. 2nd ed. Barcelona: La Gaya Ciencia.

Gaja, F. (2008) 'El "*tsunami* urbanizador" en el litoral mediterráneo. El ciclo de hiperproducción inmobiliária 1996–2006', *Scripta Nova*, 12 (270). [online] Available at: http://www.ub.edu/geocrit/sn/sn-270/sn-270-66.htm

García-Ayllón, S. (2015) 'La Manga case study: Consequences from short-term urban planning in a tourism mass destiny of the Spanish Mediterranean coast', *Cities*, 43: 141–151.

González Reverté, F. (2008) 'El papel de los destinos turísticos en la transformación sociodemográfica del litoral mediterráneo español', *Boletín de la Asociación de Geógrafos Españoles*, 47: 79–107.

Hall, C. M. (2005) 'Reconsidering the geography of tourism and contemporary mobility', *Geographical Research*, 43 (2): 125–139.

Hall, C. M. (2014) 'Second home tourism: An international review', *Tourism Review International*, 18 (3): 115–135.

Hall, C. M. (2015) 'Second homes planning, policy and governance', *Journal of Policy Research in Tourism, Leisure and Events*, 7 (1): 1–14.

Hall, C. M. and Müller, D. K. (2004) 'Introduction: Second homes, curse or blessing? Revisited'. In C. M. Hall and D. K. Müller (eds) *Tourism, Mobility and Second Homes: Between Elite Landscape and Common Ground*. Clevedon, UK: Channel View Publications, 3–14.

Karayiannis, O., Iakovidou, O. and Tsartas, P. (2013) 'Historic, symbolic aspects and policy issues of the second home phenomenon in the Greek tourism context: The Cyclades case study'. In Z. Roca (ed.) *Second Home Tourism in Europe: Lifestyle Issues and Policy Responses*. Farnham, UK: Routledge, 173–197.

Land Law 19/1975 (1975) Law of May 2 of 1975, amending the Law on Land Regime and Urban Planning. Available at: https://www.boe.es/buscar/doc.php?id=BOE-A-1975-9250

López de Lucio, R. (1999) 'Programas de actuación urbanística, planes parciales y proyectos de urbanización'. In L. Moya (ed.) *La práctica del planeamiento urbanístico*. Madrid: Síntesis, 139–203.

Lundgren, J. O. J. (1974) 'On access to recreational lands in dynamic metropolitan hinterlands', *Tourism Review*, 29 (4): 124–131.

Müller, D. K. (2004) 'Mobility, tourism and second homes'. In A. Lew, C. M. Hall and A. M. Williams (eds) *A Companion to Tourism*. Oxford: Blackwell, 387–398.

Müller, D. K. (2014) 'Progress in second-home tourism research'. In A. Lew, C. M. Hall and A. M. Williams (eds) *The Wiley Blackwell Companion to Tourism*. Chichester, UK: Wiley, 389–400.

Mullins, P. (1992) 'Cities for pleasure: The emergence of tourism urbanization in Australia', *Built Environment*, 18 (3): 187–198.

Municipality of Cambrils (2005) Urban Development Plan (POUM21) for the municipality of Cambrils. Available at: http://dtes.gencat.cat/rpucportal/AppJava/cercaExpedient.do?reqCode=veureDocument&codintExp=220287&fromPage=load

Muñoz, F. (2007) 'Paisajes aterritoriales, paisajes en huelga'. In J. Nogué (ed.) *La construcción social del paisaje*. Madrid: Biblioteca Nueva, 293–337.

Nogué, J. (2007) 'Territorios sin discurso, paisajes sin imaginario. Retos y dilemas', *Ería*, 73–74: 373–382.

Papatheodorou, A. (2004) 'Exploring the evolution of tourism resorts', *Annals of Tourism Research*, 31 (1): 219–237.

Pié, R. (2005) 'Ara toca fer ciutat'. In Col·legi d'Arquitectes de Catalunya (ed.) *Debat Costa Brava*. Girona: COAC, 50–87.

Prévost, A. and Robert, S. (2016) 'Local spatial planning practices in four French Mediterranean coastal territories under pressure', *Land Use Policy*, 56: 68–80.

Quero, D. (2004) 'La urbanización del turismo, un punto de vista clásico', *Las Nuevas Formas del Turismo*, 5: 197–214.

Roca, Z. (2013) *Second Home Tourism in Europe: Lifestyle Issues and Policy Responses*. Farnham, UK: Routledge.

Romano, B. and Zullo, F. (2014) 'The urban transformation of Italy's Adriatic coastal strip: Fifty years of unsustainability', *Land Use Policy*, 38: 26–36.

Rovira Soto, M. T. and Antón Clavé, S. (2014) 'De destino a ciudad: La reformulación urbana de los destinos turísticos costeros maduros: El caso de la Costa Daurada central', *Architecture, City and Environment*, 9 (25): 392–373.

Sanz-Ibáñez, C., Wilson, J. and Anton Clavé, S. (2017) 'Moments as catalysts for change in the evolutionary paths of tourism destinations'. In P. Brouder, S. Anton Clavé, A. Gill and D. Ioannides (eds) *Tourism Destination Evolution*. New York: Routledge, 81–102.

Serrano, J. M. (2003) 'Las viviendas de segunda residencia en la sociedad del "bienestar". El caso de un país turístico: España', *Cuadernos de Turismo*, 12: 53–76.

Smith, R. A. (1991) 'Beach resort: A model of development evolution', *Landscape and Urban Planning*, 21 (3): 189–210.

Terkenli, T. S. (2004) 'Tourism and landscape'. In A. Lew, C. M. Hall and A. M. Williams (eds) *A Companion to Tourism*. London: Blackwell, 339–347.

Ursic, S., Misetic, R. and Misetic, A. (2016) 'New perspectives on sustainable development of second homes in Croatia: Strategic planning or proliferation of building?', *Procedia- Social and Behavioral Sciences*, 216: 80–86.

Visser, G. (2004) 'Seond homes and local development: Issues arising from Cape Town's De Waterkant', *GeoJournal*, 60 (3): 259–271.

Williams, A. M. and Hall, C. M. (2000) 'Tourism and migration: New relationships between production and consumption', *Tourism Geographies*, 2 (1): 5–27.

Williams, A. M. and Hall, C. M. (2002) 'Tourism, migration, circulation and mobility. The contingencies of time and place'. In C. M. Hall and A. M. Williams (eds) *Tourism and Migration. New Relationships Between Production and Consumption*. Dordrecht: Kluwer, 1–52.

Wolfe, R. I. (1952) 'Wasaga Beach: The divorce from the geographic environment', *The Canadian Geographer*, 1 (2): 57–66.

4

SECOND HOMES AND THE COMMONS

Terms for second home leaseholds and collective action in Kvarken Archipelago, Finland

Kristina Svels and Ulrika Åkerlund

Introduction

In the shallow Kvarken Archipelago, on the west coast of Finland, pristine land is continuously created due to land elevation. As a result of land ownership structures after the Great Partition in the eighteenth century, emergent land accrues to common-pool ownership and is managed collectively by village commons. The archipelago constitutes a complex resource system where multiple users access resource units for extractive and recreational purposes, and where multiple property regimes overlap. As the landscape is becoming increasingly attractive for recreational purposes, its value has shifted from rather worthless to highly valuable over the last century. In the common-pool property, second home plots are leased, creating significant revenue for the community of part-owners. The commons, however, are viscous institutions where old power relationships are locked in path dependency, and conflictual situations emerge when more stakeholders in the post-productive society seek access to the resource system.

This chapter will focus on the management of the common-pool property in the archipelago. It aims to explore terms for second home leaseholds in the common-pool resource system and opportunities for collective action participation of second home owners. We pose the following research questions: What are the implications for second home ownership on leaseholds in the common-pool resource, in terms of:

1   Control over property and use rights to the resource.
2   Factors for conflict within the common-property community and other stakeholders using the resource.
3   Opportunities to participate in collective action.

First, the geological/environmental context and the second home patterns in Kvarken Archipelago are described. We then frame the chapter within common-pool resource theory and the concept of collective action in management of the commons. Next, after shortly describing the methods, we turn to present the results, first explaining the studied commons' management regimes and terms for second home leaseholds on the common property. The chapter then goes on to scrutinise opportunities for collective action to resolve conflictual situations before we finally explore one case in more detail where conflicts are particularly present. In concluding this chapter we discuss the inability of the commons to adapt to changes in society, and factors for path dependency and conflictual situations.

Land elevation and second homes in Kvarken Archipelago

On the West Coast of Finland, in the region of Ostrobothnia, the land- and seascapes are in continuous change due to an ongoing land elevation following the compression of the earth's crust during the last Ice Age. Emergent land, also called accretion area, is the visible result of land elevation as former water areas are converted to solid land. The land elevation within the study area is approximately 8–9 mm/year which due to the shallow sea level results in an annual land growth of roughly 1 km sq. Visible traces of the land elevation are the natural creation of skerries and shifting shorelines which causes the need for dredging waterways and moving harbours and berths outwards to the sea. Due to the unique geological formations caused by the ice masses, and the traces of land elevation, Kvarken Archipelago was in 2006 listed as a UNESCO World Heritage site, as an extension to the World Heritage High Coast in Sweden (UNESCO World Heritage Centre 2006). The World Heritage status does not imply immediate juridical conservation protection measures but is considered in regional and municipality planning processes in Ostrobothnia, adding a level of regulation structures to the management of the resource system.

Socially, the studied area in Finland has been in close connection to Sweden for centuries, and was part of the Swedish kingdom until 1809. The early purpose-built second homes in the Ostrobothnian archipelago is one legacy from the Swedish time. Traditions and cultural traces are still well linked between Ostrobothnia and the east coast of Sweden, making public and private transnational cooperation part of the overall regional development. Second homes in the studied municipalities have a long history. The initial off-mainland stays in Ostrobothnia were huts used for means of livelihood such as fishing and cattle grazing (Harjula 2007). Cattle huts existed from the late seventeenth century and fishing hamlets (saunas) in the outer archipelago were established during the 1800s (Kellari 2012). Not only were the users' days occupied by work but recreational time was indubitably more frequent than at their homestead. In Sundom archipelago (Vaasa) the fishing saunas were still used for their original purpose until the 1960s (Höglund & Uhlgrén 2008). These two types of huts later became second homes through refurbishment and subsequently used as seasonal dwellings. As early as the late eighteenth century the first known purpose-built summer residences in Finland emerged on the coast outside Vaasa by traders and other affluent citizens (Harjula 2007; Viljanen Rossi 2014; Vuori 1968). More frequently the working class started to build summer houses in the Vaasa archipelago during the 1920s and 1930s (Harjula 2007). Until the 1950s ownership of a summer house was nonetheless quite rare in Finland and an advantage for the well-off social classes (Eklund 1989). The second home construction boom occurred in Ostrobothnia during the 1960s and 1970s when new second homes were primarily purpose-built rather than converted from other types of dwellings (Jansson & Müller 2003). These dwellings were simple constructions without electricity and running water.

Kvarken Archipelago is today an attractive second home landscape. Table 4.1 presents population and second home statistics for the four study municipalities. The greater part of second home plots are privately owned; however, about 14% of the stock are built on leasehold plots owned by the commons. The majority of second home owners and users of leased property in Ostrobothnia have a close connection to the region. They are either residents of the second home municipality or reside in the neighbouring municipalities. The interest from "outsiders",

Table 4.1 Second homes in the studied municipalities

	Korsholm	*Korsnäs*	*Malax*	*Vaasa*	*Total*
Inhabitants	19,296	2,221	5,576	67,001	94,094
Second homes	3,412	1,900	1,000	1,224	7,536

Source: Statistics Finland (2014) and municipality estimations of second homes.

people without any previous connection to the region, is increasing. The contemporary second home patterns in Ostrobothnia are marked by the transformation of the small summer houses built during the boom to bigger, well-equipped year-round properties through renovation or replacement (Jansson & Müller 2003). Amenities such as electricity and running water are becoming more frequent and road connection to the plot is preferred by many second home owners in the younger generations. At the same time in the inner archipelago, land elevation results in un-navigable waterways and shore properties overgrown by vegetation, making them less attractive. The need for dredging and landscape reformation is common. Shallow areas are abandoned as the properties become uninteresting due to lack of passage to water and a deteriorated scenery.

Theoretical backdrop

Complex resource systems

Natural and built resources, for example, land and water areas, game populations, production forests, roads, wells and irrigation constructions, are increasingly understood as existing within systems. Resource systems are multi-layered, or mixed, as they comprise a variety of resource units, ownership types and users (Ostrom 1999; Fennell 2011). Access and use rights of resources can be formal or informal and are controlled in property rights regimes (Steins & Edwards 1999). Four general classes of resource units to which property rights are bound within a resource system are defined (Carlsson 2008): 1) open access resources which are freely accessible for many users, 2) public or state resources, such as national parks, where access is controlled by government bodies, 3) private resources where access is strictly exclusive, and 4) common-pool resources where access is shared within an exclusive group of users. Within these classes there are also toll resource units where access is controlled through fees, for example entrance fees or boat mooring leases at marinas.

Most natural resource systems, such as archipelagos, rivers or forests, are complex systems which contain several or all of the resource classes, are used by multiple user groups for extractive and/or non-extractive purposes, and are managed under a mixture of property regimes (Steins & Edwards 1999). Naturally, the range of users or user groups perform varying degrees of interaction and influence over the economic and social coordination, management and governing of property and use rights in a complex resource system. Therefore, the crucial resource management issue is balancing multiple interests.

Governing common-pool resources

The concept of governance presents an umbrella term to describe different kinds of steering and coordination between multiple agents. Coordination ranges from hierarchical systems to decentralised, self-organising systems taking forms such as networks, regimes or partnerships

(Rhodes 1997; Kooiman 2003) within which decision-making processes include, for example, informal norm development and stakeholder involvement (Holmgren et al. 2010). Common-pool property regimes, usually referred to as the commons, represent a distinct form of governance where coordination is managed within a group of part-owners. There are many different types of commons organisations, with varying levels of constitution. In most aspects their management functions are significantly autonomous (Ostrom 1990; Hysing 2009); however, in most instances the state still holds a regulative position through legislation on management of the commons (Ostrom 1990; Ostrom et al. 1994; Holmgren et al. 2010; Lidestav et al. 2013).

Rules relating to access and use of resource units, as well as membership criteria are stipulated by the commons' part-owner community, comprising physical and/or juridical persons (for example, government and non-government organisations). Part-owners hold varying entitlements and decision-making power, usually based on the size of their shares in the common-pool resource. Three levels of management have been identified (Ostrom 1990): the legislative level controlled by the state, the collective-choice level on which part-owners have a direct influence through the General Assembly (GA), and the operational level where an executive committee authorises the day-to-day implementation on decided rules and control functions.

Commons are, per definition, collaborative institutions; however, as they often manage complex resource systems with a diverse part-owner community, where different property rights regimes coexist, collective action situations are not always frictionless (Steins & Edwards 1999; Sandström et al. 2013). Through collective action, property and use rules are negotiated, at many levels, however ideally, in a functioning common at the collective-choice level. Collective action is encouraged through a group's shared interests, and influenced by the size and productivity of the resource system (e.g. realised value, scarcity and accessibility of the resource units), and social and human capital within the part-owner community (Lidestav et al. 2017). It is delimited by e.g. alienation of certain user groups, locked power relations and conflict situations (Heinmiller 2009; Sandström et al. 2013).

Management of the commons and collective action situations are also influenced by contextual changes in the natural environment or societal changes such as industrialisation, changing resource value recognition or institutional change (Lidestav et al. 2017). Successful commons need to be able to adapt to changes. However, most commons are inherently viscous institutions restricted by path dependency. Path dependency is a constraint to development and adaptation as well as a constraint to collective action (Heinmiller 2009). To understand path dependency, the historical-institutional development of the organisation and decisions made in the past must be considered. Path dependency stems from positive feedback loops discouraging change, for example vested interests of certain part-owners, especially if combined with a strong hierarchy/ concentration of power. Furthermore, management regime levels are normally nested, which means that changes in one management level are either the results of or demands for changes in patterns in other levels (Steins & Edwards 1999). This means that changes are costly and reduce the probability of adaptation.

Recreational resources: The value of second home tourism

Second home tourism in relation to the commons is a so far overlooked area of research. In complex resource systems, second homes figure in a mixture of private/open access and common-pool property regimes. Even though the majority of research on commons considers regimes where the main resource value is productive, such as in timber extraction or water irrigation, almost all natural resource systems hold some level of recreational value that may or may not be realised within the common-pool community. Second home plots can make up the recreational resource itself, for example as leaseholds on common-pool land property. Second home associations are often represented as stakeholders in collective management actions, for example in the management of roads, beaches, lakes or other recreational resources.

In Finland and other Nordic countries, a public access regime, the legally protected Right of Public Access, has developed, comprising practically all natural areas. This right is not stated in one single law but draws from several legislative moments in the Finnish constitution (Tuunanen et al. 2012). It is strongly rooted in the Nordic tradition of outdoor recreation and is in the general discourse principally taken for granted (Fredman et al. 2013). The tourism sector in general benefits widely from this, relying on collective control of the natural resource units while exploiting the tourism revenue stream privately (Healy 1994; Sandell & Fredman 2010). The commons play a significant role in sustainable tourism development, stipulating environmental and moral ethics to delimit overuse of resources (Kaltenborn et al. 2001; Holden 2005).

In the Nordic countries, second home tourism has been called an "endemic" phenomenon (Gallent & Tewdwr-Jones 2001), closely intertwined with national history and identity. Even though second homes per definition are used on a temporal basis, they often represent and embody strong attachments to the place where they are located (Tuulentie 2007a). In Finland second homes play an important part in the imagery of the country's cultural landscape (Vepsäläinen & Pitkänen 2010), reflecting the significance of outdoor recreation and "traditional" activities (Hiltunen et al. 2013). Studies have shown that second homes are and continue to be highly valued by a large part of Finnish society (Pitkänen et al. 2014). Many second homes are passed down generations through inheritance and are strongly related to family roots and place-identity. It has even been questioned whether they are not truly to be considered as "first", or at least "alternate" homes (Kaltenborn 1998). Second home owners thus often develop strong feelings of attachment to the place where their second home is located, and it is fair to assume that they also develop strong opinions about their use rights to the natural resources in that area. Attractive second home areas have sometimes developed into contested spaces where conflicts arise between permanent and temporary residents (Janoschka & Haas 2013). As groups compete for shared resources, second home owners have been blamed for displacing local residents. The extent to which this has happened has however been debated (Marjavaara 2007; Hoogendoorn & Marjavaara, this volume). More often, second homes are seen as a generally contributing factor for local development, and second home owners are increasingly seen as active participants in local development and decision-making (Tuulentie 2007b; Rinne et al. 2014).

Method

The study presented in this chapter draws from fieldwork conducted in the five World Heritage municipalities in Kvarken Archipelago: Vaasa, Malax, Korsnäs, Korsholm and Vörå. Several commons organisations exist, both constitutionalised and more loosely managed privately owned commons, within the study site. For this study one constitutionalised common in each municipality was chosen. Basic criteria for selection were water area size, and number of part-owners. Data was originally collected for a wider purpose, and in the present chapter, four commons are included in the analysis (Figure 4.1): Sundom commons (Vaasa), Över- and Yttermalax commons (Malax), Molpe village commons (Korsnäs) and Björkö commons (Korsholm). As Maxmo archipelago commons (Vörå) divested their second home leaseholds when deciding to deposit all their assets into a foundation in 2000 they are excluded from the analysis.

Interview data make up the study's empirical material. The interview respondents comprise representatives of the commons' executive committees, and second home leaseholders in each common. All 5 semi-structured interviews with commons representatives and 12 with second

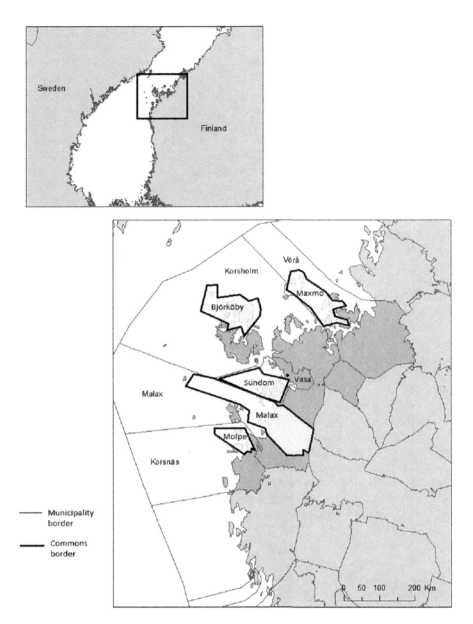

Figure 4.1 Map of commons.

home owners were carried out in 2014–2015. Representatives for the constitutionalised commons were asked about their management functions and principles, their organisational second home leasehold management system, and their perceptions of their own role in the local society. Second home owners were asked about how they value their second home, what the leasehold system means for them in terms of ability to develop their property and participation in decisions on resource management, control and transfer or property, and if and in what ways they seek to participate in collective action. A thematic qualitative analysis was conducted where the data was categorised into pre-determined themes. The themes were based on theorisation of common property management, specifically inspired by design principles or factors for successful governing of the commons (Ostrom 1990; Ostrom et al. 1994), and collective action in commons management (Steins & Edwards 1999; Heinmiller 2009; Sandström et al. 2013). The themes are:

1   Historical-institutional development of the commons, focusing on a) the external context within which the commons developed, and b) the internal composition of stakeholders. This explains the context within which the commons' management regimes have been developed.
2   Stakeholder interests, focusing on experiences and opinions of second home owners regarding for example terms of leasehold contracts, rights and obligations related to second home plots.
3   Collective action by second home owners and other stakeholders, including a) the social and human capital among part-owners and other local stakeholders, and b) platforms through which initiatives have been taken.

Results

Management regimes

In Kvarken Archipelago the water areas, including grazing meadows, shore areas and islets, remained in collective ownership after the large redistributions of land, first in the late 1700s and later in the 1920s, and commons organisations were established. At this time there was little state intervention in the ways the commons managed themselves and they developed organically depending on local contextual factors, for example composition of part-owners, size of the resource system and means of livelihood. In 1940 management of the commons was regulated in Finnish law, and subsequently developed into the *Law of the Commons* (18.8.1989/758), which lays down general rules for decision-making, transfer of property rights, distribution of dividends and other management issues. The larger commons adopted statutes as stipulated in the law and became constitutionalised, however statutes vary somewhat depending on which version of the law they are based upon and how strictly the legal text is adhered to. Figure 4.2 illustrates the three management regime levels of the commons organisations.

As emergent land accrues to the landowners, land elevation yearly adds to the common-pool resource stock, and today the commons own almost half of the water area in Kvarken

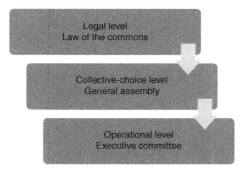

Figure 4.2   Management regime levels.

Archipelago. Part-ownership in the commons is based on ownership of private land properties in the villages and scaled according to hide (in Swedish *mantal*): the old measure for taxation of land properties (Jones 1987). Shares are thus formally tied to private land, and normally passed in inheritance to following generations. Membership can, technically, be acquired through purchasing a land property with tied shares; however, there is a reluctance to divest shares in this manner and they are now largely separated from the land properties. Individuals with no previous family connections to the village thus have very limited means of acquiring membership in the commons. Through inheritance and out-migration a sizeable proportion of part-members now reside outside of the local area.

The shares provide the basis of power distribution in the part-owner community. Most decisions are taken at the collective-choice level, through voting procedures at the General Assembly (GA). Deciding on issues of importance, for example election of executive committee, distribution of dividends or special leasehold agreements, is executed by using a proportional register of votes (scaled to shares). In the matter of routine management issues a voting per capita is most commonly used. The electoral register is proportional to individual sizes of shares meaning that small-scale owners hold an inferior position and are often ruled over by a few large shareholders. These power relations are quite cemented within the part-owner communities and sharply delimit collective action initiatives. This can partly be explained by the historical context within which the commons have developed, and partly by the social and human capital existing within the part-owner communities.

Kvarken Archipelago has traditionally been a small-scale farming and fishing society. The majority of individual part-owners hold very small shares as a result of several partitions, whereas a few landowners are still holding larger unsplit properties constituting a fair amount of shares. Originally, the collectively owned land in the archipelago was considered rather worthless, as it did not yield a high production value and was not well suited for agriculture. Forest properties yielded a high value and thus it followed that larger property owners had a power position superior to small-scale farmers and fishermen, whose interests were in the water areas. However, as tourism and second homes developed and became increasingly demanded, its recreational value has now been realised, and the commons are able to draw revenue from tourism service provision and second home leaseholds. The management regimes put down originally are, due to the proportional voting procedures, locked in path-dependency where the voting system cements its own existence.

Second home leaseholds

The studied commons lease altogether just over 860 second home plots, normally properties of 2,000 m^2 (Table 4.2). Normally the second home building itself is the private property of the leaseholder but can occasionally belong to the commons. Lease prices vary between €100 and 420 per annum, in some commons including a property taxation fee, whereas in others this is added on top. Principally, leases are only available for part-owners in the common; however, exemptions to this rule are made if no part-owners are willing to rent the plot. In Björkö commons non-part-owners are allowed to lease a plot for a higher price than the part-owners.

Contract engineering is stipulated through the commons' statutes, as regulated in the *Law of the Commons* (18.8.1989/758). Since the commons are granted some degree of freedom in formulating statutes, the contracts' designs differ somewhat. There are primarily three ways in which the leasehold contracts regulate the leaseholders' rights in relation to their second home: through length of the contract, transfer rights, and management of the plot. The length of leasehold contracts differs between 5 years, the most common span, and 30 years. The reason

Table 4.2 Second home leaseholds (2015)

	Björkö	Molpe	Sundom	Malax
Total area, ha (water area)	26,513 (20,206)	13,210 (8,600)	21,591 (15,585)	47,049 (20,410)
Part-owners in common	638	960	1,320	4,742
Number of second home leaseholds	176	60	460	170
Length of second home lease contracts (years)	30	5	5	5
Price (€) of second home lease (2000 m²)	Part-owner 160/ non-part-owner 420	100	420	120

for adopting shorter contracts can be traced to the Law of the commons (§ 15) stating that renewing contracts longer than five years needs a GA consent, which would make the process complicated. Normally, the renewal process is automatic given that the leaseholder is not guilty of serious neglect or disturbance. However, it is inconvenient for the second home owner as bank loans and building permissions are usually not permittable for such short contracts, which can have restrictive consequences when it comes to the upkeep of the property.

In the case of transferring a leasehold contract, the right to make decisions is held entirely by the commons. Transferring within the family through inheritance is normally not a difficult issue, given that the heir is a part-member. When a second home is sold to a third party, the executive committee holds the right to approve the new leaseholder. This means that the second home owner has, in principle, no control over the transfer of his/her private property (the building). It could also delimit the chances of selling the property for its "normal" market value, as the number of potential buyers is decreased.

The leaseholders are obliged to maintain the second home property in good condition during their lease. Within most commons the conduct of eliminating vegetation is free upon the leaseholders' judgement; in others the conduct is strictly controlled and the leaseholder needs to ask permission even for rather small alterations. The same control conduct is due in dredging operations although this is anchored in legal matters. The decision of dredging is legally taken by the property owners, in these cases the commons. The reason for dredging as well as where to place the sediment has to be decided by the commons together with the leaseholders. The work leaseholders invest in developing the second home property are not necessarily reduced from the yearly leasing fee or refunded when selling the second home leasehold property.

Collective action

Social and human capital among the part-owner community and other stakeholders in the area comprise the social resources needed to support development, such as networks, trust, reciprocity, exchanges, and levels of knowledge and skills among stakeholders. In a broad sense, knowledge regarding the commons is poor among the public. The perception is that older landowner generations are aware and informed about its history and meaning and their rights to the common-pool resource. Younger generations, if not landowners themselves, are quite unaware of this institution and the way the water resource is managed in Finland. The importance of the management regime, e.g. dividends logic, property rights, transfers and managerial procedures such as voting, is fairly unknown even within the part-owner community. This means that conflicts arise and sometimes become rather infected when part-members feel they have been wronged or marginalised, and that likelihood of changes are even lower as individuals do not understand how they could engage to bring changes about.

The level of knowledge about management of the commons is tightly related to the amount of networking and exchange that goes on between stakeholders. The GAs are usually attended by a fraction of the part-owner communities, notably by those with a higher level of knowledge, and holding a larger part of shares. Between the part-owner community and other users of the resource system, local boating and fishery associations are important mediators. As these associations are maintaining the shallow waterways, and the attractiveness of the resource system, some of the commons' dividends are set aside to compensate this work. However, according to the respondents, the associations deserve greater support from the commons than is perceived at the moment.

Other networks with an increasing importance are second home associations (SHA). In most areas in Ostrobothnia these institutions are scarce, only in one of the studied municipalities (Sundom village in Vaasa) a SHA is active. Its history is rather contested. The organisation re-emerged in 2015 after an interruption of over 10 years. Infected relationships and a lack of engaged individuals made the early SHA suffer and brought the activities to an early end. The renewed SHA has been well-received by the common as they felt a need for establishing a mutual forum of communication with the second home leaseholders rather than having one-to-one discussions. As most second home leaseholders hold just a fraction of the shares, the SHA could function as a mediator between the common and second home owners regarding leasehold fees and contracts but also practical matters such as upkeep of common roads, beaches and the archipelago waterways.

Sundom commons – A conflictual case

Among the studied cases, Sundom commons stands out as particularly conflictual. Located just south of the city of Vaasa, Sundom archipelago stretches from easy access and picturesque inner skerries to stony islets out at sea, and is an attractive second home area. In the analysis, several factors underlying these conflicts were identified. These are the attractiveness of Sundom archipelago as a recreational resource at the urban fringe, the prevalence of strong local elites in Sundom village, and the strong path dependency within the common's management regime, manifested in its dividend logic, voting system and social and human capital within the part-owner community. These factors develop into conflicts when they collide with the interests of less influential stakeholders in the area, primarily second home leaseholders wishing to protect their property and use rights, and members of the local boat and fairway association seeking compensation for maintenance work performed in the archipelago.

Sundom commons has the highest number of second home leaseholds in the area. Given the high demand for second homes, they also charge the highest prices. This means that Sundom commons enjoys a large and steady stream of revenue. The distribution of shares among the part-owners in Sundom commons is rather uneven, with a few individuals controlling a major part of the shares. As major decisions are taken at the GA by a proportional voting process, the few large shareholders can be understood as a local elite group in the organisation with a mandate to make decisions in their own favour. An example of a major issue is the common's dividend logic, which differs from the other studied commons, as dividends are not primarily reinvested into maintenance of the resource system but paid to part-owners as cash refunds on a regular basis. These refunds are scaled to the size of shares, which means that large shareholders make personal profit from this system. This of course in turn implies that their interests in terms of changing the system are vested. The largest part-owners own land and forest parcels away from the water areas and, according to some respondents, they thus have little "real interest" in the archipelago from where they draw the revenue. The dividends logic is viewed by many as a pure business strategy on behalf of large shareholders.

The power of the local elite is manifested at the operational level in several instances. The common has adopted statutes which are based on an early legislation on common-pool property management and have not been revised since the 1980s. The statutes adhere strictly to the written legal text and use rights at the second home leasehold are strictly controlled. An example is the maintenance of the second home plot, which is the responsibility of the leaseholder. When making alterations such as cutting trees on the plot, permission needs to be granted by the executive committee, and the wood produced is subject to a fee. Also, power is manifested during the renewal of leasehold contracts when leaseholders are required to appear before the committee to sign paper copies in person. The normal procedure in other commons is to use postal services and sign contracts at home.

The superiority of the local elite group is further strengthened by the concentration of human and social capital to the larger shareholders. As noticed earlier, knowledge about what the commons are, and especially how its management regime works, is rather low among smaller shareholders. Among the large shareholder families, network connections and knowledge seems to be higher, and some respondents expressed that the sons of executive committee members are being "groomed" for future committee service. Whether this is true or not, it can be noted that age and gender relations in the executive committee are unbalanced, as all members are males from the older generation. In one instance, a female has been up for election to the committee. However, despite winning the highest number of single votes, she lost the election in proportion of shares.

As proposed by Heinmiller (2009), the vested interests of the stakeholders combined with the concentration of decision-making power in the local elite group suggest that Sundom commons is locked in a situation of path dependency. The management regime put down originally dictates the way in which decisions can be made, and positive feedback loops encourage strong stakeholders to keep making decisions which cement the current regime. However this lock-in situation also means that the management regime is not developing and adapting to changes in society. Several respondents have started to believe that some major changes are bound to come through in the near future. One reasoning behind this is that the business logic is becoming too heavily dependent on administration, and that fees for dividend refund are becoming too large. Put simply, the common organisation is having an increasingly difficult time managing their increasingly commercial activities on an operational level.

Conclusions

This chapter presents second home leaseholds in a common-pool resource system, as well as empirically studied opportunities, rights and duties for second home leaseholders in the Kvarken Archipelago setting. As the society is undergoing a transformation the old traditional system of local power steering and social control collides with modern society's pattern of increased mobility. Family arrangements get blurred and ownership of property scattered around the world. These processes imply that villages are no longer a cohesive community. The post-productive society has also changed the values of natural resources implying the right of public access being transformed into a phenomenon where people regard their use rights more or less as universal. Visitors become locals when moving out to their second homes, bringing their "outside" opinions into local situations.

In the area where emergent land belongs to common ownership the commons institution in itself represents an important part of the local society. The role of the commons creates an important social factor among villagers and seasonal visitors. In this study Sundom commons is an exception where the power structure of the commons is more noticeable and demonstrates power in a more visible way than in the other three cases. The four examples are divided between creating advantages for their own good or for the good of local villages and the archipelago. Sundom belongs to the first category where revenue and profit is openly discussed, both locally and in the media, and is the cause of discontent among the second home community.

As constitutionalised commons tend to become village power institutions, some local societies are more affected than others. We have discussed second home leaseholders, SHAs and boat clubs as a few examples. Conflicts generally rise between second home leaseholders and the commons concerning fees and terms in regard to transfer of second home leasehold contracts. The infected interactions also create opportunities for collective action and conflict resolution among the stakeholders, one being the SHA. As in the Sundom case, the SHA creates a role of a mediator of conflicts and future development. There is room for more SHAs in Ostrobothnia in order to balance the voices of the commons against the ones of the second home leaseholders. There is furthermore an educational gap to be filled regarding the lack of awareness of the commons among part-owners and other natural resource stakeholders.

References

Carlsson, L. (2008) 'Omstridd natur i teori och praktik'. In C. Sandström, S. Hovik and E. I. Falleth (eds) *Omstridd natur: Ttrender och utmaningar i Nordisk naturförvaltning*. Umeå: Boréa, 33–59.

Eklund, E. (1989) 'Skärgårdspolitikens förändrade villkor', *Nordenskiöld Samfundets Tidskrift*, 49: 65–76.

Fennell, L. A. (2011) 'Ostrom's law: Property rights in the commons', *International Journal of the Commons*, 5 (1): 9–27.

Fredman, P., Stenseke, M., Sandell, K. and Mossing, A. (2013) *Friluftsliv i förändring*. Naturvårdsverket: Rapport nr 27.

Gallent, N. and Tewdwr-Jones, M. (2001) 'Second homes and the UK planning system', *Planning Practice and Research*, 16 (1): 59–69.

Harjula, A. (2007) *Gerby-Västervik, saariston kulttuuri-maisemainventointi*. Vasa: Österbottens museum/Vasa stadsplanering.

Healy, R. G. (1994) 'The "common pool" problem in tourism landscapes', *Annals of Tourism Research*, 21 (3): 596–611.

Heinmiller, T. B. (2009) 'Path dependency and collective action in common pool governance', *International Journal of the Commons*, 3 (1): 131–147.

Hiltunen, M. J., Pitkänen, K., Vepsäläinen, M. and Hall, C. M. (2013) 'Second home tourism in Finland: Current trends and eco-social impacts'. In Z. Roca (ed.) *Second Home Tourism in Europe: Lifestyle Issues and Policy Responses*. Farnham, UK: Ashgate, 165–198.

Höglund, K. and Uhlgrèn, A. (2008) *Sundomin saariston rakennusinventointi*. Vaasa, Finland: Österbottens Museum.

Holden, A. (2005) 'Achieving a sustainable relationship between common pool resources and tourism: The role of environmental ethics', *Journal of Sustainable Tourism*, 13 (4): 339–352.

Holmgren, E., Keskitalo, C. H. and Lidestav, G. (2010) 'Swedish forest commons – A matter of governance?', *Forest Policy and Economics*, 12 (6): 423–431.

Hysing, E. (2009) 'Statslös samhällsstyrning? Governance i svensk skogspolitik'. In G. Hedlund and S. Montin (eds) *Governance på Svenska*. Stockholm: Santérus Academic Press, 107–127.

Janoschka, M. and Haas, H. (eds) (2013) *Contested Spatialities, Lifestyle Migration and Residential Tourism*. London: Routledge.

Jansson, B. and Müller, D. (2003) *Fritidsboende i Kvarken*. Umeå, Sweden: Kvarkenrådet.

Jones, M. (1987) 'Land uplift, land tenure and the cultural landscape in Maxmo, Finland', *Bidrag till kännedom av Finlands natur och folk*, 135. Helsinki, Finland: Finska Vetenskaps Societeten, 235–247.

Kaltenborn, B. P. (1998) 'The alternate home–motives of recreation home use', *Norwegian Journal of Geography*, 53 (2): 121–134.

Kaltenborn, B. P., Haaland, H. and Sandell, K. (2001) 'The public right of access – Some challenges to sustainable tourism development in Scandinavia', *Journal of Sustainable Tourism*, 9 (5): 417–433.

Kellari, S. (2012) Stenig, karg och okonstlad – Kivinen, karu ja koruton. Master's Thesis. Oulu School of Architecture, Oulu University, Oulu, Finland.

Kooiman, J. (2003) *Governing as Governance*. London: Sage.

Lidestav, G., Poudyal, M., Holmgren, E. and Keskitalo, E. C. H. (2013) 'Shareholder perceptions of individual and common benefits in Swedish forest commons', *International Journal of the Commons*, 7 (1): 164–182.

Lidestav, G., Bogataj, N., Gatto, P., Lawrence, A., Stjernström, O. and Wong, J. (2017) 'Forests in common and their contribution to local development'. In E. C. H. Keskitalo (ed.) *Globalisation and Change in Forest Ownership and Forest Use: Natural Resource Management in Transition*. Basingstoke, UK: Palgrave Macmillan.

Marjavaara, R. (2007) 'The displacement myth: Second homes in the Stockholm archipelago', *Tourism Geographies*, 9 (3): 296–317.

Ostrom, E. (1990) *Governing the Commons: The Evolution of Institutions for Collective Action*. Cambridge: Cambridge University Press.

Ostrom, E. (1999) 'Private and common property rights'. In B. Bouckaert and G. De Geest (eds) *Encyclopedia of Law and Economics*. Cheltenham, UK: Edward Elgar, 332–379.

Ostrom, E., Gardner, R. and Walker, J. (1994) *Rules, Games and Common-Pool Resources*. Ann Arbor, MI: University of Michigan Press.

Pitkänen, K., Puhakka, R., Semi, J. and Hall, C. M. (2014) 'Generation Y and second homes: Continuity and change in Finnish outdoor recreation', *Tourism Review International*, 18 (3): 207–221.

Rhodes, R. (1997) *Understanding Governance: Policy Networks, Governance, Reflexivity and Accountability*. Buckingham: Open University Press.

Rinne, J., Paloniemi, R., Tuulentie, S. and Kietäväinen, A. (2014) 'Participation of second home users in local planning and decision-making – A study of three cottage-rich locations in Finland', *Journal of Policy Research in Tourism, Leisure and Events*, 7 (1): 98–114.

Sandell, K. and Fredman, P. (2010) 'The right of public access: Opportunity or obstacle in nature tourism in Sweden?', *Scandinavian Journal of Hospitality and Tourism*, 10 (3): 291–309.

Sandström, C., Wennberg DiGasper, S. and Öhman, K. (2013) 'Conflict resolution through ecosystem-based management: The case of Swedish moose management', *International Journal of the Commons*, 7 (2): 549–570.

Statistics Finland (2014) Population statistics for Korsholm, Korsnäs, Malax, Vaasa and Vörå municipalities. Retrieved from: www.stat.fi (accessed 21 October 2014).

Steins, N. A. and Edwards, V. M. (1999) 'Platforms for collective action in multiple-use common-pool resources', *Agriculture and Human Values*, 16 (3): 241–255.

Tuulentie, S. (2007a) 'Settled tourists: Second homes as a part of tourist life stories', *Scandinavian Journal of Hospitality and Tourism*, 7 (3): 281–300.

Tuulentie, S. (2007b) 'Local participation as a prerequisite for socially sustainable tourism: Case studies from the Ylläs and Levi ski resorts in Northern Finland'. In J. Jokimäki, M-J. Kaisanlahti-Jokimäki, S. Tuulentie, K. Laine and M. Uusitalo (eds) *Environment, Local Society and Sustainable Tourism*. Arctic Centre Reports Nr. 50. Rovaniemi, Finland: University of Lapland, 75–88.

Tuunanen, P., Tarasti, M. and Rautiainen, A. (eds) (2012) *Jokamiehenoikeudet ja toiminen toisen alueella. Lainsäädäntöä ja hyviä käytäntöjä*. Suomen Ympäristö 30/2012. Helsinki, Finland: Ympäristöministeriö.

UNESCO World Heritage Centre. (2006) 30COM 8B.27 – *Extension of properties inscribed on the World Heritage list* (Kvarken Archipelago/High Coast).

Vepsäläinen, M. and Pitkänen, K. (2010) 'Second home countryside: Representations of the rural in Finnish popular discourses', *Journal of Rural Studies*, 26 (2): 194–204.

Viljanen Rossi, R. (2014) *Hietalahden villa ja Bragen alue. Kulttuuriympäristöselvitys 2014*. Vaasa, Finland: Ostrobothnian Museum.

Vuori, O. (1968) *Huvilaväestön sosiaalinen käyttäytyminen*. Turku, Finland: Turku University.

5

RIGHTS TO THE RURAL

Comparison of political and property/ land rights of second home owners in Canada, Finland and Poland

Greg Halseth, Kati Pitkänen, Czesław Adamiak and Mia Vepsäläinen

Introduction

Second home use and ownership is a long-established topic of inquiry across a number of disciplines and literatures. One understudied area of research, however, involves the various sets of community and property rights and obligations that are tied to second home ownership and how these may vary by jurisdiction. In this chapter we examine a framework of community and property rights that apply to second home owners in Canada, Finland and Poland. In these countries with very different political regimes and heritage, non-local second homes are an increasingly important part of contemporary lifestyles and rural landscapes. In particular, we focus on two key issues: property rights with respect to the use and development of the property, and community rights with respect to participation in land-use planning and voting in local government elections. Based on the comparison, we discuss the consequences of different political systems to second home ownership.

The chapter is organised in four sections. Following this introduction, there is a background section that sets out the general directions of the multiple dwelling and property rights literature. The second substantive section includes a literature review on the dominant research themes in each of the Canadian, Finnish and Polish second home literature. The third section compares the three case study countries across two key issues: property rights and community rights. The final section is a discussion of the consequences of these different rights regimes for second home ownership.

Multiple dwelling and property and community rights

Multiple dwelling, including second homes, has become increasingly popular in contemporary Western societies (McIntyre et al. 2006). Besides labour mobility, this has been largely due to leisure- and tourism-related mobility and retirement migration. People increasingly choose to spend their lives living in multiple locations to pursue their quality of life goals and recreational interests. In the multiple dwelling and second homes literature it has been argued that the current administrative definitions and practices have not been able to respond to how people lead their lives (Hall 2015). The importance of mobility in everyday lives is largely disregarded while the political discourse favours the idea of terrestrial registration of the population (Ellingsen 2017).

The mobile life arrangements, however, have consequences not only for the lives of the multiple dwellers but also the locations where this mobility occurs. Researchers have argued that the hegemonic discourse of a singular place of living generates an inadequate picture of population distribution (Adamiak et al. 2017; Müller & Hall 2003). In countries such as Canada, Finland and Poland, second homes are often associated with mobile lifestyles consisting of a secondary property in a rural area, and a permanent residence in an urban area. While the registered population has increasingly concentrated in urban areas, a large number of people own and use a second home in the countryside leading to a substantial redistribution of the population during holiday seasons. Moreover, the change in ownership structures of rural properties is reflected in the changing values, behaviour and knowledge of the use of natural resources (Hiltunen et al. 2013).

The transformations linked to increasingly mobile lifestyles also challenge existing theory on residential mobility and property rights, political practices that tie property ownership to bundles of rights and obligations, and planning practices critical to managing the resulting social, economic, environmental and land-use pressures. Law is an important site for the production of mobilities; it enables or prevents mobility as it constructs the institutional context (e.g. nations, regions, home), and defines social relations (e.g. citizen, alien) (Cresswell 2006). In terms of multiple dwelling and second homes, the registration of one place of permanent residence is the premise for different formal and informal residential and civil rights in most jurisdictions. In many of those same jurisdictions, however, property ownership also entitles some rights that enable second home owners' public participation. Such political and civil rights are not necessarily based on local registration, but are governed at the regional or state level, and they will, of course, vary by jurisdiction.

There is a limited, but theoretically rich, property rights literature (Blomley 2010a). Property rights are the product of the expectations, and the rules governing those expectations, that societies have for the institutions of property and property ownership. These expectations and rules exist within the economic, social and political constructions of those societies. Included in the understanding of property rights are the ability to have and hold property, to use that property within some range of acceptable limits, and to exclude others (if one chooses) from the use and enjoyment of that owned property (Blomley 2010b).

The problem of space and property is made even more complex in settler societies such as Canada where one socio-legal system is replaced with another. Collisions of past and current practices can linger for generations (Blomley 2014) and underscore ongoing debate and contention about the very meaning of property and property rights. Finland, in contrast, is an example of a Nordic society balancing between historically strong private property rights on one hand and public control on the other, also with a strong legacy of common rights and free passage on private and public lands. In Poland, the post-war communist regime discriminated against private property, yet did not manage to completely eliminate it as happened in other communist countries. After the democratic transformation, the domination of a liberal discourse has led to prioritisation of private property rights over public control (Izdebski 2013).

While the property rights literature has experienced increased interest, much of that interest remains within urban settings, within developing countries, and on specific topics such as Indigenous/Aboriginal rights. In this paper we seek to extend not only the literature on second homes, but also on the property rights and community rights of non-local second home property owners in rural areas.

Second homes in Canada, Finland and Poland – National contexts and literatures

This section includes a review of the dominant research themes in each of the Canadian, Finnish and Polish second home literatures. In each of these countries, second homes are an important part of the history, culture, economy and land use (Halseth 1998; Kowalczyk 1994; Pitkänen 2011), and yet in each there has been limited attention to the topics of property and community rights.

Canada

The Canadian second home literature is well established and has covered a number of topic areas. However, it has not explored in depth those topics connected with the legal and political rights of second home owners. That said, the Canadian literature has considerable strength in studies of the iconography of rural amenity landscapes and the lifestyles that grew up around the Canadian second home or "cottage" (Bunce 1994; Luka 2010). In this sense, the idealised imagery associated with the rural countryside has been defined and re-defined by people who may only occasionally visit these rural places.

Another strength in Canadian research is with the settlement structure and socio-demographic makeup of second home areas. Classic Canadian models of the city's countryside or the urban field usually have their outer limits described by the commuting zone within which people are willing to travel for weekend recreation activities and to access second home properties (Bryant et al. 1982). Within this geography, studies have explored the specific socio-demographic makeup of second home areas and second home owners (Wolfe 1965; Lehr et al. 1991). The desire to seek respite from urban life, the need for the financial assets to afford such properties and the connection to the iconography of rural retreat lifestyles has since become a central part of much second home research in Canada. More recent concern has turned to how this idealised image is being impacted by rising demand and scarcity of supply to enhance the elite status of cottage property (Halseth 2004).

Perhaps the most extensive body of second home research in Canada looks at its land use and planning implications. Much of this focuses on the historical development, morphological form and evolving housing styles of second home landscapes (Wolfe 1951; Svenson 2004). Part of this groundbreaking work was to put second homes onto the research agenda by demonstrating their importance in rural areas, but another part was to develop a definitional framework of second homes. Additional work focused on land-use planning tools for tracking and managing second home development and conversion into year-round residences. In terms of the political and property rights, Beck and Hussey (1989) explored property rights in terms of a planning interest in converting public waterfront lands to private property for sale to second home developers, while Halseth's (1998) study included land-use planning debates that highlighted the participation of second home owners and cottager associations.

Finally, some writers have looked at the question of second home ownership within large planned resort developments (Chipeniuk 2005). Research has highlighted the continuing importance of second home property ownership, that second home owners are relatively more affluent than the Canadian population generally, and that the planning of large resorts challenges the capacity of small communities to manage the resulting disruptive and transformative impacts.

Finland

In Finland, along with other Nordic countries, the ownership and use of second homes is particularly common. Because of this, second homes have become an important topic for rural and regional development and policies. During past decades, a large number of development reports, studies and surveys have been published. These studies have often focused on the importance of second homes to rural development including rural service use and accessibility as well as their economic, social and environmental impacts. Second homes are recorded in the nation-wide cadastral register as well as the population information system, and changes in the second home stock and the value of second home transactions are reported annually (Statistics Finland, National Land Survey). In addition to these, the Finnish Islands Committee (under Ministry of Agriculture and Forestry) commissions a second home barometer, a follow-up survey providing information on the use of second homes, their equipment and second home related spending.

The Finnish academic literature on second homes is well established. Second homes have been a popular topic of research especially since the 2000s, although the first second home studies date back to the 1960s and 1970s. Popular topics in Finnish second home literature have been the distribution and spatial development of second home areas (e.g. Pitkänen 2011), and the economic, social and environmental impacts of second homes (Hiltunen et al. 2013). Likewise, researchers have looked at motives, cultural meanings and iconography of second home landscapes (e.g. Vepsäläinen & Pitkänen 2010) and studied how the current second home culture is changing and what second home futures may look like (e.g. Pitkänen et al. 2014). More recently, the perspective has shifted from rural second homes into seeing second homes as a part of a broader phenomenon of multiple dwelling and multi-local lifestyles. Researchers have looked at mobility patterns and environmental consequences of hypermobile lifestyles (e.g. Adamiak et al. 2016) and transborder second home ownership and mobilities (Hannonen 2016). Traditional dichotomies between rural and urban, local and outsider, home and away have been questioned and researchers have increasingly focused on the challenges of multi-level and multi-sector governance of multiple dwelling (Vepsäläinen et al. 2015).

The legal and political rights of second home owners have not been explicitly studied or dealt with in the academic literature. However, some development studies and reports have been commissioned by different ministries to find solutions to rural policy issues and facilitate decision-making. Reports have studied the cost of non-local second home owners to municipal economies by listing second home owners' rights and obligations in terms of using local public services and infrastructure (e.g. Sisäasiainministeriö 2006). In addition, studies have looked at second home owners' democratic rights and access to local decision-making as a response to the policy debate on dual citizenship (Aho & Ilola 2008) which would give individuals the possibility to be full members of two municipalities. The need for more academic research on legal and political rights has recently been emphasised (Rinne et al. 2014).

Poland

The number of second homes in Poland has been growing since the 1960s, and this growth accelerated significantly in the 1990s. Yet, the increasing importance of second homes and the development of rural areas have not been reflected by sufficient academic interest, let alone studies of legal regulations and policy practices. There is very sparse statistical information on the numbers or distribution of second homes (Czarnecki & Frenkel 2015), and studies on second homes have been mostly performed on regional scales, usually within the suburban zones of large cities (Kowalczyk 1994).

Research on second homes in Poland is mostly performed by geographers, thus one of the key issues is their location and impacts on the spatial structure of settlements, landscapes and the environment. In the 1970s and 1980s, several publications raised the problems of planning second home settlements (Śliwińska-Ładzińska 1981). After the political and economic change of the 1990s, and the subsequent withdrawal of public authorities from planning activity, geographers turned to describing the effects of unplanned and spontanuous second home development in rural and natural areas (Mika 2013; Adamiak 2016). Other studies treat second homes as a part of tourism infrastructure and are often placed within tourism models (Włodarczyk 2009) where the development of second homes is seen as a part of a tourism colonisation process, which can later lead to tourism urbanisation through the conversion of second homes into primary residences or other uses (Makowska-Iskierka 2011).

A relatively new aspect in Polish research is the economic contribution of second homes to rural areas. Heffner and Czarnecki (2015) studied several locations and identified positive impacts of second home development on the economies of rural areas: an increase in the income of local enterprises, farmers and authorities, the development of new infrastructure, and a slowing rural depopulation. They, as well as Adamiak (2014), found that the main sources of income for local communities from second homes was generated by grocery shopping, land purchases, the construction of new second homes, as well as property taxes. A significant part of second home owners' contribution to local economies is through the informal sector and the direct sale of food or the provision of services (Heffner & Czarnecki 2015). On the other hand, second homes are seen to be only a supplementary source of resources for rural residents, and their contribution to local economy is highly dependent on local context (Adamiak 2014; Czarnecki 2014).

Comparison

This third section compares the three case countries across two key issues: property rights (ability to have, use, develop, and exclude others) and community rights (participation in local planning, voting in local elections and tax obligations) (Table 5.1).

Property rights

All three countries have strong private landowner rights that are protected by common law and provincial legislation (Canada) or constitution and several other sets of laws (Finland, Poland). In general, no differentiation is made between permanent and second home property owners. Some differences, however, exist in terms of who can buy land, where and what type of land or properties can be bought by private people. In Poland, only active farmers are allowed to buy farm land; however, farmsteads no longer in farming use, as well as building plots not registered as farm land, can be bought as second homes. These restrictions have been tightened in 2016 in reaction to the opening of the Polish property market. Poland had to equalise the regulations for European Union (EU) residents with those for Polish residents, so the regulations for all were tightened in order to prevent foreign residents from buying out the land. There are no similar restrictions in Canada. In Finland no restrictions exist, although foreigners have been allowed to buy second homes without restrictions only since 2000, as a consequence of the accession of Finland into the EU and Schengen area.

In all three countries, second home development and construction are mostly governed at the local level by land-use plans and building permit regulations. Provincial, regional and national regulation overrides local plans in some cases, such as for protected areas, roads and energy networks. In Poland, for instance, owners of agricultural land/properties cannot change the use of the land or build anything more than extending existing farmhouses or building new constructions related to farming which also limits the rights of second home owners. Most areas of Canada have similar restrictions in place to protect agricultural lands from non-farm development. In Finland, the general principle is that land-use planning should not restrict

Table 5.1 Rights and obligations with respect to the use and development of the property

	British Columbia	Finland	Poland
Right to own and purchase land	• Same rights for permanent and second home owners • No restrictions on buying different types of land/properties	• Same rights for permanent and second home owners • No restrictions on type of land/properties • No restrictions to non-residents since 2000	• Same rights for permanent and second home owners • Special restrictions on buying farming land (and forests) • Same rights for all EU citizens since 2016
Rights to develop and construct	• Governed mostly at local level: community plans, zoning, development permits and building regulations • Provincial regulation applies in some cases (forest and water areas, protected areas, infrastructure networks) • Seasonal properties generally not differentiated from other properties	• Governed mostly at local level: town plans and municipal master plans, building permits and building regulations • Regional land-use plans override local plans in some cases (roads, energy, etc., infrastructure networks, protected areas, commercial areas) • Seasonal properties differentiated from other properties in land-use plans and registering the intended use of property in cadastre/building permits	• Governed mostly at local level: zoning plans and planning permissions • Additional regulation applies in some cases (agricultural and forest land, protected areas) • Seasonal properties differentiated from other properties in land-use plans
Conversion into permanent home	• Generally few restrictions on conversion of second homes to permanent residences • Regulated by building permits, and availability of adequate water and sewer services	• Building permission needed for converting second home into a permanent residence • One can register permanent place of residence at second home even without conversion	• No permission needed for converting second home into a permanent residence • One can register their permanent place of residence in any of their properties
Land areas, shoreline access and water rights	• Private property rights prevent trespassing over private property • Shoreline and water rights owned by the government as "crown land" • Crown land/water areas are freely accessible	• Everyman's right guarantees free access of all land and water areas • Shoreline owned by landowners and water rights held by partnerships of local landowners	• Landowners can restrict access to their properties • State-owned areas are freely accessible • Shoreline owned by landowners • Water rights held by state (excluding small ponds) • Free access to shores

property owners' rights. Authority over second home development is increasingly given to local municipalities who, after a recent bill by the government, no longer have to consult regional environmental authorities when clearing building permits.

Second homes are differentiated from other properties and land use in the three countries in similar ways. In Canada, local land-use plans and zoning bylaws specify permitted uses. In some cases, areas may be designated for second home development based on the availability of services or the sensitivity of the environment. However, most rural plans and zoning do not distinguish between full- and part-time housing occupancy in its "residential" land-use categories. In terms of building regulations, both seasonal and permanent dwellings must be built to the same standards. In Finland, local land-use plans set aside plots and areas reserved for seasonal use only and the intended use of a building is registered in the building permit and cadastre (e.g. permanent home or second home). If no land-use plan exists, landowners can commission their own plan or apply for an "exception" permit. Regulations and technical demands for building a second home are less strict than for permanent houses. It has been held important that second home ownership remains affordable and accessible to most people. In Poland, the municipal council may evaluate zoning plans ("local plan of spatial management") for any area, with detailed regulations on type of allowable construction and land use. Zoning plans may include areas for residential buildings and areas for individual recreation/summer houses. If there is no zoning plan for a given area, one needs to obtain a planning permission which is based on general rules. This planning control is quite weak and may be easily avoided, which has resulted in the uncontrolled dispersion of second homes in some areas (Adamiak 2016).

Moving permanently to one's second home is a topic that has been debated, especially in Finland and Canada. In Finland, converting a second home into a permanent residence requires permission from the municipality in order to change the registered use of the building. It has been raised as a potential violation to people's rights that some municipalities clear permits easily whereas some decline most permits or clear only temporary permits. Municipalities near major urban areas which are facing land-use pressure have especially been reluctant to support urban sprawl and low-density development (Vepsäläinen et al. 2015). People can in practice register as permanent residents at their second home at the registry office even without local government permission. In such cases, however, they are considered either as living illegally at their second homes or homeless which limits their rights to access certain services. In Poland, one can register their permanent place of residence in any of their properties. Registered residence does not need to be the place where one actually spends the most time. One can move to a second home permanently, even if it is built on an area designed for recreation housing. In Canada, there is no similar registration process for people or building use. As a result, and when coupled with relatively permissive rural residential zoning, the conversion of second homes to permanent residences is limited more by the availability of adequate water and sewer services. In some regions, this has created significant problems with urban sprawl and in others it has created considerable rural community conflict.

In Canada and Poland, landowners have a right to prevent trespassing and roaming on their property. Crown and state areas, however, are freely accessible. In Finland the everyman's right, which is based on customary law, guarantees free access to all land and water areas and no difference is made between private and public land. In all three countries, shoreline and water areas are freely accessible to anyone. In Canada, shorelines and water areas are owned by the province. In British Columbia (BC), the provincial government removed the ability of property owners to hold water rights in the 1950s in order to protect public access to shorelines and watercourses. In Finland, the shoreline is owned by landowners and water rights are held by partnerships of local landowners. Private owners, however, cannot restrict shoreline access due to the everyman's right. In practice, intensive second home developments on shorelines have restricted public access as private buildings and their immediate surroundings are within the laws of private peace. Similarly in Poland, if a private property borders a lake/river, landowners must grant free access to the shoreline for anyone. All water areas and consequently water rights, except for very small ponds, are owned by the state and freely accessible.

Community rights

Second home owners have similar possibilities for taking part in the local development processes and land-use planning in all three countries (Table 5.2). In BC and Finland, all property owners have a special right to be consulted and informed of plans and developments near their property. In Canada, provincial legislation designates processes for the general notification of the area's population of planning/development debates and for the specific notification of property owners within close proximity to any lands where the use designation may be changing. In Finland, second home owners have been influential, especially in appealing against developments threatening local landscape and quality of nature values (e.g. wind farms, peat production, mining). In Poland, stakeholders must be consulted, but the municipal councils in charge of the plans do not have to take their opinions into account.

Table 5.2 Rights to the local community

	British Columbia	Finland	Poland
Land-use planning and building	• Everybody can participate • Property owners (does not differentiate between permanent and second homes) have special rights of notice, participation, and to be consulted	• All stakeholders can participate in the preparation of land-use plans and appeal against them • Property owners or holders (does not differentiate between permanent and second homes) are always consulted/informed	• Municipal councils consult all stakeholders (does not differentiate between permanent and second homes), but do not need to take their opinions into account
Voting in local elections, democratic rights	• Residents and property owners are eligible to vote • Second home property owners are eligible for one vote per property	• Only residents are eligible to vote • Second home committees set by some local governments	• Only residents are eligible to vote
Property taxation, importance for local economies	• Local government highly dependent on property tax for operating revenue • Property tax based on real market value • No differentiation between permanent and second homes	• Local government less dependent on property tax revenue • Property tax based on taxation value (size of land area and floor area of buildings) • Higher tax rates for second homes	• Local government less dependent on property tax revenue • Property tax based on size of land area and floor area of buildings • Higher tax rates for second homes

Canada differs significantly from Finland and Poland in terms of second home owners' democratic rights to vote in local government elections. Historically, local government voting was limited in Canada only to those who held property in the jurisdiction. Many decades ago this was expanded to include all residents living within the jurisdiction. As long as one meets the basic eligibility criteria of age, one is also eligible to vote in a local government jurisdiction if they own property within that jurisdiction. Seasonal home property owners, therefore, do qualify as a property owner to vote in local government elections where their second home property is located but they get only one vote per seasonal-use property. In Finland, property owners have the status of a member of a municipality, which, however, does not give them the right to vote in local elections. Thus, in Finland, and likewise in Poland, only permanent residents of the municipality are eligible to vote in local government elections. These are EU (in Finland this also includes Norwegian and Icelandic) citizens registered in the municipality and citizens of other countries under some circumstances. In Finland, the lack of democratic rights of second home owners has been acknowledged as a problem and some municipalities have set an elected second home committee to work as an advisory board for the municipal council.

Canada also differs from the other two countries in terms of taxation. In BC, local governments depend upon property taxation for the bulk of their operating revenues. Properties are taxed based on their real market value and there are no differences between permanently and seasonally occupied properties. There are reductions in property taxes based on age (for those over 65 years) and for homeowners (this being the one place where property owners must declare a "permanent residence" to earn the property tax reduction). In Finland and Poland, property tax has less importance for local government budgets while personal income tax brings the biggest revenues. In both these countries, the property tax is calculated based on the size of the land area and floor area of buildings. Property tax rates are established by the municipal council and the top limit is set by central government. In both countries, properties registered in cadastre (Finland) and/or building permits (Finland and Poland) intended for second homes, have higher tax rates than other types of buildings. Different taxes for different types of buildings have meant that in Poland second homes are often built formally as permanent residences or registered as farms. In Finland, old farm houses or former residential buildings converted to second home use are often registered as empty dwellings to avoid paying the higher tax. In Finland, there have been debates over the possibility of second home owners to register as double-citizens of multiple municipalities, sharing their personal income tax between permanent and second home municipalities. Thus far, however, such initiative has been deemed legislatively and bureaucratically too demanding.

Discussion

Based on the comparison of property rights and community rights linked to second home ownership, this discussion will concentrate on three matters: implications for individual rights, implications for planning and policy development, and authority over second home development.

Individual rights

In terms of implications for individual rights, ownership of second home property in all three countries is not restricted. In Finland and Poland, there were limitations for foreigners before EU membership, and in Finland today there are debates about foreign ownership of second home property. The only notable exception to individual rights of ownership is in Poland where one has to be a farmer to own certain types of rural property.

In each country, there are generally strong ownership rights embedded in law, with environmental protection being one of the few ways by which these may be overridden. The conversion of second home properties to permanent residences (or vice versa) has proven difficult to regulate in each of the three countries. In Poland and Finland, registration of permanent residency provides one, however imperfect, way by which to manage or at least track such processes.

The most notable implication for individual rights is with respect to local government voting. In Canada, as a taxpayer and local voter, second home owners can exert considerable influence over local matters. In Finland and Poland, in contrast, second home owners are "invisible people" who must use more indirect means to exert influence on local matters.

Implications for planning and policy development

In each of the three countries, second home development is largely associated with high amenity landscapes – along watercourses and in mountain areas. Additionally, there are historic cases of second home ownership as suburban "retreats". While such geographies influence current and future land-use planning, the allocation of public and private use rights is also important. As noted, these differ between the three countries based largely on the heritage of customary laws and practices. How these customary laws and practices impact public access to amenity landscapes is a significant matter in second home area planning and policy development.

The availability and readiness of various tools to track and manage development and change is also important in planning and policy development for second home areas. While land-use plans as well as zoning and building regulations were noted in each of the three countries, differences in the importance of recreational land planning and property taxation to local governments can influence their attention to second home development. In cases of property conversion, it is proving increasingly difficult to maintain a differentiation between different types of properties. Even in those jurisdictions where properties and land uses are registered, there can be differences in the legal registration versus the actual use of properties.

Second home owners differed across the three countries in terms of their local political power, and their ability to influence local planning and policy development. In Canada, through their property tax and voting rights, second home owners are an essential part of the local power landscape. In Finland and Poland, while less directly influential, increasingly high numbers of second homes in some rural areas provide a foundation for their influence in planning and policy development. In Finland, in particular, the vast number of second homes has made them an important rural policy issue at the national level.

Authority over second home development

In all three countries, authority over second home development rests at the local level. As a result, different municipalities will manage and plan such development based on their own priorities. Across the three countries, there were different tools available to local governments for tracking and managing second home development and ownership. Depending upon the context, second home development, and the more intensive conversion of second homes to permanent residences, will occur based on local circumstances. This results in considerable unevenness both within and across national contexts and increasing concern for the equitability of ownership rights.

Conclusions

This initial study of property rights and community rights for second home owners in Canada, Finland and Poland has identified similarities and differences. In Finland, the context is messy and difficult to change, with rights systems based on both statutory laws and a long history of customary law. In Canada, the system is newer, simpler and retains strong (British origin) common law rights around private property ownership. In Poland, regulations and practices are often not suited to mobile lifestyles and multiple residences (a "slippage" linking back to the communist era when second homes were often purchased/rented informally to avoid strict property market controls).

Regulations across countries differ on two axes. The first is the rootedness of second homes in the regulatory system and the (economic) importance of second homes (highest probably in Finland). The second is the place of property in the regulatory system. This is probably highest in Canada where voting rights can still be tied to property, and where the property tax is so important in local budgets.

This initial comparison invites additional studies of property rights and community rights in these and other national settings. For example, there is a need to explore eligibility to use local services, and the implications of different semi-formal rights and customary laws. It would also be interesting to compare countries with different second home development characteristics, such as those with stricter control over rural land use (UK), higher foreign ownership (Spain), a more egalitarian tradition of second homes (Czechia), or with tighter restrictions on second home development (Switzerland). We hope this chapter inspires such additional research.

References

Adamiak, C. (2014) 'Importance of second homes for local economy of a rural tourism region', paper presented at International Antalya Hospitality Tourism and Travel Research Conference, December 9–12. [online] Available at: http://www.onlinehotel.pro/projects/IHTRC/Proceedings-IAHTTRC.pdf#page=372

Adamiak, C. (2016) 'Cottage sprawl: Spatial development of second homes in Bory Tucholskie, Poland', *Landscape and Urban Planning*, 147: 96–106.

Adamiak, C., Pitkänen, K. and Lehtonen, O. (2017) 'Seasonal residence and counterurbanization: The role of second homes in population redistribution in Finland', *GeoJournal*, 82 (5): 1035–1050.

Aho, S. and Ilola, H. (2008) Kahden kunnan asukkaat – Lisää osallisuutta? Lapin yliopiston matkailun ja liiketoiminnan tiedekunnan julkaisuja. B. Tutkimusraportteja ja selvityksiä 1, Rovaniemi.

Beck, R. L. and Hussey, D. (1989) 'Politics, property rights, and cottage development', *Canadian Public Policy/Analyse de Politiques*, 15 (1): 25–33.

Blomley, N. K. (2010a) 'Property, liberty and the category', *Geoforum*, 41 (3): 353–355.

Blomley, N. K. (2010b) 'Cuts, flows, and the geographies of property', *Law, Culture and the Humanities*, 7 (2): 203–216.

Blomley, N. K. (2014) 'Making space for property', *Annals of the Association of American Geographers*, 104 (6): 1291–1306.

Bryant, C. R., Russwurm, L. H. and McLellan, A. G. (1982) *The City's Countryside: Land and Its Management in the Rural-Urban Fringe*. London and New York: Longman Group Limited.

Bunce, M. (1994) *The Countryside Ideal: Anglo-American Images of Landscape*. London and New York: Routledge.

Chipeniuk, R. (2005) 'Planning for the advent of large resorts: Current capacities of interior British Columbia mountain communities', *Environments*, 33 (2): 57–69.

Cresswell, T. (2006) 'The right to mobility: The production of mobility in the courtroom', *Antipode*, 38 (4): 735–754.

Czarnecki, A. (2014) 'Economically detached? Second home owners and the local community in Poland', *Tourism Review International*, 18 (3): 153–166.

Czarnecki, A. and Frenkel, I. (2015) 'Counting the "invisible": Second homes in Polish statistical data collections', *Journal of Policy Research in Tourism, Leisure and Events*, 7 (1): 15–31.

Ellingsen, W. (2017) 'Rural second homes: A narrative of de-centralisation', *Sociologia Ruralis*, 57 (2): 229–244.

Hall, C. M. (2015) 'Second homes planning, policy and governance', *Journal of Policy Research in Tourism, Leisure and Events*, 7 (1): 1–14.

Halseth, G. (1998) *Cottage Country in Transition: A Social Geography of Change and Contention in the Rural-Recreational Countryside.* Montreal: McGill-Queen's University Press.

Halseth, G. (2004) 'The "cottage" privilege: Increasingly elite landscapes of second homes in Canada'. In D. Mueller and C. M. Hall (eds) *Tourism, Mobility and Second Homes: Between Elite Landscapes and Common Ground.* Clevedon, UK: ChannelView Publications, 35–54.

Hannonen, O. (2016) Peace and Quiet Beyond the Border: The Trans-Border Mobility of Russian Second Home Owners in Finland. PhD. Social Sciences and Business Studies No 118, University of Eastern Finland, 18, Joensuu, Finland.

Heffner, K. and Czarnecki, A. (2015) 'Linking locally: Second home owners and economic development of the rural community'. In P. Dannenberg and E. Kulke (eds) *Economic Development in Rural Areas: Functional and Multifunctional Approaches.* Farnham, UK: Ashgate, 185–210.

Hiltunen, M. J., Pitkänen, K., Vepsäläinen, M. and Hall, C. M. (2013) 'Second home tourism in Finland – Current trends and eco-social impacts'. In R. Zoran (ed.) *Second Home Tourism in Europe: Lifestyle Issues and Policy Responses.* Farnham, UK: Ashgate, 165–198.

Izdebski, H. (2013) *Ideologia i zagospodarowanie przestrzeni* [Ideology and Land Management]. Warsaw: Lex.

Kowalczyk, A. (1994) *Geograficzno-społeczne problemy zjawiska "drugich domów"* [Geographical and Social Problems of "Second Homes" Phenomenon]. Warsaw: WGiSR UW.

Lehr, J. C., Selwood, J. and Badiuk, E. (1991) 'Ethnicity, religion, and class as elements in the evolution of Lake Winnipeg resorts', *The Canadian Geographer*, 35 (1): 46–58.

Luka, N. (2010) 'Of McMansions, timeshare cottages, and zebra mussels: Dispatches from the second-home settings of Central Ontario'. In K. B. Beesley (ed.) *The Rural-Urban Fringe in Canada: Conflict and Controversy.* Brandon, MB: Rural Development Institute, Brandon University, 199–219.

McIntyre, N., Williams, D. and McHugh, K. (2006) 'Power and the politics of place'. In N. McIntyre, D. Williams and K. McHugh (eds) *Multiple Dwelling and Tourism. Negotiating Place, Home and Identity.* Wallingford, UK: CAB International, 135–237.

Makowska-Iskierka, M. (2011) *Procesy urbanizacyjne na terenach turystyczno-wypoczynkowych strefy podmiejskiej Łodzi* [Urbanization Processes on the Tourism-Recreation Areas of Łódź Suburban Zone], Łódź: ŁTN.

Mika, M. (2013) 'Spatial patterns of second homes development in the Polish Carpathians'. In J. Kozak, K. Ostapowicz, A. Bytnerowicz and B. Wyżga (eds) *The Carpathians: Integrating Nature and Society towards Sustainability.* Heidelberg, Germany: Springer, 497–512.

Müller, D. K. and Hall, C. M. (2003) 'Second homes and regional population distribution: On administrative practices and failures in Sweden', *Espace, Populations, Sociétés*, 21 (2): 251–261.

Pitkänen, K. (2011) Mökkimaisema muutoksessa: Kulttuurimaantieteellinen näkökulma mökkeilyyn. PhD. Social Sciences and Business Studies, University of Eastern Finland, Joensuu, Finland.

Pitkänen, K., Puhakka, R., Semi, J. and Hall, C. M. (2014) 'Generation Y and second homes: Continuity and change in Finnish outdoor recreation', *Tourism Review International*, 18 (3): 207–221.

Rinne, J., Kietäväinen, A., Tuulentie, S. and Paloniemi, R. (2014) 'Governing second homes: A study of policy coherence of four policy areas in Finland', *Tourism Review International*, 18 (3): 223–236.

Sisäasiainministeriö. (2006) *Mökkiläiset kuntapalvelujen käyttäjinä.* Saaristoasiain neuvottelukunta, Efeko Oy, Sisäasiainministeriön julkaisuja 24, Helsinki.

Śliwińska-Ładzińska, W. (1981) *Urbanistyczne problemy domów wakacyjnych w Polsce* [Urbanistic Problems of Vacation Houses in Poland]. Warsaw-Łódź: PWN.

Svenson, S. (2004) 'The cottage and the city: An interpretation of the Canadian second home experience'. In D. Mueller and C. M. Hall (eds) *Tourism, Mobility and Second Homes: Between Elite Landscapes and Common Ground.* Clevedon, UK: ChannelView, 55–74.

Vepsäläinen, M. and Pitkänen, K. (2010) 'Second home countryside: Representations of the rural in Finnish popular discourses', *Journal of Rural Studies*, 26 (2): 194–204.

Vepsäläinen, M., Strandell, A. and Pitkänen, K. (2015) 'Muuttuvan vapaa-ajan asumisen hallinnan haasteet kunnissa', *Yhdyskuntasuunnittelu*, 53 (2): 13–38.

Włodarczyk, B. (2009) *Przestrzeń turystyczna – Istota, koncepcje, determinanty rozwoju* [Tourism Space: Essence, Concepts, Determinants of Development], Łódź: UŁ.

Wolfe, R. I. (1951) 'Summer cottagers in Ontario', *Economic Geography*, 27 (1): 10–32.

Wolfe, R. I. (1965) 'About cottages and cottagers', *Landscape*, 15 (1): 6–8.

6

NATIONAL MEXICAN TOURISM POLICY AND NORTH AMERICAN SECOND HOME OWNERS IN MEXICO

Local tourism development and Mexican identity

Helene Balslev Clausen and Mario Alberto Velázquez García

Introduction

Tourism has increasingly become a core part of the economic growth strategies for many Latin American countries. Thus the states have an interest in the planning process of tourism-related activities, however this is not a linear and unidirectional process, rather it involves different time lapses, spaces and actors. One of the main drivers for the Mexican State has been to develop tourism policies to address and regulate the increasing tourism demand (e.g. remove barriers to growth), promote initiatives to attract investment (e.g. reduce environmental regulation), avoid market failures (e.g. support governance arrangements to enhance industry coordination) and reconstruct the Mexican identity. The central state may achieve this by imposing an audit culture and rules about spending and activities, or by promising or withholding central resources from local and non-state actors so that a pattern of reliance is established, which consolidates the central government's influence (Bevir & Richards 2009). Since the middle of the last century the tourism industry has played a pivotal role of the *intentionality* of the Mexican State (Berger 2006). Scholars normally assume tourism activities as *given* without questioning their origins. However, the Mexican State's narrative does not include transnational mobilities as second home owners, or international tourists as imperative social actors in the elaboration of tourism policies and the reconstruction of the Mexican identity. This chapter explores the interactions and relations between the Mexican national tourism policies and the norms and values of these transnational communities of North American second home owners in Mexico. Even though this group does not partake *intentionally* in the policy process, we argue that this transnational group significantly shapes the decisions made by policy actors. Limited attention in the tourism field has so far been given to the influence of North American second home owners in Mexico (Clausen 2008; Croucher 2012), and how the action arena is constructed, which is the social space where actors interact, solve problems and exchange goods and services.

Our analytical framework takes its point of departure in a sociological perspective of public policy using the social construction of reality as defined by Schneider and Ingram (1993).

Second home owners in Mexico are conceptualised as temporary visitors who admire, buy and consume cultural attractions and objects. In contrast, this chapter seeks to demonstrate how shared attributes of the North American community play a pivotal role in reinventing and creating practices and meanings of Mexican culture and identity to generate a particular view about locations, activities and the national Mexican identity in these tourism destinations. Thus they partake in the construction of the reality of tourism in Mexico.

The two empirical settings, Álamos in the State of Sonora in northern Mexico and Taxco in the State of Guerrero in central Mexico, illustrate the potential value of the theoretical frameworks and temporal approach for research on tourism policy activity. Both empirical locations are integrated into the national tourism policy program *Pueblos Mágicos* (Magical Villages) launched in 2001.

Second home owners in Mexico

In a Mexican context, North American second home owners cannot be considered only individual actors, rather they are to be perceived as a collective actor, and with substantial economic and cultural influence in the construction of whole regions. This transnational group plays a key role in the analysis of tourism policies from a sociological perspective due to: 1) Its significant economic, social and cultural capital and private properties in tourist locations. Thus their influence is important in any policy planning process related to tourism (Clausen & Velázquez 2011). 2) They often have tourism-related businesses, such as hotels, restaurants, travel- and real estate agencies, which is why tourism policy programs need to consider this group among the potential *beneficiaries* (Hall 2007; Baud & Ypeij 2009). 3) This type of second home owner constitutes the most significant group in the majority of the tourism destinations not necessarily in numbers but in economic terms (Clausen & Velázquez 2010). 4) These North Americans have a noteworthy cultural capital, which turn them into significant social agents of change when defining the locality's identity or even reconstructing whole areas' identities (Clausen & Velázquez 2011).

A framework for analysis

Social construction of reality

Context matters, and local characteristics and historical and sociopolitical processes work together to shape policy and its outcomes (Honadle 1999). Thus, paying analytical attention to differences in context and how these disparities shape decisions made by policy actors are essential. Ingram and Schneider proposed the notion 'social construction of problems and issues' as a tool to analyse how a set of actors in specific situations and times, ascribe meaning to phenomena. By regarding policy design as a phenomenon in the becoming of identity (that is, subjected to different views, interests and perspectives), the social construction perspective may reveal how different local actors and power constellations are perceived and stereotyped within specific social situations (Schneider & Ingram 1993, 2005). Ingram, Schneider and Deleon (2007) argue that policymakers can socially construct a target population in positive and negative terms and distributive benefits and sanctions that perpetuate these social constructions. The Mexican government's construction of a national cultural identity and norms based on a specific majority group, despite considerable ethnic minorities and transnational groups with strong social, cultural and economic capital, demonstrates this proposition of different treatment of different populations through social constructions. Yet, policies rooted in social constructions can also overreach stimulating opposition and mobilisation among those minority populations (Ingram et al. 2007). This has implications for the development of tourism policies. In our case, this entails the study of how second home owners' complex interaction processes and power relations are reflected in the national tourism policies as the *Pueblos Mágicos* program (Magical Village Program).

The social construction approach acknowledges that policies are instructive goals and means to be implemented by the local administration. The institutional environment comprises the rules, procedures, practices and behaviours that characterise social organisations, and provide stability over time (Lowndes & Roberts 2013). Thus, it is significant in shaping the cultural and social regularities through which the opportunities and constraints for action emerge. Both politicians and social actors seek to benefit from the resources available by mobilising a set of action strategies to participate in policy processes. Whereby, it becomes highly important to understand how decision makers define the problem, and prioritise the initiatives and distributed impacts that can emerge from different intervention strategies (Ingram et al. 2007). From a sociological perspective, policy is an action arena where different actors' interests, values, norms and visions about reality prevail and a social space in which actors interact, solve problems and negotiate and exchange services and goods on local levels, arising from the diverse interests and views on tourism development held by the involved actors (Carrión 2000). As such, tourism has become a political, economic and sociocultural ordering tool, allowing various groups (governments, civil society, private companies) to legitimise action aiming at generating, altering and reconstructing the history of a region (Velázquez & Clausen 2012). Consequently, the design of sustainable policies will reflect the norms and values of these groups and realised outcomes will depend on the relative social positions and power structures among stakeholders (Ingram et al. 2007). In terms of our analysis, this means that the *intentionality* of the North American second home owners is key and needs to be taken into consideration when analysing tourism policies. This is particularly the case with the reciprocal relationship between policy actors and these transnational actors' cultural norms, values and interests. In addition, this group's cultural and socio-economic attributes enable them to dispute national social actors' interests as well as the Mexican State's visions about how and which kind of tourism development should be considered for the region. Thus, we argue that even though these second home owners do not *intentionally* partake, they do participate in the construction and shaping of sustainable tourism policies and the Mexican identity and culture.

The Mexican State

The active involvement of the state in the development of tourism in Mexico is not a new phenomenon. Promoting tourism has been on the federal agenda since the 1920s, and this historical dimension has been extensively studied (e.g. Pick et al. 2001; Clancy 2001; Berger & Wood 2010). Berger (2006) notes that the early development of tourism in Mexico was closely linked to the United States, fuelled by a strategic interest in restoring economic and political stability in the aftermath of the Mexican Revolution (1910–1920). State incentives promoting mass tourism exploded in the late 1960s and early 1970s (Pick et al. 2001). Subsequently, national policies by National Trust Fund for Tourism Development (FONATUR) focused on the private sector in the development and implementation of tourism policy, which partnered the government and private sector with responsibility for tourism marketing and program development. Mexico succeeded to transform into one of the most popular mass tourism destinations in the world. Internationally well-known resorts like Cancún, Acapulco, Cabo San Lucas and Huatulco are results of these developments.

National tourism program Pueblos Mágicos

The turn of the new millennium marks a shift in the appreciation in the tourism policies of the relationships between sustainable development and cultural tourism. The Mexican strategic policy program *Pueblos Mágicos* (Magical Villages Program), launched by the Mexican Ministry of Tourism (SECTUR) in 2001, aims at reinvigorating rural regions through cultural tourism. On a more critical note, the emphasis is on the touristification of local cultural assets and heritage, implicitly imposing market preferences and growth logic on sustainable development processes (Clausen & Gyimóthy 2016). The *Pueblos Mágicos* program is designed to promote the "true authentic Mexico" to tourists (SECTUR 2006a) and to boost emergent Mexican destinations with dormant cultural potentials. According to the program's guidelines, a *Pueblo Mágico* is a place that possesses symbolic attributes, legends, historically important events, and day-to-day life. In other words, MAGIC (uppercase in the original), that emanates from all its cultural manifestations with great opportunities for tourism (SECTUR 2006a). Experiencing the "authentic" Mexico should be sufficiently comfortable as the village has to be situated within 200 kilometres from, or two hours driving distance from, a consolidated tourist destination (a source market) and this site should be accessible via reasonably good roads (SECTUR 2006b). This clause rules out most villages in the mountains in the States of Oaxaca and Chiapas in the South of Mexico despite their cultural and historic assets. Since the launch in 2001, 131 villages have been integrated in the program by 2016. Most of them owe their nomination to indigenous origins, colonial legacy, the preservation of traditional organisational principles, or to being sites of significant events in Mexican history. An important cornerstone of the program is to address the needs and views of the local community by involving them in tourism development projects. However, the touristification logic of *Pueblos Mágicos* development program must be explicitly addressed. The intentions are to build a funding framework to accentuate "authentic" Mexican elements in selected localities. Nonetheless, both selection criteria and conservation guidelines are defined along a tourism market rationale; that is, developing communities in the vicinity of tourism resorts which possess attractive (market-viable) cultural and historic assets for potential visitors (Clausen & Gyimóthy 2016). This has implications for sustainable tourism as it means prioritising the preferences of second home owners as opposed to the well-being of the hosts, which is potentially at odds with the principles of the sustainable development goals. Thus, how have the North American second home owners shaped the tourism social reality? As suggested by Hall and Jenkins (2005), assessments of tourism-related government institutions should be more fully systematic about their theoretical basis, such as by linking them to interpretations of governance, power and values. By reinserting the analysis of public policies as a social issue, it becomes pivotal to take into account that decisions made by the State, particularly within tourism, are situated in an action area with actors who have diversified interests, norms, values and positions. Policies become the mechanisms of the State to promote a specific construction of reality related to a bundle of public concerns (Ingram et al. 2007). However, these are not unilateral decisions within the State, rather they are responses to major social agreements that sociology defines as institutions or shared norms.

The next section turns to a brief historical description of the two empirical settings to enable an understanding of how the localities became attractive tourism destinations as well as an analysis of how North American second home owners shape tourism policies and their outcome as well as the role of the cultural norms and values in influencing decisions of policy actors in formulating these policies. The analysis draws upon a longitudinal case study of the implementation of the *Pueblos Mágicos* program in the community of Álamos and Taxco and policy and historical documents from Mexico supplemented by secondary sources.

North American second home owners in Álamos and Taxco and community attributes

Reconstructing Álamos and the Mexican imaginary (culture and identity)

Álamos is a town in northern Mexico and is home to one of Mexico's most important silver mines, as well as having one of the most famous mints in all of Spanish America. In the past, all of these things attracted a large number of people coming from different regions of Mexico, and even Europe and South Asia. However, with the closure of the mine and the mint, and the transfer of the state's seat of power to Hermosillo, to say nothing of the frequent pillaging that the town suffered during the Mexican Revolution in the beginning of the twentieth century, most of the people emigrated, leaving the previously flourishing city essentially abandoned. One of the first groups to move away were the owners of the large mansions in the city centre. The houses were shuttered, and with that, the locality lost its early splendor, and it became nothing more than a footnote in Mexican history. Historical material and the few statistics available agree that most of those who remained were poor families, and the population did not exceed 500 people. However this was not the only abandonment this region suffered; the absence of the Mexican State's *intentionality* was demonstrated by the lack of specific programs or policies seeking to reinvigorate the old mining industry or generate new sources of employment. Àlamos became one of the many towns that the Mexican State did not invest in solving the existing problems: unemployment, migration and lack of economic growth.

In the late 1940s, a visionary North American William Levant Alcorn bought one of the mansions in the centre as a second home and started to restore the centre's mansions for selling or renting to North American tourists. He formed part of the increasing number of North Americans who considered Mexico as an option for buying a second home. Despite this group's enormous influence on future Mexican tourism destinations, these migration flows have attracted little research attention (Clausen 2008). Although it is beoynd the scope of this paper, it is however necessary to point out one of the factors that explain this group's mobility to a town like Álamos. These second home owners bought locations with desirable characteristics, such as idyllic beaches, palm trees, sun, lush vegetation and colonial houses (Clausen 2008). An image constructed through films, books and songs from the US (Velázquez 2008). Yet, it is not only about fulfilling authentic Mexican imaginings, but also practical issues influenced their desicions. The favourable conversion between the US dollar and Mexican peso was an essential element in the decision making process (Clausen 2008).

Tourism has become the main economic activity in the central area of the city, and tourism activities and services, such as hotels, restaurants, transportation and cultural events, increased and were mainly owned by the North American second home owners. In 2000, Álamos had 12 lodging establishments, and by 2015 this reached 35 (Sistema Municipal de Base de Datos (SIMBAD) 2010a). Whereas, restaurants and food stalls reached 13 in 2000 and in 2010 there were 17 (SIMBAD 2010b). Tourism is an engine of regional growth, reinvigorating the economy and to such an extent that the resident Mexicans remained in Álamos instead of migrating to the US for employment. In 1950, the population was 24,525 persons, increasing to 29,091 in 1980 and then in 2010 Álamos had 25,848 residents (Instituto Nacional de Estadística y Geografía (INEGI) 1980, 2010). Today, the town is notable for having a historic city centre with colonial houses, cobblestone streets and beautiful gardens. Surrounded by verdant mountains, the town is also famous for its picturesque landscapes. Yet, the local government did not consider the presence of North American immigrants to be "relevant", (Clausen & Velázquez 2010), and the federal authority, the National Institute of Anthropology and History (INAH), did not supervise or control the reconstruction of the historic centre or mansions in the town. This is not the only town in Mexico where this same category of immigrant is present. Groups of North Americans have established communities in various cities in states like Yucatán, Quintana Roo, Guanajuato, Jalisco, Baja California, Sonora and Sinaloa. An indirect indicator of this growing interest on the part of the North Americans for selecting Mexico as their residence is the sustained expansion of the North American real estate companies that operate in the United States but that specialise in or have a portfolio of properties located in Mexico. The State's lack of intervention and absence of policies aiming at preserving historic buildings relate to the fact that northern Mexico was not percieved as having attractive national heritage as colonial buildings with historic value. These were considered to be located in central or southern Mexico. In 2000, Álamos and its restored 188 mansions were declared "national heritage" by the INAH (Diario Oficial de la Federación 2000). In the declaration, a brief historical overview is provided:

> During the nineteenth century the population was the scene of several battles, among which the liberated on January 7, 1866 in which the General Republican Angel Martinez defeated the imperialist forces led by José Tanquilino Almada and Quiroz … in January 1910, during the political tour of Don Francisco I. Madero, the city of Alamos was considered in the working program … this city has had important characters, among which Justina Almada, Felix Almada, Jose Rafael Campoy, Alfonso Ortiz Tirado, Ramon Corral.
> *(Diario Oficial de la Federación 2000: 81)*

It is noteworthy that the declaration, which legitimates the nomination of national heritage, only emphasises Mexican heroes and artists in order to justify INAH's nomination, whereas foreigners (such as the foreign communities during the town's glorious mining period or North American William L. Alcorn conserving the mansions, or his capacity to reinvigorate the town's economic growth through tourism) are totally nonexistent. From a sociological perspective in line with Ingram et al. (2007), the Mexican State's social construction of target population is the Mexicans, as its aim is to conserve national heritage and thus cannot be arbitrary. Significant historic Mexican personalities and events constitute the main narrative of the Mexican State's territory.

The set of cultural and artistic events at the internationally recognised tourism attraction, the cultural festival Dr. Ortiz, include film screenings, painting and photography exhibits, which surpass what other similar-sized towns in the region offer. Additionally, open-air classical music concerts are held periodically at one of the town's hotels (certainly, one of northern Mexico's most expensive establishments). The music and art Dr. Ortiz festival emerged as an initiative from a small group within the North American second home owners. In the beginning of the 1980s, they started inviting friends who were musicians and artists. The majority of the second home owners have a university degree or specialised knowledge within art or cultural studies (Clausen & Velázquez 2010). As suggested by Ostrom (2007) this group then has attributes of a shared cultural understanding of events related to classical music, art and crafts. It becomes an annual event and within a few years the festival presents different music and art exhibitions with a huge audience mainly from the US and apart from occupying all the town's hotels, also several private mansions are rented to visitors during the event (Clausen 2008). In 1984, the regional authorities inscribed this event as the festival Alfonso Ortiz Tirado, who is a well-known personality born in Álamos. In the official declaration from the Mexican State the festival is described as:

> In 1984, after inaugurating the Costumbrista Museum Sonora, in Álamos, the State Department of Museums of the State of Sonora, conceived the celebration of a tribute to Dr. Alfonso Ortiz Tirado, a native of the city of portals (Álamos) … On January 24,

1985, on the anniversary of birth of the tenor (Ortiz Tirado) … a performance was
held for the first time … a literary-musical event in the Auditorium of Costumbrista
Museum and around 100 people attended. The following year there were a huge influx
of persons and the auditorium and hallways were totally packed. In 1987 and 1988
even more people attended and filled the surrounding courtyards … In these four years,
guest artists came from Hermosillo and the neighboring town, Navojoa. In 1990, due
to the huge success the festival was held for three days from Wednesday 24 to Sunday
28 January … then acquired the name Festival Dr. Alfonso Ortiz Tirado, Alamos.

(Plan Municipal de Desarrollo 2003–2006: 33)

Similar to the INAH nomination of the centre as national heritage, this official historical documentation emphasises only significant Mexican artistic personalities, whereas the ones who took
the initiative to begin the festival, the second home owners, are absent. The North Americans
then become passive *contenders* (Ingram & Schneider 1993) as their presence and activities are
not benefited directly by the tourism policies. Still, they bring with them cultural norms and
practices, that when incorporated into organisational forms and put to use, are adapted by the
Mexican State. No specific acts alter or inhibit their behaviour, and the only actors integrated
are the Mexicans. As suggested by Ingram and Schneider (1993), the Mexican State succeeds in
and socially constructs target populations in positive terms and distributes benefits that perpetuate these social constructions.

Moreover, this does not impede the group of North American immigrants from limiting the
exercise of their influence and power, which has been obtained. The second home owners have
not only created a touristification of the town but also founded locally based NGOs to solve
social issues and alleviate poverty in the region. Three nonprofit organisations aim at providing
financial support to pregnant or single mothers with limited resources, and financial support to
marginalised families' children for school supplies, and a third nonprofit seeks to document the
history of Álamos through interviews and photos. In other words, the second home owners are
actively engaged in reconstructing the history of Álamos (Clausen 2008), not as passive and temporary staff, but as active members, and what Ingram and Schneider (1993) define as *determinants*.
Then, the group of North Americans owns the majority of the mansions in the historic centre, as
well as the town's tourism-related businesses, such as hotels and restaurants, which situates them
in a role of active agents to potentially shape and define the tourismscape and tourism reality of
Mexico. Despite their role as non-residents and second home owners, they are not only visitors
but creators of the very same tourism reality they themselves seek to experience and live within.
This has also led to another "imported" cultural practice – the "estudiantinas". These are musi-
cal groups originally from colonial Mexico and a Spanish tradition. The second home owners
pooled economic ressources among their North American networks and organised a group of
musicians, who play during the festival Dr. Ortiz. This has turned into an outstanding regional
tourism attraction. However, these characteristics defining the identity and culture of Álamos,
also specified in the *Pueblos Magicos* program as the "*authentic*" Mexico, are inscribed into the
narrative of the town even though they do not form part of the cultural heritage in this region.

North American second home owners reinvented
silver as Mexican identity in Taxco

Taxco's population was indigenous ethnic groups. The Spanish conqueror founded the town
because of the silver mines, which became the largest mines in Nueva España. Taxco had two
eras of splendor, economic growth and commercial activity of silver, during the sixteenth and

eighteenth centuries. Jorda de Borda, a Spanish major and urban planner in Taxco, introduced a water system, and constructed roads and bridges (Babini & Hernandez 2012). However, similar to Álamos, Taxco suffered immediately with the Mexican Revolution: people migrated, the mining industry closed down and Taxco became a ghost town. At the end of the Revolution (1920), Taxco only had 2.371 inhabitants (Babini & Hernandez 2012), whereas the population was 13,016 in 1899. In 1926, William Spratling, a North American architect and author, visited Mexico and in 1929 he became a second home owner in Taxco even though it was a ghost town. Spratling was quickly introduced to the artistic circles in Mexico, and his activities in promoting the art of Diego Rivera in New York led to his participation in the first exhibitions of Mexican art in the US (Mark 2000). Even though Taxco had been a site of silver mines for centuries, it had never been considered a location where jewelry and objects were made and designed (Mark 2000). Subsequently, in 1931 Spratling began designing works in silver, based primarily on pre-Columbian and traditional motifs. He hired local silversmiths to produce the designs and start the shop, Las Delicias, and was insistent on the high quality of the materials and techniques used in the production (Mark 2000). Several friends started investing in second homes in Taxco. However, the creation of an international artistic community in Taxco mainly from the US as well as from other Mexican regions is not the result of any State program or initiative facilitating these transnational mobilities. The same problem persisted in Taxco as in Álamos: the centralised Mexican State's lacked interest in solving socio-economic problems in the rural regions.

Spratling established the first school of silversmiths in collaboration with local Mexican residents. Soon Las Delicias designed mirrors, lamps and wooden furniture as well as silver jewelry. In 1938, Spratling had 100 artisans working in the shop, all designing new models (Mark 2000). In 1940, more than 400 artisans worked for Spratling (Salvador n.d.). The importance of the silver jewelry was immediately reflected in the number of tourists, which increased, as did the number of North American second home owners in Taxco. In 1960, the population reached 43,567, increasing to 75,912 in 1980, and even more in 2015 to 104,053 persons (INEGI 2015). In 1953, the local authorities acknowledged Spratling and his influence by declaring him the municipality's "Favorite Son and Father of Silver" and naming a street to honor him (Schmid 2014; Mark 2000). In 1990, the INAH declared Taxco a national heritage site and in the official nomination published on March 19, 1990, the justification for the nomination was:

> [T]he population of Taxco de Alarcon, was founded in 1528, and has a prehispanic history. This is situated 13 kilometers southwest of the old town of Taxco, which was the seat of Nahua prehispanic groups … (it was) one of the first mining areas; and were discovered by Hernán Cortés, being the first conqueror Rodrigo Castañeda and Miguel Diaz de Aux … the location was scene of major events during the struggle for Mexico's Independence, … highlighting the battle against the Royalist Army of the 12th of March and November 2nd, 1811 … in January 1821, Taxco hosted the Convent of San Bernardino, the Augustine Colonel Iturbide, who with Fray Agustin Leon Leal and other supporters interviewed General Vicente Guerrero, which resulted in the Treaty of Iguala and the historic treaty of Acatenpan … during the French intervention, the General Porfirio Diaz takes the population October 28, 1863.
>
> *(Diario de la Federación 1990: 35)*

Similar to Álamos, the significant events are dedicated to Mexican personalities and the town becoming nothing more than a footnote in Mexican history is left out. The national heritage focuses on selected events to inscribe the town in the national identity and culture's narrative, thereby legitimising the decision declaring the town's national heritage.

> This town was the place of birth and residence of playwriter Juan Ruiz de Alarcon who was at the Universal Theater during the Golden Age ... Also the theologian and priest Hernando Ruiz de Alarcon, who created the testimony of indigenous culture ... Among other important figures from Taxco are: Joaquín Velázquez Cárdenas of Leon, an important astronomer, Colonel Francisco Hernández who fought in the Army of the South next to Morelos, the Rayon, Nicolas Bravo and Juan Alvarez.
>
> *(Diario de la Federación 1990: 35)*

The Mexican State's social construction of target population is the Mexicans, whereas the key player, Spratling, is absent. Despite his pivotal role in reinvigorating the regional economy, Mexican identity and culture, the Mexican State's narrative only emphasises revolutionary events and significant Mexican personalities as innovators for visual and artistic identity. Nonetheless, the local authorities celebrate Spratling as the "Father of Silver". The municipality and the state of Guerrero acknowledge the contribution to the Mexican identity and culture through the silver jewelry:

> It was definitely the presence of the North American William Spratling that prompted the craftsmanship that distinguishes taxqueños. Taking advantage of local talent and combining it with two jewelers, he founded in the third decade of the twentieth century, June 27, 1931, the first organized silversmith shop called Las Delicias, where the artistic movement that marks the revival begins Mexican contemporary silversmiths and Taxco crafts silver becomes famous. Since then, Taxco has been projected to the world as the town of goldsmiths and jewelers with more artistic sensibility silversmiths of Mexico ... The first silversmith contest was organized among members of the workshop Las Delicias in 1932 ... In 1953, the silversmith Antonio Pineda celebrates Taxco which is known as the National Fair Silver by the Federal Government of the Republic and the state of Guerrero. National authorities established the annual award of National Award, which consists of a prize, a gold medal and a diploma for the best craftsmanship of silver: the National Contest Platería ... In 1974 it was held in Taxco: World Fair Silversmith, with 40 countries participating.
>
> *(Gobierno de Guerrero n.d.)*

Similar to the case study about Álamos with the festival Ortiz Tirado, Taxco also reinvigorates certain cultural products and creates specific cultural and artistic events, which generate economic growth. The transnational second home owners become triggers for community and regional development and reconfigure the locations' identities within new cartographies, given the fact that Spratling's silver designs draw upon pre-conquest Mesoamerican motifs, and that his designs facilitated Mexican artisans creating designs in non-European forms.

The analysis of the empirical cases illustrates that the transnational second home owners and entrepreneurs in these tourism locations constructed and reinvented certain characteristics considered *authentic* Mexican, which shape the narrative of the Mexican State's identity and culture reflected in the tourism policy program *Pueblos Mágicos*.

Final reflections

The analysis about the Mexican government's social construction of a particular set of cultural norms, values and images as a generalised national set of cultural identity has shed light on how tourism policy and transnational mobilities alter existing power constellations and in specific times and situations ascribe meaning to a specific phenomenon. This paper pays the most analytical attention to the second home owners, suggesting that this group's cultural norms and ideas about Mexico shape the social reality of tourism. However, that said we do not suggest that other factors are insignificant in determining Mexican tourism policy. Ostrom (2007) asserts that policy actors' decisions in action arenas can be influenced by the attributes of the community including culture and values within which the actors are situated. Our analysis illustrates how attributes of a transnational community can shape policymakers' actions despite their lack of official acknowledgement and acceptance of this group's resources. Policy actors socially construct a tourism reality represented in the attributes of their community for their own policy purposes as shown in the national tourism policy *Pueblos Mágicos* program. Moreover, the analysis addresses the importance of exploring the role of transnational groups or communities, which are imagined to be outside or "irrelevant" by the Mexican State in the reinventing and reinvigoration of cultural practices and development of one of the State's most significant productive activities: tourism.

Pueblos Mágicos program is shaped by North American second home owners' ideas even though it does not correspond with the Mexicans' perceptions of the social reality; these are perceptions of the social tourism reality. In most towns, the *Pueblos Mágicos* program has generated significant economic growth, job creation, mitigated rural to urban migration and fostered economic opportunities. As argued by Ingram et al. (2007), the cases Álamos and Taxco demonstrate that policymakers can socially construct target populations in positive terms to distribute benefits that perpetuate these social constructions. This has implications for development of sustainable tourism policies and the State's involvement in coordinating and directing tourism activities in destinations as they evolve over time. It also allows central governments to retain or re-centralise its control. The case studies show that shared cultural norms and values also play a significant role in understanding political and governance dynamics related to tourism.

References

Babini, B. A. and Hernández, T. J. (2012) 'Una aproximación al imaginario urbano y social de Taxco de Alarcón. Primeros setenta años del siglo xx', *Topofilia*, 3 (2). [online] Available at: http://148.228.173.140/topofiliaNew/assets/tres2catorceab.pdf

Baud, M. and Ypeij, A. (2009) 'Cultural tourism in Latin America: An introduction', In M. Baud and A. Ypeij (eds) *Cultural Tourism in Latin America. The politics of space and imagery*. Leiden, the Netherlands: Brill, 1–22.

Berger, D. (2006) *The Development of Mexico's Tourism Industry: Pyramids by Day, Martinis by Night*. New York: Palgrave Macmillan.

Berger, D. and Wood, A. (2010) *Holiday in Mexico: Critical Reflections on Tourism and Tourism Encounters*. Durham, NC: Duke University Press.

Bevir, M. and Richards, D. (2009) 'Decentering policy network: Lesson and prosperities', *Public Administration*, 87: 132–141.

Carrión, F. (ed.) (2000) *Desarrollo cultural y gestión en centros históricos*. Quito: Flasco.

Clancy, M. (2001) *Exporting Paradise: Tourism and Development in Mexico*. New York: Pergamon.

Clausen, B. H. (2008) *Juntos pero no revueltos. Un estudio de caso sobre los inmigrantes norteamericanos en un pueblo mexicano*. Copenhagen: Copenhagen Business School.

Clausen, B. H. and Velázquez, G. M. (2010) 'La posición social y espacial en una ciudad turística. Las luchas simbólicas de Álamos, Sonora', *PASOS. Revista de Turismo y Patrimonio Cultural*, 8 (1): 47–59.

Clausen, B. H. and Velázquez G. M. (2011) 'En búsqueda del México auténtico. Las comunidades norteamericanas en ciudades turísticas de México'. In T. Mazón Martínez, R. Huete and A. Mantecón (eds) *Construir una nueva vida. Los espacios del turismo y la migración residencial*. España: Milrazones, 61–80.

Clausen, B. H. and Gyimothy, S. (2016) 'Seizing community participation in sustainable development: Pueblos Mágicos of México', *Journal of Cleaner Production*, 111: 318–326

Croucher, S. (2012) 'Privileged mobility in an age of globality', *Societies*, 2 (4): 1–13

Diario Oficial de la federación (1990) *Gobierno Federal Mexicano*, 441 (1) (1 de junio de 1990). [online] Available at: http://www.dof.gob.mx/index.php?year=1990&month=06&day=01

Diario Oficial de la federación (2000) *Gobierno Federal Mexicano*, 557 (21 de febrero de 2000). [online] Available at: http://www.dof.gob.mx/nota_detalle.php?codigo=2051078&fecha=31/12/1969

Gobierno de Guerrero (n.d.) *Platería de Taxco*. [online] Retrieved from: http://guerrero.gob.mx/articulos/plateria-de-taxco/ (accessed 25 July 2016).

Hall, C. M. (ed.) (2007) *Pro-Poor Tourism: Who Benefits?* Clevedon, UK: Channel View.

Hall, C. M. and Jenkins, J. (2005) *Tourism and Public Policy*. London: Routledge.

Honadle, G. (1999) *How Context Matters*. Hartford, CT: Kumarian Press.

Ingram, H., Schneider, A. L. and Deleon, P. (2007) 'Social construction and policy design'. In P. A. Sabatier (ed.) *Theories of the Policy Process*. Boulder, CO: Westview Press, 93–128.

Instituto Nacional de Estadística y Geografía (INEGI) (1980) *Censo de Población y vivienda 1980*. México.

Instituto Nacional de Estadística y Geografía (INEGI) (2010) *Censo de Población y vivienda 2010*. México.

Instituto Nacional de Estadística y Geografía (INEGI) (2015) *Censo de Población y vivienda 2015*. México.

Lowndes, V. and Roberts, M. (2013) *Why Institutions Matter: The New Institutionalism in Political Science*. London: Palgrave Macmillan.

Mark, J. (2000) *The Silver Gringo: William Spratling and Taxco*. Albuquerque, NM: University of New Mexico Press.

Mexican Ministry of Tourism (SECTUR) (2006a) Programa Sectorial del Turismo. Gobierno Federal Mexicano. Retrieved from: www.sectur.gob.mx/PDF/PST2007-2012.pdf Mexico (accessed 1 June, 2016).

Mexican Ministry of Tourism (SECTUR) (2006b) Pueblos Magicos. Reglas de Operación. Retrieved from: www.sectur.gob.mx/wb2/sectur/sect/Pueblos M%e1gicos (accessed 1 June 2016).

Ostrom, E. (2007) 'Institutional rational choice: An assessment of the institutional analysis and development framework'. In P. A. Sabatier (ed.) *Theories of the Policy Process*. Boulder, CO: Westview, 12–64.

Pick, J. B., Hettrick J., Butler, E. and Katsumi, F. (2001) 'Tourism in Mexico: Its development, dependency, and spatial patterns'. In *Designing the 21st Century*, Latin American Organization Working Paper, San Diego, CA: The Business Association of Latin American Studies, 295–305.

Plan Municipal de Desarrollo, (Programa Institucional) 2003–2006, Hermosillo, México.

Salvador, R. A. (n.d.) 'Taxco: Más de doscientos años de tradición platera', *Correo del maestro*. [online] Retrieved from: http://www.correodelmaestro.com/publico/html5082014/capitulo5/Taxco_mas_de_doscientos_anios_de_tradicion_platera.html (accessed 1 July 2016).

Schmid, A. (2014) Mexico's Silver City Struggles: Fair Trade – A Solution for the Silversmiths in Taxco? Master's Thesis. Universidad de las Américas Puebla, Cholula, Mexico.

Schneider, A. and Ingram, H. (1993) 'Social construction of target populations. Implications for politics and policy', *American Political Science Review*, 87 (2): 334–247.

Schneider, A. L. and Ingram, H. M. (2005) 'Introduction: Public policy and the social construction of deservedness.' In A. Schneider and H. Ingram (eds) *Deserving and Entitled: Social Constructions and Public Policy*. Albany, NY: State University of New York Press, 1–28.

Sistema Municipal de Base de Datos (SIMBAD) (2010a) *Establecimientos de hospedaje*. México: Instituto Nacional de Geografía y Estadística.

Sistema Municipal de Base de Datos (SIMBAD) (2010b) *Establecimientos de preparación y venta de alimentos*. México: Instituto Nacional de Geografía y Estadística.

Velázquez, G. M. (2008) 'La construcción de la imagen de México en Estados Unidos desde una perspectiva de riesgo', *Frontera Norte*, 20 (39): 37–67.

Velázquez, G. M. and Clausen, H. B. (2012) 'Tepoztlán, una economía de la experiencia íntima', *Latin American Research Review*, 47 (3): 134–154.

7

RECREATIONAL SECOND HOME GOVERNANCE IN CHINA

Policy implementation and structural framework

Yuefang Wu and Honggang Xu

Introduction

Contemporary China is becoming increasingly flexible with respect to second homes, due to loosening controls on individual mobility. The paradigm of mobility in China in the past few decades has shifted from production-led migration to consumption-oriented mobility. The growth of consumption-led mobility, in particular tourism-induced mobility, has greatly diversified mobility patterns, leading to the emergence of second home mobility, residential tourism and other patterns of multiple dwellings in places outside of one's permanent residence (Xu & Wu 2016). These semi-permanent forms of mobility, as examples of "in-between" mobility (Åkerlund 2013), are unique in the continuum of human mobility in the Chinese context. Second home mobility is important in understanding the changes. On the one hand, it is reflective of the increasingly compressed modernity in China, which has forced individuals into the vortex of globalisation while posing significant challenges to developing a more democratic and flexible governance framework to adapt to the changes. On the other, it reveals changes in the relationships between the individual, family, society and government. Second home mobility involves an individual's desire to flee the "boredom of home" to a destination "anywhere, as long as it is away from here". The intense desire to seek a better quality of life in another place under the impetus of consumerist culture has highlighted crises in the relationships between families and communities, and questions the traditional social management approaches.

In fact, second homes have been both a blessing and a curse in global development. For example, the issue of second home ownership in Wales has provoked continuous and heated debate ever since the 1970s (Gallent et al. 2005). International studies of second home ownership have taken into consideration the scopes of multiple stakeholders, including owners, users, community residents, enterprises and governments. Their different objectives, values and costs with regard to second home development, and the economic, social and political impacts, are core issues for academic investigation. Second home owners are also tourists in a sense, but the influence of their unique behaviours are divergent from other recreational or business tourists; for example, second home tourism will increase demand for a destination's real estate, which then leads to different social and economic influences.

Despite the scale and quantity of second home development in China, research on the governance structure and policy impacts is still lacking, and the current urban governance structure has been developed for a static and immobile society rather than responding to the increase in fluidity. This chapter examines the global practice of second home governance, and concentrates on the governance framework in China. As the chapter unfolds, in-depth analysis is conducted vertically on the complex governance relationships from the macro to the micro levels, while horizontally, it looks at the different institutional fields such as land use and urban planning, second home communities and social infrastructure development.

Second homes and their governance in developed countries

Governance is, by its very nature, the act of governing, and its definitions tend to suggest a recognition of changes in political practices involving, among other things, increasing globalisation, the rise of networks that cross the public–private divide, the marketisation of the state and increasing institutional fragmentation (Pierre 2000a; Pierre & Peters 2005; Hall 2011). The most common focus of the key contributions to the governance debate in public policy terms is 'the role of the state in society' (Pierre 2000b: 4). Therefore, the core concept in governance in public policy terms is the relationship between state intervention (also referred to as public authority) and societal autonomy (self-regulation). Governance is a term often used in tourism to describe network-based modes of management over activities or resources whose values are recognised and sometimes contested. With the increase of international tourism mobility, studies on governance focusing on border-crossing population movement have increased. Hall (2011) conducted a series of studies on the governance of tourism and second homes, and presented implications for policy analysis. He differentiated four governance structures derived from the literature (Pierre & Peters 2000, 2005), which include hierarchies, markets, networks and communities (Hall 2011), and he also pointed out that the structure of governance is important in understanding the power relations embedded in tourism place-making (Hall 2007).

One area of the study of tourism that is of increasing public and academic interest with respect to governance and policy implications is that of international second homes (Hall & Müller 2004; Paris 2011; Hall 2015). As pointed out by Åkerlund, Lipkina and Hall (2015: 79) 'both ownership, and promotion and production of second home spaces are framed with complex governance relationships from the macro (supra- and international) to the micro (regional and local) level'. On the other hand, the establishment of supranational governance frameworks such as the EU has facilitated the mobility of populations and capital within member countries, but in the meantime it has complicated the governance structure. The EU has sought to encourage tourism and human mobility through policies and international visa regimes in addition to agreements between countries such as fiscal and social welfare agreements, as well as enabling supra- and international non-governmental bodies (Åkerlund et al. 2015).

However, increasing tensions over policies as well as between different levels of governance have been noted (Åkerlund et al. 2015; King et al. 2000). Research on the governance of second homes has focused on the governing structure and processes concerning legislation, planning practices and land use. For example, Persson (2015) studied legislation containing special provisions for land and water management with regard to natural and cultural assets, and found that alternative pragmatic attitudes within planning practice have developed and are apparently increasing. In the meantime, since a large number of second homes or summer cottages are located in rural and peripheral areas, studies have increasingly focused on the impacts on rural areas and policy frameworks. For example, Gallent et al. (2005) focused on the patterns of concentration and how policies might respond to any specific housing, social or economic problems that second homes might introduce to rural communities, and produced a framework for policies to address second home planning, taxation and spending. In the meantime, although researchers have been aware of the value of incorporating second home ownership in regional and local development plans (Brida et al. 2011; Müller et al. 2004; Paris 2011), significant issues still exist with respect to the political representation and voting rights bestowed on second home owners as a result of being either a non-permanent resident or citizen of the second home jurisdiction.

Second homes in China

Mobility is not a common theme in the historical development of Chinese society. Since the 1950s, domestic population management has been officially dominated by the fundamental household registration system, known as *hukou* in Chinese. The three major functions of the *hukou* system which are influential for population migration include: 1) Household registration and social management. This concerns the registration of individuals at a relatively stable residency, and the governance over an individual is based on registering the *hukou* with the public security organisation. In other words, if one fails to register in a temporary community outside of one's permanent residence, they are excluded from official identification and public management, and further, are left out of the public welfare system (Solinger 1985, 2000); 2) Distinctions between rural and urban status, and constraints on movement. *Hukou* has been effective in locking in rural-urban inequalities (Afridi et al. 2015; Li, Chen & Li 2015), as the rural population is deprived of the freedom to move from villages to urbanised areas, reinforcing the inequalities in public welfare between those of different status; and 3) Territorialised welfare and social infrastructure provisions tied to the locality.

This system has failed to address the increasing needs of the mobile population that is gaining in motility through education, work, leisure or health. The above characteristics of the *hukou* system have been major obstacles to the realisation of free and individualised mobility in contemporary China. In fact, this institutional designation is deeply rooted in the traditional belief in an earth-bounded China (Fei 1984), where the fundamental norms in Chinese society have not advocated for the free mobility of individuals (Wu 2009). Thus the current policies and regulatory structures are much better geared to immobility than to the mobility of people between different jurisdictions, or to multiple dwellings.

However, the reality of globalisation has pulled Chinese society into the whirling vortex of modernity, with increasing mobility being the norm. This transition in mobility initially emerged in the labour market, with rural-to-urban peasant worker migration pushed by markets as a result of the reform and opening-up policies. The emergence of new personal freedoms in China since the late 1990s has led to the development of consumption-led mobility promoting the search for a "peripatetic lifestyle", but it has not resulted in changes in formal political agendas.

Thus, despite the institutional trend towards forward-thinking development, increasing lifestyle mobility has grown into a prominent issue, and second home ownership has followed in this process. The development of second home ownership in China has been facilitated by three major forces (Xu & Wu 2016): The first of these is the use of second homes as a means of investment in the rapidly growing Chinese real estate market over the past two decades. Secondly, with the increasing health demands of the ageing population in China, a second home provides supplementary housing for retirement migrants to access "the best of both worlds" by dwelling in different places in different seasons. As well, it is becoming a trend for adult children to express their filial piety by economically supporting their parents in a second home so that they can enjoy a healthy retirement. Thirdly, second home ownership is in line with the lifestyle changes, emergence of a middle class and a consumerist society, and the deepening influence of modernity in every walk of Chinese life.

Second homes are characteristically located in places with good amenities or that provide an alternative or unique lifestyle. In general, in the past three decades, second home ownership has increased in both form and quantity, and is part of a large-scale movement from city centres to peripheral areas, from metropolises to rural spaces, and from spaces of production to spaces of consumption (Xu et al. 2009). In one way, Chinese recreational second homes can be categorised into: (1) vacation second homes (for short holidays), (2) lifestyle-migration second homes (for short stays for commercial reasons), and (3) retirement-migration second homes (for longer stays on a seasonal basis) (Xu et al. 2009). Second home ownership has grown into a much-debated issue. It acts as an important factor boosting urban tourism, rapidly changing land use patterns and physical landscapes.

Apart from the economic impacts of second home speculation on housing price inflation, however, the spatial and social dimensions of its influence are causing it to become a major concern, as the negative impacts include rural gentrification, socio-spatial separation, and inequality in land use for different social cohorts (Xu & Bao 2006). In the meantime, the clear distinctions between second home owners and local communities has led to the formation of second home migrant enclaves, with resulting parallel societies (Wu & Xu 2012), and the pressure of second home migrants has also added to the pressure on local infrastructures, especially for destinations which are in huge demand by elderly migrants (Zhou & Chai 2013; Huang 2013).

Concerns over the social dimensions of second home ownership usually relate to the social participation and political representation of second home owners in local communities. Much of the work in this area has pointed out the failure of second home migrants to fully integrate into local communities, and their indifference to local culture and society (Wu et al. 2013). The displacement of local communities and the failure of local governments in providing affordable housing through effective planning has further enlarged the discrepancies and aggravated the conflicts between the newcomers and the local inhabitants, and the case of Sanya, as we illustrate below, provides a vivid example.

However, the real situation regarding second home ownership in China is still difficult to determine due to the lack of official recognition of second homes as a concrete and definite concept for statistics. Moreover, the ambiguity of second home concepts has also constrained the development of second home planning legislation, resulting in further governance chaos, which is the focus of our analysis in this chapter.

Chinese second home governance: The case of Sanya

Besides the underdeveloped governing approaches for labour migrants, governance of the consumption-led population is arguably more chaotic than ever. A case study was conducted in the city of Sanya in Hainan province, which is the southernmost and only tropical city in China. Second home development in Sanya has been representative of the multi-faceted conflicts in the Chinese transitional period, and has highlighted the acute issues surrounding the ambiguity of definitions in policies and legislation, confused urban planning and chaotic land use, and seasonal community and social infrastructure development for the settlement of second home migrants.

Tourism and real estate are two pillar industries in Sanya, and second homes in Sanya have developed under the influence of both sectors. The marketing of second homes in the past two decades has shifted from the initial selling promoted for surplus properties after the bursting of the economic bubble in the middle 1990s to the establishment of a seller's market, highlighting the scarcity of amenity resources for the affluent population. The designation of Hainan as an International Tourism Island by the Chinese State Council on 29 December 2010 greatly promoted the development of second homes in Sanya. Although there are no accurate statistics on the real estate transactions, it is estimated that over 95% of the commercial properties are purchased by consumers from the off-island domestic market (Li 2013). The property usages vary, from investment properties for resale or rent, to vacation houses for weekend use by recreational commuters, to retirement second homes for prolonged stays by seasonal migrants. Currently, over 400,000 people from other provinces are estimated to visit Sanya every winter (Kuang 2016), and the number of seasonal snowbirds far exceeds the permanent residents. Thus, the seasonal influx of second home owners has posed huge challenges to the social, spatial and political environments.

The fieldwork was conducted by the authors between 12– January in 2013 and between 21 January and 8 February in 2015. Focus group interviews were conducted with the Sanya Municipal Government, the Sanya Bureau of Land and Resources, the Sanya Bureau of Tourism, and the police stations in whose jurisdictions the seasonal migrants are concentrated. The central questions focused on the policies and practices for second homes and on the management of the temporary population. Meanwhile, six agents in Sanya were interviewed to follow up on policy implementation and on the source and development of the second home market, and also to ascertain the distribution of second home communities. Secondary data was collected through documents, statistics and reports from official departments, newspapers and other media.

Urban planning and land use issues

Three significant characteristics were noted regarding second home land use in Sanya. First, it had accumulated a high rate of growth over the previous decade. According to statistics from the Sanya Real Estate Industry Association (SREIA), second home ownership attained steady growth both in prices and quantity. As shown in Figure 7.1, the average price increased by 3.8 times between the years 2005 and 2013, with the total sales area rising from 557,900 m^2 to 1,406,700 m^2 over those years. Over 100 real estate projects were developed since 2003, and the total sales area was over 13.8 million m^2. The SREIA also estimated that, setting the average residential area at 30 m^2, the current housing stock in Sanya can accommodate over 400,000 people. Moreover, annual monitoring from the SREIA showed that over 95% of the property purchasers came from off the island, and therefore, the second homes in Sanya have been housing approximately 380,000 seasonal residents yearly.

Second, the huge development of second home properties has placed unprecedented demands on urban land use in Sanya, as these kind of commercial properties are more demanding of land and open space. As they are generally positioned to focus on the leisure and holiday market, they are typically of low density and with low plot ratios, and this has added to the pressure on land use and pushed changes in urban planning, which had previously been designed for localised permanent residency.

Thirdly, the second homes are reliant on amenity resources. Since Sanya is a typical "sea, sand and sun" tourism destination, the coastal landscape and beach are the central attractions. The changes in rental costs have also followed this pattern, and the highest prices for condominiums, compounds and residential properties are also concentrated in the coastal areas. Sanya has the largest coastal-zone construction area in Hainan province, reaching 2,000 hectares in 2010 (Qiu et al. 2012). The changes in LUCC (Land-Use and Land-Cover Change) in the coastal zones due to urbanisation and tourism development are also an issue.

Regarding the first characteristic, farm land has diminished rapidly and construction land use has drastically increased, and as a result of the latter two, the newly established townships, urbanised areas and tourism facilities have been forced to concentrate in the coastal zone, which

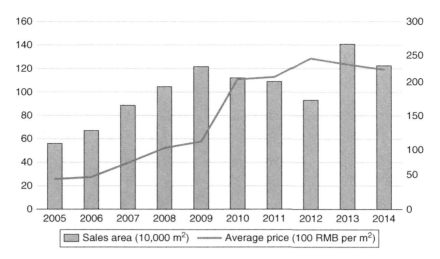

Figure 7.1 Areas and prices of property sales in Sanya (2005–2014).

Source: Derived by authors from the Registration System of Real Estate Property Transaction of Sanya.

has abundant amenity resources. This has challenged the habitat of coastal species and increased the pressure on coastal biodiversity.

Complicated problems in the governance of second home ownership have emerged. Urban planning and land use policies have failed to differentiate between housing demands for permanent residence and for second home use (Qi & Zhou 2015). In the baseline coding for planning, the *Code for Classification of Urban Land Use and Planning Standards of Development Land* (GB50137-2011), issued in 2011, residential land use was classified into three types: R1, R2 and R3. Specifically, R1 is oriented towards low-rise residential houses, R2 for multi-story, medium and high-rise residential houses, and R3 for shantytowns, decrepit houses and other temporary residential houses. This classification has focused on attributes including public infrastructure, transportation, housing environment and height of the residences, but has ignored the diversifying ownership and utilisation patterns with changes in urban development. Also, despite the huge increase in the development of second homes, no official department has provided a clear analysis of the potential influence of second homes and included it into the comprehensive regional planning process.

This indiscriminate land-use categorisation and the ambiguity of second homes as an independent planning subject has led to a serious predicament, but it does leave a space for a "breakthrough" for land use and rent-seeking for second homes from different local governments. For instance, a large number of second home owners have acquired land through local governments by claiming them to be tourism-related properties such as timeshare apartments, golf course condominiums and other kinds of extended-stay leisure accommodations. Although these properties have different tenure types and property rights validity periods compared to formal residential land usage, a clear pathway for the attainment of land for second homes has been left out. These loopholes in policies have created opportunities for operating on the margins of the legislation at the local governance level. Impetus for ignoring clear land use regulations comes from the lure of second homes as a major source of financial and taxation incomes for local governments, especially for tourist cities claiming tourism and real estate as pillar industries. Revenue seeking and wealth accumulation have underpinned government-led, pro-growth coalitions (Deng & Huang 2004; Logan 2002; Ma 2002; Qian 2007; Wu 2002), and in the case of Sanya, the real estate industry has contributed to over 50% of the financial income of the local government.

Governance on second homes also faces conflicts from different governmental levels. On the one hand, the lack of attribution of second homes to a specific governing department has resulted in cross-purposes in departmental regulations. As mentioned above, a large proportion of second homes are planned as tourism-related buildings. With regard to the planning dimension alone, tourism land use regulation involves tourism planning from the Tourism Administration, urban planning and scenic area planning from the Ministry of Housing and Urban-Rural Development, and land-use planning from the Ministry of Land and Resources. Discrepancies in tourism land use categorisation exist among different departments, where the hierarchy and content of land use policies conflict with each other. Part of the reason behind the conflicts between macro- and meso-/micro- governing levels lies in the divergent definitions and understandings of a second home, and the central government has been conservative on this issue.

Since 2005, a series of regulation and control policies have been issued by the national government to curb the overheated development in the real estate market. The *Notification on Stabilizing the Housing Price* issued by the State Council in 2005 set the tone for regulating second home transactions through measures on housing prices, land provision, supply-side structuring and market monitoring. Over the next decade, other regulatory policies were launched periodically to follow up on changes in the real estate market. For example, the *Notification on Continuing the Regulation and Control in Real Estate Market* issued by the State Council in 2013 was aimed at taking action on levying individual income taxes, increasing down payments on second homes, and restricting the entry of non-local residents into the housing market.

However, with regard to actual implementation, different coping strategies have been employed by the provincial and municipal governments. In the *Notification of Further Strengthening the Real Estate Market Regulation*, issued by the Sanya government in 2011, restrictions on the qualifications of real estate purchasers still followed the rules set by the state government, but it left a way out for non-local residents to conduct real estate transactions in places outside of the main urban areas. Meanwhile, the notifications have failed to prevent fraudulent practices by individuals to obtain a second home in places outside of their permanent residence, and the agents in local real estate markets have deployed other approaches to dodge the entry requirements for potential second home buyers. The misalignment between different governance hierarchies is most notable in the fact that although Sanya is listed as one of the five most strictly purchase-controlled cities in China (in addition to Beijing, Shenzhen, Shanghai and Guangzhou), actual transactions of second homes in Sanya have continued to rise.

Second home communities

Second home usage in Sanya is very complicated. Depending on the classification of the ownership, a second home might be considered a private home, an intermittently private home, an intermittently commercial house, or a commercial holiday home (Wu et al. 2013). Divergence exists among the three types of second home usage, which can be owner-users, owner-renters, or local residents, resulting in the diversified considerations and approaches for governance. Currently, the second home owners and long-lease users coming from other provinces in China only reside in Sanya for short periods of time, and they are reluctant to give up their citizenship registration from their permanent residency. They are considered as a "floating population" or "snowbirds" in the destination, and are supposed to apply for a temporary residence permit from the local police station. However, the majority fail to register, and thus stay uncounted in local statistics. This puts the local authorities into a difficult position, as they are ignorant of the actual situation around the population in their jurisdictions, and consequently they face multiple challenges regarding necessary public services, security and infrastructure.

In the meantime, no mature and flexible governance structure has been developed to deal with the increasing diversity in communities, but rather, a mixed population management institution is still in effect which intersects with the hierarchies of the sub-district or street offices (*jiedao* in Chinese), neighbourhood committees (*juweihui* in Chinese) and owners' committees within housing compounds. Specifically, the sub-district/street office is the basic city administrative division in charge of the local residents and those who migrate to Sanya for work or to live for a relatively stable period. The neighbourhood committee is a subdivision of the street office and the lowest unit of party organisation, and is responsible for the management details of the jurisdiction, but also concentrates on providing services for the local permanent residents, with limited public services for the registered temporary residents. The owners' committees operate within the housing compounds, and represent the property owners in a particular gated community. These communities are mainly composed of second home owners from outside of Sanya, while incorporating a minor proportion of local permanent residents.

The functions and powers of each of the governing bodies mentioned above reveal that consumption-led migrants are not in the purview of any departments, and so they are floating outside the official governance structure and are omitted from local agendas for developing appropriate social infrastructure. The paradox between the rapid growth in consumption-led mobility and the sluggish development of governance structure has led to a dilemma in managing local societies.

Conspicuous issues have emerged that challenge the capabilities of local and regional governments to adapt to the changes in an increasingly mobile society. Consumption-led mobility has led to a significant socio-spatial separation in Sanya, including separations in residential spaces, activity spaces, social networks and perceived home spaces (Wu et al. 2013). Lifestyle migrant enclaves have formed as a result of the undifferentiated urban planning as well as the natural behaviour of the seasonal migrants to seek out people from their home areas when they enter an unfamiliar place. The enclaves denote spaces of physical and structural separation that mark the arrival of migrants into urban areas (Waldinger 1993). It is a form of divergence that disturbs the existing urban fabric of a city, and causes further changes in sentiments and perceptions of the overall unity of a society (Wu et al. 2013). In the meantime, the spatial concentration of the seasonal migrants also reveals the fact that necessary social support is still absent in the scope of local governance, and it is difficult for temporary migrants to obtain public service or insurance in their new location.

Last but not least, with the dwelling patterns of second home migrants, the issues of social participation and political representation are becoming more prominent. Seasonal retirement migrants are creating new social networks in local communities, making closer connections with people from similar home areas and cultural backgrounds, and their demands for community self-governance and a bottom-up governance structure are growing. Snowbirds are striving for their political rights to vote and to take part in frontline management departments, including street offices and neighbourhood committees. The endeavors over six years by seasonal migrants coming from different parts of China finally resulted, in 2013, in the establishment of the Association for Old Age Caring Elsewhere. The association is regarded as a milestone in floating population management in Sanya. It is a non-governmental social organisation approved by the Bureau of Civil Affairs of Sanya, and is also supported by the branch office of Harbin Old Age Foundation in Hainan (Harbin is one of the main home cities of second home migrants, and support from the Bureau of Civil Affairs in Harbin has significantly facilitated the establishment of the self-governance association in Sanya). The association has significantly pushed forward the self-governance agenda of the temporary migrants. Services including legal consulting, entertainment and event organisation, old age education and medical services are provided. Furthermore, the association also organises volunteer activities through which the seasonal migrants are able to develop their social networks and build a sense of belonging in this previously unfamiliar place. Thus, with the absence of an official governance framework for them in Sanya, the association can be seen as a success in the grass-roots movement of the seasonal migrants to find a flexible form of governance. The association is thus a harbour for the second home migrants which helps them further build a sense of "home" and long-term commitment to Sanya as a seasonal destination.

Conclusion

Contemporary Chinese mobility has evolved within an extremely accelerated, compressed and complex discourse. The concomitant development of the multiple patterns of production-led and consumption-led mobility complicates their scopes of development under the context of compressed modernity. This research seeks a contextual understanding of how the existing frameworks of governance have dealt with the growth in second home ownership. In comparison to the academic and public interest in governance and policies with regard to international second home ownership, these still remain under-researched issues in China.

Chinese second home development has been driven by rapid growth in the real estate industry, increasing health care needs of an ageing population, and lifestyle changes with the emergence of a middle class and a consumerist society, and the deepening influence of modernity. Second home ownership has grown into a much-debated issue, but positive impacts have emerged in providing a supplementary market for local real estate and injecting a new impetus for regional economies. However, the negative influences are also significant, including the crowding-out of local inhabitants, inequalities in resource distribution, deficient affordable housing, socio-spatial separations and challenges to local livelihoods as a result of industrial restructuring. Governance for consumption-led migrants is even more chaotic compared to that for previous production-led migrants, because this pattern of movement is more fluid and covers a wider scope of governance needs. Governance frameworks from different levels are intertwined, and this can be clearly seen in the destinations.

By conducting a case study in Sanya, this research provides a closer look into the two most significant governance issues: urban planning and land use, and second home communities. For the former issue, a comprehensive policy framework is still difficult to bring about due to the ambiguity in the definitions of a "second home". In addition, the planning and land use management departments at different governance levels have failed to provide a way to integrate second home ownership into local, regional and rural planning. Moreover, the principles for governance for different governmental levels are often in conflict. The planning dilemma lies in the strong lure of second homes as a vehicle to boost the financial and taxation income of local governments.

Although the central government is still conservative regarding second home ownership, it has ultimately grown at a high rate over the past decades. In regard to governance over second home communities, concerns over the social dimension are related to the influx of a substantial temporary population compared to the permanent community. Conspicuous discrepancies exist between the growing demands for public participation and political representation and the sluggish development of a community governance structure, which has historically been geared toward a relatively immobile society. In response to the receding importance of boundaries and localities, and in the absence of governance mechanisms, kinship and other social networks that previously worked as frameworks for social interaction in traditional Chinese society have once again taken prominence to support contemporary lifestyle mobility. In addition, grass-roots political and social endeavors are also revealed from this research, as second home residents seek a bottom-up governance framework and partial autonomy.

The chapter has highlighted the need to develop a democratic, network-based governance strategy to accommodate the new structural changes in society. Second home ownership should be part of official political and social agendas in the emergence of a leisure society in China. Future research should place more importance on developing differentiated political schema and power structures, as well as approaches to realise sustainable development for consumption-led mobility.

References

Afridi, F., Li, X. S. and Ren, Y. F. (2015) 'Social identity and inequality: The impact of China's Hukou system', *Journal of Public Economics*, 123: 17–29.

Åkerlund, U. (2013) The Best of Both Worlds: Aspirations, Drivers and Practices of Swedish Lifestyle Movers in Malta. PhD. Umeå University, Umeå, Sweden.

Åkerlund, U., Lipkina, O. and Hall, C. M. (2015) 'Second home governance in the EU: In and out of Finland and Malta', *Journal of Policy Research in Tourism, Leisure & Events*, 7 (1): 77–97.

Brida, J. G., Osti, L. and Santifaller, E. (2011) 'Second homes and the need for policy planning', *Tourismos: An International Multidisciplinary Journal of Tourism*, 6 (1): 141–163.

Code for Classification of Urban Land Use and Planning Standards of Development Land GB50137 (2011). Ministry of Housing and Urban-Rural Development of the People's Republic of China (MOHURD), implemented from 1 January 2012.

Deng, F. F. and Huang, Y. (2004) 'Uneven land reform and urban sprawl in China: The case of Beijing' (in Chinese), *Progress in Planning*, 61 (3): 211–236.

Fei, X. T. (1984) *From the Soil: The Foundations of Chinese Society*. Beijing: SDX Joint Publishing.

Gallent, N., Mace, A. and Tewdwr-Jones, M. (2005) *Second Homes: European Perspectives and UK Policies*. Farnham, UK: Ashgate.

Hall, C. M. (2007) 'Tourism, governance and the (mis-)location of power'. In A. Church and T. Coles (eds) *Tourism, Power and Space*. London: Routledge, 247–269.

Hall, C. M. (2011) 'A typology of governance and its implications for tourism policy analysis', *Journal of Sustainable Tourism*, 19 (4–5): 437–457.

Hall, C. M. (2015) 'Second homes: Planning, policy and governance', *Journal of Policy Research in Tourism, Leisure & Events*, 7 (1): 1–14.

Hall, C. M. and Müller, D. (eds) (2004) *Tourism, Mobility and Second Homes: Between Elite Landscape and Common Ground*. Clevedon, UK: Channel View Publications.

Huang, H. (2013) 'The progress in foreign elderly long-stay tourism and its application to China' (in Chinese), *Tourism Science*, 27 (6): 13–24, 38.

King, R., Warnes, A. and Williams, A. (2000) *Sunset Lives: British Retirement Migration to the Mediterranean*. Oxford: Berg.

Kuang, C. X. (2016) 'Winter tourists exceeds local inhabitants in Sanya. How to manage snow-bird type city?' *Hainan Newspaper*, 12 January. [online] Retrieved from: http://www.hinews.cn/news/system/2016/01/12/030056514.shtml (accessed 24 October 2016).

Li, L. M., Chen, Y. F. and Li, S. M. (2015) 'Better city, better life, but for whom? The Hukou and Resident Card system and citizenship stratification in Shanghai' (in Chinese), *Nanjing Journal of Social Sciences*, 2: 52–60.

Li, S. H. (2013) 'The secretary of Sanya Real Estate Industry Association: Diversification of the real estate industry', *Chinese Real Estate Newspaper*, 11 March. [online] Available at: http://news.sanya.fang.com/2013-03-11/9679288.htm

Logan, J. R. (2002) 'Three challenges for the Chinese city: Globalization, migration and market reform'. In J. R. Logan (ed.) *The New Chinese City: Globalization and Market Reform*. Oxford, England: Blackwell, 3–21.

Ma, L. J. C. (2002) 'Urban transformation in China, 1949–2000: A review and research agenda', *Environment and Planning A*, 34 (9): 1545–1569.

Müller, D. K., Hall, C. M. and Keen, D. (2004) 'Second home tourism impact, planning and management'. In C. M. Hall and D. Müller (eds) *Tourism, Mobility and Second Homes: Between Elite Landscape and Common Ground*, Clevedon, UK: Channel View, 15–32.

Paris, C. (2011) *Affluence, Mobility and Second Home Ownership*. London: Routledge.

Persson, I. (2015) 'Second homes, legal framework and planning practice according to environmental sustainability in coastal areas: The Swedish setting', *Journal of Policy Research in Tourism, Leisure & Events*, 7 (1): 48–61.

Pierre, J. (ed.) (2000a) *Debating Governance: Authenticity, Steering and Democracy*. Oxford: Oxford University Press.

Pierre, J. (2000b) 'Introduction: Understanding governance'. In J. Pierre (ed.) *Debating Governance: Authenticity, Steering and Democracy*. Oxford: Oxford University Press, 1–12.

Pierre, J. and Peters, B. G. (2000) *Governance, Politics and the State*. New York, NY: St. Martin's Press.

Pierre, J. and Peters, B. G. (2005) *Governing Complex Societies: Trajectories and Scenarios*. Basingstoke, UK: Palgrave.

Qi, D. J. and Zhou, J. Y. (2015) 'Evolution of land use classification theory and practice in USA and UK', *City Planning Review*, 39 (8): 80–86.

Qian, Z. (2007) 'Institutional and local growth coalitions in China's urban land reform: The case of Hangzhou high-technology zone', *Asia Pacific Viewpoint*, 48 (2): 219–233.

Qiu, P. H., Xu, S. J., Fu, Y. and Xie, G. Z. (2012) 'Present situation of land use and its problems in coastal zone of Hainan' (in Chinese), *Tropical Geography*, 32 (6): 582–592.

Solinger, D. J. (1985) '"Temporary residence certificate" regulations in Wuhan, May 1983', *The China Quarterly*, 101: 98–103.

Solinger, D. J. (2000) 'Review', *The China Quarterly*, 163: 850–853.

Waldinger, R. (1993) 'The ethnic enclave debate revisited', *International Journal of Urban and Regional Research*, 17 (3): 444–452.

Wu, F. (2002) 'Real estate development and the transformation of urban space in China's transitional economy with special reference to Shanghai'. In J. R. Logan (ed.) *The New Chinese City*. Oxford, England: Blackwell, 154–166.

Wu, W. P. (2009) 'A review of "China on the move: Migration, the state, and the household"', *Annals of the Association of American Geographers*, 99 (2): 437–439.

Wu, Y. F. and Xu, H. G. (2012) 'A literature review of second residence tourism: Implication on mobility analysis' (in Chinese), *Progress in Geography*, 31 (6): 799–807.

Wu, Y. F., Xu, H. G. and Lew, A. A. (2013) 'Consumption-led mobilized urbanism: Socio-spatial separation in the second-home city of Sanya', *Mobilities*, 10 (1): 136–154.

Xu, H. G. and Wu, Y. F. (2016) 'Lifestyle mobility in China: Context, perspective and prospects', *Mobilities*, 11 (4): 509–520.

Xu, H. G., Wu, Y. F. and Wall, G. (2009) 'Tourism real estate development as a policy tool for urban tourism: A case study of Dali and Lijiang, China', *Journal of China Tourism Research*, 8: 174–193.

Xu, W. X. and Bao, J. G. (2006) 'A preliminary research on the spatial distribution of second home in peripheral areas: Case study of Foshan in Guangdong province' (in Chinese), *Planners*, 10 (22): 71–74.

Zhou, J. and Chai, Y. W. (2013) 'Research progress on spatial behaviors of the elderly in China' (in Chinese), *Progress in Geography*, 32 (5): 722–732.

8

THE RISE AND FALL OF THE HOUSES OF ATTEFALL

Effects of reduced building regulation in coastal municipalities with large numbers of second homes

Ingrid Persson

Introduction

Attefallshus [Attefall house] was one of the new Swedish words, together with for instance *mobilzombie*, published on the list of new expressions in the year of 2014 (Språkrådet 2014). The origin of the term "Attefall house" is connected to the non-socialist minister at the time, Stefan Attefall. A parallel phenomenon is *friggebod* [frigge shed] named after another non-socialist minister, Birgit Friggebo, in the late 1970s. The ministers' political ambitions were in both cases to reduce "bureaucratic fuss". Ordinary people should not be stopped in their ambitions to improve their property by rules without cause. So what happened?

The *friggebod* could probably be seen as a success from the start the average Swedish houseowner; after 40 years it is still a popular possibility to build one or two small complementary rooms (altogether 15 square metres) close to the ordinary building without a building permit. The dimensions are too small to correspond to an ordinary dwelling due to the building regulations, but in cases of small projects such as garages, greenhouses or guesthouses, the reform in general serves its purpose well: to reduce administration and costs.

But what about the initiative of Minister Attefall? The political ambitions in this case were extended. Besides facilitating the houseowner's private plans, the government saw a possibility to deal with a growing housing shortage, especially in the metropolitan areas of Sweden.

The Attefall reform meant for the private houseowner the possibility, without a building permit, to build at most one freestanding building with the size of 25 square metres and total height of 4 metres allowed to be a fully equipped dwelling or a complement building. It was also possible to make an extension of 15 square metres and to add 2 dormers to the main building, and to arrange another dwelling in the house. Instead of a building permit the houseowner had to send a building report [bygganmälan] to the municipality and await a starting permit [startbesked] before starting to build.

The changes of the *Planning and Building Act* according to the Attefall reform, gained legal force in July 2014, with the election of the Swedish Parliament coming up in September the same year. The reform meant more opportunities for the private houseowner to avoid a building permit from the municipality when building a complete extra dwelling that could possibly be put on the housing market. Consequently, the national association of Swedish houseowners calculated there was a possibility of 200,000 new dwellings for rent becoming available (Villaägarna 2014).

In March, Minister Attefall presented the bill to the government, and the very same day he and his colleague, the Minister of Finance, visited the first prototype of "Attefall houses", designed by the company *Sommarnöjen* [Summer Cottages] and casually placed at a square in central Stockholm (Regeringskansliet 2014). Perhaps the company's name should be understood as a hint about what was to come.

After 6 weeks of the Attefall reform in force, a nationwide newspaper published the result of a phone survey in 11 of the biggest municipalities in the country (Andersson 2014). According to the answers, 40 houseowners had reported an interest in building an Attefall house so far. In Stockholm, ten building reports were sent in to the municipality, and in Malmö, the third biggest municipality, the number was three. Answering staff said people were most interested in expanding their houses. The general opinion was: too poor information, many houseowners thought they needed no permit from the municipality at all, and the number of reports were low. Directly after, the author of this article phoned ten coastal municipalities, all known to be well-supplied with second homes (Borgholm, Falkenberg, Halmstad, Haparanda, Kungsbacka, Luleå, Sölvesborg, Tanum, Varberg, Värmdö). These municipalities stated a total volume of 260 Attefall building reports.

For coastal areas of national interest due to natural and cultural assets the Swedish Parliament has codified particular conservation regulations in the Swedish Environmental Code (1998). Statistics Sweden (2005) showed that in spite of the regulations in the Code a strong growth of second homes was going on in the areas outside the population centres in protected coastal areas. Development is not legally forbidden, since the areas are not intended to be nature reserves in general, but the municipalities must safeguard the national interests as part of a sustainable development. A previous study (Persson 2014a) analysed almost 70 current comprehensive plans, in coastal areas protected by the Code. The study showed that planning practice varies quite a lot, in spite of the same applicable legal framework. No uniformity is seen in the way Swedish coastal municipalities view vacation house development or the lack thereof, either in relation to how the concept should be used or how such development should be handled in the years to come. The concept of vacation housing has over time also been influenced by ideas of comfort and modernity (Persson 2014b).

Environmental dimensions of second homes have been discussed for instance by (Andersen et al. 2008; Goble et al. 2014; Hao et al. 2014; Huhtala & Lankia 2012; Jeong et al., García-Moruno et al. 2014; Lanza & Randazzo 2013) and in relation to housing, real estate and investment policies as well as within life course investment and consumption strategies (Bhattacharya & Kim 2011; Bianco 2006; Hall 2005; Hall & Müller 2004; Jurinsky 2010; McIntyre, Williams & McHugh 2006; Norris, Paris & Winston 2010; Oliveira et al. 2013). For second homes in relation to planning, policy and governance, see Hall (2014).

The difference in outcome of Attefall measures, as mentioned above, depends on the principles used to select municipalities in research leading up to this article. The research question is:

- What effects do the Attefall reform have for valuable coastal areas with great vacation housing?

The research design used is data triangulation of different data sources, and the method is content analysis (Denscombe 2007). The first part of this article starts out from the legal context of the Attefall reform. In the second part, inventive market acting is explored according to the easing-off building regulations. The third part deals with municipal practice and discusses national supervision as well as the results of the data analysis. The final section concludes with a discussion of the results and I argue that the Attefall reform as a side effect could be a risk to sustainable development in coastal areas.

Legal context

When the proposal of the Attefall amendments to the Planning and Building Act was circulated for consideration it proved to be controversial. The legal examiners, the Council of Legislation (Lagrådet 2014), objected strongly to the proposal as a whole, noting preparation of the proposal was too hasty and serious shortcomings in factual matters. The Council emphasised that viewpoints from other bodies, to which the proposal was submitted to, were hardly answered on grounds of fact and that many of these bodies had objected to the proposal. The Council also thought an introduction of a starting permit instead of a building permit, would not lead to any simplification in handling, but to a possibility for the building proprietor to diverge from a detailed plan. The latter could risk the legal system since the proposal allowed the Attefall house to be built without consideration of the legal plan in force. In the opinion of the Council, the right of a neighbour as property owner was diminished since according to the proposal, the neighbour would have no right to appeal against a starting permit before the municipal decision, unless the distance was too close; municipal supervision afterwards at the request of the neighbour was not enough.

The apprehension of the Council to the new legislation gained, in the main, no hearing from Parliament. A strong majority, across the party dividing lines of the Swedish Parliament, voted for the amendments in June 2014. The amendment to the Planning and Building Act came into operation from 2nd July the same year. A main argument for the bill was freedom for the houseowner. This argument was in line with the shift in political ideology since the 1980s and the emergence of New Public Management (Hall & Zapata Campos 2014). Among the policy tools are, as pointed out by Mäntysalo, Saglie and Cars (2011), public-private partnerships and market actors having an active role in detailed planning and development projects (Andersson & Magnusson Turner 2014; Christophers 2013; Holmqvist & Magnusson Turner 2014). According to the Attefall reform, private houseowners were supposed to contribute to the solution of an accumulated housing shortage, a situation the state had already tried to solve with initiatives (Hall & Vidén 2005; For international diversity of building regulations see Baiche et al. 2006; van der Heijden 2009; van der Heijden 2010; van der Heijden et al. 2007; Pedro at al. 2010).

Inventive market acting

A publisher saw a chance to commission 25 of "the most innovative architect's offices" in Sweden to contribute to new ideas of dwelling with one proposal each (Wrede & Issit 2014). The preface to the book states that the Attefall house could be seen as a step towards a more expressive architecture. One of the most spectacular ideas in the book could be the suggestion of a house in three levels including 20 capsules for individual dwelling, intended for students with inspiration from "capsule hotels" in Tokyo. Another way of stretching the mental borders is the proposal to dig down into the ground suggesting a house placed 90 centimetres below the ground level in order to maximise space. A third example of an exceptional Attefall house starts from the idea of cooperation amongst neighbours, a condition for the proposal to be thinkable at all. The house is described as chameleon-like, both house and fence at the same time, both elongated space and a way of shutting off the garden from people's view. And the location is suggested to be in small, isolated enclaves that are fenced in.

A main building is required at the property before an Attefall house is legally allowed to be built. In line with this, land parceling is not allowed after an Attefall house is being built. However, the property market found a creative solution on this matter. The Swedish public service broadcaster (Sveriges Television (SVT) 2015) reported accordingly that Attefall houses were offered for sale in form of expensive cooperative flats. This appeared to be a new way for building companies to get more dwellings in a site and by that to make more money.

The broadcaster reported further (SVT 2016) about the selling of about 50 prefabricated Attefall houses from a company as an example of different solutions in the housing market. As could be expected, the comment from a left-wing representative was that Attefall houses were no solution to a shortage of flats with right of tenancy, and for people with ordinary incomes. Likewise expected was the idea of a liberal political representative that Attefall houses were a possibility to achieve more independence, for people and actors as they allowed them to build as they wanted.

A municipally owned housing company in central Sweden found another way of using Attefall houses (Ljungmark 2016). The size and design with lower costs as a result could be useful in times of housing shortage for categories such as students, immigrants and other more temporary dwellers. The company accordingly decided to build 100 Attefall houses for rent to refugees and others in need of a temporary dwelling. In this case the houses were not intended to be complements to any main buildings since ten houses were planned to be built in the same area at the same time. Regular building permits therefore were needed. The Attefall house is, in this case, just a name of a product aimed at the market, a prefabricated design. The MD of the company also stated, that the size of 25 square metres would be a suitable dwelling for four adults or two adults with up to three children.

Municipal practice

National supervision

As part of the follow-up to legal adoption, the National Board of Housing, Building and Planning (Boverket 2016a) reported the result of a questionnaire to the county administrative boards and the municipalities; 86% of the 290 Swedish municipalities answered. As part of the questionnaire, municipal experiences of the Attefall reform so far were asked for. Most answering municipalities, 52% (Boverket 2016b), found the legislation simple to interpret and to apply. But the rest of the municipalities experienced difficulties and obscurities concerning legal application.

A problem pointed out by the building committees, concerning Attefall measures, was that the applicants did not understand that a mandatory report to the committee meant reconsideration, a need to send in documents and to await the starting permit from the municipality. The municipalities therefore asked for an enlarged guidance to the public. It was not unusual that several discussions were needed between the building proprietor and the municipality staff to reach alternative solutions at the local spot. But 57% of the municipalities did not at any time refuse to execute a starting permit.

The municipalities in general expressed that building proprietors felt cheated by the talk of exception from building permit, since the costs and the handling seemed to be as heavy as an ordinary building permit. The majority of the building committees and building proprietors thought the legislation to be far too bureaucratic, especially according to the starting application on some occasions the main building was also under construction.

The municipalities also highlighted a wish to obtain an integrated application across municipal borders, since different interpretations were made in different municipalities. There were, however, examples of coordination and officials in charge of the matters meeting for discussions. A number of indistinct scenarios occurred and many questions were dealt with on an *ad hoc* basis. New issues were also emerging that were not expected. Guidance for the municipalities to interpret the legislation in the same way within the country were asked for as important and urgent.

One motive to the Attefall reform was to lower the housing queue. The Board stated that in comparison to the big housing shortage, above all in the metropolitan areas, the changing of the law had a marginal effect. According to the questionnaire (Boverket 2016a) the outcome was 434 new buildings in the whole country, meaning that 8% of the starting permits concerned complete dwelllings for permanent living (434 of 5,247) during the first half-year (2014).

Another reason to change the law was to simplify the legislation according to the individual and to widen the freedom to decide over their own property. The Board called attention to the continually high number of incoming questions about Attefall houses, and doubted the law had led to the intended simplification for the individual property owner. According to the Board (Boverket 2016c), Attefall measures are not included in statistics from Statistics Sweden concerning already commenced dwellings. There are no other statistics showing the actual building of those kinds of houses so far.

Analysis of data sources

Four data sources are used in the analysis:

1   Basic data from the Board's questionnaire (Boverket 2015)
2   Basic data from the Swedish public service broadcaster's questionnaire (SVT 2015)
3   Own questionnaire to 14 municipalities
4   Own selection of starting permit lists from 5 municipalities

The Board published open data from the planning- and building questionnaire (Boverket 2015), providing the first source of data analysed by the author. The data for 2015 is further analysed from a coastal perspective. According to percentage of answers, 81% of municipalities within valuable coastal areas (municipalities with restrictions according to the Environmental Code, see Persson (2014a)), participated in the questionnaire (54 of 67). The percentage of answers for the rest of the Swedish municipalities was 94% (210 of 223). The total number of *building reports* were 13,556 during 2015; 45% of them were located in valuable coastal areas and the rest in remaining municipalities.

A little less than half of the building reports were thus handled by coastal municipalities representing, in this questionnaire, a fifth of the answering municipalities. Seven of the top ten municipalities, handling most Attefall matters, were coastal municipalities. The municipality of Norrtälje had the highest number of all building reports but no complementary dwellings were reported. The second highest position of building reports were held by the Värmdö municipality, one complementary dwelling reported. The highest numbers of building reports concerning complementary dwellings were 110 in Gotland and 57 in Varberg.

The Swedish public service broadcaster (SVT 2015) carried out a questionnaire to all Swedish municipalities and asked for the total number of *starting permits* and of complementary dwellings during the period of 2014–07–01 to 2015–04–30. The author of this article has shared the basic data and analysed it further, providing a second data source.

According to the percentage of answers, 73% of municipalities within valuable coastal areas, participated in the questionnaire (49 of 67). The percentage of answers for the rest of the Swedish municipalities was 71% (158 of 223). The total number of starting permits connected to Attefall housing was 5,150 in the whole country. Half of the matters were the responsibility of the 49 coastal municipalities, and the other half was spread among the remaining 158 municipalities. The coastal municipalities represented hardly a quarter of the answering municipalities, but handled as many Attefall starting permits as the remaining three quarters. Eight of the top ten municipalities handling most starting permits were coastal municipalities. Concerning starting permits of complementary dwellings in the 49 coastal municipalities the number was 228 projects; the other 158 municipalities handled 281 projects. That means that 45% of all starting permits concerning complementary dwellings were handled by coastal municipalities.

The results of the two questionnaires are not comparable, partly because they refer to different periods of time, and partly because one is referring to building reports (Boverket 2015) and the other to starting permits (SVT 2015). But the result of each analysis indicates the same, a situation of coastal municipalities handling a great many more Attefall related matters than other municipalities.

The author's own questionnaire about the handling of Attefall building reports provided a third data source, and this was sent to selected municipalities (Borgholm, Falkenberg, Halmstad, Haparanda, Karlskrona, Kungsbacka, Luleå, Norrtälje, Strömstad, Sölvesborg, Tanum, Varberg, Värmdö, Västervik. Tanum was left out because of a divergent reporting system) within areas protected by the Environmental Code representing coastal areas in the west, east and north of Sweden; all the municipalities are well known for great numbers of second homes (Figure 8.1). The municipalities could supply data concerning the number of building reports during 2014 and 2015. Questions about the amount of measures concerning location in an area of special protection due to cultural and/or environmental qualities, areas of national interest of any kind, protection of public access to beaches or a suggested location too close to the neighbours, were, however, in general not possible to answer. The structure of the data seemed in general not to be adapted to these kinds of cross-regulatory information; in the same register there were seldom or never notations about these conditions. In all these cases the law however implies the municipality should change from handling a simple starting permit to handling a more demanding building permit.

To get information afterwards about changes in matters, a new search is needed in other sources. The most common answer from municipal representatives to the question of how many measures change from starting permit to building permit is therefore that information of this kind is not easily connected from other sources in the digital system. A municipal representative also explained that the reason is that the measure gets a new name in the digital system, and the two measures are not compatible.

Norrtälje municipality stated 8% and Haparanda 6% of building reports concerned the matter of protection of public access to beaches, and were therefore demanding a permit according to the Code. The majority of the other municipalities were unable to answer for the reason of lack of register information.

The amount of building reports within areas with a legal regulation plan [detaljplan], was highest in two west coast municipalities, Falkenberg and Varberg. The municipalities are known to have a good size of older regulation plans from the great expansion of second homes before the restrictions were codified in the Environmental Code. The main part of the remaining municipalities could not answer because of the register structure.

The Planning and Building Act is a decentralised law; municipalities have a large influence over its application. It is also up to the municipalities to organise their work from local routines.

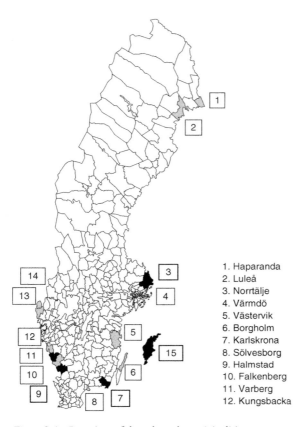

1. Haparanda
2. Luleå
3. Norrtälje
4. Värmdö
5. Västervik
6. Borgholm
7. Karlskrona
8. Sölvesborg
9. Halmstad
10. Falkenberg
11. Varberg
12. Kungsbacka

Figure 8.1 Location of the selected municipalities.

The information about the number and kind of measures is official, but not available in practice without assistance from the staff operating the digital register at the local housing and building office. They also have to prioritise in relation to other tasks, for instance ordinary building permits. The way of describing the handling situation also varies. The following quotations from two different municipalities, each with a large number of measures, show the span:

> A new type of matter [was] introduced without any big planning in advance, many uncertainties [exist] about how to handle, [one] experienced [that the legislation was] not thoroughly gone through; with a building permit check despite being something simple and facilitating the building of new dwellings. In many cases it had to do with measures carried out without any permit and afterwards injunctions, leading to further processes concerning abolitions. A lot of extra work for the staff, who are supposed to work with other things such as ordinary building permits. No larger simplification. The number of [Attefall] measures has a continuous influence on [other] remaining matters with prolonged handling.
>
> *(Informant number 1, own translation)*

We have been working with the process in general for several years; we introduced electronic service to make things more effective. The handling as a whole is run digitally and it is a faster way of handling and we also do this with [Attefall] building reports. At the website there is a guide for the electronical services. We have got negative reactions about the system not to be so user-friendly, but we bought a completed system. In the positive is that it is an easy and smart way to give feedback to the customer.

(Informant number 2, own translation)

After a building report the next step in the process of handling, is the municipality's examination of conditions according to the law, and after a decision of approval, a starting permit, is being issued. A fourth data source was constructed by asking some of the selected municipalities above, for their starting permit lists from 2015.

The municipalities represent two at the west coast, Varberg and Halmstad, two at the east coast, Karlskrona and Norrtälje. The municipality of Gotland, with the greatest number of building reports according to complementary dwellings in the questionnaire of the Board, was also asked to send in the list of starting permits. The collected lists of starting permits show that municipal handling of applications first list the dates of building reports sent in, dates of decision of starting permits, kind of measure, name of property and applicant; rarely any other place-related information is connected to the same register.

The starting permit lists of the five municipalities showed both similarities and differences in their organisation. All lists followed in principle the legal division of complementary dwelling [komplementbostadshus], complementary building [komplementbyggnad], extension [tillbyggnad], dormer [takkupa] and fit up another dwelling in the same house [inredning av ytterligare en bostad]. There are examples of additional local terms. Also divergences and inconsistencies could be found in filling in the same register according to designation of a matter, in a separate municipality or other. The explanation for this probably has to do with several members of the staff putting and/or taking information into the same register. When finding obscurities in a list the author took a renewed contact and asked for a copy of the original report form and/or drawing (Figure 8.2).

In general the address of the applicant was the same as the building site of the starting permit. Sometimes there was however a connection to a supposed permanent address elsewhere. In the latter case it could be a strong indication that the starting permit is intended for a second home. Sometimes the register contained an explicit note of the building being a second home. According to local tradition, some municipalities also separated complementary dwellings for permanent vacation use (Varberg) and several noted complementary buildings used as guest houses [gäststuga].

Two municipalities, Norrtälje and Karlskrona, stated that they did not have any applications concerning complementary dwellings. All seven complementary dwellings noted in Gotland had houseowners/applicants with addresses in the mainland of Stockholm. In Halmstad three of fifteen applicants had addresses connected to Halmstad municipality; the others had addresses outside the county, mainly in the neighbouring county. In Varberg all 47 starting permits concerning complementary dwellings were connected to second homes; none were categorised as intended for permanent dwelling. Varberg was the only municipality to specify in that way. The total number of starting permits in 2015 regarding complementary dwellings, presumably in connection to vacation housing in these five coastal municipalities, was 66 out of 69 (Table 8.1).

A comparison of the list of *building permits* sent to the Board with the list of collected *starting permits* from the five municipalities shows the best correspondence between expectation (building report) and realisation (starting permit) according to complement buildings. This indicates

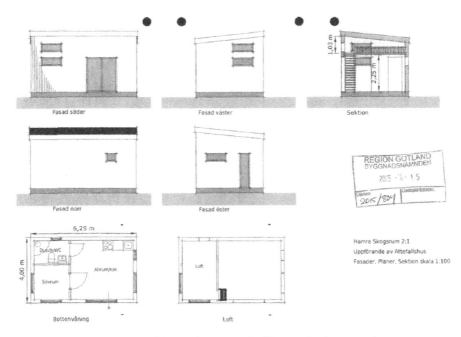

Figure 8.2 Design of an Attefall complementary dwelling, Gotland municipality.

Table 8.1 Comparison of building reports and starting permits from five municipalities in 2015

Municipality	Complementary dwelling	Complement building	Expansion of main building	Total
Building reports★				
Gotland	110	48	1	159
Halmstad	16	60	130	206
Karlskrona	10	35	42	87
Norrtälje	0	294	235	529
Varberg	57	110	166	333
Total	193	547	574	1,314
Starting permits★★				
Gotland	7	85	39	131
Halmstad	15	43	97	155
Karlskrona	0	49	27	76
Norrtälje	0	251	3	254
Varberg	47	84	0	131
Total	69	512	166	747

★ Basic data questionnaire from the National Board of Housing, Building and Planning.
★★ Basic data municipal starting lists collected by the author.

an interest in a property development of own use. The biggest difference exists according to extensions of main buildings. Further examination is needed to find out why the latter measure differentiates the most. When looking at the amount of expected complementary dwellings versus realised houses, a conspicuous difference is between Varberg (close to expectation) and Gotland (far from expectation). This would be of interest to investigate further.

Conclusion

Considering the intended effects, the Attefall reform has not been a success; there appears to be neither increased supply of dwellings in metropolitan areas nor any simplification for the individual. So what has come out of the reform? So far there has not been much information about problems within neighbourhoods or with beach protection. Presumably it is too early to say since legal cases take time and sometimes municipalities have pragmatic ways of handling such things before matters go to far.

As for the individual houseowner, an undoubted advantage is the reform supporting development of their own property, especially in attractive areas within a profitable property market; probably the reform also stimulates the local economy and building companies. The role of second homes as consumer products and part of the local economy has been discussed by, for instance, Hall and Müller (2004).

Despite not all building permits leading to starting permits, coastal municipalities especially have to handle an extensive number of Attefall measures. Their readiness to do so seems to vary and can be dependent on different elements connected to political purposes, resources and local conditions. Interchange of experiences seems necessary and the question is, which part is most suitable to do so, the local, regional or national level or a combination of all three?

Despite an apparently small matter, the effect of Attefall measures seems sometimes hard to master, when the allocation of resources is stretched. Supporting digital measures at the local administrative level vary, and seem to be designed to fit a general commercial market, rather than to facilitate current handling and control. The very fast way of changing the law, within half a year, took many municipalities with surprise, given they were already strained by a heavy load of ordinary building permits, as noted in the two quotations from municipal respondents.

As expressed by Goble et al. (2014: 1) 'The coastal environment is constantly under pressure, and management actions, policies and legislation need to ensure the protection of this unique environment'. Even a limited analysis, as presented in this chapter, indicates that Swedish municipalities in valuable coastal areas are handling disproportionately many Attefall measures. Most unsatisfying is the general lack of comprehensive readiness to evaluate the long-term effect of the Attefall reform in proportion to sustainable development of valuable coastal areas at all levels.

With elections to Parliament it was of course politically difficult to run against the "freedom for houseowner" argument. But, after all, a strong motive for the Parliament to accept restrictions supported by the Environmental Code, was the apprehension of opposition between uncontrolled growth of private second home areas versus long-term safeguarding public interests along the coast (Persson 2014a). As a whole, the Attefall reform could be suspected of having a neglected side effect by further weakening the intentions of the Environmental Code according to sustainable development.

References

Andersen, F. M., Christensen, M. S., Jensen, O. M., Kofoed N.-U. and Morthorst, P. E. (2008) 'Second-home electricity consumption', *Energy Policy*, 36 (1): 280–289.

Andersson, F. (2014) Branschen tror på en byggboom. *Dagens Nyheter*, 12 August.

Andersson, R. and Magnusson Turner, L. (2014) 'Segregation, gentrification, and residualisation: From public housing to market-driven housing allocation in inner city Stockholm', *International Journal of Housing Policy*, 14 (1): 3–29.

Baiche, B., Walliman, N. and Ogden, R. (2006) 'Compliance with building regulations in England and Wales', *Structural Survey*, 24 (4): 279–299.

Bhattacharya, R. and Kim, S.-W. (2011) 'Economic fundamentals, suprimelending and housing prices: Evidence from MSA-level panel data', *Housing Studies*, 26: 897–910.

Bianco, L. (2006) 'Malta: Housing and real esate, 1980-2005', *Architectural Design*, 76 (3): 76–81.

Boverket (2015) *Öppna data – Plan- och byggenkäten 2015*. [online] Available at: http://www.boverket.se/sv/om-boverket/publicerat-av-boverket/oppna-data/plan--och-byggenkaten/

Boverket (2016a) *PBL Kunskapsbanken – en handbok om plan- och bygglagen. PBL kunskapsbankens sidor om plan och bygglagstiftningens tillämpning under 2014*. [online] Available at: http://www.boverket.se/contentassets/45d1e0b078e54394a6c2b7d38e4187f4/uppfoljning-plan--och-bygglagstiftningens-tillampning-2014.pdf

Boverket (2016b) *Tillämpningen av de bygglovbefriade åtgärderna*. [online] Available at: http://www.boverket.se/sv/PBL-kunskapsbanken/uppfoljning/uppfoljningsteman/uppfoljningstema-bygglovsbefriade-atgarder1/bygglovsbefriade-atgarder/

Boverket (2016c) *Boverkets indikatorer nr 1 maj 2016*. [online] Available at: http://www.boverket.se/globalassets/publikationer/dokument/2016/boverkets-indikatorer-maj-2016.pdf

Christophers, B. (2013) 'A monstrous hybrid: The political economy of housing in early twenty-first century Sweden', *New Political Economy*, 18 (6): 885–911.

Denscombe, M. (2007) *The Good Research Guide: For Small-Scale Social Research Projects*. 3rd. ed. Maidenhead, UK: Open University Press.

Goble, B. J., Lewis, M., Hill, T. R. and Phillips, M. R. (2014) 'Coastal management in South Africa: Historical perspectives and setting the stage of a new era', *Ocean and Coastal Management*, 91: 32–40.

Hall C. M. (2005) *Tourism: Rethinking the Social Science of Mobility*. Edinburgh: Pearson.

Hall, C. M. (2014) 'Second homes planning, policy and governance', *Journal of Policy Research in Tourism, Leisure & Events*, 7 (1): 1–14.

Hall, C. M. and Müller, D. K. (2004) 'Introduction: Second homes, curse or blessing? Revisited'. In C. M. Hall and D. K. Müller (eds) *Tourism, Mobility and Second Homes: Between Elite Landscapes and Common Ground*. Clevedon, UK: Channel View, 65–94.

Hall, C. M. and Zapata Campos, M. J. (2014) 'Public administration and tourism: International and Nordic perspectives', *Scandinavian Journal of Public Administration*, 14 (1): 3–17.

Hall, T. and Vidén, S. (2005) 'The million homes programme: A review of the geat Swedish planning project', *Planning Perspectives*, 20 (3): 301–328.

Hao, H., Long, P. and Hoggard, W. (2014) 'Comparing property owners' perceptions of sustainable tourism in a coastal resort county', *Journal of Policy Research in Tourism, Leisure & Events*, 6 (1): 31–51.

Holmqvist, E. and Magnusson Turner, L. (2014) 'Swedish welfare state and housing markets: Under economic and political pressure', *Journal of Housing and the Built Environment*, 29 (2): 237–254.

Huhtala, A. and Lankia, T. (2012) 'Valuation of trips to second homes: Do environmental attributes matter?', *Journal of Environmental Planning and Management*, 55 (6): 733–752.

Jeong, J. S., García-Moruno, L., Hernández-Blanco, J. and Jaraíz-Cabanillas, F. J. (2014) 'An operational method to supporting siting decisions for sustainable rural second home planning in ecotourism sites', *Land Use Policy*, 41: 550–560.

Jurinsky, J. J. (2010) 'All in the family – Vacation homes and second homes in good times and bad', *Real Estate Taxation*, 37: 183–192.

Lagrådet (2014) Lagrådets yttrande, Bilaga 9, 144–151. Regeringens proposition 2013/14:127. Nya åtgärder som kan genomföras utan krav på bygglov. Stockholm: Socialdepartementet.

Lanza, S. and Randazzo, G. (2013) 'Toursit-beach protection in north-eastern Sicily (Italy)', *Journal of Coastal Conservation*, 17 (1): 49–57.

Ljungmark (2016) 'Här är områdena där Östersundshems Attefallshus ska placeras'. *Nya Länstidningen*, 30 mars. [online] Available at: http://www.ltz.se/jamtland/ostersund/har-ar-omradena-dar-ostersundshems-attefallshus-ska-placeras

McIntyre, N., Williams, D. R. and McHugh, K. (2006) 'Multiple dwelling: Prospect and retrospect'. In N. McIntyre, D. R. Williams and K. McHugh (eds) *Multiple Dwelling and Tourism: Negotiating Place, Home and Identity*. Wallingford, UK: CABI International, 313–322.

Mäntysalo, R., Saglie, I.-L. and Cars, G. (2011) 'Between input legitimacy and output efficiency: Defensive routines and agonistic reflectvity in Nordic land-use planning', *European Planning Studies*, 19 (12): 2109–2126.

Norris, M., Paris, C. and Winston, N. (2010) 'Second homes within Irish housing booms and busts: North-south comparisions, contrasts, and debate', *Environment and Planning C: Government and Policy*, 28 (4): 666–680.

Oliveira, J. A., Roca, M. N. O. and Roca, Z. (2013) 'Second homes and residential tourism: New forms of housing, new real etate market', *Revista Portuguesa de Estudos Regionais*, 32 (1): 57–72.

Pedro, J. B., Meijer, F. and Visscher, H. (2010) 'Building control of European Union countries', *International Journal of Law in the Built Environment*, 2 (1): 45–59.

Persson, I. (2014a) 'Second homes, legal framework and planning practice according to environmental sustainability in coastal areas: The Swedish setting', *Journal of Policy Research in Tourism, Leisure & Events*, 7 (1): 48–61.

Persson, I. (2014b) 'Advertising stories of second homes in the Swedish welfare state', *Tourism Review International*, 18 (3): 193–205.

Regeringskansliet. (2014) Pressmeddelanden 2010–2014 – Staffan Attefall – regering.se. [pdf] Available at: http://www.regeringen.se/contentassets/df5485bc332f4c26b23a7b89a1a3750e/pressmeddelanden-2010-2014---stefan-attefall

Språkrådet. (2014) Nyordslista 2014. [pdf] Available at: http://www.sprakochfolkminnen.se/download/18.cbc0f5b1499a212bbf1d2a/1419832595190/nyordslista+2014.pdf

Statistics Sweden. (2005) Bebyggelseutvecklingen inom kustnära områden av riksintresse enligt miljöbalken. Statistiska meddelanden 2005-12-15 NI 68 SM 0501. SCB.

Sveriges Television (SVT). (2015) Attefallshus blir dyra bostadsrätter. [online] Retrieved from: http://www.svt.se/nyheter/inrikes/attefallshus-blir-dyra-bostadsratter (accessed 22 July 2016).

Sveriges Television (SVT). (2016) *Attefallshus förvandlas till bostadsrätter*. [online] Available at: http://sveriges-radio.se/sida/artikel.aspx?programid=1637&artikel=6425661 [2016-06-22]

Swedish Environmental Code [Miljöbalk]. (1998) SFS 1998:808, Stockholm: Sveriges Riksdag. Available at: http://www.riksdagen.se/sv/Dokument-Lagar/Lagar/Svenskforfattningssamling/Miljobalk-1998808_sfs-1998-808/

van der Heijden, J. (2009) 'International comparative analysis of building regulations: An analytical tool', *International Journal of Law in the Built Environment*, 1 (1): 9–25.

van der Heijden, J. (2010) 'Privatisation of building code enforcement: A comparative study of regimes in Australia and Canada', *International Journal of Law in the Built Environment*, 2 (1): 60–75.

van der Heijden, J., Visscher, H. and Meijer, F. (2007) 'Problems in enforcing Dutch building regulations', *Structural Survey*, 25 (3/4): 319–329.

Villaägarna. (2014) Attefallshus kan ge 200 000 nya bostadstillfällen. [online] Retrieved from: http://www.villaagarna.se/Press/Pressmeddelanden/Attefallshus-kan-ge-200-000-nya-bostadstillfallen/ (accessed 22 July 2016)

Wrede, E. and Issit, M. (2014) *25 kvadrat*. Stockholm: Max Ström.

9

DISPLACEMENT AND SECOND HOME TOURISM

A debate still relevant or time to move on?

Gijsbert Hoogendoorn and Roger Marjavaara

Introduction

The displacement of permanent residents as a result of second home tourism has been a contentious debate within the field of tourism studies, town and regional planning, housing studies and tourism geography in a number of countries such as the United Kingdom, Sweden and South Africa (Coppock 1977; Gallent et al. 2005; Hoogendoorn & Visser 2015). These debates have swayed between debates of a Marxist orientation versus the results of capital accumulation of the neo-liberal economic systems (Hoogendoorn & Visser 2011a). While this debate continues, little empirical evidence is presented by researchers that displacement of local permanent residents actually takes place despite widespread claims of this in often UK-based literature and the popular media (Hoogendoorn & Visser 2015). Displacement of local permanent residents as a result of second home ownership is a serious issue related to larger issues of social justice and should be identified where applicable and addressed by governments and communities in the different political, social and geographical contexts. However, we would argue that hard empirical evidence is required first, before displacement of local permanent residents is to be considered as a fact both in public and in academic debates. Otherwise, it would be more worthwhile and practical to explore other pertinent issues around second home tourism like environmental impacts, which has seen comparatively little investigation.

Sweden has been the epicentre of second home tourism research since the re-emergence of this research foci in the late 1990s (Müller 1999; Müller & Hoogendoorn 2013). The development, updating and maintenance of an advanced database called ASTRID, has allowed researchers to do investigations with statistical testing that are almost impossible in the rest of the world due to the lack of credible macro or micro data (Hoogendoorn & Visser 2011b, 2012). Therefore, Sweden is the perfect laboratory to revisit the issue of displacement as a follow-up longitudinal study from the original work done by Marjavaara (2007a, 2007b, 2008, 2009). In the research by Marjavaara, examples of displacement in Sweden as a direct result of second home tourism were found to be largely unfounded. Rather it was found that permanent residents moved away from localities due to normal life cycle events such as higher education, economic opportunities and urbanisation was found to be the reason. Therefore, the core argument of this chapter is to reconsider whether displacement as a result of second home tourism, specifically, is viscerally evident in the case of Sweden or is it rather the case that the displacement debate should be placed on the back-burner until hard evidence can be presented.

This chapter will develop as follows: first, a historical account is provided on the displacement debate on a number of localities globally, both from a developed and developing world perspective; second, the data and methodology is presented and discussed, followed by the results section; and, third, the empirical findings are discussed, and the chapter ends with a concluding discussion.

Displacement debates

As mentioned in the introduction of this chapter, displacement of permanent residents as a result of second home ownership has been a key feature of second home tourism research since the 1970s and the purpose of this literature review is to track the development of this debate (Müller & Hoogendoorn 2013).

Coppock's (1977) seminal edited work, *Second Homes: Curse or Blessing?*, made note of second home-led invasion and succession processes and that second homes are often responsible for the hastening of out-migration from rural areas by permanent residents. Second home-induced displacement, as argued by Coppock, was often compounded by the internationalisation of the countryside where second home owners were often from foreign countries pushing local inhabitants from their homes and jobs. Shucksmith (1983) continued this debate in the 1980s by exploring the effects of second home ownership that led to displacement. These examples include the impact of second home ownership on local property values; the knock-on effect of second home investment on increased property prices for rented accommodation; second homes being responsible for the exhaustion of affordable housing stock; and municipal services being withdrawn as a result of the seasonality of second home ownership which then negatively impacts permanent residents. Shucksmith (1983: 178) argued that these processes then lead to the "*disintegration of communities*" as an end result. This debate continued into the 1990s and early 2000s, especially with the work of Gallent (1997, 2007), Gallent and Tewdwr-Jones (2001) and Gallent et al. (2003, 2005), which questioned the value of second homes in certain parts of the United Kingdom, especially in Wales, where second homes as a phenomenon have often led to social exclusion through a variety of processes very similar to what has been mentioned by Shucksmith, such as the creation of housing shortages, displacement and escalation of property prices. This development has been claimed to occur in many places throughout the world: in the United States by Jordan (1980), in Canada by Halseth (2004), in South Africa by Visser (2004), in Great Britain by Gallent and Tewdwr-Jones (2000) and Gallent et al. (2003), in Spain by Barke (1991), in Sweden by Guterstam (1984), Öhrling (1984), Gustavsson (1992), Glesbygdsverket (2001), Skärgårdarnas Riksförbund (2002), Folkesdotter (2003) and Moström et al. (2004), and in New Zealand by Keen and Hall (2004).

However, second home-induced displacement is often claimed to exist based on very little/if any empirical evidence, but rather based on anecdotal evidence from individual case studies and opinions voiced in the popular media (Hoogendoorn & Visser 2015). The seminal edited collection by Hall and Müller (2004), *Tourism, Mobility and Second Homes: Between Elite Landscape and Common Ground,* does make occasional mention of potential displacement as a result of second homes; however, it definitely does not centre on this issue. In fact, only Keen and Hall (2004) in the case of New Zealand mention the displacement as a result of second home ownership in one case study area and Müller (2004) notes that in Sweden public debate often mentions that second homes can be the reason for displacement of permanent residents. In the late 2000s a pertinent challenge against "'*displacement theory*'" came from Marjavaara (2007a, 2007b, 2008,

2009) with a four paper series, within the context of Sweden. From Marjavaara's studies it seems apparent that from the egalitarian or middle class stature of Sweden's population, second home ownership is an integral part of culture and society; the often elitist nature of second homes representing oppressive interests from elsewhere is not found in Sweden. In fact, most Swedes have access to second homes. For example, many of the reasons for out-migration from areas where second homes are prevalent in Sweden, are not significantly related to the social and economic impacts of second homes. It is rather a case of local residents deciding to migrate to urban areas as a result of broader processes within the post-productivist countryside, not specifically related to second homes. Life stage cycles also play an important role in the out-migration of permanent residents, such as retirement and the need to access health care, young people seeking education in major urban centres, but also due to the limited economic opportunities in remote areas, individuals or groups may migrate to find better and higher paying jobs. Property values also played an important role in out-migration of permanent residents: for example, Marjavaara (2007a) found that permanent residents' properties are the major reason for an increase in property prices rather than second homes. In fact the argument is rather made that permanent residents have benefitted from the presence of second home tourism and its consequent economic benefits. This is the complete opposite to what Shucksmith (1983) found in the 1980s in the UK. As a result, at least in the case of Sweden, displacement induced by second home development has very little empirical evidence; however, Marjavaara (2007a) argues that although displacement is a possibility because of second homes, there is little to no statistical evidence to support some kind of policy that would hinder the development of second homes to displace local inhabitants.

The debate concerning displacement has also been important in the developing world, especially in South Africa where Hoogendoorn (2011), Rogerson and Hoogendoorn (2014) and Hoogendoorn and Visser (2015) have very particularly reasoned against the displacement debates emerging from the UK. These authors have argued that second homes in South Africa are not necessarily situated in areas that will displace permanent residents and that in a struggling developing world economy, the economic benefits of second home ownership far outweigh potential results of displacement that could take place. Second homes are also an integral part of South African culture and society where they form part of traditional labour migration practices compounded by Visiting Friends and Relatives (VFR) travel from rural to urban areas of individuals and groups that are essentially poor, but also to the elite and wealthy that own second homes in amenity rich landscapes. Space is also not considered to be a problem in South Africa, similar to Sweden, where population densities are much lower than in, for example, the United Kingdom. Moreover, South Africa has a *Restitution of Land Rights Act of 22 of 1994* where black population groups can appeal for the restoration of their land taken away by colonial regimes and the apartheid government. While second homes may be or are present on land that was taken from indigenous groups, the main reason why land rights are restored is either to gain back tribal land which in itself would then become second home residences/settlements because of labour migration processes, or to restore agricultural land for economic purposes. However, the main purpose of land restoration is not because of second home-induced displacement, but rather because former oppressive political regimes' displaced groups and displaced residents would often like to establish second homes on those localities. Another example of a study addressing the issue in a developing world context is Wortman et al. (2016), who conclude that foreign direct investments in Mauritius created a polarisation among residents, of those who benefited from the increase in property values and those who did not.

Few researchers would argue for the presence of second homes in rural areas, if it was as directly responsible for displacement of permanent inhabitants as some commentators argue.

It is our view that nobody should be subject to forced migration; however, the hard empirical evidence needs to be provided to prove that people are directly displaced because of second homes. It is our view that second homes are often used as the scapegoat for displacement debates and have not been significant in most locations where research has been conducted (Müller 2011; Paris 2009). Also, second homes are not an entirely positive or beneficial experience for all individuals involved, depending on one's health, age and income levels (Lundmark & Marjavaara 2013). Hall (2015: 6) argues that one potential solution to the displacement debate is the definitional function of second home ownership, for example, the difference between second homes that are used for leisure/recreational purposes and second homes that are used as "investment mechanisms". Moreover, Paris (2009) makes a very good point that there are conceptual similarities between rural gentrification and displacement as a result of second home ownership. However, he argues that instead of understanding second homes and displacement as causal factors, rather it should be an empirical question or hypothesis that needs to be proven or disproven. Gallent (2013) in fact has argued that second homes can act as a positive in community development in rural areas, but nevertheless, local councils should be very wary of any form of displacement as a result of second home ownership. Second home research in a global context is still infantile and many locations across the globe have not seen significant research on the presence of second homes. It may well be that the locations where second homes directly displace individuals still need to be researched.

This study will yet again address the issue of second home-induced displacement in Sweden, simply because of the vast amount of available data in the field. This allows us to conduct enquiry into the matter from a nationwide perspective rather than producing another case study. It will also allow for utilising micro data with a longitudinal depth, not available in most countries of the world. Hence, conducting this study will contribute to the debate of second home-induced displacement and hopefully decide whether or not we have come full circle or if it's time to move on regarding this matter.

It is important to clarify and explain what second home-induced displacement really is and how we view it. The term displacement is generally used in the literature of migration to describe the process of involuntary migration or mobility (e.g. Robinson 2002). Central to the concept is the forced or involuntary movement of individuals. Factors causing this displacement can be famine, war, political instability, and industrial or infrastructure development (Boyle et al. 1998). Displacement is also used in the context of urban gentrification. Here, revitalised districts that attract individuals from the upper classes of society may force people who already live there to move because they cannot afford to buy the newly erected dwellings (Hamnet & Williams 1996). In second home research, displacement is conceptualised in a similar way. The socio-economic differences between individuals who compete for dwellings in the same location are central to the issue. Often the permanent residents occupy an inferior position, which can result in displacement. Displacement caused by second homes is generated by temporal migration whereby the displacers are seasonally attracted to a place, often in rural locations. Hence, we adopt the same definition for second home displacement as used by Marjavaara (2008): '*the process of permanent residents who leave their place of residence on an involuntary basis due to increased living costs, caused by external demand for second homes*' (p. 21).

Data and methodology

This study utilises official data from an extensive database called ASTRID (2016), created by Statistics Sweden, stored and maintained at the Department of Geography and Economic History at Umeå University, Sweden. The database contains annual micro data on every permanent resident in Sweden for the period 2003–2012 and is geo-referenced with a spatial resolution of 100 metres. Variables used in this study for the individuals are: *year of birth (> 17 years in the beginning of the period), north coordinate and east coordinate for place of residence (2003–2012), parish of residence in 2003, parish of birth, disposable income (2003–2012), highest level of education* and *occupation classification code.* Another data set is also utilised, also generated from ASTRID, which includes all second homes in Sweden for the year 2003, containing variables such as: *north coordinate and east coordinate for the property location, municipality* and *assessed property value.* The information on the properties is also linked to information concerning the owners for the year 2003. In this respect, this study uses unique nationwide data that can shed more light on the issue of second home-induced displacement. The definition of second homes follows the definition used by the Swedish national tax board and is based on the owners' statements during the annual taxation process. Accordingly, second homes are properties for recreational and secondary use based on the owners' statements. Considering that the property tax is the same for second homes and for other types of properties such as permanent residences, there is no financial incentive to declare the property with a use other than the actual one, meaning that the records are to be viewed as relatively reliable.

Individuals selected for this study are all 18 years of age or older at the start of the period (2003), meaning that they are of age and in charge of their own decisions. This limitation was done to monitor individuals who are independent and are making, more or less, conscious individual decisions regarding places to live and their own future.

The study is conducted by applying GIS tools to the data set. First, a raster layer is constructed on the annual disposable income for all permanent residents aged 18 and over, in Sweden (N=7,034,148) in 2003. Disposable income is defined as: '*the annual sum of all income after tax and negative transfers is withdrawn, plus taxable and tax free transfers*' (Statistics Sweden 2016). The raster is constructed using the neighbourhood statistics tool, creating a raster with a cell size of 1 km × 1 km, displaying the average disposable income in a specific neighbourhood of a search radius of 5 km from every individual (see Figure 9.1A).

By doing this, an extensive income landscape is constructed, displaying geographical variances in affluence. This is then done on the second home ownership data (N=489,732). However, here the location of the second home is used to display the annual disposable income for the owners, not the permanent place of residence of the owners. This is done in order to locate the economic status among second home owners to places where they are not living on a permanent basis, but still exert influence on. Finally, the difference between the two raster layers is calculated, displaying the difference in economic strength between local residents and temporal visitors (see Figure 9.1B). The logic behind this is that it has been argued in the literature of second home-induced displacement that it is the relative affluence among second home owners that drives up property prices in attractive locations. In combination with large socio-economic differences between permanent residents and second home owners, the permanent residents are often depicted as disadvantaged, leading to a situation that creates higher property taxes and increased living costs for permanent residents, which ultimately leads to the displacement and consequent out-migration of permanent residents (see Marjavaara 2008 for a broad discussion).

The final products of the calculated difference in affluence between permanent residents and second home owners are then used to locate places at significant risk of being subject to second home-induced displacement. Places with low socio-economic status among permanent residents, combined with high status among second home owners are then selected for further enquiry. Pinpointing these locations is done by selecting the most extreme cases. Here, it is done by choosing those places that have the top 10% highest difference in favour of second home

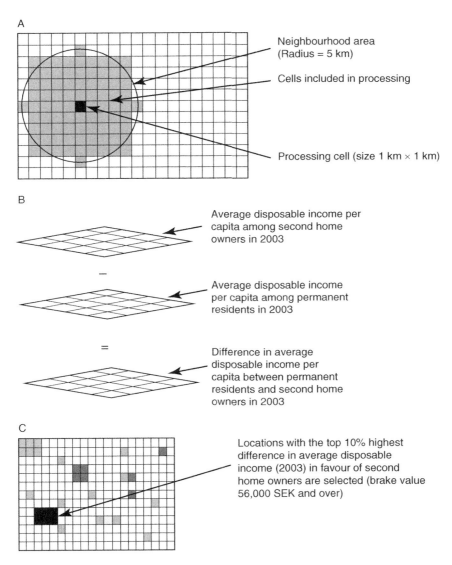

A

Neighbourhood area
(Radius = 5 km)

Cells included in processing

Processing cell (size 1 km × 1 km)

B

Average disposable income per
capita among second home
owners in 2003

–

Average disposable income
per capita among permanent
residents in 2003

=

Difference in average
disposable income per
capita between permanent
residents and second home
owners in 2003

C

Locations with the top 10% highest
difference in average disposable
income (2003) in favour of second
home owners are selected (brake value
56,000 SEK and over)

Figure 9.1 The selection process explained.

owners' affluence (see Figure 9.1C). In this way, those places that are theoretically most at risk of being subject to these processes are selected for further investigation (see Figure 9.2).

The brake point for areas with the highest 10% difference in disposable income starts at 56,000 SEK (1 SEK = 0.11 EUR, 0.12 USD, 0.09 GBP on 2016–05–11) and goes up to 904,700 SEK. This means that second home owners have between 4,666 and 75,392 SEK higher monthly income (on average) compared to the permanent residents in that particular location. In 2003, the average disposable income in Sweden equalled 173,279 SEK, or 14,439 SEK per month for all individuals 18 and over (Statistics Sweden 2016). Hence, second home owners in these locations have an income level that exceeds the average Swedish resident in the same age category by +32% to +622%.

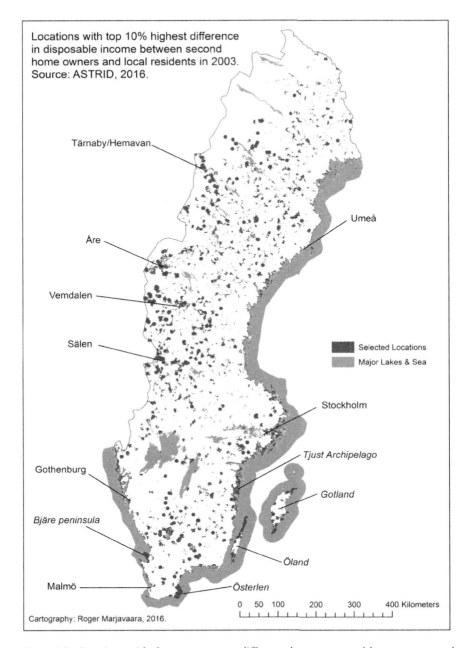

Figure 9.2 Locations with the most extreme difference between second home owners and permanent residents regarding disposable income, in 2003.

Source: ASTRID, 2016.

The locations that appear in Figure 9.2 are typically attractive second home destinations in Sweden. These are mainly located along the seashore in the southern part of the country, which is the most populous. This is especially evident on the islands of Öland and Gotland in the Baltic Sea, but also in the archipelago of Stockholm and Tjust. Furthermore, some hot spots appear in

104

the southern part of the country, especially east of the city of Malmö, where the area of Österlen is located. This part has been an attractive second home destination since the early 1900s and has been studied by Hägerstrand in the 1950s (Hägerstrand 1954). Furthermore, other attractive locations are the Bjäre peninsula, north of Malmö, which attracts some of the "rich and famous" individuals in the country. Other locations with profound difference in economic status between locals and second home owners are typically attractive ski resorts in the Swedish mountain range. These are Sälen, Vemdalen, Åre and Tärnaby/Hemavan. Other locations are spread across the country in locations that are not typically attractive, but rather are places where the second home owners are significantly more affluent than the locals.

After the selection process has been completed in terms of location selection, migration dynamics among the permanent residents are considered. For example, what is the out-migration ratio from these areas and who are the ones who migrate? How many of the original population stock are still there ten years later? Compared to other empirical attempts to address this issue, this study departs from the affluence inequality between the two populations, rather than for example Marjavaara (2007a, 2007b, 2009), who departed from the relative increase of the second home's property value, contributing to the novelty of this study.

Limitations of this study are the influence of foreign second home owners in Sweden, who are not included in the statistics at hand. In certain places, especially close to neighbouring countries like Norway, Denmark and Germany, the share of foreign ownership can be substantial (Müller 1999). Another limitation is that displacement is an issue that is difficult to isolate. The true reason for leaving an area is often complex and often related to a variety of social, cultural and psychological reasons, and is much more complex than blaming second homes specifically for the fate of permanent residents. Further, when asked, individuals can and do give reasons for their migration that may or may not correspond to real reasons. Therefore, the strengths of this study are that it looks at the issue once again, using register data, but tweaking the methodology by departing from difference in affluence and in doing so sheds new light on the issue.

Results

During the study period (2003–2012) the population of Sweden has increased significantly. For those over 17 years of age, the increase has been 8.2%, from a population of 7,034,148 to 7,612,807 individuals (See Table 9.1). At the same time, the number of individuals living permanently in the selected locations with affluent second home owners has also increased, at a rate of 9.6% or some 81,000 individuals. This means that the rate of population increase is in fact higher in the selected locations than in the nation as a whole, despite the fact that second home owners in the locations are significantly more affluent than the locals and hence, can impose a displacement effect in these localities. The relative share of the selected area's population in Sweden has also increased during the period, from 12% to 12.2%. This is rather remarkable considering the rural nature of these localities, which are generally suffering from an ageing population and out-migration resulting in a general population decline. On top of that, it is not the expected development one would assume occurring in localities suffering from second home-induced displacement, where properties are converted from permanent residencies to temporal residencies, leading to decreasing population figures.

The net figure regarding population numbers for the different localities is one thing, but the migration rate and a socio-economic profile for those who leave is perhaps more interesting in this context. Looking at the propensity to migrate in the selected localities compared to Sweden as a whole (see Figure 9.3), one can conclude that the likelihood of migrating is higher among the Swedish population as a whole than for individuals living in the selected localities. Figure 9.3

Table 9.1 Population development in Sweden and second home areas 2003–2012

	Sweden total population, >17 yrs	Sweden index	Second home areas total population	Second home areas index	Second home areas share of Sweden total
2003	7,034,148	100.0	845,287	100.0	12.0%
2004	7,072,152	100.5	851,449	100.7	12.0%
2005	7,113,429	101.1	857,490	101.4	12.1%
2006	7,159,703	101.8	863,835	102.2	12.1%
2007	7,230,368	102.8	872,685	103.2	12.1%
2008	7,313,074	104.0	883,234	104.5	12.1%
2009	7,403,144	105.2	896,643	106.1	12.1%
2010	7,484,343	106.4	909,897	107.6	12.2%
2011	7,549,756	107.3	919,088	108.7	12.2%
2012	7,612,807	108.2	926,396	109.6	12.2%

Source: ASTRID, 2016.

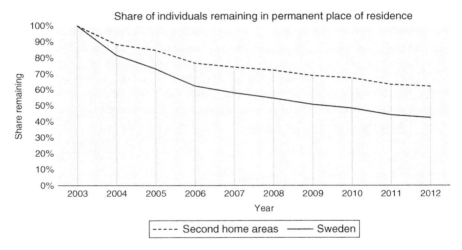

Figure 9.3 Non-migrating population in whole Sweden and second home areas (2003–2012).
Source: ASTRID, 2016.

shows a "survival-graph" of the share of individuals remaining in the same location throughout the whole period (2003–2012), meaning that they stay put in the same permanent place of residence (100 m × 100 m square). This applies to the 7,034,148 individuals living in the whole of Sweden in 2003. Looking at Figure 9.3, one can note a sharp decline for the share not moving during the first three years, declining to 62.5% in 2006. This is then somewhat stabilised during the rest of the period, terminating at a rate of 42.5%, meaning that a majority of the individuals do not live in the same place as they did in the beginning of the period.

Concerning the population living in the selected localities, the pattern is similar. There is a significant decline during the first three years, followed by a period of relative stability. However, compared to the nation, the decrease is significantly less dramatic. During the first three years the share not moving drops down to 74.4% and terminates on a share of 62.3%. Hence, a majority living in the selected localities is less likely to migrate. The difference between the two groups at the end of the period is 19.8%. This is of course not the pattern of observation one would expect to find in a place suffering from a displacement of local inhabitants. In fact, one would expect the opposite pattern: a situation with a decline in population numbers and a higher rate of people migrating.

What then is the profile of the individuals moving in and out from the selected localities of enquiry compared to the ones who do not leave? In a displacement situation, one would expect a significant difference between the individuals moving out from the area, compared to the ones that stay. Theoretically, the out-migrants would be expected to be less affluent and less influential in terms of positions in society, and are displaced due to their inability to compete for properties in these areas. Hence, a comparison between the groups is key in the enquiry of second home-induced displacement. Table 9.2 describes the socio-economic profile of in- and out-migrants and people who do not leave the selected localities. First, we can note that the share of males and females are identical among people who move in and out for the localities, with a slight overweight of females. Among the group who do not move, the share of females is much higher. Concerning age, the differences are similar as for sex. In- and out-migrants show similar patterns, with a median age slightly above the age of 30, whereas for the individuals that stay put, the age is considerably higher (median 59.67 years). The important issue in a displacement context is affluence. One way of measuring this is of course income. The difference in annual disposable income shows that in-migrants have a higher value than out-migrants in terms of median income. Still, the median income for the ones who do not move is even higher, indicating that the *stayers* are not economically disadvantageous compared to the migrant population. However, the mean income for in- and out-migrants is several times higher than for the *stayers*, indicating that there are some individuals in the migrating groups that have extremely high annual incomes.

The education level for the different groups does not differ that much. In fact, the group who stays put for the whole period has a higher degree of individuals with a doctoral degree than both in- and out-migrants. However, if one were to aggregate all post-secondary levels of education it is evident that in- and out-migrants have a higher share of highly educated people compared to the *stayers*. 43.6% of in-migrants have a post-secondary degree or higher, whereas the share is 41.9% of the out-migrants. For the *stayers*, the same share is only 34.0%. The *stayers* also have, by far, the highest share of individuals with an education level of less than nine years of compulsory schooling (14.1%).

The last variable showing the socio-economic profiles of the different groups is *occupation*. Once again, the *stayers* show a higher share of individuals on the highest level. 7.5% of the *stayers* have a managerial position, compared to 4.7% of in-migrants and 5.0% of out-migrants. However, the *stayers* also have a higher share of individuals on the top three occupational levels, compared to the in- and out-migrants. Besides this, in- and out-migrants have higher shares of individuals in service and sales occupations compared to the *stayers* and the latter group who also have a higher share of individuals in agriculture, hunting, forestry and fishing compared to the migrant population. In summary, the migrant population has a higher resemblance with each other in terms of socio-economic profiles and differ from the individuals who do not move during the period.

Discussion

The results of this study show that the selected areas of enquiry, even with their rurality and relative periphery, are not in a situation of population decline and stagnation. On the contrary, these localities are in fact showing an attractiveness that is hard to find elsewhere in rural Sweden, even with the presence of an affluence gap between permanent and temporal populations.

Table 9.2 Socio-economic profile of out-migrants and stayers in selected locations, 2003–2012

	In-migrants	Out-migrants	Stayers (2012)
# Individuals	550,565	531,528	473,941
Sex			
Male	49.7%	49.7%	47.4%
Female	50.3%	50.3%	54.6%
Age			
Median	31.00	36.00	59.67
Mean	36.38	40.91	60.00
Stdv.	16.46	17.66	15.41
Disposable Income★			
Median	167,700 SEK	159,400 SEK	212,900 SEK
Mean	3,074,000 SEK	1,814,900 SEK	264,785 SEK
Stdv.	2,030,760 SEK	110,049,000 SEK	875,739 SEK
Education			
Ph.D.	1.3%	1.3%	1.6%
Post-secondary 2–4 yrs.	32.6%	32.8%	27.6%
Post-secondary < 2 yrs.	9.7%	7.8%	4.8%
Secondary	41.8%	43.3%	42.7%
Compulsory 9–10 yrs.	10.9%	9.7%	9.1%
Compulsory < 9 yrs.	4.0%	5.0%	14.1%
Occupation			
Management positions	4.7%	5.0%	7.5%
Occupations requiring detailed higher competence	19.5%	20.5%	19.5%
Occupations requiring university qualifications or equivalent	17.8%	17.9%	18.2%
Occupations in administration and customer service	10.3%	10.5%	9.8%
Service workers and sales occupations	24.7%	22.7%	18.0%
Occupations in agriculture, hunting, forestry and fishing	0.9%	1.0%	2.7%
Occupations in construction and manufacturing	6.6%	6.9%	8.9%
Occupations in machinery manufacturing and transportation, etc.	7.2%	7.8%	8.8%
Occupations requiring shorter training or introduction	7.8%	7.1%	6.2%
Military occupations	0.5%	0.5%	0.4%

★1 SEK = 0.11 EUR, 0.12 USD, 0.09 GBP on 2016–05–11.
Source: ASTRID, 2016.

The attractiveness of these localities is expressed in the positive population development in the area, an increase of permanent residents that is higher than for the nation as a whole. Further, the area of enquiry is increasing its share of the nation's population volume despite the disadvantageous preconditions. This is of course not a situation that one would expect to find in an area suffering from extensive second home-induced displacement. Rather, one would expect a significant population decline due to the out-migration of permanent residents, which in turn are replaced by temporal inhabitants that are not registered as permanent residents.

It is also interesting to note that the individuals residing in the selected areas of enquiry are less prone to migrate, compared to the nation's population as a whole. The results show that a majority of the permanent residents in the selected localities do not change their permanent place of residence during the period, whereas a majority of the nation's population do. In a displacement situation, the observed patterns would be expected to be the opposite: a situation of relocation of permanent residents out from the area or away from the most sought locations within the area. In both cases, it would have been recorded in the register data, but it's not, supporting an argument of a non-existing second home-induced displacement process.

Further, the results show little or no difference between out- and in-migrants in terms of socio-economic compositions. The in-migrants are slightly more affluent than out-migrants and somewhat younger. This can be taken as an indication of displacement, but then it would be due to rural gentrification rather than affluent second home owners and temporal mobility. It's noteworthy that the *stayers* are the most affluent group in the area (median disposable income), indicating that the area has a permanent population that is somewhat economically robust and could be argued to be able to withstand external competition for properties.

Finally, the occupational status among individuals shows that there are minimal differences between the groups. In fact, the out-migrants have a higher share of individuals in occupations of the highest status and societal influence, compared to the in-migrants, and the *stayers* have the highest of all groups, even in the group with managerial positions.

Conclusion

A general conclusion of this study is that there is little or no existing empirical evidence to support that second home-induced displacement of permanent residents occurs, even in areas with the most extreme preconditions for this. This is yet another study pointing in this direction in the Swedish context. However, this study gives indications of a gentrification process in these rural localities, where in-migrants gradually are shifting the profile of the area. However, this is not caused by temporal mobility or second home tourism, but can rather be caused by second home owners making their temporal home their permanent home upon retirement (Marjavaara & Lundholm 2016). In this respect, we argue that it is time to move on and study and discuss more urgent matters regarding second homes situated in the rural countryside, at least in the case of Sweden, or discuss more general trends of migration and rural gentrification.

It is important to mention that the lack of evidence of displacement as a result of second home ownership is not unique to Nordic countries as a whole. In the egalitarian societies of Scandinavia, second home ownership is part of the culture and the evidence of elite capture of high amenity landscapes is limited in comparison to many developing and developed world countries around the globe. Nevertheless, in extremely unequal societies such as South Africa, the poor often have secondary residences in landscapes that are essential to their personal well-being, culture heritage and family and therefore second home tourism should be considered in terms of its particular spatial and cultural contexts and not in a "one size fits all" fashion, as has been evident especially in the spatially specific contexts of the United Kingdom.

However, second home ownership around the world has led (at least according to anecdotal evidence) and will lead to the displacement of local permanent residents in certain localities and should be remedied as soon as possible, especially where elite capture of high amenity landscapes are taking place. In the case of Sweden though, the lack of evidence of this issue is paramount to the debate around displacement, despite the increasing inequalities in Swedish society since the 2008 economic downturn and the refugee crisis that is affecting Europe at present. Therefore, at least in the case of Sweden, the displacement debate is not relevant at present and it may be more important to focus on debates that are empirically relevant. For example, one such empirically relevant research focus could be second home ownership that is a burden for individuals that have inherited it from their family and struggle to maintain its upkeep (Lundmark & Marjavaara 2013). It is important to acknowledge that not all second homes are the same and that there are cases of ownership that are problematic and troublesome. Another urgent matter is the development potential that comes as a result of the temporal presence of second home owners in rural areas. Building on the arguments of Robertsson and Marjavaara (2015) we would argue that rural communities must focus on the benefits of being attractive for second home ownership, rather than focusing on permanent population numbers, which are often not in favour of these localities. Finally, this study also shows the interrelationship between temporal and permanent mobility that cannot be disregarded. Therefore, studies of second homes, tourism, migration and interrelated societal processes must be interlinked to other subfields of geography and not studied in isolation.

References

ASTRID (2016) Geo-Referenced Database, Generated by Statistics Sweden, Containing All Properties and Individuals in Sweden 2003–2012, Department of Geography and Economic History, Umeå: Umeå University.

Barke, M. (1991) 'The growth and changing pattern of second homes in Spain in the 1970s', *Scottish Geographical Magazine*, 107 (1): 12–21.

Boyle, P., Halfacree, K. and Robinson, V. (1998) *Exploring Contemporary Migration*. Harlow, UK: Pearson Education.

Coppock, J. T. (1977) *Second Homes: Curse or Blessing?* Oxford: Pergamon.

Folkesdotter, G. (2003) 'Sweden'. In N. Gallent, M. Shucksmith and M. Tewdwr-Jones (eds) *Housing in the European Countryside: Rural Pressure and Policy in Western Europe*. London: Routledge, 44–59.

Gallent, N. (1997) 'Improvement grants, second homes and planning control in England and Wales: A policy review', *Planning Practice & Research*, 12 (4): 401–410.

Gallent, N. (2007) 'Second homes, community and a hierarchy of dwelling', *Area*, 39 (1): 97–106.

Gallent, N. (2013) 'The social value of second homes in rural communities', *Housing, Theory and Society*, 31 (2): 174–191.

Gallent, N. and Tewdwr-Jones, M. (2000) *Rural Second Homes in Europe: Examining Housing Supply and Planning Control*. Aldershot, UK: Ashgate.

Gallent, N. and Tewdwr-Jones, M. (2001) 'Second homes and the UK planning system', *Planning Practice and Research*, 16 (1): 59–70.

Gallent, N., Mace, A. and Tewdwr-Jones, M. (2003) 'Dispelling a myth? Second homes in rural Wales', *Area*, 35 (3): 271–284.

Gallent, N., Mace, A. and Tewdwr-Jones, M. (2005) *Second Homes: European Perspectives and UK Policies*. Aldershot, UK: Ashgate.

Glesbygdsverket. (2001) *Planering för åretruntboende i kust och skärgård*. Östersund, Sweden: Glesbygdsverket.

Gustavsson, A. (1992) *Sommargäster och bofasta: Kulturmöte och motsättningar vid Bohuskusten*. Etnologiska institutionens småskriftsserie. Uppsala, Sweden: Uppsala Universitet.

Guterstam, B. (ed.) (1984) *Framtid för skärgården: En rapport om skärgårdsproblematiken i vår tid*. Stockholm: Naturia Förlag.

Hägerstrand, T. (1954) 'Sommarflyttningen från sydsvenska städer', *Plan*, 6 (8): 3–9.

Hall, C. M. (2015) 'Second homes planning, policy and governance', *Journal of Policy Research in Tourism, Leisure and Events*, 7 (1): 1–14.

Hall, C. M. and Müller, D. K. (eds) (2004) *Tourism, Mobility and Second Homes: Between Elite Landscape and Common Ground*. Clevedon, UK: Channel View Publications.

Halseth, G. (2004) 'The "cottage" privilege: Increasingly elite landscapes of second homes in Canada'. In C. M. Hall and D. K. Müller (eds) *Tourism, Mobility and Second Homes: Between Elite Landscape and Common Ground*. Clevedon, UK: Channel View Publications, 35–54.

Hamnet, C. and Williams, P. (1996) 'Social change in London: A study of gentrification'. In V. Robinson (ed.) *Geography and Migration*. Cheltenham, UK: Edward Elgar, 267–282.

Hoogendoorn, G. (2011) 'Low-income earners as second home tourists in South Africa', *Tourism Review International*, 15 (1/2): 37–50.

Hoogendoorn, G. and Visser, G. (2011a) 'Economic development through second home development: Evidence from South Africa', *Tijdschrift voor economische en sociale geografie*, 102 (3): 275–289.

Hoogendoorn, G. and Visser, G. (2011b) 'Researching second home tourism in South Africa: Methodological challenges and innovations'. In C. M. Hall (ed.) *Fieldwork in Tourism: Methods, Issues and Reflections*. London: Routledge, 188–198.

Hoogendoorn, G. and Visser, G. (2012) 'Stumbling over researcher positionality and political-temporal contingency in South African second home tourism research', *Critical Arts*, 26 (3): 254–271.

Hoogendoorn, G. and Visser, G. (2015) 'Focusing on the curse and not the blessing of second homes: Evidence from South Africa', *Area*, 47 (2): 179–184.

Jordan, J. W. (1980) 'The summer people and the natives: Some effects of tourism in a Vermont vacation village', *Annals of Tourism Research*, 7 (1): 34–55.

Keen, D. and Hall, C. M. (2004) 'Second homes in New Zealand'. In C. M. Hall and D. K. Müller (eds) *Tourism, Mobility and Second Homes: Between Elite Landscape and Common Ground*. Clevedon, UK: Channel View Publications, 174–195.

Lundmark, L. and Marjavaara, R. (2013) 'Second home ownership: A blessing for all?', *Scandinavian Journal of Hospitality and Tourism*, 13 (4): 281–298.

Marjavaara, R. (2007a) 'The displacement myth: Second home tourism in the Stockholm Archipelago', *Tourism Geographies*, 9 (3): 296–317.

Marjavaara, R. (2007b) 'Route to destruction? Second home tourism in small island communities', *Island Studies Journal*, 2 (1): 27–46.

Marjavaara, R. (2008) Second Home Tourism: The Root of Displacement in Sweden? PhD. Department of Social and Economic Geography, Umeå University, Umeå, Sweden.

Marjavaara, R. (2009) 'An inquiry into second-home-induced displacement', *Tourism, Planning and Development*, 6 (3): 207–219.

Marjavaara, R. and Lundholm, E. (2016) 'Does second-home ownership trigger migration in later life?', *Population, Space and Place*, 22 (3): 228–240.

Moström, J., Nilsson, D. and Schibbye, K. (2004) *Slutredovisning av miljövårdsprojektet indikatorer för levande kust och skärgård: Att mäta förutsättningarna för framtida kulturarv*. Riksantikvarieämbetet 2004: 3. Stockholm: Riksantikvarieämbetet.

Müller, D. K. (1999) German Second Home Owners in the Swedish Countryside. PhD. Kulturgeografiska Institutionen, Umeå University, Umeå, Sweden.

Müller, D. K. (2004) 'Second homes in Sweden: Patterns and issues'. In C. M. Hall and D. K. Müller (eds) *Tourism, Mobility and Second Homes: Between Elite Landscape and Common Ground*. Clevedon, UK: Channel View Publications, 244–258.

Müller, D. K. (2011) 'The internationalization of rural municipalities: Norwegian second home owners in Northern Bohuslän, Sweden', *Tourism, Planning and Development*, 8 (4): 433–445.

Müller, D. K. and Hoogendoorn, G. (2013) 'Second homes: Curse or blessing? A review 36 years later', *Scandinavian Journal of Hospitality and Tourism*, 13 (4): 353–369.

Öhrling, P. (1984) 'Utredningen om Södermanlands kust och skärgård'. In B. Guterstam (ed.) *Framtid för skärgården: En rapport om skärgårdsproblematiken i vår tid*. Stockholm: Naturia Förlag, 11–19.

Paris, C. (2009) 'Re-positioning second homes within housing studies: Household investment, gentrification, multiple residence, mobility and hyper-consumption', *Housing, Theory and Society*, 26 (4): 292–310.

Robertsson, L. and Marjavaara, R. (2015) 'The seasonal buzz: Knowledge transfer in a temporary setting', *Tourism Planning & Development*, 12 (3): 251–265.

Robinson, J. (ed.) (2002) *Development and Displacement*. Oxford: Oxford University Press.

Rogerson, C. M. and Hoogendoorn, G. (2014) 'VFR travel and second homes tourism: The missing link?', *Tourism Review International*, 18 (3): 167–178.

Shucksmith, M. (1983) 'Second homes: A framework for policy', *Town Planning Review*, 54 (2): 174–193.

Skärgårdarnas Riksförbund (2002) *Vitbok för boende i skärgården*. Runmarö, Sweden: Skärgårdarnas Riksförbund.

Statistics Sweden (2016) Statistical database concerning individual average disposable income for 2003. [online] Available at: www.scb.se (accessed on 5 November 2016).

Visser, G. (2004) 'Second homes: Reflections on an unexplored phenomenon in South Africa' In C. M. Hall and D. K. Müller (eds) *Tourism, Mobility and Second Homes: Between Elite Landscape and Common Ground*. Clevedon, UK: Channel View Publications, 196–214.

Wortman, T., Donaldson, R. and van Westen, G. (2016) '"They are stealing my island": Residents' opinions on foreign investment in the residential tourism industry in Tamarin, Mauritius', *Singapore Journal of Tropical Geography*, 37 (2): 139–157.

PART III

Development and commercialism

10

FROM COMMON GROUND TO ELITE AND COMMERCIAL LANDSCAPE

Dieter K. Müller and C. Michael Hall

Introduction

The history of second homes in many countries reveals its roots as an early form of tourism allowing urban elites to flee newly urbanised places and enjoy the summer months in the countryside (Cross 1992; Pihl Atmer 2001, 2002). Hence, the anticipated positive impact of staying in the countryside for the visitors' health was an important driving force for early second home tourism and mirrored historic Greek and Roman practices (Coppock 1977). In the late nineteenth century and the first decades of the twentieth century, second home settlements spread along the available transport corridors outside the larger cities in many parts of northern Europe (Ljungdahl 1938), North America and Australasia. In the Swedish case a first wave of rather luxurious mansions in the Stockholm archipelago was followed by a second wave of more simple cabins widening the availability of second homes to a wider group of society (Pihl Atmer 2001). To a certain extent these cabins were thought of as alternative to camping and tents, since they were constructed in a way that allowed moving them to other locations to be relatively easy (Nordin 1993). Hence, in the Swedish context, the cabins were constructed on leased land, while in Australia the land was often public "Crown" land (Selwood & Tonts 2004).

Another reason for the development of the second home stock is migration-linked urbanisation (Müller 2004, 2010). Households moving into cities converted their previous primary residences into second homes or they inherited properties from previous generations. This implies a maintained link to the place of origin and upbringing. However, this is not always without complications because of the emotional dimensions of ownership and the sometimes collective management of inherited second homes (Jansson & Müller 2004; Flemsæter 2009).

However, the greatest growth of second home ownership in many countries, at least in the Western world, is related to the increase of car ownership and individual mobility, while international second home ownership has been facilitated by the growth of budget airlines serving secondary and regional airports and low-cost aeromobility (Barnett 2007; Gössling et al. 2009; Paris 2009; Gallant 2015; Adamiak et al. 2016). Furthermore, public programmes stimulating investment in real estate as a form of social policy aimed at creating tourism opportunities for wider groups of society contributed to the dissemination of the second home phenomenon in some jurisdictions (Müller 2010; see also Hannonen, this volume; Opacic & Koderman, this volume). As a result of such a range of, often overlapping, economic and social forces, second home development has accelerated dramatically leading to what Rogers (1977) described as the "invasion of the countryside". Nevertheless, despite many critical comments, second homes have been an important form of domestic mass tourism in many countries and hence a significant part of the common ground and cultural history (Towner 1995; Fountain & Hall 2002; Löfgren 2002; Pitkänen 2008; Rye 2011).

Towards elite landscapes

Despite their popularity, second homes disappeared from the research agenda and public debate during the 1980s and reappeared during the 1990s (Müller 2011b). Müller (2002a) claims several reasons for their reappearance. Ageing populations in Western countries and a restructuring of the labour market towards white-collar employment generated groups of people who had the possibility to spend time in places away from their primary residence and work place. Moreover, in Europe greater political integration paved the way for international second home ownership implying the discontinuation of most restrictions for foreign property ownership (Buller & Hoggart 1994; Müller 1999, 2011a; Lipkina & Hall 2014; Åkerlund et al. 2015; Hannonen et al. 2015; Honkanen et al. 2016). Other countries, such as Malaysia, have also sought to encourage second home tourism (Wong & Musa 2014). Finally, many local and regional governments have increasingly seized tourism and second homes as a tool for regional development (Hall 2015), further putting focus on the second home phenomenon.

A consequence of these changes and the growing affluence among certain groups implies that second homes are increasingly treated as real estate commodities (Paris 2009, 2010; Rye 2011), although second homes are also discussed as an escape from commodification (Chaplin 1999). However, Müller (2002b, 2005) shows that there is an increasing polarisation of second home ownership in Sweden entailing a segregation in leisure space. This does not imply, however, that all second home owners are rich. Instead, the situation certainly varies between different countries and, in many cases, includes a broad cross section of society and sometimes even includes members of some of the lowest socio-economic groups (Adamiak, this volume; Hoogendoorn 2011).

Nevertheless, local and regional government often desire increasing numbers of second home owners because of their ability to spend money locally (Hall 2015). Somewhat surprisingly this nexus between second home tourism and regional development has not yielded a lot of academic attention, at least regarding the economic impacts of second home research. However, a number of studies confirm earlier insights indicating significant economic impacts on the economy and labour market, not least because of home construction and maintenance as well as other second home services (Mottiar 2006). Overvåg (2010) therefore sees second home development in the Norwegian mountains as a way of re-resourcing rural lands, and Hoogendoorn and Visser (2010) discuss the role of second homes in local economic development in small towns in South Africa showing that it alters the economic development of rural areas. In fact, some countries have identified second home owners as a valuable asset and try to attract them through attractive taxation schemes (Åkerlund 2013; Wong & Musa 2014; Åkerlund et al. 2015). This can also be the case with respect to retirement and residential tourism (King et al. 2000; Janoscka & Haas 2013). Indeed, there may be significant connections in the life course of second home development between different owner relationships to the second home commencing with investment and then transforming over time to occupation and eventual use as a retirement property (Hall 2015), but there is an urgent need for further empirical research on long-term owner strategies with respect to second homes.

Economic impacts also occur on different levels (Gallent et al. 2005). For example, greater competition for housing and speculation are sometimes accompanied by house price inflation.

However, housing acquisition, maintenance and improvements have positive impacts on the local economy as do general expenditures by second home owners. Depending on the tax system, local councils can sometimes benefit from property tax. With respect to environmental impacts, Gallent et al. (2005) distinguish between those caused by new development and those by building conversion. Attempts to attract second homes do not always cause positive impacts. A change towards private interests, often focusing on sustaining the rural idyll, and a lack of attention to broader community housing issues puts other goals related to social and ecological dimensions at risk (Kondo et al. 2012). However, Norris and Winston (2009) warn of a rural policy-led development strategy resulting in the potential overdevelopment of rural housing with long-term consequences for the rural economy, housing market and environment. Cho and colleagues (2003) demonstrate the impact of second home development on housing prices implying that inflation effects can also exclude households from purchasing property in certain locations.

Commercial second home tourism

Historically, second home research mainly focused on second homes as private property and family projects (Jaakson 1986). Relatively little research has been conducted addressing the role of second homes as investments and objects for property speculation (Paris 2009, 2010). There is strong evidence that second home owners' use of their property may be accompanied by rental incomes (Tress 2002; Haldrup 2004; Opačić 2009). Indeed, in some countries rental incomes have been important ways of financing private second home investment (Barke & France 1988; Priemus & Mandič 2000; Skak 2004; Komppula et al. 2008). Nicod et al. (2007) argue however that renting out often aims at managing costs rather than at making a profit.

Many destinations welcome the presence of commercial second homes. This is in contrast to previous experiences where second homes were seen as containing "cold beds" that blocked a more sufficient use of local accommodation capacities (cf. Palmer & Mathel 2010; Müller 2013). Today there seems to be a more positive connotation of second homes. They are sometimes treated as a core part of the national accommodation supply and indeed a core element of the product itself (Hjalager et al. 2011). In the case of Norway, it is reported that second homes play a

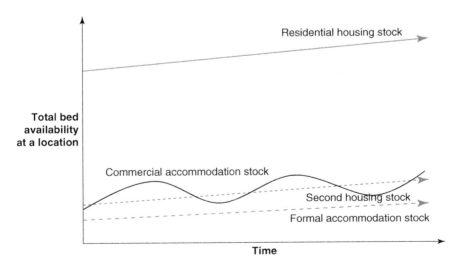

Figure 10.1 Commercial second homes in the informal accommodation sector.

significant role for the provision of touristic accommodation in mountain resorts, where the total number of second homes often outnumbers available hotel rooms. Flognfeldt and Tjørve (2013) even claim that second homes increasingly substitute traditional hotels, which today are mainly service and entertainment centres for the surrounding second homes and visitors. Understanding the way second homes are utilised within specific destination contexts is thus a precondition for gaining an improved comprehension of resort cycles and evolution (Strapp 1988).

A prerequisite for this development is of course the establishment of online booking systems allowing the offering of second home properties to other households and users. Current ideas of a sharing economy further support the potential to rent out second homes (Belk 2014; Sigala 2017), although there are concerns about the implications of this for rental housing markets (Guttentag 2015). This situation further blurs previous boundaries between hotels and other commercial accommodation and private accommodation, such as second homes. Figure 10.1 illustrates these issues by highlighting that although there is a relatively constant availability of bed nights at a location in terms of the formal accommodation sector, second homes and the permanent housing market, the total commercial accommodation stock available to visitors varies seasonally as second home beds, along with rooms and properties in the permanent market made available for rental, are added to that of the formal accommodation sector. From a destination perspective, the availability of commercial accommodation at periods of peak demand can be advantageous for tourism. However, given that there is only a finite amount of stock available, the use of commercial second homes, which may be converted from permanent housing stock, can place pressures on long-term rental markets and property prices.

Conclusion

Hence, in conclusion one can note that second home tourism has undergone significant changes. Second homes represent now a diversified supply of private homes that more or less are used by their owners only, but are increasingly available on a rental market as well. These conditions may occur simultaneously and in the same localities, though market mechanisms entail that commercial second homes are mainly available in popular tourist destinations and resorts. However, this short review indicates that "second homes" has to be seen as an umbrella term covering many different forms of second home tourism with their discrete impacts, challenges and opportunities (Hall et al. 2004).

As a consequence, research has to be more accurate in grasping the geographical conditions for second home tourism in order to contribute to theorising about it in a meaningful way. The current situation implies a blurring of boundaries with other fields of research such as housing and population studies (Paris 2010). Hence, the role of second home research should increasingly also contribute to other fields of research rather than being an isolated branch of research itself.

References

Adamiak, C., Hall, C. M., Hiltunen, M. and Pitkänen, K. (2016) 'Substitute or addition to hypermobile lifestyles? Second home mobility and Finnish CO_2 emissions', *Tourism Geographies*, 18 (2): 129–151.

Åkerlund, U. (2013) 'Buying a place abroad: Processes of recreational property acquisition', *Housing Studies*, 28 (4): 632–652.

Åkerlund, U., Lipkina, O. and Hall, C. M. (2015) 'Second home governance in a European context: In and out of Finland and Malta', *Journal of Policy Research in Tourism, Leisure & Events*, 7 (1): 77–97.

Barke, M. and France, L. A. (1988) 'Second homes in the Balearic Islands', *Geography*, 73 (2): 143–145.

Barnett, R. (2007) 'Central and Eastern Europe: Real estate development within the second and holiday home markets', *Journal of Retail & Leisure Property*, 6 (2): 137–142.

Belk, R. (2014) 'You are what you can access: Sharing and collaborative consumption online', *Journal of Business Research*, 67 (8): 1595–1600.

Buller, H. and Hoggart, K. (1994) *International Counterurbanization: British Migrants in Rural France*. Avebury, UK: Ashgate.

Chaplin, D. (1999) 'Consuming work/productive leisure: The consumption patterns of second home environments', *Leisure Studies*, 18 (1): 41–55.

Cho, S. H., Newman, D. H. and Wear, D. N. (2003) 'Impacts of second home development on housing prices in the Southern Appalachian Highlands', *Review of Urban & Regional Development Studies*, 15 (3): 208–225.

Coppock, J. T. (1977) 'Second homes in perspective'. In J. T. Coppock (ed.) *Second Homes: Curse or Blessing?* Oxford: Pergamon, 1–16.

Cross, A. W. (1992) *The Summer House: A Tradition of Leisure*. Toronto: Harper Collins.

Flemsæter, F. (2009) 'From "home" to "second home": Emotional dilemmas on Norwegian smallholdings', *Scandinavian Journal of Hospitality and Tourism*, 9 (4): 406–423.

Flognfeldt, T. and Tjørve, E. (2013) 'The shift from hotels and lodges to second-home villages in mountain-resort accommodation', *Scandinavian Journal of Hospitality and Tourism*, 13 (4): 332–352.

Fountain, J. and Hall, C. M. (2002) The impact of lifestyle migration on rural communities: A case study of Akaroa, New Zealand. In C. M. Hall and A. M. Williams (eds) *Tourism and Migration: New Relationships between Production and Consumption*, Dordrecht, the Netherlands: Kluwer, 153–168.

Gallent, N. (2015) 'Bridging social capital and the resource potential of second homes: The case of Stintino, Sardinia', *Journal of Rural Studies*, 38: 99–108.

Gallent, N., Mace, A. and Tewdwr-Jones, M. (2005) *Second Homes: European Perspectives and UK Policies*. Avebury, UK: Ashgate.

Guttentag, D. (2015) 'Airbnb: Disruptive innovation and the rise of an informal tourism accommodation sector', *Current Issues in Tourism*, 18 (12): 1192–1217.

Gössling, S., Ceron, J. P., Dubois, G. and Hall, C. M. (2009) Hypermobile Travellers. In S. Gössling and P. Upham (eds) *Climate Change and Aviation*. London: Earthscan, 131–149.

Haldrup, M. (2004) 'Laid-back mobilities: Second-home holidays in time and space', *Tourism Geographies*, 6 (4): 434–454.

Hall, C. M. (2015) 'Second homes: Planning, policy and governance', *Journal of Policy Research in Tourism, Leisure & Events*, 7 (1): 1–14.

Hall, C. M., Müller, D. K. and Keen, D. (2004) 'Second home tourism impact, planning and management'. In C. M. Hall and D. K. Müller (eds) *Tourism, Mobility and Second Homes: Between Elite Landscape and Common Ground*, Clevedon, UK: Channel View, 15–33.

Hannonen, O., Tuulentie, S. and Pitkänen, K. (2015) 'Borders and second home tourism: Norwegian and Russian second home owners in Finnish border areas', *Journal of Borderlands Studies*, 30 (1): 53–67.

Hjalager, A. M., Staunstrup, J. K. and Ibsen, R. (2011) 'Trade and value developments in the Danish second-home sector: Implications for tourism policies', *Tourism Economics*, 17 (3): 677–691.

Honkanen, A., Pitkanen, K. and Hall, C. M. (2016) 'A local perspective on cross-border tourism. Russian second home ownership in Eastern Finland', *International Journal of Tourism Research*, 18 (2): 149–158.

Hoogendoorn, G. (2011) 'Low-income earners as second home tourists in South Africa?', *Tourism Review International*, 15 (1–2): 37–50.

Hoogendoorn, G. and Visser, G. (2010) 'The role of second homes in local economic development in five small South African towns', *Development Southern Africa*, 27 (4): 547–562.

Jaakson, R. (1986) 'Second-home domestic tourism', *Annals of Tourism Research*, 13 (3): 367–391.

Janoschka, M. and Haas, H. (eds) (2013) *Contested Spatialities, Lifestyle Migration and Residential Tourism*. London: Routledge.

Jansson, B. and Müller, D. K. (2004) 'Second home plans among second home owners in Northern Europe's periphery' In: C. M. Hall and D. K. Müller (eds) *Tourism, Mobility and Second Homes: Between Elite Landscape and Common Ground*. Clevedon, UK: Channel View, 261–272.

King, R., Warnes, T. and Williams, A. (2000) *Sunset Lives: British Retirement Migration to the Mediterranean*. Oxford: Berg.

Komppula, R., Reijonen, H. and Timonen, T. (2008) 'Vacation-home owner's willingness to lease through an intermediary–A case study in two Finnish ski resorts'. In T. Keller and T. Bieger (eds) *Real Estate and Destination Development: Successful Strategies and Instruments*. Berlin: Erich Schmidt Verlag, 285–299.

Kondo, M. C., Rivera, R. and Rullman, S. (2012) 'Protecting the idyll but not the environment: Second homes, amenity migration and rural exclusion in Washington State', *Landscape and Urban Planning*, 106 (2): 174–182.

Lipkina, O. and Hall, C. M. (2014) 'Russian second home owners in Eastern Finland: Involvement in the local community'. In M. Janoschka and H. Haas (eds) *Contested Spatialities of Lifestyle Migration*, London: Routledge, 158–173.

Ljungdahl, S. (1938) 'Sommar-Stockholm', *Ymer*, 58: 218–242.

Löfgren, O. (2002) *On Holiday: A History of Vacationing*. Berkeley, CA: University of California Press.

Mottiar, Z. (2006) 'Holiday home owners, a route to sustainable tourism development? An economic analysis of tourist expenditure data', *Journal of Sustainable Tourism*, 14 (6): 582–599.

Müller, D. K. (1999) *German Second Home Owners in the Swedish Countryside: On the Internationalisation of the Leisure Space*. Umeå: Department of Social and Economic Geography.

Müller, D. (2002a) 'German second home development in Sweden'. In C. M. Hall and A. M. Williams (eds) *Tourism and Migration: New Relationships between Production and Consumption*. Dordrecht, the Netherlands: Kluwer, 169–185.

Müller D. K. (2002b) 'Second home ownership and sustainable development in northern Sweden', *Tourism and Hospitality Research*, 3 (4): 345–355.

Müller, D. K. (2004) 'Second homes in Sweden: Patterns and issues'. In C. M. Hall and D. K. Müller (eds) *Tourism, Mobility and Second Homes: Between Elite Landscape and Common Ground*. Clevedon, UK: Channel View, 244–258.

Müller, D. K. (2005) 'Second home tourism in the Swedish mountain range'. In C. M. Hall and S. Boyd (eds) *Nature-Based Tourism in Peripheral Areas: Development or Disaster?* Clevedon, UK: Channel View, 133–148.

Müller D. (2010) 'Second homes in Sweden: Between common heritage and exclusive commodity'. In B. Hermelin and U. Jansson (eds) *Placing Human Geography: Sweden through Time and Space*. Stockholm: SSAG, 185–207.

Müller, D. K. (2011b) 'The internationalization of rural municipalities: Norwegian second home owners in Northern Bohuslän, Sweden', *Tourism Planning and Development*, 8 (4): 433–445.

Müller, D. K. (2011b) 'Second homes in rural areas: Reflections on a troubled history', *Norsk Geografisk Tidsskrift*, 65 (3): 137–143.

Müller, D. K. (2013) 'Progressing second home research: A Nordic perspective', *Scandinavian Journal of Hospitality and Tourism*, 13 (4): 273–280.

Nicod, P., Mungall, A. and Henwood, J. (2007) 'Self-catering accommodation in Switzerland', *International Journal of Hospitality Management*, 26 (2): 244–262.

Nordin, U. (1993) 'Second homes'. In H. Aldskogius (ed.) *National Atlas of Sweden: Cultural Life, Recreation and Tourism*. Stockholm: SNA, 72–79.

Norris, M. and Winston, N. (2009) 'Rising second home numbers in rural Ireland: Distribution, drivers and implications', *European Planning Studies*, 17 (9): 1303–1322.

Opačić, V. T. (2009) 'Recent characteristics of the second home phenomenon in the Croatian littoral', *Croatian Geographical Bulletin*, 71 (1): 33–66.

Overvåg, K. (2010) 'Second homes and maximum yield in marginal land: The re-resourcing of rural land in Norway', *European Urban and Regional Studies*, 17 (1): 3–16.

Palmer, A. and Mathel, V. (2010) 'Causes and consequences of underutilised capacity in a tourist resort development', *Tourism Management*, 31 (6): 925–935.

Paris, C. (2009) 'Re-positioning second homes within housing studies: Household investment, gentrification, multiple residence, mobility and hyper-consumption', *Housing, Theory and Society*, 26 (4): 292–310.

Paris, C. (2010) *Affluence, Mobility and Second Home Ownership*. London: Routledge.

Pihl Atmer, A. K. (2001) *Livet som levdes där måste smaka vildmark: Sportstugor och friluftsliv 1900–1945*. Stockholm: Stockholmia.

Pihl Atmer, A. K. (2002) *Sommarnöjen vid vattnet*. Stockholm: Bonniers.

Pitkänen, K. (2008) 'Second-home landscape: The meaning (s) of landscape for second-home tourism in Finnish Lakeland', *Tourism Geographies*, 10 (2): 169–192.

Priemus, H. and Mandič, S. (2000) 'Rental housing in Central and Eastern Europe as no man's land', *Journal of Housing and the Built Environment*, 15 (3): 205–215.

Rogers, A. W. (1977) 'Second homes in England and Wales: A spatial view'. In J. T. Coppock (ed.) *Second Homes: Curse or Blessing?* Oxford: Pergamon, 85–102.

Rye, J. F. (2011) 'Conflicts and contestations: Rural populations' perspectives on the second homes phenomenon', *Journal of Rural Studies*, 27 (3): 263–274.

Selwood, J. and Tonts, M. (2004) 'Recreational second homes in the south west of Western Australia'. In C. M. Hall and D. K. Müller (eds) *Tourism, Mobility and Second Homes: Between Elite Landscape and Common Ground*. Clevedon, UK: Channel View Publications, 149–161.

Sigala, M. (2017) 'Collaborative commerce in tourism: Implications for research and industry', *Current Issues in Tourism*, 20 (4): 346–355.

Skak, M. (2004) 'Restricting ownership of vacation homes', *Tourism Economics*, 10 (4): 435–447.

Strapp, J. D. (1988) 'The resort cycle and second homes', *Annals of Tourism Research*, 15 (4): 504–516.

Towner, J. (1995) 'What is tourism's history?', *Tourism Management*, 16 (5): 339–343.

Tress, G. (2002) 'Development of second-home tourism in Denmark', *Scandinavian Journal of Hospitality and Tourism*, 2 (2): 109–122.

Wong, K. M. and Musa, G. (2014) 'Retirement motivation among "Malaysia my second home" participants', *Tourism Management*, 40: 141–154.

11

UNCERTAIN BENEFITS

How second home tourism impacts community economy

Adam Czarnecki

Introduction

Besides construction and maintenance services, the retail sector of the host community is often seen as a main beneficiary of second home tourism. Large, recurrent, less seasonally dependent and differentiated demand for locally provided goods is considered important not only in terms of income and job creation/retention but fairly much widely with regard to the local economy structure, robustness and flexibility, but also to the community's well-being and development. However, this highly positive view has been widely criticised and/or undermined either for being insufficient in quantitative terms (amount of income and number of jobs) and qualitative terms (income structure and quality of jobs created). In light of these positive and negative impacts of (second home) tourism on the economy of the host community, provided by the previous evidence-based research, it is important to refer to local people's opinions in order to examine whether and to what extent they differ from researchers' views based on empirical and experiential evidence. As many have argued, long-term economic and social sustainability is achievable solely with active participation and involvement of the local stakeholders (Hall 2008). Tourism can bring revitalisation of small, monofunctional, rural communities as long as it is embedded locally, i.e. utilising local natural, human and economic resources and preferably with an umbrella of the local social capital.

This study aims to examine whether and how local people's opinions on the (beneficial) influence of second home tourism on the community's economy differ from or concur with evidence-based impacts proved by the research so far. This objective is supplemented by the attempt to determine local people's characteristics, here treated as a socio-demographic background and the explanatory precondition shaping their views, attitudes and assessment of such economic impacts.

Literature

There are a substantial number of studies on the economic impacts of tourism (including second home tourism) on the host community (Velvin et al. 2013; Scanlon et al. 2014; Oliveira et al. 2015). The majority see the local retail sector (besides the accommodation services) and basic services as the main beneficiary of the tourist movement worldwide, taking advantage of tourists' local spending both in terms of size and diversity of demand (Müller 1999; Das & Rainey 2010). Visitor spending is an integral part of tourism although the amount of spending definitely varies according to the tourist commodity bundle – sometimes significantly. As many researchers have argued, the impact of spending on host communities has increased along with the role of shopping in tourism activities (Timothy 2005; Tosun et al. 2007). The increasing importance of shopping activities also acts as an important factor in strengthening linkages between tourism and other economic sectors, providing them with the opportunity to expand the market for local products (Jaafar et al. 2015).

The importance of tourist expenditures for the local economy is often considered by researchers and analysts at the micro scale, i.e. individual businesses and groups of businesses (with a common interest; certain segments, with linked activities) or in a wider sense – treating (local) sellers or service providers as distinct industries/sectors. For the former, income, turnover, profit (business growth), employment, cooperation, information sharing and matched investments as well as less tangible development opportunities are used as critical points in examining the impact, while for the latter there is also healthy competence (Kreag 2001), strength, diversification (Choi et al. 2016) and robustness of the economy considered as the ability to survive financial leakages and crises.

It is not surprising that, in terms of economic impacts, a number of researchers have seen income creation for local businesses as the critical benefit of tourism development (Nielsen et al. 2009). Its importance is not only due to the improvement in the financial situation (in a narrow sense) but also due to its role in expanding and multiplying development opportunities – job creation, product diversification, increase in market share, market reorientation, productivity improvement and investment (Andereck et al. 2005) thus contributing to general economic growth. Although in some cases tourists' (second home owners') demand can bring sufficient profits to local enterprises to be considered as the main source of income, more often, both in highly urbanised tourism-based communities and "traditional" rural ones, it provides what can be regarded as an additional income. In the case of highly urbanised communities, such revenues usually supplement the main "permanent"/year-round incomes ensured by supplying the local market, while in rural communities tourism-related revenues are often ancillary to main incomes from farming activity or paid work. Thus, by serving potent local markets or by combining various sources of income in weak economies (pluriactivity), local retailers and service providers can balance revenue flows, secure their funding and thus combat downsides of low/insufficient demand and seasonality.

Many have argued that the seasonality of tourism is the main challenge for the host community (especially in small economies) and for particular industries involved, i.e. the retail sector (Vanegas & Croes 2003). Indeed, seasonality in demand for tourism and consequently for other associated necessary products (basic commodities and services) influences not only incomes but also income-dependent characteristics, i.e. shaping employment fluctuations causing underemployment, lower productivity, and/or unemployment during off-seasons (Kreag 2001) and also potential investment. The significance of seasonality differs among various forms of tourism and, as some studies have shown, it is felt considerably less in an economic sense by the local suppliers of food products and everyday necessities for second home owners. Even though shopping itself is not the core activity for second home owners (being an example of tourist shopping rather than shopping tourism, according to Timothy 2005), they inevitably purchase basic commodities, infrequent goods and services or sometimes even not excluding 'tourist deviations from the daily routine shopping tourism intended for non-profit purposes' (Choi et al. 2016: 3). This is more likely to happen since the average length of stay and number of visits over the year is significantly longer in second home tourism than in the traditional form, and this simply induces higher (accumulated) and more diversified demand and local spending driven both by utilitarian and hedonistic motivations.

Particularly important in regards to profitability are certain tourism-related advantages for the retail sector and local food production systems, namely that: 1) products produced locally can command higher prices sold locally to tourists than when exported and incur lower costs because of relatively lower or absent transport or insurance costs; and 2) some perishable goods can only be sold to tourists in the domestic market because of insufficient export capability and international marketing expertise (Mihalić 2002). Obviously, besides seasonality, revenues from tourism are highly dependent upon various preconditions of consumer behaviour and spending patterns that can be either positive (reflecting high integration with the local economy) or negative, i.e. disadvantageous patterns discordant with the local supply/offer, resulting in excessive imports of goods and thus contributing to weak indirect effects and causing financial leakages from the local system (Vanegas & Croes 2003; Czarnecki 2014). Such unfavourable consumer behaviour can be mitigated at least to some extent by active and responsive management within the retail sector, including marketing strategies and segmentation of the target group (through positioning strategies, and the resultant merchandise ranges, locations, pricing, service levels and promotions) (Larke et al. 2016). These can help to meet the demand of visitors and tourists better and thus create more economic benefits. However, at the same time, other circumstances such as local market specificity and business profile need to be taken into account. This is due to the fact that overemphasis on tourist segments is unlikely to be cost effective and could also impinge upon the domestic customer experience, especially when the locals or external markets constitute the major part of the customer base (Larke et al. 2016).

Increased revenues are critical resources for employment growth in the local economy. However, the role of second home tourism has been emphasised as a local job-retention factor rather than as a job-creation driver. Even though its significance in this particular regard has been thus perceived as limited, in fact it unquestionably plays an important role in declining, peripheral communities (losing basic services) as it keeps the employment at a (more or less) stable level and consequently it maintains access to services/retailers for local people and improves their living standards. Here, similarly, the positive view of the impact on the local labour market has often been criticised and undermined by contradicting any tangible benefits in terms of quantity of new jobs, as well as in qualitative terms with second home tourism providing part-time, seasonal employment with high insecurity and low wages in comparison to jobs generated by other industries. Low wages are also seen as a main obstacle and weakness with regard to indirect effects, since they have very limited capacity to translate into significant spending by the locals (Das & Rainey 2010). In a contrasting view, some have argued that despite these limitations, jobs provided by the tourism sector are particularly important for young people just entering the labour market, since this provides them with an opportunity to gain first work experience and professional training locally, which is seemingly more important than financial aspects.

Furthermore, in a broader sense, second home tourism positively impacts the community's economy through large and more diversified demand for commodities and services in a way that can be a basis for undertaking entrepreneurial initiatives among locals and thus newly established businesses that take advantage of previously unsatisfied tourist demand (e.g. specialist shops and services) (Hall 1994). Second home tourism may induce large and diverse demand for local products, both general merchandise (provided by groceries and supermarkets), accessories (specialist shops), food/agricultural produce directly from farms (farmers' markets, cooperatives, etc.) and various types of services. Though, as previous research shows, compared to traditional tourists, second home owners are a more significant target group for the retail sector than for gastronomy services, mainly due to their daily practices, i.e. purchasing food from groceries and catering for themselves rather than going to restaurants like regular tourists do (Eriksen & Ahmt 1999). Nevertheless, business growth and saturation of the local market somehow naturally enhances the local economy structure to be more diversified (Kreag 2001) and also induces and creates grounds for wider cooperation between retailers and producers (in farming, food processing, handcrafts) and service providers within the local economy, which is also reflected more indirectly in the well-being of the local community as a whole (Muresan et al. 2016). This has also been shown by Ritchie and Inkari (2006), who stressed the decisive role of tourism in providing local people with facilities and services that would be impossible otherwise. As a result, by enriching the economic structure (especially of rural economies that are often dependent on one industry) it becomes more balanced and multifunctional and hence more stable and resilient to external changes, as opposed to specialised or monofunctional economies.

Greater diversity and cooperation between local businesses protects the local economy against financial leakages, making the system more self-sufficient at least in terms of not importing goods and services, which is particularly important given how dependent retailers are on imported products that they then sell to their customers (Rattanasuwongchai 1998; Irshad 2010). The newly established businesses representing previously non-existent sectors of the rural economy are particularly important for poor, inefficient monofunctional communities that are highly dependent upon external markets as the only supplier for farming activity and are the main goods and services providers for individuals. In addition, in tourism regions, capital erosion is not only due to the weakness of the local economy and dependence on imports (and sometimes labour), but is also due to the growing and intense (albeit seasonal) investment in the local retail and service sectors by external owners (Vanegas & Croes 2003). Seasonal shops operating during the holiday period are often seen as typical in such locations, from which they export the profits, thus depriving locals of potential revenue (Rattanasuwongchai 1998). As a result, not only do business owners lose their potential profits, but the reduced tax revenue restricts local council budgets. In contrast, in terms of long-term development it is more likely that tourist spending will contribute more significantly to the "purely" local retail sector in "typical" rural areas, in which shops are usually small-scale family businesses (of more traditional character, growing slowly and organically) but at the same time being strongly embedded locally, and having a durable impact on the area (Irshad 2010; Chuang 2013). On the other hand, for local residents in small communities, new businesses may improve accessibility in spatial terms but also to some new products unavailable outside the summer period, thus contributing to the viability of such communities. However, at the same time it means higher prices, which rise rapidly in the peak season (Ritchie & Inkari 2006) and contribute to the increase in the cost of living for the locals (Kreag 2001).

On the other hand, it is crucial for further local economic development to contrast the whole evidence-based research presented above with the perceptions of stakeholders with the greatest interest in this issue. Whether and how they consider the impact and significance as a potential or insufficient advantage depends in fact on the actual utilisation of this opportunity for business owners and more broadly for the local retail and service sectors. According to Lankford and Howard (1994: 122) 'for a tourism based economy to sustain itself in local communities, the residents must be willing partners in the process. Their attitudes toward tourism and perceptions of its impact on community life must be continually evaluated'. Hence, the local people's voice is crucial and should be heard and taken into consideration when reorienting economic activities towards tourist demand.

In general, as previous studies have shown, no matter whether directly or indirectly involved with tourism and tourism-related activities, local people's attitudes towards tourism development are positive and supportive. However, certain differences in view can be seen with regard to its economic benefits for the community (Ritchie & Inkari 2006). There is no doubt that the local community perceives the impact of tourism (in the economic sense) more positively when it sees tangible benefits for itself (mainly in terms of increasing income and job creation). On the other hand, the perception turns negative if the potential benefits are considerably reduced by the costs (including those of social and natural character) (Ritchie & Inkari 2006). Residents who achieve convincing benefits from tourism, through employment or wages, usually consider this industry as an advantageous and pro-development activity in contrast to those who, either directly or indirectly, do not take this opportunity and do not derive any benefit from it (Sirakaya et al. 2002).

A theory of social representation (Moscovici 1981) is a valuable technique for analysing the perception of the importance of tourism for the local population. This helps to identify, recognise and learn more about local people's attitudes. According to the theory, underpinning their perception of its impact, residents have conceptions of tourism that are formed by direct experience, social interaction and other sources of information, such as the media (Moscovici 1981). These conceptions are resistant to change, as they form a frame of reference in which new information is further processed and interpreted. If residents perceive the distribution of benefits as unfair, it can lead to a reduction in overall public support for the further development of tourism (Ritchie & Inkari 2006). In addition, the more benefits (especially direct) from tourism are geographically dispersed (in different locations), the greater increase in social support and a certain reputation and recognition of the importance of tourism also develops among locals, which is more likely in remote, underdeveloped communities with no opportunities, even seasonally.

As research shows, in small economies, indirect effects and multipliers are significantly lower, since there are many leakages due to monofunctional structure and weak linkages between retailers, service providers and local producers, resulting in unsatisfied demand (Vanegas & Croes 2003). But at the same time profits are achievable only for certain social or geographical groups (Ap & Crompton 1998; Ritchie & Inkari 2006; Chuang 2013). Thus, benefits remain unobservable for most local residents, since the revenues, e.g. from tourism, are not distributed equally or evenly transferred to meet the community needs.

Method

The data for Poland was collected from direct interviews with second home owners and local people, while for Finland this was done entirely by postal survey. The direct interviews in Poland were carried out in 20 selected municipalities in 2009. In total, 398 interviews with second home owners and 200 interviews with local people were completed, which gave respectively, 20 and 10 direct interviews in each of the communities surveyed. The Finnish postal survey was conducted in 2013 and included questionnaires mailed out to 1,000 second home owners whose cottages were located in 20 selected municipalities and to 500 local residents from the same municipalities. The sample prepared by the Population Register Centre (Väestörekisterikeskus) included respondents from both groups who were adults but not over 80 years of age. Here, the response rate was very high, and for second home owners accounted for 46.7% and for local residents 31.2%. Then, as the main research method, a forward stepwise regression analysis was applied in order to create an explanatory model of local people's perception of the positive effects of second home tourism on the community's economy.

Research results

The proportions of locals selling goods and services to second home owners were similar in both countries but relatively low, i.e. 19.2% in Finland and 17.0% in Poland. For the Finns, it was clearly more common to sell services (mainly construction/renovation and maintenance: 13.5%) while for their Polish counterparts it was goods (the great majority agricultural produce: 11.5%). As far as revenues from providing second home owners with goods and services are concerned, local residents in Finland admitted to earning a total of €276,482 (over the 12 months surveyed), of which sales of services accounted for the great majority, i.e. around 89%, while Poles declared total earnings of PLN 266,681 (€64,106), of which sales of services similarly accounted for 92%. Individually, total revenues differed significantly, from €90 to €201,000 for Finnish locals, with a median value of €500, while for Poles it was far less extreme – from PLN 20 to PLN 60,000 (i.e. from €5 to €14,423) with a median of PLN 450 (€108). As the medians indicate, the majority of revenues in both populations were closer to the lower figure than the highest (Table 11.1).

One may attempt to assess the importance of revenues from supplying second home owners, which is in fact to measure the proportion of total annual household income gained from these services. As mentioned above, respondents were not encouraged to put exact figures on their total incomes and revenues/turnovers (except for those from supplying second home owners), but just to place their incomes among five categories for Finns and four for Poles. This did not make it possible to measure the average proportion for the population surveyed but only within the subsequent income categories. In order to do this, the average value of the income for each income category was calculated as a baseline reference to measure the contribution.

The research showed that for Finns approximately 86% of the total revenue from supplying second home owners was earned by local residents in the second quintile, which could be described as wealthy households (with a net annual household income ranging from €60,000 to €120,000), even though this group was very small relative to the population surveyed (only four people). Bearing this in mind, the contribution to the total income per capita was very high for services as well as for goods and services (considered as a unified category), i.e. 81.2% and 66.0% respectively. This means these earnings were unusual compared not only to other income groups but to the total income base. Apart from the most affluent household income group of Finns (incomes higher than €120,000), the contribution to local people's incomes varied widely, from moderately wealthy (approximately 25%) to a very low-income group (3.4%). The situation was slightly different for their Polish counterparts, for whom the revenues were more equally distributed among income categories, with the majority accounting for 36% for the relatively poor third-quartile income group (PLN 18,000 to PLN 36,000), although here this group was the largest (32 people). Furthermore, the proportions of total household income varied significantly, ranging from 3.8% for the wealthiest group to 16.7% for the moderately wealthy group.

Table 11.1 Sales and earnings of Finnish and Polish locals

	Finnish locals			Polish locals		
	Total	Goods	Services	Total	Goods	Services
No. of suppliers	31	16	22	69	46	33
Percentage of suppliers	19.9%	10.3%	14.1%	17.2%	11.5%	8.2%
Earnings (in € and PLN)	276,482	29,190	247,292	266,381	21,380	245,301
Average per supplier (in € and PLN)	8,919	1,824	11,241	3,861	465	7,433
Median per supplier (in € and PLN)	525	250	700	450	200	1,000

Source: Own study.

In order to meet the research objective, the results (evidence-based spending/financial inflows) were matched with the locals' perceptions of economic and development benefits resulting from second home tourism. Hence, local residents were asked to express their opinions of the opportunities to serve second home owners with goods and services. The answers ranged from 0 (no opportunities) to 5 (very good opportunities). For Finns, there was a prevalence of negative views, since two-thirds rated them as lacking or very weak possibilities (0 & 1) while only 16.0% found them good (4) or very good (5). For their Polish counterparts, the distribution of answers was significantly different, with 43.3% considering such economic opportunities to be non-existent or very weak while 35.2% saw them as good and very good. Therefore, comparing those two populations, one can find generally negative assessment among Finns while Poles' views are more diverse and polarised. The factors behind respondents' characteristics and attitudes to second homes' potential contribution to the local economy need to be identified in order to learn more about the reasons that can consequently help interpret the findings.

By using forward stepwise regression analysis, an explanatory model was selected that best suited the data set variance. It included several valid explanatory variables extracted as the main factors influencing respondents' views and opinions. For Finnish locals, the value of the coefficient of determination (R^2) was 0.5456, i.e. the proportion of the total variance explained by the model was 54.56%, which was quite high bearing in mind how difficult it is to predict a human behaviour (Lancaster 1975). The F-test statistics value was 11.41 ($p < 0.05$), confirming that the outcome of the analysis was statistically significant, since it explained the greater variance of the dependent variable than its mean (median) – respectively 1.4 and 1. As shown in Table 11.2, four variables were included in the model, i.e. those with a statistically significant beta coefficient (i.e. with a significant t-value – higher than 0) and the p-value is less than 0.05: evidence-based sales of goods and services to second home owners, respondent's opinions on social relationships with second home owners, respondent's gender and respondent's opinions on the influence of second home phenomenon on the community infrastructure improvement.

Despite the fact that regression analysis cannot indicate the direction of cause-effect relationships but only identify the linkage itself, in some cases the direction seems to be quite obvious. Thus, it is very likely that the respondents' opinions on the economic opportunities resulting from second homes are highly dependent upon facts and actual actions, i.e. sales to second home owners. The higher the rate of social contact with second home owners, the higher the evaluation of economic opportunities, which in fact proves an interplay between social and economic relationships (transactions) particularly visible at the local scale. Furthermore, respondents' gender was influential, showing more positive views on economic opportunities among local women and then linking those views with opinions on the impact of second home tourism on the infrastructure improvements in the municipality (namely roads).

The next step is to formulate a regression equation, which in this case is described as follows:

$$\hat{Y} = 1.79 + 1.103956 * x_1 + 0.288684 * x_2 + 0.236736 * x_3 + -0.637630 * x_4$$

Thus one can consider the most positive scenario by predicting how locals assess second homes as an economic opportunity if they sell goods and services, have well-established and valued social contacts, are female and are most positive on the influence of second homes on the local infrastructure. Following that:

$$\hat{Y} = 1.79 + 1.103956 * 1 + 0.288684 * 5 + 0.236736 * 5 + -0.637630 * 1 = 4.88$$

Table 11.2 Preconditions behind the locals' opinions on opportunities to supply Finnish second home owners with local goods and services (progressive regression analysis)

	BETA	Standard error BETA	B	Standard error B	T(76)	Statistical significance
	R= .73869251 R2= .54566663 Correct. R2= .49784206					
	F(6,57)=11.410 p<0.00000 Standard error: .97571					
Constant			1.793	0.515	3.478	0.001
Respondent's sales goods & services	0.363	0.133	1.104	0.404	2.730	0.008
Influence of SH on local roads	0.265	0.097	0.289	0.106	2.729	0.008
Importance of SH for social contacts	0.231	0.095	0.237	0.097	2.446	0.018
Respondent's gender	−0.232	0.092	−0.638	0.254	−2.510	0.015
Respondent's education	−0.147	0.092	−0.198	0.123	−1.601	0.115
Respondent's sales of goods	0.208	0.131	0.752	0.475	1.584	0.119

Source: Own study.

Here the value close to the highest range ('5') indicates very good economic opportunities for locals supplying second home owners.

On the other hand, if there are no sales, non-existent social ties, the respondent is male and has a negative opinion on second homes' influence on the infrastructure, the following equation was calculated:

$$\hat{Y} = 1.79 + 1.103956 * 0 + 0.288684 * 0 + 0.236736 * 0 + -0.637630 * 2 = 0.51$$

Here the conditions are not fulfilled at all and the predicted value of assessment will be between "non-existent" and "very weak".

The same was measured for Polish locals for whom the value of coefficient of determination (R^2) was 0.5644, i.e. in this case the proportion of the total variance explained by the model was 56.44% higher than for their Finnish counterparts. The F-test statistics were 23.05 (while $p < 0.05$), confirming the statistical significance of the outcome as it explained more variance of the dependent variable than its mean (median) − respectively 3.2 and 3. This time eight statistically significant variables (with t-value higher than 0 and p-value lower than 0.05) were included in the regression model (Table 11.3), i.e. opinions on the influence of second homes on the community development (in general) and on the infrastructure improvement (roads), the size and type of the locality, respondent's household size, number of permanent residents in the municipality, farm size (where the respondent was a farmer), the respondent's economic activity and the leisure traditions of the locality (essentially the time when the first holiday homes were located there).

Based on value of b coefficients, it can be said that the respondent's views on the importance of second homes for community development, infrastructure improvements and economic opportunities resulting from second homes overlapped to a large extent (in most cases). The larger the locality (small town or central village) and the larger the municipality (based on the number of inhabitants), the more positive the opinions expressed by respondents on economic opportunities were. Representatives of larger households (two to three people or more) and/or for the owners of small farms and/or for working people (especially entrepreneurs) were more likely to find second homes as an income opportunity.

Finally, the longer the leisure tradition of the village the higher the evaluation of the average level of economic opportunities was.

In consequence, a regression equation was formulated as follows:

$$\hat{Y} = 3.416257 + 0.364458 * x_1 + -0.572637 * x_2 + -0.200020 * x_3 + 0.253921 * x_4$$
$$+0.168031 * x_5 + -0.268235 * x_6 + -0.113770 * x_7 + -0.115794 * x_8$$

Thus, considering the most positive scenario/model predicting how the locals assess second homes as an economic opportunity, if they express very good opinions on second homes in the community's development and infrastructure improvements, they are members of a four-person or larger household, they are small farmers, working people (self-employed), and live in a small town or central village, or in a relatively large municipality with a long leisure tradition. Following this:

$$\hat{Y} = 3.416257 + 0.364458 * 5 + -0.572637 * 1 + -0.200020 * 1 + 0.253921 * 3$$
$$+0.168031 * 4 + -0.268235 * 1 + -0.113770 * 1 + -0.115794 * 5 = 4.94$$

Here the outcome value was slightly lower than the highest value within the range of actual assessment and it confirmed that, by meeting the above criteria, the economic opportunities will be evaluated as nearest to '5' – very good. On the other hand, for members of single

Table 11.3 Preconditions behind the locals' opinions on opportunities to supply Polish second home owners with local goods and services (progressive regression analysis)

	BETA	Standard error BETA	B	Standard error B	T(76)	Statistical significance
		R= .75129158 R2= .56443904 Correct. R2= .53994967				
		F(14,249)=23.048 p<0.0000 Standard error: 1.0444				
Constant			3.416	0.595	5.740	0.000
Community development opportunities resulting from SH	0.365	0.045	0.364	0.045	8.021	0.000
Type of settlement	−0.289	0.048	−0.573	0.095	−6.029	0.000
Traditional second home area	−0.185	0.044	−0.200	0.048	−4.190	0.000
Number of permanent residences	0.129	0.043	0.254	0.085	2.987	0.003
Respondent's household size	0.105	0.047	0.168	0.076	2.219	0.027
Respondent's farm area	−0.180	0.051	−0.268	0.076	−3.516	0.001
Respondent's economic activity	−0.112	0.053	−0.114	0.054	−2.093	0.037
Influence of SH on local roads	−0.090	0.044	−0.116	0.057	−2.049	0.042
Respondent's education	0.066	0.046	0.094	0.065	1.435	0.152
Respondent's job position	−0.077	0.047	−0.062	0.038	−1.632	0.104
Respondent's sales of services	−0.042	0.044	−0.185	0.191	−0.969	0.333
Respondent's household income	0.061	0.047	0.127	0.099	1.286	0.200
Influence of SH on recreational facilities	−0.056	0.045	−0.062	0.050	−1.235	0.218
SH negative effects	0.049	0.043	0.202	0.176	1.147	0.252

Source: Own study.

households, small farmers, those living in a small village, with negative opinions on the influence on community development, and indicating various negative effects of second homes, the formula will be as follows:

$$\hat{Y} = 3.416257 + 0.364458 * 0 + -0.572637 * 3 + -0.200020 * 4 + 0.253921 * 1$$
$$+0.168031 * 1 + -0.268235 * 3 + -0.113770 * 7 + -0.115794 * 0 = -0.28$$

Thus, if the conditions are not fulfilled the predicted value of the respondent's opinion on economic opportunities will be non-existent.

Conclusions

The analysis has proved similar proportions of local suppliers of goods and services to second home owners in both surveyed countries, although the distributions of revenues had significantly different patterns. In Finland, an asymmetric financial inflow allocation with the highest share for wealthy households was recognised as opposed to more equal with a slight prevalence for relatively poor households observed in Poland. What is more, second home tourism income differential (considered individually) was significantly larger among Finnish than Polish suppliers. At the same time, this study has shown that locals' opinions on economic benefits for the receiving community resulting from the provision of second home owners were far more positive and less polarised among Poles than among their Finish counterparts who, in majority, recognised development advantages to a very limited extent while their assessment was highly differentiated. Therefore, referring to earlier research in the field, this analysis has proved a common tendency of the positive perception of (second home) tourism if the respondents' attitudes are reinforced by actual (evidence-based) financial benefits or their indirect effects associated with the quality of life improvements (Fredline 2004). Furthermore, it was also confirmed that outcomes on local people's perspective were basically in line with previous studies showing a prevalence of negative views and/or opinions undermining widely considered favourable influence (unseen benefits) for the community in the case of small economies with uneven distribution of positive effects among local society members and exclusion of certain groups/individuals out of the process (economic linkages with second home owners). On the other hand, the research results have proven that more equal distribution of revenues among the locals significantly revises their viewpoint, turning it to more positive and confident, as well as more aware of existing or potential advantages and gains (Tosun 2002; Ritchie & Inkari 2006).

It is interesting that in this regard locals in Finland did not consider second homes to be an important but rather a supplementary community development factor. In Poland, on the other hand, they were seen as an unquestionable asset, like other objective development preconditions such as good transport access, proximity to a large city and highly rated environmental amenities that can create an economic opportunity. This is all the more unexpected as the scale and popularity of second homes between the two countries differs significantly in favour of Finland. Hence, this confirms that even in Finnish communities with large concentrations of holiday homes, where the phenomenon may be a critical development resource for local authorities, the economic effect is perceived as insufficient. In Poland with a relatively low number of secondary residences, they are nevertheless seen as a potential and actual advantage (especially in remote communities), taking into account the positive, evenly distributed benefits, albeit of a very limited scope.

References

Andereck, K. L., Valentine, K. M., Knopf, R. C. and Vogt, C. A. (2005) 'Residents' perceptions of community tourism impacts', *Annals of Tourism Research*, 32 (4): 1056–1076.

Ap, J. and Crompton, J. L. (1998) 'Developing and testing a tourism impact scale', *Journal of Travel Research*, 37 (4): 120–130.

Choi, M. J., Heo, C. Y. and Law, R. (2016) 'Progress in shopping tourism', *Journal of Travel & Tourism Marketing*, 33 (S1): 1–24.

Chuang, S.-T. (2013) 'Residents' attitudes toward rural tourism in Taiwan: A comparative viewpoint', *International Journal of Tourism Research*, 15 (2): 152–170.

Czarnecki, A. (2014) 'Economically detached? Second home owners and the local community in Poland', *Tourism Review International*, 18 (3): 153–166.

Das, B. R. and Rainey, D. V. (2010) 'Agritourism in the Arkansas Delta byways: Assessing the economic impacts', *International Journal of Tourism Research*, 12 (3): 265–280.

Eriksen, L. and Ahmt, T. (1999) 'Measuring and modelling the regional impact of tourism in Denmark', *International Journal of Tourism Research*, 1: 313–327.

Fredline, L. (2004) 'Host community reactions to motorsport events: The perception of impact on quality of life'. In B. W. Ritchie and D. Adair (eds) *Sport Tourism: Interrelationships, Impacts and Issues*. Clevedon, UK: Channel View Publications, 155–173.

Hall, C. M. (1994) *Tourism and Politics: Power, Policy and Place*. Chichester, UK: John Wiley.

Hall, C. M. (2008) *Tourism Planning* 2nd. ed. Harlow, UK: Prentice Hall.

Irshad, I. (2010) *Rural Tourism: An Overview*. Edmonton, CA: Rural Development Division, Government of Alberta.

Jaafar, M., Bakri, N. M. and Rasoolimanesh, S. M. (2015) 'Local community and tourism development: A study of rural mountainous destinations', *Modern Applied Science*, 9 (8): 399–408.

Kreag, G. (2001) *The Impacts of Tourism*. Duluth, MN: Sea Grant Minnesota.

Lancaster, K. J. (1975) 'The theory of household behaviour: Some foundations', *Annals of Economic and Social Measurement*, 4 (1): 5–21.

Lankford, S. V. and Howard, D. R. (1994) 'Developing a tourism impact attitude scale', *Annals of Tourism Research*, 21 (1): 121–139.

Larke, R., Kilgour, M. and John, S. P. (2016) 'Tourist growth and the implications for retail marketing strategy: Insights from Japan', *Journal of Travel & Tourism Marketing*, 33 (5): 658–670.

Mihalić, T. (2002) 'Tourism and economic development issues'. In R. Sharply and D. J. Telfer (eds) *Tourism and Development: Concepts and Issues*. Clevedon, UK: Channel View Publications, 81–111.

Moscovici, S. (1981) 'On social representations'. In J. Forgas (ed.) *Social Cognition: Perspectives on Everyday Understanding*. London: Academic Press, 181–209.

Müller, D. K. (1999) 'German second home owners in the Swedish countryside'. *Gerum kulturgeografi*, 2. Umeå: Department of Social and Economic Geography, Umeå University.

Muresan, I. C., Oroian, C. F., Harun, R., Arion, F. H., Porutiu, A., Chiciudean, G. O., Todea, A. and Lile, R. (2016) 'Local residents' attitude toward sustainable rural tourism development', *Sustainability*, 8 (1): 100.

Nielsen, N. C., Kromann, D. S., Kjeldsen, C. and Just, F. (2009) 'Second homes: A possible pathway to rural development?', paper presented to the WorkGroup on Multifunctional Landscapes at the ESRS Conference, Vaasa, 17–20 August.

Oliveira, J. A., Roca, M. N. O. and Roca, Z. (2015) 'Economic effects of second homes: A case study in Portugal', *Economics and Sociology*, 8 (3): 183–196.

Rattanasuwongchai, N. (1998) 'Rural tourism: The impact on rural communities II. Thailand', *Food and Fertilizer Technology Center for the Asian and Pacific Region*. [online] Available at: http://www.agnet.org/library.php?func=view&id=20110726131206

Ritchie, B. W. and Inkari, M. (2006) 'Host community attitudes toward tourism and cultural tourism development: The case of the Lewes District, Southern England', *International Journal of Tourism Research*, 8 (1): 27–44.

Scanlon, K., Sagor, E. and Whitehead, C. (2014) *The Economic Impact of Holiday Rentals in the UK, A Project for HomeAway*, final report, November 2014, London: London School Economics.

Sirakaya, E., Teye, V. and Sönmez, S. (2002) 'Understanding residents' support for tourism development in the central region of Ghana', *Journal of Travel Research*, 41 (1): 57–67.

Timothy, D. J. (2005) *Shopping Tourism, Retailing and Leisure*. Clevedon, UK: Channel View Publications.

Tosun, C. (2002) 'Host perceptions of impacts: A comparative tourism study', *Annals of Tourism Research*, 29 (8): 231–253.

Tosun, C., Temizkan, S. P., Timothy, D. and Fyall, A. (2007) 'Tourist shopping experiences and satisfaction', *International Journal of Tourism Research*, 9 (2): 87–102.

Vanegas Sr., M. and Croes, R. R. (2003) 'Growth, development and tourism in a small economy: Evidence from Aruba', *International Journal of Tourism Research*, 5 (5): 315–330.

Velvin, J., Kvikstad, T. M., Drag, E. and Krogh, E. (2013) 'The impact of second home tourism on local economic development in rural areas in Norway', *Tourism Economics*, 19 (3): 689–705.

12

UNDERVALUING A SECTOR

The enigma of micro-enterprise self-contained accommodation in Australia

Clare Keogh, Anton Kriz and Lisa Barnes

Introduction

Self-contained house or apartment accommodation available for short-term rental is an understudied but uniquely important sector of the Australian tourism economy. Privately owned micro-enterprise self-contained accommodation (MSA) includes three broad groups: second home holiday rentals, private investment short-term lets and self-managed superannuation fund (SMSF) vacation rentals. Often outnumbering traditional forms of visitor accommodation such as hotels, motels and backpackers in popular tourism regions, self-contained accommodation is growing rapidly with the development of online booking platforms. MSA properties vary greatly in size, building type, target markets and returns on investment. As this chapter identifies, critical of all to commercial success is owner motivation in relation to personal commercial interests which seem to vary considerably. While these MSA operations appear very small in size and are often overlooked by private and public tourism organisations, collectively they provide a substantial regional economic contribution to Australian tourism destinations.

Our empirical research identifies that MSA properties do not feature in destination-organised development initiatives. They are dismissed as lifestyle oriented and unable to participate in strong cluster partnerships (Getz & Carlsen 2005; Thomas 2007; Thomas et al. 2011). However, this study has found that not all MSAs are lifestyle driven. Rather, we identified and uncovered uneven MSA engagement levels in destination initiatives. Significantly, regional stakeholder ignorance of the MSA sector may have stimulated overseas online platforms to fill gaps in harnessing the unrealised potential value of MSAs as well as encouraging additional destination-linked networks and activities. This chapter is an exploration of the importance of MSAs to Australian regional economies.

We use a comparative case study as a way of exploring the nature of MSAs. The chapter investigates three important Australian tourism regions of New South Wales (NSW): Central Coast, Hunter Wine Country and Byron Bay. Analysis of qualitative interviews and secondary information is used to develop deep and rich insights of MSA relational issues. Our findings highlight challenges and opportunities associated with MSA clusters and provide practical understanding for government and business to improve economic outcomes. What is clear from the research is that such destinations lack insight of MSAs, particularly their value and importance to their regional economies. Interestingly, operators like Airbnb, with their market imperative, have been quick to fill this important gap.

This chapter starts with an investigation of MSA definitions and the broad literature. This includes understanding aspects around geographic networks and clustering. The article then moves onto research methods and a detailed review of the context of the three regional destinations. Further sections address preliminary analysis and findings around stakeholder perceptions, followed by conclusions and implications for both academia and policymakers.

Definitions

Definitions take on considerable importance when they are somewhat idiosyncratic concerning indigenous national jargon and dimensions. Accordingly, there is no universal term in literature for privately owned short-term rental self-contained accommodation properties. While the recently introduced term "commercial second home" encapsulates many short-term rental properties, not all MSAs can be referred to as "homes". "Commercial second homes" combine two key concepts: "commercial homes", explaining the notion of people paying to stay in private residences such as "bed and breakfasts" (Lashley 2009; Hall & Rusher 2004) and another notion of "second homes" describing non-commercial summer residences that traditionally are representative of Nordic and later French citizens retreating to summer villas in warmer months (Müller 2002; Coppock 1982).

Scandinavian second homes accessed by 40% of the population are not usually commercially rented (Müller 2002). In contrast, literature from other countries, for example the UK, New Zealand, Australia and Poland, finds privately owned vacation properties and retirement homes widely available for short-term rental (Hall 2014; Paris 2014; Adamiak 2016; Czarnecki & Frenkel 2014). A review of commercial holiday home rental websites finds numerous terms to describe this category of short-term rental holiday accommodation (see Table 12.1).

With terminology of the sector so problematic (Lynch et al. 2009), the Australian government agency term of "self-contained accommodation" is adopted here. This also reflects the micro-enterprise self-contained accommodation (MSA) acronym used. The NSW state government tourism organisation, Destination NSW (DNSW), identifies "self-contained accommodation" as a term for promoting short-term rental of a range of property types, which captures cottages, villas, homes, apartments, cabin and lodges (DNSW 2015a). The nature of these properties as described means they are predominantly run by micro operators, such as individuals or couples for a potential income or additional income source. This research on micro excludes larger enterprise initiatives providing broader commercial accommodation property outcomes.

Regional destinations and complexity of clusters, networks and organisations

Regional tourism destinations are complex with network linkages between multiple stakeholders adding an array of views, interests and vertical and horizontal contextual challenges (Graci 2012). Such geographic concentrations are often linked to clusters. The cluster concept draws on the Marshallian concept of firm agglomeration in industrial districts (Krugman 1994). Marshall, like Porter (2003, 2013) that followed, broadly defined clusters as groups of related or linked firms in geographic areas. Tourism clusters are promoted by the United Nations World Tourism Organization (UNWTO) as 'drivers of economic development and environmental sustainability' (United Nations Industrial Development Organization (UNIDO) 2013). This view of tourism aggregation and its benefits around clusters is supported by the World Bank, Organisation for Economic Co-operation and Development (OECD) and the European Commission (EC)

Table 12.1 Examples of differing terminology

Variation in holiday letting terms	Location	Private and public online examples
Terms:	Terms used by:	Examples:
Self-contained accommodation (cottages, villas, apartments, homes, cabins, lodges, farm-stay)	Australian state tourism organisations	www.visitnsw.com.au
Holiday houses, holiday accommodation	Australian regional tourism operators	www.byron-bay.com/houses
Holiday lets, short-term rentals	Australian local government authorities	www.gosford.nsw.gov.au
Self-catering accommodation	UK tourism	www.visitengland.com
Vacation rentals, vacation lettings, vacation homes	USA tourism	www.usa-vacation-homes.com www.vrbo.com/vacation-rentals
Gites	France tourism	www.gites-de-france.com
Bachs	New Zealand tourism	www.bachcare.co.nz
Small-scale accommodation sector	Tourism Research Australia	www.tra.gov.au/aboutus/Small-scale-accommodation-survey.html
Summer houses	Nordic tourism	www.icelandicsummerhouses.com
Holiday homes, holiday rentals	International online booking agents	www.airbnb.com.au www.stayz.com.au

(Shakya 2009; EC 2008; OECD 2001). Notable authors recognise the fillip that clusters provide for regional advancement in developed and developing countries through increased competiveness and improved economic performance (Lindqvist *et al.* 2013; Delgado, Porter & Stern 2010; Porter 2003).

National and state governments have embraced cluster development in recent decades as a way of broadly enhancing regional competitiveness (Porter 1998). Key aspects include skilled labour access, supplier savings, shared infrastructure costs, knowledge absorption, adoption and diffusion, enhanced innovation, shared marketing and a collective voice (Connell et al. 2014; Lazzeretti, Sedita & Caloffi 2013; Navickas & Malakauskaite 2009). When tourism firms cluster in a geographic place, they are often termed "tourist destination regions". These arbitrary boundaries often do not reflect Australian government administrative notions and the concept in Australia of a Regional Tourism Organisation (RTOs). Adding to such confusion is the idea that RTOs can include Local Tourist Associations (LTAs) (Dredge & Jamal 2015).

There is no single definition of what constitutes a tourism "destination" (Tinsley & Lynch 2001). Destination, like clusters, are endemic to some form of regional boundary capable of providing an enhanced visitation experience (Bornhorst et al. 2010). Destination choice is important with tourists making decisions between a range of concepts including villages, towns, states and nations where tourists travel to receive unique place-based exposure and benefits (Keating & Kriz 2008). Destination resources are organised by a number of organisations and networks to maximise destination competiveness (Ritchie et al. 2005). Tourist organisations coordinating destination marketing and other development efforts are funded from a mix of private and public sources and are subject to different interests and agendas (Dredge 2006). Destination management involves the well-being of all destination aspects, emphasising leadership, teamwork and provision of effective tourism network management (Bornhorst et al. 2010; Crouch & Ritchie 1999). Such efforts will be variable, but overall enterprise engagement should be working toward positive influence on regional tourism development (Novelli et al. 2006; Michael 2003). MSAs are an important stakeholder in how destinations perform, albeit they may not be as visible as resorts, hotels and other more identifiable place-based assets.

Changing role of clustering and destination management in Australia

Government funding in Australia has been historically directed toward supporting regional destination development initiatives through marketing, infrastructure funding and training. "Initiatives" are classified as deliberate interventions by stakeholders, aimed at improving a region's competiveness through a collaboration of cluster members working to develop mutually beneficial resources and activities (Lindqvist et al. 2013). "Cluster initiatives" are organised efforts 'to increase the growth and competitiveness of clusters within a region, involving cluster firms, government and/or the research community' (Ketels 2013: 1). Regional development initiatives are applied worldwide by governments and policymakers as development tools to improve regional competiveness (Hall & Teal 2013; Ketels & Memedovic 2008).

Regional tourism initiatives to assist destination development rely on the network relationships of cluster managers or facilitators to share information and coordinate endeavours (UNIDO 2013). Australian regional development bodies and intermediaries federally and at a state level place great emphasis on supporting destination structures. However, lack of resource support means these structures are increasingly having to generate their own funding (Dredge & Jenkins 2007). Occasionally some are more formally organised with the aim of taking advantage of economies of scale, networks, innovation, knowledge and joint marketing campaigns. Explaining how enterprises can or do access these benefits and clusters has only moderately been discussed in literature (Connell et al. 2014; Michael 2003).

More formal clusters have facilitators and operate under accepted and collaborative governance arrangements (Ffowcs-Williams 2012). Notably, tourism literature has little on "cluster facilitators" or "cluster managers" and instead focuses on the concept of "destination management". In Australia, as in many western economies, government authorities have historically been responsible for the marketing and management of tourism destinations and this has meant often by default that they become surrogate coordinators of tourism clusters and their internal networks. Tourism cluster intervention by governments in the 1990s supported the view that authorities have a responsibility to be more proactive and responsible for place-based resident outcomes (Porter 1998). This is changing with a neoliberal government moving toward bottom-up community-based tourism (Dredge & Jamal 2015; Hall 1999, 2014).

Governance reversal of traditionally run tourist boards in regional Australia is underway (Wray 2015) with a decreasing number of firms engaging in cluster initiatives. This includes a decline in cooperative web-based advertising campaigns (DNSW 2015a). Tourism cluster management is no longer driven by state and local authorities but by a complex organisational management structure with private or public–private partnerships (Valente et al. 2015). There has been additional turbulence with tourism regions competing for declining funds. Increasingly place-based membership bases are also moving rapidly online as disruptive aggregators take advantage of available but underutilised rooms and accommodation assets. It is apparent that many destinations and regions lack a vision and common goal (Haugland et al. 2011). NSW RTOs are typical. They are currently undergoing a review and revision as part of a shake-up and reallocation of destination management plans (DNSW 2015b). The role of destination organisers and drivers in managing tourism enterprise engagement and networks is unclear. This brings us to the changing importance of micro-enterprise in such destinations.

Micro-enterprise engagement in tourism destination initiatives

There is no single accepted definition of small enterprises, or micro-enterprises, with a lack of academic consensus and country-by-country variations (Thomas et al. 2011). The European Economic Commission defines a micro-business as holding fewer than 10 employees whereas the New Zealand government defines "small business" as less than four employees (Hall & Rusher 2004). This study adopts the Australian Bureau of Statistics (2013) definition of micro-businesses. These enterprises employ less than five people and, in many instances, none.

Evidence from Australian tourism cluster websites indicates low levels of micro-enterprise involvement in RTO cluster marketing activities (VisitNSW 2015; Airbnb 2016; Stayz 2016). While studies have found micro-enterprise working collectively in tourism regions to develop a product and/or improve individual firm growth (Michael 2003; Tinsley & Lynch 2001, 2007), most such studies focus on processes of collaboration, cooperation and participation (Thomas 2007; Hall 1999). What is recognised is that not all micro-cluster member firms participate in cluster initiatives designed to develop tourism destinations. Why and how firms engage in their tourism cluster initiatives is the focus of this research.

Literature of destination relational engagement, in particular from a micro-enterprise perspective, is intriguingly absent. This is critical in understanding what drives or inhibits micro-enterprise engagement in destinations, given the apparent and potential size of the sector and the burgeoning role of such actors in an expanding online and sharing economy. Tourism research on micro-enterprises has found that a sizable number of operators are in the sector simply for lifestyle benefits (Lashley & Rowson 2002). But this is a limited view of the motivations of such enterprise actors and there is a clear need for more studies with a focus on the role of small firms in destination development, management and marketing (Zehrer & Hallmann 2015). The Australian Department of Industry has found 'a strong argument for government to facilitate collaboration and healthy clustering behaviour among groups of small enterprises' (Grace 2014: 1). Such efforts are seen as particularly important, given a large proportion of the 280,800 tourism businesses in 2012 were rated as non-employing (Weir 2013). While many studies have concentrated on large industries, the context of this study is opening up interesting potential fields of research. The non-employment numbers belie the multipliers, spillovers and benefits that micro-enterprises and their tourists bring.

According to Lashley (2009: xvi), commercial homes for the purpose of tourism are 'grossly under-researched'. The Australian "holiday house" is a prominent feature of tourist regions. This is a complex accommodation sector that comprises many small and unique businesses throughout Australia. Fortunately, questions like whether 'supporting tourism infrastructures are sufficiently sensitive' (Lynch et al. 2009: 184) to these micro-organisations are now being asked. Other gaps include data about operator numbers (Hall & Rusher 2004), sector behaviour (Thomas et al. 2011) and sector size (Michael 2003). Preliminary research has revealed that a key weakness of the MSA accommodation sector is that there is no recognised industry body which represents the interests of the owner/operators involved (Hall 2011). With only a few exceptions, there is scant research focusing on small tourism and micro-business clusters.

Case studies of three NSW regions

Tourism is important in Australia, with visitor expenditure contributing $107 billion to the economy in 2014–15 (Australian Bureau of Statistics 2016). New South Wales (NSW), the country's largest tourism state, employs 267,000 people, both directly and indirectly (NSW

Government 2015). This comparative case study adopts a qualitative (Charmaz 2006) theory-building approach to investigate three regional tourism destinations in NSW. Case studies have the potential of gaining deep and rich insights (Yin 2003). The key here is to ask "how" and "why" destination networks develop and secondly to probe stakeholders about the importance of the sector and its potential for development. Qualitative case studies are accepted as more suitable for approaching how and why as well as more explorative questions. Using three cases adds robustness and more potential generalisability than a single case (Yin 2003; Eisenhardt 1989). Cases drawn from NSW tourism regions include Central Coast, Ballina-Byron Coast and Hunter Valley Wine Country. Figure 12.1 highlights the location of the destinations in New South Wales (NSW), Australia.

Tourism is a critical contributor to growth in all three regions. A high number of MSA properties collectively form the critical mass of the tourism product in each of the destinations shown on the map. While historically the sector has largely been unregulated in NSW, this situation has recently changed following a NSW Land Environment Court ruling in May 2013. The court declared holiday rentals to be 'a prohibitive development use in residential areas' (Land and Environment Court (LEC) 2013). Such a ruling created much uncertainty and prompted the local government of Gosford City Council in the Central Coast region to initiate a variation to the local environmental plan (LEP) to allow "short term holiday letting" without development consent. This ruling had important additional consequences for MSAs limiting them in this region to no more than four bedrooms and a maximum of eight guests. Threat of closure was the sanction if the MSA was subject to genuine neighbour complaints (Gosford City Council 2013). Other councils followed the "Gosford model", with the exception of Byron Shire Council. Byron chose subsequently to introduce the strictest regulations on their MSA operators. They now restrict holiday lets to a "maximum 90 days" per year (Byron LGA 2016). Such regulatory environmental uncertainty is fostering uncertainty amongst MSA operators. It makes sense to provide a background analysis of each region given the notable variations geographically, environmentally, economically and socially in all three.

NSW Regional Destination Map

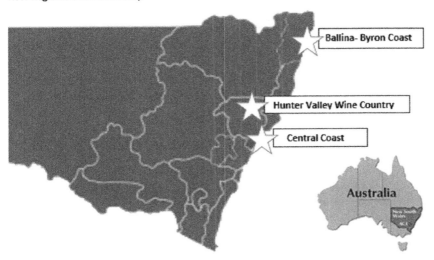

Figure 12.1   Regional case locations: New South Wales, Australia.

Central Coast region

Central Coast has over 325,000 residents with a large commuter population. Its beachside, waterways, flora and fauna and rural offerings attract many domestic weekender tourists, predominantly from Sydney. The region is flanked by two local government authorities, Gosford and Wyong. These two local government areas (LGAs) were merged into one during 2016. The forced state merger has brought disruption to local government activities and strategic tourism initiatives. Currently, under the split LGAs, the region has tourism offices at Kariong (southern end of the Coast) and The Entrance (northern end of the Coast) run by Wyong council (Central Coast Tourism (CCT) 2016; Wyong Shire Council 2016) in what is a private–public partnership. The average length of stay on the Central Coast has changed over the last three decades with the region attracting more short-stay weekend tourists than traditional summer holiday longer-stay visitors (CCT 2016). The region does have a number of larger hotels and resorts, like Crowne Plaza at Terrigal and Kooinda Waters at Wyong. However, self-contained holiday accommodation collectively forms the critical mass of the region's tourism product. Gosford Council estimates there are 3,000 self-contained properties on the Central Coast. No accurate numbers of MSAs are currently available. The sector is seasonal and fluctuates by as much as 50% as evidenced by a review of activity around commercial online advertising (Stayz 2012, 2013, 2014, 2015, 2016; Airbnb 2016).

The Hunter Valley Wine region

Hunter Valley Wine Country is a pristine rural region two hours north of Sydney. Home to Australia's oldest vineyards, this region attracts tourists from all over Australia (Hunter Valley Visitor Centre (HVVC) 2013). The management of the Hunter Valley Wine Country region has undergone significant turbulence in recent years. In June 2013, the Cessnock Council withdrew funds of $400,000 per year from the cluster management organisation called Hunter Valley Wine Country (HVWC). Cessnock Council indicates this funding withdrawal was due to several complaints from ratepayers regarding a perceived adequate lack of financial return. One month later the HVWC merged with the local wine growers' association and became a private sector funding organisation called Hunter Valley Wine & Tourism Association (HVWTA). In September 2015, this further developed into a private–public partnership between Cessnock and Singleton Councils and HVWTA. The new entity is chaired by an ex-NSW tourism minister. No published estimates of self-contained properties are available in the region. However, more MSAs advertise in the Hunter Valley Wine region official accommodation guides than the equivalent on the Central Coast (HVWTA 2015a, 2015b). MSAs are therefore acknowledged as substantive with vineyard cottages a feature of this region's advertising campaigns.

Byron-Ballina region

The Byron-Ballina region, serviced by Ballina-Byron airport, is a coastal strip of surf beaches and hinterland, but like the Central Coast has two independent LGAs. Byron Bay and Ballina Shire Councils each attract two very different visitor market segments. Ballina Shire supports tourism through its funding of the visitor information centre. Byron is an iconic Australian landmark for surfers and international tourists. It is the Eastern most point of the Australian land mass. The Byron visitor information centre relies on private funding. Byron's visitors range from backpackers to wealthy celebrities and is the only internationally recognised NSW destination outside the capital (Sydney). Lesser-known Ballina attracts domestic family and retiree visitors.

Large seafood wholesalers have been historically present with the "Big Prawn", a remnant of the wild catch in the area. Byron Bay has attracted a lot of alternative lifestyle seekers and is a strong base for aspects like the "green movement". The area is close to the South East Queensland metropolitan community and features large concerts such as a blues festival.

The endowments of a place-based destination ensure that no two areas are essentially alike with one size not fitting all (Tödtling & Trippl 2005). The three regions here provide an interesting cross section of NSW regions and have been purposively selected as high MSA providers compared to most. All have been predominantly subject to two local government authorities. Each region selected has also been subject to the impacts of three different RTOs. The dynamics are changing as witnessed by legislation and other variations occurring in the place-based dynamics.

Design and methods

The chapter reports also on primary data collected in 2016. This included in-depth qualitative interviews from the three NSW respective regions. Key stakeholders, organisers and intermediaries from each region were interviewed to analyse how each destination and respective MSA were functioning. Fifteen elite interviewees were selected based on their broader tourism expertise (Welch et al. 2002). These respondents were identified as key actors with expert knowledge and/or experience in the respective region and cluster, whether as state and local government, institution or key business, and/or related tourism industry group or body. Experts interviewed included a NSW state tourism ex-director, a mayor, two RTO directors, a LTA manager, a local government economic development and tourism manager, a tourism educator and also a tourism development manager. SMA-letting agents in each regional case were also interviewed.

Data collected from interviews was then transcribed and coded and underwent thematic content analysis using NVIVO software. Relevant attributes like age, gender and title were assigned to each interviewee. The semi-structured interviews lasted approximately an hour. Recall was aided through prompt transcription. The majority of interviews had two interviewers present. This was particularly important for ensuring consistency (Flyvbjerg 2011; Kriz et al. 2014).

Semi-structured interviews were used with a guide or protocol. This allowed the interviewee to illustrate and expand on ideas that were not always specific to MSAs and their impact on a destination. This proved beneficial as it quickly became clear that most interviewees were more aware of tourism and the destination rather than the specifics of MSAs. This lack of understanding of the sector was interesting to the interviewees themselves as the interviews unfolded. The criterion of theoretical saturation (Charmaz 2006) guided the recruitment. This is a two-stage study with the first stage around the fifteen key stakeholder interviews described in this chapter. A discussion specific to MSA operator perceptions will follow in later articles.

MSA findings and analysis

This section outlines the results of secondary data collection and interviews with key stakeholders. First, this section describes the types of MSA operations identified. Second, the research analysis reviews branding and naming issues for MSAs. Third, the focus shifts to engagement opportunities. Fourth, what is apparent is the increasing impact of the online platform. Stakeholders are aware that there is key movement. Finally, and concomitantly, despite the increasing online activity, the research identifies what appears as an enigmatic invisible sector. Despite the substantive economic impacts, MSAs particularly are going largely "under the radar" to levels of government, private stakeholders and intermediaries. Only when crisis occurs, as discussed earlier with rulings in the Gosford and then Byron cases, does the MSA sector seem to get any recognition (albeit negative).

MSA operations

The research finds MSA operators are not exclusively targeting tourist accommodation. Operators are also targeting business clients, as well as those visiting friends and family, and in the Central Coast case, operators are even targeting staff/patients visiting local hospitals. The research has identified three broad segments of self-contained accommodation. Firstly, one style of MSA called second homes, either available for rent all year or infrequently because owners are using the home intermittently for their own leisure. The second MSA segment includes investment dwellings available for short-term rental, for example property investments never intended as a home. This second category has homes used by large-scale corporates, such as serviced apartments, cabins or resort holiday lets but these are excluded from the research. This study focused only on privately owned micro-enterprise self-contained investments. A third, newer category is properties purchased by operators of privately managed pension funds. These are regulated by the federal taxation office and known in Australia as self-managed superannuation funds (SMSF). These properties under Australian tax law cannot be used by owners. MSAs in all three regions have a number of properties that move from short-term rental to permanent rental, particularly in the investment and SMSF segments. MSA rental agents interviewed reported flows of up to 25% of properties moving from short-term rentals to permanent furnished rentals. According to them, this is linked closely with rental return fluctuations. As permanent rental accommodation becomes scarce, it encourages MSAs to shift away to that market for better returns.

The respondents have identified a number of variations on self-contained accommodation. This seems to have implications related to their motivation for rent-seeking. Motivation is discussed later in the findings and appears to identify key variations that accentuate the complexity of the sector. It also has implications for networks and clustering that will be discussed. The next section outlines secondary data and expert interviewee perceptions of destination initiatives around cluster and network engagement.

Confusion around branding the destination

A key resource initiative available to tourism enterprises is the regional brand which attracts NSW state government investment and promotion. The interviews and investigations of government and stakeholder literature reveals confusion for the MSA operator about the destination branding and identification. Inconsistency at state and local levels, with changes around regional tourism operations, adds to the confusion. Multiple names and perceptions around what constitutes regional boundaries dilutes the effectiveness of destination marketing (see Table 12.2).

Central Coast is a key case with respondents identifying that the two councils often confuse regional promotion as they focus on individual council areas (Gosford vs Wyong and subregions). As the respondents highlighted, operators then choose to default to more localised names in accommodation listings, for example Terrigal or Avoca. In the Hunter Valley Wine region case, this means operators are choosing to use locality names, such as Pokolbin, Hermitage or Lovedale in advertisements. Interestingly, this is happening despite over a century of investment in the "Hunter Valley" brand. Notably, in the third case of Ballina-Byron Coast, a key stakeholder noted that the name of Ballina-Byron was only really being used by the local airport

Table 12.2 Confusion for MSAs: multiple name and regional boundary perceptions

Case	Tourist	Council	Local	Geopolitical State and Federal	State Destination NSW name	Federal Bureau of Statistics (ABS)	Geographic delineations	Notes
	Visitor perception of region name	Name of governing local authorities	Names stakeholders promote	State electoral areas for members of parliament (MPS)				
The Central Coast Region	"Central Coast"	Gosford & Wyong (merged in 2017)	Central Coast RTO, Terrigal, Avoca, The Entrance	4 MPS: Gosford, Wyong, Terrigal, The Entrance	Central Coast Region	ABS Central Coast	Central Coast stretch of 19 beaches	Hawkesbury MSA identify as central
Hunter Valley Wine Region	"Hunter Valley"	Cessnock & Singleton (borders Maitland)	Hunter Valley Alliance, Pokolbin, Lovedale, Rothbury, Broke, The Hermitage	2 MPS: Cessnock, Maitland	HVWC in Hunter Region	ABS Hunter Region (includes Newcastle & Maitland)	Australia's oldest wine growing region. Area serviced by a light airport	Some Maitland local government area wineries identify as Hunter Valley
Ballina-Byron Coast	Domestic visitor: "Ballina–Byron"; International: "Byron"	Ballina & Byron (borders Lismore & Tweed)	Byron, Ballina, Lennox Head	1 MP: Lismore, Northern Rivers Region	North Coast Region, previously Northern Rivers Region	ABS Northern Rivers Region	Stretch of coastline promoted by Byron-Ballina airport	State MP proposes name of "Green Coast" region

and interstate visitors. A secondary data search of most other promotional literature identified that the region is marketed as either Byron or Ballina.

Stakeholders highlighted a proposal by the state member to launch a "Green Coast". Destination place was identified by respondents as a topical issue with a large amount of parochialism and egos. MSAs as identified by stakeholders will then default more locally and focus on their sub-regional branding.

Confusion and conflicting names make engagement in tourism initiatives unattractive. Lack of common purpose makes harnessing MSA support difficult. The secondary data confirmed that the majority of MSAs on online platforms are using local town names. The Hunter Valley MSAs were an exception and were sticking with their traditional, more historical branding (Airbnb 2016; Stayz 2016). The table below highlights the multiplicity of names at various stakeholder and intermediary levels.

Uneven levels of MSA destination initiative engagement

Regional NSW tourism destination initiatives indicate low MSA engagement. In 2016, the Central Coast visitor information centre accommodation website, a key tourism cluster resource, marketing activity centre and networking group (VisitCC 2015), listed only a few MSAs out of the local government authority's estimation of a total of 3,000 (Gosford City Council 2013). Stakeholders highlighted that there were several reasons for the absence. One significant reason was the fragmented and micro nature of the industry which made resourcing the sector difficult. Expending resources on such a category against more vocal and established clients is a challenge. In contrast, preliminary research has revealed there are less SMA accommodation operators in the Hunter Valley, but this region has many more SMAs listed with the local visitor information centre (HVWC 2016). It is important to highlight, as stakeholders also identified, that the variation can be linked back to funding models and varying strategic and tactical approaches to destination marketing in these regions. Path dependency around regions, including key variations in institutional intermediaries, became a key theme of the research.

Interviews reveal three totally different local government authority attitudes to tourism marketing, with these directly impacting MSA operators and related marketing initiatives. Key Byron stakeholders, for example, do not support destination marketing, whereas Ballina funds the tourism office. As an elite interviewee and key stakeholder identified:

> Byron Shire council doesn't do anything in marketing … It's separate and marketing is only done through another organisation (private organisation Destination Byron). The problem is they never have enough money.

Central Coast and Hunter Wine Country tourism organisations have differing arrangements, with both having intermediaries that enjoy public funds and that also generate revenues from commercial interests.

Visitor information centres – key network resources for MSA and marketing activities – operate differently in each case, influencing MSA network activity. The Central Coast has low levels of MSA members and no planned marketing campaigns. Byron, which has been privately operated for 16 years, uses a Booking.com online reservation platform. This is in contrast to the southern part of the region, where Ballina Council runs the visitor information centre, supporting a website and visitor guide. Destination tourism network functions in Ballina are organised by the business chamber, not the visitor centre, unlike the other destinations. Central Coast, as discussed, is now in a complex scenario with a new merged Central Coast Council. There is an expectation that the Council may bring the tourism marketing activities within their domain rather than have a separate body outside. Hunter Valley Wine region visitor information centre in Pokolbin was similarly taken over by Cessnock Council in 2015, as described by a key informant:

> [T]aking over the visitors' centre, we have changed things here now. We do have a fee for service for the sustainability of the centre, around the two hundred dollars a year. They get their brochures and everything, but if they have emergency or specials on we can put them on a specials board. We've changed the centre round so that we have expos to support the smaller operators.

The Hunter Valley Tourism Alliance, a new private–public association, was launched in August 2015, with a high profile founding team, including an ex-state tourism minister, three vineyard owners and a large property developer. The alliance emerged out of frustration. All founding members have high profiles but also are time-poor. No major campaign has occurred since the launch:

> The association alone they are down to one and half people. They had seven in the team two and half years ago .... Running the association .... the thinking has got small too, because no one's thinking more than a few months ahead.

Getting traction for MSAs under such regional dynamics and tensions appears challenging. The state government cooperative marketing schemes have a minimum entry fee of $50,000. This grant level is unaffordable to individual MSAs. High entry fees necessitate regional tourism organisations liaising with larger cashed-up organisations. Byron-Ballina, Hunter Valley Wine and Central Coast all draw on state cooperative funds, but with a commencing rate of AU $50,000, the focus is not on MSAs. Even coordinating MSAs into a broader group or cluster is seen as a difficult activity. Hunter Valley Wine Country is the exception. Collectively, they have organised MSAs to advertise in their accommodation guide. From years 2006 to 2012, the Hunter Valley Wine Country accommodation directories listed 110–121 SMA rentals. This dropped to 82 properties in 2013 and then further dropped to 47 in 2013. This seemed to coincide with a withdrawal of council funds.

> When we looked at the old funding model, there was no minimum and there was no matched dollar funding. With the [new program] the minimum is $50,000 and the maximum is $500,000. That cuts out any businesses that don't have the capacity to raise those types of funds.

Other key stakeholders that were interviewed supported this sentiment.

MSA rental motivation influencing rental activity

Interviews with real estate letting agents in all three cases confirmed three types of MSA operator: second home owner, investment holiday renter and a property purchased with self-managed superannuation funds. Owners' motivations for letting their property actually vary on a continuum from what appears to be low interest to high interest. Figure 12.2 identifies that toward the left of the continuum, owners generally have minimal interest in seriously renting a property. These are second homes that are regularly used by families. In Australia, there are tax-gearing benefits for advertised rental properties (Australian Taxation Office 1985). The losses are compensated through capital gain and an income offset. As the family life cycle changes and adolescents move away, such properties often revert to full-time tenancy. One respondent that handles hundreds of such properties expanded on this in some detail:

> Where they actually sit on that spectrum does vary and change depending on what's going on in their lives. Typically, people come up, get all excited, and buy a holiday rental property when they're up here and when the kids are often young; use it for a couple of years, and then kids have sport and they find they can't actually come up here because [of other reasons].

On the right of the continuum, owners are much more motivated. These can be highly geared investments that necessitate high rental incomes to pay off mortgages. Interviews with agents in all three regions highlight that MSAs move across the spectrum depending on personal circumstances. This is represented by the dual circular arrows across the top of the figure.

> At the other end of the spectrum there are those owners who have a high mortgage, they are after every single thing they can. They really want to maximise their return on the property ... and every one sits somewhere on that spectrum and most people are probably somewhere in the middle. They are looking for a reasonable return and a degree of usage.

Owners' engagement in a destination initiative is often linked to MSA owners' motivational behaviour (Figure 12.2).

> There are some owners out there who if they have bought a property and it's all about owner usage. As long as there is some money coming through, they couldn't really care. ... And for some of them, from a taxation point of view, the property has got to be available for rent and it's not being rented hardly at all they still get the tax benefits of it by having it available.

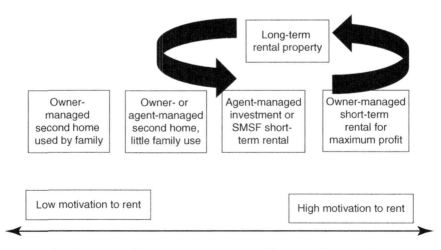

Figure 12.2 Continuum of owner motivation to rent self-contained accommodation property.

Respondents report MSA operators have previously been board members on Central Coast and Hunter Valley Wine Tourism. Interestingly, this did not lead to a strong voice for the sector.

Emerging digital online MSA platforms

Respondents noted a change in the sector with the growth of online marketing platforms, such as Stayz. A search of the sharing economy websites, such as Airbnb and Wimbu, identified that over 50% of rentals were self-contained. An independent search of Stayz found that the Central Coast lists more than 1,000 such properties, followed by Byron-Ballina with 750, and Hunter Valley Wine Country with 700. A similar Airbnb search found Byron Bay-Ballina had 600 listings, Central Coast 260, and Hunter Valley Wine Country 220. There has been a rapid growth of these peer-to-peer platforms. Known as the sharing economy, this sector in America has sales revenues of approximately US $335 billion (Saul & Anthony 2014). These initiatives are not simply online, but providers are also now developing online chat and peer review networks. These are now migrating to group level meetings in respective regions. Coupled with such activity is the rise in online specialist blogs. These include the vacation rental marketing blog (see www.vacationrentalmarketingblog.com).

Respondents were less aware of MSAs but were cognisant of the power of these disruptors. The meta-mediaries like Airbnb seem to have found a gap that previously was unrecognised. Like Uber, they are overcoming and circumventing some of the broader institutional impediments through their market power and political clout. These rapidly changing dynamics will impact MSA engagement. As one respondent suggested, 'Airbnb is appealing for those international visitors'. What the respondent was not realising is that on the supply side Airbnb is largely built on MSA operators.

MSA is largely an invisible sector

The lack of awareness of the sector corresponds to the respondents' lack of understanding of the size of the MSA sector. One Central Coast stakeholder indicated that MSA properties have no real champions at regional management level.

> I am not saying it (self-contained accommodation) doesn't get mentioned, but at board level and I've been at most (board meetings), I've never heard it mentioned.

Interestingly, the interviews themselves were alerting the stakeholders to the size and nature of the sector. Many of the respondents then acknowledged the incredible level of ignorance of what suddenly dawned on them was more than simply size. They realised the multiplier effect and that certain food and hospitality providers would effectively be non-profitable in many locations without MSA activity.

In summary, the research shows an overwhelming lack of understanding of the importance of MSAs in the regions. The researchers expected a level of ignorance, but not as comprehensively across most stakeholders. Those intermediaries that were marketing MSAs, however, were definitely more enlightened. They were aware of the potential multipliers and also how failure in this sector would lead to acute issues in the sector. One can only speculate on why such a sizable contributor to the tourism economy is not as prominent as expected. As discussed earlier, the micro nature of the enterprises seems an important element. A lack of cohesive marketing, which is also associated with the current political turbulence and the inability to achieve a united regional brand in two regions and accepted strategic approach, is not helping.

Conclusion and contribution

The chapter has provided an exploratory view of an important but largely ignored sector of the Australian economy. The existence of champions, observed by Hall (1999), to promote the development of regional cluster networks, seems to be seriously lacking. What is apparent is that Airbnb is seeing opportunities in this apparent market failure. Unfortunately, in some instances, the MSA sector only gains traction when confronted with negative publicity and broader policy issues. The aim of the chapter is to help "shine a light" on what is a very important economic driver of some Australian regions. Defining and classifying MSAs is an important start.

Various combinations of private–public partnerships between local government authorities, private enterprise and not-for-profit associations exist in the regions studied and analysed. Airbnb has launched regional online networks to help fill a gap in engagement and encourage more collaboration within the regional clusters and sectors. Whether the micro-enterprises actually want to engage, given their varying motivations, is an unanswered question. As discussed, motivation is key, and not all MSAs are interested in engaging in collaborative platforms. It will be interesting to go from stakeholder perceptions of this changing sector to seeing micro-enterprise perceptions themselves. Airbnb and Stayz have identified the immense potential of what to date has been a rather invisible MSA sector.

More research is required to investigate MSA–operator online networks and determine if there is a role for online networks and supporting marketing interventions. One thing is clear from the study: if a region itself is having difficulty with its identity, it is unlikely that it will be sufficiently capable of assisting MSAs to take advantage of such opportunities. Future research needs to try and value the sector and provide more intelligence on the regional economic importance of MSAs. The sector is certainly undervalued economically but also inadequately supported from a tourism product and place perspective.

It truly is an enigma that such an important contributor is so absent in key stakeholder minds. How this can be redressed is beyond the scope here. What is apparent is that players like Airbnb are filling this gap. It appears the digital economy in this instance is not only shining a light but also coming to the rescue. The question for the destination is what this may mean regarding the uniqueness of their place.

References

Adamiak, C. (2016) 'Cottage sprawl: Spatial development of second homes in Bory Tucholskie, Poland', *Landscape and Urban Planning*, 147: 96–106.

Airbnb (2016) *NSW Rentals*. [online] Retrieved from: https://www.airbnb.com.au/s/New-South-Wales?ss (accessed 21 February 2016).

Australian Bureau of Statistics (2013) *Defining Small Business*. [online] Retrieved from: http://www.abs.gov.au/AUSSTATS/abs@.nsf/mf/1321.0 (accessed 2 July 2016).

Australian Bureau of Statistics (2016) Tourism Satellite Account 2014–15 (ABS Cat. No. 5249.0) [online] Available at: www.abs.gov.au

Australian Government, Australian Taxation Office (1985) Taxation Ruling IT 2167 – Income tax: rental properties – non-economic rental, holiday home, share of residence, etc. cases, family trust cases. [online] Available at: http://law.ato.gov.au/atolaw/view.htm?docid=ITR/IT2167/nat/ato/00001

Bornhorst, T., Ritchie J. R. B. and Sheehan, L. (2010) 'Determinants of tourism success for DMOs & destinations: An empirical examination of stakeholders' perspectives', *Tourism Management*, 31 (5): 572–589.

Byron LGA. (2016) *New Rules for Holiday Letting*. [online] Retrieved from: http://www.byron.nsw.gov.au/media-releases/2016/04/12/new-rules-for-holiday-letting-to-come-into-effect (accessed 30 April 2016).

Central Coast Tourism (CCT) (2016) *Central Coast Destination Management Plan for the Visitor Economy 2013 to 2017*. Kariong, NSW: CCT Inc. Publishing.

Charmaz, K. (2006) *Constructing Grounded Theory: A Practical Guide through Qualitative Analysis.* London: Sage.

Connell, J., Kriz, A. and Thorpe, M. (2014) 'Industry clusters: An antidote for knowledge sharing and collaborative innovation?', *Journal of Knowledge Management*, 18 (1): 137–151.

Coppock, J. T. (1982) 'Geographical contributions to the study of leisure', *Leisure Studies*, 1 (1): 1–27.

Crouch, G. I. and Ritchie, J. R. B. (1999) 'Tourism, competitiveness, and societal prosperity', *Journal of Business Research*, 44 (3): 137–152.

Czarnecki, A. and Frenkel, I. (2014) 'Counting the "invisible": Second homes in Polish statistical data collections', *Journal of Research in Tourism, Leisure and Events*, 7 (1): 15–31.

Delgado, M., Porter, M. and Stern, S. (2010) 'Clusters and entrepreneurship', *Journal of Economic Geography*, 10 (4): 495–518.

Destination NSW (DNSW) (2015a) *Welcome to Destination NSW.* [online] Retrieved from: http://www.destinationnsw.com.au/ (accessed 24 July 2015).

Destination NSW (DNSW) (2015b) *Destination Management Planning.* [online] Retrieved from: http://www.destinationnsw.com.au/tourism/business-development-resources/destination-management-and-marketing/destination-management-planning (accessed 24 July 2015).

Dredge, D. (2006) 'Networks, conflict and collaborative communities', *Journal of Sustainable Tourism*, 14 (6): 562–581.

Dredge, D. and Jamal, T. (2015) 'Progress in tourism planning and policy: A post-structural perspective on knowledge production', *Tourism Management*, 51: 285–297.

Dredge, D. and Jenkins, J. (2007) *Tourism Planning and Policy.* Milton, Qld.: Wiley & Sons.

Eisenhardt, K. M. (1989) 'Building theories from case study research', *The Academy of Management Review*, 14 (4): 532–550.

European Communities (EC) (2008) *The Concept of Clusters and Cluster Policies and Their Role for Competitiveness and Innovation.* Luxembourg: Office for Official Publications of the European Communities.

Ffowcs-Williams, I. (2012) *Cluster Development: The Go-To Handbook: Building Competitiveness through Smart Specialisation.* Nelson, N.Z.: Cluster Navigators.

Flyvbjerg, B. (2011) 'Case study'. In N. K. Denzin and Y. S. Lincoln (eds) *Qualitative Research.* 4th ed. Thousand Oaks, CA: Sage, 301–316.

Getz, D. and Carlsen, J. (2005) 'Family business in tourism: State of the art', *Annals of Tourism Research*, 32 (1): 237–258.

Gosford City Council (2013) *Gosford City Council Planning Proposal and Development Control Plan (DCP) – Short Term Holiday Letting of Dwellings in GCC LGA.* [online] Retrieved from: http://www.gosford.nsw.gov.au/ (accessed 3 March 2014).

Grace, J. (2014) 'Supporting SME competitiveness in an industry agglomeration', paper presented at TCI Network Oceania Australasian Cluster Conference, 30 May.

Graci, S. (2012) 'Collaboration and partnership development for sustainable tourism', *Tourism Geographies*, 15 (1): 25–42.

Hall, C. M. (1999) 'Rethinking collaboration and partnership: A public policy perspective', *Journal of Sustainable Tourism*, 7 (3–4): 274–289.

Hall, C. M. (2011) 'A typology of governance and its implications for tourism policy analysis', *Journal of Sustainable Tourism*, 19 (4–5): 437–457.

Hall, C. M. (2014) 'Second homes planning, policy and governance', *Journal of Policy Research in Tourism, Leisure and Events*, 7 (1): 1–14.

Hall, C. M. and Rusher, K. (2004) 'Risky lifestyles? Entrepreneurial characteristics of the New Zealand bed and breakfast sector'. In R. Thomas (ed.) *Small Firms in Tourism: International Perspectives.* Hoboken, NJ: Taylor and Francis, 83–98.

Hall, T. and Teal, G. (2013) 'Understanding the changing nature of cluster drivers', *GSTF Business Review (GBR)*, 2 (4): 81–93.

Haugland, S. A., Ness, H., Grønseth, B.-O. and Aarstad, J. (2011) 'Development of tourism destinations: An integrated multilevel perspective', *Annals of Tourism Research*, 38 (1): 268–290.

Hunter Valley Visitor Centre (HVVC) (2013) *Cessnock City Council: Hunter Valley Visitor Centre Strategy 2013 – 2017.* [online] Retrieved from: http://www.huntervalleyvisitorcentre.com.au/media/filer_public/d0/30/d0300352-b1b1-4caf-9a6d-176c68622c53/hvvc_strategy_final.pdf *(accessed 20 July 2013).*

Hunter Valley Wine and Tourism Association (HVWTA) (2015a) *Hunter Valley Wine Country Membership Prospectus 2015–2016 HVWC.* Pokolbin NSW: HVWTA.

Hunter Valley Wine and Tourism Association (HVWTA) (2015b) *Hunter Valley Wine Country Accommodation Guide 2015–2016 HVWC*. Pokolbin NSW: HVWTA.

Keating, B. and Kriz, A. (2008) 'Outbound tourism from China: Literature review and research agenda', *Journal of Hospitality and Tourism Management*, 15 (1): 32–41.

Ketels, C. (2013) 'Recent research on competitiveness and clusters: What are the implications for regional policy?', *Cambridge Journal of Regions, Economy and Society*, 6: 269–284.

Ketels, C. and Memedovic, O. (2008) 'From clusters to cluster-based economic development', *International Journal of Technological Learning, Innovation and Development*, 1 (3): 375–392.

Kriz, A., Gummesson, E. and Quazi, A. (2014) 'Methodology meets culture: Relational and guanxi-oriented research in China', *International Journal of Cross Cultural Management*, 14: 27–46.

Krugman, P. (1994) 'Competitiveness: A dangerous obsession', *Foreign Affairs*, 73 (2): 28–44.

Land and Environment Court (LEC) (2013) *Land and Environment Court of NSW 2013 Judicial Newsletter*. [online] Available at: http://www.lec.justice.nsw.gov.au (accessed 21 June 2014).

Lashley, C. (2009) 'Forward'. In P. Lynch, A. L. McIntosh and H. Tucker (eds) *Commercial Homes in Tourism: An International Perspective*. London: Routledge, xiv–xvi.

Lashley, C. and Rowson, B. (2002) 'Big firms waiting to grow? Franchisees in the pub sector', *Strategic Change*, 11 (8): 411–424.

Lazzeretti, L., Sedita, S. R. and Caloffi, A. (2013) 'Founders and disseminators of cluster research', *Journal of Economic Geography*, 14 (1): 21–23.

Lindqvist, G., Ketels, C. and Sölvell, Ö. (2013) *The Cluster Initiative Green Book 2.0*. Stockholm: Ivory Tower Publishers.

Lynch, P., McIntosh, A. J. and Tucker, H. (eds) (2009) *Commercial Homes in Tourism: An International Perspective*. London and New York: Routledge.

Michael, E. J. (2003) 'Tourism micro-clusters', *Tourism Economics*, 9 (2): 133–145.

Müller, D. K. (2002) 'Reinventing the countryside: German second-home owners in southern Sweden'. *Current Issues in Tourism*, 5 (5): 426–446.

Navickas, V. and Malakauskaite, A. (2009) 'The impact of clusterization on the development of small and medium-sized enterprise (SME) sector', *Journal of Business Economics and Management*, 10 (3): 255–259.

New South Wales Government (2015) *Invest in NSW: Industry Strengths and Capabilities*. [online] Retrieved from: http://www.industry.nsw.gov.au/export-from-nsw/key-industry-sectors/tourism/industry-strengths-and-capabilities (accessed 8 October 2015).

Novelli, M., Schmitz, B. and Spencer, T. (2006) 'Networks, clusters and innovation in tourism: A UK experience', *Tourism Management*, 27 (6): 1141–1152.

Organization for Economic Cooperation and Development (OECD) (2001) *Innovative Clusters*. [online] Retrieved from: http://www.oecd-ilibrary.org/science-and-technology/innovative-clusters_9789264193383-en (accessed 16 August 2014).

Paris, C. (2014) 'Critical commentary: Second homes', *Annals of Leisure Research*, 17 (1): 4–9.

Porter, M. (1998) 'Clusters and the new economics of competition', *Harvard Business Review*, 76 (6): 77–90.

Porter, M. (2003) 'The Economic Performance of Regions', *Regional Studies*, 37 (6–7): 549–578.

Porter, M. (2013) 'Development strategies for the 21st century: Social progress and competitive growth', paper presented at Social Progress Imperative, Asuncion, Paraguay. [online] Retrieved from: http://www.isc.hbs.edu/pdf/20130905SPI_and_Comp_Paraguay_Michael_Porter.pdf?sf16883440=1 (accessed 20 June 2014).

Ritchie, J. R. B., Crouch, G. I. and Ritchie, J. R. (2005) *Competitive Destination: A Sustainable Tourism Perspective*. Wallingford, UK: CABI Publishing.

Saul, B. and Anthony, M. (2014) 'The next digital transformation: From an individual-centered to an everyone-to-everyone economy', *Strategy & Leadership*, 42 (5): 9–17.

Shakya, M. (2009) *Clusters for Competitiveness: A Practical Guide & Policy Implications for Developing Cluster Initiatives*. Washington, DC: International Trade Department, The World Bank.

Stayz (2012) *Central Coast Accommodation*. [online] Retrieved from: http://www.stayz.com.au (accessed 12 October 2009).

Stayz (2013) *Central Coast Accommodation*. [online] Retrieved from: http://www.stayz.com.au/accommodation/nsw/central-coast?view=list (accessed 20 November 2013).

Stayz (2014) *Central Coast Accommodation*. [online] Retrieved from: http://www.stayz.com.au/accommodation/nsw/central-coast?view=list (accessed 19 October 2014).

Stayz (2015) *Central Coast Accommodation*. [online] Retrieved from: http://www.stayz.com.au/accommodation/nsw/central-coast?view=list (accessed 20 November 2015).

Stayz (2016) *Central Coast Accommodation*. [online] Retrieved from: https://www.stayz.com.au/accom-modation/nsw/central-coast (accessed 28 June 2016).

Thomas, R. (2007) 'Tourism partnerships and small firms: Power, participation and partition', *The International Journal of Entrepreneurship and Innovation*, 8 (1): 37.

Thomas, R., Shaw, G. and Page, S. (2011) 'Understanding small firms in tourism: A perspective on research trends and challenges', *Tourism Management*, 32 (5): 963–976.

Tinsley, R. and Lynch, P. (2001) 'Small tourism business networks and destination development', *International Journal of Hospitality Management*, 20 (4): 367–378.

Tinsley, R. and Lynch, P. A. (2007) 'Small hospitality and tourism businesses in Pushkar, India: Destination development through communication networks', *World Journal of Tourism Small Business Management Revue*, 1: 83–94.

Tödtling, F. and Trippl, M. (2005) 'One size fits all? Towards a differentiated policy approach with respect to regional innovation systems', *Research Policy* 34 (8): 1203–1219.

United Nations Industrial Development Organization (UNIDO) (2013) *United Nations Development Organisation Approach to Cluster Development.* Vienna, Austria: Clusters and Business Linkages, UNIDO.

Valente, F., Dredge, D. and Lohmann, G. (2015) 'Leadership and governance in regional tourism', *Journal of Destination Marketing & Management*, 4 (2): 127–136.

VisitCC (2015) *Central Coast Accommodation*. [online] Retrieved from: https://visitcc.com.au (accessed 7 October 2015).

Weir, R. (2013) *Strategies to Assist Tourism Industry Small and Medium Enterprises to Engage with Asian Markets.* Canberra: Department of Industry, Tourism Research Australia.

Welch, C., Marschan-Piekkari, R., Penttinen, H. and Tahvanainen, M. (2002) 'Corporate elites as inform-ants in qualitative international business research', *International Business Review*, 11 (5): 611–628.

Wray, M. (2015) 'Drivers of change in regional tourism governance: A case analysis of the influence of the New South Wales Government, Australia, 2007–2013', *Journal of Sustainable Tourism*, 23 (7): 990–1010.

Wyong Shire Council (2016) *Wyong Shire Local Government Authority*. [online] Retrieved from: https://www.wyong.nsw.gov.au (accessed 20 March 2016).

Yin, R. K. (2003) *Case Study Research: Design and Theory*. 3rd ed. Thousand Oaks, CA: Sage.

Zehrer, A. and Hallmann, K. (2015) 'A stakeholder perspective on policy indicators of destination competi-tiveness', *Journal of Destination Marketing & Management*, 4 (2): 120–126.

13

AUSTRALIAN HOLIDAY HOMES

Places of escape and sites of investment

Chris Paris

Introduction

This chapter provides a comparative historical analysis of the evolution of second homes in Australia, relating the changing nature of second home ownership to the international literature and the changing national socio-economic context (Paris 2011, 2014). It explores overlapping dimensions of Australian second homes (typically called "holiday homes" in Australia) as items of private leisure consumption *and* as sites of capital investment in contemporary land, housing and commercial holiday markets. Examples are largely drawn from my research on second home "hot spot" local government authority areas (LGAs).

Early second home developments from the 1930s to the early 1960s were typically informal structures in unregulated environments, often involving self-construction of modest cottages or "shacks" on Crown Land. Many "holiday homes communities" were developed on previously undeveloped places, typically by the coast or inland rivers and lakes, as places of escape from a rapidly modernising world, albeit only made possible by the enhanced affluence and mobility of that very world (Marsden 1969; Murphy 1977). Second home ownership grew substantially during the 1950s and 1960s for family recreational use, but increasingly with formally built structures regulated by new systems of planning and building control.

The context and content of Australian second home ownership changed in the 1970s, as 'the weekender was being turned into the holiday home' (White 2005: 136). Contemporary commentators predicted substantial growth of second home ownership but actual growth has been much lower; rather, it has changed and diversified within a changing context. The Australian housing system has undergone transitions affecting dwelling types, tenure and costs, also flowing into leisure-related investment in dwellings. Rapid population growth and metropolitan expansion changed urban-regional geographies; some holiday home places were overwhelmed by suburbia but others were newly created by large-scale developers.

Holiday homes have become increasingly focused in coastal areas, moved up-market, and emerged into a hybrid form of dwelling ownership involving use for private leisure *and* commercial letting. These changes have generated new debates about holiday homes and local communities, including the fiscal basis of local government, land use planning and conflicts between "permanent" and "temporary" residents.

Theoretical perspectives on Australian second homes

This chapter builds on a substantial body of research and commentary on second homes, including recent overviews by Müller and Hoogendoorn (2013) and Paris (2011, 2014). My perspective is comparative historical analysis, with second home ownership conceptualised as a social phenomenon that has evolved ecologically through human interactions (Paris 2014). There are many differences in the concept of second homes between places and over time, and in the words used to describe second homes. Whilst most research has been country-specific, globalisation and massively increased mobility have contributed to internationalisation of second homes with transnational second home ownership identifiable in most countries. Research on second homes has focused largely on leisure and tourism, with little recognition that such dwellings are also part of housing markets, while housing researchers have paid little attention to second homes (Paris 2014). But second homes represent an arena of interaction between housing and leisure markets within changing socio-economic contexts.

The term "holiday home" is used almost exclusively in Australia rather than "second home". One advantage of using the term "holiday home" is that it recognises the hybridity of second homes – as elements of both leisure *and* housing markets – and the flexibility and fluidity of use inherent in dwelling ownership which combines private consumption and commercial investment. It recognises that these are not particular types of dwellings, that "second homes" are not a tenure category, and that the use of dwellings can and does vary over time. Dwellings that were constructed for use as holiday homes may subsequently be used primarily as holiday lettings, or sold to a household which then resides permanently, and subsequently subdivided with part occupied by the owners and the other part let to holiday makers. The permutations are almost endless and have come over the last few years to include other forms of use, especially Airbnb.

The overlapping and ambiguous uses of the terms "second homes", "holiday homes" and "holiday accommodation" are not confined to Australia, but are widespread in the scholarly literature. This ambiguity reflects diversity of dwelling use and widespread socio-economic changes in the context of the production, ownership and use of this form of housing *and* leisure provision. Many scholars have discussed the increasing commodification and commercialisation of second homes, recently including Rye (2011), but this just represents an intensification and expansion of longstanding elements in the history of second homes. Thus, references in the literature to "traditions" of holiday home ownership often are unreflective and inaccurate descriptions of dwelling uses of recent origin in changing contexts and circumstances (Paris 2013).

The Australian case demonstrates how rapidly a "tradition" can be created, how quickly such traditions have been developed and changed, and how the same words can be used to describe fundamentally different kinds of relationships. These developments are explored below through an analysis of Australian census data relating to second homes, especially for the period 1971–2011. I also use a range of historical and empirical evidence to reconceptualise relations between leisure and tourism, on the one hand, and local, national and transnational housing markets on the other hand.

The Australian case illustrates some data problems that complicate attempts to measure the incidence and dimensions of second home ownership. For a review of general data issues, see Paris (2011); for the Australian case, see Paris et al. (2014). There is no current official estimate of the number of second homes, so comparative analysis usually has to utilise data on occupied/ unoccupied dwellings or counts of permanent/non-permanent residents, from censuses and local government records, as indicative or proxy data on second homes. Other estimates have derived from surveys relating to housing and social phenomena, indicating that in 2006 around 214,000 Australian households, about 3% of the total, owned dwellings acquired primarily for use as holiday homes (Paris 2011). The ABS considered including questions on holiday homes in the 2016 census but did not do so. The Australian census of 1971, however, contained counts of dwellings thought to be holiday homes, providing a baseline for comparison with best estimates derived from the 2011 census (Paris et al. 2014).

Second homes in Australia: A distinctive case?

The story of second homes in Australia has many similarities to developments in other affluent "new world" countries, with most second homes being newly constructed rather than represent-ing changing use of older dwellings (Marsden 1969). But the Australian case has differed from the USA or Canada cases in four distinctive ways: the timing of second home developments; the settlement of Australia and the establishment of a self-governing nation state was much more recent; population growth and change has involved a much higher level of net in-migration; and, the pattern of colonial settlement and subsequent development was concentrated almost entirely in coastal centres ("settlement" is used in Australia in two ways: (a) objectively to refer to the establishment of physical settlements, and (b) euphemistically to refer to colonial invasion and displacement of indigenous populations).

Mass second home ownership and developer-driven second home developments both emerged 10 years later in Australia than in the USA and Canada (Council of Planning Librarians 1975; Ragatz 1973; Wolfe 1977). The Australian economy has been driven largely by primary production since the nineteenth century. Manufacturing industry initially was related to pri-mary production and food processing, but expanded after 1945 in a heavily regulated and pro-tected environment with strong Commonwealth and state government support. Australia was relatively prosperous compared to most European countries from the 1880s gold rushes to the late 1920s. The economy suffered during the 1930s depression but quickly achieved prosperity during the post-war boom. Australia had one of the highest home ownership rates in the world by the 1960s due to strongly supportive government policies and the prosperous and expanding economy (Kemeny 1981; Paris 1993).

The Australian population grew steadily in the early twentieth century, with immigrants mostly from the UK and Ireland, reflecting the determination of governments to block non-white immigration. Post-war immigration up to the 1960s included a million UK immigrants on the Assisted Migration Scheme, displaced persons from across Europe and substantial migra-tion from southern Europe. Britain and Europe remained major sources of immigration after 1970, but immigration from other areas grew rapidly, especially from the Asian Pacific region (including New Zealand), India and the Middle East. The changing migrant mix led to greater ethnic and cultural diversity than the white Anglo-Irish Australia of the 1950s (Hugo 2013) and Asian-Australians were on the brink of overtaking European-Australians (Colebatch 2011). The population almost doubled between 1945 and 1970, increasing by another 50% between 1981 and 2011 to 21.5 million; half were migrants or children of migrants, compared to 20% in the USA (Hugo 2013). Like most developed countries, Australia experienced significant changes in household formation patterns from the 1970s onwards, with many more "non-family" single person and couple households.

Australian population growth occurred in a distinctive urban and regional geography, radiat-ing out from a few coastal colonial centres, currently State capital cities, with a high degree of urban concentration but little inland settlement. Sydney and Hobart were established first, fol-lowed by Adelaide, Melbourne, Brisbane and Perth. The population concentrations of the early twentieth century lost ground in relative terms after 1945, with falling shares in New South Wales (NSW), Victoria, South Australia (SA) and Tasmania, and strong growth in Queensland,

Western Australia (WA) and the Northern Territory. The national capital, Canberra, grew most rapidly of all in relative terms after 1970 and will soon overtake the population of Tasmania.

Post-war Australian urbanisation was at very low population and housing densities by world standards, fuelled by increasing car ownership, with extensive suburban expansion from the 1960s onwards. The overall settlement pattern remained dominated by capital cities in 2011: 62% of the population lived in cities of 1 million or more and 14% in cities of 80,000 or more. The vast arid and semi-arid inland is sparsely populated, apart from Canberra and a few other inland centres. New forms of coastal urban development emerged in the 1970s, related to life-style choices, tourism and a preference for living in warmer coastal areas. Mullins (1985, 1991, 1994) reviewed the impacts of population shifts through "sun-belt" migration, especially to SE Queensland, with emergent "tourist urbanisation" on the Gold Coast.

Australian second homes from the 1930s to the 1960s

Second homes in Australia up to the 1920s were the preserve of wealthy households, located in high amenity coastal areas and cooler upland regions like the Adelaide Hills (Hertzberg 1978). But a new "tradition" emerged in the 1930s when people affluent enough to own cars con-structed self-built cottages or "shacks". Shack owners celebrated simplicity and the Australian tradition of bush living. Two years before Australia entered the Second World War, the Adelaide *Chronicle* newspaper considered the simple pleasures of shack life:

> The word "shacks" brings to me memories and dreams – weeks in the hills, or by the sea, days spent in bathers, shorts or unpretentious slacks under the still hot sun or among fresh winds – surfing, sunbathing, fishing, shooting, or, by the lazy or highly intelligent, just loafing.
>
> *(Anon (R. J. C.) 1937)*

Other wealthy holidaymakers travelled by sea to hotels and small resorts within easy range of Sydney or Melbourne in the 1930s and 1940s, as many regional roads remained unsealed before mass car ownership (Ryan 1965). Victor Harbor and Port Elliott were established resorts in SA by the 1930s, reputedly with 'the finest promenades in the whole of Australia' (White 2005: 108).

The early scholarly writing on the growth of second home ownership in Australia contrasted local experience with developments in Europe, drawing parallels with other settler capitalist soci-eties, especially the USA, Canada and New Zealand (Marsden 1969; Murphy 1977; Robertson 1977). Growing affluence, car ownership and increased paid leisure time were important drivers of the growth of second home ownership in the 1950s and 1960s. Access to cars increased four-fold: from 1 in every 14 Australians in 1946 to 1 in every 3.5 by 1960 (White 2005).

The growth of second home ownership was primarily for private family use, typically "shacks" in SA, WA and Tasmania, and modest newly built housing in coastal areas of NSW and Queensland (Cook 1977; Mosley 1965). An emphasis on self-building, rusticity and lack of sophisticated amenities echoed commentary from the inter-war period. Many shacks were assembled on Crown Land, with little or no security of tenure, in an era with no significant planning or environmental regulations or restrictions.

The development of holiday homes involved the creation of many new "places" in previously undeveloped localities, especially coastal strips near Sydney (Murphy 1977) and Melbourne (Frost 2004) or more remote coastal areas where farming families sought refuge from the summer heat. There was also extensive shack development along the River Murray in SA and other inland developments near lakes, as water was '*the* multi-function recreational resource, activities on, under or by it appealing to all ages' (Marsden 1969: 67; emphasis in original), and 'for the masses, a seaside cottage became the most usual form of summer vacation home' (Herzberg 1978: 19).

Marsden (1969: 69) described most holiday homes in Queensland as 'new structures rather than converted farm or fishing cottages, and very few, apart from commercial flats, were architect designed'. These coastal "holiday homescapes" created a new type of land use within weekend commuting distance of urban centres; their coastal geography testified 'to the lessened belief in the therapeutic qualities of the mountain air and spa water promoted by nineteenth century medical topographers' (Marsden 1969: 67).

Marsden (1969: 57–8) noted ambiguities in the term "holiday home" over 40 years ago, proposing a fourfold typology of the use of holiday homes:

1   Private holiday homes: used at weekends and holidays by owners, family and friends, including diverse dwelling types and usually located within "generally acceptable recreational commuting times".
2   Intermittently commercial holiday homes: mainly for private use but occasionally let to others especially during high seasons.
3   Intermittently private: often purchased for possible future retirement but mainly used as commercial lettings with some private use.
4   Commercial: investment properties generally let and maintained by agents.

The "dramatic increase in the ownership of second homes" from the early 1950s to the mid-1960s, especially in coastal NSW and Queensland, slowed down substantially in the late 1960s (Robertson 1977: 119). Despite this slackening rate of growth, Robertson (1977) expected that the proportion of Australian households with second homes would increase from the recorded level of 5–6% in 1971 to 20% by the end of the century.

The 1971 Australian census was the last to identify holiday homes, providing a benchmark against which to assess subsequent developments. Census enumerators identified unoccupied and occupied dwellings and tried to assess why some dwellings were unoccupied. Table 13.1 shows that just over half of all unoccupied dwellings were newly built, for sale or let, or temporarily vacant; most were in major urban areas, least in rural areas.

Table 13.1 Unoccupied private dwellings, Australia 1971

| | Urban-rural variations | | | |
	Major urban	Other urban	Rural	Total
Reason unoccupied	%			
Newly built	10	4	2	6
For sale or to let	28	19	10	20
Temporarily vacant	35	26	18	27
Holiday home	10	40	40	27
Other/NS	9	6	22	12
Vacant for repair	5	3	3	4
Condemned	3	2	5	4
Total ('000)	143	94	102	339

Major urban: 100,000<; Other urban: 25,000–99,999; rural < 24,999
Source: Commonwealth Bureau of Census and Statistics (1975).

About a quarter (27%) of the unoccupied dwellings were considered to be holiday homes. These were concentrated in other urban and rural areas (40% in each); unoccupied dwellings classified as "other and not stated" were *heavily* concentrated in rural areas, suggesting that many also were holiday homes. There were small variations between States and Territories in the proportion of unoccupied dwellings considered to be holiday homes: highest in Tasmania (43%), and least (23–24%) in WA and Queensland.

The growth of Australian second home ownership between 1945 and 1971 occurred in a white Anglo-Irish culture, and was driven predominantly by middle-aged Australians who had grown up during the Depression of the 1930s and experienced sacrifices and deprivations of the Second World War. But all of these dimensions were to change rapidly as Australian society and economy changed in the 1970s and 1980s, and holiday homes were transformed from "shacks to mansions" within a generation (Paris 2011; White 2005).

Australian holiday homes since the 1970s: Post-Fordist second home ownership

Our study of second homes in SA was developed and completed between April 2013 and June 2014 (Paris et al. 2014). During that same period, the last two major car manufacturers still making cars in Australia, Ford and GM Holden, both announced that production would shortly cease. The ending of Australian car production is symptomatic of larger changes in economy and society, all of which affected the changing nature of second home ownership.

The long post-war boom ended in the mid-1970s and the growth of second home ownership was arrested by the same processes affecting Australian society and housing: economic restructuring, demographic change, the shift to neo-liberalism across Australian politics and society, and growing socio-economic polarisation. As in many other wealthy countries, there have been major transformations in Australian housing policies and markets since the 1970s, with a switch away from the "social project" of mass home ownership to commodified systems of housing production and ownership (Forrest & Hirayama 2014; Rolnik 2013). As in other societies, too, there have been significant demographic changes, as falling birth rates and increasing longevity resulted in substantial falls in average household size (Hugo 2013).

The effects of these changes have been to arrest the growth of home ownership and the emergence of long-term private renting. Home ownership in Australia fell from 71% of households in 1971 to 67% in 2011 as the public policies that had promoted the growth of mass home ownership were replaced with supply-side subsidies (Beer et al. 2011; Flood & Baker 2010). The small public housing sector was in near-terminal decline, although there was modest growth of a small "community" housing sector, but the strongest growth in the private rented sector was fuelled by tax breaks for wealthy investors. Booming capital city house prices were further inflamed by extensive overseas purchase of Australian residential property (Paris 2017).

Table 13.2 shows that the number of unoccupied dwellings increased more substantially between 1971 and 2011 (175%) than occupied dwellings (114%). Although a comparison of the proportions of unoccupied dwellings at the 1971 and 2011 censuses is not exactly like-for-like, this is a well established proxy for measuring changing volumes of second homes, especially when informed by LGA data on non-permanent residents (Paris et al. 2014). Based on the census and considering previous detailed research on the characteristics of second home owners (Paris et al. 2009), I estimate that around 6–7% of Australian households, primarily middle-aged and older affluent households, owned holiday homes in 2011. The number of holiday homes had increased significantly by 2011, driven by overall growth in population and households, but growth in the proportion of Australian households with second homes was *much* lower than was predicted in the 1970s.

Table 13.2 Occupied and unoccupied Australia private dwellings in 1971 and 2011

Occupied and unoccupied dwellings by State & Territory 1971 and 2011

	1971				2011			
	Occupied	Unoccupied	Total	Unoccupied %	Occupied	Unoccupied	Total	Unoccupied %
	('000)				('000)			
NSW	1,357	125	1,481	8.4	2,471	265	2,736	10.7
Victoria	1,010	89	1,099	8.1	1,945	247	2,192	11.3
Queensland	513	51	564	9.1	1,547	178	1,725	10.3
SA	342	31	373	8.2	619	84	703	11.9
WA	284	28	313	9.0	794	109	903	12.1
Tasmania	110	13	123	10.8	193	33	226	14.4
NT	17	1	18	5.1	61	9	70	12.4
ACT	38	2	40	4.7	129	10	139	7.3
Australia	3,671	340	4,011	8.5	7,759	935	8,694	10.7

Sources: Commonwealth Bureau of Census and Statistics 1975; Australian Bureau of Statistics 2012.

Table 13.2 indicates that the increase in the number of unoccupied dwellings was higher in the more southerly States, especially SA and Tasmania. This partly reflects the timing of the census in winter, when holiday homes in southern states are unlikely to be occupied midweek apart from Alpine areas, while many are let to tourists in Queensland or northern NSW (Paris et al. 2014). It also reflects the changed nature of second home ownership in Australia, increasingly focused in coastal areas as developers drove the growth and change since the 1970s, and emerged as a hybrid form of ownership for leisure use *and* investment.

Many of the new second home places developed in the 1960s have subsequently been overtaken by suburbia as cities expanded outwards, or in the case of Adelaide, as the city expanded to the seaside. Others have been incorporated into new, larger communities, such as the Sunshine Coast to the north of Brisbane. State governments have removed or are removing many shack settlements from National Parks and Crown Land. Some other early post-war holiday home developments have endured, though shacks are increasingly replaced with more substantial dwellings. In most cases new legislation has resulted in transfer of title from annual leasehold to more secure forms of tenure, but this has been accompanied by the imposition of stricter environmental planning regulations and building control.

The wider environmental context has also changed as Australian metropolitan areas have expanded massively, by low-density developments catering for a rapidly growing population fuelled by high levels of in-migration. There has been extensive development in coastal "sea change" and peri-urban areas, reflecting wider socio-economic and demographic changes (Burnley & Murphy 2004). The changes in public policies and increasing socio-economic polarisation have resulted in holiday homes increasingly becoming forms of investment rather than spaces for family leisure, underpinned by a tax regime favouring property investment by affluent households. Greater affluence for some Australians and enhanced mobility for most has resulted in complex patterns of seasonal movement and migration for leisure purposes (Bell & Brown 2006; Charles-Edwards et al. 2008; Hugo, Feist & Tan 2013). Holiday homes are a vital element of tourist accommodation in many areas. In some popular areas they are the *only* form of holiday rental accommodation, as in the Yorke Peninsula (Paris et al. 2014).

Demand for seasonal rental holiday homes in Australia has distinctive peaks compared to northern hemisphere tourism, due to the coincidence of summer holidays and the Christmas and New Year period. Holiday home tourism peaks in late December and early January, and around Easter. The peak effect is most concentrated in the southern states (SA, Victoria and Tasmania) where cool and dismal winters contrast with the more pleasant weather encountered in much of NSW, Queensland and Western Australia. The high degree of metropolitan dominance explains the spatial focus of second home places, especially within relatively easy access to main population concentrations in SA, Tasmania and WA.

Current issues and policy debates

The impacts of holiday homes on local governments in SA

The SA research examined the impacts of second home ownership and retirement migration on local governments, focusing on 11 participating LGAs with high levels of holiday homes, using qualitative and quantitative methods (Paris et al. 2014). Figure 13.1 shows the study of LGAs located in coastal areas, including four case study areas (Alexandrina, Kangaroo Island, Robe and Yorke Peninsula). The other participating LGAs were located along the River Murray waterway (Gerard-Loxton Waikerie, Mid Murray, Murray Bridge) and a booming wine region (Clare-Gilbert Valley).

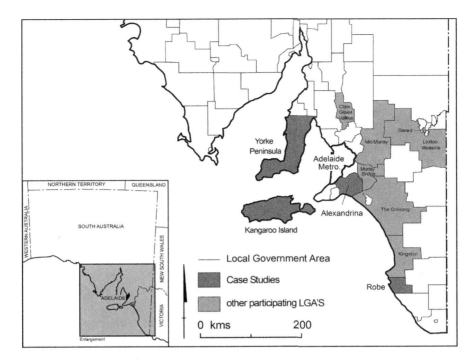

Figure 13.1 Local Government Areas participating in the South Australian study.

Source: Paris et al., 2014.

Quantitative methods included analyses of census data relating to holiday homes, socio-economic characteristics of permanent residents in second home LGAs, and changing relations between population and dwellings from 2001 to 2011. Multivariate census data analysis assessed the significance of retirement migration in SA between 2006 and 2011. The research also collected and analysed primary quantitative data from LGAs and utility providers on seasonality of service use and examined LGA data on non-resident ratepayers (NRRs).

Qualitative methods included fieldwork in "hot spot" LGAs, with interviews exploring a range of issues:

- Seasonal population variations
- Impacts on LGA service provision and businesses
- Relations between permanent residents and second home owners
- The extent and impacts of retirement migration, including second home owners
- Concerns about second homes and retirement migration
- The changing nature of holiday homes and their geographical distribution.

A Delphi workshop refined our analysis of the impacts of second homes and retirement migration.

Growth of holiday homes in coastal areas

The study showed that growing affluence had enabled strong growth of holiday home ownership driven by investment potential and amenity factors. The number of holiday homes had increased at a faster rate than the total of occupied dwellings, from around 10,000 in 1971 to at least 30,000 in 2011. Most of the growth in holiday homes after 1971 was in coastal areas, with little growth along the River Murray. Holiday homes had gone strongly up-market as shacks were replaced and superseded by large and expensive houses. The few exceptions were areas of shacks with little or no prospect of obtaining freehold title. There was evidence of gentrification in Robe, with demolition of decent older dwellings and replacement by much larger new buildings. Some developments are fully developer-led and linked to other forms of development, especially marinas. Some other areas, especially within the coastal zone of Alexandrina within commuting distance of metro Adelaide, contain a mix of holiday homes and permanent residences.

Hybrid character of holiday homes and impacts on local housing markets

Any conceptual differences between "second homes" as sites of family leisure and commercial "holiday rentals" had become blurred: holiday homes were sites of leisure and amenity *and* business premises used for commercial letting. The creation of the Australia-wide Holiday Rental Industry Association in 2013 highlighted the emergence of a new business sector that had been paid little attention. The emergence of this hybrid type of dwelling use has not been recognised in State and Territory planning systems, and any basis for distinguishing between holiday accommodation and permanent residences within building codes had become redundant. Holiday homes were a vital form of tourist accommodation, the *main* form in some LGAs, but this was rarely acknowledged in local planning and tourism strategies.

The main "housing" issue was the development of distinctive local housing markets, with growing proportions of large and expensive holiday homes left empty for much of the year, but little or no other rental housing. In many cases, these are in areas with few if any permanent residents, as at Black Point in Yorke Peninsula. But whole local housing markets have been transformed in other cases, notably in Robe where a growing amount of high value housing is empty for much of the year and available for holiday letting at high costs, with little or no other rental accommodation and strong house and land price inflation.

The housing market impacts vary between places, partly as a function of wider development processes. Robe's development is constrained by planning and environmental factors. Similar constraints affected some second home hotspots in Yorke Peninsula but much more land is available for development in high amenity locations in Alexandrina, and Kangaroo Island has no significant development pressure, so there was much less rapid land price inflation in these cases. Large parts of all case study LGAs remain unaffected by holiday home development: inland Yorke Peninsula, Robe and Kangaroo Island are similar to most of country Australia, with falling permanent populations and rapid ageing.

Changing local housing markets reflect the mismatch between the incomes and wealth of permanent residents and second home owners. This in turn affects attitudes to holiday homes and aspirations for the future of local areas. Positively, the growth of second home ownership has been a vital element in sustaining and growing local businesses. Some second home hotspots have more substantial restaurants and local supermarkets than would exist locally on the basis of the permanent population alone, especially Robe. The study found strong evidence of different attitudes to aspects of development: some holiday home owners oppose the provision of facilities for tourists near "their" beaches and others seek to privatise public spaces. But second home owners and permanent residents often share opposition to some proposed developments such as wind farms or mining. Other differences between permanent residents and second home owners related mainly to concerns about noise, litter and over-occupation of holiday homes during peak visitor periods.

Variations between second home places

Census data showed differences between coastal LGAs and those along the Murray River in terms of the socio-demographic and economic characteristics of permanent populations: generally there were older populations and fewer children in coastal LGAs, and more retirement migration. But there were also demographic differences *within* the two groups of coastal and non-coastal LGAs and clear differences *between* the case studies in terms of the demographic characteristics of their in-migrants and the effects of demographic change between 2001 and 2011. The resident population of Alexandrina increased substantially through an influx of people of all ages, though its age distribution was more like that of the other case studies than SA as a whole. There was no evidence of net in-migration to other case studies; rather, the number of occupied private dwellings *fell* in Robe and Yorke Peninsula. There was strong growth in the number of *unoccupied* dwellings in these cases, especially Kangaroo Island: should we think of the construction of new dwellings that remain largely unoccupied as a form of "ghost" in-migration?

Environmental considerations and impacts also varied considerably between holiday home LGAs, including dealing with the legacy of shacks in environmentally sensitive places and concern regarding what types of new development should be permitted and what environmental constraints should be applied. But there were many clear and growing risks of inundation through tidal surges, river floods and possible future sea level rise.

Mobility, migration and retirement: Impacts on localities

There was no evidence of large-scale retirement migration to second homes by baby boomers in SA between 2006 and 2011. Most over-65s were ageing in place or moving over short distances, usually within the Adelaide metro area. The main impacts of retirement migration were felt in places that receive aged in-migrants, as many also have rapidly ageing populations due to out-migration by younger people.

Growing second home ownership and retirement migration have occurred within a wider context involving other processes of social, demographic and economic change, especially economic restructuring, changing housing markets and the continued expansion of metropolitan Adelaide. Population mobility and seasonality affect the ability of LGAs to cope with dramatic seasonal variations in demand for council services (waste collection, local road maintenance and parking). The growth of second home ownership by NRRs has had perceived negative impacts on many LGAs as the allocation of Grants Commission funding does not allow for the impacts of seasonal population fluctuations (McKenzie et al. 2008; Paris et al. 2009, 2014). The State Government gets Land Tax from NRRs, local businesses get more demand for their services, but LGAs just get extra costs of seasonality of service demand. The Delphi workshop raised the suggestion that Grants Commission allocations should be based on the count of dwellings within an area, not "permanent" population.

Wider implications of the SA study

Many aspects of this study are more widely applicable across Australia. The lack of evidence regarding baby boomer relocation corresponds to doubts about the extent to which this is happening across Australia (Alexander 2012) and whether there is likely to be widespread retirement migration to second homes as suggested by Hugo et al. (2013). The limited evidence of such movement is consistent with the literature on older Australians' housing preferences and relations between migration and the life course: retirees use their second homes more than previously, but few move to them full-time and many return to their previous areas of residence (Charles-Edwards & Bell 2015; Pinnegar et al. 2012; Sander & Bell 2014).

The Alexandrina case study differed from the other three case studies but had many similarities with much coastal development across Australia. The southwards extension of metropolitan Adelaide has opened up opportunities for "sea change" retirement (or pre-retirement) moves, with better access to hospital and medical facilities than would be possible in Robe or most of Kangaroo Island and Yorke Peninsula. There was strong local opposition to the notion that Alexandrina is an extension of metropolitan Adelaide, but its growth is *clearly* related to overall metropolitan region growth.

The evidence of holiday homes going up-market confirms trends already considered elsewhere (Paris 2011) and apparent almost universally. A "national professional association for Australia's holiday rental industry", the Holiday Rental Industry Association (HRIA), was established in 2014, highlighting the economic significance of holiday homes in terms of tourist accommodation. It claimed that the holiday rental industry generated over $30 billion to the national economy and supported over 200,000 jobs (HRIA 2014). Australian holiday homes had evolved from being primarily privately used dwellings into investments with professionally managed commercial businesses.

The LGA concerns about funding support for local services in the South Australian study are relevant throughout Australia. Another concern of wider relevance was raised in Robe when LGA representatives questioned the validity of the 2011 census population numbers, suggesting that the recorded population was an undercount. The increased use of holiday homes by people who do not live in Robe on a "permanent" basis but are there *more often*, generating increased demand for services, are not included within the census count of permanent residents. This is consistent with the literature on temporary mobility and population circulation as people use second homes more but do not move there permanently.

Finally, environmental and land-use planning issues reviewed in the South Australian study are of Australia-wide significance in ongoing research on housing and local government in Australia (Beer et al. 2014). Environmental planning systems have struggled to cope with the dual nature of dwelling use and blurred distinction between private and commercial uses of holiday homes. The NSW Land and Environment Court determined that short-term renting of homes within a particular residential zone in Gosford was unlawful. The case involved complaints by neighbours that a large house was let to groups of revellers involving large congregations of people, public drunkenness and nudity (Gadens 2014). This case focused on the distinction between "residential dwelling" and "holiday letting" within planning ordinances. Such debates over dwelling use have resulted in contested planning decisions, leading to reviews of land use zoning and dwelling categorisation in many states (Paris et al. 2014).

The Gosford case also highlights the dilemma for LGAs that wish to encourage tourism, with holiday rentals being a major source of visitor accommodation, but *also* wanting to maintain "quiet enjoyment" within residential areas. Such dilemmas may not be resolved easily or permanently, and attempted resolutions may vary between and within States, Territories and LGAs. These considerations are amplified by the growth of part-time letting of whole houses through Airbnb. Many uncertainties remain, but we can be certain that this issue will not go away, and is most problematic where a growing proportion of retirees live in areas with large proportions of holiday rentals.

Conclusions

Australian second home ownership has been transformed since the 1960s, from low-cost vernacular structures into commoditised forms with high levels of investor activity. Self-built shacks and cottages have given way to commercially driven upmarket housing sold as holiday homes, with growing numbers of commercial developments of large, expensive houses, often with marinas or other leisure facilities. Despite such changes, large, new holiday homes are still often called "shacks" by their owners or in real estate marketing.

These changes have reflected changing social and economic relationships between people and physical environments, including built environments. Most of these changes have been ecological, rather than planned, though public planning policies have been one factor affecting some of the change. Australian holiday homes in the twenty-first century have evolved into a hybrid form of dwelling ownership for leisure use *and* investment.

No commentators writing about second homes in the 1960s and 1970s anticipated these developments, though Marsden (1969) captured the ambiguous nature of second homes in his fourfold categorisation. This chapter has argued that the balance between those four categories has shifted *fundamentally* from predominantly "private holiday homes" around 1971, towards "intermittently private" and "commercial" by 2011.

Robertson's prediction of substantial growth in the proportion of Australian households with second homes did not eventuate. But he was writing at the end of the long boom before any appreciation of the coming change in economy and society. There are many parallels between the changed situation in Australia and Europe and North America, within globalised housing and leisure markets, as demonstrated in the international literature (Müller & Hoogendoorn 2013; Paris 2011, 2014; Rye 2011). The shift in household formation patterns, with many more one- and two-person households, combined with changing leisure and tourism preferences, has reduced demand for "family" holiday homes.

Australian second homes are increasingly investment goods rather than family retreats, reflecting wider socio-economic change and the financialisation of home ownership. Like second homes worldwide, they are interchangeable with other dwellings in terms of use as permanent or non-permanent homes, and they will continue to relate ambiguously to housing and leisure markets.

Acknowledgements

My research on second home and retirement migration in SA was conducted at Adelaide University, assisted by the Local Government Research and Development Scheme, with inputs from many colleagues, especially Sandy Horne.

References

Alexander, S. (2012) *Has the Tide Turned on Coastal Growth?* [Blog] idblog. Retrieved from: http://blog.id.com.au/2012/australian-demographic-trends/has-the-tide-turned-on-coastal-growth (accessed 1 March 2013).

Anonymous (R. J. C.) (1937) 'Escaping from the city'. *The Adelaide Chronicle*, 30 September: 50.

Australian Bureau of Statistics (2012) 2011 Census Data. Available at: http://www.abs.gov.au/websitedbs/D3310114.nsf/Home/Census

Beer, A. and Faulkner, D. with Paris, C. and Clower, T. (2011) *Housing Transitions through the Life Course: Aspirations, Needs and Policy.* Bristol: Policy Press.

Beer, A., Morris, A. and Paris, C. (2014) *Housing and Local Government in Australia in the 21st Century.* Sydney: Australian Centre for Excellence in Local Government.

Bell, M. and Brown, D. (2006) 'Who are the visitors? Characteristics of temporary movers in Australia', *Population, Space and Place*, 12 (2): 77–92.

Burnley, I. and Murphy, P. (2004) *Sea Change: Movement from Metropolitan to Arcadian Australia*, Sydney: University of New South Wales Press.

Charles-Edwards, E., Bell, M. and Brown, D. (2008) 'Where people move and when: Temporary population mobility in Australia', *People and Place*, 16 (1): 21–30.

Charles-Edwards, E. and Bell, M. (2015) 'Seasonal flux in Australia's population geography: Linking space and time', *Population, Space and Place*, 21 (2): 103–123.

Colebatch, T. (2011) 'Asian migration a tour de force'. *The Age*, 17 June. [online] Retrieved from: http://www.theage.com.au/national/asian-migration-a-tour-de-force-20110616-1g62x.html (accessed 8 October 2014).

Commonwealth Bureau of Census and Statistics (1975) *Census of Population and Housing, 30 June 1971*, Canberra: Commonwealth Bureau of Census and Statistics.

Cook, B. G. (1977) Holiday Homes in South Australia: A Study of the Distribution of Holiday Homes and Holiday Home Owners with Reference to the Yorke Peninsula. Master's Thesis, Flinders University, Adelaide, Australia.

Council of Planning Librarians (1975) *Second Homes, Vacations Homes: Potentials, Impacts and Issues. An Annotated Bibliography*. Chicago: Council of Planning Librarians.

Flood, J. and Baker, E. (2010) *Housing Implications of Economic, Social, and Spatial Change. For the Australian Housing and Urban Research Institute Southern Research Centre, September 2010, AHURI Final Report No. 150*. Melbourne: Australian Housing and Urban Research Institute.

Forrest, R. and Hirayama, Y. (2014) 'The financialisation of the social project: Embedded liberalism, neoliberalism and home ownership', *Urban Studies*, 52 (2): 233–244.

Frost, W. (2004) 'A hidden giant: Second homes and coastal tourism in south-eastern Australia'. In C. M. Hall and D. Müller (eds) *Tourism, Mobility and Second Homes*. Clevedon, UK: Channel View Publications, 162–173.

Gadens (2014) 'Many holiday-house lettings unlawful', *Gadens*. [online] Available at: http://www.gadens.com.au/publications/Pages/Many-holiday-house-lettings-unlawful-%E2%80%93-Important-Land-and-Environment-Court-decision-for- landlords.aspx

Herzberg, S. E. (1978) Planning for Second Homes with Particular Reference to Rural Properties in the Mt Lofty Ranges. Master of Urban and Regional Planning Thesis, University of Adelaide, Adelaide, Australia.

Holiday Rental Industry Association (HRIA) (2014) 'Holiday homes contributing $31 billion to national economic growth', Media Release, 12 February. [online] Available at: http://www.hria.com.au/news/160870/Holiday-homes-contributing-31-billion-to-national-economic-growth.htm

Hugo, G. (2013) 'The changing demographics of Australia over the last 30 years', *Australasian Journal on Ageing*, 32 (S2): 18–27.

Hugo, G., Feist, H. and Tan, G. (2013) 'Temporary mobility and regional Australia', *Australian Population and Migration Research Centre Policy Brief*, 1 (5).

Kemeny, J. (1981) *The Myth of Home Ownership*. Melbourne: Routledge.

McKenzie, F., Martin, J., Paris, C. and Reynolds, J. (2008) 'Fiscal policy and mobility: The impact of multiple residences on the provision of place-based service funding', *Australasian Journal of Regional Studies*, 14 (1): 53–72.

Marsden, B. (1969) 'Holiday homescapes of Queensland', *Australian Geographical Studies*, 7 (1): 57–73.

Mosley, J. G. (1965) 'Outdoor recreation'. In J. L. Davies (ed.) *Atlas of Tasmania*. Hobart, Australia: Lands and Surveys Department, 97.

Müller, D. and Hoogendoorn, G. (2013) 'Second homes: Curse or blessing? A Review 36 Years on', *Scandinavian Journal of Hospitality and Tourism*, 13 (4): 353–369.

Mullins, P. (1985) 'Social issues arising from rapid coastal tourist urbanisation', *Australian Urban Studies*, 13 (2): 13–19.

Mullins, P. (1991) 'Tourism urbanisation', *International Journal of Urban and Regional Research*, 15 (3): 326–342.

Mullins, P. (1994) 'Class relations and tourism urbanisation: The regeneration of the petite bourgeoisie and the emergence of a new urban form', *International Journal of Urban and Regional Research*, 18 (5): 491–608.

Murphy, P. (1977) 'Second homes in New South Wales', *Australian Geographer*, 13 (5): 310–316.

Paris (1993) *Housing Australia*. Melbourne: Macmillan Australia.

Paris, C. (2011) *Affluence, Mobility and Second Home Ownership*. London: Routledge.

Paris, C. (2013) 'Second home ownership in the United Kingdom and Ireland since the global financial crisis', In Roca, Z. (ed.) *Second Homes in Europe: Lifestyle Issues and Policy Responses*. Aldershot, UK: Ashgate, 3–32.

Paris, C. (2014) 'Critical commentary: Second homes', *Annals of Leisure Research*, 17 (1): 4–9.

Paris, C. (2017) 'The super-rich and transnational housing markets: Asians buying Australian housing'. In R. Forrest, S.Y. Koh and B. Wissink (eds) *Cities and the Super-Rich: Real Estate, Elite Practices and Urban Political Economies*. Basingstoke, UK: Palgrave Macmillan, 63–83.

Paris, C., Jorgensen, B. and Martin, J. (2009) 'The ownership of many homes in Ireland and Australia: Issues for states and localities', *Australasian Journal of Regional Studies*, 15 (1): 65–80.

Paris, C. and Thredgold, C. with Jorgensen, B. and Martin, J. (2014) *Second Homes and Changing Populations, Impacts and Implications for Local Government in South Australia*. Adelaide: Centre for Housing, Urban and Regional Planning (CHURP), The University of Adelaide.

Pinnegar, S., van den Nouwelant, R., Judd, B. and Randolph, B. (2012) *Understanding Housing and Location Choices of Retiring Australians in the "Baby Boom" Generation*, Sydney: City Futures Research Centre. [online] Available at: www.cityfutures.net.au (accessed 20 June 2013).

Ragatz, R. (1973) 'The expanding market for vacation homes', *Real Estate Review*, 3: 15–19.

Robertson, R. W. (1977) 'Second-home decisions: The Australian context'. In J. T. Coppock (ed.) *Second Homes: Curse or Blessing?* Oxford: Pergamon, 119–138.

Rolnik, R. (2013) 'Late neoliberalism: The financialisation of homeownership and housing rights', *International Journal of Urban and Regional Research*, 37 (3): 1058–1066.

Ryan, B. (1965) 'The dynamics of recreational development on the South Coast of New South Wales', *Australian Geographer*, 9 (6): 331–348.

Rye, F. (2011) 'Conflicts and contestations. Rural populations' perspectives on the second homes phenomenon', *Journal of Rural Studies*, 27 (3): 263–274.

Sander, N. and Bell, M. (2014) 'Migration and retirement in the life course: An event history approach', *Journal of Population Research*, 31 (1): 1–27

White, R. (2005) *On Holidays*. Melbourne: Pluto Press Australia.

Wolfe, R. W. (1977) 'Summer cottages in Ontario: Purpose-built for an inessential purpose'. In J. T. Coppock (ed.) *Second Homes: Curse or Blessing?* Oxford: Pergamon, 17–34.

14

FROM SOCIALIST YUGOSLAVIA TO THE EUROPEAN UNION

Second home development in Croatia and Slovenia

Vuk Tvrtko Opačić and Miha Koderman

Introduction

Second home development in the Socialist Federal Republic of Yugoslavia (1945–1991) started gaining momentum in the 1960s (Jeršič 1968; Pepeonik 1977) when this type of accommodation was becoming increasingly acceptable in Yugoslav socialist society. As the Yugoslav currency was experiencing high inflation rates in the absence of a free market economy, this was the period in which investment in private ownership of second home real estate was one of the most rational ways of saving surplus capital. Additional factors in the purchase of such dwellings were favourable housing loans and low land prices in depopulated rural areas of the country. Although it is, in general, hard to associate the state socialist form of government with privately owned real estate such as second homes, some political and ideological systems favoured specific forms of leisure activities. This was the case with second homes, which were considered an area of tolerance for some communist regimes due to the lack of commercial tourism being offered (Vágner et al. 2011). In this regard, Yugoslavia resembled other Eastern European countries with state socialist political systems, which were established after World War II and ceased to exist by the late 1980s or the early 1990s.

As constituent republics of the former Yugoslavia, Croatia and Slovenia shared the same socio-economic context of second home development. Although this development still showed some similarities after the collapse of socialist Yugoslavia in 1991, the challenges the two countries faced in the period of transition from a centrally planned to a market economy and contemporary capitalism in the years that followed were considerably different. Slovenia passed the transition period much sooner and became a full member of the European Union (EU) and North Atlantic Treaty Organization (NATO) in 2004. Furthermore, the country adopted the Euro as its currency and entered the Schengen Area in 2007. In addition to its early entry into the Euro-Atlantic integration, Slovenia managed to attract substantial foreign investment during the 1990s, which, compared to Croatia, indicated a faster and easier introduction of the free market economy. After the breakup of the former Yugoslavia, the development of Croatia, on the other hand, was strongly influenced by the Croatian War of Independence (1991–1995), which significantly affected the national economy, held back foreign investment and generally slowed down the processes of Euro-Atlantic integration. The country did not enter the period of social and economic transition until the cessation of hostilities and the consolidation of the economy at the end of the 1990s, and only became a full member of NATO and the EU after long negotiations in 2009 and 2013, respectively.

Today, both countries represent particularly interesting cases for in-depth research in post-socialist second home development as they remain the only two (of the seven) independent countries located on the territory of the former Yugoslavia that have passed the unstable period of transition relatively successfully. These two countries were often referred to as role models for other former Yugoslav republics (Bosnia and Herzegovina, Serbia, Kosovo, Montenegro and the former Yugoslav Republic of Macedonia), some of which are still striving to attain political and economic stability 25 years after the breakup of the once commonly described "Land of the South Slavs".

The main objective of this study is therefore to analyse second home development in Croatia and Slovenia in the context of other former socialist European countries. Second home development is further examined in both countries during the time of state social-ism and in the period of political and economic transition, as well as in the recent years of the modern market economy. Detailed analysis of the recent period was performed mostly by using data obtained from the last two censuses in Croatia (2001 and 2011) and Slovenia (2002 and 2011). The study examined the contemporary second home development in a total of 556 towns and municipalities in Croatia and 210 municipalities in Slovenia, as well as within individual physical geographical regions of both countries. According to the tradi-tional regionalisation of Croatia (Rogić 1983) and Slovenia (Perko & Orožen Adamič 1999), the countries share three physical geographical regions: the Pannonian-Peripannonian, the Dinaric and the Mediterranean regions, while the northern part of Slovenia also covers the Alpine region.

Second home development in the Yugoslav period

Although Coppock (1977: 5) pointed out that 'second homes do not, at first glance, seem likely to be a significant feature of life in eastern Europe, where levels of car ownership are much lower and there is much public provision for leisure', second homes became increasingly popu-lar in many areas of the Yugoslav socialist republics of Croatia and Slovenia after World War II. This process was similar to most Eastern European ex-socialist countries, e.g. Czechoslovakia (Gardavský 1977; Bičík & Fialová 1997; Vágner et al. 2011); Poland (Kowalczyk 1993, 2003); Bulgaria (Marinov 1986, 1994); and the USSR (Struyk & Angelici 1996; Nefedova & Pallot 2013). However, the economic and political situation in Croatia and Slovenia was somewhat different, as the two countries enjoyed a higher standard of living, better traffic connections and greater openness to Western influences.

In the early post-war socialist Yugoslavia, owning a second home seemed (much like tourism) too reminiscent of class distinction, and thus conflicted with the proclaimed socialist ideology of the time (Vukonić 2005). Some of the former elite summer residences, located in attractive and exclusive locations of the Croatian Littoral and the Slovenian Alps, owned by wealthy landlords, were nationalised in the 1950s and became facilities for vacations of the state's new socialist elite (Rogić 2006). In this regard, Yugoslavia was not an isolated case; in the USSR 'more elaborate dachas were built for the top Party officials and other members of the apex of the Soviet elite' (Nefedova & Pallot 2013: 95).

In parallel with the development of tourism, second homes started to evolve in the 1960s, spurred not only by state promotion of the Croatian Littoral for tourism and marketing purposes, but also by a more liberal attitude towards private ownership of (second) real estate units (Pepeonik 1977; Klarić 1989; Miletić 2011; Opačić 2012). In order to ensure social stability, the authorities introduced the so-called socialist self-management model, which allowed investment in privately owned (second) real estate. In Yugoslav socialist society, owning a second home was motivated by saving, perhaps even more so than in capitalist societies (Gosar 1984, 1989; Poljanec-Borić 1991). In the climate of high inflation and a non-existent free market on one hand and affordable housing loans on the other (Mikačić 1994, 2007), the population was encouraged to construct second homes.

In the 1970s and 1980s, urban areas in ex-Yugoslavia experienced an increase in the standard of living (Duda 2005), which, along with the standardisation of working hours and increasing negative aspects of the urban lifestyle, brought about larger tourism and second home demand. Additionally, increased urbanisation led to a decline in interest in agriculture, leaving many small towns and villages, especially those on islands and in mountainous areas depopulated (Nejašmić 1991). That, in turn, led to an increase in the supply of older, uninhabited houses and adjoining agricultural facilities, which made them even more affordable to the urban population. The reason for such low prices for land in the 1970s, especially agricultural land, lies in the fact that it was determined on the basis of its agricultural and not recreational value.

During the 1980s, land and real estate prices experienced a sharp growth resulting in a slower second home construction rate in the Croatian Littoral (Klarić 1989). The reasons for this lay in intensive industrial and tourism development in littoral areas, combined with a growing demand for second homes and increasing spatial planning restrictions.

A high number of second homes in both countries proves that second home development grew massively during the era of socialist Yugoslavia (Opačić 2009b). The 1971 Census of Population and Dwellings registered the so-called "dwellings for rest and recreation" as an integral part of the housing stock for the first time. In this year, the absolute number of second homes, as well as their share in the housing stock of both countries, was relatively small – in Croatia, 22,946 second homes were registered (1.98% of the housing stock), while in Slovenia the number of second homes was 4,281 (0.93% of the housing stock) (Federal Bureau of Statistics of the Socialist Federal Republic of Yugoslavia 1972).

Since 1971, the number of second homes has shown continuous exponential growth throughout both Yugoslav republics, and in many areas a typical second home landscape has been formed (Opačić & Koderman 2016) with numerous, mostly negative, physiognomic (Opačić 2009a), economic (Opačić 2008), sociocultural and environmental spatial implications. In 1981, Croatia registered 84,317 second homes (6.10% of the housing stock), while in Slovenia their number was 18,965 (3.24% of the housing stock) (Federal Bureau of Statistics of the Socialist Federal Republic of Yugoslavia 1984). During the 1980s, the share of second homes in the housing stock of both countries doubled. According to the data from the 1991 census, 176,845 second homes were recorded (9.98% of the housing stock) in Croatia, while in Slovenia their number reached 26,374 (3.86% of the housing stock) (Croatian Bureau of Statistics 1995; Bureau of Statistics of the Republic of Slovenia 1994). In the period from 1970 to 1990, the strong growth in the number of second homes correlates with the dynamics of tourism development in both countries (Opačić & Mikačić 2009), primarily on the Croatian coast and islands and also in the Slovenian Alps.

In Yugoslavia, the number of second homes was highest along the Croatian coast and islands (Pepeonik 1983; Miletić 2011; Opačić 2012), in the Slovenian Alps (Gosar 1984, 1989; Koderman 2014) and in attractive parts of rural recreational areas of larger cities, especially around the current state capitals of Zagreb and Ljubljana (Miletić 2011; Opačić 2012; Koderman 2014). Other popular second home locations included spa tourism destinations, mountainous and hilly areas (Gosar 1987; Salmič & Koderman 2013), as well as locations along riverbanks and lakes (Klarić 1989; Koderman & Salmič 2013).

The period of socialist Yugoslavia in Croatia and Slovenia was marked by a dominant type of second homes – family holiday houses intended for the rest and recreation of their owners/users. In contrast to elite villas and summer houses which had dominated before World War II, second homes in socialist times were not as luxurious or large – they were smaller and humbler dwellings, intended for use by a wider circle of interested parties (Pepeonik 1983).

Second homes in the 1960s and the 1970s were the result of adaptation and conversion of the abandoned housing and agricultural stock (vineyard cottages, stables, shepherd shelters, fisherman sheds) into secondary residences. In the 1970s and 1980s, when the supply of abandoned houses and agricultural buildings suitable for conversion into second homes became depleted, the most desirable areas in both countries experienced intense construction of family holiday houses. In the 1970s, family holiday houses were smaller and had an infrastructure inferior to that of second homes because they were converted old houses, but as time went on (e.g. in the 1980s), bigger and more luxurious family holiday houses began to be constructed (Opačić 2009b). The process of conversion and adaptation of existing old structures would then move on to somewhat less desirable locations (Opačić 2012).

In the period of socialist Yugoslavia, the main motivation for the acquisition of a second home was the relaxation and recreation of the owner and their family and friends, as spending family holidays in a second home was more affordable in comparison to hotel accommodation. The demand for the acquisition of second homes in the socialist period was exclusively domestic (Opačić & Koderman 2016), as foreign citizens were not allowed to own real estate in socialist Yugoslavia. Therefore, the majority of second home owners were residents of major Yugoslav cities.

In the late 1980s, a specific form of second homes in leading Croatian and Slovenian second-home areas started evolving – multi-apartment recreational complexes, which appeared either as detached structures in towns and villages or as part of planned multi-apartment resorts (Opačić 2012). The appearance of such collective recreational housing in leading coastal and mountain tourism destinations in both countries can be recognised as the final phase of second home development in socialist Yugoslavia (Opačić & Koderman 2016).

Characteristics of second home development in independent Croatia and Slovenia

The new developmental context

With the fall of state socialism and the disintegration of Yugoslavia in 1991, the newly formed independent states entered the period of transition from a centrally planned to a free market economy. Slovenia, where the process of achieving independence was interrupted by a short military conflict (also referred to as the Ten-Day War) with the Yugoslav People's Army, weathered the challenges of the socio-economic transition relatively quickly in comparison to Croatia, where the Croatian War of Independence had many direct and indirect impacts that negatively affected economic development. In this regard, the tourism sector, whose development is usually closely connected with second homes, was particularly affected.

In Slovenia, the beginning of the process of privatisation and increased foreign investment started in the 1990s, but Croatia, on the other hand, did not experience such transitional processes until its economic recovery in the first decade of the twenty-first century. Tourism became one of the main pillars of the Croatian economic revitalisation, which was especially evident in the coastal part of the country.

Second home development was positively influenced by increased strengthening of private property together with the emergence of private enterprise (Rogić 2006). As a consequence of the re-establishment of a free real estate market, a considerable increase in prices in the most popular tourism and second home areas was recorded. At the same time, domestic and foreign demand for secondary houses and apartments increased after the opening of the real estate market to foreigners, especially after admission to the EU. Moreover, international second home demand from other members of the EU was further boosted by the expansion of the highway network. Domestic second home demand in Croatia and Slovenia, however, still prevails over foreign interest (Opačić & Koderman 2016).

In Croatia, a slight increase in the number of second homes was recorded in the period from 1991 to 2001, with a total of 182,513 second home dwellings identified (9.72% of the housing stock) (Croatian Bureau of Statistics 2003). In the inter-census period 2001–2011, the number of second homes in Croatia significantly increased as well as their share of the housing stock (altogether a total of 249,243 second homes were recorded, while the share of the housing stock reached 11.09%) (Croatian Bureau of Statistics 2013).

For the interpretation of the 2011 census data on second homes in Slovenia, several methodological explanations are of crucial importance. The 2002 census was the last terrain census of buildings and dwellings in Slovenia and according to its results, 31,681 buildings in Slovenia (or 4.1% of the housing stock) were categorised as second homes (Statistical Office of the Republic of Slovenia 2002). In 2011, the Statistical Office conducted a register-based census, according to which only 20,740 buildings (or 2.5% of the housing stock) were categorised as second homes (Statistical Office of the Republic of Slovenia 2011). Its main sources were the Central Population Register of the Ministry of the Interior, Building Cadastre and Real-Estate Register of the Surveying and Mapping Authority and the Land Registry (managed by the Supreme Court of the Republic of Slovenia). Compared to the results of the 2002 census, it can certainly be said that the number of second homes in the Register of Real Estate is underestimated. This fact was also pointed out in the analysis of the Statistical Office of the Republic of Slovenia, which registered many dwellings that were categorised as second homes in 2002 but had their categorisation changed to vineyard cottages in 2011 (especially in the Pannonian-Peripannonian region of Slovenia, which shows a significantly smaller share of these dwellings) (Statistical Office of the Republic of Slovenia 2015). These methodological clarifications have to be taken into account when interpreting the data from the 2011 census and in potential comparisons with the previous census from 2002.

Although the majority of second homes in Croatia and Slovenia can still be found in the form of family houses (mostly built in the socialist period of Yugoslavia), multi-apartment recreational complexes are becoming a more distinctive element of the second home landscape in the coastal and island areas of Croatia, as well as in the coastal and Alpine areas of Slovenia. Mountain and lakeshore resorts became popular locations for building multi-apartment recreational complexes in amenity-rich traditional tourist and second home destinations in other former socialist European countries, for example, in the Czech Republic (Vágner et al. 2011).

Within the context of second home development, the building lobby of private enterprises achieved a position of great power in the late 1990s and early 2000s and often became a key participant in spatial and urban planning at the local level (Opačić 2009b). Multi-apartment recreational complexes transformed many local communities in terms of their physiognomy and functionality, as well as in other economic, socio-cultural and environmental aspects.

The motives for the acquisition of apartments in multi-apartment recreational complexes can be found in the fact that many investors cannot bear the financial cost of the construction or purchase of a family house and therefore decide to buy collective secondary housing. At the beginning of the 2000s, the increase of real estate prices was influenced not only by the growth of foreign second home demand, but also by the growing practice of legal and illegal renting of second homes to potential tourists – the so called "Zimmer Frei" phenomenon. In this way, some second home owners arguably created unfair competition for the hotel sector and other registered accommodation providers, who pay regulatory local and national taxes. Several littoral areas of both countries and the Alpine parts of Slovenia have faced this problem in the last two decades. Although relaxation and recreation of the owners and their family and friends remains the prime motive for the ownership of second homes, commercial (renting) or speculative motives (investments in real estate) for their acquisition have become more prominent in this period. As pointed out by Vágner et al. (2011: 201), the commercialisation and increasing internationalisation of second home development has also 'led to a boom in this new market segment of real estate agencies'.

The above processes have gradually transformed second home ownership from a relatively widespread societal phenomenon in socialist Yugoslavia with fairly common availability of these dwellings into an increasingly exclusive ownership in the newly formed independent states of Croatia and Slovenia. Similar trends can be observed in Russia in the 1990s, where a growing inequality of income distribution created the so-called phenomenon of "new Russians" (Struyk & Angelici 1996) or Russia's "*nouveau riche*", who constructed mansion-type second homes 'adorned with turrets and towers that reference medieval fortresses, surrounded by high walls, fences and secure gates' (Nefedova & Pallot 2013: 101). Some of them tend to buy traditional second homes (known as *dachas*) from elderly pensioners and renovate them in a luxurious style (Struyk & Angelici 1996). According to Halseth (2004), many rural communities have been disrupted by such exclusive zones of second home properties. In this way, second home landscapes are turning more and more into playgrounds of the elite (Hall & Müller 2004).

As has been the case elsewhere in Europe (Paris 2013), the financial crisis of 2007–2008 has significantly affected the real estate market in both countries. The inflated prices of real estate in most hotspot second home destinations decreased to their fair values, while at the same time the real estate market became less active. The recession in Croatia and Slovenia lasted longer (until 2015 and 2014, respectively); therefore, some second home facilities remain unsold to this day.

Spatial distribution of second homes

Spatial distribution of the number of second homes in Croatia and Slovenia has not changed very much from the socialist period. Figure 14.1 shows the administrative units of Croatia and Slovenia according to the share of second homes in the housing stock and in physical geographical regions in 2011.

It is clearly evident that the Mediterranean region of Croatia is the "hotspot" second home area in the country. In general, the towns and municipalities with the highest share of dwellings for secondary use are located in this region and almost 70% of all second homes in Croatia can be found here (Table 14.1). Second homes make up a clear majority of the housing stock in 18 towns and municipalities. Most of them are located on islands that are connected with the mainland by bridge: Vir (municipality of Vir), Pag (town of Novalja) and Krk (municipalities of Malinska-Dubašnica and Dobrinj). In these administrative units, the share of second homes exceeds 60% of the housing stock.

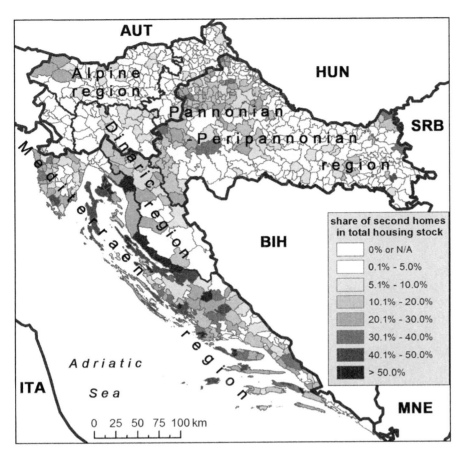

Figure 14.1 Shares of second homes in the housing stock at municipal level in physical geographical regions of Croatia and Slovenia in 2011.

Sources: Croatian Bureau of Statistics, 2003, 2013; Statistical Office of the Republic of Slovenia, 2002, 2011.

In 2011, a higher number and a higher share of second homes in the housing stock were recorded in the towns and municipalities of the Northern Croatian Littoral (the regions of Istria and Kvarner) in comparison with the Southern Croatian Littoral (Dalmatia region). In comparison to Istria and Kvarner, Dalmatia is located further away from the leading national and international centres of second home demand. These two regions were excluded from the zone of direct military operations in the first half of the 1990s, and therefore second home development here took place more spontaneously than in Dalmatia. In addition, because of the advantages of the proximity to centres of demand and better transport accessibility, the construction of multi-apartment recreational complexes in the Northern Croatian Littoral began earlier and was stronger than in the Southern Croatian Littoral (Opačić & Koderman 2016).

Important second home areas can also be found in the Pannonian-Peripannonian region of Croatia, where more than 28% of all second homes were located in 2011. These areas include towns and municipalities with high numbers and shares of secondary dwellings, mostly in the hilly regions of Hrvatsko Zagorje and Zagreb County, which are both strongly influenced by the domestic second home demand that originates in the broader area of Croatia's capital city. Similar concentration of second homes can be found in the vicinity of other national capitals

Table 14.1 Number and share of second homes in the housing stock in Croatian physical geographical regions in 2001 and 2011

Type of region	Number of municipalities	Census year	Total number of dwellings	Number of second homes	Share of second homes in housing stock (%)	Share of second homes by regions (%)
Mediterranean region	201	2001	658,537	114,603	17.4	62.8
		2011	874,908	172,244	19.7	69.1
Dinaric region	24	2001	49,648	4,265	8.6	2.3
		2011	55,452	5,479	9.9	2.2
Panonian region	331	2001	1,168,941	63,645	5.4	34.9
		2011	1,316,550	71,520	5.4	28.7
CROATIA (total)	556	2001	1,877,126	182,513	9.7	100.0
		2011	2,246,910	249,243	11.1	100.0

Source: Croatian Bureau of Statistics, 2003, 2013.

and urban agglomerations across Eastern European countries, for example in Prague (Bičík & Fialová 1997) and several Polish cities, such as Łódź, Warsaw, Poznań and Kraków (Kowalczyk 1993). The flat areas of the Pannonian-Peripannonian region have recorded the lowest number and share of second homes in the housing stock of the country.

As can be seen in Table 14.1, the housing stock of Croatia shows a higher share of second homes in the Dinaric region than in the Pannonian-Peripannonian region. Owing to its rich natural amenities, the Dinaric region has experienced considerable growth in tourism in the last decade. However, since this mountainous peripheral region has been characterised by prominent depopulation and an ageing population, there are plenty of abandoned houses that are being converted into second homes.

The greater number of second homes, as well as their higher share in the housing stock, has marks most significant difference in second home development between Croatia and Slovenia. There are several obvious reasons for a lower number and share of second homes in Slovenia – they can be found in the location, size and landscape characteristics of this country: Compared to Croatia, where the combined coastline lengths of its 1,246 islands and the mainland coastline comes to a total of 6,278 kilometres (Croatian Bureau of Statistics 2015), Slovenia has a modest 46.6 kilometres of the Adriatic Sea coastline (Perko & Orožen Adamič 1999). The country is strongly characterised by the mountainous region of the Alps, while it also covers three other geographical regions found on the territory of both countries. It therefore shows a higher degree of landscape diversity in a smaller area than its southern neighbour.

As outlined in Table 14.2, some municipalities in the Alpine region show a substantial proportion of dwellings intended for secondary use. These account for around one quarter of all dwellings in municipalities with a well-developed tourist infrastructure and a long tradition as mountain resorts (the municipalities of Kranjska Gora, Bohinj and Bovec). In the 2011 census, the highest number of dwellings for secondary use in Slovenia was recorded in its Alpine region with over 43% of all second homes located in this region. Although the Dinaric region of Slovenia has an attractive mountainous landscape, it nevertheless remains overshadowed by the tourism and second home development of the Alpine region.

Second homes also represent an important share of the housing stock of certain municipalities in the Pannonian-Peripannonian region of Slovenia, which are known for their spa resorts (Podčetrtek, Zreče, Šmarješke Toplice) or for their wine-growing areas (Mokronog-Trebelno,

Table 14.2 Number and share of second homes in the housing stock in Slovenian physical geographical regions in 2002 and 2011

Type of region	Number of municipalities	Census year	Total number of dwellings	Number of second homes	Share of second homes in total housing stock (%)	Share of second homes in regions (%)
Mediterranean region	15	2002	75,639	2,911	3.8	9.2
		2011	89,122	2,732	3.1	13.2
Dinaric region	34	2002	102,871	7,194	7.0	22.7
		2011	111,484	4,009	3.6	19.3
Panonian region	76	2002	209,470	11,046	5.3	34.9
		2011	223,442	4,949	2.2	23.9
Alpine region	85	2002	389,792	10,484	2.7	33.1
		2011	420,608	9,050	2.2	43.6
SLOVENIA (Total)	210	2002	777,772	31,681	4.1	100.0
		2011	844,656	20,740	2.5	100.0

Source: Statistical Office of the Republic of Slovenia, 2002, 2011.

Semič, Podlehnik). Second home developmental characteristics of Slovenia's Mediterranean region are similar to those of Croatia; however, the share of second homes is significantly lower here due to a high level of urbanisation and permanent residences.

Conclusion and perspectives

The chapter has presented the main features of second home development in Croatia and Slovenia during the time of the Socialist Federal Republic of Yugoslavia, as well as in their last 25 years as independent states. This recent period was marked by different stages of transition, which included the disintegration process of socialist Yugoslavia in 1991, along with wars that affected several regions of Croatia, the two countries' economic transition from a centrally planned to a free market economy, their Euro-Atlantic integration (joining the EU and NATO) and, finally, the global economic crisis. The main trends of second home development in both periods are summarised in Table 14.3.

Much like other second home areas across Eastern Europe, Croatian and Slovenian second home hotspots, especially in littoral areas, which can be recognised as part of the expanding leisure "European Sun Belt", will continue to strengthen in the foreseeable future. Similar processes that have appeared here can also be found in other popular regions, particularly in the mountain and lakeshore resorts.

The expansion of second homes after the recovery of the real estate market in recent years and stable but moderate growth of prices can also be anticipated. In line with European practices, the taxes for owning second homes in both countries are likely to increase significantly, turning second homes from a "necessity" into a "luxury". Leading second home areas can also expect a stagnation of the self-managed construction of family holiday houses on account of the construction of multi-apartment recreational buildings.

One of the key factors leading to the further internationalisation of second home development will be an increase in retirement second home migrations. This, together with potential buyers from the active population, will strongly modify the international second home demand in Croatia and Slovenia and shift the character of the second home phenomenon from a recreational, leisurely activity into a commercially entrepreneurial one.

Table 14.3 Trends of second home development in Croatia and Slovenia in the Socialist Federal Republic of Yugoslavia (until 1991) and in their period of independence (after 1991)

Features	In Socialist Yugoslavia	In Independent Croatia and Slovenia
Developmental dynamics	High growth of second homes	Slower growth of second homes
Prices and financing	Low prices of real estate and land	Increase in real estate and land prices
	Favourable loan conditions for the construction and adaptation	Often unattainable loans for domestic demand
Availability of second homes	Widely available	Mostly available to the elite
Type of demand	Exclusively domestic	Mostly domestic as well as international
	Relaxation and recreation with family and friends	
Motive for acquisition	Saving surplus capital in conditions of high inflation rates	Commercial and speculative motives
	Family holiday houses	
Morphological types	Converted and adapted abandoned houses	Multi-apartment recreational buildings
Mode of construction	Self-managed construction according to owner's ideas	
		Construction according to building lobby's ideas
	Croatian coast and islands	
	Slovenian Alps	
Locations	Parts of attractive rural areas, along lakes and river banks, in hilly areas and spa destinations	

References

Bičík, I. and Fialová, D. (1997) 'Second homes: Case study Kocába region', Acta Universitatis Carolinae, *Geographica, 32*, supplementum: 247–253.

Bureau of Statistics of the Republic of Slovenia (1994) *Census of Population, Households, Dwellings and Agricultural Holdings in the Republic of Slovenia 1991: Documentation 617.* Ljubljana, Bureau of Statistics of the Republic of Slovenia.

Coppock, J. T. (1977) 'Second homes in perspective'. In J. T. Coppock (ed.) *Second Homes: Curse or Blessing?* Oxford: Pergamon, 1–16.

Croatian Bureau of Statistics (1995) *Census of Population, Households, Dwellings and Agricultural Holdings in the Republic of Croatia 1991: Documentation 888.* Zagreb, Croatian Bureau of Statistics.

Croatian Bureau of Statistics (2003) *Census of Population, Households and Dwellings in the Republic of Croatia 2001.* Zagreb: Croatian Bureau of Statistics.

Croatian Bureau of Statistics (2013) *Census of Population, Households and Dwellings in the Republic of Croatia 2013.* Zagreb: Croatian Bureau of Statistics.

Croatian Bureau of Statistics (2015) *Statistical Yearbook of the Republic of Croatia.* Zagreb: Croatian Bureau of Statistics.

Duda, I. (2005) *U potrazi za blagostanjem: O povijesti dokolice i potrošačkog društva u Hrvatskoj 1950-ih i 1960-ih.* Zagreb: Srednja Europa.

Federal Bureau of Statistics of the Socialist Federal Republic of Yugoslavia (1972) *Census of Population and Dwellings in the Socialist Federal Republic of Yugoslavia 1971: Book 1.* Beograd: Federal Bureau of Statistics of the Socialist Federal Republic of Yugoslavia.

Federal Bureau of Statistics of the Socialist Federal Republic of Yugoslavia (1984) *Census of Population, Households and Dwellings in the Socialist Federal Republic of Yugoslavia 1981: Table 196*. Beograd: Federal Bureau of Statistics of the Socialist Federal Republic of Yugoslavia.

Gardavský, V. (1977) 'Second homes in Czechoslovakia'. In J. T. Coppock (ed.) *Second Homes: Curse or Blessing?* Oxford: Pergamon, 63–74.

Gosar, A. (1984) 'Vacation cottages in the part of the Slovene Alps', *Geographica Iugoslavica*, 5: 85–90.

Gosar, A. (1987) 'Učinki počitniških bivališč na preobrazbo slovenske kulturne pokrajine, Pokrajinski učinki človekovih dejavnosti na življensko okolje', *Geographica Slovenica*, 18: 183–204.

Gosar, A. (1989) 'Second homes in the alpine region of Yugoslavia', *Mountain Research and Development*, 9 (2): 165–174.

Hall, C. M. and Müller, D. K. (2004) 'Introduction: Second homes, curse or blessing? Revisited'. In C. M. Hall and D. K. Müller (eds) *Tourism, Mobility and Second Homes: Between Elite Landscape and Common Ground*. Clevedon, UK: Channel View Publications, 3–14.

Halseth, G. (2004) 'The "cottage" privilege: Increasingly elite landscapes of second homes in Canada'. In C. M. Hall and D. K. Müller (eds) *Tourism, Mobility and Second Homes: Between Elite Landscape and Common Ground*. Clevedon, UK: Channel View Publications, 35–54.

Jeršič, M. (1968) 'Sekundarna počitniška bivališča v Sloveniji in Zahodni Istri', *Geografski vestnik*, 40: 53–67.

Klarić, Z. (1989) 'Sekundarne rezidencije u Jugoslaviji – Prostorni raspored i utjecaj na okolinu', *Geografski glasnik*, 51: 75–90.

Koderman, M. (2014) 'Razvoj počitniških bivališč v alpsko-jadranskem prostoru Slovenije'. In K. Vodeb (ed.) *Trajnostni razvoj turističnih destinacij alpsko-jadranskega prostora*. Koper, Slovenia: Založba Univerze na Primorskem, 27–41.

Koderman, M. and Salmič, S. (2013) 'Prebivati ob "jezeru bliz' Triglava": Prostorska analiza počitniških bivališč v občini Bohinj'. In M. Blatnik, I. Mrak, I. Potočnik Slavič, B. Rogelj and T. KožELj (eds) *Gorenjska v obdobju glokalizacije*. Bled, Ljubljana: Znanstvena založba Filozofske fakultete, 111–126.

Kowalczyk, A. (1993) 'Second homes in Poland', *Geographica*, 28 (2): 37–45.

Kowalczyk, A. (2003) 'Second homes twenty years later: The case of the commune Jadów', *Geographica*, 38 (1): 181–191.

Marinov, V. (1986) 'Vtorite žilišta za otdih v B'lgarija, Godišnik na Sofijskija universitet "Kliment Ohridski", Geologo-geografski fakultet, knjiga 2', *Geografija*, 80: 148–166.

Marinov, V. (1994) 'Vlijanie na vtorite žilišta v'rhu razvitieto i teritorialnata organizacija na otdiha i turizma (po primera na Sofija i nejnija rajon za kratkotraen otdih), Godišnik na Sofijskija universitet "Sv. Kliment Ohridski", Geologo-geografski fakultet, knjiga 2', *Geografija*, 85: 389–409.

Mikačić, V. (1994) 'Otočni turizam Hrvatske', *Društvena istraživanja*, 3 (4–5): 517–529.

Mikačić, V. (2007) 'Utjecaj rezidencijalnog turizma na primorski prostor Hrvatske'. In Lj. Bajs, J. Čelant-Hromatko, M. Jakovčić, M. Maradin, V. Prelogović and R. Vuk (eds) *Zbornik radova 4. hrvatskog geografskog kongresa*. Zagreb: Hrvatsko geografsko društvo, 321–336.

Miletić, G.-M. (2011) *U potrazi za drugim prostorom: sociologijski aspekti sekundarnog stanovanja u Hrvatskoj*. Zagreb, Croatia: Institut društvenih znanosti Ivo Pilar.

Nefedova, T. and Pallot, J. (2013) 'The multiplicity of second home development in the Russian Federation: A case of "seasonal suburbanization"?' In Z. Roca (ed.) *Second Home Tourism in Europe: Lifestyle Issues and Policy Responses*. Aldershot, UK: Ashgate, 91–119.

Nejašmić, I. (1991) *Depopulacija u Hrvatskoj: Korijeni, stanje, izgledi*. Zagreb, Croatia: Globus, Institut za migracije i narodnosti.

Opačić, V. T. (2008) 'Ekonomsko-geografski utjecaji i posljedice vikendaštva u receptivnim vikendaškim područjima – Primjer otoka Krka', *Ekonomska misao i praksa*, 17 (2): 127–154.

Opačić, V. T. (2009a) 'Fizionomske implikacije vikendaštva u receptivnim naseljima – Primjer Malinske na otoku Krku', *Geoadria*, 14 (2): 273–310.

Opačić, V. T. (2009b) 'Recent characteristics of the second home phenomenon in the Croatian littoral', *Hrvatski geografski glasnik*, 71 (1): 33–66.

Opačić, V. T. (2012) *Vikendaštvo u hrvatskom priobalju: Jučer, danas, sutra*. Zagreb, Croatia: Hrvatska sveučilišna naklada.

Opačić, V. T. and Koderman, M. (2016) 'Changes in pattern of second home development in countries arising from Socialist Federal Republic of Yugoslavia'. In N. Drešković (ed.) *Book of Proceedings of International Tourism and Hospitality Management Conference*. Sarajevo: Faculty of Science, University of Sarajevo, 484–494.

Opačić,V.T. and Mikačić,V. (2009) 'Second home phenomenon and tourism in the Croatian littoral – Two pretenders for the same space?', *Tourism*, 57 (2): 155–175.

Paris, C. (2013) 'Second home ownership since the global financial crisis in the United Kingdom and Ireland'. In Z. Roca (ed.) *Second Home Tourism in Europe: Lifestyle Issues and Policy Responses*. Aldershot, UK: Ashgate, 3–31.

Pepeonik, Z. (1977) 'Stanovi za odmor i rekreaciju u Jugoslaviji', *Geographica Slovenica*, 5: 181–194.

Pepeonik Z. (1983) 'Prostorni raspored i osnovne značajke stambenih objekata za odmor i rekreaciju u SR Hrvatskoj', *Geografski glasnik*, 45: 91–103.

Perko, D. and Orožen Adamič, M. (eds) (1999) *Slovenija: Pokrajine in ljudje*. Ljubljana: Mladinska knjiga.

Poljanec-Borić, S. (1991) 'Simbolika vikendice'. In S. Marković and M. Dragičević (eds) *Zbornik radova*. Zagreb, Croatia: Institut za turizam, 211–224.

Rogić, I. (2006) 'Odnos spram kuće za odmor u Hrvatskoj u strategiji urbanizacije 1945–2005', *Društvena istraživanja*, 15 (1–2): 3–26.

Rogić,V. (1983) 'Nacrt uvjetno homogene regionalizacije SR Hrvatske', *Geografski glasnik*, 45: 75–89.

Salmič, S. and Koderman, M. (2013) 'Prostorska analiza počitniških bivališč v Občini Kranjska Gora', *Geografski vestnik*, 85 (1): 9–24.

Statistical Office of the Republic of Slovenia (2002) *Census 2002: Dwellings for Leisure and Recreation by Number of Rooms, Useful Floor Space and Type of Building and Total Useful Floor Space, Municipalities, Slovenia*. Ljubljana: Statistical Office of the Republic of Slovenia.

Statistical Office of the Republic of Slovenia (2011) *Registry-Based Census 2011: Dwellings Reserved for Seasonal or Secondary Use by Type of Building and Number of Rooms, Municipalities, Slovenia, Multiannually*. Ljubljana: Statistical Office of the Republic of Slovenia.

Statistical Office of the Republic of Slovenia (2015) *Stanovanja, Slovenija, 1. januar 2011 – končni podatki*. [online] Retrieved from: http://www.stat.si/StatWeb/glavnanavigacija/ podatki/prikazistaronovico?Id Novice=4771 (accessed 10 October 2015)

Struyk, R. J. and Angelici, K. (1996) 'The Russian dacha phenomenon', *Housing Studies*, 11 (2): 233–250.

Vágner, J., Müller, K. M. and Fialová, D. (2011) 'Second home tourism in light of the historical-political and socio-geographical development of Czechia and Sweden', *Geografie*, 116 (2): 191–210.

Vukonić, B. (2005) Povijest hrvatskog turizma, Zagreb: Prometej, Hrvatska akademija znanosti i umjetnosti, Znanstveno vijeće za turizam.

15

STRETCHING THE BOUNDARIES

Building the Russian dacha dream

Olga Hannonen

Introduction

It is a hot summer day. City dwellers are eager to leave the city. At the bus station in Petrozavodsk, the capital of the Republic of Karelia, people are queuing for the bus for about half an hour. They are carrying bag-trolleys, buckets, baskets and plastic bags full of provision. I am among the passengers heading to Luchevoe-1, one of the dacha settlements 30 kilometres away from Petrozavodsk.

The bus is full. I am standing next to Vanya, a university student, who is going to visit his grandmother for a weekend. I am heading to Luchevoe-1 to meet my aunt, who has a dacha there. Vanya's grandmother, Galina, turns out to be a dacha neighbour of my aunt, so I immediately ask for an interview. Galina is on of the rare dacha owners who do not cultivate every centimetre of her land. Her dacha plot is covered with lawn, still a rare element on dacha plots in Russia.

Luchevoe-1 is one of five dacha locations that I have visited during my fieldtrip in Petrozavodsk. The area appeared in the 1970s as specially designed for a dacha settlement. Luchevoe-1 is an agglomeration of 13 garden cooperatives or garden partnerships (*sadovodcheskoe toverishchestvo*). A garden cooperative is one of the most widespread forms of the dacha in Russia. The contemporary official term would be translated into English as "non-commercial gardeners' partnerships". Following other scholars (Caldwell 2011; Galtz 2000; Kasatkina 2011; Lovell 2003), I deliberately use the term "garden cooperative" to refer to the origin of such garden communities. Among other terms that are interchangeably used in the literature are garden settlement (Nefedova & Pallot 2013) and garden plot dachas (Struyk & Angelici 1996). Divisions in cooperatives within the big dacha settlement of Luchevoe-1 are defined by different enterprises that handed out 600 m^2 land plots to their workers to engage in productive leisure through supplementary agriculture and build modest summer houses. One of the latest garden cooperatives in Luchevoe-1 was formed in 1991.

The dacha is referred to as 'the Russian equivalent of the summer second home' (Selwood 2006: 118), though it significantly differs from European and Scandinavian second home traditions, and from Russian second homes abroad (see Hall & Müller 2004; Hannonen 2016; Lipkina 2013). A dacha is a house with a plot of land in a rural area that is used intermittently, the owner of which is a permanent urban resident who spends a week to a year there (Lovell 2003;

179

Nefedova 2012). Dacha is an umbrella term that 'encompasses various types of housing, including small houses on small agricultural lots (averaging 600 m²) in special dacha cooperatives, and village houses with yards that have been purchased by city people' (Brumfield & Ruble 1993: 289) (see Figure 15.1). Thus, dacha in Russia represents various types of dwellings on a plot of land for temporary stay and recreation (Chernykh 1993; Nefedova 2012; Nefedova & Pallot 2013).

Dacha as a form of summer recreation and a 'second home out of town' has nowhere else 'been so deeply embedded in cultural memory and social practice' (Lovell 2003: 5–6) as in Russia. A number of works on Russian dacha history, ethnography, culture and folklore such as "Summerfolk" (Lovell 2003), "Dacha Idyll" (Caldwell 2011) and "Dacha Kingdom" (Baschmakoff & Ristolainen 2009) present in great detail the history of the dacha, as well as the significance of dachas in Russian culture and everyday life. Thus, I will not engage in a deep discussion about the history and praise of the cultural and recreational importance of dachas. Instead, I will focus on the construction of the dacha space by contemporary dacha dwellers or *dachniks*. A dacha user or owner is referred to as *dachnik* in the Russian language and this is used in this chapter to define dacha dwellers.

Nowadays dacha remains popular among city dwellers. Despite the absence of official statistics on the number of dachas in Russia, the study of Russian Opinion Foundation (FOM 2013) estimates that about 30% of Russian city dwellers have a dacha (in its broad understanding) and 28% would like to have one. The Russian Public Opinion Research Centre (VCIOM) reports that about half of Russians visited a dacha in 2015. Thus, for the great majority of the Russian population dacha is the most popular summer destination.

Today the dacha has taken on the form of a "survival strategy" for Russians, be it for food production, bigger living spaces, an escape from polluted cities or a place to take kids during the summer season or spend retirement (Caldwell 2011; Polukhina 2014). The dacha is also a complexly constructed leisure space. It is a space of constant negotiations between private and public, between passive leisure and previously imposed (and nowadays the culturally embedded

Figure 15.1   Dachas in a garden cooperative of Luchevoe-1.

180

practice of) active leisure in a form of land cultivation, between a liberating second home and strictly regulated recreation space. The aim of this chapter is to look at how contemporary dacha dwellers have been interpreting, negotiating and deviating from the prescribed leisure code in order to live out their dacha dream. In order to achieve this goal, I employ the concept of space as a form of social organisation both by the state and individuals.

There are a number of reports on circumventing the state regulations by dacha users (see Lovell 2003; Caldwell 2011; Galtz 2000; Kasatkina 2011). However, other than to note the fact, these studies do not provide a more detailed analysis on how informal practices became a personal strategy in building the dacha dream and forming a unique out-of-the-city space. I use the term dacha space both as a general category of leisure space in the countryside that is opposed to the city space, and as a private portion of a common leisure space, an individually crafted space on the provided land plot. Thus the focus is both on building a dacha space as a shared leisure space, and a personal one, and negotiations between the two.

The chapter is structured in the following way: first, I define in more detail different dacha forms to emphasise distinct features of the garden cooperatives that are in focus in this chapter. The next section outlines the Soviet leisure code through the concepts of space, its ideological and practical construction, as well as the nature of informal practices. The next section provides information about the data and research area. The results sections present the empirical findings, followed by the conclusions.

Defining dacha

Garden cooperatives

Dachas as a collective term include five types of summer houses: a "classic dacha", a garden settlement, a vegetable allotment, a rural house and a "cottage" or "mansion" (Nefedova 2012; Nefedova & Pallot 2013). For some other typologies, see Lovell (2003) and Struyk and Angelici (1996). The empirical material for this chapter was collected predominantly in garden cooperatives that represent non-elite dachas that are owned by former Soviet "working class". Garden cooperatives were introduced in 1949 with the purpose of food supply, health promotion and cultural recreation for urban workers and introduction to work for teenagers (Kasatkina 2011; Standard Regulation of Workers' Garden Partnership 1966). The state allocated land to enterprises and institutions for distribution among their workers free of charge. Today garden cooperatives are the most widespread form of dacha in Russia. The cooperatives were formed in the following way: one cooperative represents one enterprise that divided 600–800 m^2 shares among its workers. Depending on the size of a particular organisation, the number of shares and members in each cooperative varied. In my research case, the number of individual land plots in cooperatives varied between 80 and 200 plots. The membership in a cooperative was compulsory to receive a land plot. Land cultivation and growing agricultural produce was a binding obligation in garden cooperatives.

Norms and restrictions were prescribed in Regulations for a Garden Cooperative and individual plans for each cooperative. It was prohibited to build houses suitable for living. Only one store shed 6–10 m^2 in size for equipment and rest during work on the plot but not for an overnight stay was allowed until 1966. The control over construction of these sheds was accompanied by an inspection to ensure proper use of plots in garden cooperatives (Decree N2991 of the Council of Ministers of the USSR 1952). The amount of fruit trees, berry bushes and vegetables grown on a single plot was also defined and controlled (Kasatkina 2011; Nefedova 2012).

In 1966 the regulations were softened and summer houses 25 m^2 in size with mansard and a 10 m^2 terrace were allowed. My respondents have unanimously informed me that 36 m^2 is the maximum size of a house. The type of building materials, however, were left to the personal choice of dachniks. The land plot was limited to 600 m². Each cooperative had plans for the location of houses and other buildings on individual plots. Fences between the plots were not allowed, only from the street side (Figure 15.1). Bathhouses and garages were forbidden (Standard Regulation of Workers' Garden Partnership 1966; Kasatkina 2011). The cultivation of the plot was compulsory: 'We had to report to the cooperative that we are not doing nothing, but sweating, everything was in the name of labour' (Female, Luchevoe-2). Any violation of these regulations could lead to an exclusion from the cooperative (Standard Regulation of Workers' Garden Partnership 1966).

In 1985 the regulations were modified. They provided even more detailed description of building regulations. The construction of mansions on garden plots was prohibited, and the maximum height of 6.5 m² for the house was introduced. The use of unofficially obtained building materials and unofficial workforce, as well as unauthorised land grab were also forbidden. To facilitate the distribution and increase the popularity of dachas, dachniks were allowed to obtain a loan for dacha construction. The size of the garden plot became smaller, from 400 to 600 m², but fences were formally allowed if a general meeting of the cooperative granted such a permission. By the end of the 1980s, houses of 50 m² in size were allowed (not including terraces and verandas), and other restrictions on space planning of the plot were lifted (Decree N1079 of the Central Committee of the CPSU and the Council of Ministers of the USSR 1987; Lovell 2003). The regulations for garden cooperatives were significantly softened by the end of the Soviet time, and were completely abandoned in the 1990s.

Other dacha types

A "classic dacha" is the oldest form of dacha that appeared before the Soviet times. The number of classic dachas rapidly increased after the October Revolution in 1917, when plots of land were distributed to members of leading organisations and institutions. Classic dachas differ from other dacha types by having bigger plots (from 1200 to 5000 m²) that are not intended for land cultivation (Nefedova 2012; Nefedova & Pallot 2013).

Another form of dacha, vegetable allotments, are formally small plots (from 200 to 600 m²) for growing agricultural produce. These vegetable allotments are very distant from dachas by their nature and 'would not normally qualify for inclusion in a study of second homes were it not for the fact that in Russia there is often a gap between what is permitted by law and what happens in reality' (Nefedova & Pallot 2013: 99). Rapid construction of summer houses on vegetable allotments in the post-Soviet period made them only slightly different than garden cooperatives. These types of plots, however, cannot be private property.

Another type of dacha, a rural house, became an alternative to a shortage of dacha plots in the Soviet time. Until 1989, a city dweller could not officially purchase a house in a rural area, thus they were acquired unofficially through shadow housing market arrangements. There are no official statistics on the number of rural houses that are owned by the city dwellers (Nefedova 2012). For this reason, it is harder to find owners of this dacha type. Among my informants only one is a rural house owner. The cottage or mansion is the most recent type of dacha. It is a well-equipped dwelling for year-round use that is usually big in size. The cottage as a type of dacha should not be confused with the term's meaning in other countries. Cottages become an additional housing unit for city dwellers that are used intermittently. Nowadays all these types are referred to as dachas in spoken language and official documentation (see also Kasatkina 2011). In this chapter the terms "dacha", "garden cooperative" and "dacha cooperative" are used interchangeably.

Today the relationship with and the ownership of the dacha can vary. Second home ownership in Russia is still undergoing a privatisation process. This means that individuals who were given the rights to use the land during the Soviet era are being granted full ownership with the right of disposition (Kasatkina 2011; Struyk & Angelici 1996). A specially designed, simplified privatisation for dachas is known as dacha amnesty and allows de facto owners to claim official ownership of the dwelling and the plot based on the provision of evidence of land or house occupancy (Dachnuiu amnistiiu prodlili 2015).

An overview of dacha types demonstrates that informality is strongly interrelated with the phenomenon. In order to better understand the informality of dacha life and formation of personal bypass routes, it is important to outline Soviet life at that time and the nature of restrictive regulations to which the dacha was conditioned.

Leisure code

The theoretical framework for the study is built upon theoretical approaches to space, spatial organisation and control that enhances the understanding of the organisation of dacha space. To understand the dacha leisure code and the grounding ideas behind it, it is important to look at the ideological stand and societal conditions in the Soviet and post-Soviet times.

The dominant ideology of Marxism-Leninism predefined the collective organisation of leisure and recreation. According to Marx, the city is the centre of production, consumption, government, learning and commerce. The city, through its infrastructure, has to maintain a healthy and malleable workforce, simultaneously keeping under control the movement to and from work space (Zieleniec 2007). Controlled leisure was an integral component in the process of forming a productive and healthy Soviet worker. As part of the soviet welfare system, enterprises and institutions distributed land to their workers to engage in compulsory agriculture. This process was facilitated by the Soviet realities of the supply crisis in the post-war period (World War II) that according to Lovell (2003: 163) prepared the ground for 'the "mass" dacha of the later Soviet period'.

The supply crisis called for new ways of food production and redistribution. Individual land cultivation and food production were actively encouraged by trade unions and soviets at the local level through distribution of land to workers, though not yet under the label of productive leisure. Facing starvation, city dwellers seized the opportunity to cultivate land and grow their own produce (Lovell 2003). In such a manner, when garden cooperatives were officially introduced in 1949 with the aim to solve the problem of food supply, they rapidly gained popularity among Soviet workers and became the most widespread type of Soviet dacha by the end of the 1980s (Kasatkina 2011). Garden cooperatives helped the Soviet state both to shift the responsibility for food supply from the state to individuals, and to promote it as a form of active leisure. The popularity of dachas in the post-Soviet period is explained by their role in alleviating food shortages. As one of my respondents notes: 'Then came 1990s […] the food was harder to get' (Female, Luchevoe-1). In the period of economic turbulences in the 1990s, the dacha possession in Russia peaked due to the possibility of engaging in subsistence agriculture, and using it for recreation (Southworth 2006).

In order to control the actions and facilitate the economic development, or in this case, food supply, there is a need for strict disciplinary control over the populations, or the "eye of power". The culmination of the control over the space and its inhabitants is a "disciplinary society", in which everyday living, work and leisure, are also organised and controlled. According to Michael Foucault (1977, 1980) who theorised about the nineteenth-century city, city problems such as overcrowding, poor sanitation and diseases were solved with moral training of society through education and rational recreation. The latter presumed a "beneficial" use of leisure (Zieleniec 2007). Foucault's ideas were reflected in the eye of communist power from the beginning of the twentieth century in the Soviet Union through organised and controlled leisure and leisure space in the form of dachas. To facilitate dacha construction and land cultivation, organisations provided collective transportation from the city to the dacha site during the weekends. Caldwell (2011) defines such a form of control as a body regime: 'In the logic of socialist body regimes, gardening and cottaging represented additional techniques through which the state could cultivate individual citizens' bodily performances and harness them for the benefit of the nation' (Caldwell 2011: 42). In such a manner, these healthier and more efficient bodies would perform 'the greater productivity of the socialist state' (Caldwell 2011: 41). Moreover, Caldwell (2011) argues that the restrictions were aimed at keeping the role of the state as the centre of people's lives, and preventing any possible replacement by dachas.

The control over space the dacha space in this case, is one of the forms of execution and consolidation of power. According to Harvey (2012), real estate or private property becomes a commodity in the market through which power is maintained. At the same time '[i]t creates a tension between ownership and use of space for private and collective purposes, and the domination of space by the state' (Zieleniec 2007: 109). It is important to note that distributed plots of land were given to Soviet workers for use without any right to property, as the latter was not in line with the ideological stand of that time. In order to prevent any personal attachment to dacha plots, strict spatial planning with very limited privacy and a number of limitations were enforced (Kasatkina 2011).

This conflict between state domination of space and personal use, and of land plots (portions of common dacha space), resulted in the formation of a developed system of informal solutions that is known as *blat* in the Russian language. 'Blat networks channelled an alternative currency – an informal exchange of favours' (Ledeneva 2009: 257). In this chapter the term is used in its narrowest sense as an individual's ability to obtain goods and services that they cannot influence or get personally. In other words, the use of informal services from formal organisations and the utilisation of personal networks.

The nature of informal networks is very diverse and may be driven by friendship, family, professional circles, membership in associations, interaction in business life, or leisure activities. The Soviet shortage economy provided fertile ground for developing informal networks and strengthening *blat* practices in the dacha sector. The distribution of dacha stock and obtaining building materials in many cases took place through personal contacts. This study shows that the developed practice of exchanging favours in the city was revived when the possibility of getting a dacha plot appeared (see the results section for more details).

According to Ledeneva (2009: 261), the power of informal networks 'can be effectively conceptualised as the know-how of the Soviet system and the reverse side of the over-controlling centre'. The conflict between imposed and desirable was resolved through 'finding creative ways to circumvent official rules and unfortunate circumstances' (Caldwell 2011: 182). The utilisation of informal contacts is embedded so deeply in cultural practice that even in post-Soviet times dacha dwellers use *blat* (Lovell 2003).

Caldwell's (2011: 143) empirical study reveals that imposed regulations were perceived differently in the city than in the dacha communities. As in regard to dacha spaces, her informants claimed 'not to feel the effects of these regulations on their behaviour or feelings'. Thus, there is a clear distinction between city and dacha spaces. Rules and norms are interpreted and followed differently out of the city. I argue that dacha is a distinct space that is constructed through constant negotiating and borders between private and public, as well as imposed and desired. The results section outlines how the prescribed norms were accepted and followed on the ground.

Data

The empirical data consists of 15 interviews collected in July 2012 in five locations outside the city of Petrozavodsk, the Republic of Karelia. The interviews were conducted in the following dacha locations: Luchevoe-1 (four cooperatives), Luchevoe-2 (one cooperative), Besovets (one cooperative), Mashezero (one cooperative), and the village of Lekhnavolok. The distance from the city to these locations varies between 14 and 40 kilometres. The majority of the interviews (N=14) have been collected in dacha cooperatives. Only one respondent femal has another type of dacha, a house in a village. All in all, 17 dachniks took part in the interviews, 5 males and 12 females, born between 1933 and 1958. Most of the respondents are pensioners with quite modest incomes. A monthly income for a household of two persons is about 20–40 thousand rubbles (about €285–570). For a single person, it is even less.

The garden partnerships in this research case refer to late Soviet and post-Soviet periods, and were formed between 1977 and 1995. Thus, the periods of ownership, dacha acquisition and their use vary significantly among the respondents. The interviews were collected through a snowball effect. I asked friends and relatives who have dachas around Petrozavodsk, and they guided me further to their friends and dacha neighbours. The interview guide consists of nine sections: acquiring the plot, cultivating the plot, infrastructure, dacha life, services, social interactions, feelings and plans about the dacha, family and background information. All interviews were conducted in Russian. I am responsible for transcription and further translation of the interviews. The interview data was analysed thematically, using an inductive approach to the data.

Results: Building the dacha dream

Acquiring the plot

Personal networks played an important role in acquiring the dacha plot. While the plots were distributed through organisations and trade unions to their workers and members, over half of the respondents did not have any connection to the distributing institution. Some of the respondents, who were "outsiders" to the distributing organisation, followed formal rules and joined the garden cooperative after someone terminated a membership and the plot was vacant. Others skilfully utilised developed personal networks. Two of the most vivid examples come from the cooperative of a clothing factory in Luchevoe-1. Three ladies, L., N. and K., had dachas in this cooperative, but only L. was working at the clothing factory, and was entitled to acquire a plot. It turned out that L. was a friend of K.'s sister. K. herself worked at the liquor distillery and in the time of food shortages exchanged alcohol for meat products with N., who worked at the meat processing plant. This network of friends and food exchange in the city led to the invitation to N. and K. to join the garden cooperative.

Another respondent shares her story:

> My husband had a classmate. This is a clothing factory, and his [*classmate's*] mom worked at this factory. We have nothing to do with sewing. […] There were some vacant plots, and we got here somehow, by chance.
>
> *(Female, Luchevoe-1)*

These two examples demonstrate how personal networks worked in the shortage economy and were utilised in the process of dacha acquisition in the Soviet time. In post-Soviet time, "outsiders" in newly formed garden cooperatives were still a common practice. The use of personal networks to acquire a dacha plot became a first step in building one's dacha dream. However, the dacha itself was yet to be constructed.

Constructing the dacha

In the Soviet times, actual construction of the summer house and other structures on the plot was regulated by the Standard Regulations and individual plans of cooperatives. Once becoming a member of a cooperative, the member had to follow its rules. As one of my respondents recalls, individual actions were limited to the shape of the roof; otherwise, everything was planned. The realities of the shortage economy and enforced limitations are nowadays still seen in the design of individual summer houses. Restrictions on the size and location of a house did not result in uniformity of the external appearances of dachas (Figure 15.1). Poor supply of building materials resulted in a number of "making do" (Caldwell 2011) strategies and searches for "alternate routes" (Female, Luchevoe-1) by dachniks. Dachas were erected literally from anything that could be used. This was the situation in which the use of personal networks and other informal practices reached its climax. Several of my respondents talked about collecting building materials for their dachas from the sites of demolished buildings in the city:

> If you see a wood board somewhere, you grab it. The buildings were demolished, I made a deal with the guys, and got the materials mostly from there [*demolishing sites*].
>
> *(Male, Mashezero)*

> The bricks for the stove are collected in old houses.
>
> *(Female, Luchevoe-1)*

The purchase of building materials was another strategy:

> Nothing was available. We were queuing for a plasterboard in turns. We all, dachniks, worked in the same organisation, and queued in turns for roof slates, for plasterboards or for paint.
>
> *(Female, Luchevoe-2)*

Official purchase of building materials was troublesome. One respondent remembered how she saw nails for sale and purchased as many as she could physically carry. Another respondent told me about purchasing small wood boards in a handicraft shop for interior finishing. Everyone had their own story.

An executive commission controlled the construction of dachas and the acquisition of building materials. My respondents informed me about strict inspections that required them to provide evidence of the acquisition of (and not stealing) building materials. Even drivers delivering some materials had to have receipts in case of inspection (Female, Luchevoe-1). Many dachniks still have a folder full of receipts and checks for building supplies. There is a clear distinction between the Soviet-time regulations and a construction "freedom" in the 1990s. Nowadays the plans of cooperatives are used as a recommendation rather than an obligation.

Despite the strict regulations on the size and type of buildings on individual plots, there are a number of deviations from these rules both in size and location:

> We were told to have six per six meters, but we have a little bit bigger house, seven per eight metres. [...] Well, we decided to take a chance.
>
> *(Female, Luchevoe-1)*

According to the plan, our house was supposed to be by the road. I told them that I would not place my house there, as it would shade the whole plot. I would put it only here, and let them deal with us.

(Female, Luchevoe-1)

Forbidden bathhouses were constructed as small sheds to be less visible to the eye of inspection. Bathhouses were illegal even in villages due to their location on the shore, though later they were recognised (Female, Lekhnavolok). The executive commission that checked the correspondence of buildings with the regulations reported a number of violations. Officials and local authorities 'proved to be powerless to prevent all the numerous violations people committed in their desire to have proper summer house' (Kasatkina 2011: 17). Since all the restrictions were lifted in the 1990s, all the violations are now openly shared by the respondents. Due to the high pressure of executive control, the violations and informal practices are morally justified by the respondents as being natural solutions. Under the conditions of great imbalance between state demands and supply, dacha spaces were crafted in an individual way.

Private vs public

The location of land plots right next to each other did not provide any possibilities to enlarge individual space. However, those who had their plots next to a forest or a green zone (green zone or green line refers to preserved areas for example, around lakes and areas for fire safety purposes and socialisation) seized the opportunity to move the boundary of the plot a bit further. In some cases, attempts to enlarge the plot from the side of the road resulted in forced correction of the boundary. Others, more fortunate dachniks, legalised their illegal land grabs:

We have 1200 m². We have a corner site and grabbed a piece of the forest. [...] The plot is now privatised and all [*1200 m²*] is documented. As we have a corner site we could grab from both sides, and took four meters from each side.

(Male, Besovets)

As formal delimitations between land plots in many cooperatives were absent, and are absent even nowadays in some cooperatives, borders of a land plot were left to dacha owners' own interpretation. One of the owners told me a story about how a part of his plot was cut off, as it turned out that he had some extra land. He was fortunate to be able to keep the shed that officially stands outside a formal border of his land plot.

Any formal separation between the garden plots in the form of a fence was prohibited. The only "natural" borders between plots are ditches, which are a common practice in different cooperatives. Some of my respondents had only a vague idea where their territory ends, as it's neither officially nor unofficially marked. Fences between dacha plots nowadays indicate the change from the old Soviet practice of shared public dacha space to the new post-Soviet tradition of private property. Thus, more recent owners tend to put up fences around their property, while many primary owners see fences as disruptions of the social order in their cooperative:

We do not have fences, we have communism. [...] Nobody set up a fence, why should I? People would say: "Why are they fencing off? What do they have?"
To set up a fence I have to do the land surveying.

(Female, Luchevoe-2)

The latter point indicates a vague understanding of the boundaries between private property and someone else's territory imposed and inherited from Soviet times (see also Kasatkina 2011). While some would like to have more privacy, not to be observed and judged on their summer outfits, others consider fences to be a negative feature of newcomers.

Without any delimitations between plots, dachniks ended up living under constant surveillance of their neighbours. The small size of a land plot does not provide enough privacy. Individuals were observable and controlled at their dachas. Dachniks in fact never left their working community, and private city life (in one's own apartment) became collective at the dacha (Polukhina 2014). Such an open planned living at the dacha has put additional social pressure on individuals, as certain forms of (mis)behaviour are openly commented on and even criticised. The examples in my research case vary from unfriendly commentaries from neighbours about overgrown grass on a plot to open insults about the use of external workers on the plot, to threats about being excluded from the cooperative. The head of one of the cooperatives explained to me that she has to provide information on poorly cultivated and neglected plots to the Federal Service for Veterinary and Phytosanitary Surveillance (Rosselkhoznadzor). She granted a second chance to three dachniks that year, but two were forced to sell their dachas. This is another example of ever-present control over leisure, which, however, depends on the heads of the cooperatives and varies between cooperatives.

Membership in a cooperative is not compulsory nowadays. Since 1998, membership in a cooperative has been separated from the land ownership (Kasatkina 2011). Many new dacha owners who purchased dachas in existing cooperatives are not members. This is an example of how personal vs community space, and control over individual dachas, are renegotiated. A similar situation is observed with fences, which are a more common feature in cooperatives that appeared in the 1990s, or around plots with new owners.

Soviet inheritance vs modern life demands

Albeit a number of violations, the imposed frameworks of spatial organisation of individual plots are deeply rooted in dacha communities and in leisure practices. The majority of dacha owners see their dachas as a site of productive leisure. They grow agricultural produce on their plots, though admit that it is not of economic benefit, and they invest more than they receive. This is an example of the inherited Soviet leisure code.

Moreover, limited choice and supressed desires still guide the behaviour of dachniks. When I asked my respondents about the dacha of their dreams, they hesitated to answer. It turned out to be a difficult question for many respondents. They see their current dacha, which they managed to construct and inhabit circumventing certain regulations, as their best achievement, the dream dacha.

Dacha owners are quite limited in their desires for any change. A possible dream dacha is an improved version of the present one, renovated or painted, with cultivated land. Many dachniks do not want modern life facilities at their dachas, such as running hot water and indoor toilets. They prefer to have 'something different from the city', 'to have simplicity' (Females, Luchevoe-1). This again indicates a different perception of the dacha space as a contrast and opposition to life in the city.

Conclusions

This chapter has presented an analysis of how the dacha space has been constructed and renegotiated by the state and by individuals. The organised and controlled leisure space to support healthy and moral Soviet citizens met the ideological demands of the period. Spatial arrangements of leisure sustained the regime delimiting personal space. Rules and regulations, however, were met and interpreted differently at the dacha.

Dacha represents a contradiction. On the one hand, 'dacha emerges as oases of "one's own"' (Caldwell 2011: 145), de facto becoming private property. On the other hand, dacha is regulated public property that is subjected to greater control and public observation than life in the city. Attempts to resolve this conflict of control over space are revealed in numerous examples of bypassing the spectrum of regulations in acquiring the land plot, constructing the dacha, to inhabiting the dacha space. Common dacha space is very fragmented. The spatial organisation of garden cooperatives was imposed, while personal space on land quarters was individually crafted. The latter was accompanied by constant negotiation between permissible vs possible. Individual solutions are vividly noticeable through the spatial arrangements of single land plots and the design of summer houses (see Figure 15.1).

Following the study of Caldwell (2011), who emphasised the dichotomy between the city and the countryside with regards to obeying formal rules, this study confirmed that dachas represent a unique space for renegotiating the norms. As a place of constant negotiations between imposed and desired, dachniks stretched the boundaries and created their own 'zone of the actually permissible' (Galtz 2000: 64).

This study shows that spacial order at the dacha cooperatives is complexly produced through imposed regulations and control over productive leisure, as well as individuals' interpretations and implementations of rules. Moreover, the omnipresent public privacy functions as a form of symbolic control and shapes additional norms and practices at the dacha. Thus, more recent dacha owners are more outspoken about public vs private property through physical delimitations of individual space with fences, and suppressing the public through non-membership in cooperatives.

Regulations are, however, imbedded in the way dachas are perceived by the respondents. Individual solutions of breaking through or breaking free exist only along strict norms. As a result, nowadays many respondents do not know what to do with the unexpected dacha freedom. Many still do not know the official boundaries of their plots and do not have their dachas in private ownership.

The study of spatial arrangements of dachas along with the ideological and sociopolitical situation and theoretical approaches to space help to better explain the unofficial solutions and practices of dacha owners. Under the pressure of the state, numerous violations were somehow morally justified as the only solutions to meet the strict regulations and requirements. As a result, contemporary dachas with their individual troublesome histories are the dream come true.

It is time to leave Luchevoe-1 and go back to the city. As I enter the bus, a lady hands me over fresh strawberries from her dacha garden, the symbol of her fulfilled dacha dream.

References

Baschmakoff, N. and Ristolainen, M. (2009) *The Dacha Kingdom: Summer Dwellers and Dwellings in the Baltic Area*. Helsinki: Gummerus Printing.

Brumfield, W. C. and Ruble B. A. (1993) *Russian Housing in the Modern Age: Design and Social History*. Cambridge: Cambridge University Press.

Caldwell, M. (2011) *Dacha Idylls: Living Organically in Russia's Countryside*. Berkley, CA: University of California Press.

Chernykh, O. I. (1993) 'Dachnoe stroitel'stvo Peterburgskoi gubernii XVIII – Nachala XIX vv.', SPb: Rossiiskaia akademiia khudozhestv.

Dachnuiu amnistiiu prodlili (2015) 'Dachnuiu amnistiiu prodlili na tri goda', *Rossiiskaia gazeta*, 4 March. [online] Retrieved from: http://www.rg.ru/2015/03/04/amnisia-site.html (accessed 30 March 2015).

Decree N2991 of the Council of Ministers of the USSR (1952) 'Sovet Ministrov SSSR. Postanovlenie ot 3 iiulia 1952g. N2991 O Vozvedenii v Kollektivnykh Sadakh Predpriiatii, Uchrezhdenii I Organizatsii g. Moskvy i Moskovskoi Oblasti' [Decree N2991 of the Council of Ministers of the USSR on July 3, 1952 on Construction in Collective Gardens of Factories, Enterprises and Institutions of Moscow and Moscow Region]. [online] Retrieved from: www.libussr.ru (accessed 5 June 2016).

Decree N1079 of the Central Committee of the CPSU and the Council of Ministers of the USSR (1987) 'Tsentral'nyi Komitet KPSS, Sovet Ministrov SSSR. Postanovlenie ot 19 sentiabria 1987g. N1079 O Dopolnitel'nykh Merakh po Razvitiiu Lichnykh Podsobnykh Khoziaistv Grazhdan Kollektivnogo Sadovodstva I Ogorodnichestva' [Decree N1079 of the Central Committee of the CPSU and the Council of Ministers of the USSR on September 19, 1987 on Additional Measures for Personal Subsidiary Plot Development of Citizens of Collective Gardens and Allotments]. [online] Retrieved from: www.libussr.ru (accessed 5 June 2016).

FOM (2013) *O Dachakh i Dachnikakh*. [online] Available at: http://fom.ru/Rabota-i-dom/11029 (accessed 15 May 2016).

Foucault, M. (1977) *Discipline and Punish*. London: Penguin.

Foucault, M. (1980) 'The Politics of Health in the Eighteen Century.' In C. Gordon (ed.) *Power/Knowledge – Selected Interviews and Other Writings (1972–1977)*. London: Harvester Wheatsheaf, 63–77.

Galtz, N. R. (2000) Space and the Everyday: An Historical Sociology on the Moscow Dacha. PhD. The University of Michigan.

Hall, C. M. and Müller D. K. (eds) (2004) *Tourism, Mobility and Second Homes: Between Elite Landscape and Common Ground*. Clevedon, UK: Channel View Publications.

Hannonen, O. (2016) *Peace and Quiet beyond the Border: The Trans-Border Mobility of Russian Second Home Owners in Finland*. Tampere, Finland: Juvenes Print.

Harvey, D. (2012) *Rebel Cities: From the Right to the City to the Urban Revolution*. London: Verso Books.

Kasatkina, A. (2011) Public and Private in Contemporary Russia: The Case of Garden Cooperatives. Master of Arts. Central European University, Budapest, Hungary.

Ledeneva, A. (2009) 'From Russia with Blat: Can informal networks help modernize Russia?', *Social Research*, 76 (1): 257–288.

Lipkina, O. (2013) 'Motives for Russian second home ownership in Finland', *Scandinavian Journal of Hospitality and Tourism*, 13 (4): 299–316.

Lovell, S. (2003) *Summerfolk: A History of the Dacha, 1700–2000*. Ithaca, NY: Cornell University Press.

Nefedova, T. (2012) 'Gorozhane i dachi'. [City Dwellers and Dachas], *Otechestvennye zapiski* 3 (48). [online] Retrieved from: www.strana-oz.ru/2012/3/gorozhane-i-dachi (accessed 10 March 2014).

Nefedova, T. and Pallot, J. (2013) 'The multiplicity of second home development in Russian Federation: A case of "seasonal suburbanization"?' In Z. Roca, M. Nazaré Roca and J. Oliveira (eds) *Second Home Tourism in Europe: Lifestyle Issues and Policy Responses*. Surrey, UK: Ashgate, 91–121.

Polukhina, E.V. (2014) 'The peculiarities of social order in the space of post-Soviet Dacha: Work, generations, and gender', *Labirint*, 4: 22–31.

Selwood, J. (2006) 'Second homes Russian/Ukrainian style', *Prairie Perspectives*, 9 (1): 118–142.

Southworth, C. (2006) 'The Dacha debate: Household agriculture and labour markets in post-Soviet Russia', *Rural Sociology*, 71 (3): 451–478.

Standard Regulation of Workers' Garden Partnership (1966) 'Tipovoi Ustav Sadovodcheskogo Tovarishchestva Rabochikh i Sluzhashchikh. Utverzhden na Osnovanii Postanovleniia Soveta Ministrov RSFSR i VTSSPS ot 18 marta 1966g. N261' [Standard Regulation of Workers' Garden Partnership. Ratified by the Decree N 261 of the Council of Ministers of the RSFSR and the All-Union Central Soviet of Trade Unions on March 18, 1966]. [online] Retrieved from: http://www.libussr.ru (accessed 5 June 2016).

Struyk, R. and Angelici, K. (1996) 'The Russian Dacha phenomenon', *Housing Studies*, 11 (2): 233–250.

Zieleniec, A. (2007) *Space and Social Theory*. Los Angeles, CA: Sage.

16

SECOND HOME TOURISM IN SICILY

Development, current trend and future outlook

Serena Volo

Introduction and background of the study

Patterns of tourism and leisure behaviour involving second homes have been studied comprehensively across several geographical areas and historical timeframes (Coopock 1977; Gartner 1987; Go 1988; Kaltenborn 1997; Gallent & Tewdwr-Jones 2000; Müller 2002, 2004, 2013; Frost 2004; Hall & Müller 2004; Gallent et al. 2005; Hall 2014; Anabestani 2014; Volo 2015). Traditionally conceived as a retreat for social elites, Italian second homes served as places to escape everyday life and restore health; generally located in areas with favourable climate, these dwellings were an expression of a luxurious lifestyle. The democratisation of second home tourism happened with the economic boom that followed the Second World War, when the desired characteristics of second homes changed and an increasing number of less affluent citizens started seeking a summer or weekend retreat (Volo 2014). With a wider second home market, less well-known settings were discovered and less luxurious homes built. Thus, the Italian middle class invested in affordable properties close to their permanent residence in order to use them on a more regular basis. Modern second homes were seen in the same light as their historical predecessors: they both represented an escape from everyday life, an opportunity for relaxation, a chance to be in contact with nature and with family or friends. However, the more contemporary phenomenon includes further motives: real estate investment opportunity, flavouring multiple identities, experiencing different locations and cultures, and retiring in a more suitable place (e.g. Williams & Hall 2000, 2002; Mazón 2006; Bieger et al. 2007; Marjavaara & Müller 2007; Paris 2011; Casado-Diaz et al. 2014). Indeed, second home tourism has been growing in recent decades, and due to the increased mobility of tourists, the character of the demand has shifted. A more or less stable regional and seasonal migration has been replaced by an increasingly international and flexible demand (Hall 2014; Paris 2012; Volo 2014). Additionally, second homes are increasingly owned, rented or used by multiple dwellers on the basis of home or time sharing and, in many regions around the world, this form of tourism is thriving, assuring exploitation of a large number of properties originally built as weekend retreats or vacation homes.

In this changing landscape, numerous studies have addressed the European second home tourism phenomenon and substantial academic research has been carried out with regard to different aspects: the motives for ownership; the interpretations and meanings of the experience; the mobilities and encounters; the spatial and temporal patterns and issues; the economic, social and environmental impacts; and, the policies, planning and governance concerns (Marjavaara 2007; Módenes Cabrerizo & López Colás 2007; Paris 2009; Vepsäläinen & Pitkänen 2010; Norris et al. 2010; Müller 2013, 2014;Velvin et al. 2013; Persson 2015). However, within Italian second home research, studies have focused mostly on estimations of tourist flows in small destinations, ignoring the underlying motivations and behavioural patterns of second home owners, their interaction with the local community and the possible future usage of these dwellings.

This chapter addresses issues related to the development, current trends and future usage of second homes in Sicily by reviewing and discussing the available but fragmented studies conducted on the island and by framing them within contemporary international debate. Indeed, the geographical area targeted is an ideal second home tourism laboratory, with a high second home presence and considerable unregulated exploitation for both private usage and commercial rentals. As old problems permeate second home tourism in Sicily, new challenges ought to be faced by planners, policymakers and tourism stakeholders. This study contributes to bridging the shores between traditional and contemporary consumption practices and highlights future research areas that will become increasingly significant at regional and national levels.

The study area: Origins and development of second homes in Sicily

Located in the Mediterranean Sea, Sicily is an Italian region and island well-known as a tourist destination, and that appears to be in its growth phase since the late 1990s, attracting both domestic and international visitors. The island offers natural beauty and a bundle of culture, art and history, having been home to some of the greatest civilisations and cultures throughout history. Tourism has been a significant factor in the economic development of Sicily and has been designated, especially during the last twenty years, by local and regional authorities as an important economic sector on which to focus development initiatives (Volo 2008).

In the Sicilian tourism landscape a special role is attributed to second home tourism, often seen more as a curse than a blessing. Indeed, second home tourism is very heterogeneous across the different regions of Italy, and each region has its own history and its own characteristics that shape how the second home tourism reality plays out and how second home tourists experience their home and their stay. The development of second homes in Sicily occurred alongside the history of the emancipation of the region and its inhabitants. Left impoverished after the Second World War, Sicily slowly started to rebuild its economy and witnessed a strong migratory flow. As the whole nation took the first steps towards rebuilding its real estate stock, Sicily lagged behind. Only in the late 1960s did the region witness the redevelopment of its major cities and, with the economic boom of the 1980s, the less affluent middle class saw in the seaside cottage a way to step up the ladder of society (Macchiavelli 2011).

Characterised by mass emigration and a lack of industrial strengths, Sicily intensively developed the construction industry in which low educated workers could easily find a source of income, and organised crime could find an opportunity for money laundering. Thus, the development of the construction industry fostered a rapid and unplanned real estate development that on one side favoured a few entrepreneurs and, on the other, it was – for many in the workforce – the only reasonable alternative to emigration. In the midst of this unregulated development, the middle class sought to own a little piece of coastline, and numerous properties were built without respecting the almost non-existent regulatory frameworks (Volo 2011; Romita 2013). In the late 1990s, Sicily was left with a high number of second homes, mostly located within commuting distance from the major cities, and heavily characterised by a strong seasonal migration, whether for private or commercial use. Similar to other southern Italian regions, Sicily witnessed the development of residential tourism characterised by often undeclared, unregulated private houses in which families could dwell during the summer months and that ensured the owners a financial investment and a means for social distinction (Romita 2013). In the early years of the new millennium, stakeholders, journalists and researchers started to raise awareness about the issues that surround this form of tourism. The predominant outcome of the uncontrolled construction seems to be negative, as the seasonal overcrowding favours environmental, economic and social drawbacks.

The scholarly debate around Sicilian second home tourism

The negative character attributed to second home tourism is evident in the multiplicity of designations; indeed, both academic and nonacademic literature refer to it as hidden, ignored, unmeasured, unobserved or undetected tourism (Manente & Scaramuzzi 1999; Volo 2004a; Parroco & Vaccina 2005; De Cantis & Volo 2006; Volo & Giambalvo 2008; Romita 2013; De Cantis & Ferrante 2013). An array of Italian regional studies focused on the issue of estimations of unregistered tourism accommodations (Macchiavelli 1995; Manente & Scaramuzzi 1999; Giambalvo & Parroco 2004; Parroco & Vaccina 2005; Tomaselli & Vaccina 2006; Mendola 2006; Guizzardi & Bernini 2012).

The literature that investigated second homes in Sicily focused almost exclusively on the unreported economic activity associated with second home tourism (Ferrante et al. 2006), on the statistical estimations of its effect on local or regional economies (Tomaselli & Vaccina 2006), and on its contribution to the load placed on the local and regional public infrastructures (Giambalvo & Parroco 2004; Parroco & Vaccina 2005). The investigators have rarely described the historical origins, development or geographical patterns of second home tourism. Furthermore, it appears that the attitudes of second home owners, their reasons for ownership, place attachment and identity issues have been largely ignored in the Sicilian region, whereas other Italian regions have recently witnessed a few investigations on these aspects of second home consumption (Volo 2011; Romita 2013; Perri 2013).

The available body of literature that investigates Sicilian second homes can be framed into three areas of concerns, which are discussed below: (a) conceptual definitions and estimates of statistically unreported activity; (b) the spontaneous and unregulated market supply; and (c) the choices of second home renters.

Conceptual definitions and estimates of statistically unreported activity

The inevitable inadequacy of tourism statistics is amply described in literature (Volo 2004a; Vaccina & Parroco 2013; Guizzardi & Bernini 2012; Aroca et al. 2013, 2016). Indeed, due to the mobile nature of the phenomenon, tourists are considered to be a statistical population that is difficult to reach (Mendola & Milito 2013). Available studies on second homes in Sicily focus on the unmeasured tourism activity (De Cantis & Ferrante 2013), in which the emphasis resides on the inability of official statistics to measure the physical presence in the second homes at any given time and to record the exact usage of the second home (personal use, unpaid guests or rentals). In line with this approach, three approaches have been used in measuring second home tourism in Sicily: (a) comparison of different statistical sources, (b) use of indirect indicators of presence in the territory, and (c) *ad hoc* surveys (De Cantis et al. 2015). The first approach consists of a comparison between official statistics collected from the supply side (statistics collected from officially registered accommodations and gathered by the Italian National Statistical Institute) and those collected from the demand side (two surveys have been used for this purpose: a survey conducted by the Italian National Statistical Institute and the Bank of Italy frontier survey on tourists' behaviours). The results of studies using these methods show, for Sicily as a whole, a rough estimate of four unmeasured overnight stays for each recorded night a tourist spent at the destination (Giambalvo & Parroco 2004; De Cantis et al. 2015). The second approach consists of using indirect measures of physical presence at the destination (the so-called Becheri-Gambassi model, see Volo 2004a; also used by Macchiavelli 1995); several studies were undertaken in small seaside destinations using both direct and indirect indicators such as the consumption of electricity and the production of solid waste. Results show a range of variability between 14 and 24 unmeasured overnights for each 10 officially recorded (Ferrante & De Cantis 2013). The third approach consists of *ad hoc* surveys that are specifically designed to estimate tourists staying in non-officially registered accommodations (second homes). Several studies used this approach at both the small local seaside town level and the regional level. The results show a range of variability between 17 and 22 unmeasured overnights for each 10 officially recorded (De Cantis et al. 2015).

The three methods described above have been applied to various areas in Sicily during the period 2004–2009, and the results support the contribution of second homes to tourism flows. Finally, the limitations of the indirect estimates and the time-consuming and costly procedures of the *ad hoc* survey discourage a systematic replication for management purposes. However, while acknowledging the effort made by the various research groups in Sicily, one wonders about the reasons that inhibited them from creating a systematic database that could be appropriately updated or modified for different contexts and used by policymakers at the destination. It is also surprising that the studies did not relate their findings to the stock of second homes registered in the Italian census, thus de facto ignoring a valuable source of statistical data on the Sicilian housing market.

The spontaneous and unregulated market supply

A second area of concern with reference to Sicilian second homes is that of rented properties offered in an unregulated marketplace; second homes indeed create a parallel supply of accommodations that enter into competition with the official market of accommodation establishments. A few studies have pointed out this relevant issue, highlighting the effect on market prices and competition that this parallel market could create (Volo 2004b; Oliveri & Vaccina 2013). The factors that have stimulated the spontaneous and unregulated second homes market were the growth of tourism flows unaccompanied by an adequate modification of supply; the pressure of high maintenance costs and growing property taxes on second home owners; and a marketing push from real estate intermediaries that, with an increasing number of outlets in the territory, were able to organise attractive seasonal rentals (Volo 2004b).

Past studies emphasise the variety of these offers that include private rooms, houses, apartments, cottages, villas and any other type of private dwelling offered for temporary use to tourists and not registered in the appropriate lists of the tourism authorities (Giambalvo & Parroco 2004). It was noticed, however, that the accommodations offered, by either individuals or real estate agencies, appear less standardised than those offered by the official hospitality operators, including apartments close to the shores, traditional fishermen's houses and beautiful villas in rural zones. The dimension of these lodgings are variable and the prices that both the agencies and the individual owners practice are very structured so as to distinguish at a minimum between five different levels: very low season, low season, medium, high and very high season (Volo 2004b; Oliveri & Vaccina 2013). This showed a sophisticated offer of authentically portrayed dwellings with weekly differentiated prices and a complex yield management that not even the official accommodation sector practices (Volo 2004b; De Cantis & Volo 2005).

Moreover, additional services such as boat tours, rental of bikes or motorbikes and transportation services are offered to those renting the property, thus creating an even more personalised experience for the tourists. Second home seasonal rentals are introduced to tourists in simple ways: word-of-mouth and online offers drive the offerings of individual owners, whereas advertising and personal sales are used mostly by real estate agencies (Volo 2004b).

The real estate agencies operate like tourism intermediaries, offering a structured distribution system and an organised managerial structure with good communication skills. The negative effects of this parallel unregulated market have been neglected for a long time, with a more recent interest of the hotel associations to unveil the market share of second home properties in the tourism market place. A close investigation of this spontaneous tourism supply shows the variety of services that second home owners propose to satisfy a demand that would otherwise be unmet by the limited official accommodation (Volo 2004b, 2010). Past literature shows that so-called hidden, unmeasured, unobserved or undetected tourism has emerged and it is traceable and visible to the interested public within the region (public administration, fiscal authorities and tourism institutions), which nevertheless seem to ignore the phenomenon and overlook the opportunity to relate the amount of second home supply to the available officially registered accommodations at the destination.

The choices of second home tourists: Owners, non-paying guests and renters

In the general tourism literature, limited attention has been paid to Sicily as a tourism destination, and very little is known about the decision making process that brings tourists to the island and their choices and behaviour once at the destination. Only a handful of studies have looked at the demand for Sicilian holidays, and those refer to: the image of the destination (Volo 2004c), the relationship between seasonality patterns and the development of tourism (Volo 2010), the contribution of cultural heritage to reducing tourism seasonality (Cuccia & Rizzo 2011), the wine tourists' motivations (Asero & Patti 2011), and the more recent analysis of the determinants of tourism demand (Asero & Tomaselli 2015; Provenzano 2015).

Similarly, in the second home panorama, available research includes only investigations of the economic expenditures and essential traveler information associated with users of second homes (Giambalvo & Parroco 2004; Parroco & Vaccina 2005; Tomaselli & Vaccina 2006). The *ad hoc* surveys carried out in various seaside destinations in Sicily include no specific mention of users' motives for second home stays and no behavioural details were scrutinised. However, indirect estimates indicate some characteristics about second home renters (1) they tend to stay about two weeks or more, (2) they travel by car and (3) they spend relatively less than those staying at hotels or other registered accommodations. Their preference for a second home rental often relates to the ability to accommodate larger parties, the possibility of local flavour, non-standardised accommodations, and the simplicity in locating the offerings online (Volo 2008). Still, it is likely that the share of second home tourism generated by Sicilian residents is higher than that generated by non-residents and therefore more accurate studies on the behavioural choices of users ought to be undertaken (Volo & Giambalvo 2008). Furthermore, available studies concentrate almost exclusively on paying guests, completely ignoring the point of view of the owners of second homes, who are never surveyed directly or in-depth.

Overall, in the Italian literature very limited attention has been posed on the behavioural choices of second home users, whether owners, non-paying guests or renters. Thus, the underlying motivations and behavioural patterns of second home usage, the social role of second homes and the users' interaction with the local community have been almost totally neglected (a few exceptions are Volo 2011; Romita 2013). Conclusively, in order to align the findings of Italian second home studies with those of the extensively available international literature, there is a need to shift the understanding of second home tourism and the research approach used by Italian scholars.

Conclusions, managerial implications and future outlook

The central challenge reported in the Italian literature is the lack of relevant and credible data on tourists using second homes. Similarly, with reference to Sicily, past studies describe and evaluate the strengths and weakness of the different methodological approaches in order to estimate the tourists' presence in a given territory. Likewise, the international literature acknowledges a lack of available statistics on second homes or vacation properties and the usually unreported economic activity associated with them (Hall & Müller 2004; Czarnecki & Frenkel 2015; Aroca et al. 2013, 2016), but it also acknowledges the multifaceted nature of the phenomenon and its changing features in the increasingly mobile marketplace (Paris 2011; Halfacree 2012; Duncan et al. 2013). As shown in this brief review, the Italian literature has focused almost exclusively on the unreported economic activity associated with second home tourism, on the statistical estimations of its effect on local or regional economies, and on its contribution to the load placed on the local and regional public infrastructures. This section attempts to bridge the shores between traditional and contemporary consumption practices and highlight future research areas that will become increasingly significant at regional and national levels.

The neglected second home users: Avenues for research

In the studies that focus on Sicilian second home tourism, investigators have rarely described the historical origins, development or geographical patterns of second home tourism and to the extent that they have, it has been poorly described. Available, albeit sparse, data on the housing stock has not been used to assist with the estimation of second home usage. Furthermore, the visibility of second home rentals in the marketplace collides with the hidden nature of rentals portrayed by some of the literature. Indeed, to the attentive observer the phenomenon is traceable and to the inquisitive researcher it is measurable. The challenge that remains is to connect the missing piece, which – as appears from this review of literature – is the *second home user*, whose behavioural choices and usage habits have not been surveyed. More surprisingly, applied tourism researchers have often tried to suggest planning and marketing policies despite the fact that the experience, attitudes and consumer behaviour of second home tourists have not been investigated.

Considering the issues discussed above and in light of the international debate on second homes (Müller 2013; Paris 2009, 2013; Hall 2014, 2015a; Osbaldiston et al. 2015), several interesting paths of research emerge: (a) There is a need, within the Italian context, to re-frame the operational definition of second home tourism: to move from a *hard* one, that is based on the operational needs of the statisticians, to a *soft* one that is user-centred and involves the different scopes and usages, and three different categories of users: the owners and their close family, nonpaying guests (usually relatives and friends of the owners) and paying guests. (b) Greater attention should be devoted to comprehensive studies that, starting from the knowledge on the available real estate, could distinguish destinations with a high concentration of second homes from those less affected by the phenomenon and trace a relationship between different types of usage (private or rentals) and the accommodation structure of destinations; this will help distinguish, within the vast second home stock, the character of the market by categorising properties and understanding their different contribution to accommodating domestic or international guests. (c) Further investigations should also open a more attentive lens to capture possible positive effects of this form of tourism that have so far been neglected. Indeed, second homes are unquestionably seen as places and spaces of new lifestyle mobilities and identities, and numerous international studies have depicted second homes from different angles, presenting a fluid image of users' motivations, mobilities and locations (Paris 2012; Hall 2014; Müller 2014). It would be beneficial to both Italian scholars and policymakers to move towards a softer, more fluid and multifaceted conception of second homes. This effort will in turn help to better understand the phenomenon and to meet the needs of users, economic planners, destination officials and tourism operators.

From the construction industry boom to novel consumption practices

In a recently published international review, the need for a deeper understanding of the temporal and spatial dimension of the second home phenomenon is highlighted (Hall 2014). The relevance of the changing tourism landscape (higher levels of mobility, the disintermediation of offering, the co-creation of experiences) cannot be ignored. Scholars interested in understanding the second home phenomenon ought to comprehend the influences that second homes' novel uses and their related mobilities have, at different levels and at different points in time, in the big picture of tourism destinations' development (Notarstefano & Volo 2012; Volo 2016). Implicitly suggesting a longer-term perspective, some of the ideas that are worthy of investigation require an integration of different perspectives. The notion of contemporary fluid *mobilities* can help to assess the new components of the production and *co-creation* dimensions of second home tourism. Such a vision needs to be developed to ensure proper destination offerings, which can contribute to the long-term sustainability of vacation home destinations. Furthermore, tourism governance seen under the light of the new mobility paradigm (Sheller & Urry 2006; Hall 2015b) ought to include traditional tourism agents, housing entities, providers of public services, territorial space planners and many more stakeholders that can create or reshape altogether the identity of the destination. In the Italian and Sicilian second home market there is a strong need to reconcile the conflict between second home users and stakeholders to move forward in understanding how to integrate contemporary consumption practices of second homes into tourism policies.

A more mature academic interest in the topic could also open up opportunities for international, cross-cultural comparisons. Undeniably, second or multiple homes are places and spaces of new lifestyle mobilities and identities that ought to be compared and integrated, rather than simply measured and dissected.

Concluding thoughts

In order to contribute to an understanding of the role, structure and development of second home tourism in Sicily, this study: (a) introduced the study area's characteristics, by defining the supply of second homes in Sicily, tracing origin, structure and development of the phenomenon, (b) presented and discussed past literature on Sicilian second homes by identifying three major areas of interest and highlighting the shortcomings of existing investigations, and (c) discussed future research needs in light of the international debate on second home tourism.

The study highlights the inquisitor role of past scholars with respect to the negative effects of second homes on tourism destinations' development and emphasises the lack of investigations on the use, motivations, behaviours and preferences of second home users. Thus, despite the large number of studies on second home tourism in specific areas of Sicily, there is still a need for further investigations at destination level. Indeed, with a more comprehensive representation of the phenomenon, managerial and planning issues related to second homes can be more substantively addressed.

References

Anabestani, A. (2014) 'Effects of second home tourism on rural settlements development in Iran (case study: Shirin-Dareh Region)', *International Journal of Culture, Tourism and Hospitality Research*, 8 (1): 58–73.

Aroca, P., Brida J. G. and Volo, S. (2013) 'Applying weights to correct distortions in a non-random sample: An application to Chilean tourism time series data', *Tourism Economics*, 19 (2): 453–472.

Aroca, P., Brida J. G. and Volo, S. (2016) 'Tourism statistics: Correcting data inadequacy', *Tourism Economics*, 1–14: doi:10.5367/te.2015.0500.

Asero, V. and Patti, S. (2011) 'Wine tourism experience and consumer behavior: The case of Sicily', *Tourism Analysis*, 16 (4): 431–442.

Asero, V. and Tomaselli, V. (2015) 'Research note: Analysing tourism demand in tourist districts – The case of Sicily', *Tourism Economics*, 21 (5): 1111–1119.

Bieger, T., Beritelli, P. and Weinert, R. (2007) 'Understanding second home owners who do not rent – Insights on the proprietors of self-catered accommodation', *International Journal of Hospitality Management*, 26 (2): 263–276.

Casado-Diaz, M., Casado-Diaz, A. B. and Casado-Diaz, J. M. (2014) 'Linking tourism, retirement migration and social capital', *Tourism Geographies*, 16 (1): 124–140.

Coppock, J. T. (1977) *Second Homes: Curse or Blessing?* Oxford: Pergamon.

Cuccia, T. and Rizzo, I. (2011) 'Tourism seasonality in cultural destinations: Empirical evidence from Sicily', *Tourism Management*, 32 (3): 589–595.

Czarnecki, A. and Frenkel, I. (2015) 'Counting the "invisible": Second homes in Polish statistical data collections', *Journal of Policy Research in Tourism, Leisure and Events*, 7 (1): 15–31.

De Cantis, S. and Volo S. (2005) 'L'offerta turistica eoliana: Tassi di utilizzo e fatturato delle strutture ricettive'. In A. M. Parroco and F. Vaccina (eds) *Isole Eolie: Quanto turismo?!* Padova, Italy: Cleup, 121–184.

De Cantis, S. and Volo, S. (2006) 'Flussi turistici ufficiali. Il ciclo di vita e la stagionalità'. In V. Tomaselli and F. Vaccina (eds) *Turismo a Cefalù: Dimensioni statistiche ed effetti socio-economici*. Padova, Italy: Cleup, 83–106.

De Cantis, S. and Ferrante, M. (2013) 'Tourism statistics and unobserved tourism: Empirical evidences in Sicily', *DIEM*, Dubrovnik International Economic Meeting, 1 (1), Rujan, 2013.

De Cantis, S., Parroco, A. M., Ferrante, M. and Vaccina, F. (2015) 'Unobserved tourism', *Annals of Tourism Research*, 50: 1–18.

Duncan, T., Cohen, S. A. and Thulemark, M. (2013) *Lifestyle Mobilities: Intersections of Travel, Leisure and Migration*. Farnham, UK: Ashgate.

Ferrante, M. and De Cantis, S. (2013) 'Indirect measurement of unobserved tourism. The municipal solid waste (MSW) as an indicator of human pressure'. In A. M. Oliveri and S. De Cantis (eds) *Analysing Local Tourism: A Statistical Perspective*. Maidenhead, UK: McGraw-Hill Education, 73–86.

Ferrante, M., Notarstefano, G., Purpura A. and Scuderi, R. (2006) 'Comportamento di spesa del turista: Un approccio micro-econometrico'. In V. Tomaselli and F. Vaccina (eds) *Turismo a Cefalù: Dimensioni statistiche ed effetti socio-economici*. Padova, Italy: Cleup, 155–186.

Frost, W. (2004) 'A hidden giant: Second homes and coastal tourism in south-eastern Australia'. In C. M. Hall and D. K. Müller (eds) *Tourism, Mobility and Second Homes: Between Elite Landscape and Common Ground*. Clevedon, UK: Channel View, 162–173.

Gallent, N. and Tewdwr-Jones, M. (2000) *Rural Second Home in Europe: Examining Housing Supply and Planning Control*. Hampshire, UK: Ashgate.

Gallent, N., Mace A. and Tewdwr-Jones M. (2005) *Second Homes: European Perspectives and UK policies*. Hampshire, UK: Ashgate.

Gartner, W. C. (1987) 'Environmental impacts of recreational home developments', *Annals of Tourism Research*, 14 (1): 38–57.

Giambalvo, O. and Parroco A. M. (2004) 'Analisi dei mercati turistici regionali e sub-regionali', *Collana di Studi Statistici per il Turismo*, 1, Padova, Italy: Cleup.

Go, F. (1988) 'Holiday homes in Europe', *Travel and Tourism Analyst*, 3: 20–33.

Guizzardi, A. and Bernini, C. (2012) 'Measuring underreporting in accommodation statistics: Evidence from Italy', *Current Issues in Tourism*, 15 (6): 597–602.

Halfacree, K. (2012) 'Heterolocal identities? Counter-urbanisation, second homes, and rural consumption in the era of mobilities', *Population, Space and Place*, 18 (2): 209–224.

Hall, C. M. (2014) 'Second home tourism: An international review', *Tourism Review International*, 18 (3): 115–135.

Hall, C. M. (2015a) 'Second homes planning, policy and governance', *Journal of Policy Research in Tourism, Leisure and Events*, 7 (1): 1–14.

Hall, C. M. (2015b) 'On the mobility of tourism mobilities', *Current Issues in Tourism*, 18 (1): 7–10.

Hall, C. M. and Müller, D. K. (eds) (2004) *Tourism, Mobility, and Second Homes: Between Elite Landscape and Common Ground*. Clevedon, UK: Channel View Publications.

Kaltenborn, B. P. (1997) 'Nature of place attachment: A study among recreation homeowners in Southern Norway', *Leisure Sciences*, 19 (3): 175–189.

Macchiavelli, A. (1995) 'An experiment to calculate the number of tourists in holiday resort flats' paper presented at Second International Forum on Tourism Statistics, Venice, 30 May – 2 June 1995.

Macchiavelli, A. (2011) *Le abitazioni di vacanza nella funzione turistica territoriale*. Milano, Italy: Franco Angeli.

Manente, M. and Scaramuzzi, I. (1999) *Le case dei turisti. Dimensioni e qualità del ricettivo residenziale nelle spiagge veneziane*. Bologna, Italy: Il Mulino.

Marjavaara, R. (2007) 'The displacement myth: Second home tourism in the Stockholm Archipelago', *Tourism Geographies*, 9 (3): 296–317.

Marjavaara, R. and Müller, D. K. (2007) 'The development of second homes' assessed property values in Sweden 1991–2001', *Scandinavian Journal of Hospitality and Tourism*, 7 (3): 202–222.

Mazón, T. (2006) 'Inquiring into residential tourism: The Costa Blanca case', *Tourism and Hospitality Planning and Development*, 3 (2): 89–97.

Mendola, D. (2006) 'La stima del turismo non ufficiale: Il disegno campionario, la scheda d'intervista ed alcuni primi risultati'. In V. Tomaselli and F. Vaccina (eds) *Turismo a Cefalù: Dimensioni statistiche ed effetti socio-economici*. Padova, Italy: Cleup, 13–30.

Mendola, D. and Milito, A. M. (2013) 'Sampling in local tourism quantification: Critical issues and field experience'. In A. M. Oliveri and S. De Cantis (eds) *Analysing Local Tourism: A Statistical Perspective*. Maidenhead, UK: McGraw-Hill Education, 53–64.

Módenes Cabrerizo, J. A. M. and López Colás, J. L. (2007) 'Second homes in Spain: Socio-demographic and geographical profiles', *Population*, 62 (1): 157–171.

Müller, D. K. (2002) 'Reinventing the countryside: German second-home owners in southern Sweden', *Current Issues in Tourism*, 5 (5): 426–446.

Müller, D. K. (2004) 'Second homes in Sweden: Patterns and issues'. In C. M. Hall and D. K. Müller (eds) *Tourism, Mobility and Second Homes: Between Elite Landscape and Common Ground*. Clevedon, UK: Channel View Publications, 244–258.

Müller, D. K. (2013) 'Progressing second home research: A Nordic perspective', *Scandinavian Journal of Hospitality and Tourism*, 13 (4): 273–280.

Müller, D. K. (2014) 'Progress in second-home tourism research'. In A. A. Lew, C. M. Hall and A. M. Williams (eds) *The Wiley Blackwell Companion to Tourism*. Oxford, UK: John Wiley and Sons, 389–400.

Norris, M., Paris, C. and Winston, N. (2010) 'Second homes within Irish housing booms and busts: North-South comparisons, contrasts and debates', *Environment and Planning C: Government and Policy*, 28 (4): 666–80.

Notarstefano, G. and Volo, S. (2012) 'Measuring the impact of tourism: A "territorial" approach', *Rivista Italiana di Economia Demografia e Statistica*, 66 (2): 235–247.

Oliveri, A. M. and Vaccina, A. (2013) 'Unobserved tourism and observable on-line tourism accommodation supply'. In A. M. Oliveri and S. De Cantis (eds) *Analysing Local Tourism: A Statistical Perspective*. Maidenhead, UK: McGraw-Hill Education, 127–143.

Osbaldiston, N., Picken, F. and Duffy, M. (2015) 'Characteristics and future intentions of second homeowners: A case study from Eastern Victoria, Australia', *Journal of Policy Research in Tourism, Leisure and Events*, 7 (1): 62–76.

Paris, C. (2009) 'Re-positioning second homes within housing studies: Household investment, gentrification, multiple residence, mobility and hyper-consumption', *Housing, Theory and Society*, 26 (4): 292–310.

Paris, C. (2011) *Affluence, Mobility and Second Home Ownership*. London: Routledge.

Paris, C. (2012) 'Multiple homes'. In S. Smith, M. Elsinga, L. F. O'Mahony, O. S. Eng, S. Wachter and G. Wood (eds) *The International Encyclopedia of Housing and Home*, Vol. 5. Oxford: Elsevier, 1–5.

Paris, C. (2013) 'Second home ownership in the United Kingdom and Ireland since the global financial crisis'. In Z. Roca (ed.) *Second Home Tourism in Europe: Lifestyle Issues and Policy Responses*. Aldershot, UK: Ashgate, 3–32.

Parroco, A. M. and Vaccina, F. (eds) (2005) *Isole Eolie. Quanto turismo?!* Padova, Italy: Cleup.

Perri, A. (2013) 'Residential toots tourism in Italy'. In Z. Roca (ed.) *Second Home Tourism in Europe: Lifestyle Issues and Policy Responses.* Aldershot, UK: Ashgate Publishing, 53–68.

Persson, I. (2015) 'Second homes, legal framework and planning practice according to environmental sustainability in coastal areas: The Swedish setting', *Journal of Policy Research in Tourism, Leisure and Events,* 7 (1): 48–61.

Provenzano, D. (2015) 'A dynamic analysis of tourism determinants in Sicily', *Tourism Economics,* 21 (3): 441–454.

Romita, T. (2013) 'Lifestyle and consumption of do-it-yourself residential tourists in Italy'. In Z. Roca (ed.) *Second Home Tourism in Europe: Lifestyle Issues and Policy Responses.* Aldershot, UK: Ashgate Publishing, 263–284.

Sheller, M. and Urry, J. (2006) 'The new mobilities paradigm', *Environment and Planning A,* 38 (2): 207–226.

Tomaselli, V. and Vaccina F. (eds) (2006) *Turismo a Cefalù: Dimensioni statistiche ed effetti socio-economici.* Padova, Italy: Cleup.

Vaccina, F. and Parroco, A. M. (2013) 'Statistical information and local tourism'. In A. M. Oliveri and S. De Cantis (eds) *Analysing Local Tourism: A Statistical Perspective.* Maidenhead, UK: McGraw-Hill Education, 17–24.

Velvin, J., Kvikstad, T. M., Drag, E. and Krogh, E. (2013) 'The impact of second home tourism on local economic development in rural areas in Norway', *Tourism Economics,* 19 (3): 689–705.

Vepsäläinen, M. and Pitkänen, K. (2010) 'Second home countryside. Representations of the rural in Finnish popular discourses', *Journal of Rural Studies,* 26 (2): 194–204.

Volo, S. (2004a) 'A journey through tourism statistics: Accuracy and comparability issues across local, regional and national levels'. In *SCORUS 24th Biennial Conference on Regional and Urban Statistics: Understanding Change.* SCORUS, 210–216.

Volo, S. (2004b) 'Il Marketing Mix dell'offerta turistica sommersa'. In O. Giambalvo and A. M. Parroco (eds) *Analisi dei mercati turistici regionali e sub-regionali. Costumi sociali risorse economiche per una politica di sviluppo sostenibile del territorio.* Padu, Italy: Cleup, 203–210.

Volo, S. (2004c) 'The role of roots in the perception of a destination: An exploratory study on Sicily', *Journal of Hospitality and Leisure Marketing,* 11 (2–3): 19–29.

Volo, S. (2008) 'Real estate supply and demand issues in a seaside destination'. In P. Keller and T. Bieger (eds) *Real Estate and Destination Development in Tourism: Successful Strategies and Instruments.* Berlin, Germany: Erich Schmidt Verlag GmbH and Co, 193–214.

Volo, S. (2010) 'Seasonality in Sicilian tourism demand – An exploratory study', *Tourism Economics,* 16 (4): 1073–1080.

Volo, S. (2011) 'Comity or conflict? A qualitative study on host-guest relationship in second home tourism', *Tourism Analysis,* 16 (4): 443–460.

Volo, S. (2015) 'Second home'. In J. Jafari and H. Xiao (eds) *Encyclopedia of Tourism.* Cham, Switzerland: Springer.

Volo, S. (2016) 'Eudaimonic well-being of islanders: Does tourism contribute? The case of the Aeolian Archipelago', *Journal of Destination Marketing and Management,* 6 (4): 465–476.

Volo, S. and Giambalvo, O. (2008) 'Tourism statistics: Methodological imperatives and difficulties: The case of residential tourism in island communities', *Current Issues in Tourism,* 11 (4): 369–380.

Williams, A. M. and Hall, C. M. (2000) 'Tourism and migration: New relationships between production and consumption', *Tourism Geographies,* 2 (1): 5–27.

Williams, A. M. and Hall, C. M. (2002) 'Tourism, migration, circulation and mobility: The contingencies of time and place'. In C. M. Hall and A. M. Williams (eds) *Tourism and Migration: New Relationships between Production and Consumption.* Dordrecht, the Netherlands: Kluwer, 1–52.

17

CHANGING SOCIAL STRUCTURE OF SECOND HOME OWNERS IN POLAND

Czesław Adamiak

Introduction

Among the research problems often undertaken by second home researchers is the access to second homes: to what degree is second home ownership reserved for certain groups of people and what socio-economic factors determine the possibility to own a second home? Answers to these questions might explain to what extent second home ownership reflects social inequalities, and help in understanding the practices of second home use, and the relations between second home owners and local residents, and to foresee the future development of second home ownership.

This chapter takes a dynamic perspective on this topic. It analyses the changes in the social structure of second home ownership during the past two decades. Such a time period is expected to enable us to identify how global trends, like increasing inter- and intraregional inequalities, internationalisation, commercialisation and the economic crisis, affect second home ownership. The study uses data from Poland, a country which experienced these processes in a specific and accelerated version, after the dismantlement of the communist political system in 1989.

The research question posed in this chapter is thus, how has the social structure of second home owners in Poland changed during the last decades? To answer this question, I have performed two concise empirical analyses based on two sets of data. First, I use the results of general social surveys of large representative samples of the Polish population to analyse the structure of second home owners by their demographic, socio-economic and geographical characteristics. Second, I go down in the scale of the study to a region of Bory Tucholskie in northern Poland. I use information obtained during extensive field study, including surveys with second home users, to look more in-depth at the differences between consecutive generations of second home owners. These two analyses are preceded by the presentation of the previous research on social composition of second home owners, and recent transformations in the social structure of Poland.

Social structures of second home owners

A household's possibility (and propensity) to own a second home is usually related to some economic, demographic and geographical factors. The importance and strength of influence of these factors differ between countries, as a result of different traditions, socio-economic conditions and legal systems. There are numerous studies which describe the social structures of second home owners in various countries (e.g. Clout 1977; Struyk & Angelici 1996; Di et al. 2001; Dijst et al. 2005; Módenes Cabrerizo, López Colás & Robertson 2007; Norris & Winston 2010; Adamiak et al. 2015). Most of them distinguish three major dimensions in which the specific character of second home owners can be described: their economic position, place of residence and demographic situation.

The position of a household in the socio-economic hierarchy of the society is recognised as one of the most important factors deciding their access to second homes. Most second homes belong to higher economic strata of the societies: members of the high or middle class, entrepreneurs or professionals, with a relatively high level of education and income (Clout 1977; Struyk & Angelici 1996; Kremarik 2002; Halseth 2004; Dijst et al. 2005; Modenes et al. 2007; Norris & Winston 2010). Economic availability of second homes varies between countries, due to different historical conditions, characteristics of real estate markets, and traditions of second home ownership. For example, in the Scandinavian countries, broad access to second homes is partially a result of the tradition of supporting this form of tourism in the framework of the welfare state (Müller 2007), and an egalitarian tradition of second homes in the Czech Republic comes from the pre-war movement of tramping, born among urban workers (Vágner 2001). On the other hand, in the UK, scarce resources of attractive locations and restrictive planning regulations in rural areas make second homes a kind of good reserved for the wealthiest families (Paris 2010).

The place of residence is another factor that determines households' chances to have a second home. Second home owners are most commonly the inhabitants of cities, especially large ones (Clout 1977; Dijst et al. 2005; Norris & Winston 2010). In European countries, they are typically residents of densely developed central urban areas of these cities (Modenes Cabrerizo et al. 2007). This does not apply to the countries where living in a single family home is an indicator of high economic status, as in North America and Ireland, where detached house settlements inhabited by more affluent populations are characterised by higher rates of second home ownership than poorer, dense urban environments (Jaakson 1986; Norris & Winston 2010).

The last major factor that decides on households' access to second homes is demography. Ownership of second homes is more common among couples (with or without children) than among single persons, and the chances of acquiring one are determined by family life cycle: the acquisition and maintenance of a second home requires savings and stable professional position, so most owners of second homes are married couples in their upper-middle age (Godbey & Bevins 1987; McHugh et al. 1995; Di et al. 2001; Dijst et al. 2005; Modenes Cabrerizo et al. 2007; Oxley et al. 2008; Norris & Winston 2010). In countries with common second home use, the demography seems to be a more important factor deciding on second home ownership than the economic position. It does not mean, however, that young families do not have access to second homes. Instead, they often use second homes owned by their parents (Adamiak et al. 2015).

The above characteristics of second home owners are based on surveys conducted in various countries. The common problem with such data is that it provides static snapshots of a dynamic reality of the social structures of second home owners. Such quantitative studies are not effective in noticing rare phenomena, which may have serious impacts, or be the preludes of wider processes. Other studies using qualitative approaches point at increasing diversification of the phenomenon of second homes in terms of the patterns of their uses, locations and technical characteristics, and also social characteristics of the owners. This increasing variation of forms and uses of second homes makes it even harder to describe typical owners of them. The diversification within the group of second home owners reflects the increase in social inequalities, internationalisation and changing patterns of division of life between various locations (Pitkänen & Vepselläinen 2008; Paris 2010).

Social structure and second home ownership in Poland

In order to understand the structure and changes of second home ownership in Poland, it is necessary to introduce the Polish case in terms of demographical, geographical (urban-rural) and economic structure of the population. Particular attention should be given to the period of post-communist transformation after 1989, when the transition from an authoritarian to democratic political system, and from a centrally planned to free market economy, led to important changes in the socio-economic structure of the society, and also impacted the demographic and urbanisation processes.

The number of Polish residents increased from 24 to 38 million between 1946 and 1990 as an effect of a high natural increase during the whole communist period. Later, the rate of births fell down to one of the lowest levels in Europe, which in a few decades will make Poland one of the oldest populations in Europe (Central Statistical Office of Poland (GUS) 2016). The demographic structure is further undermined by emigration: its latest high wave happened as a result of opening the Western European labour market after Poland's accession to the EU in 2004. In terms of urban-rural population distribution, Poland is one of the least urbanised countries in Europe, with 39% of the population still living in rural areas. The urbanisation is also relatively late as the urban population did not outnumber rural population until the 1960s. After a period of rapid increase of the urban population since the 1990s, the rural-to-urban migration has been balanced by suburbanisation processes, which started as a result of post-communist transformation (Sýkora & Stanilov 2014). Relatively recent rural history of many urban residents and strong cultural ties to the rurality in Poland are factors that may foster second home ownership.

The current socio-economic structure of Polish society is a result of the evolution typical of industrialising societies on the one hand, and, on the other hand, processes of the establishment of the communist political system after the Second World War and its consequent dismantlement after 1989. Despite the official ideology, communist society was characterised by social inequalities, though on the top of the social structure previous economic elites were replaced by high communist party representatives (nomenklatura), who became de facto owners of the means of production. The privileged position was also held by the intelligentsia, a typical Eastern European class or social group, which includes employees and freelancers performing jobs which usually need higher education. Labourers and peasants (farmers) remained at the bottom of the social hierarchy (Domański 2015). Compared to the capitalist countries, and both before 1945 and after 1989, the communist society was characterised by little inequality in incomes. Instead, the class position manifested in other privileges, such as the access to rationed goods. For example, party representatives and professionals were the first to obtain new flats in state-owned housing, which produced new patterns of residential segregation in cities (Węcławowicz 2007). They also had better opportunities to travel abroad, which enabled taking advantage of the shadow market trade and purchasing imported goods (Podemski 2005). Communist social stratification also determined access to second homes. Immediately after the Second World War, previous suburban houses of wealthy and middle-class urban families were transformed into residential houses and for other uses. Soon after, new second homes appeared, mostly owned by the members of the nomenklatura, which was a reflection of Soviet social practices (Lovell 2003). Second homes also became accessible for wider groups of intelligentsia since the 1960s and grew in popularity through the 1970s and 1980s. This growth was enhanced by the increasing number of cars in private hands due to growing incomes, but also constrains in foreign travels in the 1980s, and restrictions on building single family houses in the suburbs. During the economic depression that preceded the political transformation, second homes were also seen as a protection against shortages in the supply of food products (Kowalczyk 1994).

After the change of political power in 1989, the hasty introduction of new economic rules, labelled as "shock therapy", effected a quick improvement of macroeconomic indicators, but brought economic hardship to large groups of the population, including farmers and employees of restructured or bankrupt industries. These processes altered the socio-economic structure of the society mostly by widening the income gap between the socio-economic strata. Those who gained were part of the intelligentsia, managers and mostly a new class of private entrepreneurs. On the other hand, those who lost were farmers (whose economic situation improved again after joining the EU and the Common Agricultural Policy in 2004) and labourers affected by the sudden appearance of the unemployment phenomenon (Domański 2015). The liberalisation of trade, property and building regulations facilitated buying and building second homes on rural properties, and in the early 1990s the newly established property market enabled the buying of recreation plots virtually for free before the prices stabilised in the mid-1990s (Adamiak 2014). On the other hand, the same factors enabled them to construct detached houses in suburban areas, which for many eliminated the need to own rural second homes. Also, international tourism trips and other ways of consumption became available, competing with second homes for the potential owners' money and time.

Second home owners according to nationwide social surveys

There is no reliable and complete statistical information on the number and distribution of second homes in Poland. The statistical office does not collect such data (Czarnecki & Frenkel 2015), but the numbers can be estimated based on the nationwide general social surveys which ask the respondents about the ownership of various consumer goods, including second homes. A survey "Social Diagnosis: The conditions and quality of life of the Poles" has been performed every 2–3 years on random samples of 3–12 thousand residents of Poland since 2000 (Czapiński & Panek 2015). In every round of the survey, the respondents were asked, among other questions, about the ownership of a "summer house". Before the "Social Diagnosis", in the years 1991–1997, the same research team conducted similar surveys called "Quality of life of the Poles during the social change 1991–1997" (Czapiński 1998). In this case, however, the question about the ownership of summer houses was only asked in the 1995 round.

The comparison of the shares of households owning second homes at various time points informs about the pace of increase of second home ownership across years. Taking into account analytical weights of cases included in the data set, the rate of second home ownership rose from 2.5% in 1995 to 3.3% in 2000, 4.2% in 2005, 4.5% in 2009, and 4.9% in 2013. It means that the number of second homes (or, to be precise, households owning summer houses) doubled in that time from about 300 to over 600 thousand. In another nationwide survey, Polish Panel Survey POLPAN, carried out in 1988 (Słomczyński et al. 1988), 1.3% of the respondents answered they had summer houses (this survey differed methodically from the "Social Diagnosis" surveys; hence its results were not included in further analysis). This means that the 1990s and early 2000s are the period with the quickest growth in the second home stock. After that time, the growth decelerated.

The social structure of second home owners in Poland is similar to the ones observed in other countries. There is a relative domination of couples with or without children, living in large cities, and relatively affluent. In further analysis, three categorical variables were taken into account as representative for three dimensions of social characteristics of second home owners: structure of a household as an indicator of the demographic dimension, size of place of residence, and belonging to the highest quarter, lowest quarter, or middle half of the population in terms of income per capita. These were all included in a logit model, which enabled the identification of the independent impacts of each factor on the odds of a household having a second home. It enabled us to reduce the confusion caused by possible correlation between the explaining variables, e.g. the fact that big city residents also have frequently higher incomes than rural residents might confound the independent influences of income and place of residence on second home ownership. The results of modelling were presented as the estimated marginal means, and the original coefficients are not presented for the ease of interpretation (Table 17.1). The estimated marginal means should be read as the rates of second home ownership among respondents characterised by a certain value of the variable in question, with the assumption that all other explaining variables hold the reference values. Thus, the table does not show actual rates of ownership of all members of the groups. Instead, for instance, the rates for household types present the expected ratios of second home ownership among residents of small cities, fitting in the middle half of the population in terms of income per capita in different household type groups. (Table 17.1)

The results of logit modelling show that all three variables had significant independent influence on the households' chances to own a second home at all three time points in the analysis. In terms of demographic characteristics of the household, couples without children were most probable to have a second home, followed closely by couples with children, though the difference between those two categories is not statistically significant. Other households, including single persons, single parents with children, multi-generational households and households other than families, had twice (and statistically significantly) less chances to have a second home than the previous two groups. Over time, the basic difference remains the same, though the relative distance between couples with or without children, and other households, shrinks, which means it is more and more common among "other households" to own a second home.

In terms of place of permanent residence, the inhabitants of largest cities (over half a million population) are the most probable to have second homes, and the chances decline with the decreasing settlement size. The residents of the largest cities are more than six times more probable to own a second home than those who live in rural areas. This distance has decreased since 1995, when it was over ten to one, because of fast growth in second home ownership

Table 17.1 Expected marginal probabilities of owning a second home

Variable and value	1995	2003	2013
Household type:	★★★	★★★	★★★
couple without children (reference value)	1.96% (ref.)	2.54% (ref.)	4.42% (ref.)
couple with children	1.61%	3.41%	4.18%
Other	0.57% ★★★	1.23% ★★★	2.09% ★★★
Place of residence:	★★★	★★★	★★★
city >500 thousand inhabitants	7.37% ★★★	9.55% ★★★	9.90% ★★★
city 100–500 thousand inhabitants	2.58%	4.72% ★★	7.32% ★★★
city <100 thousand inhabitants (reference value)	1.96% (ref.)	2.54% (ref.)	4.42% (ref.)
rural area	0.70%	1.05% ★	1.51% ★★★
Income per capita:	★★★	★★★	★★★
highest quarter (over 3rd quartile)	5.86% ★★★	5.67% ★★★	9.11% ★★★
medium half (between 1st and 3rd quartile, reference value)	1.96% (ref.)	2.54% (ref.)	4.42% (ref.)
lowest quarter (below 1st quartile)	0.24% ★	0.98% ★	3.49%

Significance of impact of variables: ★★★ $p < 0.001$, ★★ $p < 0.01$, ★ $p < 0.05$.
Expected probabilities assuming other variables hold reference values

among rural residents (over twofold), and relatively slow increase for the largest city dwellers (by one-third). Even quicker than in the case of rural areas was the increase in second home ownership among the residents of small- and medium-sized cities. For them, the rate of second home ownership raised two- to threefold, and, as a result, the residents of cities between 100 and 500 thousand are now almost as probable to have a second home as those who live in the largest cities, while in the 1990s there was a large gap between these groups.

The dependence of second home ownership on the per capita income of the household follows the expectations: the members of the highest earning quarter of the sample are the most likely to have a second home, and they significantly differ in that from the middle half and the lowest quarter. Since 1995, the expected rates of ownership for all groups increased, but the quickest increase happened in the least affluent group (over 14 times), with a moderate increase in the medium half (over twice), and for the richest quarter of the sample the chances to own a second home rose only by half.

The above analysis shows that the factors that affect second home ownership remain stable, but the relative distance between groups, which are the most and least privileged in this regard, is narrowing (even though in absolute percentages it widens at some points). It might be an indicator of decreasing elitism of second home ownership and growing accessibility of this kind of good. However, the results of this analysis may be undermined by its two major drawbacks. First, in the description of second home owners, I am limited to the available secondary data. It would be desirable to look at more precise characteristics of the respondents, such as their age, level of education and profession, but they are unavailable in the results of the survey that are used. Second, the data is cross-sectional in character, so it says who owns second homes at some points in time, while in fact, to learn about their accessibility, one should rather ask who acquires them, how, and in what circumstances. Some of the changes in the structure of the group of second home owners presented above might not be an effect of new people gaining access to second homes, but rather of changes in the characteristics of the same persons, e.g. transition from couple to single family as an effect of a divorce or spouse's death, decrease in household incomes after retirement and permanent move from an urban to suburban location. Part of these reservations will be tackled in the next part of the chapter, in which I will analyse primary data gathered during the field study in the Bory Tucholskie region.

Second home owners in Bory Tucholskie

Bory Tucholskie (Tuchola Pinewoods) is a region located in northern Poland, in the Kujawsko-Pomorskie province, 40–90 km north of the closest large city, Bydgoszcz (c. 360 thousand inhabitants). The name of the region derives from coniferous forest that covers almost half of the area, and is a part of the largest forest complex in Poland. Apart from it, the major recreation resources in the area are water bodies: numerous lakes, rivers and reservoirs. The first second homes were built here in the 1960s, but the most rapid development happened during recent decades. According to the analysis of cartographic sources, aerial photographs and field research, the number of purpose-built second homes in the area grew from c. 400 in the mid-1980s, to c. 950 in the mid-1990s and 2.5 thousand in 2013 (Adamiak 2016). Additionally, there are c. 400 farms converted to second homes in the area.

To trace the changes in the structures of the owners of second homes in the region, I performed extensive field study, including the inventory of second homes, observation, interviews with local stakeholders and analysis of cartographic sources and planning documents, and a survey among the owners of second homes. The survey sample included 255 respondents. It was not random due to the lack of an address list of second home owners. The survey was carried out personally during the summer of 2013. The owners of second homes were asked, among other questions, about the time, motives and circumstances of the acquisition of second homes. They were also asked about the background information of their socio-demographic position.

According to the results of the survey, the current owners of second homes have mostly acquired them on their own: they bought undeveloped plots of land and built houses on them. A secondary market of second homes and transfers of ownership through inheritance started later. Hence, the majority of second home owners are their first owners. The most "experienced" household surveyed possessed their second home since 1966, and the most recent owners acquired their properties in the year of the survey. I divided the respondents into three arbitrarily designed generations, according to the date of acquisition of a second home or a plot on which the second home was later constructed. First generation includes those who acquired their homes before 1990, so under the communist regime. It is the smallest group, with 19% of respondents. The second group owned their homes since the 1990s, so they bought them during the most dynamic period of the systemic transition, and before the highest peak in the number of acquisitions, which happened at the turn of the 1990s and the 2000s. The members of the third group, the most numerous group (44% of the total sample), acquired their second homes after 1999. These three generations of second home owners were compared in terms of their social structures (Table 17.2).

The age of respondents clearly differentiates older and younger generations of second home owners. Half of the first generation are people aged 65 and older, while the two younger generations consist mostly of middle-aged persons (the question was about the age of the respondent who answered the survey). The average size of a household is quite stable over time, though among the older generation of owners both small (1–2 persons) and large (5 persons and more) households prevail, while in the newest generation 3–4 person families are most common. In all three groups, households with children predominate (though in the case of the older generation the persons under 19 may be grandchildren of the initial owners), and in the two younger generations, they form over 80% of all households. On the other hand, most households in the two older generations consist of at least one retiree.

There are no major differences in the structure of the places of permanent residence of second home owners between the generations. In all three of them, about half of the respondents come from the nearest big city Bydgoszcz. A temporal dispersion of places of origin of owners occurred in the 1990s. One visible, though still weak, tendency is the increase in the number of owners who reside outside of Poland. In many cases, they are Poles who had emigrated to Western Europe, and treat the use of a second home as a form of seasonal return migration or seasonal retirement migration.

In all three generations, the new owners of second homes had a higher average level of education than the majority of the population. The share of owners with university education (of at least one household member) was about 80%, and slightly decreased in the last decade. This is unusual considering the fact that the share of people with university education in the country has been increasing: from 6.5% in 1988 to 10.2% in 2002 and 17.0% in 2011 (GUS 2003, 2012). It suggests that the relative importance of higher education for the ownership of second homes was reduced in the period of analysis. The occupation structure changed significantly across the three generations. Until the 1980s, professionals (intelligentsia) were present in every three out of four households owning second homes in Bory Tucholskie, and this proportion fell to 40% after 2000. The categories whose share increased were the entrepreneurs (from 2% to 16%), and various middle-income categories: technical, clerks, machine operators and assemblers.

Table 17.2 Characteristics of three generations of second home owners in Bory Tucholskie

Variable and value	Date of acquisition of second home or plot		
	Before 1990	1990–1999	After 1999
Age of respondent			
18–30	4%	13%	3%
31–50	30%	24%	49%
51–65	20%	48%	44%
over 65	46%	16%	5%
Size of household			
1–2 persons	37%	39%	31%
3–4 persons	20%	25%	45%
5 and more persons	44%	36%	24%
At least one child (up to 18) in the household			
Yes	59%	82%	83%
No	41%	18%	17%
At least one retiree in the household			
Yes	74%	61%	33%
No	26%	39%	67%
Place of residence			
Bydgoszcz	50%	38%	51%
Other city over 100 thousand inhabitants	30%	37%	29%
Other places in Poland	20%	24%	16%
Outside Poland	0%	1%	4%
At least one member of the household has university degree			
Yes	78%	83%	74%
No	22%	17%	26%
Occupation (one household may be counted more than once, so percentages do not add up to 100%)			
Entrepreneurs	2%	13%	16%
Managers	2%	6%	5%
Professionals	73%	50%	40%
Technicians and associate professionals	31%	36%	41%
Clerical support workers	11%	9%	15%
Services and sales workers	9%	3%	8%
Skilled agriculture, forestry and fishery workers	0%	0%	1%
Craft and related trades workers	7%	6%	6%
Plant and machine operators and assemblers	7%	14%	10%
Elementary occupations	0%	3%	0%
Armed forces	0%	3%	1%

Conclusion

Second home ownership has rapidly developed in Poland during recent decades. It can be estimated that the number of second homes has doubled since 1995, reaching more than 600 thousand in 2013. This chapter described the recent transformations in the social composition of the group of second home owners based on two sources of information: the results of nationwide social surveys and field research in the Bory Tucholskie region.

The study has identified changes in the structure of second home owners after 1989. Before that date, the ownership of second homes was limited to families living in large cities (Warsaw in particular), with relatively high earnings (though the difference in incomes was smaller than now, in general), high level of education, and representing occupations either related to the government (nomenklatura) or others requiring higher education (intelligentsia). The major change since the 1990s, besides numerical increase, was the relatively fast increase in second home ownership among all groups that previously had limited access to them. These were households other than families, with low or middle income, entrepreneurs and representatives of lower-middle-class jobs. Perhaps the most visible change was the dispersion of second home ownership in geographical terms, as the residents of smaller cities almost reached the residents of the largest cities in the rates of second home ownership. It can thus be claimed that second homes became more egalitarian, accessible for wider groups of the members of the middle class.

Nonetheless, the increase in the general number of second homes does not provide a full picture of the changes in the social structure of second home owners. There is also a growing diversity within this group, manifested by the increasing diversity in the locations and technical forms of second homes. Before the 1990s, they were typically small, wooden and not winterised summer houses, located on small plots of land and similar to each other. Nowadays, there is also a growing stock of large houses not different from the year-round residential houses, often located on large plots of land in attractive natural areas.

A new phenomenon for Poland is the internationalisation of second home ownership. It is not yet a significant issue in numerical terms, yet the study region is not among the most attractive ones from the point of view of foreign tourists. The internationalisation in the study area is usually a form of return migration, often in late life, of Poles who had emigrated to other countries and want to come back to Poland without leaving their jobs, new families or pension eligibility in Western European countries. This phenomenon is likely to increase, considering the high number of Poles who live in foreign countries and still maintain contact with Poland.

The Polish case presented in this chapter cannot be treated as representative for all countries, or even for Central and Eastern Europe. Besides the transformation of the political and economic system, the Polish situation is specific because of relatively little access to second homes before the 1990s, and the agrarian structure with the domination of small private farms, which created a supply of cheap land plots after the deregulation of the property market in the 1990s. Still, there are some commonalities between Poland and other countries. It is in general more and more common to have some kind of a second home. There are also processes occurring that increasingly differentiate the group of second home owners in social terms, which is manifested in the diverging forms and locations of second homes. It is needed then to investigate the internal variety of the group of second home owners, rather than treat them as a socially homogenous group.

References

Adamiak, C. (2014) Rozwój zjawiska drugich domów w Polsce na przykładzie Borów Tucholskich. PhD. Nicolaus Copernicus University, Toruń, Poland.

Adamiak, C. (2016) 'Cottage sprawl: Spatial development of second homes in Bory Tucholskie, Poland', *Landscape and Urban Planning*, 147: 96–106.

Adamiak, C., Vepsäläinen, M., Strandell, A., Hiltunen, M. J., Pitkänen, K., Hall, C. M., Rinne, J., Paloniemi, R. and Åkerlund, U. (2015) *Second Home Tourism in Finland: Perceptions of Citizens and Municipalities on the State and Development of Second Home Tourism*. Helsinki, Finland: Finnish Environment Institute.

Central Statistical Office of Poland (GUS) (2003) *Ludność, stan i struktura demograficzno-społeczna*, Warsaw: GUS. [online] Available at: http://stat.gov.pl/cps/rde/xbcr/gus/ludnosc_stan_i_struktura_demograficzno_spoleczna.pdf

Central Statistical Office of Poland (GUS) (2012) *Raport z wyników – Narodowy Spis Powszechny Ludności i Mieszkań 2011*, Warsaw: GUS. [online] Available at: http://stat.gov.pl/cps/rde/xbcr/gus/lud_raport_z_wynikow_NSP2011.pdf

Central Statistical Office of Poland (GUS) (2016) *Ludność. Stan i struktura ludności oraz ruch naturalny w przekroju terytorialnym. Stan w dniu 31 grudnia 2015 roku*, Warsaw, GUS. [online] Available at: http://stat.gov.pl/obszary-tematyczne/ludnosc/ludnosc/ludnosc-stan-i-struktura-ludnosci-oraz-ruch-naturalny-w-przekroju-terytorialnym-stan-w-dniu-31-grudnia-2015-roku,6,19.html

Clout, H. D. (1977) 'Résidences secondaires in France'. In J. T. Coppock (ed.) *Second Homes: Curse or Blessing?* Oxford: Pergamon, 47–62.

Czapiński, J. (1998) *Jakość życia Polaków w czasie zmiany społecznej 1991–1997. Raport końcowy z realizacji projektu badawczego: Związek między obiektywnymi i subiektywnymi wskaźnikami jakości życia w okresie transformacji systemowej*. Warsaw: Uniwersytet Warszawski.

Czapiński, J. and Panek, T. (2015) *Diagnoza Społeczna 2015. Warunki i jakość życia Polaków – raport*. Warsaw: Rada Monitoringu Społecznego.

Czarnecki, A. and Frenkel, I. (2015) 'Counting the "invisible": Second homes in Polish statistical data collections', *Journal of Policy Research in Tourism, Leisure and Events*, 7 (1): 15–31.

Di, Z. X., McArdle, N. and Masnick, G. S. (2001) *Second Homes: What, How Many, Where and Who*. Joint Center for Housing Studies, Harvard University. [online] Available at: http://www.jchs.harvard.edu/publications/homeownership/di_n01-2.pdf

Dijst, M., Lanzendorf, M., Barendregt, A. and Smit, L. (2005) 'Second homes in Germany and the Netherlands: Ownership and travel impact explained', *Tijdschrift Voor Economische En Sociale Geografie*, 96 (2): 139–152.

Domański, H. (2015) *Czy są w Polsce klasy społeczne?* Warsaw: Wydawnictwo Krytyki Politycznej.

Godbey, G. and Bevins, M. I. (1987) 'The life cycle of second home ownership: A case study', *Journal of Travel Research*, 25 (3): 18–22.

Halseth, G. (2004) 'The "cottage" privilege: Increasingly elite landscapes of second homes in Canada'. In C. M. Hall and D. K. Müller (eds) *Tourism, Mobility and Second Homes: Between Elite Landscape and Common Ground*. Clevedon, UK: Channel View, 35–54.

Jaakson, R. (1986) 'Second-home domestic tourism', *Annals of Tourism Research*, 13 (3): 367–391.

Kowalczyk, A. (1994) *Geograficzno-społeczne problemy zjawiska "drugich domów"*. Warsaw: WGiSR UW.

Kremarik, F. (2002) 'A little place in the country: A profile of Canadians who own vacation property', *Canadian Social Trends*, 11 (8): 12–14. [online] Available at: http://www.statcan.gc.ca/access_acces/archive.action?loc=/pub/11-008-x/2002001/article/6196-eng.pdf

Lovell, S. (2003) *Summerfolk: A History of the Dacha, 1710-2000*. Ithaca: Cornell University Press.

McHugh, K. E., Hogan, T. D. and Happel, S. K. (1995) 'Multiple residence and cyclical migration: A life course perspective', *Professional Geographer*, 47 (3): 251–267.

Módenes Cabrerizo, J. A., López Colás, J. and Robertson, G. (2007) 'Second homes in Spain: Socio-demographic and geographical profiles', *Population (English Edition)*, 62 (1): 157–171.

Müller, D. K. (2007) 'Second homes in the Nordic countries: Between common heritage and exclusive commodity', *Scandinavian Journal of Hospitality and Tourism*, 7 (3): 193–201.

Norris, M. and Winston, N. (2010) 'Second-home owners: Escaping, investing or retiring?' *Tourism Geographies*, 12 (4): 546–567.

Oxley, M., Brown, T., Lishman, R. and Turkington, R. (2008) *Rapid Evidence Assessment of the Research Literature on the Purchase and Use of Second Homes*. Fareham, UK: National Housing and Planning Advice Unit.

Paris, C. (2010) *Affluence, Mobility and Second Homes Ownership*. London: Routledge.

Pitkänen, K. and Vepsäläinen, M. (2008) 'Foreseeing the future of second home tourism. The case of Finnish media and policy discourse', *Scandinavian Journal of Hospitality and Tourism*, 8 (1): 1–24.

Podemski, K. (2005) *Socjologia podróży*. Poznań, Poland: UAM.

Słomczyński, K. M., Białecki, I., Domański, H., Janicka, K., Mach, B. W., Sawiński, Z., Sikorska, J. and Zaborowski, W. (1988) Struktura społeczna w Polsce. POLPAN 1988: Komputerowy zbiór danych, Warsaw: IFiS PAN.

Struyk, R. J. and Angelici, K. (1996) 'The Russian dacha phenomenon', *Housing Studies*, 11 (1): 233–250.

Sýkora, L. and Stanilov, K. (2014) 'The challenge of postsocialist suburbanization'. In K. Stanilov and L. Sýkora (eds) *Confronting Suburbanization. Urban Decentralization in Postsocialist Central and Eastern Europe*. Oxford: Wiley–Blackwell, 1–32.

Vágner, J. (2001) 'Vývoj druhého bydlení v Česku'. In I. Bičík (ed.) *Druhé bydlení v Česku*. Prague: Univerzita Karlova, 42–54.

Węcławowicz, G. (2007) *Geografia społeczna miast, Uwarunkowania społeczno-przestrzenne*. Warsaw: PWN.

PART IV

Community, culture and identities

18

COMMUNITY, CULTURE
AND IDENTITIES

Dieter K. Müller and C. Michael Hall

Introduction

Research has often portrayed second homes as part of cultural heritage with strong relations to identity, work and sometimes community cohesion (Müller 2010). Although awareness of the cultural dimensions of second homes has existed for many years, the cultural turn in the social sciences has meant that issues related to second homes as a form of symbolic consumption have become a popular research topic (Nelson 2002; Vepsäläinen & Pitkänen 2010; Pitkänen 2008, 2011; Schier et al. 2015), while economic approaches (for example) highlighting the impact on business and local households, have been relatively rare (Müller 2011; Hall 2014).

Gallent et al. (2005) divide second home tourism impacts into social, economic and environmental dimensions. In this chapter, however, mainly the social and cultural dimensions of second home ownership in relation to host communities are reviewed. Nevertheless, some notes should be made on economic impacts given their significance for communities and the role that second homes play within them. Gallent et al. (2005) note a growing competition for housing and speculation as well as house price inflation as a result of second home development. Such concerns have also been expressed in the Australian context (Paris 2010). Housing acquisition, maintenance and improvements influence the local economy as do second home owners' overall consumption. Depending on the tax system, local councils can sometimes benefit from increased property tax returns (Frost & Lawrence 2006; Mottiar 2006; Hoogendoorn & Visser 2010a, 2010b, 2011; Hall 2015). Deller et al. (1997) show, however, that impacts on households should not be overestimated. Similarly, Norris and Winston (2009) warn of a rural policy-led development strategy resulting in an overdevelopment of rural housing with long-term consequences for the rural economy and environment. Second homes also alter the rural economy and increasingly contribute to a restructuring towards leisure, tourism and services, replacing or complementing traditional sectors like agriculture (Nelson 2002; Hoogendoorn & Visser 2010a, 2010b).

Second homes in communities

During the 1970s, second homes were often presented as a negative contribution to communities. Rogers (1977) depicted the arrival of second home owners in the countryside as an

215

"invasion", and Jordan (1980) saw second home owners in the countryside as an annoyance, producing among other things "fake" cultures. In contrast, Wolfe (1952) and Halseth (1998) were more nuanced and noted that second home owners often had little to do with permanent local communities, and instead created a "community inside communities".

Nevertheless, the potential displacement of permanent populations as a result of second home ownership has been prominent in public debate and scientific literature alike. Several earlier studies state that rural populations are displaced by second home owners (Gallent et al. 2005). In Swedish studies, however, no support for this claim could be found and the emergence of second home tourism is instead primarily explained as a result of rural decline (Müller 2004; Marjavaara 2007, 2009). In the UK, poor access to rural housing as a result of poor planning and housing policy has been identified as a major reason for conflict (Paris 2010). In research on residential tourism, it has also been argued that conflict is caused by xenophobia and social envy rather than about actual displacement (Barke & France 1988; Lipkina & Hall 2014; Honkanen et al. 2016).

However, narratives of community impact vary as do expectations towards second home owners. The latter cannot be depicted everywhere as consumers of only rural areas. In the Nordic countries, it is sometimes noted that second home owners are previous villagers that left the countryside for work, lifestyle or education (Müller 2010; Adamiak et al. 2015). Here the relation to local community sometimes remains unproblematic and friendly. It has been shown, too, that second home owners engage in rural affairs as well as social associations and clubs (Kelly & Hosking 2008; Nordin & Marjavaara 2012). They function as a temporary competence asset and assist the local population in various matters (Robertsson & Marjavaara 2015; Nordbø 2014). In this context, Huijbens (2012) makes an interesting observation, distinguishing between those with previous ties to the second home destination who may be less engaged in the development of the area, and newcomers who are there to pursue an active lifestyle (see also Fountain & Hall 2002). The latter are more active in matters of local development too, and contribute to sustaining rural cultural life as well.

Farstad and Rye (2013) also reject the social polarisation of permanent dwellers and second home owners in their work on second homes in Norway. They argue that second home owners share a "not in my backyard" approach to development with the majority of permanent residents. Therefore, second home owners create more "backyards" that have to be defended against interests promoting undesired development. Rural residents' attitudes concerning second home tourism vary however. Where second home owners seemingly contribute to positive development, permanent residents are inclined to grant access to social life and recreational assets (Farstad 2011). A problem in this context is that administrative structures hinder second home owners from being recognised as citizens of rural destination municipalities (Müller & Hall 2003; Farstad 2011; Rinne et al. 2014; Hall 2015; Kietäväinen et al. 2016). This is despite second home owners sometimes hardly differing from permanent residents, not least regarding how they identify with the region and their sense of place attachment (Nordin & Marjavaara 2012; Vágner & Fialová 2012), as well as sometimes exceeding the number of permanent residents (Kietäväinen et al. 2016).

Nevertheless, the arrival of second home owners in a rural setting may have impacts on the social fabric. Hay (2017) reports on the transformation of rural towns in South Africa. Here the more liberal sexual orientation of the second home owner group stands in strong contrast to the traditional and conservative rural community. Kaltenborn et al. (2009) also showed that second home owners tended to be more positive towards environmental protection and against extractive industries and development, differentiating them from the local population (Fountain & Hall 2002; Kondo et al. 2012).

A lot of second home development happens, however, outside traditional communities in resorts and more or less planned second home settlements. Here, second home areas are highly segregated (Müller 2002, 2005). This can also apply in the Canadian case, where recent second home development often occurs in mountain resorts (Nepal & Jamal 2011). The result of such a resort-led development strategy is gentrified communities with only loose relations to rural towns. Nevertheless, the income generated by second home development is usually welcomed by communities. In the case of residential tourism in Spain, Huete et al. (2008) show that community stakeholders have a mostly positive outlook on second home development, especially given a general increase in wealth associated with recent change.

Motivations and identities

An important topic in the second home literature is the question of why people own second homes. Jaakson (1986) offered a groundbreaking account of motives for second home ownership, allocating second home motivation not least to the microcosm of the family. Accordingly, back-to-nature, identity, surety, continuity, creative work, elitism and conservative aspirations were among the reasons listed. More recent research, including international second home ownership, has added motives such as investment and speculation (Paris 2010) and safety (Hannonen et al. 2015).

McIntyre et al. (2006a) provide another important research contribution to this field by addressing and reviewing the meaning of second home ownership in the context of multiple dwelling. They address Urry's (2000) mobility paradigm, suggesting 'a need to reset the pendulum swing initiated by Urry (2000) and others which privileges "movement" over "pause" or "dwelling"' (McIntyre et al. 2006b: 322). Instead, it is argued that people still relate to places, though multiple place attachments and relationships are common. Similarly, Gallent (2007) argues that evidence for dwelling hierarchies are lacking but at the same time people may be at home in several places. This is also confirmed in studies of place attachment that indicate limited differences between "primary" and "secondary" dwellers (Kaltenborn 1997a, 1997b; Stedman 2006). Hence, Kaltenborn (1998) suggests addressing second homes as "alternate homes".

Pitkänen (2008) provides another perspective arguing that the physical, experiential and cultural dimensions of idealised second home landscapes are closely intertwined, and that the second home landscape is produced through the second home owners' everyday performances. Life at second homes is often inspired by stereotypical images of rural life, and its surroundings are often used for traditional leisure activities (Vepsäläinen & Pitkänen 2010). However, environmental preferences are not always manifested in action (Pitkänen et al. 2011). Similar results are reported from Norway, where recent urbanisation and renewed representations of the rural as idyllic entail important preconditions for recreational consumption of the countryside (Rye & Gunnerud Berg 2011).

Besides these cultural explanations for second home use, there are also authors that highlight the role of increased affluence and consumption lifestyles in the growing interest in second home ownership (Norris & Winston 2010; Paris 2010; Walters 2014). This can be seen in combination with urbanisation, where rural second homes offer a compensation for dense living conditions in urban areas (Módenes & López-Colás 2007; Stradell & Hall 2015a, 2015b). However, Hoogendoorn (2011) argues that affluence is not a precondition for such a development. Instead, in the case of South Africa, poor urban workers often retain a link to their rural place of origin. Even in an international context, second homes can manifest the existence of the homeward links of a diaspora (Timothy 2002; Duval 2004).

Future second home cultures

The future of second homes is seldom discussed. However, Pitkänen and Vepsäläinen (2008) show that the media depict a future in which multiple dwelling is frequent, while the second home remains an important part of contemporary media presentations of desirable homes and lifestyles, in some cases reinforcing the role of the second home in national and regional identities (Collins & Kearns 2008; Rudman et al. 2009; Lagerqvist 2014; Walters 2014; Walters & Carr 2015). A further internationalisation of the second home landscape and regional differentiations in development can be expected (Paris 2010). However, there are no signs that second home tourism will go out of fashion. Most second home owners are happy with their second home lives (Lundmark & Marjavaara 2013). Instead, even though administration and governance often lag behind (Hall 2015), it seems that second homes are important nodes in the mobile lives of many households all over the world (Coles & Hall 2006; Coles et al. 2006). This situation challenges ideas of community as being a container for a place-based discrete population. Increasing multiple dwelling implies that communities can be seen as nodes and anchors for bundles of individuals' time-space trajectories. As a result, second home communities and the second home itself may be even more important to individuals and families than the so-called primary home. Thus, as Marjavaara (2012) shows, second homes are often the destination for many individuals' final journeys.

References

Adamiak, C., Vepsäläinen, M., Strandell, A., Hiltunen, M. J., Pitkänen, K., Hall, C. M., Rinne, J., Hannonen, O., Paloniemi, R. and Åkerlund, U. (2015) *Second Home Tourism in Finland: Perceptions of Citizens and Municipalities on the State and Development of Second Home Tourism*. Reports of the Finnish Environment Institute 22, Helsinki: SYKE.

Barke, M. and France, L. A. (1988) 'Second homes in the Balearic Islands', *Geography*, 73 (2): 143–145.

Coles, T. and Hall, C. M. (2006) 'The geography of tourism is dead. Long live geographies of tourism and mobility', *Current Issues in Tourism*, 9 (4–5): 289–292.

Coles, T., Hall, C. M. and Duval, D. T. (2006) 'Tourism and post-disciplinary enquiry', *Current Issues in Tourism*, 9 (4–5): 293–319.

Collins, D. and Kearns, R. (2008) 'Uninterrupted views: Real-estate advertising and changing perspectives on coastal property in New Zealand', *Environment and Planning A*, 40 (12): 2914–2932.

Deller, S. C., Marcouiller, D. W. and Green, G. P. (1997) 'Recreational housing and local government finance', *Annals of Tourism Research*, 24 (3): 687–705.

Duval, D. T. (2004) 'Mobile migrants: Travel to second homes'. In C. M. Hall and D. K. Müller (eds) *Tourism, Mobility and Second Homes: Between Elite Landscape and Common Ground*. Clevedon, UK: Channel View, 87–96.

Farstad, M. (2011) 'Rural residents' opinions about second home owners' pursuit of own interests in the host community', *Norsk Geografisk Tidsskrift*, 65 (3): 165–174.

Farstad, M. and Rye, J. F. (2013) 'Second home owners, locals and their perspectives on rural development', *Journal of Rural Studies*, 30 (1): 41–51.

Fountain, J. and Hall, C. M. (2002) 'The impact of lifestyle migration on rural communities: A case study of Akaroa, New Zealand'. In C. M. Hall and A. M. Williams (eds) *Tourism and Migration: New Relationships between Production and Consumption*. Dordrecht, the Netherlands: Kluwer, 153–168.

Frost, W. and Lawrence, M. (2006) 'Taxes and host–tourist tensions in Australian coastal resorts', *Current Issues in Tourism*, 9 (2): 152–156.

Gallent, N. (2007) 'Second homes, community and a hierarchy of dwelling', *Area*, 39 (1): 97–106.

Gallent, N., Mace, A. and Tewdwr-Jones, M. (2005) *Second Homes: European Perspectives and UK Policies*. Avebury, UK: Ashgate.

Hall, C. M. (2014) 'Second home tourism: An international review', *Tourism Review International*, 18 (3): 115–135.

Hall, C. M. (2015) 'Second homes: Planning, policy and governance', *Journal of Policy Research in Tourism, Leisure & Events*, 7 (1): 1–14.

Halseth, G. (1998) *Cottage Country in Transition: A Social Geography of Change and Contention in the Rural-Recreational Countryside.* Montreal: McGill-Queen's Press-MQUP.

Hannonen, O., Tuulentie, S. and Pitkänen, K. (2015) 'Borders and second home tourism: Norwegian and Russian second home owners in Finnish border areas', *Journal of Borderlands Studies*, 30 (1): 53–67.

Hay, A. (2017) 'Second home tourism: Social and economic change in developing countries like South Africa'. In D. K. Müller and M. Więckowski (eds) *Tourism in Transitions: Recovering Decline, Managing Change.* Cham, Switzerland: Springer, 97–116.

Honkanen, A., Pitkänen, K. and Hall, C. M. (2016) 'A local perspective on cross-border tourism: Russian second home ownership in Eastern Finland', *International Journal of Tourism Research*, 18 (2): 149–158.

Hoogendoorn, G. (2011) 'Low-income earners as second home tourists in South Africa?', *Tourism Review International*, 15 (1–2): 37–50.

Hoogendoorn, G. and Visser, G. (2010a) 'The economic impact of second home development in small-town South Africa', *Tourism Recreation Research*, 35 (1): 55–66.

Hoogendoorn, G. and Visser, G. (2010b) 'The role of second homes in local economic development in five small South African towns', *Development Southern Africa*, 27 (4): 547–562.

Hoogendoorn, G. and Visser, G. (2011) 'Economic development through second home development: Evidence from South Africa', *Tijdschrift voor economische en sociale geografie*, 102 (3): 275–289.

Huete, R., Mantecón, A. and Mazón, T. (2008) 'Analysing the social perception of residential tourism development'. In C. Costa and P. Cravo (eds) *Advances in Tourism Research.* Aveiro, Portugal: IASK, 153–161.

Huijbens, E. H. (2012) 'Sustaining a village's social fabric?', *Sociologia Ruralis*, 52 (3): 332–352.

Jaakson, R. (1986) 'Second-home domestic tourism', *Annals of Tourism Research*, 13 (3): 367–391.

Jordan, J. W. (1980) 'The summer people and the natives: Some effects of tourism in a Vermont vacation village', *Annals of Tourism Research*, 7 (1): 34–55.

Kaltenborn, B. P. (1997a) 'Nature of place attachment: A study among recreation homeowners in Southern Norway', *Leisure Sciences*, 19 (3): 175–189.

Kaltenborn, B. P. (1997b) 'Recreation homes in natural settings: Factors affecting place attachment', *Norsk Geografisk Tidsskrift*, 51 (4): 187–198.

Kaltenborn, B. P. (1998) 'The alternate home-motives of recreation home use', *Norsk Geografisk Tidsskrift*, 52 (3): 121–134.

Kaltenborn, B. P., Andersen, O. and Nellemann, C. (2009) 'Amenity development in the Norwegian mountains: Effects of second home owner environmental attitudes on preferences for alternative development options', *Landscape and Urban Planning*, 91 (4): 195–201.

Kelly, G. and Hosking, K. (2008) 'Nonpermanent residents, place attachment, and "sea change" communities', *Environment and Behavior*, 40 (4): 575–594.

Kietäväinen, A. T., Rinne, J., Paloniemi, R. and Tuulentie, S. (2016) 'Participation of second home owners and permanent residents in local decision making: The case of a rural village in Finland', *Fennia-International Journal of Geography*, 194 (2): 152–167.

Kondo, M. C., Rivera, R. and Rullman, S. (2012) 'Protecting the idyll but not the environment: Second homes, amenity migration and rural exclusion in Washington State', *Landscape and Urban Planning*, 106 (2): 174–182.

Lagerqvist, M. (2014) 'The importance of an old rural cottage: Media representation and the construction of a national idyll in post-war Sweden', *Journal of Rural Studies*, 36: 33–41.

Lipkina, O. and Hall, C. M. (2014) 'Russian second home owners in Eastern Finland: Involvement in the local community'. In M. Janoschka and H. Haas (eds) *Contested Spatialities of Lifestyle Migration.* London: Routledge, 158–173.

Lundmark, L. and Marjavaara, R. (2013) 'Second home ownership: A blessing for all?', *Scandinavian Journal of Hospitality and Tourism*, 13 (4): 281–298.

McIntyre, N., Williams, D. and McHugh, K. (eds) (2006a) *Multiple Dwelling and Tourism: Negotiating Place, Home and Identity.* Wallingford, UK: CABI.

McIntyre, N., Williams, D. and McHugh, K. (2006b) 'Multiple dwelling: Prospect and retrospect'. In N. McIntyre, D. Williams and K. McHugh (eds) *Multiple Dwelling and Tourism: Negotiating Place, Home and Identity.* Wallingford, UK: CABI, 313–322.

Marjavaara, R. (2007) 'The displacement myth: Second home tourism in the Stockholm Archipelago', *Tourism Geographies*, 9 (3): 296–317.

Marjavaara, R. (2009) 'An inquiry into second-home-induced displacement', *Tourism and Hospitality Planning & Development*, 6 (3): 207–219.

Marjavaara, R. (2012) 'The final trip: Post-mortal mobility in Sweden', *Mortality*, 17 (3): 256–275.

Módenes, J. A. and López-Colás, J. (2007) 'Second homes and compact cities in Spain: Two elements of the same system?', *Tijdschrift voor economische en sociale geografie*, 98 (3): 325–335.

Mottiar, Z. (2006) 'Holiday home owners, a route to sustainable tourism development? An economic analysis of tourist expenditure data', *Journal of Sustainable Tourism*, 14 (6): 582–599.

Müller D. (2010) 'Second homes in Sweden: Between common heritage and exclusive commodity'. In B. Hermelin and U. Jansson (eds) *Placing Human Geography: Sweden through Time and Space*. Stockholm: SSAG, 185–207.

Müller, D. K. (2002) 'Second home ownership and sustainable development in northern Sweden', *Tourism and Hospitality Research*, 3 (4): 345–355.

Müller, D. K. (2004) 'Second homes in Sweden: Patterns and issues'. In C. M. Hall and D. K. Müller (eds) *Tourism, Mobility and Second Homes: Between Elite Landscape and Common Ground*. Clevedon, UK: Channel View, 244–258.

Müller, D. K. (2005) 'Second home tourism in the Swedish mountain range'. In C. M. Hall and S. Boyd (eds) *Nature-Based Tourism in Peripheral Areas: Development or Disaster?* Clevedon, UK: Channel View, 133–148.

Müller, D. K. (2011) 'Second homes in rural areas: Reflections on a troubled history', *Norsk Geografisk Tidsskrift – Norwegian Journal of Geography*, 65 (3): 137–143.

Müller, D. K. and Hall, C. M. (2003) 'Second homes and regional population distribution: On administrative practices and failures in Sweden', *Espace, populations, sociétés*, 21 (2): 251–261.

Nelson, P. B. (2002) 'Perceptions of restructuring in the rural west: Insights from the "cultural turn"', *Society & Natural Resources*, 15 (10): 903–921.

Nepal, S. K. and Jamal, T. B. (2011) 'Resort-induced changes in small mountain communities in British Columbia, Canada', *Mountain Research and Development*, 31 (2): 89–101.

Nordbø, I. (2014) 'Beyond the transfer of capital? Second-home owners as competence brokers for rural entrepreneurship and innovation', *European Planning Studies*, 22 (8): 1641–1658.

Nordin, U. and Marjavaara, R. (2012) 'The local non-locals: Second home owners associational engagement in Sweden', *Tourism*, 60 (3): 293–305.

Norris, M. and Winston, N. (2009) 'Rising second home numbers in rural Ireland: Distribution, drivers and implications', *European Planning Studies*, 17 (9): 1303–1322.

Norris, M. and Winston, N. (2010) 'Second-home owners: Escaping, investing or retiring?', *Tourism Geographies*, 12 (4): 546–567.

Paris, C. (2010) *Affluence, Mobility and Second Home Ownership*. London: Routledge.

Pitkänen, K. (2008) 'Second-home landscape: The meaning(s) of landscape for second-home tourism in Finnish Lakeland', *Tourism Geographies*, 10 (2): 169–192.

Pitkänen, K. (2011) 'Contested cottage landscapes: Host perspective to the increase of foreign second home ownership in Finland 1990-2008', *Fennia*, 189 (1): 43–59.

Pitkänen, K., Puhakka, R. and Sawatzky, M. (2011) 'The role of nature in the place meanings and practices of cottage owners in northern environments', *Norsk Geografisk Tidsskrift*, 65 (3): 175–187.

Rinne, J., Kietäväinen, A., Tuulentie, S. and Paloniemi, R. (2014) 'Governing second homes: A study of policy coherence of four policy areas in Finland', *Tourism Review International*, 18 (3): 223–236.

Robertsson, L. and Marjavaara, R. (2015) 'The seasonal buzz: Knowledge transfer in a temporary setting', *Tourism Planning & Development*, 12 (3): 251–265.

Rogers, A. W. (1977) 'Second homes in England and Wales: A spatial view'. In J. T. Coppock (ed.) *Second Homes: Curse or Blessing?* Oxford: Pergamon, 85–102.

Rudman, D. L., Huot, S. and Dennhardt, S. (2009) 'Shaping ideal places for retirement: Occupational possibilities within contemporary media', *Journal of Occupational Science*, 16 (1): 18–24.

Rye, J. F. and Gunnerud Berg, N. (2011) 'The second home phenomenon and Norwegian rurality', *Norsk Geografisk Tidsskrift*, 65 (3): 126–136.

Schier, M., Hilti, N., Schad, H., Tippel, C., Dittrich-Wesbuer, A. and Monz, A. (2015) 'Residential multi-locality studies: The added value for research on families and second homes', *Tijdschrift voor economische en sociale geografie*, 106 (4): 439–452.

Stedman, R. C. (2006) 'Understanding place attachment among second home owners', *American Behavioral Scientist*, 50 (2): 187–205.

Strandell, A. and Hall, C. M. (2015a) 'Impact of the residential environment on second home use in Finland – Testing the compensation hypothesis'. *Landscape and Urban Planning*, 133: 12–33.

Strandell, A. and Hall, C. M. (2015b) 'Corrigendum to "Impact of the residential environment on second home use in Finland – Testing the compensation hypothesis" [Landsc. Urban Plan. 133 (2015) 12–23]', *Landscape and Urban Planning*, 137: 165–167.

Timothy, D. (2002) 'Tourism and the growth of urban ethnic islands'. In C. M. Hall and A. M. Williams (eds) *Tourism and Migration: New Relationships between Production and Consumption*. Dordrecht, the Netherlands: Kluwer, 135–151.

Urry, J. (2000) *Sociology beyond Societies: Mobilities for the Twenty-First Century*. London: Routledge.

Vágner, J. and Fialová, D. (2012) 'Impacts of second home tourism on shaping regional identity in the regions with significant recreational function', *Tourism & Management Studies*, 1: 285–294.

Vepsäläinen, M. and Pitkänen, K. (2010) 'Second home countryside: Representations of the rural in Finnish popular discourses', *Journal of Rural Studies*, 26 (2): 194–204.

Walters, T. (2014) 'The luxury of leisure and pleasure at the New Zealand second home', *Annals of Leisure Research*, 17 (1): 97–112.

Walters, T. and Carr, N. (2015) 'Second homes as sites for the consumption of luxury', *Tourism and Hospitality Research*, 15 (2): 130–141.

Wolfe, R. I. (1952) 'Wasaga Beach: The divorce from the geographic environment', *The Canadian Geographer*, 1 (2): 57–66.

19

SECOND HOMES, THEIR USERS AND RELATIONS TO THE RURAL SPACE AND THE RESIDENT COMMUNITIES IN CZECHIA

Dana Fialová, Jiří Vágner and Tereza Kůsová

Introduction: Theoretical background

Research on relations between second home users and other actors in rural areas follows the concept of community development suggested by Giddens (1991) and Wellman (1996), where the local community is perceived as a potential collective agent. The development of communication and cooperation inside local communities has been studied, for instance, by Gans (1968), Wellman (2001) and Day (2006), who described potential conflicts between a traditional rural local community and incomers from cities bringing features of an urban lifestyle. Relations between residents and tourists can be also influenced by their relations to the territory used. As far as the local community structure is concerned, crucial actors are traditionally defined as the residents, the local authorities, entrepreneurs and civic associations. Various actors have different visions for the use of an area, its function and future development. They also perceive diverse territorial identities which also differ in their formation process.

Reconceptualisations of territorial identities were introduced to contemporary geographical discourse in the 1980s (e.g. Knight 1982; Paasi 1986, 2009; Giddens 1991; Raagmaa 2002; Fukuyama 2006) as well as in Czech scientific literature (Vencálek 1998; Chromý 2003; Zich 2003; Chromý et al. 2009; Semian 2012). The territorial identity can be conceptualised as two complementary parts (Paasi 1986, 2009): 1) the territorial consciousness of inhabitants, their sense of belonging to a territory and their perception of it, and 2) territorial images formulated and reproduced by various agents. Territorial identity is thus continuously reproduced through socio-spatial, politico-economic and cultural changes. In the contemporary discourse, territorial identities are often related to the territorial development of various areas (Antonsich 2010), sometimes accenting tourist potential for development (Kneafsey 2000; Light 2001). Territorial identities in development strategies are often seen as narratives reinterpreted for different purposes by different actors in regional development (Frisvoll & Rye 2009). Nevertheless, the importance of the reshaping of territorial identity by different actors (residents versus second home owners and users, versus organised and individual tourists, versus municipality representatives) has not been studied sufficiently.

The relations of people to a territory are a natural component of life. The areas with changing environmental, socio-economic and socio-cultural conditions and those with specific historical development play different roles in the processes shaping peoples' territorial identity. The different spatial relations are mostly suggested for two groups of identity creators: the residents and the second home users, which reflects the finding that second home users become an important part of local communities (Hall & Müller 2004; Müller 2011).

In relation to the cottage, locality and community are created over a long time and passed on through generations, and the level of attachment by second home owners is often very high (Kaltenborn 1997; Clendenning & Field 2006; Stedman 2006; Kelly & Hosking 2008; Matarrita-Cascante et al. 2010; Fialová & Vágner 2014). According to Stedman (2006), the locals are more attached to the community, and the attachment of second home owners is fostered through meanings of environmental quality and escape from everyday cares. Although some researchers (Halseth 1993, 2004; Halseth & Rosenberg 1995; Green et al. 1996; Marcouiller et al. 1996; Aronsson 2004) stress the social difference and isolation of second home owners from the locals, more recent research has confirmed a relatively high frequency and quality of contacts (Clendenning & Field 2006; Nordin & Marjavaara 2012; Pitkänen et al. 2014; Fialová & Vágner 2014; Robertsson & Marjavaara 2015). Thus, the time spent in the second home can be richer in terms of social life than time spent in the area of their permanent home (Jarlöv 1999). The theoretical framework for this chapter comes from Fialová and Vágner (2014).

Recent research on territorial identity in rural areas of Czechia (Chromý et al. 2009; Chromý & Skála 2010; Chromý et al. 2010) has focused on the opinions of members of local authorities and on the residents. However, second home users have been rather neglected despite their being significant or even dominant agents. This also required the acquisition of primary data for the survey, described in the next section.

This research focuses specifically on community development in the municipalities with a significant share of the second home population. The main aim, with the use of empirical data, is to demonstrate and discuss linkages between second home users and residents as crucial agents in the rural development of specific recreational areas. First, quantitative data from the Census, the Cadastre Office and a survey are used to introduce the significance of second homes in the settlement system and rural area all over Czechia, and also to explain the selection of model areas for the next case studies. Second, the importance of second home users in shaping territorial identity is observed. Finally, the social ties are examined through the use of different methods in the case studies.

The Czech countryside has been transforming itself into a multifunctional environment in which the recreational function, significantly represented by second homes, prevails in many localities and even regions (Frantál & Martinát 2013). As a result, several research questions were formulated: Whether in general and how second home users influence the rural area, how they perceive it, whether and how they participate in the creation of the social capital, whether they identify themselves with the place they use and how they shape its territorial identity.

Methods

The first research stage proceeded from the quantitative statistical data on the population, second homes and residential dwellings provided by the State Administration of Land Surveying and Cadastre (ČÚZK) and the Czech Statistical Office (Census). The absolute data was related to the area, population and dwellings (see Figure 19.1).

For a detailed analysis of phenomena and activities associated with second homes, results of a survey conducted by the CVVM Agency (Sociological Institute of Academy of Sciences,

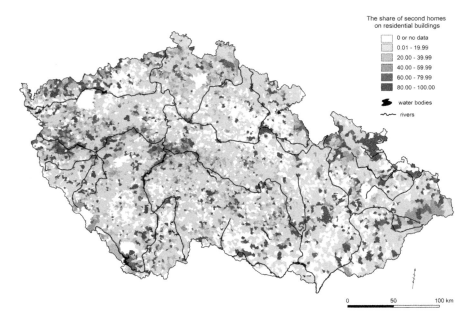

Figure 19.1   The share of second homes on residential buildings.

Source: Vágner and Fialová (based on 2005 data from Czech Office for Surveying, Mapping and Cadastre 2005).

Czech Republic) were used. The questionnaire survey was prepared by the authors. A total of 1,013 respondents over 18 were surveyed. A quota survey was used with respect to geographical characteristics all over Czechia as well as the respondents' structure of demographic and socio-economic characteristics.

Subsequently, two sorts of case studies (regional identity and social ties surveys) were conducted. This was followed by qualitative field research, predominantly in the form of questionnaire surveys and in-depth interviews with the agents.

For the purpose of a regional identity study, eight case-study regions were selected based on the share of second homes in a number of residential dwellings. Second homes in Czechia are classified as a) cabins and recreational homes – buildings built primarily for recreational purposes; or b) cottages – primarily built for another (mostly residential) function (Fialová & Vágner 2005a). Long-term unoccupied flats used for recreational purposes were taken into account too.

During the selection of case-study regions, the geographic location was also considered. Case-study regions represent an area with sparse settlement in the inner periphery of the amenity-rich hinterland of Prague, which had been depopulated during the Second World War, with a subsequent large-scale population exchange. Four case-study regions are peripheral areas with bad accessibility, weak economic power and not fully exploited recreational potential, which are, however, very valuable from an environmental point of view (amenity-rich areas). Three case-study regions represent attractive hilly and mountainous regions visited by a high number of tourists. For a more detailed location and description of the study regions, see Fialová and Vágner (2014).

One hundred respondents were interviewed in each case-study region; the ratio of the residents and second home users reflected the share of second homes. The surveys were conducted in 2010 and 2011, mostly in the summer recreation season (when the frequency of second home use is the highest), in the form of structured interviews by qualified field workers trained by the authors. The asked questions focused on perceived identity relating to three hierarchical levels of the territory (methodologically based on recent research by Chromý 2004; Fialová et al. 2010). The highest level was represented by the case-study region as a whole, i.e. (larger) neighbourhood of the residence/second home, the second level by the municipality (village) and the lowest by the place (locality) which means the close neighbourhood of the resident/second home (settlement, a part of the municipality). Emotional relations to the territory and generation ties were surveyed as well as the identification of the singularity of the territory of their symbols and functions. The respondents were asked about the most painful problems, especially in the residents versus second home users relations, and about their involvement in rural life. They also expressed views of their satisfaction and potential future use of the territory. The basic identifiers of gender and age group concluded the surveys.

The structure of the respondents was as follows: a total of 734 questionnaires were obtained from 440 residents (60%) and from 294 second home users. Both men (47%) and women (53%) were interviewed. More than 60% of people were above 46 years of age. The closed questions in the questionnaire were analysed with simple descriptive statistics and complemented with an analysis of the open questions and with other findings obtained from the analysis of the interviews.

For the purpose of even more detailed insight into social relationships, another case study was conducted in three model regions. The questionnaire survey in the form of interviews was conducted in August and September 2013 by qualified questioners trained by the authors, or by the authors themselves. The interviews were conducted with second home users only; as well as questions aimed at relations in the locality and ties to the residential community, primary relation data was also gathered. The respondents were asked to name particular persons who had purposely been addressed: 1) for clearing a personal or professional matter, e.g. a loan, assistance or advice, 2) for a friendly chat. The respondents also named examples of help they provided or obtained from other persons. The method of social network analysis was used for the assessment of the relationships. The survey was held in second home settlements outside of village centres, which have a residential function. The first case-study area was located at the edge of the dense recreational hinterland of Prague, which has has a traditional leisure function for several generations (Český Šternberk). The other two case-study areas were two municipalities (Dlouhá Voda and Česká Ves) situated in a peripheral part of Czechia: in Silesia near the Polish border (Bruntál region), but which has been used for recreation for several decades (Kůsová et al. 2017). The interviews were conducted in 80% of second homes situated in both peripheral villages (51 respondents in Česká Ves and 30 in Dlouhá Voda). In Český Šternberk, the sample included 37% of second homes (39 respondents). Even though interviews were held with only one person in each second home, the responses usually related to the whole family.

Results and discussions

Second homes in rural areas

Second home tourism in Czechia has traditionally been a significant phenomenon. Some 12% of households own a second home (with the number of owners twice as high in big cities), and a quarter of the population use a second home regularly. Second homes cover 20% of all dwellings in Czechia (Figure 19.1) (Vágner & Fialová 2009).

In different numbers and at varying intensities, second homes are spread practically all over Czechia. Nevertheless, the main concentration zones of cabins and purpose-built second homes include the southern hinterland of Prague and outskirts of the biggest cities. Secondary zones are represented by the banks of water reservoirs. The other form of second homes, cottages converted from primarily non-recreational dwellings, are concentrated in border and peripheral (hilly) areas with a large number of abandoned houses after the expulsion of Germans after WWII, as well as in rural areas depopulated due to the controlled communist (and post-communist) urbanisation process.

The data was provided by the Czech Office for Surveying, Mapping and Cadastre (ČÚZK), which keeps records of all real estate, classified by functional usage. We focused on residential dwellings as well as second homes denoted as individual recreation dwellings in the register (Bičík et al. 2001). CVVM results indicated that 16% of the population in Czechia regularly use second homes, i.e. 9% cabins and recreational houses, 4% cottages (primarily built for non-recreational purposes) and 3% garden allotment cabins, which are not included in regular counts of second homes. Further responses arose from a sample of 170 respondents who reported regular use of second homes. About 42% of them commute less than 20 km. Commuting over 100 km is exceptional (8%). The average commuting distance is around 30 km and is quite stable compared to the surveys conducted in 2003 (Vágner & Fialová 2004).

Second home users commute for around 20–25 years on average, but 15% have been using a second home for more than 30 years. The share slightly decreased, which is probably due to a high proportion of pensioners who are not able to commute regularly any longer. At the break of the millennium, 36% of owners were in post-productive age (Vágner & Fialová 2004). The summer season from May until September is dominant. No visit between November and February was declared by 40% of respondents.

Plans for future use (in 10 years) are crucial for second home perspectives. Only two-thirds want to maintain the status quo and use the second home only for leisure. The interest in conversion to permanent dwelling seems to have decreased (5%). About 10% presume no further use and only 1% think about renting. The results do not agree with an extensive field and questionnaire survey (n = 4153) held 13 years ago (Vágner & Fialová 2004). At that time, the option of permanent dwelling was considered by 19%. However, the question had not indicated an exact time but "near time horizon". It is also possible that after more than a decade, the potential for residential function of second homes is somewhat lower than before. Older research was carried out in the boom of the suburbanisation period, while recent studies took place in a period of almost saturated demand for suburbanisation dwellings with changing society and residential preferences. Many second homes had already been converted into homes with a residential function (Ouředníček & Temelová 2012), which was also proven in other post-communist countries (Leetmaa et al. 2012; Nuga et al. 2015; Sýkora & Kiril 2014). The transformation is also strongly differentiated regionally.

Territorial identity

The respondents in the case-study regions evaluated their own perceived identity relating to the different hierarchical levels of the territory commonly used in their everyday lives. As far as the municipality level is concerned, an important finding emerged, namely that one-third of second home users consider themselves locals. This is because of the high share of long-term cottage users that have close ties to local life in the case-study regions (80% of the residents and 65% of the second home users have stayed in the municipality more or less regularly for at least 20 years, which means for more than one generation). The questionnaire survey revealed quite a stable population with 30% of people born locally.

The residents live in the area mainly because of their ancestors, family roots and relationships. A big share of the second home users (30%) had also known the place of second home since their childhood. The importance of friendship was declared by 40% of respondents. Social and family ties are among the most important factors of the ownership, use and location of second homes.

The respondents explained their spatial ties on the following scale: strong, rather strong, rather weak, weak, and related to three hierarchical levels of territory. Both groups of respondents (second home users even more clearly) have declared stronger relations to closer and smaller-area units. Both groups of interviewed persons declared that the regions are unique because of their environmental quality, landscape, nature and calmness. They are also proud of these features of the regions.

The respondents were also asked to characterise and give their opinion of their residence/second home territory (Figure 19.2). The second home users mostly declared that the area is appropriate for recreation (55%) and also a place where people have closer relations to each other (20%). The residents had similar opinions. However, their main reason for presence was comfortable living (36%). Closer interpersonal contacts where people help each other were mentioned as the highest value by 20% of the respondents in both groups, which indicates the high importance of a good social climate for living and recreation.

Social relations

The questionnaire survey (2011) made it possible to collect opinions about the quality of social relations among residents and second home users and between those two groups. Generally, the relations seem to be perceived more positively by second home owners. The final results appear very optimistic because more than two-thirds of the population declared good relations and only about 5% of locals feel there are bad relations between residents, and also between residents and second home owners (Table 19.1). However, a part of the respondents feel a trend of worsening relations, which may be seen as a potential problem. Similar results are also shown by a CVVM survey (2014). Some 70% of ties were assessed as very good or fairly good, with almost no differences between particular groups. Only 3–5% assessed the ties as bad or fairly bad, which seems to be positive for social peace. The results strongly agree with the surveys conducted in cottage areas all over Czechia in 2011.

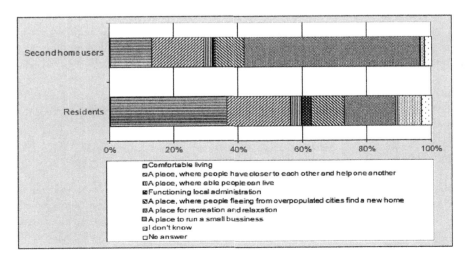

Figure 19.2 The characteristics of the residence/second home territory and opinions of it.

Table 19.1 Social relations among residents, second home owners and between the groups

Social relations	Opinions of residents			Opinions of second home owners		
	residents vs residents	residents vs SHO	SHO vs SHO	residents vs residents	residents vs SHO	SHO vs SHO
Very good and good	68.8%	69.8%	71.8%	76.2%	72.7%	77.5%
Rather bad and very bad	5.5%	4.4%	1.0%	1.4%	4.5%	0.7%

Note: SHO – second home owners.

The residents and second home owners declared similar interests in participating in traditional social events such as funfairs, balls and sports events. The chief organisers of social events are traditional clubs and associations – volunteer fire brigades, soccer teams and game-keepers in the Czech countryside (Kůsová 2013). Our survey indicated high activity from second home users, not only in regard to participation, but also in the organisation of social events in cooperation with active local residents.

The results given above about quite stable, good relations were confirmed by surveys using primary relation data based on social networking. However, when it comes to linkages between second home users' and residents' communities, a separation of groups was observed, arising naturally from the physical distance between recreational settlements and village residential centres. The densest contact networks were indicated between neighbours. The residents who lived permanently in recreational localities represented the most active agents in local life. Socio-economic features, such as profession or education, were not proven to have any strong relevance for stronger contacts between second home users. The highest frequency and quality of ties were indicated in the groups who had shared the space for a long time. Such users have a long-term, inherited local identity. Narrow ties are also often kept out of the surveyed recreational space. The quality of the ties is also visible physically in the exterior of nearby public buildings (Kůsová et al. 2017).

Second home users used to be considered a burden for the municipality (Gallent & Tewdwr-Jones 2000; Fialová & Vágner 2005b). This statement was agreed on by 40% of the mayors, mostly in the municipalities with extremely high concentrations of second homes and with some new forms close to commercial tourism, e.g. holiday apartments in mountain resorts. In our survey, however, this negative opinion was not confirmed by second home users or 80% of the residents, which was rather surprising. Half of the respondents (as well as half of the residents) declared that long-term second home owners should also have a chance to become representatives of municipal councils! The CVVM survey (2014) indicated that about one-third would agree to enter the council, with a recent increase also for cabin owners, approaching the percentage of cottagers.

Conclusions

As stated in the introduction, relations between residents and tourists can also be influenced by their relations to the territory used. As far as the local community structure is concerned, crucial actors are traditionally defined as the residents, the local authorities, entrepreneurs and civic associations. Various actors have different visions for the use of the area, its function and future development. They also perceive diverse territorial identities, which also differ in their formation process.

Our research pointed out that second home owners and users are additional significant agents with a considerable influence, especially on social life in the rural space and local community, and it is necessary to take them into account, especially in areas with a higher concentration of second homes. The quantitative data has indicated specific territories where detailed field surveys have been conducted in the form of interviews with the agents and questionnaire surveys. The data has been analysed and explained with the use of both quantitative and qualitative methods with respect to their characteristics. Although the generalisation of the results is rather problematic, in fact a joint community of residents and second home users has been found in most surveyed regions, rather than separate groups of residents and second home users with strongly different interests. The similarity of social behaviour and perceived identity relating to the territory was high, especially in the regions with a higher share of cottages with long-term stays of the second home users.

As a result, our results contradict general statements (frequently shown in the media) about antagonistic relations between the local population and the "invaders from cities". Likewise, social conflicts between the rural hosting and the visiting second home populations were expected according to key researchers of this issue (Doxey 1975; Farstad & Rye 2013). Similar conflicting results were also obtained from users of more or less separated cabin and recreational home localities or holiday villages (Horáková & Fialová 2014). Our research has shown that long-term cottage users are for the most part no longer considered allochthonous elements in the rural space, which used to cause social conflicts.

Further research should focus on those regions where second home users are less involved in the local and rural life (cabin and recreational home users). Other studies might explore the formation of social capital in various types of countryside (as defined by Bourdieu 1986, Coleman 1988, and Putnam 1993), following the pilot studies drawn up by Pileček (2010) and Pileček and Jančák (2010) in the Czech countryside.

Importantly, the differences between second homes and primary residences seem to be more blurred than in the past. Due to this, the concept of multiple dwelling (McIntyre & Pavlovich 2006) has become common in developed societies. Second home commuting is replaced with semi-migration or circulation processes (Williams & Hall 2002; Flognfeldt 2004; Overvåg 2011). These principles, as well as the theory of hetero-local identities as described by Halfacree (2012), have not been examined in the rural space of Czechia yet and, therefore, become challenges for future research.

Acknowledgement

The text was supported by the project GA ČR P410/12/G113 at the Historical Geography Research Centre.

References

Antonsich, M. (2010) 'Exploring the correspondence between regional forms of governance and regional identity: The case of Western Europe', *European Urban and Regional Studies*, 17 (3): 261–276.

Aronsson, L. (2004) 'Place attachment of vacation residents: Between tourists and permanent residents'. In C. M. Hall and D. K. Müller (eds) *Tourism, Mobility and Second Homes: Between Elite Landscape and Common Ground*. Clevedon, UK: Channel View Publications, 75–86.

Bičík, I., Vágner, J. and Fialová, D. (2001) *Druhé bydlení v Česku*. Prague: Katedra sociální geografie a regionálního rozvoje PřF UK v Praze.

Bourdieu, P. (1986) 'The forms of capital'. In J. G. Richardson (ed.) *Handbook of Theory and Research for the Sociology of Education*. New York: Greenwood Press, 46–58.

Chromý, P. (2003) 'Formování regionální identity: Nezbytná součást geografických výzkumů'. In V. Jančák, P. Chromý and M. Marada (eds) *Geografie na cestách poznání*. Praha: Katedra sociální geografie a regionálního rozvoje PřF UK v Praze, 163–178.

Chromý, P. (2004) *Historická a kulturní geografie a nové přístupy v regionálním studiu*. Dizertační práce. Univerzita Karlova v Praze, Přírodovědecká fakulta, katedra sociální geografie a regionálního rozvoje, Prague, 60 p. + suppl.

Chromý, P., Kučerová, S. and Kučera, Z. (2009) 'Regional identity, contemporary and historical regions and the issue of relict borders. The case of Czechia', *Regions and Regionalism*, 9 (2): 9–19.

Chromý, P. and Skála, J. (2010) 'Kulturněgeografické aspekty rozvoje příhraničních periferií: analýza vybraných složek územní identity obyvatelstva Sušicka', *Geografie*, 115 (2): 223–246.

Chromý, P., Jančák, V., Marada, M. and Havlíček, T. (2010) 'Venkov – žitý prostor: Regionální diferenciace percepce venkova představiteli venkovských obcí Česka', *Geografie*, 116 (1): 23–45.

Clendenning, G. and Field, D. (2006) 'Seasonal residents: Members of community or part of the scenery?' In G. Green, S. Deller and D. Marcouiller (eds) *Amenities and Rural Development: Theory, Method and Public Policy*. Cheltenham, UK: Edward Elgar, 215–236.

Coleman, J. (1988) 'Social capital and the creation of human capital', *American Journal of Sociology*, 94 Supplement: 52–120.

Czech Office for Surveying, Mapping and Cadastre (2005) Database on number of dwellings in cadastre units. Prague: Author.

Day, G. (2006) *Community and Everyday Life*. New York: Routledge.

Doxey, A. (1975) 'A causation theory of visitor – resident irritants: Methodology and research inference', Sixth Annual Conference Proceedings of *the Travel Research Association*, San Diego, CA, 195–198.

Farstad, M. and Rye, J. F. (2013) 'Second home owners, locals and their perspectives on rural development', *Journal of Rural Studies*, 30: 41–51.

Fialová, D. and Vágner, J. (2005a) 'Struktura, typologie, současnost a perspektivy druhéhobydlení v Česku', *Geografie*, 109 (2): 73–81.

Fialová, D. and Vágner, J. (2005b) 'Druhé bydlení v periferních oblastech'. In M. Novotná (ed.) *Problémy periferních oblastí*. Univerzita Karlova v Praze. Přírodovědecká fakulta. Katedra sociální geografie a regionálního rozvoje, 74–80.

Fialová, D. and Vágner, J. (2014) 'The owners of second homes as users of rural space in Czechia', *Acta Universitatis Carolinae Geographica*, 49 (2): 21–28.

Fialová, D., Chromý, P., Kučera, Z., Spilková, J., Štych, P. and Vágner, J. (2010) 'The forming of regional identity and identity of regions in Czechia – Introduction to the research on the impact of second housing and tourism', *Acta Universitatis Carolinae – Geographica*, 45 (1): 49–60.

Flognfeldt, T. (2004) 'Second homes as a part of a new rural lifestyle in Norway'. In C. M. Hall and D. K. Müller (eds) *Tourism, Mobility and Second Homes: Between Elite Landscape and Common Ground*. Clevedon, UK: Channel View Publications, 233–243.

Frantál, B. and Martinát, S. (eds) (2013) *New Rural Spaces: Towards Renewable Energies, Multifunctional Farming and Sustainable Tourism*. Brno, Czech Republic: Institute of Geonics.

Frisvoll, S. and Rye, J. F. (2009) 'Elite discourses of regional identity in a new regionalism development scheme: The case of the "Mountain Region" in Norway', *Norsk Geografisk Tidsskrift*, 63: 175–190.

Fukuyama, F. (2006) 'Identity, immigration and democracy', *Journal of Democracy*, 17 (2): 5–20.

Gallent, N. and Tewdwr-Jones, M. (2000) *Rural Second Homes in Europe*. Hampshire, UK: Ashgate.

Gans, H. J. (1968) *People and Plans: Essays on Urban Problems and Solutions*. New York: Basic Books.

Giddens, A. (1991) *Modernity and Self-Identity: Self and Society in the Late Modern Age*. Cambridge: Policy.

Green, G. P., Marcouiller, D., Deller, S. D., Erkkila, D. and Sumathi, N. R. (1996) 'Local dependency, land use attitudes, and economic development: Comparisons between seasonal and permanent residents', *Rural Sociology*, 61 (3): 427–445.

Halfacree, K. (2012) 'Heterolocal identities? Counter-urbanisation, second homes, and rural consumption in the era of mobilities', *Population, Space and Place*, 18 (2): 209–224.

Hall, C. M. and Müller, D. (eds) (2004) *Tourism, Mobility and Second Homes: Between Elite Landscape and Common Ground*. Clevedon, UK: Channel View Publications.

Halseth, G. (1993) 'Communities within communities: Changing "residential" areas at Cultus Lake, British Columbia', *Journal of Rural Studies*, 9 (2): 175–187.

Halseth, G. (2004) 'The "cottage" privilege: Increasingly elite landscapes of second homes in Canada'. In C. M. Hall and D. K. Müller (eds) *Tourism, Mobility and Second Homes: Between Elite Landscape and Common Ground*. Clevedon, UK: Channel View Publications, 35–54.

Halseth, G. and Rosenberg, M. (1995) 'Cottagers in an urban field', *The Professional Geographer*, 47 (2): 148–159.

Horáková, H. and Fialová, D. (2014) *Transformace venkova. Turismus jako forma rozvoje*. Plzeň, Czech Republic: Nakladatelství a vydavatelství Aleš Čeněk, s.r.o.

Jarlöv, L. (1999) 'Leisure lots and summer cottages as places for people's own creative work'. In D. Crouch (ed.) *Leisure/Tourism Geographies: Practices and Geographical Knowledge*. London: Routledge, 231–237.

Kaltenborn, B. P. (1997) 'Nature of place attachment: A study among recreation homeowners in Southern Norway', *Leisure Sciences: An Interdisciplinary Journal*, 19 (3): 175–189.

Kelly, G. and Hosking, K. (2008) 'Nonpermanent residents, place attachment, and "sea change" communities', *Environment and Behavior*, 40 (4): 575–594.

Kneafsey, M. (2000) 'Tourism, place identities and social relations in the European rural periphery', *European Urban and Regional Studies*, 7 (1): 35–50.

Knight, D. B. (1982) 'Identity and territory: Geographical perspectives on nationalism and regionalism', *Annals of the Association of American Geographers*, 72 (4): 514–531.

Kůsová, T. (2013) 'Volný čas a sociální kapitál: Prostorová diferenciace spolkové aktivity v Česku', *Geografie*, 118 (4): 372–391.

Kůsová, T., Fialová, D. and Hučínová, M. (2017) 'Sociální vazby v lokalitách druhého bydlení' *Geografie*, 122 (2): 236–256.

Leetmaa, K., Brade, I., Anniste, K. and Nuga, M. (2012) 'Socialist summer-home settlements in post-socialist suburbanisation', *Urban Studies*, 49 (1): 3–21.

Light, D. (2001) '"Facing the future": Tourism and identity-building in post-socialist Romania', *Political Geography*, 20 (8): 1053–1074.

McIntyre, N. and Pavlovich, K. (2006) 'Changing places: Amenity coastal communities in transition'. In N. McIntyre, D. R. Williams and K. E. McHugh (eds) *Multiple Dwelling and Tourism. Negotiating Place, Home and Identity*. Wallingford, UK: CABI, 262–277.

Marcouiller, D. W., Green, G. P., Deller, S. C. and Sumathi, N. R. (1996) *Recreational Homes and Regional Development: A Case Study from the Upper Great Lakes States*. Madison, WI: University of Wisconsin.

Matarrita-Cascante, D., Stedman, R. and Luloff, A. (2010) 'Permanent and seasonal residents' community attachment in natural amenity-rich areas', *Environment and Behavior*, 42 (2): 197–220.

Müller, D. K. (2011) 'Second homes in rural areas: Reflections on a troubled history', *Norsk Geografisk Tidsskrift – Norwegian Journal of Geography*, 65 (3): 137–143.

Nordin, U. and Marjavaara, R. (2012) 'The local non-locals: Second home owners associational engagement in Sweden', *Turizam: Znanstveno-stručni časopis*, 60 (3): 293–305.

Nuga, M., Metspalu, P., Org, A. and Leetmaa, K. (2015) 'Planning post-summurbia: From spontaneous pragmatism to collaborative planning?', *Moravian Geographical Reports*, 23 (4): 36–46.

Ouředníček, M. and Temelová, J. (eds) (2012) *Sociální proměny pražských čtvrtí*. Prague: Academia.

Overvåg, K. (2011) 'Second homes: Migration or circulation?', *Norsk Geografisk Tidsskrift – Norwegian Journal of Geography*, 65 (3): 154–164.

Paasi, A. (1986) 'The institutionalization of regions: A theoretical framework for understanding the emergence of regions and the constitution of regional identity', *Fennia*, 164 (1): 105–146.

Paasi, A. (2009) 'The resurgence of the region and regional identity: Theoretical perspectives and empirical observation on regional dynamics in Europe', *Review of International Studies* 35 (1): 121–146.

Pileček, J. (2010) 'Koncept sociálního kapitálu: Pokus o přehled teoretickýchvýchodisek a aplikačních přístupů jeho studia', *Geografie*, 115 (1): 64–77.

Pileček, J. and Jančák, V. (2010) 'Je možné měřit sociální kapitál? Analýza územní diferenciace okresů Česka', *Geografie*, 115 (1): 78–95.

Pitkänen, K., Adamiak, C. and Halseth, G. (2014) 'Leisure activities and rural community change: Valuation and use of rural space among permanent residents and second home owners', *Sociologia Ruralis*, 54 (2): 143–166.

Putnam, R. D. (1993) *Making Democracy Work: Civic Transitions in Modern Italy*. Princeton, NJ: Princeton University Press.

Raagmaa, G. (2002) 'Regional identity in regional development and planning', *European Planning Studies*, 10 (1): 55–76.

Robertsson, L. and Marjavaara, R. (2015) 'The seasonal buzz: Knowledge transfer in a temporary setting', *Tourism Planning and Development*, 12 (3): 251–265.

Semian, M. (2012) 'Searching for the territorial shape of a region in regional consciousness: The Český Ráj (Bohemian Paradise), Czech Republic', *Moravian Geographical Reports*, 20 (2): 25–35.

Stedman, R. C. (2006) 'Understanding place attachment among second home owners', *American Behavioral Scientist*, 50 (2): 187–205.

Sýkora, L. and Kiril, S. (2014) 'The challenge of postsocialist suburbanization'. In S. Kiril and L. Sýkora (eds) *Confronting Suburbanization: Urban Decentralization in Postsocialist Central and Eastern Europe.* Malden, MA: Wiley-Blackwell, 1–32.

Vágner, J. and Fialová, D. (2004) *Regionální diferenciace druhého bydlení v Česku.* Prague: Katedra sociální geografie a regionálního rozvoje PřF UK v Praze.

Vágner, J. and Fialová, D. (2009) 'Objekty druhého bydlení na úhrnu obytných staveb'. In T. Hrnčiarová (ed.) *Atlas krajiny České republiky.* Prague: Ministerstvo životního prostředí České republiky, 55.

Vencálek, J. (1998) *Protisměry územní identity.* Český Těšín, Czech Republic: Olza.

Wellman, B. (1996) 'Are personal communities local? A dumptarian reconsideration', *Social Networks*, 18 (4): 347–354.

Wellman, B. (2001) 'Physical place and cyber-place: The rise of networked individualism', *International Journal for Urban and Regional Research*, 25 (2): 227–252.

Williams, A. M. and Hall, C. M. (2002) 'Tourism, migration, circulation and mobility: The contingencies of time and place'. In C. M. Hall and A. M. Williams (eds) *Tourism and Migration: New Relationships between Production and Consumption.* Dordrecht, the Netherlands: Kluwer, 1–52.

Zich, F. (2003) *Regionální identita obyvatel v pohraničí.* Prague: Sociologický ústav Akademie věd ČR.

20

DO SECOND HOME OWNERS ONLY PLAY A SECONDARY ROLE IN COASTAL TERRITORIES?

A case study in Charente-Maritime (France)

Caroline Blondy, Christine Plumejeaud,
Luc Vacher, Didier Vye and Caroline Bontet

Introduction

In a context of globalisation, coastlines are mostly characterised by their high economic and demographic attractiveness. Among the populations present, second home owners occupy a particular place and belong to an emerging category, namely "multiresidents" (McIntyre et al. 2006), among whom they are distinct insofar as their mobility is linked to leisure (Duchêne-Lacroix 2013).

Although they fully participate in the residential and tourist attractiveness of coastal areas (more than a million second homes on the French coast), they are also the subject of considerable debate and controversy. Often associated with a pejorative image of "closed shutters" or "empty beds" and deemed guilty of unfairly competing with commercial accommodation, this is a population which is both residential and tourist (Sacareau et al. 2010), and an expression of the new arts of dwelling in our contemporary societies (Stock 2006). Via home owner status, the secondary resident 'lives, resides and is rooted in a place' (Dubost 1998: 12) but is also a 'passer-through who resides and a resident who passes through' (Urbain 2002: 516) defined by his spatial mobility between here and elsewhere. This duality lies in the origin of questions about the impact of this population's presence on territories: Are they a "blessing" or a "curse" (Coppock 1977) to the extent that they bring change such as rising house prices, gentrification, tensions with the "local" populations (Dubost 1995; Müller & Hoogendoorn 2013; Paris 2009; Brida et al. 2011; Gallent et al. 2005)? These tensions with local populations would also appear to be generated by two opposing visions of regional development, one specific to permanent residents who are positive about to economic development, another specific to second home owners, who prefer the status quo and are defenders of preservation within an idealised environment (Müller 2002; Overvag & Berg 2011).

Stigmatisation can also be fuelled by the notion that the second home is a distinctive sign of elite populations (Pinçon & Pinçon-Charlot 1989) whose acquisition strategies sometimes permit tax evasion (Paris 2011). Faced with this somewhat accusative discourse, a more harmonious relationship between secondary residents and host territories can be demonstrated (Hall & Müller 2004; Roca 2013; Müller & Hoogendoorn 2013) emphasising the recurrence of occupancy and loyalty towards the territory (Urbain 2002). Furthermore, "local populations" and "secondary residents" are not categories which are always in opposition since, faced with regional development issues, they can join forces as part of a "not in my backyard" (NIMBY) mindset (Farstad & Rye 2013). Moreover, even if second home owners belong to social groups which are higher up the socio-economic scale than the national average (Atout France 2010), we are witnessing a democratisation of the acquisition of second homes (Módenes & López-Colás 2007). However, this opposition must be qualified to the extent that most studies covering attachment in the places concern rural areas (Clout 1971; Hoggart & Buller 1995; Perrot & La Soudière 1998; Urbain 2002), whose residential and tourist attractiveness is less marked than on the coasts. Coastal gentrification is as much related to the increase of permanent residents (Buhot 2009; Marjavaara 2007) as the arrival of secondary residents, some of whom may become permanent residents in the future (Duhamel 2000; Cribier 1994; Bésingrand 2005). Finally, regarding the economic impact, second home owners are considered to be populations which make a significant contribution to the in-place economy of the territories (Davezies 2009).

We therefore hypothesise that, far from being "secondary", this category of actor fully participates in the dynamics of coastal and tourist territories. Are they really less rooted in a place than a principal resident when they are by definition owners, which is far from being the case for all of the year-round residents? Is this particular act of putting down roots reflected in a specific investment in the territory of the second home? By accommodating their entourage, is it not the case that the second home owner is also playing a role in the attractiveness and promotion of the tourist destination?

To answer these questions, we will build on the results of a survey conducted by the University of La Rochelle in partnership with local institutions and businesses in 10 *commune*s (the French word for municipality) along the Charente coastline. First, we will describe the context of this study, the methodology used and the scientific value of the main themes selected. In a second step, we will present and interpret the initial findings in order to assess in what way second home owners are effectively full participants in coastal tourist areas.

Methodology

Despite a sharp revival in interest since the late 1990s, especially in the English-language literature (Hall & Müller 2004; McIntyre et al. 2006; Roca 2013), the relationship between owners of second homes and their host territory remains poorly understood (Duchêne-Lacroix 2013; Bonnin & Villanova 1999). This is particularly true for their relationship with the environment, which for some peculiar reason has been little studied (Müller & Hoogendoorn 2013). The rare French-language studies have primarily been conducted in the context of international tourism mobility (Duhamel 2000) or were concerned with a particular category of the population, especially the retired (Cribier 1994). The few recent studies on the French coast tend to focus on property (Aguer & Vergeau 2009; Lefèvre & Frayssinet 2011) or on the analysis of regional disparities in this phenomenon (Roca 2013). The same goes for grey literature whose approach remains more quantitative (e.g. Atout France 2010). Although a number of surveys covering multi-residency are underway, including those of the Family and Housing survey conducted by Institut National de la Statistique et des Etudes Economiques (INSEE) (French National Institute of Statistics and Economic Studies) and Institut National des Etudes Démographiques (INED) (French National Institute of Demography), these are not focused on second home owners or on coastal areas. Only surveys of owners can provide a detailed and nuanced interpretation of their uses and their representations (Roca 2013). However, these surveys or interviews are difficult to conduct because of this population's intermittent presence in the territory, which may limit the size of the sample (Brida et al. 2011). The study launched in Charente-Maritime in 2012 and completed in 2013 endeavoured to respond to this challenge.

Context of the study

This study builds on previous research conducted at the "departmental" level (The *Departement* is the third level of French Territorial Administration (Level 1 = State, Level 2 = Region)). In 2008, use of Fichier des Logements par COMmune (FILOCOM) data (housing files for each municipality) was initiated by Charente-Maritime Tourism (CMT) in partnership with INSEE and the Poitou-Charentes Region. It resulted in the publication in 2009 of factsheets presenting the situation of second homes in the *department* and in the region. This study focused on the second home as a property and its characteristics (location, number, changes, profile). It shows that the base of second homes in the *department* has expanded faster than the national average, underlining the attractiveness of certain areas such as the Île de Ré, the Marennes-Oléron sector and the Royan area where the proportion of second homes in the housing stock is significant at 54%, 47% and 43% respectively. This increase was still visible between 2007 and 2010 (Figure 20.1). Indeed, there was a rise from 73,000 second homes in the department in 2007, i.e. 21% of the total housing stock, to 89,000 second homes (24% of the total housing stock).

This preliminary study therefore justified our choice of field. However, although this research highlighted the significant presence of second homes in the provision of tourist accommodation, it did not enable the scale of this practice in the local tourism system to be highlighted. In fact, the study did not detail the profile of owners or how they use their properties (occupancy, lending, leasing, tourism practices). Yet this data provides an insight into the tourism systems and the activities of players who drive them. It is also possible to assess the role of second home owners in the in-place economy and to tailor the policies or actions of regional development and so better meet the needs of this population, especially in terms of services or activities.

The study was born out of a convergence of interests between institutional players, local authorities and researchers at the University of La Rochelle (ULR). In 2012, the University of La Rochelle teamed up with *Charente-Maritime Tourisme* (CMT), the *Chambre de Commerce et d'Industrie* of La Rochelle (CCILR) and that of Rochefort-Saintonge (CCIRS) to investigate second home owners and uses of their property. In fact, owners are the people who theoretically know most about use of their property by themselves but also by others (lending or leasing).

The themes selected, in agreement with the various partners, were as follows:

- perception of quality of life (value assigned to the property and satisfaction gained);
- practices and consumption of the owner (occupancy, activities performed, expenditure);
- description of the property (location, sleeping capacity);
- socio-economic profile of owners, with particular attention paid to their motivation in becoming owner of this property.

Giving secondary residents a voice: A methodological challenge to be met

The first phase of the survey entailed contacting the owners by post, while asking for their telephone number for participation in the second phase. To ensure its effectiveness, the postal survey could not have too many questions; the telephone survey aimed to flesh out the responses obtained by post, addressing more sensitive or more complex issues.

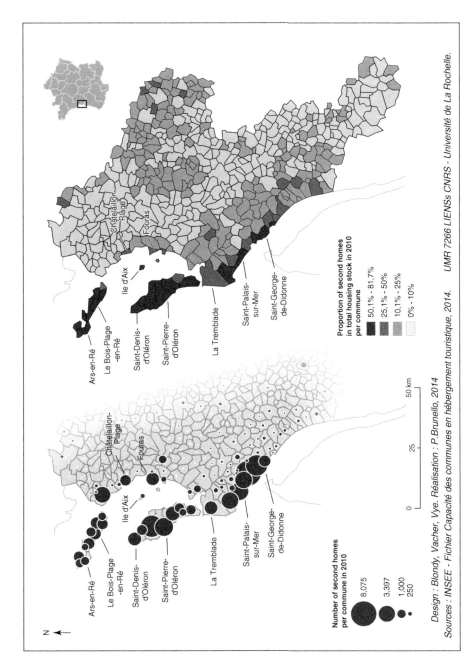

Figure 20.1 The presence of second homes on the Charante coast (France) in 2010.

Contacting owners by post raises at least two questions: the choice of address (the secondary or principal home?) and the period when the letter is sent out, bearing in mind that the aim is to ensure the best possible rate of return for the survey. The choice of principal home seemed more relevant to the extent that the *Atout France* (2010) study revealed a figure of 30 nights of occupancy on average by the owner. For practical reasons and representativeness, only owners whose principal home is located in France were surveyed. They represent the majority of the target population and in 2007, 95% of the stock of second homes in Charente-Maritime belonged to this group (Observatoire des clientèles CMT 2008). The postal contact period (mid-June) avoided the major school holidays in France, when the owners would have been absent.

To determine the principal home of the owners, two possibilities were tested. The first approach entailed cross analysing the files of the digital land register (MAJIC III) and that of property tax. This cross analysis made it necessary to filter out owners of multiple residences, as well as to retain only one owner for co-owned residences. The second possibility was to use the file for the household waste collection tax, which lists all second homes for which a single owner is identified. However, this type of file is not available in all *communes*. In the end, a substantial effort to combine the results obtained via these two methods made it possible to establish a list of addresses of owners of principal homes sampled according to a geographic origin criterion.

At the end of this postal survey, the telephone survey was intended to flesh out the initial answers given by the respondents agreeing to be called. It was therefore necessary to consolidate the answers by the same owner to the postal and telephone questionnaires within a single database for conducting the telephone interview on the basis of responses provided by post. The database and the software for the telephone survey developed for this purpose were then used to cross analyse the results of these two surveys.

At the same time, focus groups were organised in one of the test *communes* (Châtelaillon-Plage). Two groups totalling 17 people (14 households) were brought together in July 2013 for more than two hours so they could express themselves freely. We therefore combined a quantitative and qualitative approach in order to better identify profiles, practices and representations.

The success of the study: Second home owners pleased to be given a voice?

Questionnaires were sent out in ten test *communes* selected for their representativeness in respect to the different territorial contexts of the Charente coast: mainland or island coastline, and tourist resorts whether or not part of an urban area (Figure 20.1). The decision to give owners a voice proved a success: second home owners showed a willingness to express themselves through a high rate of return (34%) but also through the addition of *verbatim* contributions or even letters accompanying the questionnaire on its return (Blondy, Vacher & Vye 2016). Of the 12,919 questionnaires sent out, 4,662 were collected of which 4,648 were judged usable and were duly processed. 1,487 respondents wished to be contacted by phone to continue the exchange. More than 700 of them were able to be contacted and continued to express their views. The focus groups also met with considerable success. It is worth noting that the secondary residents were responsive in respect to this study. This population, which is said to shine more by its absence than by its presence in the territories, seems to belie these stereotypes. Should we not then conclude that they are not such "secondary" players after all and that they feel an investment in the place where their property is located? We will try to offer some answers to this question.

Analysis of results

To verify that the secondary residents are full participants in the functioning of the coastal tourist territory, we questioned them about their different forms of investment in it. The notion of investment is primarily economic: acquiring a second home is first for owners a way to increase their property assets which their families may inherit. Once acquired, they maintain their property, stay there regularly, and consume goods and services, thus supporting the local economy of the tourist area. This economic dimension was part of the survey, but the focus here will be more on the results related to the emotional and social investment of the secondary resident.

The bond between the secondary resident and the tourist place

We wanted to assess a form of attachment to the territory, a *topophilia* (Tuan 1961; Stock 2003), that is to say, the emotional bond between a person and a place. It is a place in which the individual feels good, a kind of "home" which they want to return to, where they have their habits, where they make an emotional investment. But what is the best way to gauge this attachment to a place by an individual as a second home owner?

We should start by restating the obvious: the location of the secondary residence is a place associated with holidays and leisure, thus, before becoming a property owner, the secondary resident has visited the place as a tourist many times. Our study shows that in 8 out of 10 *communes*, this is the primary reason cited for their familiarity with the place when acquiring their property. This figure, which is consistently above 40%, is particularly high in the popular tourist *communes* of Royan (Saint-Palais-sur-Mer and Saint-Georges-de-Didonne). Prior tourist experience could be a strong determinant in the acquisition of their second home. Moreover, in each of our *communes* surveyed, over 88% of respondents consider their second home to be a place of relaxation, a place to break free from the constraints of everyday life, a place of individual or collective '*recreation*' (Équipe MIT 2002), like any tourist place. In fact, the discourse on the break with the principal home's living environment came up regularly in the focus groups organised: staying at the second home permits 'a change of air, a different pace of life, a chance to stroll leisurely to the market and walk back along the seafront' (an owner participating in Focus Group no. 1, 17 July 2013, Châtelaillon-Plage (Charente-Maritime)).

It is also, for the vast majority of owners (61% to 84% depending on the *commune*), a place of reunion, especially family gatherings. In a context of increasing geographical dispersion of families, the second home emerges as the centre of family life, making it possible to strengthen family ties, but also as a marker of family identity and history (Clément & Lelièvre 2005), hence the qualification of "family home" that is often attributed. In addition, many home owners have family ties. Whatever the *commune* tested, at least one secondary resident in five declared himself to be a child or grandchild of a resident (secondary or permanent). It is, in general, the second reason for past familiarity with the place after the tourist experience. This attachment by descent is also reinforced by the fact of inheriting their second home, which concerns around one owner in four in the three *communes* in our sample (Ars-en-Ré, Châtelaillon and Fouras). (Data from the telephone survey (702 owners were called, 632 were used) of Ile d'Aix, where the number of respondents was too low, was excluded from analysis of the survey).

In addition, home owners, who are mostly seniors (about half of them between 60 and 74 years), regularly accommodate children and grandchildren. Topophilia can therefore be passed on from generation to generation, as confirmed by certain practices: children sometimes decide to choose the *commune* where their parents have a second home to get married; this is the case for at least three households participating in Châtelaillon-Plage focus groups. This practice can be a strong marker for setting down roots in the place. Furthermore, according to the home owners participating in focus groups, it is the children or grandchildren who justify the presence of the second home or the decision to keep it within the family fold.

Another criterion can be used to measure attachment to the place: the rhythms and time-scales of stays. In particular, returning to a place over several years is a sign of strong attachment. Our investigation thus raised the question of the year in which the residence was acquired, even if the home owners may have been visiting the place for much longer, as a tourist or descendants of secondary or permanent residents. However, in eight out of ten *communes*, the secondary residents surveyed had been owners for longer than the national average, which is 15 years (Atout France 2010). The average tenure was even 19 years in Ars-en-Ré and 23 years on the Île d'Aix. This average conceals an opposition between two categories of secondary residents. First, the "new owners", that is to say the secondary residents who have acquired their property since 2001, i.e. approximately ten years. They illustrate the recent dynamics of the residential attractiveness of the Atlantic coast, in general, and the department of Charente-Maritime, in particular, and are the group most represented in nine out of our ten test *communes*, even accounting for half of all owners interviewed in three *communes*: Châtelaillon-Plage, La Tremblade and Saint-Denis-d'Oléron. This majority category coexists with the category of "rooted" residents, who have had their second home for at least one generation (before 1991, i.e. 22 years minimum). The latter represent up to a third of secondary residents in Ars-en-Ré (34%), Fouras (30%) and Saint-Georges-de-Didonne (32%).

Participation in local life

This concerns analysis of the different forms of participation by second home owners in local life. However, allowance should be made for a representativeness bias. In fact, merely by returning the questionnaire, respondents are demonstrating that they are more immediately interested in and committed to collective action than the average population.

Participation in an association is a good indicator of local investment by secondary residents. This level of investment is extremely interesting, with one second home owner in four participating in an association in their *commune* of secondary residence in the majority of *communes* surveyed. This value is important because we can easily imagine that of the 45% of French citizens aged over 18 belonging to an association at the national level (Prouteau & Wolff 2013), most do so in the *commune* of their principal home. The profile of owners who are older and better educated than the national average (Atout France 2010) partly compensates for their discontinuous presence in a place. Indeed, Prouteau and Wolff (2013) have shown that the propensity to be a member of an association increases significantly with age and level of education. However, second home owners have an average age of 61 years versus 57 years for owners of principal homes (FILICOM 2007), and 60% are over 60 years of age. In our survey, 70% of respondents were aged over 60.

In most *communes* surveyed, over 40% of members of a local association participated in a home owner association, a type of structure intended to defend rights and interests, which is a much higher proportion than at the national level (12.5% for Prouteau & Wolff 2013). Moreover, 20% of secondary residents in the survey are members of organisations which work to protect the environment and heritage. The proportion of members in home owner associations is often inversely proportional to the proportion of members in environmental protection associations. In fact, in the surveyed *communes* on the Île d'Oléron, where 50% of membership of associations concerns the defence of the interests of owners, environmental protection associations represent less than 20% of memberships. However, in the two *communes* of the Île de Ré where "green" associations are better represented (25% to 36% of membership), home owner associations are less popular (less than 20% of memberships). However, secondary residents surveyed on the Île d'Oléron seem more concerned than their counterparts on the Île de Ré about environmental protection in the *commune* hosting their second home: 17% to 19% were not at all satisfied with the environmental protection in the *communes* of Oléron, whereas this figure was 8% in both Île de Ré *communes*, and the proportion of "very satisfied" which reached 13% on Ré was below 5% on Oléron. Strangely, membership in environmental associations seems to develop when the situation for heritage protection stabilises, whereas when this aspect is problematic, it tends to find expression through the more general question of defending the owner's interests.

Although involvement in local associations is significant, the assertion of involvement in the life of the *commune* of the secondary residence is more so. For all *communes* surveyed, people saying they were as much or more involved in their *commune* of secondary residence in relation to their principal home represented between 25% and 55% of respondents. For the *communes* surveyed on the Île de Ré and Île d'Oléron, the proportion was consistently greater than 50%. These values demonstrate a willingness to be considered as a real player in the territory.

Contribution of the attractiveness of the tourist area

Second home owners have a key role in the dynamics of attractiveness through their welcome and the image of a place they offer. Non-commercial accommodation in France is the leading form of tourist accommodation, accounting for 66.7% of overnight stays in 2013. Although overnight stays in a household's secondary residence accounted for 16.8% of this value, staying with relatives and friends made up 47.8% of overnight stays (DGCIS 2013), i.e. almost half of all tourist overnight stays. A portion of these nights concerned the principal homes of family and friends (Blondy et al. 2013), but a significant portion also took advantage of their second home, especially in tourist areas.

On the Charente coast, only 2% of second home owners said they never "welcome visitors" to their property while one in two declared that they regularly accommodate friends or family. The second home is therefore clearly a place of sociability where family and friends are welcomed, and each property can sleep six to seven people on average. Moreover, the second home, seen as a relaxing place for almost all of those surveyed, is also considered a place of reunion for the vast majority of second home owners (70% in the majority of *communes*, with rates exceeding 80% on the Île de Ré). This act of welcoming others contributes to the attractiveness of the area since getting friends and family to visit often means praising the quality of the places. And conversely, the attractiveness of the tourist place compared to the place of the principal residence, even when it is located nearby, impacts the arrival of relatives and friends: 'When we're in Niort, no-one comes to visit, but when we're in Chatelaillon, everyone turns up as if by magic' (an owner living in Niort, an inland city in the Poitou-Charentes region, and participating in Focus Group No. 2, 25 July 2013, Châtelaillon-Plage (Charente-Maritime)). These newly discovered places can be visited again in the context of commercial accommodation or can even encourage people to buy a property so as to enjoy the places more regularly and more independently.

Owners of second homes on the Charente coast declared that they stay in their property for between 75 and 94 days per year, depending on the *communes* surveyed (Figure 20.2). However, the little existing data on the occupancy rate of second homes reveals much lower values nationally: 30 days by the owner (Atout France 2010). On the Charente coast, our survey shows that in 2013 the values are at least three times higher, reaching or exceeding three months occupancy, particularly on the Île de Ré. (The initial results of the 2013 survey did not permit us to

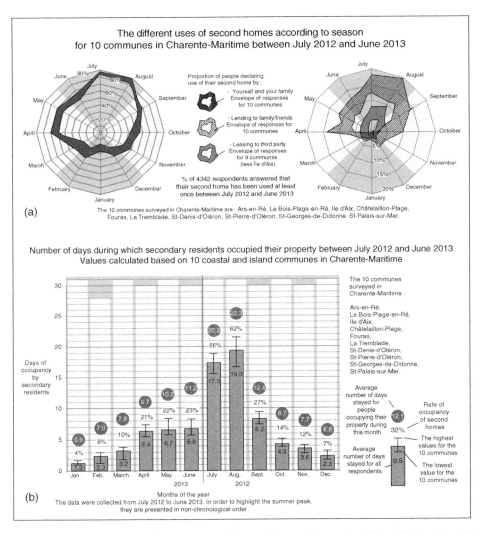

Figure 20.2 Analysis of monthly occupancy of second homes. Conception: Blondy, Vacher, Vye, 2014. (a) Source: Enquête Residénces secondaires Charente-Maritime 2013, UMR LIENSs CNRS Université de La Rochelle, Charente-Maritime Tourisme, CCI La Rochelle, CCI Rochefort et Saintonge.

calculate a total number of days of occupancy for lending or leasing for each commune due to the low response levels. Deployment of the survey at the departmental level should make this possible.) Visits are highly seasonal. With between 16 and 21 days average occupancy, July and August are the months when occupancy is highest: between 80 and 90% of second home owners stay in their property during this period. Between December and February, only 20–30% of owners (depending on the *commune*) reported that they use these properties, which often have poor or non-existent heating systems. When the properties are well equipped, as presumably they are on the Île de Ré, where the price of land is high, the occupancy rate of the owners during the winter months can reach 40% on weekends or the Christmas and New Year period. Occupancy is therefore clearly seasonal in nature, although this aspect should be qualified.

The use of second homes for tourist accommodation is supplemented by the fact that the property is generally lent out to family or friends. The 2013 survey indicates that about a third of residents surveyed in each *commune* lent out their second home in 2013. The summer peak remains the preferred time for this loan (which is the case for one residence in ten), and the study of timescales (Figure 20.2) indicates that in winter, the second home is mainly used by the owners, if it is used at all.

Many homes are leased out for part of the year, to help cover the maintenance costs and taxes related to the property. This leasing period is generally in summer. Over this period, depending on the *commune*, between 4% and 13% of respondents declared having leased out second homes at least once in the month. The importance of the summer period compared to the rest of the year is even greater for acts of leasing than for lending. For spring or early autumn, a few lets of second homes extend the season and the functioning of these coastal areas to a degree. However, many lets are not declared and therefore escape taxation (Sacareau et al. 2013). As a result, home owners tend to say little or nothing about operations, which are certainly underestimated in this study.

Conclusion

Although still incomplete, the study concerning the use of second homes in Charente-Maritime already enables a better understanding of the complex relationship which these actors have with the tourist area by giving a voice to the owners. It also provides an unprecedented insight into this study's purpose for several reasons. First, its magnitude is a guarantee of reliability, with more than 4,000 respondents in the *communes* on the Charente coast presenting representative territorial contexts. It is also unique because it covers original themes by focusing on the uses, expectations and representations that these players have of their property and their living environment.

It was thus possible to analyse three forms of investment in the place by these populations. First, the importance of emotional investment as reflected in the expression of a strong attachment to the place. This is explained by the positive role assigned to the property (as a place for holidays and/or family reunions). It sometimes takes root in the long term; familiarity with the place may date back some time to when the second home owner was a tourist in the place or a descendant of a secondary or permanent resident. Second, we have also identified a significant participation in local life. There is a real desire for recognition as a distinct resident within the tourist area, whether they are long-standing or new owners, heirs or recent buyers of a property. At the same time, this participation is complex to define, between the defence of specific interests related to their status as owner and an investment in the community when environmental issues are to the fore. Finally, second home owners are key players in increasing the attractiveness of the coastal tourist area thanks to a significant presence in the territory (almost 3 months with a strong presence, from April to September). Also, by welcoming relatives and friends, they contribute to the promotion of the destination although it is focused on their circle of friends and family and does not effect any real spread of occupancy over the year.

References

Aguer, O. and Vergeau, E. (2009) 'Les résidences secondaires: Une composante du développement et de l'attractivité de la région', *Décimal – INSEE Poitou-Charentes*, 288 (February): 1–6.

Atout France (2010) 'La résidence secondaire en France, fonctionnement économique, mise en marché, services d'intendance', *Paris: Editions Atout France*, 24: 113.

Bésingrand, D. (2005) La mobilité résidentielle des seniors sur la façade atlantique de l'Europe. PhD. Université d'Angers, Angers, France.

Blondy, C., Vacher, L. and Vye, D. (2013) 'A qualified reading of the impact of tourism on island areas: The role of local populations in visits to tourist locations and perception of their environmental quality'. In S. Favro and C. A. Brebbia (eds) *Island Sustainability II*. Ashurst, UK: WIT Press, 63–79.

Blondy, C., Vacher, L. and Vye, D. (2016) Les résidents secondaires, des acteurs essentiels des systèmes touristiques littoraux français?, Territoire en mouvement Revue de géographie et aménagement [En ligne], Articles, mis en ligne le 20 avril 2016. [online] Available at: http://tem.revues.org/3344

Bonnin, P. and Villanova, R. (eds) (1999) *D'une maison l'autre: Parcours et mobilités résidentielles*. Paris: Créaphis.

Brida, J. G., Osti, L. and Santifaller, E. (2011) 'Second homes and the need of policy planning', *Tourismos: An International Multidisciplinary Journal of Tourism*, 6 (1): 141–163.

Buhot, C. (2009) 'Embourgeoisement et effet littoral. Recompositions socio-spatiales à La Rochelle et à l'Île de Ré', *Journal of Urban Research, Special*, 1. [online] Available at: http://articulo.revues.org/1034

Clément, C. and Lelièvre, E. (2005) 'Familles recomposées et ancrage résidentiel', *Espaces et Sociétés*, 2: 79–97.

Clout, H. D. (1971) 'Second homes in Auvergne', *Geographical Review*, 61 (4): 530–553.

Coppock, J. T. (ed.) (1977) *Second Homes: Curse or Blessing?* Oxford: Pergamon Press.

Cribier, F. (1994) 'La migration de retraites des Parisiens, l'apport des enquêtes biographiques, Espace, Populations', *Sociétés*, 12 (1): 75–83.

Davezies, L. (2009) 'L'économie locale "résidentielle"', *Géographie Économie Société*, 11 (1): 7–53.

DGCIS (Direction générale de la compétitivité, de l'industrie et des services) (2013) *Report for the year 2013*. Ivry-sur-Seine, France: DGCIS.

Dubost, F. (ed.) (1995) *Les résidences secondaires, nouvelles orientations. Final Report*. Février: Groupe de prospective sur l'avenir des espaces ruraux, DATAR.

Dubost, F. (ed.) (1998) *L'autre maison, la résidence secondaire, refuge des générations*. Paris: Editions Autrement.

Duchêne-Lacroix, C. (2013) 'Eléments pour une typologie des pratiques plurirésidentielles et d'un habiter multilocal, e-migrinter', *Poitiers*, 11: 151–164.

Duhamel, P. (2000) 'Vivre à Majorque. La sédentarisation des résidents secondaires', *Revue Espaces*, 176: 33–37.

Équipe MIT (2002) *Tourisme 1, lieux communs*. Paris: Belin.

Farstad, M. and Rye, J. F. (2013) 'Second home owners, locals and their perspectives on rural development', *Journal of Rural Studies*, 30: 41–51.

FILICOM (Fichier des logements à la commune) (2007) *Report for the year 2007*. Bron, France: CEREMA.

Gallent, N., Mace, A. and Tewdwr-Jones, M. (2005) *Second Homes: European Perspectives and UK Policies*. Ashgate, UK: Aldershot.

Hall, C. M. and Müller, D. K. (2004) 'Introduction: Second homes, curse or blessing? Revisited'. In C. M. Hall and D. K. Müller (eds) *Tourism, Mobility and Second Homes, Between Elite Landscapes and Common Ground*. Clevedon, UK: Channel View Publications, 3–14.

Hoggart, K. and Buller, H. (1995) 'British home owners and housing change in rural France', *Housing Studies*, 10 (2): 179–198.

Lefèvre, M. and Frayssinet, D. (2011) La qualité des résidences secondaires, une question majeure pour le tourisme en Languedoc-Roussillon, INSEE Languedoc-Roussillon, Collection Repères/Synthèse, 7: 9.

McIntyre, N., Williams, D. R. and McHugh, K. E. (eds) (2006) *Multiple Dwelling and Tourism, Negotiating Place, Home and Identity*. Wallingford, UK: CABI.

Marjavaara, R. (2007) 'The displacement myth: Second home tourism in the Stockholm Archipelago', *Tourism Geographies*, 9 (3): 296–317.

Módenes, J.-A. and López-Colás, J. (2007) 'La résidence secondaire en Espagne: Profils sociodémographiques et territoriaux', *Population*, 62 (1): 161–177.

Müller, D. K. (2002) 'Reinventing the countryside: German second-home owners in Southern Sweden', *Current Issues in Tourism*, 5 (5): 426–446.

Müller, D. K. and Hoogendoorn, G. (2013) 'Second homes: Curse or blessing? A review 36 years later', *Scandinavian Journal of Hospitality and Tourism*, 13 (4): 353–369.

Observatoire des clientèles CMT (2008) Faites connaissance avec les différentes clientèles de la Charente-Maritime. [online] Available at: https://pro.en-charente-maritime.com/Creer-et-developper/J-analyse-mon-territoire/Les-clienteles-touristiques/

Overvag, K. and Berg, N. G. (2011) 'Second homes, rurality and contested space in Eastern Norway', *Tourism Geographies*, 13 (3): 417–442.

Paris, C. (2009) 'Re-positioning second homes within housing studies: Household investment, gentrification, multiple residence, mobility and hyper-consumption', *Housing, Theory and Society*, 26 (4): 292–310.

Paris, C. (2011) *Affluence, Mobility and Second Home Ownership*. London: Routledge.

Perrot, M. and de La Soudière, M. (1998) 'La résidence secondaire: Un nouveau mode d'habiter la campagne?' *Ruralia*, 2. [online] Available at: https://ruralia.revues.org/34

Pinçon, M. and Pinçon-Charlot, M. (1989) *Dans Les Beaux Quartiers*. Paris: Seuil.

Prouteau, L. and Wolff, F. C. (2013) 'Adhésions et dons aux associations: Permanences et évolutions de 2002 à 2010', *Economie et statistiques*, 459: 27–57.

Roca, Z. (ed.) (2013) *Second Home Tourism in Europe, Lifestyle Issues and Policy Responses*. London: Ashgate.

Sacareau, I., Vacher, L. and Vye, D. (2010) 'Attractivité touristique et attractivité résidentielle du littoral charentais: Lorsque les Anglais brouillent la donne', *Sud-Ouest Européen*, 29: 7–22.

Sacareau, I., Vacher, L. and Vye, D. (2013) 'La résidence secondaire est-elle un objet aux confins du tourisme? Réflexions à partir de l'exemple des résidences secondaires des Britanniques en Poitou-Charentes'. In P. Bourdeau, H. François and L. Perrin-Bensahe (eds) *Fins et confins du tourisme*. Paris: L'Harmattan, 177–193.

Stock, M. (2003) 'Topophilia'. In J. Lévy and M. Lussault (eds) *Dictionnaire de la géographie et de l'espace des sociétés*. Paris: Belin, 930–931.

Stock, M. (2006) 'L'hypothèse de l'habiter poly-topique: Pratiquer les lieux géographiques dans les sociétés à individus mobiles', *EspacesTemps.net*. [online] Retrieved at: http://espacestemps.net/document1853.html (accessed 26 February 2006)

Urbain, J.-D. (2002) 'Le résident secondaire, un touriste à part?', *Ethnologie Française*, 3: 515–520.

Tuan, Y.-F. (1961) 'Topophilia', *Landscape*, 11 (1): 29–32.

21

HOST COMMUNITY PERCEPTIONS OF INTERNATIONAL PERMANENT TOURISTS

The case of Didim, Turkey

Imren Uysal Waller* and Richard Sharpley

Introduction

The phenomenon of northern Europeans retiring to southern Europe is not new (Dwyer 2002; King et al. 2000). Residents of colder, northern European countries have long sought to migrate south to warmer climates, although, until the latter years of the twentieth century, few people had the means to do so. However, reflecting broader political–economic transformations, the last three decades have witnessed remarkable growth in north–south migration within Europe. For example, in 1990 an estimated 62,069 British expatriates were living in Spain; by 2013, this figure had risen to 381,025 (Royal Statistical Society (RSS) 2014).

A variety of factors have underpinned this contemporary manifestation of mobility, not least the more general desire of Western populations to live in warmer climates (Cohen 2008). At the same time, the image of the country or destination (often previously visited on holiday), the opportunity to buy a larger or more luxurious home in a country with lower property prices and the attraction of a lower cost of living have all driven its growth. Hence, a number of commentators refer to this phenomenon as lifestyle migration (Benson & O'Reilly 2009a; Cohen et al. 2015; Torkington 2012) or mobility based upon people's 'belief that there is a more fulfilling way of life available to them elsewhere' (Benson & O'Reilly 2009b: 608). Yet, such lifestyle migration is a broad concept. It embraces not only those seeking to retire elsewhere but also younger people looking for a "new life"; equally, it includes both permanent and semi-permanent migrants. Therefore, it is often considered within the broader context of tourism and second home ownership, an issue that has long attracted attention within the academic literature (Coppock 1977; Hall & Müller 2004; Hall & Williams 2002; Helderman et al. 2006; Jaakson 1986; Müller 2004).

Irrespective of the nature of and motives for this north-south migration within Europe, however, it is typically manifested in the development of often substantial communities of what are referred to here as permanent or semi-permanent tourists in destination areas. It is not surprising, therefore, that such tourist-migration and its associated impacts on local society and culture in destination areas have long been explored in the academic literature (e.g. Girard & Gartner 1993; Helderman et al. 2006; Marjavara 2007, 2009; O'Reilly 2003, 2007). It is also not surprising that, in the southern European context (significant research has also been undertaken in Scandinavian countries where there exists an established tradition of second home ownership) much of the research has focused predominantly on Spain (e.g. Haug, Dann & Mehmetoglu 2007; Rodriguez 2001) and to a lesser extent France (Benson 2010). What is surprising, perhaps, is that one country yet to benefit from academic scrutiny in this context is Turkey. Despite the evidence of increasing overseas property ownership in the country, particularly in or near popular holiday destinations, second home ownership in the country in general has been overlooked, and little, if any, attention has been paid to interactions between permanent tourists and local host communities in particular.

More specifically, research undertaken by Bahar, Laciner, Bal and Özcan (2009) reveals that growing numbers of British, Scandinavian and German tourists have in recent years started to buy properties in Turkey for the purposes of both extended holidays/semi-migration and for retirement. The demand is clearly illustrated by official data from Turkey's Land Registry Directorate's Foreigner Affairs Unit, cited by Wallork (2011: 1):

> British [and] German are the top foreign buyers of property in Turkey. Foreign buyers from 89 countries have purchased approximately 111,200 properties across Turkey. British people are the most prolific buyers with 35,249 British people owning 24,848 properties, followed by Germany and Greece.

In other words, there is clear evidence of significant and growing demand, principally among central and northern Europeans, in purchasing properties in Turkey. This, in turn, suggests that the need exists for systematic research into the phenomenon, particularly given the potential scale of overseas ownership of properties in Turkey. Indeed, as noted above, this need has already been recognised within Turkey. According to the International Strategic Research Organisation (ISRO) in Turkey, sponsored by The Scientific and Technological Research Council of Turkey (TUBITAK): 'There are many scholarly studies of settled migrants in several Mediterranean countries like Spain, Greece, Italy and Malta. Yet, the issue remains relatively untouched in the case of Turkey' (ISRO 2008: 2). Hence, an initial project entitled *Integration of Settled Foreigners in Turkey with the Turkish Community: Issues and Opportunities* was undertaken by ISRO. It was, however, based primarily on quantitative data collection and, as a consequence, the study concluded that:

> There is not a clear understanding of the "settled foreigners" concept amongst the Turkish public. A sophisticated understanding regarding the issue does not exist, either. Not only are settled foreigners perceived as a homogenous group, but also their reasons for coming to the country, their needs and their interests are perceived as common.
>
> *(ISRO 2008: 7)*

Thus, despite some initial work, there remains a lack of knowledge and understanding of the consequences of increasing international tourist-migration into Turkey and, in particular, how this is perceived by local residents in areas where permanent tourist communities have become established. The purpose of this chapter is to address this significant gap in the literature. Drawing on research undertaken among stakeholders in the second home property sector in Didim, Turkey, it explores local people's perceptions of and responses to permanent tourists, focusing in particular on issues related to the extent of their integration and cultural exchange with the local community. In so doing, it seeks to contribute to the tourist migration/second home literature in general and the understanding of the permanent tourist phenomenon in Turkey in particular. The first task, however, is to review briefly the concept of the "permanent tourist" and understandings of so-called host–guest relations as a framework for the subsequent research.

Permanent tourists: Towards a definition

As observed above, a number of terms are employed in the literature to describe the phenomenon of people migrating overseas to live in properties purchased as either their principal or second homes, including: "lifestyle migration" (Benson & O'Reilly 2009a); "lifestyle mobility" (Cohen et al. 2015), "retirement migration" (King et al. 2000) and, more generally, second home ownership (Hall & Müller 2004). Similarly, these migrants are variously referred to as, for example, "lifestyle migrants" (Benson & O'Reilly 2009b), "residential tourists" (O'Reilly 2003, 2007) or "settled foreigners" (ISRO 2008; Bahar et al. 2009).

For the purposes of this study, however, the term "permanent tourist" is employed in order to differentiate the target group (those migrating from other countries to retire in Turkey) from other types of migrants referred to in the above definitions, such as temporary tourists, semi-permanent migrants or those migrating to live and work in Turkey. The term "permanent tourists" is adopted from Cohen (1974: 537), who defines these individuals as 'persons who, though deriving their income in their country of origin, prefer to take up semi-permanent residence in another country'. Here, the main emphasis is on the fact that permanent tourists are not working in the host country, the principal basis for differentiating the phenomenon of permanent tourists from, for example, residential tourists and lifestyle migration. However, also in this study, the duration of permanent tourists' residence in the destination is considered to involve relatively longer periods of time than temporary tourists while socio-cultural self-identification as permanent tourists, irrespective of whether they own their property or not, is also a factor.

Host–guest relations and host perceptions of tourism

Given the nature of tourism, it is almost inevitable that tourists meet and interact with members of the local community in the destination or, more succinctly, that a relationship exists between local people as "hosts" and tourists as "guests". The nature of that relationship varies according to a number of factors, not least the role of the host (de Kadt 1979; Sutton 1967) but, significantly, it has long been claimed that a balanced or harmonious relationship between hosts and guests is of fundamental importance to the success of tourism (Zhang, Inbakaran & Jackson 2006). Putting it another way, the development of tourism inevitably incurs some degree of impact on the local environment and society and that, should members of the local community perceive the costs of tourism to outweigh the benefits they receive, they may withdraw their support for tourism (Lawson et al. 1998). That is, a "happy host" (Snaith & Hailey 1999) is essential to the successful development of tourism and, hence, not only is it important to ensure the positive outcomes of tourism for the host community are optimised (and costs minimised), but that the "voices" of the local community should inform tourism planning and management.

Consequently, host community perceptions of tourism have been a popular and enduring focus of research or what McGehee and Anderek (2004: 132) describe as 'one of the most systematic and well-studied areas of tourism'. A comprehensive review is beyond the scope of this chapter (see, for example, Deery, Jago & Fredline 2012; Easterling 2004; Harrill 2004; Nunkoo, Smith & Ramkissoon 2013; Sharpley 2014) although a number of key points are of relevance here, not least the fact that over the last three decades the research has evolved significantly in terms of scope, theoretical underpinning and conceptual design. Indeed, since Ap (1990) lamented the narrow, descriptive nature of the research then, much of which typically reflected a "tourism impact" focus (McGehee & Anderek 2004: 132) that identified and described local communities' experiences of and responses to tourism's economic, social and environmental impacts, tourism perceptions have been increasingly adopted. Within this broader perspective, the research has developed along two distinctive but related paths. First, significant attention has been paid to identifying, measuring and comparing the variables which may determine the local community's perceptions of tourism, such variables being both intrinsic to the individual and extrinsic, or related to, the destination community as a whole (Faulkner & Tideswell 1997). However, as Andriotis and Vaughan (2003) note, these variables-based studies tend to view the local community as homogeneous; that is, they overlook the potential for different groups or clusters within destination communities to have varying perceptions of tourism. Hence, the second research path has focused on segmentation or cluster analysis (for example, Fredline & Faulkner 2000; Pérez & Nadal 2005). In addition, recent studies have explored local community perceptions within the broader context of residents' quality of life/well-being (Andereck & Nyaupane 2011; Kim et al. 2013) while attempts have also been made, albeit unconvincingly (Pearce et al. 1996), to apply theoretical frameworks, particularly social action theory, to the research.

Nevertheless, the host perceptions research continues to suffer a number of limitations (Deery et al. 2012; Sharpley 2014). Typically, for example, it is based on "one-off" case studies, most usually in the developed world (much of the research emanates from North America), and often focuses on domestic tourism in untypical destinations (Nunkoo & Gursoy 2012). Hence, not only have larger mainstream international tourism destinations been excluded, but the validity and generalisability of outcomes is limited (Huh & Vogt 2008). At the same time, not only does the research focus on perceptions of, rather than responses to tourism, but studies that explore the local community's perception of and interaction with tourists themselves are relatively rare. However, the research is most criticised for the predominant use of quantitative methods which, according to some, renders the outcomes simplistic and theoretically fragile (Woosnam 2012); the research is unable to explain or predict local community perceptions or responses to tourism. Or, as Moufakkir and Reisinger (2013: xiii) observe 'perception studies tend to reduce the reality of the … [host] … gaze to what is visible; yet we know what is visible is not the whole truth'. As a consequence, it has been suggested that a multi-dimensional, qualitative approach should be adopted that, in general, has the potential to explain not only how but why the local community perceives and responds to tourism (Deery et al. 2012); that is, to reveal more of, if not the "whole truth". As the chapter now discusses, the research among the local community in this study was, thus, based on qualitative methods in order to elicit a deeper, more nuanced picture of their perceptions of permanent tourists.

The research

As noted in the introduction, the research was undertaken in Didim, a small town located on the Aegean coast in the Western part of Turkey. It was selected for the research because it is not only a popular tourism destination but also home to an established community of international permanent tourists. According to Turkey's Office of National Statistics (TUIK 2016), Didim's population increased from 42,266 in 2007 to 73,000 in 2015, primarily as a consequence of incoming migration. This growth includes both domestic and international migration. Although according to a newspaper report, in 2016 British migrants accounted for 25% of the town's population (Londra Gazete 2016).

Given the specific purpose of the research to critically explore the local community's perceptions of permanent tourists, respondents were purposefully sampled from the local Turkish community in Didim. They were identified and contacted through the first author's existing contacts and, in total, 13 members of the local community participated in the research, including representatives of different age groups as well as people who had either been born and always lived in Didim or who had lived in the town for at least ten years. The sample also included a mix of genders and political backgrounds as well as different professions, including stakeholders in the second home property sector, local government officials, the religious community (e.g. imams), the coach of a local football team and other businessmen and workers from the region.

The semi-structured interviews were conducted (in Turkish) during August 2013. Each interview took approximately 50–60 minutes; all interviews were, with the respondents' consent, digitally recorded and subsequently transcribed and translated into English.

As observed above, previous host perception research is considered to be limited by the predominant employment of quantitative data collection methods. Hence, the use of qualitative interviews sought to generate a deeper understanding of the local community's perceptions and experiences of permanent tourists in Didim (McGregor & Murnane 2010; Silverman 2006). As discussed in the remainder of the chapter, this approach indeed yielded rich data with respect to the local community's perceptions of permanent tourists, of their expectations and level of adaptation to and integration with the host community in Didim.

Research outcomes

General perceptions of permanent tourists

From the interviews, a number of broad findings emerged which suggest that the local community in Didim has generally positive perceptions of permanent tourists in their town. From a practical perspective, there was a belief among most respondents that the majority of "outsiders" buying properties in Didim are primarily British people aged over fifty and, to a lesser extent, Turkish retirees, with both being from lower income groups. The respondents were also of the opinion that most of these now permanent tourists had previously holidayed in the region before deciding to buy a property there, and that the main reasons for British migrants choosing Didim is that housing there is relatively cheap compared with other touristic regions in Turkey. At the same time, they also felt that the small size of the town and its relaxed atmosphere also attracted permanent tourists.

More specifically, the respondents claimed that although they recognised that the culture of the permanent tourists is dissimilar to their own, they are nevertheless happy to host them. This, perhaps, reflects generally positive attitudes towards tourism (both seasonal and permanent) and, in particular, its contribution to the local economy in Didim. For example, many local businesses have responded to opportunities offered by the British community; prices are displayed in British currency, and products, such as fish and chips, are widely available. Indeed, a local Turkish bakery produces steak and kidney pies for the foreign residents. Hence, all respondents, including those who were not working in the tourism industry, were positively disposed towards British permanent tourists and expressed no negative opinions.

Such an outcome is unsurprising; research has long revealed a correlation between economic benefits/dependency and positive attitudes towards tourism (Pizam 1978; Brougham &

Butler 1981). Equally unsurprising was evident concern among respondents regarding the increase in the number of property developments in Didim in response to the demand from permanent tourists, an increase that has, they felt, degraded the environment. Interestingly, however, many respondents expressed the view that this problem has arisen because of poor practice on the part of property developers rather than because of permanent tourists themselves; that is, the local community does not "blame" the permanent tourists for the excessive property development.

Indeed, the respondents also claimed that the number of permanent tourists living in Didim has fallen in recent years, resulting in another interesting outcome from the study with regards to the manner in which the local community has taken advantage of the surplus supply of cheap buildings. In most other case studies from around the Mediterranean, the influx of permanent tourists has tended to lead to an increase in house prices and the costs of products and services (Benson & O'Reilly 2009a; Helderman et al. 2006; Hall & Müller 2004; O'Reilly 2003, 2007; King et al. 2000). In the past, this also occurred in Didim. In recent years, however, and perhaps as a consequence of the 2008 global financial crisis, international demand for homes in the town demand has reduced. As a consequence, surplus properties are now being bought by Turkish nationals from outside of the local area. These changes have impacted existing permanent tourists/second home owners as it seems to have emphasised the divisions between the two communities and created pressures owing to the different expectations of permanent tourists and the increasing Turkish population. Further research intends to investigate this issue more deeply but, following the objectives of this study, a number of more specific findings emerged from this study.

Permanent tourists: Impacts on society, culture and religion

As noted above, despite recognised cultural differences, most interviewees were positive about British permanent tourists in Didim. Indeed, some suggested that the presence of British permanent tourists improved the social life of the local community, with many migrants involving themselves in and supporting the wider community by, for example, setting up charitable organisations and supporting the poor in the region.

Others, however, commented that social and cultural changes had occurred owing to the presence of British permanent tourists, particularly in the lifestyle of local Turkish families. Specifically, they suggested that British permanent tourists needed to be more aware of the host culture, particularly towards younger people who, some respondents suggested, are more susceptible to foreign influences or acculturation. More generally, the main criticism of permanent tourists related to their perceived excessive alcohol consumption and the consequential social issues such as neighbours being too noisy and being disrespectful towards the host community. Indeed, the perceived general pattern of behaviour of some, if not all, permanent tourists (for example, socialising outdoors with other permanent tourists, frequent and excessive drinking, and being noisy and carefree within sight and hearing of their Turkish neighbours) gives the local community the impression that even though they are permanent home owners/residents in Didim, they behave no differently from temporary visitors on extended holidays.

Overall, however, the research revealed no consensus as to how the presence of permanent tourists was perceived to influence or impact the social lives of the local community. That is, opposing viewpoints were often expressed by respondents. Even the local religious community offered different opinions: the town's two imams (both of whom participated in interviews) held differing views on British permanent tourists in Didim. For example:

Extract 1:

Interviewer: What do you think about these people who bought property here? What type of needs do they have here and what should be done in response?

Respondent 4:   now … I have information about that when we compare England and here. I have been told that [here] we allow them more freedom than in England. For example, I heard that while they drink like that in England they can't go shopping or walk around the streets very comfortably in England and make people uncomfortable but here they behave very comfortably while they are drunk.

Interviewer: Do you think they have been given too much freedom here?

Respondent 4:   Yes, too much freedom. I always hear that. [They have] been given too much. This is what I see and this is what I heard all the time. These things can make us uncomfortable and unhappy with this behaviour because they influence for our families and children negatively.

The other imam, however, emphasised that these differences should be seen as adding cultural richness to local society rather than bringing about social change or problems:

Extract 2:

Interviewer: Do you think there have been any cultural changes in the region? [since British permanent tourists arrived?]

Respondent 3:   No there haven't been any cultural changes [since they arrived]. I believe and see that this brings more cultural richness into our society.

One of the interesting points to emerge from these exchanges is that even though both imams are religious leaders within the same community, their perceptions of international permanent tourists vary significantly. One explanation may be that one respondent claims that he was told by some British tourists about cultural life in Britain and hence, came to conclusions about their behaviour in Turkey. In other words, it is important to note that residents' perceptions are influenced by their own socio-cultural environment. Here, the respondent's individual social relations with British permanent tourists and the knowledge he has thereby gained appear to have influenced his perceptions. This supports Pearce et al.'s (1996) criticism of social exchange theory, often used to frame research in host community perceptions of tourism, that residents' perceptions are often derived socially rather than from individual knowledge.

Another respondent claims that there are few if any differences in the attitudes and observed behaviour of the British permanent tourist community and that of many local people. Consequently, for this respondent, the British population does not cause any problems:

Extract 3:

Interviewer: Turkey is mainly Muslim while the British are from a Christian culture; does this cause any cultural clashes or issues?

Respondent 10:   No, there aren't any clashes or issues [related to this] because Turkey is not like that. For example, last month we had Ramadan. Some local people were fasting and praying but others were also drinking [alcohol] and going to entertainment areas [bars]. So we can't have any clash with English people because our own nationals also drink alcohol; they do the same things as English people usually do … So our nation drinks like them. Everyone lives their own religion the way they want to.

This response points to the fact that Turkey is not a typical Muslim nation, its society being culturally and socially polarised due to Turkey's secular structure, which has been established since 1923 (Yashin 2002; Lewis 1955, 1996).

Varying and opposing perceptions were also expressed by other respondents with regards to aspects of permanent tourists' presence and behaviour in Didim, as will now be discussed.

Perceptions of permanent tourists' adaptation to local life

Adaptation, like any other form of social behaviour, is a difficult concept to measure as it's relative, and viewpoints change depending on who is being interviewed, and behaviour is multidirectional and multidimensional (Moufakkir & Reisinger 2013; Griffiths & Sharpley 2012). Nevertheless, respondents generally expressed the belief that most permanent tourists showed little signs of adaptation to the host culture. However, this did not appear to be an issue for many respondents because they did not expect British permanent tourists to adapt to the local lifestyle; they believed that because most permanent tourists were aged over 50, adapting to the host culture would be difficult for them. Some respondents also commented that there were in fact some permanent tourists who had adapted, but these reflected the individual's personal circumstances, such as marriage to a member of the local community.

Having said that, most respondents stated that in terms of general lifestyle, such as shopping habits, eating local cuisine and other everyday activities, British permanent tourists have learnt how to live in Didim alongside the local community but did so in their own manner. For example, it was revealed in the interviews that permanent tourists go to the local village Pazar (open village market) and had learnt practical behaviour, such as taking sufficient small change with them to the market, just like locals. Conversely, the expectations of some members of the local community differ from those of permanent tourists. They had greater expectations and, hence, were more critical of permanent tourists:

Extract 4:

Interviewer: What do you think about these people who bought property here? What type of needs do they have here and what should be done in response?

Respondent 9: First of all, when English people settle in other countries, they should have learnt about their [hosts'] culture. Secondly, if they come to my country I believe that they should learn at least a basic level of our language in order to cope.

Interviewer: So you are saying they do not learn the native language?

Respondent 9: Look, these people don't. For example, Gordon Miller [Football coach] lived in Turkey for nine years and did not speak a word. … Even I tried to adapt to them; I tried to speak with them in English, like "good, hello" … because we live in same residence with English people. I do not understand them. What type of problem do they have not learning the our language? … They are extremely nationalistic! Why do they think they are better than anybody else? Why they do not learn the basic native language, especially when they want to live here?

However, another respondent had a completely different perception about the English community in Didim. He said that he has English friends because he visits English bars to hear their stories and that he has known some of them for ten years.

Extract 5:

Interviewer: So do you have a good friendship [with them]?

Respondent 8:   Yes, English people are known for being cold but they are not … In most cases, English people's relations with local people are good, socially and culturally. Most English people interact with locals and go to restaurants and bring money to local businesses. They are integrating with locals. They don't separate themselves from locals or create their own enclaves.

Interviewer: What do you think about their culture? Are they different from local people?

Respondent 8:   They are culturally different from us. We are a Muslim nation.

Interviewer: Do you think this causes problems?

Respondent 8:   No, definitely not. That does not cause any problems. People should respect each other and their differences. You can be a non-believer or Christian or Muslim; you need to respect that.

Interviewer: Shall we say that the English population here do not cause any cultural problems?

Respondent 8:   Yes, certainly. They do not cause any cultural problems here. Apart from that they are contributing to the local economy.

Interviewer: Very briefly I was wondering who adapts to whom in Didim? What do you think?

Respondent 8:   No one adapts to anyone. Everybody lives in their own way. If we think about it then the English community are more likely adapt here.

Interviewer: Do they learn Turkish?

Respondent 8:   No they don't. Especially English community are like that … . They do not learn Turkish. They are very certain on that.

Interviewer: Do you think because they think it is not easy for them to learn?

Respondent 8:   I know some of them tried [to learn it] but most of them do not want to learn Turkish.

To summarise the above respondent's view, British and local Turkish people get on well with and accept each other. The British community are willing to learn the local lifestyle but language is an issue; they do not learn it. It is interesting to see that Extract 4 mentioned Gordon Miller, a British football coach who lived and worked in Turkey for years and who did not learn any Turkish. It is important to state that these perceptions may be influenced by their own individual experiences or socially, such as through the national media or the role of one famous person.

Local perceptions of close friendship with permanent tourists

Most respondents indicated that they did not have close friendships with permanent tourists, primarily because of the language barrier. Some hosts felt that permanent tourists did not want to have deeper social contact because of their lack of effort to learn the language. Respondent 5, an elderly Turkish woman, revealed that even though one permanent tourist had lived in the same apartment block for four years, their British neighbour (who is of the same age and gender) has never learnt any Turkish and whenever they had a problem in the apartment they had to provide a translator.

Extract 6:

Interviewer: What do you think about their [permanent tourists] social and cultural life in here?

Respondent 5: My neighbour, I don't think she has any social life … she walks around by herself and then goes to bed. Hello or good morning is all she has to say or to learn these two words not more but she cannot speak a word …

Interviewer: So you are saying that she has been living with you for two years but she can't speak a single word of Turkish?

Respondent 5: No 4 years by now, and all she has to learned are two words and asks [me] how are you? But she couldn't … It is important to learn other culture's language, especially if you are living with them.

Interestingly, however, most respondents did not consider learning the local language an issue. Indeed, most did not expect permanent tourists to do so. Rather, most local people put more effort into speaking English to accommodate the permanent tourists. For example, Respondent 7 stated that Didim's local government used to send bills in English to British permanent tourists.

Conclusion

In summary, then, despite living permanently in Didim, most permanent tourists enjoy only superficial relationships with the local community, the principal reason being the language barrier. Many respondents were critical about the lack of desire on the part of permanent tourists to learn Turkish, yet they nevertheless felt that permanent tourists have made an effort to learn how to live in the location, particularly with regards to obtaining goods and services. At the same time, however, these superficial relationships may reflect differing lifestyle expectations between the two groups; certainly, the research suggested that although some local people make an effort to interact with and get to know the migrant community, permanent tourists appear less willing to engage with the indigenous community. Generally, however, the situation is summed up by one respondent: 'No one adapts to anyone; everybody lives in their own way'.

Nevertheless, and despite the cultural differences between them, almost all respondents expressed the view that they are very happy to host British permanent tourists in Didim. Indeed, given their demographic characteristics (specifically, their age), permanent tourists are not expected to adapt to the local culture and society; the local community is happy to accept them, in a sense, as permanent "outsiders". In other words, though residing permanently in Didim, permanent tourists often behave similarly to seasonal tourists, but this appears to be generally accepted by the local community, perhaps because they recognise the economic benefits. However, reflecting their individual political and religious beliefs, the research did reveal differing perceptions on the part of respondents. In other words, the research suggests that it is difficult to generalise the perceptions of the local community with regard to permanent tourists, though it may be concluded, as no overall negative perceptions emerged from the interviews, that local people are generally happy to accept the "status quo" of the two culturally and socially distinctive communities living alongside each other.

At the same time, however, differing opinions and perceptions were evident among respondents, even within the religious community, supporting the argument in the literature that the 'whole truth' (Moufakkir & Reisinger 2013) can only be revealed through a deeper understanding of the local community's social world. Equally, revealing that "truth" also necessarily requires understanding of the perceptions of the permanent tourist community (Griffiths & Sharpley 2012); hence, this research presents only a partial picture. Nevertheless, it has revealed (perhaps surprisingly) a relatively stable and harmonious relationship between the local community and permanent tourists based upon the former group's acceptance of the expectation and behaviours of the latter.

References

Andereck, K. and Nyaupane, G. (2011) 'Exploring the nature of tourism and quality of life perceptions among residents', *Journal of Travel Research*, 50 (3): 248–260.

Andriotis, K. and Vaughan, R. (2003) 'Urban residents' attitudes toward tourism development: The case of Crete', *Journal of Travel Research*, 42 (2): 172–185.

Ap, J. (1990) 'Residents' perceptions research on the social impacts of tourism', *Annals of Tourism Research*, 17 (4): 610–616.

Bahar, H. I., Laciner, S., Bal, I. and Özcan, M. (2009) 'Older migrants to the Mediterranean: The Turkish example', *Population, Space and Place*, 15 (6): 509–522.

Benson, M. (2010) 'The context and trajectory of lifestyle migration: The case of the British residents of southwest France', *European Societies*, 12 (1): 45–64.

Benson, M. and O'Reilly, K. (2009a) *Lifestyle Migration: Expectations Aspirations and Experiences*, London: Routledge.

Benson, M. and O'Reilly K. (2009b) 'Migration and the search for a better way of life: A critical exploration of lifestyle migration', *The Sociological Review*, 57 (4): 608–625.

Brougham, J. and Butler, R. (1981) 'A segmentation analysis of resident attitudes to the social impact of tourism', *Annals of Tourism Research*, 8 (3): 569–589.

Cohen E. (1974) 'Who is a tourist? A conceptual clarification', *Sociological Review*, 22 (4): 527–555.

Cohen, E. (2008) *Explorations in Thai Tourism: Collected Case Studies*. Bingley, UK: Emerald.

Cohen, S., Duncan T. and Thulemark, M. (2015) 'Lifestyle mobilities: The crossroads of travel, leisure and migration', *Mobilities*, 10 (1): 155–172.

Coppock, J. (1977) *Second Homes: Curse or Blessing?* Oxford: Pergamon.

Deery, M., Jago, L. and Fredline, L. (2012) 'Rethinking social impacts of tourism research: A new research agenda', *Tourism Management*, 33 (1): 64–73.

de Kadt, E. (1979) *Tourism: Passport to Development?* New York: Oxford University Press.

Dwyer, P. (2002) 'Movements to some purpose? An exploration of international retirement migration in the European Union', *Education and Ageing*, 15 (3): 353–377.

Easterling, D. (2004) 'The residents' perspective in tourism research: A review and synthesis', *Journal of Travel & Tourism Marketing*, 17 (4): 45–62.

Faulkner, B. and Tideswell, C. (1997) 'A framework for monitoring community impacts of tourism', *Journal of Sustainable Tourism*, 5 (1): 3–28.

Fredline, E. and Faulkner, B. (2000) 'Host community reactions: A cluster analysis', *Annals of Tourism Research*, 27 (3): 763–784.

Girard, T. and Gartner, W. (1993) 'Second home second view: Host community perceptions', *Annals of Tourism Research*, 20 (4): 685–700.

Griffiths, I. and Sharpley, R. (2012) 'Influences of nationalism on tourist-host relationships', *Annals of Tourism Research*, 39 (4): 2051–2072.

Hall, C. M. and Williams, A. (eds) (2002) *Tourism and Migration: New Relationships between Production and Consumption*. Dordrecht, the Netherlands: Kluwer.

Hall, C. M. and Müller, D. (eds) (2004) *Tourism, Mobility and Second Homes: Between Elite Landscape and Common Ground*. Clevedon, UK: Channel View Publications.

Harrill, R. (2004) 'Residents' attitudes toward tourism development: A literature review with implications for tourism planning', *Journal of Planning Literature*, 18 (3): 251–266.

Haug, B., Dann, G. and Mehmetoglu, M. (2007) 'Little Norway in Spain: From tourism to migration', *Annals of Tourism Research*, 34 (1): 202–222.

Helderman, A. C., Ham, M. and Mulder, C. (2006) 'Migration and home ownership', *Tijdschrift voor Economische en Sociale Geografie*, 97 (2): 111–125.

Huh, C. and Vogt, C. (2008) 'Changes in residents' attitudes toward tourism over time: A cohort analytical approach', *Journal of Travel Research*, 46 (4): 446–455.

International Strategic Research Organisation (ISRO). (2008) *Integration of settled foreigners in Turkey with Turkish Community: Issues and opportunities*. Ankara, Turkey: ISRO.

Jaakson, R. (1986) 'Second-home domestic tourism', *Annals of Tourism Research*, 13 (3): 367–391.

Kim, K., Uysal, M. and Sirgy, J. (2013) 'How does tourism in a community impact the quality of life of community residents?', *Tourism Management*, 36: 527–540.

King, R., Warnes, T. and Williams, A. (2000) *Sunset Lives: British Retirement Migration to the Mediterranean*. Oxford: Berg Publishers.

Lawson, R., Williams, J., Young, T. and Cossens, J. (1998) 'A comparison of residents' attitudes towards tourism in 10 New Zealand destinations', *Tourism Management*, 19 (3): 247–256.

Lewis, B. (1955) 'Turkey: Westernization'. In G. von Grunebaum (ed.) *Unity and Variety in Müslim Civilization*. Chicago, IL: University of Chicago Press, 311–331.

Lewis, B. (1996) 'Islam and liberal democracy: A historical overview', *Journal of Democracy*, 7 (2): 52–63.

Londra Gazete. (2016) 'Didim'de 12 bin İngiliz yaşıyor', *Londra Gazete*, 7 February. [online] Retrieved from: http://www.londragazete.com/2016/02/07/didimde-12-bin-ingiliz-yasiyor/ (accessed 7 May 2016).

Marjavaara, R. (2007) 'Route to destruction? Second home tourism in small island communities', *Island Studies Journal*, 2 (1): 27–46.

Marjavaara, R. (2009) 'An inquiry into second-home-induced displacement', *Tourism and Hospitality Planning & Development*, 6 (3): 207–219.

McGehee, N. and Anderek, K. (2004) 'Factors predicting rural residents' support for tourism', *Journal of Travel Research*, 43 (2): 131–140.

McGregor, S. and Murnane, J. (2010) 'Paradigm, methodology and method: Intellectual integrity in consumer scholarship', *International Journal of Consumer Studies*, 34 (4): 419–427.

Moufakkir, O. and Reisinger, Y. (eds) (2013) *The Host Gaze in Global Tourism*. Wallingford, UK: CABI.

Müller, D. (2004) 'Mobility, tourism and second homes'. In A. Lew, C. M. Hall and A. Williams (eds) *A Companion to Tourism*. Oxford: Blackwell, 387–398.

Nunkoo, R. and Gursoy, D. (2012) 'Residents' support for tourism: An identity perspective', *Annals of Tourism Research*, 39 (1): 243–268.

Nunkoo, R., Smith, S. and Ramkissoon, M. (2013) 'Resident attitudes to tourism: A longitudinal study of 140 articles from 1984 to 2010', *Journal of Sustainable Tourism*, 21 (1): 5–25.

O'Reilly, K. (2003) 'When is a tourist? The articulation of tourism and migration in Spain's Costa del Sol', *Tourist Studies*, 3 (3): 301–317.

O'Reilly, K. (2007) 'Intra-European migration and the mobility-enclosure dialectic', *Sociology*, 41 (2): 277–293.

Pearce, P., Moscardo, G. and Ross, G. (1996) *Tourism Community Relationships*. Oxford: Pergamion Press.

Pérez, E. and Nadal, J. (2005) 'Host community perceptions: A cluster analysis', *Annals of Tourism Research*, 32 (4): 925–941.

Pizam, A. (1978) 'Tourist impacts: The social costs to the destination community as perceived by its residents', *Journal of Travel Research* 16 (4): 8–12.

Rodriguez, V. (2001) 'Tourism as a recruiting post for retirement migration', *Tourism Geographies*, 3 (1): 52–63.

Royal Statistical Society (RSS) (2014) 'How many British immigrants are there in other countries?', RSS. [online] Available at: https://www.statslife.org.uk/social-sciences/1910-how-many-british-immigrants-are-there-in-other-people-s-countries (accessed 26 May 2016).

Sharpley, R. (2014) 'Host perceptions of tourism: A review of the research', *Tourism Management*, 42 (1): 37–49.

Silverman D. (2006) *Interpreting Qualitative Data*. 3rd ed. London: Sage Publications.

Snaith, T. and Haley, A. (1999) 'Residents' opinions of tourism development in the historical city of York', *Tourism Management*, 20 (5): 595–603.

Sutton, W. (1967) 'Travel and understanding: Notes on the social structure of touring', *International Journal of Comparative Sociology*, 8 (2): 217–233.

Torkington, K. (2012) 'Place and lifestyle migration: The discursive construction of "glocal" place-identity', *Mobilities*, 7 (1): 71–92.

Turkey's Office of National Statistics (TUIK) (2016) Population of Didim-Aydin *TUIK*. [online] Retrieved from: http://www.nufusu.com/ilce/didim_aydin-nufusu (accessed 23 June 2017).

Wallwork, N. (2011) 'British buyers top foreign purchasers in Turkey', *Turkey Property News*. [online] Available at: http://www.propertyforum.com/property-in-turkey/british-buyers-top-foreign-purchasers-in-turkey-figures-show.html

Woosnam, K. (2012) 'Using emotional solidarity to explain residents' attitudes about tourism and tourism development', *Journal of Travel Research*, 51 (3): 315–327.

Yashin, Y. N. (2002) *Faces of the State: Secularism and Public Life in Turkey*. Princeton, NJ: Princeton University Press.

Zhang, J., Inbakaran, R. and Jackson, M. (2006) 'Understanding community attitudes towards tourism and host-guest interaction in the urban-rural border region', *Tourism Geographies*, 8 (2): 182–204.

22

THE MORAL DILEMMA OF SECOND HOME OWNERS' POSITION IN THE HOST COMMUNITY

Maja Farstad

Introduction

Second home owners have certain desires and perceived needs in their host communities related to their second home ownership. Consequently, they may dislike, or disagree with, initiatives that threaten the surroundings of their second homes; with administration of the local infrastructure and economic issues such as taxes and charges; or with the sometimes unequal treatment of second home owners and local residents (Farstad 2011). A significant proportion of second home owners pursue these desires and needs, and the accompanying requests have to be handled in one way or another by the local authorities. Either they end up being complied with or not. Largely, it seems to be up to local government to decide how second home owners' requests should be met, except that widespread national laws eliminate the possibility of offering second home owners local suffrage.

Decisions on, and execution of, second home owners' position in the host community are, like policy and public allocation in general, heavily influenced by moral considerations (Jenkins 2008). In this chapter, the aim is to highlight the moral aspects related to second home owners' position in the host community. "Position" refers to second home owners' situation when it comes to assigned rights, influence, further privileges and general regard towards this group. I will clarify the existing multitude of moral considerations both among year-round residents and second home owners in this matter, and argue that no perspective is right or wrong, as this is rather a moral dilemma, where any solution may bring about unfortunate results from various perspectives (For a clarification of the multitude of life situations covered by the concept of "year-round residents", as well as by the concept of "second home owners", see e.g. Pitkänen, Adamiak & Halseth 2013; Farstad 2015).

First, I give an account of the formalised and practised position of second home owners, as the situation appears to be in most countries. Then, I present the lay perspectives of involved actors (second home owners and year-round residents, respectively), mainly based on my PhD work (Farstad 2015), which dealt with second home owners' position in their host communities in Norway. Subsequently, scholars' use of sedentarist and mobility approaches is mentioned, since both these approaches to social organisation may be used to direct and legitimate the policy concerning second home owners' positions. Finally, moral implications of policies based on these approaches are discussed.

On second home owners' formal position in the host community

Second home owners are not registered as inhabitants of the host municipality unless their regular residence is in the same municipality. This has certain juridical consequences for them, but, at the same time they maintain many rights through national legislation, such as the right to necessary health- and care assistance, and general rights of ownership. Citizenship is a useful concept when it comes to clarifying the consequences that follow from not having one's formal address in the host municipality. Citizenship may be defined as 'a bundle of rights and obligations that formally define the legal status of a person within a state' (Turner 2001: 11). Since municipalities function as local governments, there are also similar bundles of rights and obligations at the local level. Each municipality has a geographically defined territory that frames its political and administrative entity, and many citizen-based, individual rights and obligations (such as municipal suffrage, various taxes and charges) are distributed at this level. These obligations and rights do not involve second home owners. One exception is the property tax that many municipalities have introduced, as this tax is based on real estate and not on inhabitants as such.

When it comes to the concept of rights related to the welfare legislation, a division may be drawn between benefits that individuals have legal claim to receive and benefits that may be acquired by competing for limited resources (Kjønstad 2003). The latter type of distribution depends on budgetary priorities, and the individual's opportunity to get access to various benefits depends on which characteristics are emphasised when it comes to the distribution (Kjønstad 2003). Second home owners risk receiving low priority in cases where there are no legal claims, since year-round settlement in general seems to be given a higher priority as a result of municipalities' ascribed responsibility for their own inhabitants' welfare. In the Norwegian case, there are many examples where second home owners have systematically lost in the competition for limited resources. Examples include lower priority when it comes to hunting privileges, higher costs for ski lift access, and higher electricity prices. In one Norwegian municipality it was suggested that year-round residents should be given first priority when it came to long ferry queues (Farstad 2011).

The most important limitation related to second home owners' formal status is, however, that by public law, local suffrage is only applicable to the municipality where the individual is formally registered as an inhabitant. Hence, as a second home owner the individual is not a member of the local, formal, *political* community, and does not have a formalised right to influence local policy.

Still, it is possible for second home owners to influence local decisions through channels other than the voting booth. For example, there are no rules for how municipal authorities should treat second home owners beyond the general rules that are in place in the municipality. There is considerable variation between municipalities when it comes to who is considered to have legitimate interests in local decisions, and hence, who should be actively involved in the consultative processes. For example, in Norway, a survey conducted among mayors (Kroken et al. 2010) revealed a high variation between municipalities when it comes to taking second home owners' perspectives into account in local development processes. Further, previous research shows that kinship and other social connections together with high social status are conditions that may contribute to second home owners' influence on decision makers (at the single individual level) (Mottiar & Quinn 2003; Farstad 2011).

The significance of morality

When focusing on lay understandings of how second home owners should be treated, formally and informally, in their rural host community, "should" is an important word as it reveals that moral considerations are at stake, and not merely expectations based on what is perceived to be normal practice. This involves considerations of who/how many people qualify to be recipients of various local goods and privileges. Jenkins (2008) points to how the stereotypes of "the deserving" and "the undeserving" are important in this context. These stereotypes are used both by various levels of governments and in everyday thinking, to ensure that "the deserving" will not lose (the scarce) resources for the benefit of "the undeserving" (Jenkins 2008).

Any system or decision that favours second home owners may be interpreted as a recognition of the *moral value* of second home owners (Sayer 2005b). While unconditional recognition refers to recognition of a human's value in itself, conditional recognition is based on individuals' behaviour, characteristics and achievements (Sayer 2005a, 2005b). According to Sayer (2005b), recognition is sought after as a necessary source of self-respect and self-confidence in itself (so-called "internal goods") (Sayer 2005b). However, recognition is in many cases also important in a more material way, since it is closely related to the allocation of various local goods and privileges. Year-round residents are automatically recognised by the authorities in various ways through their citizenship. In the case of second home owners, both absence of economic calling-ins (taxes and charges) and gained privileges (such as influence, rights, as well as having one's needs taken into account) are relevant and often longed for external goods.

Sayer's (2011) theory on morality contends that the basis of individuals' moral considerations is quite complex, as ethical dispositions and emotions are strongly influenced by every social relationship that the individual has been and is involved in. The ethical dimension of everyday life is based on emotions, practical thinking, learned and often unconscious good behaviour (virtues), duties, and other aspects characterising human social interaction (Sayer 2011). At the same time as individual morality is influenced by a multitude of factors, each individual possesses a range of values (Sayer 2011) that vary from person to person in terms of their importance to subjective well-being. Moreover, different values may manifest themselves under different conditions, but that also depends on the practical considerations of each individual (Sayer 2011). Thus, Sayer (2011) describes the morality of everyday life as imperfect in every aspect, since it does not follow fixed principles, but is led by practical thinking as much as by rules. However, there are also certain shared moral standards, and even though such moral beliefs and practices differ with time and space and between cultures, reciprocity is a social norm that can be seen as more or less universal (Smith 2000; Fry 2006).

Moral perspectives of year-round residents

There is a broad range of opinions about what position second home owners should have in the host community among year-round residents, as demonstrated in Farstad (2011). For example, on the one hand, one of the interviewees stated that, 'I want them [the second home owners] to feel welcome, and to feel that they are attended to, because of the increase in value that they are creating' (Farstad 2011: 170). Previous research has also demonstrated that year-round residents may be positive towards the presence of residents who do not have the same obvious attachment to the community as themselves (Buller & Hoggart 1994). However, on the other hand, year-round residents' assessment of second home owners' presence can also be completely different, as illustrated in the following quote from Farstad's (2011: 171) study, 'and the others actually are just visitors. ... That is the situation. They are on a visit. ... Even if some of them might have grown up here, they are still visitors. So they should behave properly'. Similar reactions towards residents with less evident belonging to the community have also been documented by previous research (Barlow & Cocklin 2003; Cloke et al. 1998; Fountain & Hall 2002). Such opinions clearly reflect symbolic construction of boundaries between "we" and "the others", where the latter is defined as non-belonging.

Findings from Farstad's (2011, 2013) studies indicate that the second home owners' impact on local resources is essential to whether year-round residents want a strong position for second home owners in the host community (Farstad 2011). Second home owners who pursue their desires and needs are perceived as a burden as long as they do not appear to contribute sufficiently to meeting the needs of the host community. On the contrary, if they are perceived as supplying the host community with sought after resources, the principle of reciprocity seems to manifest itself among year-round residents, and the tolerance towards second home owners increases considerably. Thus, it is not a strong sense of collectivity with the other year-round residents as such that leads to second home owners being defined as "the others", and of less moral worth. Rather, the findings from Farstad's (2013) study indicate that it is the perception of second home owners as a resource or a burden to the host community that determines whether they get identified as "the others" or not. This is in line with Barth's (1969) argument that identification and collective identity are generated to a large extent as by-products of the transactions and negotiations among individuals who pursue their interests (Jenkins 2008).

Year-round residents' perceptions of the second home owners' impact on local resources may depend on several conditions. First, second home owners may be perceived as a burden if there are no significant benefits from the second home owners' presence. It has become a common trend that rural municipalities pursue second home tourism as a major development strategy. Some municipalities have over time succeeded in generating significant municipal benefits from these developments, among other things in the form of more local jobs, improved infrastructure, and an extended assortment of commodities and services. This has to a large extent been obtained by motivating second home owners to a certain level of local consumption, through development and establishment of various money-generating services. In other municipalities, development has occurred more at random, by catering for the demands of eager, potential second home buyers, as well as from local property owners wanting to sell their lots. The last-mentioned type of municipality has not necessarily managed to generate a sufficient level of local consumption among the second home owners, simply because they have just a few or no places at all where second home owners can spend their money (e.g. Farstad 2011). When a large share of the second homes are remotely located and with difficult access to the area's shops and remaining services, this also contributes to a poor level of local consumption among the second home owners (Ericsson & Grefsrud 2005).

As long as the host communities are not struggling against depopulation and have substantial *social* needs that second home owners can meet through social participation (see Farstad 2013), the municipalities' earning ability will be essential to realising the second home owners' requested contribution to the host community. In addition to the fact that year-round residents' perceptions of the benefits from second home tourism may vary from person to person, there is clearly also great variation from place to place in what the local community actually gains from the second home owners' presence.

Another condition that may hinder year-round residents' benevolence towards second home owners is when class distinctions between the two groups appear as too remarkable. The relationship between year-round residents and second home owners may at best be perceived as equal. However, Rye (2012) has demonstrated that, in the Norwegian case, second home ownership is not as egalitarian as one might think. He found that in general, second home ownership is most common among people with higher wages and higher education (although, this varies a lot from place to place). A focus on reciprocity implies 'a concern with consistency and fairness, *other things being equal*' (Sayer 2011: 160; my italics). The perception that second home owners possess more capital of various kinds, and hence, more potential power than year-round residents, leads to second home owners being perceived as a threat (Farstad 2011). Potential economic benefits of second home tourism to the host community, as well as the principle of reciprocity, are then likely to be overshadowed by perceived class distinctions (Farstad 2011).

Since second home owners are usually as well off or better off than local residents with regard to general levels of prosperity, it is natural that local residents will expect reciprocal behaviour from them. If the second home owners were generally worse off than the year-round residents, it is conceivable that the social norm of reciprocity would be replaced by the social norm of solidarity, which is 'a matter of altruistic, one-sided transactions, of helping those incapable of helping themselves' (Leitner & Lessenich 2003: 329). Thus, the question of rights and other privileges for residents with less obvious belonging may very well be assessed differently if talking about, for example, vulnerable refugees, rather than second home owners.

Previous research (Farstad 2013) has also identified a third condition that can make year-round residents assess second home owners as a burden rather than an asset to the local resource base. That is, when local circumstances create the perception that increasing numbers of second home owners is an *alternative* to more permanent residents, typically in cases where local residents are hoping for more residents in their rural, local community. When compared to potential new year-round residents, the whole "package" which second home owners at best would be able to offer, makes them appear as "insufficient dwellers" rather than as a resource to the community (Farstad 2013).

Moral perspectives of second home owners

When it comes to second home owners' perspectives on what would be the morally right position for them to occupy in the host community, a broad range of perspectives exists, for example, as demonstrated in the study of Farstad (2016). Some of the interviewees said things that reflected a rather humble perspective, for example:

> I belong to the group who thinks that second home owners should interfere as little as possible in local decisions. If second home owners become engaged in what is going on, it is usually interpreted in a negative way, and the locals get angry: 'It is one thing that the second home owners are free to use our outlying fields, but the deuce, they cannot come here and tell us that they are going to govern, too'. I tend to acknowledge that way of thinking.
>
> *(Second home owner quoted in Farstad 2016: 415)*

Other interviewees' approach to second home owners' position reflected what could be labelled as a reward-collecting perspective:

> if something special should happen or be done [which concerns me], then I would have to react. But I guess the municipality has a great interest in having a positive relationship to the second home owners, because I think it leads to an additional value for them, since it is a tourist municipality and a large second home municipality. People

leave a great deal of money behind there, and I guess they are aware of that value, so to speak. At least they *should* be. And if they are not, then someone has to tell them, if it is needed (brief laughter).

(Second home owner quoted in Farstad 2016: 417)

Farstad (2016) found that the humble perspective emphasises belonging as the condition that makes people worthy of recognition. This perspective acknowledges a sense of territoriality among year-round residents, and hence, second home owners themselves are understood as outsiders. The reward-collecting perspective, on the contrary, sees contributions to the community as the condition that makes people worthy of recognition. This perspective highlights the positive impact of second home tourism on the host community, and suggests that second home owners should be rewarded for helping the host community. A third, "in-between" perspective seems to agree with the humble perspective on the relevance of belonging/second home owners' non-belonging, but at the same time emphasises the importance of ensuring that second home owners, simply by virtue of being human, do not become subject to non-recognition (Farstad 2016).

Farstad's (2016) study further indicates that both the humble and the reward-collecting perspectives are based on a perception of the host municipality as weak and dependent on the second home owners' presence and further actions. However, this perception of the host community appears to be disconnected from the actual situation of the place. Second home owners' expectations towards the host municipality seem to a large extent to depend on individual, moral dispositions. Still, it seems that some local measures – to a greater or lesser extent – may strengthen already existing lay perspectives (Farstad 2016).

A sedentarist perspective versus a mobilities paradigm perspective

There are two different approaches to social organisation: a sedentarist, territory-based approach and a mobility-based approach. Both can be used as the basis for policy concerning the position of second home owners. Ellingsen (2017: 231) refers to Gustafson (2001), and describes them as, 'one that gives predominance to residence and roots, while the other takes mobility and routes as its base'. The sedentarist perspective has traditionally been dominant both among cultures in general, and within social science (Malkki 1992). However, this perspective is increasingly being criticised for ignoring or trivialising contemporary society's considerable mobility.

'The mobility turn' challenges the supposed 'amobility' perspective of the social sciences (Sheller & Urry 2006). By emphasising society's increased mobility in all its forms, this approach fits into a broader theoretical project 'aimed at going beyond the imagery of "terrains" as spatially fixed geographical containers for social processes, and calling into question scalar logics such as local/global' (Sheller & Urry 2006: 209). Social science has also previously recognised that various types of mobility have taken place, such as removal, migration and transport, but with this theoretical turn one has started taking the movement in itself more seriously (Cresswell 2010). As a consequence, this approach invites new thoughts when it comes to understanding economic, social and political issues (Urry 2007).

Bader (2012) writes about moral arguments for open and closed borders, respectively. This can be transferred to a sedentarist versus a mobilities paradigm perspective, in relation to the question of strongly territorial citizenship. Arguments for a more flexible citizenship (open borders) focus on issues of poverty and global inequality and redistribution and include an emphasis on free movement as a superior moral human right. Arguments for a sedentarism-based, territorial citizenship (closed borders) include, among other things, the moral priority of compatriots, that fundamental civil and political rights can only be guaranteed under such conditions, and because social rights and welfare arrangements have to be defended this way (Bader 2012).

Even though the new mobilities paradigm challenges the dominant sedentarist tradition within social science, the goal has not been to eliminate the sedentarist approach (Halfacree 2012; Sheller & Urry 2006). Rather, the new mobilities paradigm seeks to transcend the division between the two approaches, acknowledging 'stability within movement and movement within stability' (Halfacree 2012: 211).

Second home owners' position in the host community: A moral dilemma

Within the research literature on second homes, many scholars argue that second home owners should get a stronger position in the host community (see Farstad 2016). If year-round residents are to keep their special position, then what about the second home owners? It is clear that in many cases they contribute positively to local development, indirectly through local consumption, but also directly through more active participation (Huijbens 2012). They contribute both economically (Farstad 2011) and socially (Farstad 2013). Many second home owners experience place or host community attachment (Clendenning & Field 2005; Tuulentie 2007; Flemsæter 2009; Pitkänen et al. 2013). In many municipalities, second home owners pay property tax in line with year-round residents, and related to that, the principle of "no taxation without participation" has been highlighted. Should not second home owners have a formalised opportunity to participate when local decisions affect their local surroundings or situation in other ways? Is it right that they must just accept every local government decision without having any means of sanctioning or influencing the process? These are completely legitimate and highly understandable questions raised on behalf of the second home owners.

However, there is another perspective if one focuses on the situation of year-round residents. This perspective has not been fronted the same way in the second homes literature, with exception of documentation of year-round residents reacting negatively to second home owners who are perceived as doing too much of whatever they like (e.g. Jordan 1980). If second home owners were to receive a stronger position, how would that affect the year-round residents? Is it right that those who are present only when it suits them are able to influence the local development? Those who are dependent on neither local jobs nor local public services? Second home owners could use their potential influence based on their narrow fields of interest, such as their immediate local surroundings, and would not have to relate to the outcomes of the remaining areas of policy. Is it right that those who have enough money to own two or more residences are entitled to have influence on two or more places, while those who can only afford to buy one residence can only have influence on one place? (Here, it should be mentioned that, at least in Norway, the introduction of so-called divided suffrage has been suggested. However, it does not seem that this suggestion has been considered seriously). Should a stronger position only include second home owners? What about, for example, camping tourists who return to the same place year after year and who also pay for local services as well as experience a sense of place attachment and feel that this is one of their "homes"? In some cases, second home owners are clearly in possession of more economic as well as social capital than the year-round residents. Thus, there is an occasionally present upper class that is potentially able to acquire influence at the expense of year-round residents. Is it right for them to be assigned more *formal* influence as well?

The recognition of increased mobility or of a need for place-based structures for the organisation of society are not morally charged issues. However, the use of one of these perspectives to lift up one affected stakeholder group while overriding another involves a moral choice. Scholars have commented that a sedentarist perspective can be morally charged (Ellingsen 2017).

The same can be said about the mobilities paradigm perspective if it is used to categorically argue for a stronger position among second home owners.

In some cases, it is considered legitimate for researchers to take a morally charged position in order to obtain so-called strong objectivity (Harding 1992). Since the organisation of contemporary society is heavily based on sedentaristic ideas, much research relating to these frames can be reasonably criticised for pursuing research questions that only fall within the priorities of such institutions and practices. Here, standpoint theories argue that strong objectivity requires that one starts from outside these frames (as the mobilities paradigm perspective does) to gain a critical view of them. However, the standpoint project is to generate scientific problems – by taking into account the "*marginal lives*" (Harding 1992). Marginal lives are then exemplified with categories such as post-colonials, people of the third world entering the first world, lesbians and gays, and lower class people (Harding 1992) – in other words, categories that evidently are vulnerable and severely repressed by other groups. Neither second home owners nor year-round residents appear to fit within this type of category.

Thus, even though it is obvious that there is more mobility now than previously, it is not obvious that a morally right consequence of this is that all mobile people must be awarded more (material or symbolical, direct or indirect) resources. Likewise, even though today's rights legislation and welfare system are largely based on the assumption that people reside only in one place, this is not necessarily the morally appropriate solution.

Either one chooses to defend existing administrative systems (to a great extent based on a sedentarist perspective) or to assert systems that are based more heavily on increased mobilities; both choices result in a particular distribution of the local resources that strikes either year-round residents or second home owners. In other words, this is a moral dilemma. Thus, social scientists cannot tell politicians, governments or civil servants what they *should do* (Bader 2012) regarding adjustments of second home owners' position in the host community. However, social science can ensure that every perspective informs the debates, it can highlight pros and cons for the host community and reveal every consequence of the existing systems, so that decision-makers at various levels can make informed and well-considered decisions in this matter.

References

Bader, V. (2012) 'Moral, ethical, and realist dilemmas of transnational governance of migration', *American Behavioral Scientist*, 56 (9): 1165–1182.

Barlow, K. and Cocklin, C. (2003) 'Reconstructing rurality and community: Plantation forestry in Victoria, Australia', *Journal of Rural Studies*, 19 (4): 503–519.

Barth, F. (1969) 'Introduction'. In F. Barth (ed.) *Ethnic Groups and Boundaries: The Social Organisation of Culture Difference*. Oslo: Universitetsforlaget, 9–38.

Buller, H. and Hoggart, K. (1994) 'The social integration of British home owners into French rural communities', *Journal of Rural Studies*, 10 (2): 197–210.

Clendenning, G. and Field, D. (2005) 'Seasonal residents: Members of community or part of the scenery?'. In G. P. Green, S. C. Deller and D. W. Marcouiller (eds) *Amenities and Rural Development: Theory, Methods and Public Policy*. Cheltenham, UK: Edward Elgar, 216–236.

Cloke, P., Goodwin, M. and Milbourne, P. (1998) 'Inside looking out; Outside looking in. Different experiences of cultural competence in rural lifestyles'. In P. Boyle and K. Halfacree (eds) *Migration into Rural Areas. Theories and issues*. Cheltenham, UK: Edward Elgar, 216–236.

Cresswell, T. (2010) 'Towards a politics of mobility', *Environment and Planning D: Society and Space*, 28 (1): 17–31.

Ellingsen, W. (2017) 'Rural second homes: A narrative of de-centralisation', *Sociologia Ruralis*, 57 (2): 229–244.

Ericsson, B. and Grefsrud, R. (2005) Fritidshus i innlandet: Bruk og lokaløkonomiske effekter. ØF-report no. 06/2005. Lillehammer, Norway: Østlandsforskning.

Farstad, M. (2011) 'Rural residents' opinions about second home owners' pursuit of own interests in the host community', *Norsk Geografisk Tidsskrift – Norwegian Journal of Geography*, 65 (3): 165–174.

Farstad, M. (2013) 'Local residents' valuation of second home owners' presence in a sparsely populated area', *Scandinavian Journal of Hospitality and Tourism*, 13 (4): 317–331.

Farstad, M. (2015) 'Hytteeierne og bygda. Interesser, moral og vern om lokale ressurser. Doktorgradsavhandling' [*Second Home Owners and the Countryside. Interests, Morality and Protection of Local Resources.*]. PhD. Norwegian University of Science and Technology (NTNU), Trondheim, Norway. Trondheim.

Farstad, M. (2016) 'Worthy of recognition? How second home owners understand their own group's moral worth in rural host communities', *Sociologia Ruralis*, 56 (3): 408–426.

Flemsæter, F. (2009) 'From "home" to "second home": Emotional dilemmas on Norwegian smallholdings', *Scandinavian Journal of Hospitality and Tourism*, 9 (4): 406–423.

Fountain, J. and Hall, C. M. (2002) 'The impact of lifestyle migration on rural communities'. In C. M. Hall and A. M. Williams (eds) *Tourism and Migration. New Relationships between Production and Consumption.* Dordrecht, Netherlands: Kluwer Academic Publishers, 153–168.

Fry, D. P. (2006) 'Reciprocity: The foundation stone of morality'. In M. Killen and J. G. Smetana (eds) *Handbook of Moral Development.* Mahwah, NJ: Lawrence Erlbaum Associated, 399–422.

Gustafson, P. (2001) 'Roots and routes. Exploring the relationship between place attachment and mobility', *Environment and Behaviour*, 33 (5): 667–686.

Halfacree, K. (2012) 'Heterolocal identities? Counter-urbanisation, second homes, and rural consumption in the era of mobilities', *Population, Space and Place*, 18 (2): 209–224.

Harding, S. (1992) 'After the neutrality ideal: Science, politics, and "strong objectivity"', *Social Research*, 59 (3): 567–587.

Huijbens, E. (2012) 'Sustaining a village's social fabric?', *Sociologia Ruralis*, 52 (3): 332–352.

Jenkins, R. (2008) *Social Identity.* 3rd ed. London: Routledge.

Jordan, J. W. (1980) 'The summer people and the natives: Some effects of tourism in a Vermont vacation village', *Annals of Tourism Research*, 7 (1): 34–55.

Kjønstad, A. (2003) 'Rettighetslovgivning og kommunalt selvstyre', *Lov og rett*, 6: 341–359.

Kroken, A., Logstein, B., Storstad, O. and Villa, M. (2010) Norske kommuner og fritids-befolkningen. Kommentert frekvensrapport. R-9/10. Trondheim, Norway: Norsk senter for bygdeforskning.

Leitner, S. and Lessenich, S. (2003) 'Assessing welfare state change: The German social insurance state between reciprocity and solidarity', *Journal of Public Policy*, 23 (3): 325–347.

Malkki, L. (1992) 'National geographic – The rooting of peoples and the territorialisation of national identity among scholars and refugees', *Cultural Anthropology*, 7 (1): 24–44.

Mottiar, Z. and Quinn, B. (2003) 'Shaping leisure/tourism places: The role of holiday home owners: A case study of Courtown, Co. Wexford, Ireland', *Leisure Studies*, 22 (2): 109–128.

Pitkänen, K., Adamiak, C. and Halseth, G. (2013) 'Leisure activities and rural community change: Valuation and use of rural space among permanent residents and second home owners', *Sociologia Ruralis*, 54 (2): 143–166.

Rye, J. F. (2012) 'En egalitær norsk hyttetradisjon?' *UTMARK* 1/2009. [online] Available at: http://www.utmark.org/

Sayer, A. (2005a) 'Class, moral worth and recognition', *Sociology*, 39 (5): 947–963.

Sayer, A. (2005b) *The Moral Significance of Class.* Cambridge: Cambridge University Press.

Sayer, A. (2011) *Why Things Matter to People.* New York: Cambridge University Press.

Sheller, M. and Urry, J. (2006) 'The new mobilities paradigm', *Environment and Planning A*, 38 (2): 207–226.

Smith, D. M. (2000) *Moral Geographies: Ethics in a World of Difference.* Edinburgh: Edinburgh University Press.

Turner, B. S. (2001) 'Outline of a general theory of cultural citizenship'. In N. Stevenson (ed.) *Culture and Citizenship.* London: Sage, 11–32.

Tuulentie, S. (2007) 'Settled tourists: Second homes as part of tourist life stories', *Scandinavian Journal of Hospitality and Tourism*, 7 (3): 281–300.

Urry, J. (2007) *Mobilities.* Cambridge: Polity Press.

23

THE FAMILY AND THE SECOND HOME

On building sandcastles, sharing places and the passing of time

Annika Strandin Pers, Maja Lagerqvist and Urban Nordin

Setting the scene

From rural idyll to cottage TERROR. Becoming a second home owner is a holiday dream for many Swedes. But a warning is in order, the rural idyll may quickly transform to a cottage war, if things turn bad. Endless renovation projects, fights regarding weeks of use and bored youngsters are only a few of the threats to the summer goodliness.
(Wållgren & Bratt Lejring 2014, June 25, translated from Swedish by the authors)

Each summer, this type of statement is widespread in Swedish media. Such representations and the commonality of second home usage in Sweden surely make a case that second home usage, as well as second home dreams and conflicts, permeate Swedish society and the idea of the Swedish summer. Strong emotions appear to be in play. A second home is often an important place for the owner. It is a place for meeting family and friends and for continuity, relaxation and creativity. However, it can also be a place for agonising meetings and of diverse, and conflicting, desires, needs and meanings. Today, more than half of the Swedish population has access to a second home through their family (Lundmark & Marjavaara 2013). Our reading of the current situation is that many second homes are being shared within families and that several generations use, or try to use, second homes jointly. Many second home owners in Sweden hope for, and expect, a continuation of the second home within the family, i.e. that younger generations will take over the second home, as shown in Lagerqvist, Strandin Pers and Nordin (2016) and Müller, Nordin and Marjavaara (2010). Moreover, research shows that the average age of Swedish second home owners has increased recently (Müller et al. 2010). This suggests that we are entering a time of generational changes and an increased number of users per second home. This can increase the pressure of time, space and resources per second home as generations change and families grow.

Aim

In the light of the suggested trend of increasing generational changes and shared usage alongside the often assumed importance of second homes for families and individuals, this chapter aims to analyse second home usage within families and across generations. We see a need to dissect and understand the emotional, social and material significance and complexity of second homes as places for individuals and families. More specifically, the chapter analyses second home users' thinking and feeling regarding their second home in relation to existing or future shared usage/ ownership and generational changes there. A life course perspective is used as a way to under- stand the challenging situations that may arise in relation to this. We are interested in situations where a large or growing number of individuals use and have bonds to the same physical place, or are taken into consideration regarding it, be it the closest family, individuals of past and future generations or an extended family. In order to analyse these matters, this chapter focuses on the following questions: (1) How do the second home users recognise the second home as a family place and how do they experience shared usage and intersection of generations there? and (2) How may experiences, claims and expectations of different users vary over the life course and how do they correlate?

Theoretical points of departure

Second homes are here approached as a type of *place*. A place can be regarded as a specific configuration of certain social practices, meanings and material dimensions, which provide both possibilities and restrictions. It is always related to other places and times and forever in a process of being created by the ways people think, feel and act regarding it (Lefebvre 1991; Massey 2005). The literature has pinpointed many reasons for using second homes and why they become important places (see Halfacree 2011). The most significant motive for this chapter is the idea that the second home is a place for the family and that it provides a sense of place, home, identity and continuity (Cohen & Taylor 1978; Hall & Müller 2004; Jaakson 1986; Williams & Kaltenborn 1999). From studies on smallholdings, we know that there can be strong emotional bonds between people and the properties where earlier generations have farmed and lived. These relations often outrun economic reasoning and affect how individuals and families act, plan and relate to these places today and onwards (Flemsæter 2009a, 2009b, 2009c; Flemsæter & Setten 2009; Grubbström 2011). In these studies, the conceptualisation of emotional relations is based on what geographer Tuan (1974: 33) termed "affective bonds". These evolve between people and places when places are ascribed with deep meaning as they are lived and experi- enced. Flemsæter (2009a, 2009b, 2009c) and others demonstrate how influential emotions such as feelings of belonging or duty are for past, present and future generations of the family with regard to their maintaining the smallholding, or at least keeping it in the family. Flemsæter and Setten (2009) conclude that in order to understand how property owners act and think regard- ing their property, we also need to understand these emotional bonds between people and places and how past and future owners are taken into consideration. This chapter expands on this by exploring the emotional bonds to second homes. Second homes can be places that are inherited, used over a long period of time and charged with family connotations, memories and values of both economic and non-economic kinds. Interestingly, a second home is supposedly a place of freedom, joy and leisure, a voluntary home. Yet there seem to be many elements that can influence and impose on it, particularly when sharing it. To share a second home implies material, social and emotional coexistence. Legislation, material and geographical dimensions, personal and others' traditions, dreams, memories, values, perceptions and resources of different kinds may shape the present existence and the possible future of the complex place that the second home can be.

Moreover, Jansson and Müller (2003) point out that people may change their permanent homes but seem less likely to change their second home; this is kept throughout the course of life, and also often within a family. A second home, and especially when kept for many years, has been described as a valued mooring providing identity, sense of place and continuity in life (Jaakson 1986; Müller et al. 2010; Williams & Kaltenborn 1999). We have elsewhere (Lagerqvist 2013, 2016) noted how second homes may provide fixed points in life and enable travelling into family or personal history, as memories can be embedded in the materiality of the second home and in the traditions of how to act there. Many users gather their lives at the second home, materially and through experience, which makes it a shrine of private or family memories (Bachelard 2000). If we consider second homes as potentially powerful and significant places with abilities to hold individual and family identity, memories, expectations and sense of place and continuity, all entrenched in a specific and limited material space, one can also assume that there could be challenges regarding social, material and emotional matters when they are to be used jointly or in times of generational changes.

Our research addresses a lack of qualitative, long-term and life course focused approaches in the second home literature (Lundmark & Marjavaara 2013). This is a way to understand how people relate to and use their second home and how motives, needs and resources for owning or using a second home may vary over different stages in life. With its longitudinal design, a life course study is able to follow the significance of past events, experiences and emotions for the individuals' later actions and decisions. As a way to avoid single-factor explanations of individual behaviour, the life course approach highlights the event trajectories of the individual in a context that takes into account the age of the individual, life phase, and the timing of events (Giele & Elder 1998). This means that we can analyse the emotional connections, ideas and usage of second homes in relation to different stages of life. The method also has the advantage of emphasising the importance of linked life, which for this study means that it is possible to make analysis that reveals the family and even more distant relatives' influence on the individual's situation.

This chapter problematises the strong meanings given to second homes by exploring the implications of these meanings when sharing a second home and in the restructuring of usage and ownership in processes of generational changes there. It provides a time perspective, where both families and individuals, and life courses, are taken into consideration. As such, it presents insights into second homes as family places where social, emotional and material aspects of these places create complex, diverse and sometimes quite challenging experiences, expectations and situations.

The interview study

This chapter is based on interviews with second home users in various parts of Sweden during 2006–2015. In all, we have conducted 6 unstructured interviews and 23 semi-structured interviews with people aged between 27 and 85 years. All in the age group up to 35 years are non-owners and are using their parents' second homes. The age group 36–45 years include both non-owners and owners. Most of these owners have inherited their second homes. The group of elderly, those over 60 years, are all owners of their second homes. About half of them had acquired their second home through their family, while the other half had bought it. The second homes in this study are quite diverse in terms of house types, economic value, location and distances to the permanent house. However, in all, a focus of the second home as a family place is a recurring theme in the respondents' narratives.

Figure 23.1 shows how the interviews can be analysed based on the respondent's position in the individual life course and how they coincide in time with other generations' life course positions. This means that users within the same age group may have different generation positions, and that these positions change over life. We have chosen to show three generations: the oldest G1, their children G2 and their grandchildren G3.

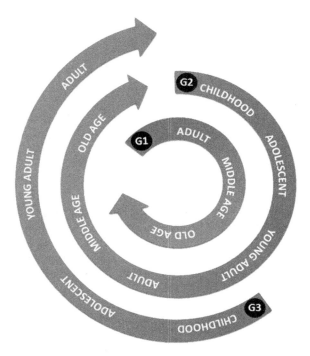

Figure 23.1 Three generations: G1, G2 and G3.

The second home as an emotionally important family place

The second home is clearly a family project. It is a place for the social life of the family. Many of the interviewees have had their second home for decades and most of the second homes are now, or have been, used by several generations at the same time. This is highlighted as significant as to why these places become such important places. One 75-year-old woman (G1) explains, 'By having children and grandchildren here, doing things here, I am getting roots here' (all quotes are translated from Swedish by the authors). As also pointed out by earlier studies on second homes, the interviewees' dreams and desires of having a place where family, both the now living and generations to come, could spend time together, was a major reason for getting and/ or continuously using the second home:

> [T]o have a place where we all could be, where our children, our grandchildren and even the children of our grandchildren could come and meet up. We are four genera-tions there now. And just to be able to spend time with them, that is what is best with it [the second home].
>
> *(Woman, 72, G1)*

The following quotes show the importance of the second home as a family place:

> *She:* This place is a way to keep the family together. This is a solid point for the children. They really like coming here. [...] It is partly for the sake of them (the children and the grand children) that we keep this cottage.

He: Yes, we would see them less often if we didn't have it! And as they have grown up here, it is great fun for them and their children to come here and go into their rooms and dig out the closets.

She: This is our own family tradition! We, the family, are what's important, not the house in itself.

(Wife, 66 and husband, 70, G1)

One common trait in the interviews is that the interviewees have spent time at a second home earlier in life, either the same one as now or another one. Several users describe the second home as the place where they grew up, although the largest part of the time of childhood was spent in the permanent home. The childhood years at the second home seem to have provided strong tracks and memories of a good childhood that many of the interviewees sought to recreate for their own children. Several users communicate an idea of how the second home is a place where children can play but also be taught about life and nature. The importance of being able to be outdoors and run free is highlighted.

Since we got kids … it just feels comfortable to stay there for a bit longer than we have done before. […] I think it is really great to be there as a child. I remember how much I liked it. So much freedom, you could just run around, into the forest, down to the beach.

(Woman, 35, G2. G1 still owns the property)

Repeatedly we met a narrative that describes second homes as very powerful, emotional and important places that are often perceived as non-replaceable:

It would definitely feel odd and empty if one was to lose it. It would be like losing something that you've always have had, and always loved, something that always have been your own. […] I have my whole childhood there.

(Woman, 27, no children, G2. G1 still owns the property)

When you were young, you took it for granted, the possibility to be there … and now, well I've been there […] every summer since I was little. That alone is something valuable. Just imagine, I've been there every year since I was born, every year!

(Woman, 35, 2 children, G2. G1 still owns the property)

Emotional bonds to the place become evident when talking to both younger and older generations. The strong feelings that may exist for the second home, a bit like in a love relationship, can be seen in the discussion about getting another place:

I would feel a bit like I was cheating! And I don't want it [a new second home] to compete with this [the family second home]. I don't think I could feel at home at a second home that you just bought somewhere, when I have this place. I would only compare the new place to this.

(Woman, 35, 2 children, G2. G1 still owns the property)

When several generations have used or are using the same place, a number of individuals and their histories, memories, traditions and practices are embedded in the one and same place. Within this, there are ideas, dreams and plans about how life should be lived and how the second home should be. These ideas do not only concern those who live there now, but also past and future generations. The citations below illuminate how several generations come to matter, and linger, at the second home:

> [T]he stuff has just been here since my parents lived here. Our son asked us just the other day why we have this particular painting from Switzerland on the wall. It is from my father's work trip and we have never even thought about taking it down! [...] My parents lived for 20–30 years after we had bought this from them and when they came to visit they were always saying things like 'have you moved the beds?!'. I bought it from them with furniture and all, and we have been very careful ... and I would say that they had been dead for many years before I dared to throw their clothes away!
>
> *(Man, 70, G1)*

> Who am I to make that decision, in the whole line of family who have lived there? Is it me who should take the decision? [...] It's such a strange thing, then I will take the decision that will affect my kids and maybe their kids that they might get in the future.
>
> *(Woman, 44, G1. Shares the property with her aunt)*

The second home becomes a place of memories and duties: 'I can see my father standing by the fire and throw in dry spruce boughs, it is important that it is as it was before, nothing should change, the dream must be kept alive' (Man, 65, G1). The fact that many of the second homes have been kept within the family through a number of years has resulted in a sense of continuity for the users. This has generated many recurring practices and ways of doing things and has embedded many memories at the second home. Things are supposed to be the same way as they always have been. The key is put under the same stone in the garden and reorganisation of the second home and its furniture is seldom made. The users learn the practices and learn to like them, and consequently they are transferred across generations. Thus, the second home is a central family place where several generations are given importance. It is important that the family has been there, is still there and will remain there. But also the story of one's own childhood creates a huge value, and anticipation for the future. All this makes the success of the handover between generations significant.

The claims, expectations and experiences of different generations

Both younger and older interviewees describe the second home as something more than a "summer cottage". It is portrayed as a place filled with memories and opportunities as well as duties. The family second home is conceptualised as a gift between generations. However, it is not without obligations, and the term gift may be misleading (see Derrida 1992).

The young owners' views of the handover between generations (building sandcastles)

The young owners (G1) with young children are optimistic about the handover and the future for the family at the second home. 'This is something that cannot be bought for money ... This is not just a holiday home. This is something nice that you can give to your children, I think' (Woman, 44, G1). They describe how their children love to be in the second home and that they think their children, due to their positive experiences and memories of summers with cousins and siblings at the second home, will be able and willing to share the ownership in the future without difficulty:

I don't think that will be a problem, we spend time together. My brother's kids are close in age to mine and they play a lot together and have a lot of fun, so following that I think they are going to want to share the second home with their cousins.

(Woman, 39, G1. Shares property with her brother)

Young non-owners' views of the handover between generations

Among the younger generations (G1 and G2), both owners and non-owners, the plans for the future include an unquestioned continuation of the place within the family. For the users where the older generation still owns the second home, there is no anticipation of problems like larger conflicts among family members, although they all stress that they are aware of such problems. However, the shift in ownership is thought of as lying several years ahead. The young adults do not seem to have begun to talk much to their parents about the takeover, neither of their own initiative or their parents, nor talked so much with their siblings about it. One reason for this is that the second home still feels very much like their parents. Many of them do however express a concern for the organisation of future use and ownership. There are concerns and reflections on how the takeover will be completed and if they will be able to manage the second home as the parents do. The concern is based primarily on the feeling that they themselves lack practical knowledge on how the second home should be cared for. Also, the younger generation (G2) sense that the older generation (G1) do not really want to give up any control over the place, that they are not fully trusted and are still seen as children.

Him: And then, in the future, we need to deal with this….

Her: I think about that a lot. As for now, they [her parents] are doing everything […] but we will need to be able to do all that. And it is an old house with, you know, old solutions for everything. And I don't really have any know-how on that. […] One just trusts that someone else, the older generation, will take care of it: 'oh, dad will deal with that!'

Him: Yeah, I think he [her dad] needs to do some sort of manual for us …

Her: Yes! I have been thinking that I need to talk to him about that, and ask him how they [her parents] will deal with this, how they are going to transfer this to us when they feel too old to cope. You need to make some plans for this!

(Woman, 35, and her husband, 36, 2 children,
G2. G1 still owns the property)

The interviews show that many of those who use their parents' second home (G2) have tried to increase their influence over the second home in connection to their own family formation. They express a sense of perceived ownership of the second home with rights to stay there and to influence maintenance and standard improvements, as they often take their future ownership for granted: 'As long as my father was alive, I just went ahead because I thought that I had an equal right to this place … because I knew it would be mine' (Woman, 44, now G1). They describe the owner generation (G1) as reluctant and hostile to change as they hold back the younger generation's attempt to get involved. This seems to create uncertainty and discord. Many also describe that even after the ownership has been taken over by the next generation, the older generation continues to influence many decisions.

In an American study, the sociologist Huggins Balfe (1999) describes the role of family second homes in creating social identity and how families managed to maintain sufficient cohesion to keep it in their possession through several generations. She stresses how the creation of traditions and routines, and clear legal structure for future generations at the same time as the family starts to share responsibilities and decisions among the different generations, simplifies the transfer of the second home to the next generation. This recurs in our study as the informants (G2) describe their own desire for how they want the common use and ownership to work, but in many cases it does not seem to work. Why is it like this? Why doesn't the sharing of the responsibility for the second home start at the stage when both generations consist of adult individuals?

The elderly owners' views on the handover (cracks in the sandcastle)

Unlike the younger owners optimistic view of the future of the family at the second home, the older generation, approaching handover, describe a different, more problematic reality. When the practical circumstances of the handover catch up with the dream of future generations taking over the second home, doubts are creeping up on how this should be done.

All practical circumstances and values associated with the gift make the handover problematic. The older generation describes the fear of triggering conflicts between the children, for example, on the basis of differences that may exist between the children in interests, personality and economic conditions. The parents are aware that the conditions for owning a second home have changed. There are many more things their children can do now, compared to when they were young. The importance of the economic value of the second home is mentioned occasionally during the interviews. This can also be a source of concern. The elderly in some cases mean that future generations will by necessity have to agree and be able to share because: 'They will probably never be able to acquire something similar to a place at this level' (Man, 65, G1). Another concern is that the children may choose a partner who does not want to stay at the second home. Perhaps the partner and his/her parents own their own second home, filled with similar dreams and memories, "gifts" that are waiting to be handed over to the next generation. Also, the elderly often carry their own sad experiences of disputes in earlier shared ownership, succession and buyouts. There are also legal frameworks regarding ownership, inheritance, co-ownership and splitting of real estate. All this influences the older generation and makes them unsure about how and when the handover should take place. This is given as a reason why they avoid starting the process and instead leave it up to their children to settle it in the future. Even the middle-aged children of the ageing owners describe how they eventually chose to defer a decision about the future of the second home as long as their parents lived. That means postponing the handover until after the death of G1 and for the adult children (G2), now middle-aged, it often means that their own children (G3) by then have become teenagers and are no longer interested in staying in the second home with the family (see Figure 23.2). Some of the oldest owners (G1) say that they will wait and see. They are not certain that their children (G2) want to take over, but hope that their grandchildren (G3) will want it in the future. There are also those that highlight that 'One must be careful not to oppress the children with demands regarding taking over the property' (Man, 61, G1. Newly purchased second home).

In many cases, some stakes in the second home have, in an early stage, been transferred to G2 for tax reasons or to get the children to feel more involved. However, in the interviews it becomes clear that this does not necessarily mean that the generational change has been simplified. Those who have transferred the house to younger generations have in some cases assured themselves that they still have the right to stay in the house as long as they live. This often means that they remain as the head of the second home.

Despite the fact that the younger generation (G2), who use their parents' second home, experience that they do not get their needs met when it comes to the standard and improvements they perceive that they need, the older generation stress that they do have to prepare for the future of the children at the second home. This has been done by renovations, repairs and new constructions to allow a joint stay on site and meeting the demands of children and grandchildren in a perspective of 10–15 years. Furthermore, the question of justice seems to be central to the older owners' perception of the changes that should take place. The ambition is that none of the children should be wronged. 'No one can say they have been treated unfairly (Man, 66, G1. Has built three smaller houses, one for each of the children, at the second home property).

In the wake of the "storm", i.e. the generational changes, the older generation express a tiredness because of all the concerns and duties regarding the second home. This is sometimes further fuelled by growing social tensions, and in some cases open antagonism, between the children. The elderly are worried about how they will cope with practical tasks such as repairs and maintenance on the house and the garden once they begin to feel their physical limits. They describe how they want the children to engage in the maintenance. They do not feel that they get the help they need in the way they see necessary. 'I won't do this alone again, the children must help. [...] I have explained to the kids that it is not certain that the summer house remain in the family when I get old' (Man, 65, G1). But as we previously noted, the younger generation experience that they are not admitted to the practicalities surrounding the second home. The adjustments undertaken by the elderly, for the young, are also not made entirely in the way that the young feel is necessary. Apparently the young and the older have quite different experiences of what is happening, and this is causing tensions.

Figure 23.2 shows three generations, G1, G2 and G3. The grey wedges show during which parts of life that the interest in the second home seems to be the greatest. The model illustrates in which phases the different generations' periods of high interest overlap and the pressure on the second home, in term of accountability, control and usage, is highest.

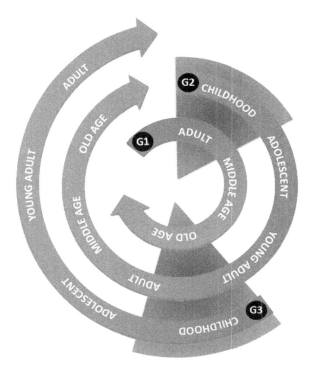

Figure 23.2 Model illustrating when the different generations' periods of high interest for the second home often overlap.

Concluding discussion: Sandcastles, sharing places and the passing of time

A combination of spatial limitations (such as restricted space) and diverse ideas of how and when to share responsibilities and decision making occurs when all three generations are in a phase of life when the interest in the second home seems to be the greatest. With a life course perspective, it becomes clear that several generations' needs and preferences regarding the second home cannot always be met when periods of high interest in the second home overlap. G1 has finally retired and has more time to spend at the second home with their children and grandchildren. They express frustration that they feel that there is a reluctance or disinterest from G2 to receive the gift that the second home represents. We also see a possible discrepancy in the oldest generation's conceptualisation of how they have created the place for the next generation and their own desire and needs to spend time there and decide over the place that they own and created. As long as they have the energy, they want to have the right to be there. G2 wants to use the second home, but in line with their own needs and ideas, and wants to control their own use. They describe that they take their future ownership for granted but that it is difficult to ascertain how the future ownership will be worked out and they do not feel they get their rightful influence over the place during the period of life when they have the greatest interest in it. If we compare the different generations' views on the handover, what the older generation interpret as the younger generation's (G2) lack of involvement may rather be an expression of dissatisfaction with how and when the gift is given and how to share the responsibility and decision making than an unwillingness to receive the gift itself. Maybe this is where the core of the problem lies. When several generations share a second home, it becomes a place where younger generations become adults much later than in other contexts.

The interviews illuminate the importance of the second home as a family place and how several generations exist and come to matter at the second home. It seems to be a project stretching from the past into the future of the family (see also Lagerqvist 2016). This means that it is not only those who live today that have to be taken into consideration when making decisions. Also those who had lived before and those who will come after are given significance. All this can also be perceived as a straight jacket that affects how users relate and act in regards to the second home. The second home can be a place of freedom and of constraints. Several of the interviewees highlight possible problems regarding how to deal with future usage and management of the second home within the family. Conflicts often start when the authority of the second home is going to be transferred between generations (see also Huggings Balfe 1999). Furthermore, many interviewees highlight the fact that they have had their second home for decades and that it has been used by several generations as significant in why these places have become so important and connected to responsibilities in regard to the family. Here we start to see similarities with the emotional bonds to family farms that Flemsæter (2009a, 2009b, 2009c), Flemsæter and Setten (2009) and Grubbström (2011) have identified. As these second homes are shared within families and over generations, they may become places with strong positive emotional bonds to their users and be a material, social and emotional resource and mooring for families. But they may also offer a problematic, constraining continuity and decreasing space and prospects per user, which eventually could break the stability and continuity for the family or parts of it. The dream of the family second home over generations may be transformed into a cracking sandcastle.

References

Bachelard, G. (2000) *Rummets Poetic*. Lund, Sweden: Skarabé: Bakhåll distributör.
Cohen, S. and Taylor, L. (1978) *Escape Attempts: The Theory and Practice of Resistance to Everyday Life*. Harmondsworth, UK: Penguin.
Derrida, J. (1992) *Given Time*. Chicago, IL: University of Chicago Press.

Flemsaeter, F. (2009a) Geography, Law and the Emotions of Property – Property Enactment on Norwegian Smallholdings. PhD. NTNU, Trondheim, Norway.

Flemsaeter, F. (2009b) 'From "home" to "second home": The emotional dilemmas on Norwegian small-holdings', *Scandinavian Journal of Hospitality and Tourism*, 9 (4): 406–423.

Flemsaeter, F. (2009c) 'Home matters: The role of home in property enactment on Norwegian smallholdings', *Norsk Geografisk Tidsskrift*, 63 (3): 204–214.

Flemsaeter, F. and Setten, G. (2009) 'Holding property in trust: Kinship, law and property enactment on Norwegian smallholdings', *Environment and Planning A*, 41 (9): 2267–2284.

Giele, J. Z. and Elder, Jr. G. H. (1998) (eds) *Methods of Life Course Research: Qualitative and Quantitative Approaches*. Thousand Oaks, CA: Sage Publications.

Grubbström, A. (2011) 'Emotional bonds as obstacles to land sale: Attitudes to land among local and absentee landowners in Northwest Estonia', *Landscape and Urban Planning*, 99 (1): 31–39.

Halfacree, K. (2011) '"A solid partner in a fluid world" and/or "line of flight"? Interpreting second homes in the era of mobilities', *Norsk Geografisk Tidsskrift*, 65 (3): 144–153.

Hall, C. M. and Müller, D. K. (eds) (2004) *Tourism, Mobility, and Second Homes: Between Elite Landscape and Common Ground*. Clevedon, UK: Channel View Publications.

Huggings Balfe, J. (1999) *Passing It On: The Inheritance and Use of Summer Houses*, Montclair, NJ: Pocomo Press.

Jaakson, R. (1986) 'Second-home domestic tourism', *Annals of Tourism Research*, 13 (3), 367–391.

Jansson, B. and Müller, D. (2003) *Fritidsboende i Kvarken*. Umeå, Vasa: Kvarkenrådet.

Kaltenborn, B. K and Clout, H. D. (1998) 'The alternate home – Motives of recreation use', *Norsk Geografisk Tidsskrift*, 52 (3): 121–134.

Lagerqvist, M. (2013) '"I would much rather be still here and travel in time": The intertwinedness of mobility and stillness in cottage living', *Fennia*, 191 (2): 92–105.

Lagerqvist, M. (2016) 'Ännu en sommar på torpet. Om arv och platstillhörighet'. In K. Gunnemark (ed.) *Sommarliv – Om minnen, drömmar och materialitet*. Göteborg: Makadam förlag, 171–185.

Lagerqvist, M., Strandin Pers, A. and Nordin, U. (2016) 'The more, the merrier? Experiences of shared usage and generational intersections at second homes in Sweden', *Tourism, Leisure and Global Change*, 1 (1): 49–61.

Lefebvre, H. (1991) *The Production of Space*. Oxford: Basil Blackwell.

Lundmark, L. and Marjavaara, R. (2013) 'Second home ownership: A blessing for all?', *Scandinavian Journal of Hospitality and Tourism*, 13 (4): 281–298.

Massey, D. (2005) *For Space*. London: Sage.

Müller, D. K., Nordin, U. and Marjavaara, R. (2010) *Fritidsboendes relationer till den svenska landsbygden*. Umeå: Kulturgeografiska institutionen, Umeå universitet.

Tuan, Y. (1974) *Topophilia: A Study of Environmental Perception, Attitudes, and Values*. Englewood Cliffs, NJ: Prentice-Hall.

Williams, D. and Kaltenborn, P. (1999) 'Leisure places and modernity'. In D. Crouch (ed.) *Leisure/Tourism Geographies: Practices and Geographical Knowledge*. London: Routledge, 214–230.

Wållgren, R. and Bratt Lejring, E. (2014) 'Från lantdröm till torpTERROR', *Aftonbladet*, 25 June. Available at: http://www.aftonbladet.se/relationer/article19117011.ab

24

FROM MAKESHIFT TO MAKEOVER

Materialising the beach shack as architectural heritage

Felicity Picken

Materials as realities of second homes and Australian coastal culture

Australia's coastal areas are significant locations for second homes and the related activities of tourism and sea change. The term "sea change" is the outcome of demographers' observations of patterns of migration to coastal areas for both lifestyle and in retirement, often following a pattern of coastal holidays before this (Burnley & Murphy 2004; Gurran & Blakely 2007; Osbaldiston 2010). Second homes have played a role in both the sea change phenomenon and in the performance of the coast as a popular holiday and leisure space. They have contributed towards establishing both of these enduring relations by encouraging populations from mainly urban areas to both access the coast and establish strong relations with these places over time (Selwood & Tonts 2006). These relations were to become so pronounced that the twentieth century marked Australian identity against the backdrop of the beach, where rituals that marked the life course were undertaken, including family "bucket and spade" tourism, courtship and marriage, retirement and then extended family visits to begin the process again (Franklin et al. 2013; Huntsman 2001). During the twentieth century, in practice and imaginary, these became significantly beach bound.

'Memories of the family beach shack (or staying at someone else's family beach shack) are strongly tied to perceptions of traditional Australian values' (Hosking et al. 2009: 35). This cultural narrative is well established among scholars of various disciplinary persuasions but these narratives are also constituted by materialities. Most notable among these in the patterns of second homes are the motor car, the post-World War II economic boom and increased disposable income, and the desirability and amenity of the places themselves – particularly their relation to the principal "suburban" home (Hall & Müller 2004; Osbaldiston & Picken 2014; Osbaldiston et al. 2015). While generally whether the second home is an apartment, villa, chalet, house, cabin or houseboat has not mattered much beyond marking regional and temporal diversity, some have taken closer account of the second homes themselves. These include, for example, the unique attributes of the New Zealand bachs and cribs (Keen & Hall 2004; Kearns & Collins 2006), midwest American cabins (Hoefferle 2013), Finnish and Canadian cottages (Periäinen 2006; Halseth 2004; Svenson 2004) as well as Australian second home shacks (Selwood & Tonts

2004; Atkinson, Picken & Tranter 2009). This chapter contributes to this discussion by drawing insights from the changing relationship between architecture, second homes and cultural heritage as made evident through the Australian beach shack.

The shack has become entwined with the rise in interest in vernacular architecture in Australia and its inherent relationship to cultural heritage. This has influenced the look and character of Australia's second home locations and how they identify with what Hall and Müller (2004) describe as "elite landscapes". Australia has a living memory of a time when this was not, so decisively, the case and provides one of the places where processes of elite landscaping, "the second homes estate", are still unfolding. This process sees the second home beach shack, and its emerging value as vernacular architecture and cultural heritage, as shaping both the symbolic and material presence of the shack on coastal landscapes. The transition of second homes is visible in the transformation of shacks, in some places ubiquitous, to second homes that are not only more elite, but also *indistinguishable* from other kinds of homes and homing arrangements. An architectural reading of these elite landscapes reveals second homes have greater *invisibility*, yet as the shack disappears, it is recast as part of a suite of vernacular devices, contributing to a global "postmodern architectural pastiche" (Soja 1996; Venturi & Brown 2004) in the invention of a shack form and aesthetic that is wholly retrospective and mostly fabricated. Simultaneously, the rise in Australian vernacular, and the "shack" as an exemplar of this, supports the recasting of the shack as cultural heritage. Through these two avenues, the erasure of the shack and the cultures it permitted is remade as new material for the development of cultural heritage and for the commercial development of more "authentic" elite landscapes.

Second homes and vernacular architecture

A survey of the scholarship concerning the architecture of second homes along Australia's coast emphasises a study into the materiality of a *receding* twentieth-century landscape. The reason for this is that the "beach shack" is the only notable, distinguishable residential form of Australian coastal landscapes. As a vernacular form of architecture, the shack materialises as an object of nostalgia. This nostalgia is fuelled and emphasised by its disappearance from the landscape. This, coupled with the habit of *not* documenting shacks at a time when their presence was more common, both frustrates and supports the emerging significance of shacks as heritage. Nevertheless, the growing status of the shack as vernacular architecture is not insignificant to its growing status as an object of national heritage.

The vernacular is associated with the quotidian, ordinary and mundane, belonging to the culture that is popular or low as 'the style of building shared by the underclass' (Drew 2006: 26). Through these associations with the lives of "folk", vernacular architecture supports the emerging interest in, and popularity of "heritage from below" (Robertson 2008; Selwood & Jones 2010) and is part of the movement towards the recognition of the heritage of sites like workplaces, domesticity and suburbia (Robertson 2008). It is described as:

> [A] building designed by an amateur without any training in design; the individual will have been guided by a series of conventions built up in his locality, paying little attention to what may be fashionable. The function of the building would be the dominant factor, aesthetic considerations, though present to some small degree, being quite minimal.
>
> *(Brunskill 2000, cited in Hoefferle 2013: 1)*

These qualities have come to resonate with various environmental and slow movements, their core value of sensitivity to surrounds (Osbaldiston & Picken 2014; Groth 2016) and with vernacular architecture's increasing value as an environmental legacy (Foruzanmehr & Vellinga 2011). At the same time, while vernacular architecture can be valued for its modesty, simplicity and resourcefulness, it can also be dismissed as redundant, out-of-date and gauche (Drew 2006). As a kind of counter architecture – that is built by the people, for the people – it has been assigned the same low, marginal or quaint social status as other "folk" cultures and crafts (Foruzanmehr & Vellinga 2011; Hoefferle 2013).

Architecture follows what, in the social sciences, is a somewhat radical view of material practices: that materials are more than "representations", or sceneries for social action. While the discipline has tended towards spatial determinism, this has increasingly been tempered with increasing cultural and social awareness (Picken 2013). Vernacular architecture is particularly demanding of this kind of awareness, since its value lies not in the globally oriented notion of "good design", but in the locally oriented social and cultural processes that are embedded into the structure. As Frank Gehry is embedded in the *Guggenheim Bilbao* and the *Dancing House*, so these situational processes are embedded in the vernacular (if more subtly).

There is no simple understanding of vernacular architecture, especially since it depends in part on the equally fluid definition of architecture. The relationship becomes troubled, for example, when architecture is defined as the 'consistency of approach in development of form and function' (Steiner 1998: 1). In this case, much of what is referred to as vernacular architecture is not architecture at all. In Australia, with some notable exceptions, there has been little interest in the vernacular until quite recently (Drew 2006). Vernacular architecture includes the buildings that the profession of architecture does not. It is a kind of counter-architecture in the sense that it is the only kind of architecture that is *without architects* (Drew 2006). These structures are more about spontaneous action than planning, and more about making-do than engineering. Even in the cases where Australian vernacular has been revered, there remains the problem that vernacular often produces built environments that are stylistically differentiated (Drew 2006). There is consensus in the impossibility of "essentializing" the vernacular which remains a category that is, effectively, constituted by multiple 'divergent architectural traditions' (Vellinga 2006, cited in Foruzanmehr & Vellinga 2011: 276).

Australian vernacular architecture encompasses rural structures like the shearing shed and other farm buildings, some industrial structures like warehouses, the veranda/sleep-out, the "Queenslander" (house) in the northeast and the shack as a second home. It also includes building materials, like corrugated iron and timber louvres and rudimentary building methods, responding to local environmental, social and economic conditions or from adaptations to these (Tiwari & Churchill 2004). Commensurately, the beach shack as Australian vernacular architecture is defined by the process through which it is constructed, the local or re-used materials and an emphasis on rough functionality that is its style per se. The emphasis on locale means that variance in the vernacular can be expected across landscapes of great climatic and geographical variation. These differences and sheer size of the Australian coast are what inspires Goad (2002) to refer to the nation more broadly as 'an archipelago of architectural cultures', but the nuances of this are of recent interest.

Vernacular shack and the shack vernacular

The shack, as vernacular architecture, is not specific to Australia but is part of those 'seasonal, temporary quarters surrounded by the natural world and comprise a category of architecture that includes shacks, camps and cabins' (Hoefferle 2013: 14). As both a process of building and a structure, they are noted to share common characteristics of resourcefulness and thrift, as well as self-reliance and the virtue that is derived from 'doing it yourself' (Hoefferle 2013: 6). Tiwari and Churchill (2004: 7) refer to these qualities as a 'particular architectural language' that includes 'the inventive and unconventional use of materials, methods of construction, the relationship between the interior of the building and the wilderness of its exterior world'. Against an existing, formal architectural cache, shacks are part of a class of structures that are highly expedient and tolerant to change (Steiner 1998). This supports a close relationship between shack and environment, including adaptions to the micro-climate, as a key functionality of shacks and, ultimately, their form (Hoefferle 2013). It also makes them challenging built heritages.

Like many vernacular styles, shacks emerged informally on the margins of a formally constituted architectural profession that tended towards internationalism rather than indigenous or setter forms (Drew 2006). Among the least "engineered" housing stock in Australia, shack development belonged to a time when less formal development could occur and leisure was not yet so commercialised. The shack was often illegal, vaguely defined accommodation that was at a minimum an improvement on a tent. When compared to the principal home, it was the comparative impermanency of the shacks that characterised their improvised nature. This informality itself described the informal nature of these earlier leisure relations with the coast; the simplicity of the shack bespoke a building that was brought into being with a primary view for *use* and that adopted re-use as a means to achieve this. As a geographical, social and material site, the shack was always "secondary" as a second home, inhabiting a second (leisure) space and made of "second-hand things". These were makeshift, unplanned and sometimes illegally constructed dwellings with an air of temporality that offered little to the architectural palette (Shaw & Menday 2013). Now, as the shack disappears and passes to nostalgia, it has gained a quaintness and vernacular interest in Australian architecture that is reasserting a shack-like presence on the coastal landscape.

Shack-styling the Australian coast

In the present day, the *symbolism* of shacks resonates more with Australians and *Australianness* than their presence does. This symbolism is increasingly imprinted onto coastal landscapes through architectural interventions and with the reinvention of coastal resorts and undeveloped land (Essex & Brown 1997). One of these interventions is the production of a nostalgia for and appreciation of a shack aesthetic. While there is a certain romanticism and nostalgia attached to the maverick shack, in reality they could not be said to have added attractiveness nor orderly development to the Australian landscape. Any aesthetic quality was attributable to their raw functionality and 'ruggedness' (Hoefferle 2013: 13). The development of this aesthetic began to attract architects, who came to the shack *after* it was formed, and to elaborate on the roughly hewn "pioneer" and casual leisure culture of coastal Australia. This former *non-style* now serves as the basis for an architectural styled revival (Hosking et al. 2009) as 'shack detailing comes to the main street' (Dawson 2009: 3) and 'readers-turned-tourists' are able to 'interpret the landscape for themselves' (Groth 2016: 447).

The "Noosa style", a design thematic for what has become Queensland's Sunshine Coast's premier beach resort embeds the vernacular into the planning process, not least in claiming to encourage architecture that is locally sensitive and specific. This specificity includes encouragement of the reinterpretation of the 'simple vernacular "weekenders" that became common in Australian coastal towns during the twentieth century' (O'Hare 2001: 102).

Likewise, at Kings Beach, on New South Wales north coast, a master-planned estate claimed to reinvent the "lost architecture" of the coastal shack. The aesthetic goal of the estate was to produce the "ultimate Australian Beachside Vernacular" via an architectural competition that effectively reinstates the shack as a cultural icon (Shaw & Menday 2013: 2948), instead of a cultural practice or material.

Such a development contributes towards the production of a more pronounced Australian vernacular in places that are now noted for their increasing dependence on international tourism and residential investment. At its architectural "worst", such embedding can become a case of "vernacular opportunism" (Drew 2006), a form of exploitation of cultural assets and heritage not unlike that exposed through the mechanisms of "staged authenticity" (MacCannell 1992) and described as part of a "neo-traditional" turn in new forms of urbanism and new price premiums (Shaw & Menday 2013). Architecturally, shacks are to be admired because they were always 'liberated from convention, because they were improvised' (Drew 2006: 39), and accidentally expedient with currents of post-modern theories of space and design (Soja 1996; Venturi & Brown 2004).

Off the main street, the appropriation and residential development of high amenity coastal space continues the formation of private, "elite landscapes" (Hall & Müller 2004). Here the term "shack" is attached to luxurious holiday or permanent coastal homes. Existing, renovated shacks are now sold as investment potential and newly built "shacks" use the term to parody and capitalise on the nostalgia surrounding shack culture and the international "market" in which the link between the aesthetic sensibility and cultural values (Hoefferle 2013) is emphasised in the pursuit of economic gain.

While these landscapes are becoming increasingly elite, they are also becoming architecturally less distinctive than when shacks signalled a significant proportion of second homes stock. As shacks have been legitimised and significantly renovated and as other second homes have come into being from within existing residential stock, the architecture of second homes becomes less obviously meaningful. In these landscapes, to speak of second home architecture is to speak of the architecture of a wide range of homes. As Selwood and Tonts (2006: 161) noted, 'The variety of coastal settlements and accommodation into which the population has gravitated ranges from the permanent to the temporary, the metropolitan to the remote periphery, the luxurious to the rudimentary and the exciting to the serene'.

Likewise, second homes become indistinguishable along the Gold and Sunshine Coasts in southeast Queensland, where towers accommodating permanent residents, tourists and second homeowners neutralise any architectural difference between hotel accommodation, principal and holiday apartments. Second homes become indistinctive among accommodations in coastal areas, part of a more uniform aesthetic that is itself criticised as a 'triumph of the International Style' (Noß 2005: 1). This is now argued to have replaced the 'irregularities and idiosyncrasies' (Hoefferle 2013: 14) that once characterised the landscapes that included the vernacular. At the same time there is a sense of inevitability in this process, a process of shack pioneering and coastal transformation. Closer to the cities, along the beaches that were once distant but are now encompassed by suburbia, a similar process had already taken place (Franklin et al. 2013).

The beach shack as cultural heritage

Globally, vernacular traditions and architecture are cultural and built heritages and their importance as heritage increases proportionately to their decline through abandonment, neglect or demolition (Foruzanmehr & Vellinga 2011; Selwood & May 2001). This is mirrored in the transition of the Australian shack. As Hosking et al. (2009: 35) notes, 'as the shack becomes an "endangered" species, nostalgia for shack culture is increasing'. While there has been a close relationship between architecture and heritage in Australia, particularly since the rise in heritage movements in the 1970s (Willis & Goad 2008), it is with the vernacular that architecture and heritage merge. Heritage movements first sought to protect Australia's colonial heritage, some of which was ordinary people's heritage, like with the *Green Bans* at The Rocks. The shack had not, at this time, attracted any significant value as Australian cultural heritage. This has become a concern of the twenty-first century where shacks are increasingly drawn into conversations about cultural heritage estates (Selwood & Jones 2010; Crafti 2006).

As Hoefferle (2013) shows in the case of the American midwest, the very definition of a shack depends upon the history of the inhabitants as much as its physical attributes. Architects agree, reading in the shack a revelation about 'the lives of ordinary people', for what it expresses about 'the spirit of the people tied to a region' and for its ability to capture 'a true common cultural identity' (Drew 2006: 27–28). Vernacular architecture, especially when it is no longer practised, becomes a form of "heritage from below" (Selwood & Jones 2010), the heritage that emerges "informally" (Selwood & May 2001), that resists authorised heritage discourses and seeks recognition at the level of community (Waterton 2005; Byrne 2008). The shack "lacks completion" (Tiwari & Churchill 2004) and its organic, adaptive nature embodies what is perceived to be an authentic, living heritage and, when used ideally, is a chrysalis for multigenerational ties (Selwood & Tonts 2006).

As a *second* home, the shack played a part in mobilising Australian populations away from the city towards the more distant coasts. These, alongside low-cost (and low-grade) hotel and motel accommodation, camping grounds and caravan parks set much of the tone for a more distinctly *Australian* beachside experience (Franklin et al. 2013). Post-World War Two, this was to play its own role in driving the desire to differentiate the nation from the UK, not least of which were those practices deemed derivative of this relationship, rather than necessary or even practical (Hartley & Green 2006). More practically, where the British model was initiated by wealthy patrons and new consumers of the seaside, Australia lacked such patronage (Fiske 1983). Coastal access was gained through opportunism, taken on seemingly abundant, undeveloped coastal land, and subsequent leisure relations were formed in many places without so distinctive a social tone, opulence or elaboration (Franklin et al. 2013). While the shack was meagre in its amateur construction, lacking style or elegance and its rudimentary materiality starkly contrasting the comparative amenity of both the holiday camp and resort towns (Paris 2009), it also offered a certain autonomy and freedom in leisure. As Griffith (2010: 4) noted, 'In Australia shacks have become our protest against the brick veneer, the place where we unwind on holiday, the workshop that feeds our soul […] the pleasure of inhabiting spaces that are at once monuments to self-expression and symbols of old-fashioned common sense'.

It is within this kind of sentiment that much of the value of the shack as a cultural heritage rests. The case of Wedge on the West Australian coast is a well-documented example of the shack as an object that is undergoing processes of becoming cultural heritage (Selwood & May 2001; Tiwari & Churchill 2004; Selwood & Jones 2010). Tiwari and Churchill (2004: 7) articulate the cultural capital that develops around the shack when they describe it as an authentic embodiment of cultural responses to specific landscapes, as a *palimpsest* 'of time and of the symbiotic relationship between human and nature'. For them, amid the 'chaotic, organic and ambiguous' patterns of shack settlements at Wedge on the West Australian coast are also culturally contrived 'glimpses of a poetic order' (Tiwari & Churchill 2004: 7); a landscape as a 'cultural field' (Howard & Pinder 2003).

Further examples of this process can be found in international examples. As both a vernacular form and as cultural heritage, there are parallels between the Australian *shack* and the New Zealand *bach* or *crib*. 'Both traditionally represent a form of "camping out" in temporary but intermittent fashion that is far from fashion-consciousness' (Thompson 1985 cited in Kearns

& Collins 2006: 229) and that expressed 'a certain pride in roughness and lack of civilisation' (Olsen 1997 cited in Hoefferle 2013: 13). Like the Australian shack, the bach served as access to leisure and tourism for ordinary people. It became 'a site of memory, a gathering place for family and friends, and a material as well as symbolic connection between land and sea' (Kearns & Collins 2006: 227). Its form was modest, amateurishly built and land tenure was also questionable or "informal" (Kearns & Collins 2006). They note a transition that is also evident across the Tasman Sea of increased property prices in coastal areas and the development of "holiday homes" that reflect this.

As cultural heritage, the shack subscribes to a new set of values and utilities and to critical heritage analyses. Like other comparable examples in other parts of the world, as the shack itself disappears from the landscape, its representational presence intensifies and diversifies. Architecture and design plays a role in re-presenting the shack and so does the heritage industry where the shack conforms to a process of *heritigisation* (Ashworth 2008). This process includes the aestheticisation of these newly recognised vernacular forms in glossy magazines, coffee table books, museum displays (Kearns & Collins 2006) and in shack holidays that are increasingly promoted as part of destination Australia.

The extent that the second holiday home or shack constitutes a significant vernacular form of Australia seems to perhaps disproportionately reflect the "luckiness" discourse of the country's identity at this time (Horne 1976). This vernacular shack does not include, for example, the shacks that made up principal homes, despite principal homes making up the vernacular in so many cases elsewhere. Instead, it is the shack as the second home – usually located near the coast or a waterway. As a principle home, the shack was formative of early urban slum development. Like the holiday shacks that were to arise during better times, many of these were close to the sea by virtue of the sea's proximity to the cities (Taussig 2000) but that is where any similarity or recognition appears to end. In the national psyche, these "shacks in Australia" are not the same as "Australian shacks". Nevertheless, the lack of pretention of the shack resonated with Australian identity, with the character of the larrikin and also the nature of the Australian landscape, since in the shack, the democratic spirit arose through a "common" of undeveloped spaces. By the 1960s, if owning a suburban home was "the great Australian dream", then the "midsummer dream" was to spend weekends and holidays at the beach shack (Hosking et al. 2009). At the same time, despite their centrality to the national narrative, wrapped in the euphoric economic boom, lucky countries tend to be based on luck and neither dream was ever realised for all.

Conclusion

In 1960, Kevin Lynch summarised a practice of making spaces *legible*, enabling people to accurately read the landscape through built and natural forms. He was advocating a universal system of spatial signs or cues, those that humans are "wired" to respond to in orienting themselves through space. Lynch's legacy is in claiming a powerful method in the readability of landscapes, underscoring a conviction that they somehow "speak" and "act". It is in this broader context that Stewart Brand (1995) asks us to consider 'how buildings learn?' and this chapter has questioned how "holiday" homes learnt to be part of the Australian coastal landscapes.

Second home "consumption" has emerged in Australian coastal places in concert with the material conditions of Australian life, people and the places themselves. As the history of architecture and its alliance with heritage continues to emphasise, most environments, of whatever kind, are best understood within the "vernacular matrix" in which they are embedded (Rapoport 2005: 158). The shack's dis-embedding from the landscape is not a wholescale dis-embedding but involves the re-embedding of both tangible vernacular shack elements and a much greater symbolic or intangible value as cultural heritage (and see Pétursdóttir 2013) and as added value for elite landscaping. In the renovation and disappearance of shacks from the landscape is also a renovation and transformation of material culture. This chapter has highlighted the materiality of second homes through insights from the architectural heritage of the shack as an Australian vernacular form.

The vernacular of the shack aligns with more general observations about the architectural heritage of Australia and of cultural heritage more broadly. Each is comprised of transplantation, adaptation, hybridisation and invention (Willis & Goad 2008) that transforms the material and symbolic landscapes. The elite landscapes of second homes in Australia are examined for the way they reappropriate the counter-elite landscapes of shack culture that they increasingly occupy as a vernacular architectural pastiche and an increasingly symbolic cultural heritage.

This revival of the shack as a "style" does not mask the fact that, with so few shacks actually remaining, Australia's coastal second homes are far less visibly ubiquitous than they used to be. This invisibility is an outcome of both the disappearance of shacks from the landscape and the indistinguishable nature of the current stock of second homes. These are now blended into coastal housing stock, into highly renovated shacks, into tower apartments and within new coastal development estates, some of which are variously denoted, designed or adorned after the style of the vernacular shack.

References

Ashworth, G. (2008) 'In search of the place identity dividend: Using heritage landscapes to create place identity'. In J. Eyles and A. Williams (eds) *Sense of Place, Health and Quality of Life.* Buckinghamshire, UK: Ashgate, 185–196.

Atkinson, R., Picken, F. and Tranter, B. (2009) 'Home and away from home: The urban-regional dynamics of second home ownership in Australia', *Urban Research & Practice*, 2 (1): 1–17.

Brand, S. (1995) *How Buildings Learn: What Happens After They're Built.* London: Penguin.

Burnley, I. and Murphy, P. (2004) *Sea Change: Movement from Metropolitan to Arcadian Australia.* Sydney: UNSW Press.

Byrne, D. (2008) 'Heritage as social action'. In G. Fairclough, R. Harrison, J. Jameson and J. Schofield (eds) *The Heritage Reader.* London: Routledge, 149–173.

Crafti, S. (2006) *Beach Houses: Down Under.* Hong Kong: Images Publishing Group.

Dawson, P. (2009) 'Freedom and the city' in *International Cities Town Centres & Communities Society Conference*, Deakin University, Geelong, Victoria, Australia 27–30 October, 2009. Retrieved from: http://www.ictcsociety.org/papers/dawson.pdf (accessed 20 June 2017).

Drew, P. (2006) 'Inspiration from below: Australian vernacular in contemporary architecture', *Architectural Theory Review*, 11 (1): 26–40.

Essex, S. and Brown, G. (1997) 'The emergence of post suburban landscapes on the north coast of New South Wales: A case study of contested space', *International Journal of Urban and Regional Research*, 21 (2): 259–287.

Fiske, J. (1983) 'Surfalism and sandiotics: The beach in Oz culture', *Australian Journal of Cultural Studies*, 1 (2): 120–148.

Foruzanmehr, A. and Vellinga, M. (2011) 'Vernacular architecture: Questions of comfort and practicality', *Building Research & Information*, 39 (3): 274–285.

Franklin, A., Picken, F. and Osbaldiston, N. (2013) 'Conceptualizing the changing nature of Australian beach tourism in a low carbon society', *International Journal of Climate Change: Impacts & Responses*, 5 (1): 1–10.

Goad, P. (2002) 'Australia, an archipelago of cultures', *World Architecture*, 7: 3–7.

Griffith, S. (2010) *Shack: In Praise of An Australian Icon.* Camberwell, UK: Penguin.

Groth, P. (2016) 'Making new connections in vernacular architecture', *Journal of the Society of Architectural Historians*, 58 (3): 444–451.

Gurran, N. and Blakely, E. (2007) 'Suffer a sea change? Contrasting perspectives towards urban policy and migration in coastal Australia', *Australian Geographer*, 38 (1): 113–131.

Hall, C. M. and Müller, D. (eds) (2004) *Tourism, Mobility, and Second Homes: Between Elite Landscape and Common Ground*. Clevedon, UK: ChannelView Publications.

Halseth, G. (2004) 'The "cottage" privilege: Increasingly elite landscapes of second homes in Canada'. In C. M. Hall and D. Müller (eds) *Tourism, Mobility, and Second Homes: Between Elite Landscape and Common Ground*. Clevedon, UK: ChannelView Publications, 35–54.

Hartley, J. and Green, J. (2006) 'The public sphere on the beach', *European Journal of Cultural Studies*, 9 (3): 341–362.

Hoefferle, M. (2013) 'Making something out of nothing: Vernacular architecture in Michigan's Upper Peninsula', *Upper Country: A Journal of the Lake Superior Region*, 1 (1): Article 3. [online] Retrieved from: http://commons.nmu.edu/upper_country/vol1/iss1/3 (accessed 21 July 2016).

Horne, D. (1976) *The Death of the Lucky Country*. Ringwood, Vic.: Penguin.

Hosking, S., Hosking, R., Pannell, R. and Bierbaum, N. (2009) *Sea Changes, Beaches and the Littoral in the Antipodes*. Kent Town, South Australia: Wakefield Press.

Howard, P. and Pinder, D. (2003) 'Cultural heritage and sustainability in the coastal zone: Experiences in south west England', *Journal of Cultural Heritage*, 4 (1): 57–68.

Huntsman, L. (2001) *Sand in Our Souls: The Beach in Australian History*. Melbourne: Melbourne University Press.

Kearns, D. and Collins, D. (2006) '"On the rocks". New Zealand's coastal bach landscape and the case of Rangitoto Island', *New Zealand Geographer*, 62 (3): 227–235.

Keen, D. and Hall, C. M. (2004) 'Second homes in New Zealand'. In C. M. Hall and D. Müller (eds) *Tourism, Mobility, and Second Homes: Between Elite Landscape and Common Ground*. Clevedon, UK: ChannelView Publications, 174–195.

MacCannell, D. (1992) *Empty Meeting Grounds: The Tourist Papers*. London: Routledge.

Noß, A. (2005) 'Australian Themes in Architecture', Hanover University. Retrieved from: http://www.nos-designs.de/downloads/Australian%20Themes%20in%20Architecture.pdf (accessed 20 June 2017).

O'Hare, D. (2001) 'Articulating the heritage tourism resource in coastal towns: A study of Noosa', paper presented at Heritage Economics: Challenges for Heritage Conservation and Sustainable Development in the 21st Century, Canberra: Australian National University, July 2001.

Olson, R. (1997) 'Up north: Regionalism, resources and self-reliance' R. T. Teske, (eds) *Wisconsin Folk Art: A Sesquicentennial Celebration*. Cedarburg, WI: Cedarburg Cultural Center, 65–78.

Osbaldiston, N. (2010) 'Chasing the idyll lifestyle: The seachange problem', *Social Alternatives*, 29 (1): 54–57.

Osbaldiston, N. and Picken, F. (2014) 'Negotiating the value of "slow" in amenity migration'. In L. Moss and R. Glorioso (eds) *Global Amenity Migration*. Vancouver: New Ecology Press, 83–97.

Osbaldiston, N., Picken, F. and Duffy, M. (2015) 'Characteristics and future intentions of second homeowners: A case study from Eastern Victoria, Australia', *Journal of Policy Research in Tourism, Leisure and Events*, 7 (1): 62–76.

Paris, C. (2009) 'Re-positioning second homes within housing studies: Household investment, gentrification, multiple residence, mobility and hyper-consumption', *Housing, Theory and Society*, 26 (4): 292–310.

Periäinen, K. (2006) 'The summer cottage: A dream in the Finnish forest'. In N. McIntyre, D. Williams and K. McHugh (eds) *Multiple Dwelling and Tourism: Negotiating Place, Home and Identity*. Wallingford, UK: CABI, 103–113.

Pétursdóttir, Þ. (2013). 'Concrete matters: Ruins of modernity and the things called heritage'. *Journal of Social Archaeology*, 13 (1), 31–53.

Picken, F. (2013) 'From designed spaces to designer savvy societies: The potential of ideas competitions in willing participation', *Environment and Planning A*, 45 (8): 1963–1976.

Rapoport, A. (2005) 'Vernacular architecture and the cultural determinants of form'. In A. King (ed.) *Buildings and Society: Essays on the Social Development of the Built Environment*. London: Routledge, 158–169.

Robertson, I. (2008) 'Heritage from below: Class, social protest and resistance'. In B. Graham and P. Howard (eds) *The Ashgate Research Companion to Heritage and Identity*. Aldershot, UK: Ashgate, 143–158.

Selwood, J. and May, A. (2001) 'Research note: Resolving contested notions of tourism sustainability on Western Australia's "Turquoise Coast": The squatter settlements', *Current Issues in Tourism*, 4 (2–4): 381–391.

Selwood, J. and Tonts, M. (2004) 'Recreational second home in the south west of Western Australia'. In C. M. Hall and D. Müller (eds) *Tourism, Mobility, and Second Homes: Between Elite Landscape and Common Ground*. Clevedon, UK: ChannelView Publications, 149–161.

Selwood, J. and Tonts, M. (2006) 'Seeking serenity: Homes away from home in Western Australia'. In N. McIntyre, D. Williams and K. McHugh (eds) *Multiple Dwelling and Tourism: Negotiating Place, Home and Identity.* Wallingford, UK: CABI, 161–180.

Selwood, J. and Jones, R. (2010) 'Western Australian battlers and coastal squatter settlements: Heritage from below versus regulation from above', *Prairie Perspectives: Geographical Essays*, 13: 78–85.

Shaw, W. and Menday, L. (2013) 'Fibro dreaming: Greenwashed beach-house development on Australia's Coasts', *Urban Studies*, 15 (14): 2940–2958.

Soja, E. (1996) *Thirdspace: Journeys to Los Angeles and Other Real-and-Imagined Places.* London: Blackwell.

Steiner, R. (1998) 'System architectures and evolvability: Definitions and perspective', paper presented at the 8th Annual Symposium of the International Council on System Engineering. [online] Retrieved from: http://members.tripod.com/Rick_Steiner/Evolarch.pdf (accessed 24 August 2016).

Svenson, S. (2004) 'The cottage and the city: An interpretation of the Canadian second home experience'. In C. M. Hall and D. Müller (eds) *Tourism, Mobility, and Second Homes: Between Elite Landscape and Common Ground.* Clevedon, UK: Channel View Publications, 55–74.

Taussig, M. (2000) 'The beach (A fantasy)', *Critical Inquiry*, 26 (2): 248–278.

Thompson, P. (1985) *The Bach.* Wellington: Government Printer.

Tiwari, R. and Churchill, L. (2004) '"Shack" architecture: A produced landscape', *Landscapes: The Journal of the International Centre for Landscape and Language*, 2 (2): 1–13. [online] Retrieved from: http://ro.ecu.edu.au/landscapes/vol2/iss2/1 (accessed 21 July 2016).

Vellinga, M. (2006). 'Engaging the future: Vernacular architecture studies in the twenty-first century', in L. Asquith and M. Vellinga (eds) *Vernacular Architecture in the 21st Century Theory, Education and Practice.* New York: Taylor & Francis.

Venturi, R. and Brown, D. (2004) *Architecture as Signs and Systems: For a Mannerist Time.* Cambridge, MA: Harvard University Press.

Waterton, E. (2005) 'Whose sense of place? Reconciling archaeological perspectives with community values: Cultural landscapes in England', *International Journal of Heritage Studies*, 11 (4): 309–325.

Willis, J. and Goad, P. (2008) 'A bigger picture: Reframing Australian architectural history', *Fabrications*, 18 (10): 6–23.

PART V

Caravanning and mobile second homes

25

CARAVANNING AND MOBILE SECOND HOMES

C. Michael Hall and Dieter K. Müller

Introduction

Although mobile homes and caravans are an important element of second home tourism, representing more than 20% of tourism accommodation in the EU for example (see Leivestad, this volume) and almost half of British second homes (Steer-Fowler and Brunt, this volume), they have not attracted anywhere near the same level of attention as permanent second homes. This may be because whereas most tourism research is focused on essentially middle-class travel and leisure behaviours, the caravan and the mobile home have long been regarded as more "working class" (Leivestad 2015), although the emergence of "grey nomads" and the use of caravans and RVs as part of retirement mobilities is potentially changing some perceptions (Onyx & Leonard 2005, 2007; Holloway et al. 2011; Patterson, Pegg & Litster 2011; Hillman 2013; Brooker & Joppe 2014; Wu & Pearce 2016). Moreover, the inherent mobility of the caravan or mobile home has made it much harder to define as a second home category, which also reflects the difficulties inherent in governing and regulating mobile dwellings (Behr & Gober 1982; Hall & Müller 2004; Löfgren & Bendix 2007). This is also because the mobile second home offers significant flexibility with respect to use and can be used for both temporary and permanent residential tourism.

Caravans, mobile homes and houseboats are also sometimes included as categories of second homes in some jurisdictions (Hall 2014a), although most research attention is given to non-mobile second homes (see Chapter 1, this volume). However, the differences between mobile and non-mobile second homes are often quite fluid because of the growth of "permanent" caravan parks and mobile home sites that are used for second homes and retirement migration (Hall 2014a, 2014b). Nevertheless, Hall (2014a) suggests that it is important to recognise that even though mobile second homes, such as caravans, have the capacity to move, the reality is that they are usually "fixed" and immobile and often situated in specifically designated sites or parked at other "homes". In addition, their use needs to be understood over time in relation to changed socio-economic and mobility circumstances (see Figure 25.1).

Negative perceptions of caravans and mobile homes

Historically, even though they are inseparable from the growth of personal auto-mobility (Belasco 1979; Rockland 1980; Østby 2014), caravans and mobile homes have tended not to be perceived positively. Negative attitudes towards mobile homes have several potential sources.

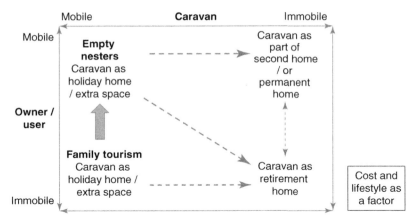

Figure 25.1   Stages of mobile practices.

Source: Hall 2014a.

From a cultural perspective, there are often negative perceptions of mobile populations and their caravans. In the British and European context, there have long been negative attitudes held towards the Romany, also referred to as gypsies or travellers, which is strongly coloured by perceptions of illegality. These images have often been reinforced by negative media portrayals (Wood & King 2001; Van Cleemput 2010; Dalsklev & Kunst 2015). While the gypsy caravan is one source of negative attitudes, another is the fact that mobile homes are a cheap form of housing and have therefore come to be associated with lower socio-economic groups and the poor (Hart et al. 2002).

Mobile homes were originally developed in the United States as a response to the impacts of the depression and the need for worker housing during the Second World War (Edwards 1977), as well as to the overall need for low-cost housing in the post-war era (Cowgill 1941; Drury 1972; Rockland 1980; Wallis 1991). However, as Edwards (1977) has argued, the perception of mobile homes as transient housing and architecture as well as being "cheap" has often meant a negative portrayal of their attributes. In the American context, this has come to be associated with a significant amount of stigmatisation and the perception and portrayal of mobile home residents as "trailer park trash" (MacTavish 2007; Kusenbach 2009; Saatcioglu & Ozanne 2013) and the homes as being insecure, poorly constructed and unsafe (Beamish et al. 2001; Fothergill & Peek 2004). Nevertheless, mobile homes, or manufactured homes as the industry prefers to describe them (Beamish et al. 2001), are one of the fastest growing parts of the American housing market and are especially important in rural areas. Aman and Yamal (2010), for example, suggest that over half of mobile homes in the United States are located in rural areas.

Saatcioglu and Ozanne (2013) suggest that mobile homes, with their standardised factory-made designs, fail to satisfy American middle-class ideals for site-built homes that are rooted in a community, noting that prestige goods are generally distinguished by their workmanship, customization and durability (Daloz 2010). However, Saatcioglu and Ozanne (2013) also observe that although mobile homes may symbolise impermanence, they are actually relatively immobile after being transported and note that less than 1% of mobile homes are moved, given the significant cost, lack of available sites due to zoning laws, and trailer park restrictions that prohibit older homes. Furthermore, American mobile home residents appear relatively intransient. The turnover rates for mobile home communities (2%–4%) are significantly less than those of apartments (50%) (Rowe 1998). Furthermore, 60% of trailer owners live in their parks for over 10 years, as compared to site-built home owners, who reside at a specific address for an average of only six years (Burkhart 2010).

The American data highlights the importance of distinguishing between the mobility of people and the mobility of housing and the home. In the majority of cases, the mobile home is a primary rather than a secondary dwelling. Moreover, they are more likely to be permanent than mobile. But this does not mean they do not serve an important role as a second home. Instead, the location of mobile homes and caravans on either private lots or in parks can become a relatively cheap way of accessing a holiday or second home (Sullivan & Stevens 1982; O'Reilly 2000), although these may still be perceived less positively by permanent populations (Sheldon & Var 1984). In addition, housing regulations may be used to prohibit the use of caravans and mobile homes as permanent structures, while the sell-off or privatisation of caravan and holiday parks by some local governments for greater financial returns is placing further pressures on the availability of sites where caravans can be located (Gurran 2008; Collins & Kearns 2010).

Mobility and identity

Yet at the same time that caravans and mobile homes are often framed negatively, there is a strong counter-veiling theme, in the United States at least, that is closely linked to more positive notions of identity (Belasco 1979; Jackson 1984). For example, White (2000: 188) argues 'After a century of development, the motor home has come to symbolize and reaffirm the unity of home, family, travel, and outdoor lifestyles more than any other possession or institution'. Like Jackson (1984), who sees the mobile home as a representative American architecture, Zelinsky (1973; in Rockland 1980) also regards nomadism and transience as an integral part of American culture and pioneering, and suggests that the desire for 'mobility receive their ideal embodiment in that superlatively American invention, the house trailer, which is virtually non-existent outside North America'. Such sentiments are clear in Rockland's own work when he suggests that, 'The RV is a natural in a country that has always felt a conflict between its desire for stability, permanence, and roots, and its desire for mobility, change, and freedom' (Rockland 1980: 10). However, it is perhaps important here to differentiate between the RV (recreational vehicles, motorhomes or trailers [equivalent to a caravan] that come equipped with the amenities and living spaces of home) and mobile or manufactured homes. Although both may serve as mobile second homes, RVs are designed to be much more mobile.

Community

Despite, or perhaps because of, their greater mobility, those who use caravans and RVs often have a strong sense of community whether when mobile or when visiting holiday parks and camping sites (Southerton et al. 2001; Foley & Hayllar 2007; Holloway et al. 2011; Triantafillidou & Siomkos 2013; Wu & Pearce 2016). Often, the regularity of return to the same location reinforces senses of attachment as well as community (Ming & McHugh 1995; Ming 1997). For example, Desrosiers-Lauzon (2011: x), suggests 'snowbirds are community builders, through their unique lifestyle – leisurely but not quite like tourists, with homeownership but unlike permanent residents – and their practice of sociability and mutual help'.

Notions of community are also important in Hardy et al. (2012, 2013), for example, who portray RVers as a form of neo-tribe, while Counts and Counts (1992) identify them as family (see also Counts & Counts 2009). Community ideas may also be reinforced by club membership, especially when that provides access to members only camping grounds (Van Heerden &

Van Heerden 2008). A sense of freedom is often reported in research on RVs and caravanning (Foley & Hayllar 2007; Mikkelsen & Cohen 2015; Kearns et al. 2017; Wilson & Hannam 2017). However, while significant, this motivation should arguably be seen with the search for a better quality of life that the social, community and place dimensions of RV-ing and caravanning can bring (Blichfeldt & Mikkelsen, 2013; Hardy & Gretzel 2011; Oliveira et al. 2017; Zhou et al. 2017). Arguably, from this perspective, the social aspects of mobile second homes mirror some of the attachments people have to the permanent second home (Stedman 2006). However, in many ways this should not be surprising. As Desrosiers-Lauzon (2011: viii) noted with respect to Canadian snowbirds in Florida, they

> share a similarly complex – or layered, or ambivalent, or ambiguous – relationship with their identity understood in terms of their locality, ethnicity, home states or provinces, or even their "natural" landscape. In this they are like most "modern people" feeling different emotions in different context; telling different stories to different audiences; using a varied repertoire of postures, statements, and attitudes on the meaning of self, place, and community in order to identify themselves and others while maintaining a sense of belonging, dignity, and personal autonomy.

Conclusions and future issues

Despite pressures on the availability of caravan sites in some countries, the caravan and RVs appear likely to remain significant parts of the mobile leisure landscape. Their size, in comparison with other second homes, is not regarded as a problem, with the lack of space and permanence regarded as positive attributes, providing, as Steer-Fowler and Brunt (this volume) note, as much an attachment with the type of space and memories of previous occasions enjoyed in them, as any relationship to particular locations. Nevertheless, the mobile home segment does seem to be changing with the RV becoming increasingly popular in many countries, such as Australia, at the expense of sedentary caravanning. As Caldicott, Jenkins and Scherrer (Chapter 28, this volume) suggest, the focus is now more on the caravan or RV itself and its serviceability as a long-term, touring, residential "home unit" rather than as a temporary, short-term holiday unit to be conveniently parked in a caravan park. It is therefore no surprise that Simpson (2008) refers to the nomadic urbanism of those who travel in their RV and caravan, taking home with them. Nevertheless, while the growth of such "freedom camping" connects back to some of the perceived motivations for RVing and caravanning, it is not without its controversies, given regulatory concerns and potential environmental impacts (Caldicott et al. 2014; Caldicott et al., this volume) with the provisioning of toilets and managing large numbers of visitors in public and private spaces becoming a significant issue in countries, such as Iceland and New Zealand, given the problems of human waste disposal and noise control (Connell et al. 2009; Collins et al. 2017; Kearns et al. 2017).

As pointed out in Figure 25.1, the caravan or motorhome is often static. Indeed, while such vehicles may have a mobile life, they are usually stationery, whether they are on the road or at a primary home. Furthermore, over their life course, they may become part of a permanent second home providing extra beds for visitors or even providing a base for the start of construction or repair of a permanent second home. When this happens, the caravan (as it tends to be caravans and trailers rather than RVs) becomes similar to the constructed mobile home. However, as noted above, this can create significant issues with respect to housing regulation and governance (see also Chapter 2, this volume) as local government seeks to control housing quality and aesthetics. This last point also reinforces that second homes, even when mobile, need to be understood within a wide lens that includes awareness of housing and social policy in the regulation of mobility, and not just tourism.

References

Aman, D. D. and Yarnal, B. (2010) 'Home sweet mobile home? Benefits and challenges of mobile home ownership in rural Pennsylvania'. *Applied Geography*, 30 (1): 84–95.

Beamish, J. O., Goss, R. C., Atiles, J. H. and Kim, Y. (2001) 'Not a trailer anymore: Perceptions of manufactured housing'. *Housing Policy Debate*, 12 (2): 373–392.

Behr, M. and Gober, P. (1982) 'When a residence is not a house: Examining residence-based migration definitions', *The Professional Geographer*, 34 (2): 178–184.

Belasco, W. J. (1979) *Americans on the Road: From Autocamp to Motel, 1910–1945*. Cambridge, MA: MIT Press.

Blichfeldt, B. S. and Mikkelsen, M. (2013) 'Vacability and sociability as touristic attraction', *Tourist Studies*, 13 (3): 235–250.

Brooker, E. and Joppe, M. (2014) 'A critical review of camping research and direction for future studies', *Journal of Vacation Marketing*, 20 (4), 335–351.

Burkhart, A. M. (2010) 'Bringing manufactured housing into the real estate finance system', *Pepperdine Law Review*, 37 (2): 427–458.

Caldicott, R., Scherrer, P. and Jenkins, J. (2014) 'Freedom camping in Australia: Current status, key stakeholders and political debate', *Annals of Leisure Research*, 17 (4): 417–442.

Collins, D. and Kearns, R. (2010) 'Pulling up the tent pegs? The significance and changing status of coastal campgrounds in New Zealand', *Tourism Geographies*, 12 (1): 53–76.

Collins, D., Kearns, R., Bates, L. and Serjeant, E. (2017) 'Police power and fettered freedom: Regulating coastal freedom camping in New Zealand', *Social & Cultural Geography*, http://dx.doi.org/10.1080/14649365.2017.1323342.

Connell, J., Page, S. J. and Bentley, T. (2009) 'Towards sustainable tourism planning in New Zealand: Monitoring local government planning under the Resource Management Act', *Tourism Management*, 30 (6): 867–877.

Counts, D. A. and Counts, D. R. (1992) 'They're my family now: The creation of community among RVers', *Anthropologica*, 34 (2): 153–182.

Counts, D. A. and Counts, D. R. (2009) *Over the Next Hill. An Ethnography of RVing Seniors in North America* 2nd ed. Toronto: University of Toronto Press.

Cowgill, D. O. (1941) *Mobile Homes: A Study of Trailer Life*. Philadelphia: University of Pennsylvania Press.

Daloz, J.-P. (2010) *The Sociology of Elite Distinction: From Theoretical to Comparative Perspectives*. New York: Palgrave Macmillan.

Dalsklev, M. and Kunst, J. R. (2015) 'The effect of disgust-eliciting media portrayals on outgroup dehumanization and support of deportation in a Norwegian sample', *International Journal of Intercultural Relations*, 47: 28–40.

Desrosiers-Lauzon, G. (2011) *Florida's Snowbirds: Spectacle, Mobility, and Community Since 1945*. Montreal: McGill-Queen's Press-MQUP.

Drury, M. J. (1972) *Mobile Homes: The Unrecognized Revolution in American Housing*. New York: Praeger.

Edwards, C. M. (1977) *Homes for Travel and Living: The History and Development of the Recreational Vehicle and Mobile Home Industries*. East Lansing, MI: Carl Edwards.

Foley, C. and Hayllar, B. (2007) 'A tale of two caravan parks: Friendship, community and the freedom thing', *Tourism Today*, 7: 7–28.

Fothergill, A. and Peek, L. A. (2004) 'Poverty and disasters in the United States: A review of recent sociological findings', *Natural Hazards*, 32 (1): 89–110.

Gurran, N. (2008) 'The turning tide: Amenity migration in coastal Australia', *International Planning Studies*, 13 (4): 391–414.

Hall, C. M. (2014a) Mobile second homes or cheap permanent homes? The problematic fluidity of caravans and motor homes as second homes. Paper presented at New Perspectives on Second Homes, June 9–11, Stockholm, Sweden. [online] Available at: https://www.academia.edu/7312722/Mobile_second_homes_or_cheap_permanent_homes_The_problematic_fluidity_of_caravans_and_motor_homes_as_second_homes

Hall, C. M. (2014b) 'Second home tourism: An international review', *Tourism Review International*, 18 (3), 115–135.

Hall, C. M. and Müller, D. (2004) 'Introduction: Second homes, curse or blessing? Revisited'. In C. M. Hall and D. Müller (eds) *Tourism, Mobility and Second Homes: Between Elite Landscape and Common Ground.* Clevedon, UK: Channel View Publications, 3–14.

Hardy, A. and Gretzel, U. (2011) 'Why we travel this way: An exploration into the motivations of recreational vehicle users', In D. Carson and B. Prideaux (eds) *Drive Tourism: Trends and Emerging Markets.* London: Routledge, 194–223.

Hardy, A., Hanson, D. and Gretzel, U. (2012) 'Online representations of RVing neo-tribes in the USA and Australia', *Journal of Tourism and Cultural Change*, 10 (3): 219–232.

Hardy, A., Gretzel, U. and Hanson, D. (2013) 'Travelling neo-tribes: Conceptualizing recreational vehicle users', *Journal of Tourism and Cultural Change*, 11 (1–2): 48–60.

Hart, J. F., Rhodes, M. J. and Morgan, J. T. (2002) *The Unknown World of the Mobile Home.* Baltimore, MD: Johns Hopkins University Press.

Hillman, W. (2013) 'Grey nomads travelling in Queensland, Australia: Social and health needs', *Ageing & Society*, 33 (4): 579–597.

Holloway, D., Green, L. and Holloway, D. (2011) 'The intratourist gaze: Grey nomads and "other tourists"', *Tourist Studies*, 11 (3): 235–252.

Jackson, J. B. (1984) *Discovering the Vernacular Landscape.* New Haven, CT: Yale University Press.

Kearns, R., Collins, D. and Bates, L. (2017) '"It's freedom!": Examining the motivations and experiences of coastal freedom campers in New Zealand', *Leisure Studies*, 36 (3): 395–408.

Kusenbach, M. (2009) 'Salvaging decency: Mobile home residents' strategies of managing the stigma of "trailer" living', *Qualitative Sociology*, 32 (4): 399–428.

Leivestad, H. H. (2015) Lives on Wheels. Caravan Homes in Contemporary Europe. PhD. Stockholm University, Stockholm, Sweden.

Löfgren, O. and Bendix, R. (2007) 'Double homes, double lives?', *Ethnologia Europaea*, 37 (1/2): 7–16.

MacTavish, K. A. (2007) 'The wrong side of the tracks: Social inequality and mobile home park residence', *Community Development*, 38 (1): 74–91.

Mikkelsen, M and Cohen, S. A. (2015) 'Freedom in mundane mobilities: Caravanning in Denmark', *Tourism Geographies*, 17 (5): 663–681.

Ming, R. and McHugh, K. (1995) 'Wintering in American sunbelt: Linking place and behaviour', *Journal of Tourism Studies*, 6 (2): 56–61.

Ming, R. C. (1997) 'Tracking "snowbirds" in Australia: Winter sun seekers in far north Queensland', *Australian Geographical Studies*, 35 (2): 168–182.

Oliveira, C., Brochado, A. and Correia, A. (2017) 'Seniors in international residential tourism: Looking for quality of life', *Anatolia*, 1–13. Available at: http://dx.doi.org/10.1080/13032917.2017.1358189

Onyx, J. and Leonard, R. (2005) 'Australian grey nomads and American snowbirds: Similarities and differences', *Journal of Tourism Studies*, 16 (1): 61–68.

Onyx, J. and Leonard, R. (2007) 'The grey nomads phenomenon: Changing the script of aging', *International Journal of Aging and Human Development*, 64 (4): 381–398.

O'Reilly, K. (2000) New Europe/Old boundaries: British migrants in Spain. *Journal of Social Welfare and Family Law*, 22 (4): 477–491.

Østby, P. (2014) 'Car mobility and camping tourism in Norway, 1950–1970', *Journal of Tourism History*, 5 (3): 287–304.

Patterson, I., Pegg, S. and Litster, J. (2011) 'Grey nomads on tour: A revolution in travel and tourism for older adults', *Tourism Analysis*, 16 (3): 283–294.

Rockland, M. A. (1980) *Homes on Wheels.* New Brunswick, NJ: Rutgers University Press.

Rowe, R. K. (1998) 'Investing in manufactured housing communities', *Urban Land*, 57 (6): 80–81.

Saatcioglu, B. and Ozanne, J. L. (2013) 'Moral habitus and status negotiation in a marginalized working-class neighborhood', *Journal of Consumer Research*, 40 (4): 692–710.

Sheldon, P. J. and Var, T. (1984) 'Resident attitudes to tourism in North Wales', *Tourism Management*, 5 (1): 40–47.

Simpson, D. (2008) 'Nomadic urbanism: The senior full-time recreational vehicle community', *Interstices: Journal of Architecture and Related Arts*, 9: 34–46.

Southerton, D., Shove E., Warde, A. and Deem, R. (2001) 'The social worlds of caravanning: Objects, scripts and practices', *Sociological Research Online*, 6 (2): 1–8.

Stedman, R. C. (2006) 'Understanding place attachment among second home owners', *American Behavioral Scientist*, 50 (2): 187–205.

Sullivan, D. A. and Stevens, S. A. (1982) 'Snowbirds: Seasonal migrants to the sunbelt', *Research on Aging*, 4 (2): −159–177.

Triantafillidou, A. and Siomkos, G. (2013) 'Summer camping: An extraordinary, nostalgic, and interpersonal experience', *Journal of Vacation Marketing*, 19 (3): 197–208.

Van Cleemput, P. (2010) 'Social exclusion of gypsies and travellers: Health impact', *Journal of Research in Nursing*, 15 (4): 315–327.

Van Heerden, N. and Van Heerden, C. H. (2008) 'Leisure motorhoming: The case of the motorhome club of South Africa', *South African Journal for Research in Sport, Physical Education and Recreation*, 30 (1): 125–136.

Wallis, A. D. (1991) *Wheel Estate: The Rise and Decline of Mobile Homes*. New York: Oxford University Press.

White, R. B. (2000) *Home on the Road: The Motor Home in America*. Washington, DC: Smithsonian Institution.

Wilson, S. and Hannam, K. (2017) 'The frictions of slow tourism mobilities: Conceptualising campervan travel', *Annals of Tourism Research*, 67: 25–36.

Wood, N. and King, R. (2001) 'Media and migration: An overview'. In R. King and N. Wood (eds) *Media and Migration: Constructions of Mobility and Difference*. London: Routledge, 1–22.

Wu, M. Y. and Pearce, P. L. (2016) 'The rally experience: Exploring motivation patterns of Australian grey nomads', *Journal of Destination Marketing & Management*, 6 (4): 407–415. Available at:https://doi.org/10.1016/j.jdmm.2016.06.008

Zelinsky, W. (1973) *The Cultural Geography of the United States*. New York: Pearson.

Zhou, L., Yu, J., Wu, M. Y., Wall, G. and Pearce, P. L. (2017) 'Seniors' seasonal movements for health enhancement', *The Service Industries Journal*, 38 (1–2): 27–47. Available at: http://dx.doi.org/10.1080/02642069.2017.1365139

26

CARAVAN CULTURES

Second homes on wheels

Hege Høyer Leivestad

Introduction

In a stellar contribution to the theoretical understanding of our physical surroundings, landscape theorist John Brinckerhoff Jackson (1984) offers a rather unique discussion of the American mobile dwelling. In *Discovering the Vernacular Landscape*, Jackson traces the mobile home back to other forms of dwellings that since colonial times have held some key features in common: their temporary nature and their inherent mobility. These were houses that were built quickly and that were easy to disassemble when land or work was found elsewhere. Jackson identifies what he argues has become specific vernacular architectures, in the shape of box houses, prefabricated homes, mobile homes and trailers. And the latter is where Jackson, in 1984 (86), sees 'the low-cost dwelling for the future', as trailers are 'lacking in solidity, lacking in permanence, lacking in charm, but inexpensive, convenient and mobile'.

What Jackson (1984) importantly pointed to more than 30 years ago was the link between the mobile dwelling's material properties and its potential mobility (see Leivestad 2015). This chapter seeks to place the European equivalent to the American trailer, the *caravan*, in a similar theoretical light, by examining its connections with various meanings and practices of (im) mobility. The caravan – a unit for sleeping and living that can be towed behind a car – holds an ambiguous position in the leisure and housing landscape of Western Europe. Frequently used as homes for travelling and often stigmatised segments of society such as shelter for the homeless and increasingly for migrant populations in the outskirts of capitals and cities, the caravan has become the subject of media reports on second rate housing, and as the cause of debates concerning land rights and building codes. At the same time, the caravan remains perhaps the most potent symbol for working-class leisure, largely a result of its popularity in the 1950s to 1970s, and the various ways in which the caravan holiday has become ridiculed in media reports and TV shows (Leivestad 2015). While the domestic caravan holiday found new resurgence in parts of Western Europe following the recession from 2007 and onwards, and camping clubs reported all-time high membership status, Walker (2009) put it as follows: 'But while caravanning is undoubtedly big business, there is one leap it has yet to make: being seen as cool'.

Despite this troublesome position in the public conscience, caravanning *is* actually big business. Camping on a campsite or caravan park is today counted for as one of the largest tourism industries in Europe, representing more than 20% of tourism accommodation in the EU

(EFCO & HPA 2016). The European Caravan Federation calculates that in 2014, almost 4 million touring caravans were in use, as well as more than 1.6 million motorhomes. In addition come all the caravans that are deregistered, but still in use as static housing on campsites and private property. Because while many caravans are inhabited seasonally as touring second homes, the varieties in usage – from static campsite dwelling to extra accommodation on farms – clearly illustrates the difficulties of the second home category itself (Löfgren & Bendix 2007; Hall & Müller 2004), as real practices blur sharp categorisations between different forms of dwellings.

Following a short historical review of some of the developments in motorised camping, and the ways in which it has been understood in the academic literature, this chapter will offer an ethnographic glimpse into the use of caravans in present-day Europe. By highlighting the connections between the material features of mobile dwellings and the sites upon which they are parked, I will show how these various practices can be understood through a notion of *potential mobility* (Leivestad 2016). The case used to illustrate this argument is based on ethnographic fieldwork on a campsite in the outskirts of a post-industrial town in central Sweden, where caravan dwellers stay during the summer season and some even live on a full-time basis. Sweden is a particularly interesting nation when it comes to motorised camping and caravanning. It is a country where camping grew to be a popular leisure form in the 1950–60s socially democratic era, and that during the past half-decade has held the position of the nation with the most caravans per capita in Europe. However, the history of the caravan itself will first take us across to the British Isles.

Family cohesion, nature and "freedom of mobility"

It was in the late 1800s that the first caravans for leisure purposes were introduced by the Scotsman William Gordon Stables, a retired navy surgeon and writer of adventure stories for boys (Pressnell 1991; Wilson 1986). *The Wanderer* was built by the Bristol Wagon Company after Gordon Stables' drawings, a result of his dream of a very own "Land Yacht". In the book *Cruise of the Land Yacht Wanderer, or, Thirteen Hundred Miles in My Caravan,* Gordon Stables (1886) describes his observations from a more than 1,300-British miles journey around his native Scotland. While *The Wanderer* has been called the first recreational caravan, horse-drawn caravans had existed in the UK for some 60 years already, first as vehicles for travelling showmen and later as dwellings for Traveller-Gypsies (Pressnell 1991). It took until the turn of the century to see the first example of a motorised caravan in Europe, but by the 1920s car camping was becoming increasingly popular among the privileged classes that could own a private car (Leivestad 2015; Wilson 1986). With a history better documented in Britain than other parts of Europe, one saw the early start of motorised camping in the 1920s and 1930s, in tandem with the movement for compulsory holidays (see Wilson 1986). But while the establishment of holiday camps was one of the initiatives taken in favour of the working classes, tents still remained the most used form of camping dwelling.

Parallel with the European beginnings, motorised camping was becoming increasingly popular in the US from the 1920s onwards, and American progress had important impacts on European developments (see Østby 2014). In large parts of Europe, the real caravanning breakthrough came with the expansion of private car use in the post-war period of the 1950s and 1960s. By then, more groups of workers were entitled to holidays and the so-called masses found their way to coastal areas that previously had been dominated by the middle classes (Löfgren 1999). Wilson (1986: 189) reports for instance that in 1955 as many as 2 million UK families went on caravan holidays. Löfgren (1999), elegantly sweeping over the historical growth of camping in the US and Sweden, discusses the important role of the car in transforming tourism, making it more privatised, but also providing the working classes with a means of discovering new areas. He importantly links the development of camping with class-based controversies regarding the right to – and use of – nature (see also Morris 2003). Löfgren's (1999) work critically shows then how the infrastructures of motorised camping and the establishment of campsites in some countries was part of a wider political and largely moral project of nature, order and family cohesion. Sweden is a prime example of such tendencies. Here, in the 1960s, during the social democratic era of Swedish politics, campsites were opened and publicly run by local municipalities with the aim of providing an affordable and well-organised recreation for the citizens. The 1960s was interestingly also a period when one first started to see regulars returning to the same campsite, privatising reserved pitches with fences and gardens (Löfgren 1999). This change, where the campsite gradually became a "home for steady regulars" came as a result of how a growing working-class affluence made the caravan less prestigious (Löfgren 1999).

Except for Löfgren's (1999) work, the limited number of academic attempts that have been made to make sense of the caravan and camping phenomenon – then mostly in terms of analysis of contemporary phenomena – have mostly been preoccupied with the American and Australian recreational vehicle (RV) culture as it has come to symbolise freedom, mobility and escape, commonly as an alternative retirement option (Counts & Counts 1992, 2009; Jobes 1984; Hardy et al. 2012, 2013; Hartwigsen & Null 1989, 1990; Hillman 2013; Onyx & Leonard 2005). In the European academic literature on camping, the cultural and social milieu of the campsite has led some scholars to see these spaces as "social worlds" setting the stage for social differentiation (Southerton et al. 2001), and in the case of Danish caravan sites, as places for domestic mundane tourism "freed from experience" (Blichfeldt 2009; Blichfeldt & Mikkelsen 2013; Mikkelsen & Cohen 2015; see also Triantafillidou & Siomkos 2013 on sociability in Greek camping). So, while the academic literature on motorised camping and caravanning in general is sparse, some threads are still visible in the existing bodies of work. One is a focus on the meanings and associations of "freedom", as these are interlinked with mobility and domestic downsizing (Counts & Counts 2009; see also Mikkelsen & Cohen 2015). Another is the attempt to understand camping and caravanning mainly within a framework of domestic tourism (see Blichfeldt & Mikkelsen 2013). In the following, I will carefully sidestep these modes of interpretation and use a case from a campsite in Sweden to discuss how mobility can be both used and problematised as an analytical category to shed light upon caravan dwelling in contemporary Europe (see also Leivestad 2017, 2015).

Potentially mobile or stereotypically still: A caravan case from Sweden

In the year 2000, when Benny and Louise, a factory worker and kindergarten employee in their forties, bought their first caravan and parked it on a pitch at Lake Camping, it was the result of several coincidences. Benny's older brother and his wife had already had a caravan at the same campsite since the 1980s, but Benny had wanted to buy a cabin, preferably cycling distance from work and their rental apartment in town. Benny soon realised however, that while the bank could grant him a loan for the cabin, he wouldn't be able to afford to make any changes to it. Later the same day, after meeting the bank, Benny and Louise went to their local caravan dealer and after three hours ended up buying a second-hand caravan model. Sixteen years later they are still parked on a pitch at Lake Camping, about five kilometres from their 90 m^2 apartment in central Lake Town, and cycling distance from Benny's workplace. While Benny had wanted a cabin, Louise had never fancied a caravan either. Her father used to have one, and she always found it to be cramped and uncomfortable. Now, however, they are on their third model, increasingly advancing in both size and comfort. Their camping season has eventually become longer and longer, starting in late April and lasting until the end of September. They go to work early in the morning, and return daytime, spending afternoons, holidays and weekends relaxing at their pitch, often together with their campsite neighbours and close family – some of whom also have a caravan at the site. During the winter season, they pay a special night fee to come out on the weekends, while not having to remove the caravan from the pitch. In the summer season they spend every night in their caravan, only dropping into their apartment in town once or twice a week to water the flowers and pick up the mail.

Lake Camping, first established as a municipal campground in the 1960s, lies on the outskirts of Lake Town in central Sweden, once a thriving centre of Swedish industry, and today rebranding as a locus for service and administration, with a population of approximately 140,000 inhabitants, not least due to a growing immigrant population. Still situated on municipal ground, Lake Camping is today a four-star rated campsite, run by a joint stockcompany registered in Stockholm as part of one of the leading camping chains in Sweden. Having gone through a long period of private ownership, which resulted in a bad reputation for the campsite due to the high number of caravans being used as social housing, the municipality regained control and rebuilt the entire site. The result was new spacious pitches with less vegetation in between, new drains and electricity and well-equipped service buildings with kitchens, showers and a sauna. During the summer season, the site, which is located far from any tourist attractions, receives motorhomers and caravanners stopping for a night or two, in addition to the more than 50 caravan dwellers on seasonal contracts. All of these seasonal caravanners, in Swedish known as *säsongare*, are from the local Lake Town area. Some even live full-time in a caravan or motorhome on the campsite, enabled by the campsite management's use of double seasonal contracts.

For several years, Benny and Louise used to take their caravan for a few weeks of travelling in Sweden during the summer holidays. But gradually, their caravan awning was so well-equipped that going away became logistically difficult. During the summer of 2011, they invested in a four-season self-standing awning that would allow them to simply disconnect the caravan when wanting to go away, something they still have not done. On the other hand, Benny's brother Kalle and his wife Lena, a couple in their fifties occupying the pitch next to Benny and Louise, would no longer use their caravan for travelling. Every spring the process of furnishing their campsite home usually required weeks of transporting furniture, the fridge and all ornaments used to decorate the awning. Still, Kalle and Lena would retell vivid memories from their years of travelling with their caravan around Sweden, and Kalle would proudly show anyone interested his detailed caravan log of all distances travelled and stops taken with their mobile unit. Inside the caravan, Kalle has all loose objects carefully secured with strings and wires, so that 'we could go tomorrow if we wanted to'.

These Lake Camping couples' domestication of the campsite has involved a gradual immobilisation of their caravan property, through furnished awnings and material instalments. Material upgrading is performed following conventional home aesthetics, with sofa groups, TV sections and a dining area in the semi-outdoors of the caravan awning, and wooden balconies, garden furniture, flagpoles and a barbeque area on the pitch. Still, mobility features in a well-kept and almost fetishised discourse of being able to geographically move one's dwelling 'whenever one wants to', and the liberty of being able to move the location of the caravan pitch. In this sense, mobility is idealised as an inherent part of the camping phenomenon, also through practices of static campsite dwelling.

I have argued elsewhere that such paradoxes can best be understood by turning attention to the way mobility, as both idea and ideal, regain meaning through material practices of home building. And here it becomes necessary to problematise the very analytical category of mobility itself. While the so-called "mobility turn" in the social sciences has provided analytical insights into various forms of movement through a holistic ambition (Hannam et al. 2006; Sheller & Urry 2006; Urry 2007), it remains problematic that mobility is seen as something "new" (Cresswell 2010) or simply as an empty category applicable to all sorts of practices (Adey 2006; Merriman 2014). As the sociologist Vincent Kaufmann (2001) argued when launching the term *motility*, it is sometimes mobility as potential, and not as realised practice, that can broaden our understandings of contemporary phenomena of people, objects and infrastructures on the move. Kaufmann finds motility useful mainly in terms of studies of transportation, where motility is a resource that needs to be activated. The caravan case, as described above, suggests however that *potential mobility* (see Leivestad 2017, 2016, 2015) is rather an idea that perhaps never is fulfilled, and often contradicted, in a wider imagining of the various potentials of the unfixed dwelling. Read this way, the caravan potential is located in its ability to move, but also in its general unfixity and the possibilities this generates for caravan dwellers.

Legal voids and blurred categories

It is the caravan's potential mobility that is the very basis of its legal existence on many campsites around Europe. The wheels that are there, but perhaps seldom used, provide campsites and caravan owners with the possibility of establishing second home facilities, and affordable housing, in spaces planned and regulated for mobile tourism activity. This was also the case at the Swedish Lake Camping. When the site was rebuilt by the municipality in the mid-2000s, all former full-time residents were also removed. Lake Camping was to be a tourist facility, not a location for social clients. Several measurements were taken in order to assure the order of the new site. As a means of preventing Roma or Traveller groups from using the site for instance, all payments were to be done upfront, and with credit cards, in addition to allowing payment for only one family at a time. This particular example illustrates the ways in which campsite owners actively play a part in discrimination and regulation of stigmatised groups' mobility, through the implementation of control and payment systems.

Lake Camping *säsongare*, such as Kalle and Lena, who were regulars at the site already during the previous ownership, would both enjoy the material changes of the site, and miss the social milieu that the more "primitive" infrastructures allowed for. But while the municipality's intention was to remake Lake Camping into a transit post for tourists, the management's flexibility and the company's need for stable incoming pitch rents have secured a stable group of both seasonal and full-time residents at the site. The camping chain's own regulations state that all their establishments are directed towards tourists and that it is prohibited to use the campsite for full-time residency, or other kinds of temporary accommodation that is not aimed at tourism. The company's regulations show that while registering with residency is not allowed, post can be sent to the reception upon agreement. However, the allowance of double contracts, one winter and one summer, in practice enable full-time residency at the site, but in contrary to the situation in the past – now mostly for working people who wish to lead a different lifestyle – and the economic means to do so after the sales of property (see Counts & Counts 2009; Hoey 2014).

The regulation of building structures is however another area where forms of caravan dwellings can be controlled. I have elsewhere – and more extensively – shown this in the case of Spain, where British caravanners transform touring caravans into permanent housing (Leivestad forthcoming, 2015). At Swedish Lake Camping, the campsite chain operates with a long list of regulations where some are explicitly directed towards the establishment of permanent building structures that may contradict the very idea of temporary tourism dwelling. While the placing of touring and permanent caravans at the campsites is regulated in the local area plan and in municipal legislation, these legislative bodies do not concern themselves with structures such as wooden terraces. Lake Camping campsite regulations, however, prohibit fences, planting of flowers and bushes on the ground, and built floors and verandas outside caravan awnings. While wooden awning flooring is allowed, it is required to be removed by the end of the contract. In practice however, the seasonal and full-time caravanners at Lake Camping have bended these regulations for years, gradually extending the built structures outside their caravans, allowing them to widen and rework the temporary nature of their mobile dwelling.

What do these seemingly mundane examples tell us, then, about the position of the caravan as second homes, in Sweden and elsewhere in Western Europe? They can certainly be connected to a much more general void in which the caravan is located in Western Europe today. Regulated as private property and not as real estate, caravans pass under the radar of much housing legislation. This legislative ambiguity – and their potential mobility as dwellings that can be moved – create a wider caravan potential. Still, there are considerable insecurities involved in investing in a caravan for long-term or full-time use. Caravans are seldom materially constructed for full-time use, and their sometimes-fragile material structures are easily worn down (see also Wallis 1991). The land whereupon the caravan is parked, where caravanners invest and build extensions, patios and domesticize as gardens, remain under the control of the campsite owner, and pitches are leased only for 6 or 12 months at a time. But it cannot be neglected that legislative voids also create economic advantages for caravan owners, provided through, for instance, avoidance of property taxes. At Lake Camping, caravans – and motorhomes – are used both as second homes close to home, but also as primary dwellings for those who have taken the step to sell houses and apartments in search of a different lifestyle. The life aspirations embedded in these arrangements, involving both a wish of domestic downsizing and the believed agency lying in owning a home that can be moved, underline the complex interconnections between class, home ownership and mobility that the caravan continues to manifest.

Concluding remarks: Ambiguous affection

In the years 2009–2015, no less than five docudramas on Swedish television featured the everyday of summer caravanning. The most popular, *Böda Camping*, airing its fourth season in 2015, follows daily life at one of Sweden's largest campsites on the island of Öland. Wrapped in humorous settings of broken awning poles, clumsy motorhomers and eccentric caravanners, the audience were introduced to staff, visiting tourists and the steady regulars of the campsite's nicest street. The "parade-street", occupied by couples that seemed mostly concerned with keeping pedantic order and inelegantly competing in sporting well-kept façades, met the stereotypical image of caravanners so frequently seen in media portrayals, in Sweden and elsewhere. It is obvious that the caravan and the cultures it carries continue to puzzle a sometimes-ignorant public. The Böda Camping series fed into an already established middle-class expectation of caravanning as paradoxically static, materialistic and essentially non-urban working class. While Lake Camping residents, such as Benny and Louise, would find the Böda series rather amusing, they found it hard to see any parallels with their own caravan reality.

There are several reasons why the caravan continues to be an object of both affection and refusal. In this chapter, I have briefly discussed some of them, using an example of a Swedish campsite to show how second homes and primary dwellings are established on a site regulated for touristic activity. For the Lake Town couples, a rather undefined notion of mobility continues to appear in a discourse surrounding the caravan lifestyle. In this chapter, I have suggested that the ways mobility appears as an idea that is continuously contradicted allow for an understanding of the caravan phenomenon through the concept of potential mobility (Leivestad forthcoming, 2017, 2015). This notion of potential mobility plays back at the unfixity of the caravan dwelling that continues to be both an asset and a challenge. I have illustrated this with examples of immobilisation of mobile dwelling, and the ways material adjustments are both enabled and constrained by regulation and legislative voids. This could, however, have been a story about the expectations of particular forms of collective sociality embedded in the camping phenomenon, and their interlinkage with how historical ideas of democracy and class were part of the campsite establishment (Löfgren 1999). It could also have been a story about how cultural ideas surrounding the role of the home and domesticity in the contemporary West form part of the caravan home aspirations that rise in furnished awnings and wheels that potentially can take you anywhere. When Jackson (1984) saw the trailer as part of a vernacular landscape, and the housing solution of the American future, his prognostication carried both economic and material factors. Such factors, and their interlinkage with issues of class, need to be taken into account when we continue to try to make sense out of the European caravan phenomenon.

References

Adey, P. (2006) 'If mobility is everything it is nothing: Towards a relational politics of (im)mobilities', *Mobilities*, 1 (1): 75–94.

Blichfeldt, B. S. (2009) 'Innovation and entrepreneurship in tourism: The case of a Danish caravan site', *Pasos. Revista de Turismo y Patrimonio Cultural*, 7 (3): 415–431.

Blichfeldt, B. S. and Mikkelsen, M. (2013) 'Vacability and sociability as touristic attraction', *Tourist Studies*, 13 (3): 235–250.

Counts, D. A. and Counts, D. R. (1992) 'They're my family now: The creation of community among RVers', *Anthropologica*, 34 (2): 153–182.

Counts, D. A. and Counts, D. R. (2009) *Over the Next Hill. An Ethnography of RVing Seniors in North America*, 2nd ed. Toronto, Ont.: University of Toronto Press.

Cresswell, T. (2010) 'Towards a politics of mobility', *Environment and Planning D: Society and Space*, 28 (1): 17–31.

European Caravan Federation and Holiday Park Association, EFCO and HPA (2016). http://www.efcohpa.eu/

Hall, C. M. and Müller, D. (2004) 'Introduction: Second homes, curse or blessing? Revisited'. In C. M. Hall and D. Müller (eds) *Tourism, Mobility and Second Homes: Between Elite Landscape and Common Ground*. Clevedon, UK: Channel View Publications, 3–14.

Hannam, K., Sheller, M. and Urry, J. (2006) 'Editorial: Mobilities, immobilities and moorings', *Mobilities*, 1 (1): 1–22.

Hardy, A., Hanson, D. and Gretzel, U. (2012) 'Online representations of Rving neo-tribes in the USA and Australia', *Journal of Tourism and Cultural Change*, 10 (3): 219–232.

Hardy, A., Gretzel, U. and Hanson, D. (2013) 'Travelling neo-tribes: Conceptualizing recreational vehicle users', *Journal of Tourism and Cultural Change*, 11 (1–2): 48–60.

Hartwigsen, G. and Null, R. (1989) 'Full-timing: A housing alternative for older people', *International Journal of Aging and Human Development*, 29 (4): 317–328.

Hartwigsen, G. and Null, R. (1990) 'Full timers: Who are these older people who are living in their RVs?', *Journal of Housing for the Elderly*, 7 (1): 133–147.

Hillman, W. (2013) 'Grey nomads travelling in Queensland, Australia: Social and health needs', *Ageing and Society*, 33 (4): 579–597.

Hoey, B. A. (2014) *Opting for Elsewhere: Lifestyle Migration in the American Middle Class*. Nashville, TN: Vanderbilt University Press.

Jackson, J. B. (1984) *Discovering the Vernacular Landscape*. New Haven, CT: Yale University Press.

Jobes, P. C. (1984) 'Old timers and new mobile lifestyles', *Annals of Tourism Research*, 11 (2): 181–198.

Kaufmann, V. (2001) *Re-Thinking Mobility: Contemporary Sociology*. Aldershot, UK: Ashgate.

Leivestad, H. H. (2015) Lives on Wheels. Caravan Homes in Contemporary Europe. PhD. Stockholm University, Stockholm, Sweden.

Leivestad, H. H. (2016) 'Motility'. In N. Salazar and K. Jayaram (eds) *The Keywords of Mobility: Critical Engagements*. Oxford: Berghahn, 133–151.

Leivestad, H. H. (2017) 'Inventorying Mobility: Methodology on Wheels'. In A. Elliot, R. Norum and N. Salazar (eds) *Methodologies of Mobility: Ethnography and Experiment*. Oxford: Berghahn.

Löfgren, O. (1999) *On Holiday. A History of Vacationing*. Berkeley, CA: University of California Press.

Löfgren, O. and Bendix, R. (2007) 'Double homes, double lives?', *Ethnologia Europaea*, 37 (1/2): 7–16.

Merriman, P. (2014) 'Rethinking mobile methods', *Mobilities*, 9 (2): 167–187.

Mikkelsen, M and Cohen, S.A. (2015) 'Freedom in mundane mobilities: Caravanning in Denmark', *Tourism Geographies*, 17 (5): 663–681.

Morris, N. (2003) Feeling Nature: Naturism, Camping, Environment and the Body in Britain, 1920–1960. PhD. University of Hull, Hull, England.

Onyx, J. and Leonard, R. (2005) 'Australian grey nomads and American snowbirds: Similarities and differences', *Journal of Tourism Studies*, 16 (1): 61–68.

Østby, P. (2014) 'Car mobility and camping tourism in Norway, 1950–1970', *Journal of Tourism History*, 5 (3): 287–304.

Pressnell, J. (1991) *Touring Caravans*. Oxford: Shire Publications.

Sheller, M and Urry, J. (2006) 'New mobilities paradigm', *Environment and Planning A*, 38 (2): 207–226.

Southerton, D., Shove E., Warde, A. and Deem, R. (2001) 'The social worlds of caravanning: Objects, scripts and practices', *Sociological Research Online*, 6 (2).

Stables, G. (1886) *The Cruise of the Land Yacht Wanderer, Or, Thirteen Hundred Miles in My Caravan*. London: Hodder and Stoughton.

Triantafillidou, A. and Siomkos, G. (2013) 'Summer camping: An extraordinary, nostalgic, and interpersonal experience', *Journal of Vacation Marketing*, 19 (3): 197–208.

Urry, J. (2007) *Mobilities*. Cambridge: Polity Press.

Walker, P. (2009) 'Recession-hit Britons abandon foreign holidays in favour of "staycations"'. *The Guardian*, 13 August. [online] Available at: https://www.theguardian.com/travel/2009/aug/13/uk-recession-travel-holidays-staycation

Wallis, A. D. (1991) *Wheel Estate. The Rise and Decline of Mobile Homes*. Baltimore and London: The Johns Hopkins University Press.

Wilson, N. (1986) *Gypsies and Gentlemen. The Life and Times of the Leisure Caravan*. London: Columbus Books.

27

CARAVAN PEOPLE AND SPACE ATTACHMENT

Martyn Steer-Fowler and Paul Brunt

Introduction: The contribution of static caravans

The recent proliferation of second home ownership in Britain has become a significant feature of contemporary tourism. Fuelled by growth in urbanisation (Williams et al. 2004) and the relentless pace of modern life during a period of increasing wealth and recreation, no longer does it remain the pursuit of the *leisure class* Rojek (2000) suggested, or the phenomenon of the *middle class* to which Jaakson (1986) refers, but has become an accessible preoccupation for *all* social groups. This has been greatly facilitated by the reinvention of the holiday park industry using business models based more on the sale and site rental of units as second homes than on traditional seasonal holiday lettings (Middleton & Lickorish 2005).

The true extent of second home ownership in Britain over the past 50 years is difficult to quantify as definitions have varied over time, and consequently so too have the properties which qualify and the regions that are included. Second homes are by instinct places where people like to retreat in private, and like most countries Britain has been unable to measure the official definition satisfactorily. Moreover, until 1994 there was no single information source to accurately reflect a pattern of growth on a comparable basis, and the data which has been gathered may not be wholly reliable. By carefully piecing together the evidence which does exist from the most reliable sources (Table 27.1), some retrospective picture of second home development can be established with reasonable accuracy.

By 1970 it was estimated that the number of British second homes had reached almost 200,000, matched by a similar number of static caravans (Dower 1977). With strong economic performance, developments in infrastructure and increasing "hyper-mobility" (Middleton & Lickorish 2005), ownership of second homes continued to rise through the decades to become an important part of modern day tourism (Quinn 2004).

The quantification of static caravans used as second homes which by their very nature are less permanent and at times portable is more problematic. The National Centre for Social Research who collects information for those who reside in mobile homes does not specifically include caravans, and the Valuation Office who is responsible for rating assessments has no breakdown between caravans owned by holiday operators or those by private individuals as second homes. Taking production figures from all manufacturers over a 12-year period together with their

Table 27.1 Comparative evidence of second home ownership in Britain from 1930 to 2007

Year	Number of second homes	Source	Notes
1930	<10,000	Gallent & Tewdwr-Jones (2001)	
1940	<15,000	Bielckus, Rogers & Wibberley (1972)	Actual growth during 1950s calculated as 5,000 second homes per year (Town and Country Planning Association 1962 Housing in Britain)
1960	50,000	Grays & Russell (1962)	Excludes estimated 90,000 static caravans in the UK (Wilson, 1959), growing at 10,000 per annum (Rogers, 1977)
1960	>50,000	Town and Country Planning Association (1962), Social Survey	Growth in demand estimated at 10,000 per annum. Forecast of 600,000 by 1982. (Town and Country Planning Association, 1962)
1965	140,000	Barr (1967)	Indicates 1% of households owned a second home
1966	144,000	Bielckus, Rogers & Wibberley (1972) – Wye College Study	Random sample of local authorities. Estimated annual growth from 1955–70 of the order of 12,000 per year
1970	180,000–200,000	Bielckus, Rogers & Wibberley (1972) – Wye College Study	Random sample of local authorities. Dower (1977) cites figures including static caravans as being between 300,000 and 400,000
1972	>160,000	Downing & Dower (1973)	Excludes estimated 154,000 static caravans
1995	223,000	National Statistics (2008) – Survey of English Housing	Excludes caravans, and second homes that are lived in by others, intending to sell, and owned abroad
2000	251,000	National Statistics (2008) – Survey of English Housing	Excludes caravans, and second homes that are lived in by others, intending to sell, and owned abroad
2004	267,000	National Statistics (2008) – Survey of English Housing	Excludes caravans, and second homes that are lived in by others, intending to sell, and owned abroad
2007	277,000	National Statistics (2008) – Survey of English Housing	Excludes caravans, and second homes that are lived in by others, intending to sell, and owned abroad

records of those for retail sale suggests there are approximately 249,000 static caravans used as second homes today. Static caravans therefore are likely to account for almost half of British second homes.

Our research

Using both qualitative and quantitative primary data collection (Steer-Fowler 2009) the initial stages of our investigation were conducted at six UK holiday park locations, and findings were grouped between the identification of consumer needs, and wider explanations as to why static caravans were chosen and how they were enjoyed.

While for some the second home may be a reference to the *physical form* such as a cottage, house or apartment, for others it can signify a *varying purpose* or *functionality* of a retreat,

Figure 27.1 "Rabbit's Corner" – Example of a static caravan.
Source: Author.

investment property, or holiday home (Jaakson 1986; Hall & Müller 2004). For the study we specifically focused on static caravans which were intended to be permanently sited as second homes (Figure 27.1), and the definition of Bielckus, Rogers & Wibberley (1972) which excludes rental property was taken as our frame of reference: 'A property which is the occasional residence of a household that usually lives elsewhere and which is primarily used for recreational purposes' (Bielckus et al. 1972: 9).

Findings

Escape

Among the principal reasons given for static caravan ownership (Table 27.2) unsurprisingly was to *escape* the effects of urban life. Distress from excessive *noise, crime, disturbance, traffic*, and *abusive* or *unruly behaviour* were frequently referred to, and there was an overall sense of relentless disruption that was hard to evade: 'I am in a terraced house and you are watching the telly if they are watching next door, I go in the garden and I have got their radio' was illustrative of the frustration.

Many also referred to escape in terms of the pressures endured in their working and domestic life. Whether retired or fully employed, for many this seemed to emanate as much from jobs awaiting them at home as from busy or demanding occupations. At the static caravan there was no requirement to enter into work, and those jobs which did exist were all the more enjoyable for the voluntary and leisurely context in which they took place; 'we usually work when we are down here' but 'we don't mind doing those jobs' one couple explained. The static caravan provided sanctuary, and a holiday environment in which it was considered natural and acceptable to have the freedom to do what they wished, when they desired:

Table 27.2 Themes arising from the reasons given for owning a static caravan as a second home

Central Themes		Divisions	Sub-Categories
Improved quality of life	*Escape*	Work Environment	Occupational work
			Work and chores at home
		Urban Environment	Stress
			Noise
			Crime/unruly behaviour
			Confinement
			Traffic & congestion
	Salvation	Quality of life	Relaxation
			Peace & quiet
			Reassurance
			Space & freedom
			Tranquillity/solitude
	Control	Routine (break)	Working life
			Domestic life
		Choice	Daily agenda
			Pace of life
	Enhancement	Change/Variety/Pride	Location
			Environment
			Activity
	Opportunity	Group	Closer to family
			Alternative to foreign holidays
		Individual	Health
			Leisure activities

I think that all week you build up the pressure in work, and I think that this is kind of the release for it … because I can do what I want down here … I can go off … I please myself … not only that but when you are home you tend to look 'well what can I do?' and find something to do, and inevitably you end up doing a bit of work around the house.

Salvation

For most owners, the static caravan provided not only a means for escape, but *salvation* in the contrast of the alternative life it contributed; 'this morning I woke up and there were birds singing … no sirens going off … it's just totally different' one interviewee explained. Typically, the contrasting environment of the static caravan was referred to in terms of 'almost all the opposites to what we have got at home': solitude, freedom, peace and quiet, and one within which an owner could relax and unwind providing a means for the stress of life at the principal dwelling to be released.

I feel totally un-overlooked … very private … there's no phone going to ring … nobody is going to knock on the door … that's the luxury. I get up in the morning and I feel really content … and I say to you 'oh another day in paradise'.

Control

A third theme to emerge was *control*. Inextricably linked with working and domestic agendas, owners suggested that they had little control of their lives within their principal dwelling, and had difficulty breaking the incessant routine and pace while they remained within the home environment. The static caravan seemed to provide an opportunity for them to break that routine and regain control, offering an environment within which they could do as they wished, when they wanted, and without the interruption of external demands and influences. One owner explained this value to be not so much in doing nothing, but having the *choice* to do as they wished, and with such choice came freedom. In the static caravan environment there was no timetable, no agenda, and time therefore became 'totally different ... you're not clock watching. Nothing really matters ... because it's no big deal, and there's no rush'.

Enhancement

Conversely, other owners talked of enjoyment of their work, and love of their domestic environment; 'we love where we live as well ... we just wanted to get away for a break' such owners exclaimed. For this group, the value of the static caravan seemed to be provided not by escape, but variety and change, commonly referring to their purchase in terms of a holiday or break from the routine of work or their schedule at home. Sometimes the regularity of change was surprising, with an almost perpetual yo-yo-ing between the principal and second home. 'When we're down here we have had enough, and when we get up home, we have had enough, then we come back' an owner explained. Each location seemed to compliment the other, the principal dwelling raising the desirability of the static caravan, which following a visit replenished the appreciation of home. The static caravan was not so much a salvation, but an *enhancement* of their lives. Not only did the static caravan provide variety therefore, but life at the owner's principal dwelling was more enhanced and enjoyable as a consequence.

Opportunity

Others specified varying personal reasons for their purchase, often in conjunction with other themes such as *escape* and *enhancement*. Ownership provided the chance for families to unite, removed from one another's personal agendas, permitting greater togetherness and sharing of quality time, which was not possible at the principal dwelling. Quite simply, second homes provided *opportunity*. Grandparents could interact with their grandchildren, and gain considerable satisfaction and pride from them enjoying the advantages of their wise investment; 'we get as much pleasure from them coming back saying they have enjoyed it', one couple explained. It was also common for interviewees to refer to childhood relationships with the area, for example 'my father used to bring us' and 'I came when I was a kid' were typical recollections.

The allure of static caravans

Emotive nature

Almost all owners described the time that they chose their static caravan in passionate terms, knowing instinctively when they had found the right one. Led by emotion, first impressions seemed fundamental to the decision process, governed by a love and feeling for the caravan as much as the functionality and utility it offered: 'as soon as I looked at it I knew it was mine' ... 'I just fell in love with it … it was like love at first sight!'; 'as we walked into it I said I like this … yeah … we both did … as soon as we walked in'; 'we just fell in love with it, and I can't explain it any more than that'. Notwithstanding the basic criteria of price, size and number of bedrooms, owners found it difficult to describe what they had been seeking, but felt 'overwhelmed' when they had found it, using phrases such as 'there was a bit of a wow factor'; 'there's a certain umm … what is it … ?'; 'this is nice … wow this is nice …'. Others, to be certain of how they felt, took a little time to reinforce their choice, but nevertheless showed considerable passion towards their purchase.

Affordability

Invariably, some owners saw a fundamental appeal of their caravan to be the ability to provide them with 'the chance of a second home', referring to *budget* and *price ceiling* as the chief constraints on further choice. 'There was no way that we could afford a proper second home anywhere, and caravans were … totally affordable' was typical of the discussion. However, there was much evidence to suggest that price was not the single attraction, and many indicated a passionate loyalty to caravans with little regard for alternative forms of property. Suggesting a chance of a more permanent second home without the constraints of a budget or price, owners were largely dismissive: 'I think I would still be looking to a caravan'; 'nothing else even crossed our mind'; 'no … never entered my mind'; 'it had to be a caravan'; 'yes, it still would have been a caravan, oh yes'. In many ways owners were suggesting that they were a certain kind of person, a group, or cohort, referring to themselves as 'the caravan type', typically exclaiming 'it's just what we like', or 'we are caravan people, aren't we … a cottage wouldn't be for me'.

Freedom

There were many obvious reasons for such loyalty. Some of those interviewed associated more conventional forms of property with worry and added responsibility. Responsibilities they were seeking to escape:

> Mentally it feels less burdensome. I think that if you take on a second home which is a building or something structural, personally I would be scared stiff of things going wrong, and maintenance and goodness knows what, that I don't know anything about. Whereas here I don't feel any burdensome responsibility … it's lovely.

The *freedom* which interviewees referred to static caravans providing appeared in a number of forms. For some, it meant the avoidance of the maintenance and upkeep more conventional types of property required, while for others it meant they provided *choice* and *opportunity* to do as they wished. Sometimes it was used to refer to connection to *nature*, which might be the coastline, countryside, the environment their plot provided, or even with the elements themselves. 'I can feel really close to the wind and the rain', one owner explained, 'and know I will never get wet'.

The value of space

Almost all who were interviewed revealed a significant appeal of the static caravan as being the orderly environment they provided. *Compact, neat, tidy,* and *uncluttered* were words regularly used. It was evident from the discussion that by virtue of the limitations of size, manufacturers had given considerable thought to ergonomics, design, and the use of space, which became a necessary requirement to keep tidy. 'If caravan builders built you a house you would probably have the best house in the world' one owner remarked, 'it's not more spacious but it feels more spacious because of the use of space'.

> you become very disciplined ... and very good at keeping it uncluttered ... we want these psychological benefits of an uncluttered appearance, and we work harder to keep it that way, and it pays off ... it all makes a difference to my frame of mind totally ... and is easier because it is in a caravan.

This emerged as central to the post-consumption appeal of caravans and the nature of the life which they provided. Despite being considerably smaller than their principal home, almost all owners felt their caravan to be spacious, and significantly more than half of those interviewed implied that the space because more limited, held a greater value to that of their principal dwelling. This led them to live quite differently, and for most a 'more enjoyable life' at their caravan. With space at a premium, owners talked of being *disciplined*, *tidier*, and *less cluttered*, and fewer possessions seemed to make for a simpler, but more satisfying life.

> Oh it's just like a sense ... to breathe! I always feel that as soon as I get down to the caravan and I'm in there then I'm ... oh! ... yeah! You've only got the things that you actually use and need. At home I always say to myself we have got a lot of stuff here we don't really use ... it's just gadgets or whatever ... it's almost like why have I got it all?

The effects of light

Surprisingly, as many as half of the interviewees referred to the abundance of light as an alluring characteristic of caravans. The 'illusion of light' was 'part of its niceness' making it *cosier*, *welcoming*, and *homely*. They referred to an uplifting feeling, freedom and cheerfulness provided by the daylight from the predominance of windows opposed to other forms of property, and often made comparisons with their home. Typically, the contrast could not be more pronounced: 'We could never grow plants in our living room ... which is quite gloomy, we would have the light on at like nine o'clock in the morning' whereas in their caravan it was 'umm ... cosier ... windows and more light coming in ... plenty of sunshine'. Another said 'at home ... umm ... it's like darker colours. My front room is like a red ... a deep red ... so everything seems more closed in', whereas in the caravan 'there are more windows ... it's lighter ... it makes you feel freer'. Such a positive effect of the daylight on the attitude of owners while they visited their caravan was not untypical.

> we had decided that it would be a caravan ... because ... light ... I could never stay in apartments ... the light. I absolutely adore the light. The lovely thing about caravans is that they feel spacious ... you have got daylight coming in, and I find daylight coming in makes an incredible difference to your mind ... if you are looking at a wall, ooh you feel hemmed in ... but if you are looking at daylight you're not somehow.

Fairytale environment

Most owners were proud to suggest static caravans to be properties in the same sense as their principal dwellings, but interestingly for those who could not, it was for reasons not of their size or limited life, but the fact that they possessed wheels and could feasibly be moved. Both owners and sellers alike were universally agreed that static caravans possessed a certain novelty; 'there's something about them' one explained because they're 'like a big doll's house'. Clearly caravans were different from conventional properties, and interviewees showed considerable post-consumption excitement in describing their life which they led in them, commonly using terms such as: *make believe*; *adventure*; *novelty*; a place where 'your childhood instincts sort of come out in you'; and life becomes a *fairytale*. An owner's time within a static caravan it seemed was spent with an expectation that it would be short lived, which seemed to further add to the novelty, and its simplification and miniaturisation made for an exciting existence; an adventure; a Disneyfication of life. 'I know it's reality … I know it's there, and everything's solid … but it's like one day I am going to wake up and it's gone … and it just seems unreal' one owner explained.

Perceived value

Invariably, their purchases were seen to provide good value, not in terms of a monetary investment consumers were quick to recognise, but in the lifestyle and quality of life that they provided for the cost incurred. Its value, one owner explained was 'the enjoyment that we got out of it … and I value that enjoyment'. Predominantly, static caravans were perceived as a *lifestyle investment*. For the relatively small number of owners who also sublet, any income was viewed as facilitating the payment of annual pitch fees, rates and running costs, rather than to provide a rate of return on the investment of the purchase price. Despite such an attraction, subletting was often seen as hindering personal use, and unless it became an essential part of affordability, owners were firm in maintaining the privacy of their home from home.

A sales perspective

Most sellers had experience of selling at a number of locations, and naturally reported some differences between owners. These were largely of character and personality rather than perception or general requirements which remained remarkably similar between regions. Their experience taught them that caravan owners were in many ways distinct, sharing characteristics quite different to those seeking conventional property. Property people were thought to be more analytical in behaviour, seeking enjoyment from the monetary return and safety of their investment, as much as any benefit from the leisurely lifestyle that caravan owners enjoyed. If customers asked about depreciation it was suggested they 'don't tend to buy'. Certainly, owners were felt to be 'like minded' but opinion was divided as to whether they could be classed as a group in other ways. On the one hand, some sellers were adamant that *caravan types* existed, confident they could be picked out from the crowd, yet others felt that caravans had become so advanced that they now appealed to audiences 'used to having a fantastic standard of living' and should not be thought of as caravans any more.

Purchaser characteristics

To further investigate the role static caravans played, data from 456 owner questionnaires was collected to provide an understanding of consumer experiences, caravan usage and reasons for purchase. In addition, respondents were asked to answer questions about themselves in order to provide personal characteristics.

The results suggested purchasers were distributed across all life stages, with the single most common being over 60 and retired. Contrary to the seller who felt that he rarely saw owners who were forty to fifty-five with teenage children, these consumers in fact accounted for one in five. Our findings were much in line with that of existing research which described owners as 'middle of the road people, ordinary guy in the street plus a few people who've got a bit' (The Tourism Company 2003: 17).

The basic results suggested owners to range between 30 and 84 years, with half the respondents aged between 49 and 65; the mean age was a little over 57 years, and 47% were retired. Households on average consisted of 2.7 people, with the 35 to 44 year age group (12.1% of owners) having the largest families, typically consisting of a couple and two children, aged 11. Only one in five couples within the most significant group of 55 to 64 year olds (36.9% of owners) were likely to have dependents remaining at home. Typically, therefore in almost seven out of ten cases owners were found to be couples over the age of 50 who did not have children or dependents to accompany them to their caravan. Significantly, more than half of owners (57.8%) gave their household income at the time of their most recent caravan purchase to be in excess of the UK national median.

The occupations of the principal wage earners were broadly distributed, and reflected a close alignment with the national average for each group. Owners on average lived 112 miles distance or 130 minutes travel time from their second homes. For almost eight out of ten, "home" was in or near a city or urban environment, and significantly, only 5% of cases were found to reside in the countryside or surroundings similar to that of their static caravan.

It was evident that before their purchase of a static caravan, owners also had considerable experience of the local area and the lifestyle caravans provided. Prior to purchase only 6.4% of respondents had never taken a holiday in a static caravan, and less than 20% had no experience of the locality in which it was sited. Two-thirds (67%) of the sample visited their caravan at least once every four weeks, and 43% used their caravan regularly on at least a fortnightly basis. The average pattern of use, having removed outliers, proved to be every 4.2 weeks. There was likewise considerable consistency in the duration of visits. Removing five outliers who suggested that they were almost residing at their second homes, the average duration of each visit was 4.5 nights, and respondents who stayed for two or three nights accounted for almost half the sample (48%).

While single occupancy accounted for 3%, for parties of two this rose to 50%. Groups of three were represented by 12%, whereas for four once again this rose to 28%. Likewise occupancies of five accounted for 5%, while six rose to 7%. Accounting for the spread of all groups, the mean average occupancy was 3.0 persons. Prior to purchase, 87% of respondents had taken regular holidays, and contrary to the routine which might be expected, destinations largely varied (86% of cases). Post-purchase, however, the number with a need for a regular holiday had reduced to 53%. Thus, for many the virtue of owning a static caravan, or its additional expense, there was less need or desire to seek holidays elsewhere.

Developing a typology

To develop the research further, a factor analysis was undertaken in order to clarify the principal reasons for purchase, from which a hierarchical cluster analysis was carried out to identify a number of purchaser types.

One particularly important characteristic central to defining groups was the purchasers' recognition of values. This was termed as their *level of engagement,* and extended to become a reflection of the overall participation owners had with their caravan, encompassing a measurement of *need, motivation* and *an individual's values.* When the levels of engagement were combined with socio-economic status, a typology could be formed to distinguish between the four principal consumer groups: *materialists, enthusiasts, pragmatists* and *devotees* (Figure 27.2).

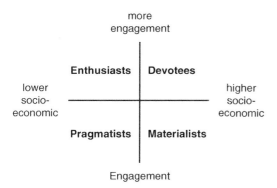

Figure 27.2 Identifying consumer types defined by the cluster analysis.

Materialists

The first group accounted for one in five purchasers, and was characterised by a comparatively high socio-economic status (A and A/B professional and senior managerial occupations) and contrastingly low level of engagement. This group was given the name *materialists*, as their purchase of a static caravan seemed to be driven neither by limited choice or overwhelming need, but by the materialistic concept of owning a static caravan for the symbolism and usefulness it might sometimes serve.

In comparison to other consumer groups, materialists were less likely to come from urban environments and had the greatest financial ability to purchase alternative forms of second homes should they desire. Consequently, static caravans did not seem to be considered essential, or even that desirable. In fact, given their time again, they indicated they would now be likely to purchase something different. Not surprisingly, therefore, they exhibited little eagerness during the purchase process, and once completed, were less inclined to partake in the customary second home activities or recognise the forms of value static caravans offered. Materialists were the least regular to use their static caravans, and when they did, they would stay for relatively short periods. For them, life at their static caravan was considered to be no better than home, and they would be likely to holiday elsewhere.

Enthusiasts

In contrast to materialists, the second type of consumer which accounted for almost one in four purchasers, was characterised by low socio-economic status (groups D and E) and high levels of engagement. This group was termed *enthusiasts*, as their purchase was driven by a passion for a static caravan which could only be met by the affordability of a static caravan. Enthusiasts were more likely to be engaged in manual occupations and reside within urban environments, and what they could purchase was limited by their means. Consequently, static caravans were perceived to be highly desirable, and given their time again they would have bought earlier in their life. Not surprisingly, enthusiasts exhibited the greatest eagerness during the purchase process, and were more inclined to desire park facilities or partake in the customary park activities and appreciate the forms of value static caravans offered. For them, the motivation to purchase was a quest for freedom and convenience, and they placed great value on the peace and quiet static caravans provided, where life and time was perceived to be more organised and valuable than that at their principal dwelling. Of all groups, enthusiasts gained greatest satisfaction from ownership, and they showed the least inclination or ability to holiday elsewhere. Not surprisingly, they were the most regular visitors, although the length of stay tended to be for only short periods. Enthusiasts' expectation was to extend their tenure, and given the opportunity they were the most likely to wish to make their caravans their principal home.

Pragmatists

The third type of consumer which accounted for more than one in three was characterised by socio-economic group C and a low level of engagement. This group was given the name *prag-matists*, for their purchase seemed to be principally driven by practical consequences, such as to be close to relatives, to reconnect with a specific location, to acquire flexibility for holidays or subsidy from letting income. Despite considerable financial means and choice being available, for the pragmatist the static caravan was the most practical and economic way of achieving specific objectives, and they showed less recognition of the freedom and the forms of value which could be offered. Not surprisingly, therefore, they were the least pre-decided on their type of purchase, and there was a greater likelihood that their enjoyment might wear off or that they would begin to regret their purchase. This might be as a consequence of their younger profile, or perhaps their children becoming disenchanted with repetitive holidays. Pragmatists were the most likely to sublet their static caravans, and consequently less regular in their use. When they did visit, they would stay for slightly longer periods, perhaps for traditional family holidays.

Devotees

The fourth consumer group was typified by owners most devoted to static caravans, the *devotees*, who represented approximately one in seven purchasers, and characterised by relatively high socio-economic status and levels of engagement. Regardless of being predominantly from professional and managerial occupations and having the financial ability to choose alternative types of second homes, devotees were the most pre-decided in their choice being a static caravan and most unlikely to ever regret their purchase. This was perhaps a reflection of their previous experience of static caravans, much of which was gained during childhood. Their purchase was considered to be good value, and despite their slightly older profile they held the greatest expectation of renewing their tenure and retaining their plot the longest. For devotees who were more likely to come from urban environments than not, life at their static caravan was considered to be more enjoyable than at home, and such pleasure was unlikely to wear off through the repetition of their visits. The emphasis for them was upon peace and quiet, and there was a significant recognition of the benefits of park facilities and appreciation of the forms of value static caravans provided.

Conclusion

While memories of former dwellings (Marcus 1992) and the effect of place attachment upon the desire to purchase a second home is well established (Stedman 2006; Aronsson 2004; Mottiar & Quinn 2003; Kaltenborn & Bjerke 2002), our study suggests that for many purchasing a static caravan is another form of attachment which exists. In what can be best understood as *space attachment,* a significant appeal of the static caravan was found to be its ability to provide a re-acquaintance with not so much location, but novel moments which could be enjoyed in them, and the inimitable lifestyle determined by its unique space. While the reasons for ownership can be conceptualised by the emergent themes of *escape, salvation, control, enhancement* and *opportunity,* static caravans established an arena in which life was miniaturised, simplified, and returned to basic values. Their limited space was seen to possess greater worth, in which living was more organised, tidier, and as a consequence more enjoyable than that in a conventional dwelling. The ambiance of light and lack of permanence suggested a fairytale environment in which living became exciting, novel and an adventure. Clearly, many of the caravan's shortcomings were perceived to be attributes, and there were significant reasons beyond just affordability that drove a decision to purchase.

Throughout the study, both owners and sellers also referred to 'caravan people' and how they could be distinguished from those who did not own: 'you can just point them out … they are a certain kind of people … you can tell a caravan owner'. What they were suggesting was that there was a *type of person* for whom the static caravan had greatest appeal, who not only shared interests and similar behaviour, but were different in personality to others. Upon analysis the data suggested they were indeed less *extraverted* and more *agreeable*, and showed greater traits of *sympathy*, *kindness*, *optimism* and *helpfulness* compared to the control data. While not conclusive, the evidence did imply that UK purchasers of static caravans may display some variation in personality, which together with an inevitable similarity in their day-to-day interests and behaviour may well enable them to be identified within the context of a caravan park.

References

Aronsson, L. (2004) 'Place attachment of vacation residents: Between tourists and permanent residents'. In C. M. Hall and D. K. Müller (eds) *Tourism, Mobility and Second Homes*. Toronto: Channel View Publications, 75–86.

Barr, J. (1967) 'A two-home democracy?', *New Society*, 7: 313–315.

Bielckus, C. L., Rogers, A. W. and Wibberley, G. P. (1972) *Second Homes in England and Wales*. Ashford, UK: Wye College, University of London.

Dower, M. (1977) 'Planning aspects of second homes'. In J. T. Coppock (ed.) *Second Homes: Curse or Blessing?* Oxford: Pergamon Press, 155–164.

Downing, P. and M. Dower (1973) *Second Homes in England and Wales*. London. Countryside Commission, HMSO.

Gallent, G. and Tewdwr-Jones, M. (2001) 'Second homes and the UK planning system', *Planning Practice & Research*, 16 (1): 59–69.

Grays, P. G. and Russell, M. (1962) 'The housing situation in 1960', Social Survey, London: Central Office of Information.

Hall, C. M. and Müller, D. K. (2004) 'Introduction: Second homes, curse or blessing? Revisited'. In C. M. Hall and D. K. Müller (eds) *Tourism, Mobility and Second Homes: Between Elite Landscape and Common Ground*. Clevedon, UK: Channel View Publications, 3–14.

Jaakson, R. (1986) 'Second-home domestic tourism', *Annals of Tourism Research*, 13 (3): 367–391.

Kaltenborn, B. P. and Bjerke, T. (2002) 'Associations between landscape preferences and place attachment: A study in Roros, Southern Norway', *Landscape Research*, 27 (4): 381–396.

Marcus, C. C. (1992) 'Environmental memories'. In I. Altman and S. M. Low (eds) *Place Attachment: Human Behavior and Environment*. New York: Plenium Press, 87–112.

Middleton, V. T. C. with the late Lickorish, L. J. (2005) *British Tourism: The Remarkable Story of Growth*. Oxford: Elsevier Butterworth-Heinemann.

Mottiar, Z. and Quinn, B. (2003) 'Shaping leisure/tourism places – The role of holiday home owners: A case study of Courtown, Co. Wexford, Ireland', *Leisure Studies*, 22 (2): 109–127.

National Statistics. (2008) *Survey of English Housing 2006/07: A report based on the 2006/07 Survey of English Housing, carried out by the National Centre for Social Research*, London: Department for Communities and Local Government.

Quinn, B. (2004) 'Dwelling through multiple places: A case study of second home ownership in Ireland'. In C. M. Hall and D. K. Müller (eds) *Tourism, Mobility and Second Homes: Between Elite Landscape and Common Ground*. Clevedon, UK: Channel View Publications, 113–130.

Rogers, A. W. (1977) 'Second homes in England and Wales: A spatial view'. In J. T. Coppock (ed.) *Second Homes: Curse or Blessing?* Oxford: Pergamon Press, 85–102.

Rojek, C. (2000) 'Leisure and the rich today: Veblen's thesis after a century', *Leisure Studies*, 19 (1): 1–15.

Stedman, R. C. (2006) 'Understanding place attachment among second home owners', *American Behavioral Scientist*, 50 (2): 187–205.

Steer-Fowler, J. M. W. (2009) Second Homes: An Empirical study of Consumer Behaviour towards a Depreciating Property Asset. PhD. University of Plymouth, Plymouth, England.

The Tourism Company (2003) Caravan Holiday Homes in Wales, conducted on behalf of the BH&HPA and Wales Tourist Board, Ledbury, UK: The Tourism Company.

Town and Country Planning Association (1962) *Housing in Britain. Social Survey.* London: Town and Country Planning Association.

Williams, A. M., King, R. and Warnes, A. M. (2004) 'British second homes in Southern Europe: Shifting nodes in the scapes and flows of migration and tourism'. In C. M. Hall and D. K. Müller (eds) *Tourism, Mobility and Second Homes: Between Elite Landscape and Common Ground.* Clevedon, UK: Channel View Publications, 97–112.

Wilson, A. (1959) *Caravans as Homes.* London: Ministry of Housing and Local Government. H.M.S.O. Cmd. 872.

28

WHEREVER I PARK MY RV, THAT'S MY HOME

Freedom camping and local community tensions in eastern Australia

Rod Caldicott, John M. Jenkins and Pascal Scherrer

Background and introduction

The caravan park, as a subsector of the tourist accommodation industry, has been traditionally perceived by the public as the symbol of caravanning. However, this symbol of caravanning is rapidly diminishing. Changing population demographics, with an increasing baby-boomer skew coupled with technological advancement in recreational vehicle (RV) manufacturing, has impacted recent caravanning developments. The focus is now more on the caravan itself and its serviceability as a long-term, touring, residential "home unit" (a mobile home) rather than as a temporary, short-term holiday unit designed for a caravan park (Caldicott 2011). As a corollary, freedom camping enables contemporary caravanners, particularly those with RVs with self-containment accreditation and having a shower, toilet and associated waste holding tanks within their vehicles (Campervan and Motorhome Club of Australia (CMCA) 2014), to pursue Ulyssean lifestyles of choice (Cohen 2011; Macbeth 2000; Onyx & Leonard 2007). Such a lifestyle, whether long or short term (and sometimes permanent), rejects the notion of containment, uniformity and conformity established by traditional caravan parks. It also rejects in some ways the distinction between a first home and second home.

For Australia's highly urbanised population, there is a well-entrenched culture of "getting away from it all" and escaping the city for the rich environments that rural and remote coastal places can offer. Domestic travel to regional inland and coastal areas is largely characterised, though not exclusively, by road travel and the use of motor cars. Camping at roadsides, in state forests, and at legislated reserves, show grounds and other public places, away from commercial caravan and camping parks, is both the legacy of an Australian tradition (Garner 2013) and a growing phenomenon (Caldicott & Scherrer 2013). For a growing segment of the Australian population, the self-contained RV that some freedom campers occupy for extended periods of time becomes their home away from home (Hardy & Gretzel 2011; Hillman 2013; Woodman 2012), their mobile first home or second home residence. They are motivated and behave, socially and economically, as mobile residents as opposed to tourists (Counts & Counts 1996; Holloway & Holloway 2011; Radel & Hillman 2013), a conceptual shift little understood and often overlooked by destination marketers, community planners and policymakers (Caldicott 2011). Beyond the baby-boomers, a new wave of campers in the form of the young family is now

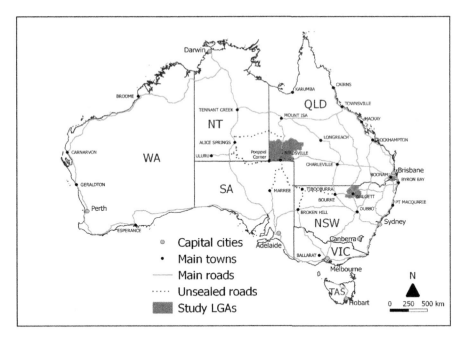

Figure 28.1 Main political and legislative boundaries and RV access corridors in Australia.
Source: Author.

choosing to freedom camp as a lifestyle choice through which to educate their children and provide cultural- and environmental-based recreational experiences (Podmore 2014). However, this wave of transient campers and caravanners, no longer reliant upon the fixed services of the caravan park, is presenting a significant and complex set of problems, impacts and planning and policy settings for local councils and communities, some of which have become very popular, if not overcrowded, freedom camping destinations.

This chapter arises from a larger study which aims to describe and explain the politics of freedom camping in four case study local government areas drawn from the states of New South Wales (NSW) and Queensland (Qld) in eastern Australia (Figure 28.1). Here we focus on local community tensions and issues associated with the phenomenon of freedom camping in one of the case studies, Byron Shire Council (Figure 28.2). We define freedom camping and its characteristics and briefly describe the lack of research on the issue of freedom camping. An overview of selected international freedom camping policy contexts is provided as a means to highlight the very diverse approaches to the freedom camping phenomenon. We then describe some of the characteristics particular to the town of Byron Bay in Byron Shire Council. We close by reflecting upon aspects of the nature of the freedom camping problem and the difficulties of finding policy resolutions within the local community, particularly with regards to the construction of space as a social and highly fluid process.

Freedom camping: Definitions and characteristics

Freedom camping involves the combination of a mobile form of accommodation and its use in a public space. Caldicott, Scherrer and Jenkins (2014) defined freedom camping as the practice

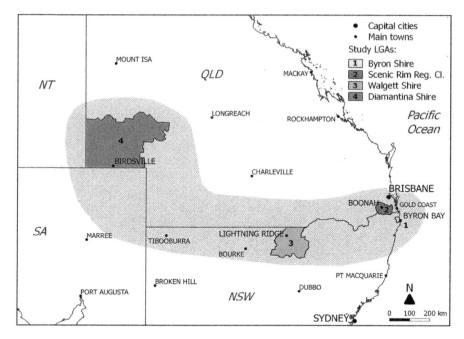

Figure 28.2   The case-study regions.
Source: Author.

whereby domestic or international travellers occupy, by deliberate choice, an RV as a mode of accommodation in an open space that is not bound by market-based commercial norms and camping and/or caravan park-based regulations. Roadside rest areas, residential streets and crown reserves are common spaces used. Freedom camping is a legal activity in Australia unless it is prescribed otherwise within site or zone specific legislation with accompanying signposting (Department of Tourism, Events, Small Business and the Commonwealth Games (DTESB) 2014).

The caravan today is giving way to broader representations of RVs, which now come in a variety of forms and can be camp-kitted 4x4 wheel drives and minivans, camper trailers, caravans, converted buses, motorhomes and fifth wheelers. The practice of camping using RVs for accommodation has been around for a long time nationally and internationally, and recent growth in Australia has increased its visual presence and impact. There is strong consumer demand for caravanning and RVs in Australia, with total RV registrations in 2014 exceeding half-a-million units and manufacturing exceeding 20,000 units of production annually for the fourth year running (Caravan Industry Association of Australia (CIAA) 2014a). Statistics for April 2015 show increases in production of 3.2% compared with April 2014 and year-to-date production 10.3% higher compared to 2014 figures (CIAA 2015a). The caravanning and camping industry generates $19.02 billion to the Australian economy annually, much of which is in regional areas, creating 53,000 direct jobs and providing valuable inward capital for Australian communities (CIAA 2016a, 2016b). This substantial growth is driving RV-related business and presenting opportunities for commercial caravan parks to promote their respective locations and facilities. Simultaneously, demand for camping locations is diversifying, with some travellers opting to freedom camp rather than stay at designated camping sites and caravan parks (Caldicott et al. 2014). Recent research discusses this diversity as an international phenomenon.

Research in Australia, the United Kingdom and the United States dismisses contentions of caravanning being homogenous and mundane (Cridland 2008; Hardy et al. 2013; Ming 1997), and reflects a new image of this phenomenon (Morgan & Pritchard 1998). Green's (1978: 432) US study revealed that the 'different types of vehicles that RVers use lend themselves to styles or modes of travel that are distinctive enough to identify and study separately'. In England, 'deeper scrutiny [of caravanning] reveals an internally differentiated set of cultural ideas, values and practices related to wider patterns of social life' (Southerton et al. 2003: 2) among, and by, caravanners. Southerton et al. (2003: 2) also contends 'it is the way that caravanning is done, and the positions taken with respect to the valuing of novelty, or routine; security and anxiety; privacy and sociability which caravanners refer to in distinguishing between themselves and others'.

Patterson, Pegg and Lister (2011: 286) identified common motivations for RVers in Australia, which included 'adventure of discovery of new places and towns, enjoyment of warmer weather, the pleasure of beautiful scenery, learning about history, meeting new people and mostly having the freedom to do what they wanted'. Freedom campers did not like to be organised, or managed and preferred to do their own thing having a great desire for 'self-fulfilling experiences that are physically challenging, meaningful and authentic' (Patterson et al. 2011: 289). This extends to different types of campsites, in remote areas as well as caravan parks, with campers indicating that as they 'were self-sufficient, facilities in caravan parks were not an issue' (Patterson et al. 2011: 290). Many prefer outback touring and some avoid the coast altogether, 'camping in out-of-the-way places … off the beaten track' (Patterson et al. 2011: 289). While at times they may be 'far-away physically, RVers are rarely [technologically] isolated from friends and family despite being in remote areas of Australia, often on trips that take several months to complete' (Patterson et al. 2011: 283) while some are never ending. Although campers may be 'relishing in the wilderness and wide open spaces that the natural and/or rural settings afforded' (Patterson et al. 2011: 292), modern mobile, digital and satellite technology substantially narrows the divides between "home and away" (Caldicott et al. 2014; Simpson 2008; White & White 2007).

Research released by the Caravan Industry Association of Australia (CIAA 2015b) found 89% of respondents indicated the caravan industry has improved in recent times with 31% attributing their more positive opinion with "better products and facilities" in the marketplace. However, products and services are not the biggest motivator for new caravanners and campers. For 49%, "a desire to see more of Australia" was the biggest factor leading them to camping and caravanning. A further 20% saw it as an opportunity for "a change in overall lifestyle", a salient point and one motivating a growing group of RVers towards full-time RV living, distinguishing them from holiday makers. However, despite the positive growth in demand for the "mobile-resident" lifestyle (Caldicott 2011), caravanning is facing an interesting dilemma. The number of caravan parks has been consistently declining since the late 1990s, as coastal beachfront lands are converted to high rise units, hotels, retirement and other commercial service facilities (Caldicott et al. 2014; Caldicott & Harris 2015; Caldicott & Scherrer 2013; Prideaux & McClymont 2006). Conversely, registrations of new caravans rose 257% between 1995 and 2005, and 17.5% between 2008 and 2012 (CIAA 2014b), while total RV manufacturing grew by 29% between 2005 and 2010 (Australian Bureau of Statistics (ABS) 2010; Recreational Vehicle Manufacturers Association of Australia (RVMAA) 2011) and overall RV production grew 5% in 2014 alone (McDonald 2014).

Additional aspects of the demand for caravans, camping, caravan parks, and so on are discussed in Caldicott et al. (2014) and Caldicott and Scherrer (2013). In brief, though, approximately 34% of caravanners always stay in caravan parks, while 16% of RVers are using only freedom camping venues, and a possible further 50% regularly swing between use of commercial and freedom camping places to varying degrees. Balfour's (2010) study of 397 domestic RVers across north Queensland rest areas revealed that 50% of RVers overnighting in rest areas also stayed in caravan parks. On average, respondents in Balfour's (2010) study spent 2.15 nights in a rest area for every night spent in a caravan park and 14% were permanently travelling. A 2015 survey of 200 campers interviewed at recognised and published freedom camping areas (see Fennell & Fennell 2017) across Queensland, New South Wales, Victoria and Tasmania reported that 'while 15% of travellers advised they were travelling for over 12 months, about 3% of those surveyed mentioned they were "permanent travellers" who had sold up their house and were enjoying travelling "forever"' (Jones 2016: 12). Against this background, and before looking at circumstances in the case study area of Byron Shire, we now turn our attention to international policy settings and issues.

The policy setting: International comparisons

Freedom camping is evident around the world, but the policy settings within which it takes place show great variations. Here we provide some examples.

New Zealand

New Zealand has a *Freedom Camping Act* (New Zealand Parliament 2011), which permits camping on public conservation lands. Exclusion zones apply where camping is specifically prohibited or restricted to self-contained vehicles. This usually occurs as a result of previous inappropriate use of a site or due to the presence of endangered species or as a means to promote equitable access to sites (New Zealand Department of Conservation (DoC) 2014). In response to the introduction of the Act, the New Zealand Motor-Camping Association (NZMCA) (2013a) developed and distributed a model Freedom Camping Bylaw to support local governments in their management of freedom camping. This bylaw specifically reminds councils that unless restricted or prohibited under a local bylaw made in accordance with section 11 of the Act, freedom camping is allowed in any local authority area unless it is prohibited by another enactment.

The *Freedom Camping Act* has not been the panacea for camping disputes, land-use contests and social conflicts that was anticipated by New Zealand legislators. On the one hand, areas of Dunedin (Porteous 2014) and Taranaki (Strongman 2014) are reporting 'it's all positive in our view' (Strongman 2014: 1). On the other hand, the Westland District Council Mayor, Maureen Pugh, said her council took exception to the Act on the premise that 'the large number of cars, station wagons and sleeper vans being used for camping has meant that our roadsides are virtually open sewers, and there is nothing we can do to control that' (Fraser 2013). Westland Council consequently passed a bylaw with a total prohibition on freedom camping on Council tenured lands. NZMCA (2013b) challenged the bylaw, on behalf of its members, taking the case to the High Court. Westland subsequently withdrew their defence and revoked the bylaw. More recently, the Christchurch mayor believes there needed to be a nationwide approach to freedom camping because there were too many sets of rules operating across the country, inviting the national government to step in and amend the *Freedom Camping Act 2011*:

> Because you can't tell a tourist coming into New Zealand that we have one set of rules in this council, another set of rules in that council, one set of rules in the South Island, another set of rules in the North Island, one set of rules for Docklands and another set of rules for council lands, and by the way, you can't tell the difference between them.
>
> *(Lianne Dalziel quoted in Stylianou 2016)*

United States

The United States similarly permits freedom camping (locally referred to as "boondocking" or "dispersed camping") on federal conservation lands (National Parks Service 2016). Much of this estate is operated by the Bureau of Land Management (BLM), although other agencies such as the US Army Corps of Engineers, US Forest Services, National Parks Service, Bureau of Reclamation, National Archives and Records Administration and the National Oceanic and Atmospheric Association all offer freedom camping opportunities. In addition, the major box store franchise Walmart offers boondocking within their carparks at select locations (Roundabout Publications 2016) as do major highway service centres (Pilot Flying J. 2016) and casinos (Moeller & Moeller 1993).

While these no/low-cost opportunities exist for freedom camping in the US, there is also a vast array of commercial sites offered by federal agencies at tariffs acceptable to the boondockers. For example, the Department of the Interior, Land and Water Resources and National Parks Service offer sites with full services through their *America the Beautiful* pass program for less than USD $20 per night. When purchased with a Seniors Card (USD $10.00 for lifetime membership post 62 years of age) the tariffs are further discounted by 50% (National Parks Service 2016). Annual passes can be purchased for the more popular BLM lands for $180. Annual pass holders are entitled to 28-day stays at one site before the occupant is required to move on, and they can go directly to another BLM site that is at least 30 miles distant. For many years, the federal lands have thus become an archipelago for many snowbirds (Ming & McHugh 1995; Simpson 2008) on their annual migration to the southern States during the colder northern winters and continue to provide affordable refuge for full-timing RVers avoiding fully commercial sites. Freedom camping options in the US are many with the totally free sites complemented by numerous low-cost commercial options diffusing demand for free sites and providing ready relief for full-time RVers (Simpson 2008). 'While little in the way of official governmental statistics exist for the senior full-time recreational vehicle community (SFTRVC), this so-called nomadic society is conservatively estimated to number between two and three million retirees who have relinquished their sedentary homes and lifestyles for a continuous year-round life on the road' (Simpson 2008: 34).

United Kingdom

In the UK, freedom camping is commonly called motor camping, off-site camping or wild camping. The latter is enshrined in the Scottish Outdoor Access Code, which was set up as a requirement of the *Land Reform (Scotland) Act 2003* (Hadfield 2015). Scotland is the only part of the UK that has specific legislation pertaining to wild camping although this is targeted toward ramblers rather than motor campers. The *Enclosure Act* (1709–1869) strongly defends property rights – private and public. The right to roam without compensation to landowners was beyond access for the public until the enactment of the *Countryside and Rights of Way Act 2000* (CROW) (UK Government 2016). This though still only permitted rights to walkers and backcountry campers – not vehicular access across private lands for motor camping. All motor camping places are required to conform to the requirements of the *Caravan Sites and Control of Development Act 1960* (UK Government 1960) with access to land, and camping, outside of registered campgrounds only with the express permission of the landowner. Effectively there is no "right" to simply stay anywhere. Under the *Criminal Justice and Public Order Act 1994*, Clause 77, campers can be asked to move on at any time and the police have powers to remove and fine those who fail to comply.

The English Department for Transport advises there is no national legislation which either specifically permits or prohibits roadside motor camping (Hadfield 2015). However, a number of clauses detailed in the primary and secondary road legislations give effect to restrictions, particularly requirements for parking at night. In addition, some local authorities have passed contrasting Traffic Regulation Orders which variously permit or prohibit overnight camping in vehicles within the area over which they have jurisdiction. Restrictions are enforced through local bylaws with associated signage which usually prohibits parking between the hours of 11.00pm and 7.00am (Whitby Gazette 2015). The police, local authorities and landowners have powers to take action where any trespassers are camping on land unlawfully (Hadfield 2015).

National Motorhome Association (NMA) campaigner, Mr Andy Strangeway, says overnight motorhome camping is an ongoing source of contention in the UK. Particular hotspots include sea-fronts in resort towns such as those of North Yorkshire (Andy Strangeway cited in Ward 2015). According to Strangeway, Yorkshire, Derbyshire and Lincolnshire all 'have provision for free overnight parking available to cars, white vans, motorhomes and heavy goods vehicles (HGVs), as is the case across every county in the UK' (Strangeway 2014b). However, responding to the North Yorks Enquirer (Ward 2015), which reported on a potential legal challenge to the North Yorkshire County Council's (NYCC) proposal to prohibit on-street parking, Strangeway warns such a bylaw would be a breach of fundamental legislation and make motor camping illegal. UKMotorhomes.net (2016) has a disclaimer on their website warning that the car and lorry parking locations within their listing are not dedicated camping sites (similar to areas in Europe) but are simply the ones 'we understand to have no regulations prohibiting overnight sleeping eating and cooking'. While Stangeway (2014b) suggests there to be 'no proposed resolution in sight' to the contest for overnight parking space, David Bowe, NYCC's director of Business Services said 'a ban prohibiting motor-caravans from overnight camping on earmarked roads is to be introduced between 11pm and 7am' (David Bowe quoted in Whitby Gazette 2015). Responding to previously introduced parking bans at other Lincolnshire carparks, Strangeway (2014a) requested of the Deputy Director, Democracy, Department for Communities and Local Government that the introduced bylaws be revoked, a position that was subsequently upheld (Northeast Lincolnshire Council 2014: 1).

The off-site camping needs of ethnic groups of Romany Gypsies and Irish Travellers are legally protected in the UK by the *Race Relations Act 1976* (Hogger 2013), but the equivalent off-site camping needs of touring motor campers are not officially recognised in UK law. Community tensions continue to surface when unauthorised motor camps are established on public land. In 2015 North Yorkshire County Council conducted surveys of residents and campers to 'explore the problem' (David Bowe quoted in Whitby Gazette 2015). Despite the strong oppositional interests to freedom camping in public parking spaces as displayed in the media, a council spokesperson said 'council could hold a public inquiry, [but] no-one had asked for one' (David Bowe quoted in Whitby Gazette 2015).

Sweden

Sweden, along with its Scandinavian neighbours, is famous for allowing public access to all land under the terms of *allemansratten* or the 'everyman's right to roam' (Nature Travels 2008). This instrument of government supports the freedom to walk, cycle, ski and camp for up to 48 hours on any land with the exception being to areas in the immediate vicinity of a private residence. Although this ancient provision fosters public walking access, and does extend to snowmobiles on frozen lakes and snow-covered fields or forests in winter, it does not support open and unvetted vehicular access across private lands. But, it is legal to vehicle camp on the sides of public roads, rest areas and parking places for up to 48 hours unless signs state otherwise. Thus, while freedom camping in a tent, associated with rambling, berry picking or backcountry hiking, is permitted on private property without permission, vehicular camping is not openly supported without the express consent of the landowner.

The Swedish Camping Owners' Association in 2010 recognised the demands of RVers for greater access to camping places and for a less regulated form of camping space. Following a survey of 1,541 respondents from RV clubs and holders of Camping Card Scandinavia, two levels of service and amenity provision were identified (Hörmander, 2017). Commercial caravan pitches for long stays were already available, but demand was growing for simpler short-term automated services such as *Stellplatz* in Germany and *Aires* in France. These 24-hour access parking places for overnight camping, with payment and services through automated kiosks, are now auspice through the Motor Caravan Destination Sweden Project (Hörmander 2017).

Australia

In Australia, there are vastly different approaches to freedom camping across the States and Territories and their local government areas and communities. Responsibility for compliance in camping, in the State of New South Wales (NSW) for example, is prescribed by the *Local Government Act (Caravan Parks, Camping Grounds and Moveable Dwellings) Regulation 2005*. In Queensland, however, the Local Government Act 2009 does not specifically define or legislate around camping. Rather, it requires local governments to develop and adhere to a planning scheme for all lands they manage. Either way, freedom camping is often vigorously criticised by commercial caravan park operators and their industry associations. They consider it to be a non-competitive and non-compliant accommodation practice when supported and facilitated by local government (councils) (Caldicott et al. 2014).

To highlight important policy positions and perspectives in the Australian context, and to develop a baseline for future discourse, Caldicott et al. (2014) observed there were four key interest groups: camping consumers represented by the Campervan and Motorhome Club of Australia Ltd; park operators represented by Caravan Industry Association of Australia Ltd; state and territory governments who have devolved camping regulatory power down to their respective local governments; and local governments that have the dual role of representing their constituents (resident communities, business communities and visitor communities) as well as regulating places and spaces visitors and locals use for freedom and commercial camping. These stakeholder groups were identified through various mediums and literatures, including: independent state parliamentary inquiries; government agency sponsored reports; and the popular press (Caldicott et al. 2014).

Individual and community perspectives on freedom camping in Australia are divided. The media sensationalises this division through an emotive portrayal of the phenomenon and its influence on regional and urban communities (Feliu 2014; Gardiner 2013a; Kinninment 2014a; Morrow 2016). Inevitably, tensions have arisen as freedom camping continues to surface as a form of "street life". Its prominence is increasingly raising the ire of commercial caravan park owners. There is no consistency across states and territories in the planning and management of freedom camping and the public spaces upon which it necessarily relies. Power struggles are surfacing within national caravanning communities and within national, state and local community governance arenas. Civic leaders concerned for their respective leisure, policy, management and regulatory environments through local councils are being urged by state governments (Department of Local Government and Communities (DLGC) 2015; DTESB 2014) to consider the needs of all types of caravanning visitors to their communities – freedom and commercial.

Summary

This brief international overview highlights the diverse and contentious policy settings for freedom camping, and the complexities of domestic and international travellers knowing what is and what is not legal and permitted within and across jurisdictions. It also shows that the planning and management of freedom camping is inherently political and must confront historical legacies associated with past planning, legislation and practices, and the economic, social and environmental nuances of the communities affected. Bianchi (2003) suggests that places are not just congruent with a particular geographical location, but rather are 'constructed out of a particular constellation of special relations, meeting and weaving together at a particular locus' (Massey 1991: 28) over time. The space is thus a lived experience extending tourism consumption into areas not previously associated with intrinsic tourism production and is forging new social alignments (Bianchi 2003), which we examine in more detail in our case study of Byron Shire below.

The case study: Byron Bay

Byron Bay is the most easterly town in New South Wales (and Australia). With 5,120 residents, it is the most populous town within Byron Shire (population 32,119). Byron Bay is accessed via Australia's most highly used highway, the Pacific Highway. It is renowned for its popularity as a backpacking destination, eclectic lifestyle, historically alternative culture, surfing, land-based whale watching, international music festivals receiving in excess of one million visitors annually, New Year's Eve and other parties and celebrations, and access to diverse natural and culturally significant attractions. Tourism, and its related services of accommodation, food, beverage and attractions, is a significant industry sector for Byron Shire, generating important employment opportunities and contributing almost 10% of GRP (Gross Regional Product) (Lawrence Consulting 2015). The number of campers and caravanners freedom camping, however, generates considerable social and political angst, particularly in the town of Byron Bay and nearby surrounds (Byron Shire Council 2014; Hansen 2015; Wilson 2012a).

The Byron Bay Township has no formal (council-approved) public camping places for freedom campers. The streets and public reserves are regularly used by freedom campers. This contributes to public unrest within Byron Shire generally, and more specifically, the inner urban Byron environs. Several private and public low-cost camping venues are available within the Shire hinterland, including a highway rest area at Tyagarah (see Figure 28.3), but they are away from the Byron town centre. Consequently, Byron Shire Council is keen to find solutions to the local tourism unrest and dichotomous local interests in freedom camping (Gardiner 2013a; Grant 2012).

Of particular concern in Byron Township is the "van-packing" or street camping culture popularised by younger international backpackers. Byron is not so much affected by grey nomads as provision for low-cost nomad camping is already a feature of Byron Shire with options open at Mullumbimby showground and also the sports reserve. As these venues are in the hinterland, at least 15 minutes' drive outside of Byron Bay, they are less attractive to the vanpackers, who prefer the limelight, nightlife and eclecticism of Byron beachside venues. Helping fuel the tension, local newspapers run sensationalist headlines such as: 'Freeloading parasites: vanpackers are "degrading" Byron Bay' (Wilson 2012a); '"Lazy, bloody mongrel" vanpackers flee Byron for the hills' (Kinninment 2014b); and, 'Byron's own "shanty town" to clean up' (Morrow 2016).

Byron Shire Council has been actively campaigning to have freedom camping totally shut down within its streets and reserves, asking the NSW government to change the *Local*

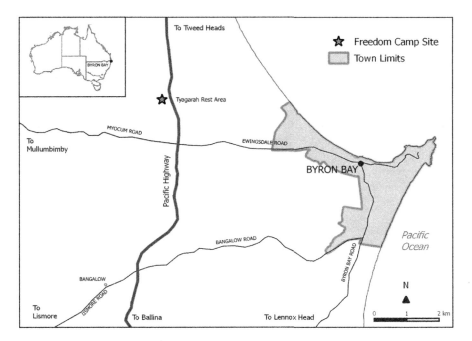

Figure 28.3 Byron Bay town limits and Tyagarah rest area on the Pacific Highway.
Source: Author.

Government Act 1993 so the Council can regulate street camping (Wilson 2012b). This follows numerous outbreaks of anti-social behaviour from vanpackers, often associated with music festivals and holiday celebrations when there are high concentrations of visitors. Such activity is typical of many coastal communities in NSW, with popular tourism destinations like Port Macquarie (Fairhurst 2014), Newcastle (Gleeson 2014) and Bondi (Walker 2014). These popular destinations experience various types of anti-social behaviour, often visually accentuated by naked public showering, public defecation, party waste, noise and temporary clothes lines strung up in public areas (Feliu 2014; Foran 2016; Gardiner 2013b; Hansen 2015).

Byron Council's governance manager Ralph James says 'the culture of street camping in our coastal towns has grown significantly over the years and has had an impact on residential amenity, as well as our tourism operators that offer a place for people to legitimately camp' (Byron Shire Council 2012c). In Byron Shire, public car parks, residential streets and vacant industrial, retail or residential blocks are being transformed into de facto camping grounds on a regular, and in some cases nightly, basis. Campers, most commonly but not limited to younger international visitors, take the liberty to pull up and stay overnight in regulated and non-regulated street parking spaces, along public foreshores or at other popular scenic or convenient vantage points within the urban environment. On some occasions, the activity is naively undertaken by the RVer as consent to occupy again, due to the observed practice at the venue. However, on other occasions, the non-compliant activity is known prior to arrival by the RVer, or is signposted on-site, but the RVers are still prepared to run the risk of being moved on by regulation officers or even face penalty through a statutory authority (Byron Shire Council 2012c, 2015b; Clement 2015a, 2015b).

Local government legislation currently prevents councils from restricting roadside and street camping as local government cannot legally regulate the use of vehicles in a road or road-related area (Byron Shire Council 2012a; Clement 2015b; Feain 2012). Clr Sally Betts of Waverly Council (Bondi, Sydney) insists 'council is hampered by "pathetic" legal powers' (Clr Sally Betts quoted in Clement 2015a). Not deterred, in 2012 Byron Shire Council was determined to stamp out the practice of freedom or street camping and approached the NSW Minister for Local Government asking for approval to amend the *Local Government Act 1993*. Their intent was to have councils empowered to regulate street camping, 'to put up no camping signs and police them' (Feain 2012: 3). Byron's request was declined by the Minister, who advised that amendment to section 632 of the Act was not considered appropriate at that time as control over parking or use of a vehicle on a road falls within the domain of road-related legislation administered by Roads and Maritime Services, with responsibilities delegated to local councils through their traffic committees (Page 2012).

In the face of little sympathy from the State government, the Shire Council commenced strategic action of their own, designed to strengthen their legal ability to enforce a strict no tolerance approach to freedom camping. Their first move was to define "street camping". Byron Shire Councilors resolved on 22 March 2012 to endorse the new definition that would enable its rangers to tackle street camping head-on (Byron Shire Council 2012b). As part one, to a seven part resolution (File No: ENG655090 #1196990 12-179), camping in Byron Shire is now defined as:

> Where any place is used as recreation, or on an outing or vacation the use of that place by a person or persons lodged in a tent or any temporary structure or other means of shelter or accommodation.
>
> *(Byron Shire Council 2012d: 1)*

Council's manager of corporate infrastructure Mark Arnold said 'the new definition would assist rangers with regulating street camping in Byron Shire' (Byron Shire Council 2012d: 1) and aim to shift visitors in camper vans and cars 'from camping in residential and beachfront locations, to using one of the many camping sites with the Shire's caravan parks' (Byron Shire Council 2012d: 1).

The definition, by exclusion, facilitates clear demarcation between homelessness and emergency accommodation provision to that of deliberate recreation, outings and vacation. Mr Arnold stressed the new definition 'will not affect people who sleep in their cars due to homelessness nor people travelling through who need to rest due to illness, tiredness and or intoxication' (Byron Shire Council 2012d: 1). The concept adopted by Byron Council in 2012 of "shifting" non-commercial campers into commercial campgrounds, while proving ineffective as a holistic solution to a local issue within a national environment, was not unusual practice at that time (e.g. see Caravanning Queensland 2015).

In a more recent attempt to manage rather than regulate freedom camping in Byron Bay, the Byron Shire in 2015 partnered with the North Coast Destination Network (NCDN) in embracing the Queensland Camping Options Toolkit model (see DTESB 2014) at a NSW regional level. NCDN facilitated a Freedom Traveller Taskforce taking carriage of the State's General Purpose Standing Committee No. 3 recommendation for consistent freedom camping guidelines. Encouraged by Byron's shifting stance to freedom camping, the NCDN sought to generate common solutions to freedom camping across 21 LGAs, most particularly the nine councils along the Pacific Highway (see Figure 28.3). Byron's stark change of attitude from the "zero tolerance" mentality recognises that the NIMBY (not in my back yard) syndrome of "fine 'em and move 'em on" is not a realistic or sustainable local solution to a national phenomenon, particularly in renowned national and international tourism hotspots like Byron Bay. NCDN executive officer Ms Belinda Novicky admitted freedom camping is a complex problem but she told News ABC, 'a policy solution can be found to satisfy both travellers and businesses' (quoted in Lowrey 2014). 'We want to make sure that we have the right facilities and that we're able to promote our holiday parks, and what they have to offer, as well as making sure that we're providing free camping that is also of interest to the emerging RV market' (Belinda Novicky quoted in Lowrey 2014).

The initiative, supported in principle by the NSW Office of Premier and the Cabinet, was not without challenges. These were duly noted to include: current legislation and diversity of views regarding regulation of freedom camping; threats to and challenges from the caravan and camping industry; difficulties in reaching agreement with Roads and Maritime Services (RMS) over roadside infrastructure and signage; and local parochialism and discontent of local residents. Participating in the NCDN Freedom Camping Taskforce survey of freedom camping (North Coast Destination Network Inc. (NCDN) 2015), 9 of 13 coastal councils advised that they did not have a current policy on low-cost or alternate camping. However, each council did confirm that they currently accommodate alternate camping across a range of locations and through a range of legislative instruments and initiatives to independently address the phenomenon.

Despite the high ideals of the NCDN to provide a circuit breaker on the freedom camping problems confronted by local communities through their destination "development" project, funding for the Freedom Traveller Taskforce was not forthcoming from their State parent and marketing agency, Destination NSW. This was a significant setback for the participating local governments in NSW, including Byron Shire. The unique window to "couple" (see Kingdon 1984, 2011) local initiatives through regional actions in support of State Legislative Council's recommendations presented a lost policy-agenda opportunity. Nevertheless, despite the Projects preliminary endorsement by the NSW Office of the Premier and Cabinet, and being totally in step with recommendations emanating from several other states, the failure to fund was a significant indication of governmental block. The multi-tiered approach, for a short time, was gathering momentum. There appeared, for the first time in Australia, to be radical progress in developing cooperative solutions across multiple councils and multiple levels of decision making, and in systematic policy-making for NSW.

Without funding for the Project, the action (or non-action) of the government agency demonstrates that freedom camping was still not seen as a high political priority for the New South Wales government. Subsequently, the NCDN Board re-instructed their executive officer to disband the Taskforce and reprioritise regional projects in line with the "marketing" focus of Destination NSW. Subsequently, Byron Shire resolved not to proceed in their quest for managing freedom camping through provision of dedicated space. Indeed, at Byron Shire Council's Ordinary meeting on 10 December 2015 (File No. I2015/1389), Council resolved:

1　Not to proceed with the Freedom Camping Site Trials at Main Beach Carpark and the Cavanbah Centre, due to prohibitive infrastructure costs, legal constraints and incompatibility with the current land use guidelines at each site.
2　That Council undertake the following actions:
　　a　Authorise staff to continue discussions with the private sector and other potential stakeholders to progress proposals and expressions of interest from operators to explore capacity for the Freedom Camping and RV markets on appropriate sites.
　　b　Continue to work with the North Coast Destination Network Freedom Camping Taskforce on a regional solution (Byron Shire Council 2015a: 26).

Despite this regional level setback in NSW, individual LGAs across Australia continue to develop innovative management strategies for their own freedom camping challenges. LGAs and private developers of freedom camping places are not assisted by an environment of systemic uncertainty and delays caused by overly prescribed and inflexible caravan and camping regulation. In spite of the challenges and the apparent market failure of commercial interests to meet the needs of a growing mobile RV resident community, enterprising local governments continue to progress a range of freedom camping initiatives balancing the needs, welfare and demands of mobile resident communities against those of their permanent resident communities.

Discussion and conclusions

Freedom camping is an age-old practice, characterised by free or open access to leisure and outdoor recreation spaces. It is an activity and experience growing in popularity among diverse population cohorts with diverse motivations, from the backpacker, to baby boomer retirees and young families, some of whom have sold their homes or left their homes for lengthy periods of time for experiences associated with a mobile lifestyle using an RV as their mobile residence or home. The growth in demand for freedom camping venues coupled with the decline in the number of commercial caravan and camping parks has led to widespread debate about the merits and impacts of freedom camping among travel groups, industry associations, local councils and state governments, and local communities.

The new prominence of caravanning and mobile homes is highlighting the recurring, but intensifying, issue of freedom camping versus commercial camping as mixed-markets from grey nomads, young families and van-packers are demonstrating their preferences for primitive style camping over traditional caravan park camping. By way of example, Cridland (2008: 71) suggests that 'until a method to determine the exact number of grey nomads travelling each year across Australia is formulated, understanding the full extent of their economic impact and the exact benefits they provide will remain problematic'. Grant (2012: 11) shares Cridland's concerns, going even further to argue 'using the state to persecute people unable to find a cheap place to stay is not a reasonable or acceptable response'. Cridland (2008) further highlights the gap in knowledge of consumer preferences, particularly with regards to the personal choice of participating in open and relaxed freedom camping over closed and rule-bound caravan parks that incur the high regulatory burdens imposed by councils.

Civic leaders concerned for their respective leisure, policy, management and regulatory environments that support freedom and commercial camping practices are grappling with the consequences of decreased RV accommodation facilities and increased host–guest hostilities toward freedom campers. This myriad of concerns has led to consideration of policies and other instruments to manage accessibility of resources for freedom campers and the legality of freedom camping. The ability of local communities to regulate or promote its practice is significantly impacted upon by diverse opinions and responsibilities spanning the jurisdictions of different levels of government, and diverse, often competing, interests.

According to Williams (2002: 365), 'reconciling competing claims on a place … is not simply a debate about which uses, meanings, and values are at stake. It also involves examining the appropriate social processes and institutions by which society orders, evaluates and decides which practices and meanings to protect and promote'. The planning and management of resources are inherently political activities, as land and water are valued for a variety of competing uses by users with diverse perceptions and motivations. The multipurpose characters of rural and regional landscapes mean it is 'perhaps inevitable that, given the finite supply of the countryside, conflicts occur between different demands on the rural resource base' (Pigram 1993: 161).

Williams (2002) clearly articulates how leisure and recreational resources, and tourist travel, present opportunities to examine matters such as the politics of place. Williams (2002: 356), for instance, uses Urry's (2000: 59) example of changing mobility with reference to the automobile:

> It reconfigures civil society involving distinct ways of dwelling, travelling and socialising in, and through, an automobilised time-space. Automobility necessarily divides workplaces from the home producing lengthy commutes; it splits home and shopping and destroys local retailing outlets; it separates home and various kinds of leisure site(s); it splits up families which live in distant places; it necessitates leisure visits to sites lying on the road network.

To further the automobile analogy to the self-contained recreational vehicle, this mode of travel integrates but transposes the "splitting" concepts of mobility vs permanent residency and leisure vs work. With the RV and the road network combined, they facilitate "new" spaces of and for leisure as freedom campers increasingly return to the highways for transit camping places and/or alternate places of domicile.

Williams (2002) asserts modern global relations were something leisure scholars had been slow to confront. He observes inequalities in leisure services and delivery, including spatial inequalities, and indeed inherent sectoral inequalities or inequalities between potential or actual users. But critically, he raises the flag of the politics of place in leisure studies and concludes, 'Modern leisure is a constituting factor in the politics of specific places by making and resisting claims on the meaning and use of spaces, claims that often collide with one another as well as with non-recreational uses and meanings' (Williams 2002: 363).

This multi-divergence of views reflects the changes that occur in public spaces, arising from what White (2012: 33) described as 'the ebbs and flows of economic development and social conflict'. White's various and cogent discussions about public space, consumption and consumer society make some telling points (White 2007, 2012). According to White (2007: 225) who was writing with reference to public spaces, consumption, and the social regulation of young people:

> The types of housing and amenity in a neighbourhood, the policing of street life, and different patterns of use of parks and pavements have always been symptomatic of broader social divisions and differences … Development is paramount, and commercially created places rather than publicly planned spaces have come to dominate.

White's arguments are persuasive with respect to public space and consumption generally. He describes public space as having several demarcations according to ownership and access, explains the influence of "institutional logic" upon access, and cites other authors, such as Harvey (1990) and Stilwell (1993), in seeing 'The construction of public space as a social process' (White 2007: 224). Elsewhere, White describes the social construction of public space being dominated by the rise of consumerism, the ongoing privatisation of public assets including public space, and the intensification of efforts to increasingly apply different forms of social regulation to effect shifts in attitudes, behaviours, access and use (White 2007, 2012). White concludes, 'Inevitably, conflict over uses, and between users, of public space leads to state and private attempts to regulate it' (White 2007: 224).

The larger study on which this snapshot of freedom camping is based is examining aspects of the politics of freedom camping. What the current literature highlights, including those studies cited in this chapter, is that the notions of home, travel and space are intricately intertwined, yet modern policy initiatives have not been able to find workable solutions to cater for freedom campers living in their mobile homes. And whereas the politics are fascinating, a much-neglected aspect of research into this phenomenon is the impact of public and private decisions and actions on the lives of people for whom their mobile residence is indeed their second or first home.

References

Australian Bureau of Statistics (ABS) (2010) *Motor Vehicle Census, Canberra*. [online] Retrieved from: http://www.abs.gov.au/AUSSTATS/abs@.nsf/DetailsPage/9309.031%20Mar%202010?OpenDocument (accessed 24 February 2012).

Balfour, C. (2010) 'RV travellers: Coming ready or not', Balfour Consulting, Townsville, Qld, Australia. [online] Retrieved from: http://www.savannahway.com.au/resources/rvtravellers.pdf (accessed 18 July 2014).

Bianchi, R.V. (2003) 'Place and power in tourism development: Tracing the complex articulations of community and locality', *Pasos*, 1 (1): 13–22.

Byron Shire Council (2012a) Management of Street Camping, Report No. 13.13 to the Ordinary Meeting on 22 March, Byron Shire Council, Mullumbimby, NSW, Australia.

Byron Shire Council (2012b) 'Management of Street Camping, Report No. 13.13, Minute 12-179, File No. ENG655090 #1196990, Byron Shire Council, Mullumbimby, NSW, Australia. 22 March. [online] Retrieved from: http://www.byron.nsw.gov.au/meetings/2012-03-22-ordinary (accessed 18 March 2014).

Byron Shire Council (2012c) 'No street camping signage goes up in the Bay', Byron Shire Council, Mullumbimby, NSW, Australia. 17 July. [online] Retrieved from: http://www.byron.nsw.gov.au/media-releases/2012/07/17/no-street-camping-signage-goes-up-in-the-bay (accessed 11 January 2014).

Byron Shire Council (2012d) 'Street camping to be redefined as Council seeks enforcement powers', Byron Shire Council, Mullumbimby, NSW, Australia, 23 March. [online] Retrieved from: http://www.byron.nsw.gov.au/media-releases/2012/03/23/street-camping-to-be-redefined-as-council-seeks-enforcement-powers (accessed 18 March 2014).

Byron Shire Council (2014) Minutes: Report 14.8 free camping in Byron Bay 28 August, Minutes of the Ordinary Meeting 28 August 2014, Byron Shire Council, Mullumbimby, NSW, Australia. [online] Retrieved from: http://www.byron.nsw.gov.au/search?query=14-419 (accessed 12 January 2015).

Byron Shire Council (2015a) Minutes 13.13 – free camping trial – Byron Bay, Minutes of the Ordinary Meeting 10 December, Byron Shire Council, Mullumbimby, NSW, Australia. [online] Retrieved from: http://byron.infocouncil.biz/Open/2015/12/OC_10122015_MIN_389.PDF (accessed 12 May 2016).

Byron Shire Council (2015b) Tough stance on illegal street camping – 10 fined, Byron Shire Council, Mullumbimby, NSW, Australia. [online]. Retrieved from: http://www.byron.nsw.gov.au/media-releases/2015/02/06/tough-stance-on-illegal-street-camping-10-fined (accessed 12 February 2015).

Caldicott, R. (2011) Supply-Side Evolution of Caravanning in Australia: An Historical Analysis of Caravan Manufacturing and Caravan Parks. Honours Thesis. Southern Cross University, Lismore, Australia.

Caldicott, R., Scherrer, P. and Jenkins, J. (2014) 'Freedom camping in Australia: Current status, key stakeholders and political debate', *Annals of Leisure Research*, 17 (4): 417–442.

Caldicott, R.W. and Harris, A. (2015) 'Freedom camping: Is it changing the face of caravanning in Australia?'. In E. Wilson and M. Witsel (eds) *Handbook and Book of Abstracts to the 25th Annual CAUTHE Conference – Rising Tides and Sea Changes: Adaption and Innovation in Tourism and Hospitality (USB)*. Gold Coast, Qld, Australia: Southern Cross University, 8. [online] Available at: http://scu.edu.au/cauthe2015/index.php/4

Caldicott, R. W. and Scherrer, P. (2013) 'Facing divergent supply and demand trajectories in Australian caravanning: Learnings from the evolution of caravan park site-mix options in Tweed Shire', *Journal of Vacation Marketing*, 19 (2): 117–131.

Campervan and Motorhome Club of Australia (CMCA) (2014) 'Leave no trace – Selfcontainment code of conduct', *CMCA*, March 2014, Newcastle, NSW, Australia. [online] Retrieved from: http://kulin.wa.gov.au/file/LeaveNoTraceRVFriendly2014.pdf (accessed 27 April 2015).

Caravan Industry Association of Australia (CIAA) (2014a) 'Caravan and campervan registrations on the rise reports BDO', *CIAA*, 14 August: Brisbane, Australia. [online] Retrieved from: http://www.caravanindustry.com.au/caravan-and-campervan-registrations-on-the-rise-reports-bdo (accessed 23 August 2014).

Caravan Industry Association of Australia (CIAA) (2014b) 'Industry facts', *CIAA*, 11 March: Brisbane, Australia.

Caravan Industry Association of Australia (CIAA) (2015a) '2015 RV production figures up 10 percent YTD', *CIAA*, Brisbane, Australia. [online] Retrieved from: http://www.caravanindustry.com.au/2015-rv-production-figures-up-10-percent-ytd (accessed 2 July 2015).

Caravan Industry Association of Australia (CIAA) (2015b) 'New research highlights changing attitudes in the caravan industry', *CIAA*, Brisbane, Australia. [online] Retrieved from: http://www.caravanindustry. com.au/new-research-highlights-changing-attitudes-in-the-caravan-industry (accessed 2 July 2015).

Caravan Industry Association of Australia (CIAA) (2016a) 'Prime Minister Turnbull; It's time to get on with business', *CIAA*, Brisbane, Australia. [online] Retrieved from: http://campaign.r20.constantcontact.com/ render?m=1103447516004&ca=872ea31e-588f-4d0a-8583-ca6b8dcc8608 (accessed 19 July 2016).

Caravan Industry Association of Australia (CIAA) (2016b) 'Who are we', *CIAA*, Brisbane, Australia. [online] Retrieved from: http://www.caravanindustry.com.au/who-is-caravanindustry (accessed 3 August 2016).

Caravanning Queensland. (2015) 'Caravanning Queensland's response to the circulating CMCA document', *Caravanning Queensland*, Brisbane, Australia. [online] Available at: http://www.freechoicecamps. com.au/caravanning-qld-document.html

Clement, J. (2015a) 'Backpacker campervan surge in Sydney's east has residents fuming and councils begging for more power to remove overnight sleepers', *Wentworth Courier*, 14 January. [online] Retrieved from: http://www.dailytelegraph.com.au/newslocal/city-east/backpacker-campervan-surge-in-sydneys-east-has-residents-fuming-and-councils-begging-for-more-power-to-remove-overnight-sleepers/story-fngr8h22-1227183700276 (accessed 29 January 2015).

Clement, J. (2015b) 'Who will send Bondi's backpackers packing? Buckpassing continues over unwanted guests', *Wentworth Courier*, 27 January. [online] Retrieved from: http://www.dailytelegraph.com. au/newslocal/city-east/who-will-send-bondis-backpackers-packing-buckpassing-continues-over-unwanted-guests/story-fngr8h22-1227198606333 (accessed 29 January 2015).

Cohen, S. (2011) 'Lifestyle travellers: Backpacking as a way of life', *Annals of Tourism Research*, 38 (4): 1535–1555.

Counts, D. R. and Counts, D. A. (1996) *Over the Next Hill: An Ethnography of RVing Seniors in North America*. Peterborough, Ontario: Broadview Press.

Cridland, S. (2008) An Analysis of the Winter Movement of Grey Nomads to Northern Australia: Planning for Increase Senior Visitation. PhD. James Cook University, Cairns, Australia.

Department of Local Government and Communities (DLGC) (2015) *Nature-Based Parks – Licensing Guidelines for Developers and Governments*, Perth, WA: DLGC.

Department of Tourism, Events, Small Business and the Commonwealth Games (DTESB) (2014) *Queensland Camping Options Toolkit: A Guide for Local Government in Developing Camping Options.* Brisbane, Qld, Australia: DTESB.

Fairhurst, T. (2014) 'Council crackdown on carpark campers', *Fairfax Regional Media, Port McQuarie News*, 6 January. [online] Retrieved from: http://www.portnews.com.au/story/2003839/council-crackdown-on-carpark-campers/?cs=12 (accessed 11 January 2014).

Feain, D. (2012) 'Byron's roadside campers are about to get the boot', *The Northern Star*, 11 January: 3.

Feliu, L. (2014) 'Byron Bay street campers fined $4250', *The Byron Echo, Echonetdaily*, Byron Bay, NSW, Australia,18 August. [online] Retrieved from: http://www.echo.net.au/2014/08/byron-bay-street-campers-fined-4250/ (accessed 16 February 2014).

Fennell, P. and Fennell, C. (2017) *Camps Australia Wide*, 9th ed., Noosaville, Qld, Australia: Camps Australia Wide.

Foran, K. (2016) 'Calls to introduce mobile showers for Byron bay's homeless', *NBN News*: Lismore, NSW, Australia, 2 March. [online] Retrieved from: http://www.nbnnews.com.au/2016/03/02/calls-to-introduce-mobile-showers-for-byron-bays-homeless/ (accessed 2 March 2016).

Fraser, R. (2013) 'Council abandons freedom camping test case', *The New Zealand Herald*, 3 April. [online] Available at: http://www.nzherald.co.nz/nz/news/article.cfm?c_id=1&objectid=10875182

Gardiner, S. (2013a) 'Byron solution is complex one', *The Northern Star*, 12 January: 12.

Gardiner, S. (2013b) 'Illegal campers trash Byron Bay', *The Northern Star*, 1 January. [online] Retrieved from: http://www.northernstar.com.au/news/illegal-campers-trash-byron-bay/1702622/ (accessed 11 January 2014).

Garner, B. (2013) *Born in a Tent: How Camping Makes us Australian*. Sydney: New South Wales University Press.

Gleeson, A. (2014) 'Council bans Horseshoe Beach camping', *Newcastle Herald*, 22 January. [online] Retrieved from: http://www.theherald.com.au/story/2035141/council-bans-horseshoe-beach-camping/?cs=303 (accessed 22 January 2014).

Grant, S. (2012) 'Purge will make Byron an insipid enclave', *The Northern Star*, 19 January: 11.

Green, F. B. (1978) 'Recreation vehicles: A perspective', *Annals of Tourism Research*, 5 (4): 429–439.

Hadfield, G. J. (2015) 'Off site camping in the UK', *motorhomeparking.com*, 3 March. [online] Retrieved from: http://www.motorhomeparking.co.uk/roads.htm (accessed 31 March 2016).

Hansen, J. (2015) 'Operation take back the Bay: How Byron Bay is getting its tranquility back', *The Daily Telegraph*, 11 January. [online] Retrieved from: http://www.dailytelegraph.com.au/news/nsw/operation-take-back-the-bay-how-byron-bay-is-getting-its-tranquillity-back/story-fni0cx12-1227178604974 (accessed 12 April 2015).

Hardy, A. and Gretzel, U. (2011) 'Why we travel this way'. In B. Prideaux and D. Carson (eds) *Drive Tourism: Trends and Emerging Markets*. New York: Routledge, 194–209.

Hardy, A., Gretzel, U. and Hanson, D. (2013) 'Travelling neo-tribes: Conceptualising recreational vehicle users', *Journal of Tourism and Cultural Change*, 11 (1–2): 48–60.

Harvey, D. (1990) *The Condition of Postmodernity: An Inquiry into the Origins of Cultural Change*. Oxford: Blackwell.

Hillman, W. (2013) 'Grey nomads travelling in Queensland, Australia: Social and health needs', *Ageing & Society*, 33 (4): 579–597.

Hogger, H. (2013) 'Weymouth park and ride put forward as possible temporary traveller site', *Dorset Echo*, 1 October. [online] Retrieved from: http://www.dorsetecho.co.uk/news/10709321.UPDATE__Weymouth_park_and_ride_put_forward_as_possible_temporary_traveller_site/ (accessed 16 February 2014).

Holloway, D. J. and Holloway, D. A. (2011) 'Everyday life in the "tourist zone"', *Journal of Media and Culture*, 14 (5). [online] Available at: http://journal.media-culture.org.au/index.php/mcjournal/article/view/412

Hörmander, L.-E. (2017) *Motorhome destination Sweden*, Gothenburg: SCR Swedish Camping. [online] Retrieved from: http://www.husbilsdestinationsverige.se/Documents/husbilsdestinationsverige/husbilsdestination-sverige-2017.pdf (accessed 19 June 2017).

Jones, P. (2016) 'The camping habits & economic value of "free-camping" travellers', *Freedom Camping Australia*, Tuncurry, NSW, 28 February. [online] Retrieved fromt: http://www.toora.org/Grey%20Nomad-Friendly%20Camping%20~%20Economic%20Benefits.pdf (accessed 28 February 2016).

Kingdon, J. W. (1984) *Agendas, Alternatives and Public Politics*. Boston, MA: Longman.

Kingdon, J. W. (2011) *Agendas, Alternatives and Public Politics*, 2nd ed. Boston, MA: Longman.

Kinninment, M. (2014a) 'Byron Shire Council rangers' blitz send "vanpackers" packing', *Northern Star*, 21 March. [online] Retrieved from: http://www.northernstar.com.au/news/van-campers-sent-packing/2205298/ (accessed 20 August 2014).

Kinninment, M. (2014b) '"Lazy, bloody mongrel" vanpackers flee Byron for the hills', *Northern Star*, 27 March. [online] Retrieved from: http://www.northernstar.com.au/news/campers-behave-badly/2211117/#.UzNQ2BEE2-I.email (accessed 27 March 2014).

Lawrence Consulting. (2015) *Local Economy, Lawrence Consulting, Toowoomba, Qld, Current for 2013/14 Financial Year*, [online] Retrieved from: http://lawrenceconsulting.com.au/ (accessed 29 October 2015).

Lowrey, T. (2014) 'North Coast councils planning new strategy to handle growth in popularity of RVs', Australian Broadcasting Commission, 17 July. [online] Retrieved from: http://mobile.abc.net.au/news/2014-07-16/rv27s-causing-headaches-for-north-coast-councils-and-caravan-p/5602078 (accessed 19 July 2014).

Macbeth, J. (2000) 'Utopian tourists – Cruising is not just about sailing', *Current Issues in Tourism*, 3 (1): 20–34.

McDonald, M. (2014) 'Australian caravan manufacturers travelling well', *Manufacturers' Monthly*, 21 November. [online] Retrieved from: http://www.manmonthly.com.au/news/australian-caravan-manufacturers-travelling-well (accessed 21 November 2014).

Massey, D. (1991) 'A global sense of place', *Marxism Today*, June: 24–29.

Ming, R. C. (1997) 'Tracking "snowbirds" in Australia: Winter sun seekers in far north Queensland', *Australian Geographical Studies*, 35 (2): 168–182.

Ming, R. and McHugh, K. (1995) 'Wintering in American sunbelt: Linking place and behaviour', *Journal of Tourism Studies*, 6 (2): 56–61.

Moeller, B. and Moeller, J. (1993) *Full-Time RVing: A Complete Guide to Life on the Open Road*. 2nd ed., Englewood, CO: Trailer Life Enterprise.

Morgan, N. and Pritchard, A. (1998) *Tourism Promotion and Power: Creating Images, Creating Identities*. Chichester, UK: Wiley.

Morrow, C. (2016) 'Byron's own "shanty town" to clean up', *The Northern Star*, APN News and Media, Lismore, NSW, 9 June. [online] Retrieved from: http://www.pressreader.com/australia/the-northern-star/20160609 (accessed 10 June 2016).

National Parks Service. (2016) 'America the beautiful passes', *National Parks Service*, Washington, DC. [online] Retrieved from: https://www.nps.gov/planyourvisit/passes.htm (accessed 31 March 2016).

Nature Travels (2008) 'Wild camping in Sweden and the right of public access', *Nature Travels*, London, 8 February [online] Retrieved from: https://naturetravels.wordpress.com/2008/02/08/wild-camping-in-sweden-and-the-right-of-public-access/ (accessed 1 April 2016).

New Zealand Department of Conservation (DoC) (2014) *Freedom camping: Where can I freedom camp?* Wellington, NZ: Department of Conservation. [online] Retrieved from: http://www.doc.govt.nz/parks-and-recreation/places-to-stay/freedom-camping/ (accessed 13 July 2014).

New Zealand Motor Camping Association Inc (NZMCA) (2013a) 'Model freedom camping bylaws', NZMCA. [online] Retrieved from: http://www.nzmca.org.nz/freedom-camping/ (accessed 25 January 2014).

New Zealand Motor Camping Association Inc (NZMCA) (2013b) 'NZMCA disputes mayor's claims over freedom camping', *Scoop Media*, 4 April. [online] Retrieved from: http://www.scoop.co.nz/stories/PO1304/S00038/nzmca-disputes-mayors-claims-over-freedom-camping.htm (accessed 12 July 2014).

New Zealand Parliament (2011) *Freedom Camping Act 2011*, Wellington, NZ: Parliamentary Counsel Office.

North Coast Destination Network Inc. (NCDN) (2015) 'Freedom camping LGA survey interim results', *NCDN*, Port Macquarie, NSW, Australia, 26 May.

Northeast Lincolnshire Council (2014) *Stage 1 Complaint Received on 31st July 2014*, Andy Strangeway, Pocklington, UK, 3 October. [online] Retrieved fromt: https://andystrangewayovernightparkingcampaigner.files.wordpress.com/2014/10/unlawful-signs-buck-beck-cleethorpes-north-east-lincs.pdf (accessed 28 July 2016).

Onyx, J. and Leonard, R. (2007) 'The grey nomads phenomenon: Changing the script of aging', *International Journal of Aging and Human Development*, 64 (4): 381–398.

Page, D. (2012) 'Street camping – Confidential annexure 12(d)', *Byron Shire Council*: Byron Bay, NSW, Australia. [online] Retrieved from: http://www.byron.nsw.gov.au/meetings/2013-09-19-ordinary/update-on-ministerial-correspondence-relating-to-street-camping (accessed 19 March 2014).

Patterson, I., Pegg, S. and Litster, J. (2011) 'Grey nomads on tour: A revolution in travel and tourism for older adults', *Tourism Analysis*, 16 (3): 283–294.

Pigram, J. J. (1993) 'Planning for tourism in rural areas: Bridging the policy implementation gap'. In D. G. Pearce and R. W. Butler (eds) *Tourism Research: Critiques and Challenges*. London: Routledge, 156–174.

Pilot Flying J. (2016) 'Amenities', *Pilot Flying J*, Knoxville, TN. [online] Retrieved from: http://www.pilot-flyingj.com/rv-amenities (accessed 31 March 2016).

Podmore, S. (2014) 'Move over, grey nomads: Younger Australians can't get enough of caravanning, camping and road trip adventures', *Herald Sun*, 24 August. [online] Retrieved from: http://m.heraldsun.com.au/travel/move-over-grey-nomads-younger-australians-cant-get-enough-of-caravanning-camping-and-road-trip-adventures/story-fnjjuxvu-1227031729587?nk=d41965e4396969d6222b300ffecd58f9 (accessed 26 August 2014).

Porteous, D. (2014) 'Freedom camping sites very popular', *Otago Daily Times*, 14 January. [online] Retrieved from: http://www.odt.co.nz/news/dunedin/288088/freedom-camping-sites-very-popular (accessed 14 January 2014).

Prideaux, B. and McClymont, H. (2006) 'The changing profile of caravanners in Australia', *International Journal of Tourism Research*, 8 (1): 45–58.

Radel, K. and Hillman, W. (2013) 'Not on vacation: Triggering travel in response to trauma', in J. Fountain and K. Moore (eds) *CAUTHE 2013: Tourism and Global Change: On the Edge of Something Big*, Christchurch, NZ: Lincoln University, 676–686. [online]. Available at: http://search.informit.com.au/documentSummary;dn=514887450792716;res=IELBUS

Recreational Vehicle Manufacturers Association of Australia (RVMAA) (2011) 'Industry stats', *RVMAA*. [online] Retrieved from: http://www.rvmaa.com.au/6147/HOME/ (accessed 11 October 2011).

Roundabout Publications. (2016) 'Walmart locator', Roundabout Publications, LaCygne, KS. [online] Retrieved from: http://www.walmartlocator.com/contact/ (accessed 31 March 2016).

Simpson, D. (2008) 'Nomadic urbanism: The senior full-time recreational vehicle community', *Interstices: Journal of Architecture and Related Arts*, 9: 34–46.

Southerton, D., Shove, E., Warde, A. and Deem, R. (2003) *Home from Home?: A Research Note on Recreational Caravanning*, Lancaster, UK: Department of Sociology, Lancaster University. [online] Retrieved from: http://www.lancaster.ac.uk/sociology/research/publications/papers/southerton-et-al-home-from-home.pdf (accessed 15 November 2012).

Stilwell, F. (1993) *Reshaping Australia: Urban Problems and Policies*. Sydney: Pluto Press.

Strangeway, A. (2014a) *Byelaw Challenge*, Pocklington, UK, 4 February 2014. [online] Retrieved from: https://lincolnshireovernightparking.wordpress.com/2014/02/04/byelaw-challenge/ (accessed 28 July 2016).

Strangeway, A. (2014b) *Skegness Standard Letter: Why I Am Camping Against Restrictions*, Pocklington, UK, 27 March 2014. [online] Retrieved from: https://andystrangewayovernightparkingcampaigner.wordpress.com/2014/03/27/skegness-standard-letter/ (accessed 28 July 2016).

Strongman, S. (2014) 'Taranaki welcomes freedom campers – its all positive in our view', *Taranaki Daily News*, 21 January. [online] Retrieved from: http://www.stuff.co.nz/taranaki-daily-news/news/9630581/Taranaki-welcomes-freedom-campers (accessed 22 January 2014).

Stylianou, G. (2016) 'Council to ban freedom campers: Got no loo, you're not welcome', *Stuff*, 28 July. [online] Retrieved from: http://www.stuff.co.nz/travel/82559656/christchurch-council-bans-freedom-camping-calls-for-government-intervention (accessed 3 August 2016).

UK Government (1960) 'Caravan sites and control of development Act 1960', *The National Archives*, London, 29 July 1960. [online] Retrieved from: http://www.legislation.gov.uk/ukpga/Eliz2/8-9/62 (accessed 31 March 2016).

UK Government (2016) 'Open access land: Management, rights and responsibilities', *Natural England*, London, 10 May 2016. [online] Retrieved from: https://www.gov.uk/guidance/open-access-land-management-rights-and-responsibilities (accessed 28 July 2016).

UKMotorhomes.net. (2016) 'UK stopovers: Motorhome stopovers in the UK and Ireland', *BM Services and UKMotorhomes.net*, London, 29 September. [online] Available at: http://www.ukmotorhomes.net/uk-stopovers/9-motorhome-stopover-listing

Urry, J. (2000) *Sociology beyond Societies: Mobilities for the Twenty-First Century*. London: Routledge.

Walker, C. (2014) 'Residents want backpackers to pack up and leave Coogee's coastal parks', *Southern Courier*, 4 March. [online] Retrieved from: http://www.dailytelegraph.com.au/newslocal/city-east/residents-want-backpackers-to-pack-up-and-leave-coogees-coastal-parks/story-fngr8h22-1226844009821 (accessed 6 April 2014).

Ward, N. (2015) 'NYCC: A sea-view in pitch darkness', *North Yorks Enquirer*, 7 April. [online] Retrived from: http://nyenquirer.uk/nycc-a-sea-view-in-pitch-darkness/ (accessed 7 April 2015).

Whitby Gazette. (2015) 'County council to clamp down on motorhomes', *Whitby Gazette*, 30 July. [online] Available at: https://andystrangewayovernightparkingcampaigner.files.wordpress.com/2015/08/council-to-clamp-down-on-motorhomes-2.jpg

White, N. R. and White, P. B. (2007) 'Home and away: Tourists in a connected world', *Annals of Tourism Research*, 34 (1): 88–104.

White, R. (2007) 'Public spaces, consumption and social regulation of young people'. In S. A. Venkatesh and R. Kassimir (eds) *Youth, Globalization, and the Law*. Stanford, CA: Stanford University Press, 223–254.

White, R. (2012) 'The making, shaking and taking of public spaces'. In C. Jones, E. Barclay and R. I. Mawby (eds) *The Problem of Pleasure – Leisure, Tourism and Crime*. London: Routledge, 32–47.

Williams, D. R. (2002) 'Leisure identities, globalization, and the politics of place', *Journal of Leisure Research*, 34 (4): 351–367.

Wilson, J. (2012a) 'Freeloading parasites: Vanpackers are "degrading" Byron Bay', *Northern Star*, 13 January: 4.

Wilson, J. (2012b) '"Vanpackers" degrading Byron Bay', *Northern Star*, 13 January. [online] Retrieved from: http://www.northernstar.com.au/news/vanpackers-degrading-byron-bay/1236498/ (accessed 13 January 2014).

Woodman, C. (2012) 'RV deduction information', *Demand Media*. [online] Retrieved from: http://www.ehow.com/info_7746859_rv-deduction-information.html (accessed 18 November 2012).

29

FOLLOW THE SUN

Retirees motorhomes' movements, meanings and practices during the winter season in the Algarve

Joana Afonso Dias and Alexandre Domingues

Introduction

Western Europe is the second largest regional destination for recreational transportation exports (International Trade Administration (ITA) 2016). The motorhome is a recreation vehicle rapidly growing in popularity in Europe (see Table 29.1) and is particularly used by third-age or young-old-age travellers enjoying the winter season (Brooker & Joppe 2013). As Lorentzein (2015) describes, a motorhome is a vehicle constructed for recreation, merging accommodation and transportation together, thereby enhancing the possibility for people to go wherever they want, whenever they want. The European region has some of the highest levels of leisure time, middle-class consumers and income outside the United States, and Europe is the second largest global recreation vehicle market after the United States (ITA 2016). In 2016 Germany had the largest motorhome market segment, with 535,428 vehicles, followed by France (402,671), Italy (217,327), Great Britain (204,792), the Netherlands (88,724) and Sweden (78,799).

The number of seniors involved in this kind of migratory movement has grown considerably in the last 20 years; an increase in mass tourism is one explanation, but this may also be the result of generally stronger finances among the main age groups (Blaakilde & Nilsson 2013), as well as the constantly growing number of retirees in Western Europe. The term "mobilities" refers not just to movement but to "movement-driven" social science in which movement or blocked movement, as well as voluntary/temporary immobilities, practices of dwelling and "nomadic" place-making are all viewed as constitutive of economic, social and political relations (Sheller & Urry 2006). Thus, mobilities need to be examined in their fluid interdependence and not in their separate spheres (such as driving, travelling virtually, writing letters, flying and walking) (Sheller & Urry 2006). As Uteng and Cresswell (2016) argue, by mobility we mean not only geographical movement but also the potential for undertaking movements – *motility* as it is lived and experienced. In this investigation, we provide data related to movements, meanings and experiences that, together, help produce the practice of driving motorhomes in the Algarve during the winter season. A number of authors (e.g. Hall 2005) proclaim the need for a stronger and more nuanced engagement with the relationality of tourism. Regarding tourism as a bundle of lines that may engage or disengage with coexisting trajectories of other things indeed blurs the figure of tourism as conventionally framed. This chapter therefore aims to remind us that travelling by motorhome, an alternative form of mobility, can be more than a means of transport.

Table 29.1 Number of registered motorhomes

	2013	*2016*	*(Δ Var %) 2013/2016*
Germany	450,000	535,428	19.0
France	353,000	402,671	14.1
Italy	206,500	217,327	5.2
Great Britain	175,000	204,792	17.0
The Netherlands	85,000	88,724	4.4
Sweden	66,000	78,799	19.4
Finland	48,000	51,022	6.3
Belgium	42,000	41,785	23.3
Switzerland	34,000	44,303	30.3
Spain	29,500	34,442	16.8
Austria	22,000	25,409	15.5
Denmark	16,000	16,508	3.2
Others	10,000	14,879	48.8
Portugal	10,000	10,223	2.2
Norway	5,700	13,658	139.6
Slovenia	4,100	4,451	8.6
Total	1,556,800	1,794,421	15.3

Source: European Caravan Federation (ECF) 2016.

Throughout this chapter the crucial intention was to obtain a better understanding of the following questions:

1 Who is the tourist travelling by motorhome to the Algarve during the winter season?
2 How do motorhome users who visited the Algarve during the winter season experience the destination? Where and how did they stay overnight?
3 How do motorhome users ascribe meaning to the phenomenon of motorhome tourism?
4 What is the level of awareness of spontaneous and stimulated ASAs and campgrounds in the Algarve?

This chapter will be presented in six sections, including the introduction. The second part provides a review of literature related to mobility, from drive tourism to motorhomes and European retirement mobility patterns, and gives a sum of previous studies on grey movers. The third part offers an overview of the study area (Algarve) and also outlines the variety of physical conditions of the south of Europe, which attract the elderly population, particularly in the winter season. The methodologies used in this article are outlined in the fourth section, definitions used are discussed, and the methods applied for the selection of motorhomes are presented. The last section presents the results regarding the level of travel motivation and planning from field surveys on movements, experiences and meanings based on grey movers surveyed in the Algarve, and also exposes the main themes discussed based on results obtained primarily from field interviews and researcher observations.

Mobility

The deep transformations associated with the current phase of globalisation have prompted scholars to search for new conceptual, theoretical and methodological approaches to make sense of contemporary social (re)configurations. The self-proclaimed "new mobilities paradigm" (Büscher et al. 2010; Hannam, Sheller & Urry 2006; Sheller & Urry 2006; Urry 2007; Sheller 2014; Uteng & Cresswell 2016) constitutes the most eloquent instance of this phenomenon, but several influential approaches in contemporary social theory are built on more or less explicit assumptions about rising and diversifying types of mobility and their role in shaping society.

Mobility is more than mappable and calculable movement; it also, it is argued, reflects meaning (Cresswell 2010) and linkage across different scales of movement. Mobility is also considered in relation to forms of place, stopping, stillness and relative immobility (Adey 2006; Hannam et al. 2006). A focus on empirical mobilities necessitates both mobile theorisation and mobile methodologies. It also gathers new empirical sensitivities, analytical orientations, methods and motivations to examine important social and material phenomena and folds social science insight into responses (Büscher & Urry 2009). The rise of mobilities in the social sciences has raised interest in a diverse range of mobile practices. Various studies have reflected on walking (Middleton 2009), running (Cook et al. 2015), cycling (Spinney 2009), driving (Laurier 2004; Landin 2015) and flying (Adey 2004), among others, from a variety of angles. The term "mobilities" refers not just to movement but to this broader project of establishing a "movement-driven" social science, in which movement, potential movement and blocked movement, as well as voluntary/temporary immobilities, practices of dwelling and "nomadic" place-making are all viewed as constitutive of economic, social and political relations. Mobility is a sum of movements, meanings and practices. Understanding mobility holistically means paying attention to all three of these aspects (Cresswell 2008).

Thus movement, in short, is getting from one place to another, which is described as physical movement. We reach meaning through discourses, narratives and stories related to movement. Mobility has been figured as freedom, as it is so often related with this touristic way of experiencing it, and finally the experience and embodied practice of movement, walking, driving, flying and sailing are a few examples of these mobile practices. Driving a motorhome can be a liberating or stressful experience. Whether we have chosen to be mobile and how we feel about doing it affects our experience of it. Getting from A to B can be very different depending on which mobile practice we use. Driving caravans, motorhomes or any recreation vehicle has played an important role, and freedom and mobility are longstanding key elements of American culture (Landin 2015). For those who choose these vehicles as their home and subscribe to a mobile lifestyle, it comes with a new community, a new set of ideals, a new shared habitus and even new kinds of cities (Bourdieu 1990).

From drive tourism to motorhome tourism

The drive market represents visitors who use some form of vehicular transport as a mode of transport to reach their destination, where their main purpose of visit is leisure, including day trips and overnight trips to one or multiple destinations. The drive tourism market derives from the network of interrelated institutions developed to support it (Scott 2002). Drive tourism is a complex phenomenon, with decisions about whether to drive, what to drive, and what role the vehicle plays in the travel experiences being influenced by a range of factors (Prideaux & Carson 2010). While the resulting multiplicity of experiences enriches tourist consumption, itineraries also offer particular rewards in the promotion of tourism as a spatial development strategy. Many recent researches into drive tourism have shown that the drive market is large but not homogeneous (Olsen 2003; Shih 2006). In essence, this encompasses forms of recreation involving at least one overnight stay away from home, typically with some form of transport incorporating accommodation, to an outdoor recreational destination. In Europe, one in six of all overnight stays were spent on a campground (Eurostat European Commission 2012). This "outdoors hospitality" appears to be particularly attractive to Europeans, North Americans, Australians and New Zealanders, though there is said be to be growing interest in China (Wu & Pearce 2014) and India (Brooker & Joppe 2013). The recreational vehicle sector has been reported as growing rapidly (Counts & Counts 2004; Onyx & Leonard 2005; Hardy et al. 2013).

The range of road-based travel encompassed by the description of drive tourism includes day trips and overnight travel in a family car or a rental car, travel in four-wheel-drive vehicles (4WD), caravanning, travel in recreational vehicles (RVs) and touring by motorcycle (Prideaux & Carson 2010). The motorhome is an example of a recreation vehicle and it is linked to "itinerant tourism", which has presented truly remarkable growth figures (Caravanning Industry Association (CIVD) 2016). In Portugal, the phenomenon does not have the dimensions of other European countries (like France, Norway and Germany) although the number of supporters and practitioners has been experiencing remarkable growth (Dias & Domingues 2016). In 2015, new registrations of recreational vehicles in Europe totalled 151,293, representing a 10% increase from 2014 (ECF 2016). The motorhome market is growing in Australia (Apostolidis et al. 2009), USA (Recreation Vehicle Industry Association (RVIA) 2015) and other countries in Europe such as Norway (Lorentzen 2015). However, there are countries in which, for different reasons, this type of tourism doesn't grow, Taiwan (Cheng & Chen 2006) for instance (RV costs; parking is a critical issue in Taiwan, as is learning to drive a large vehicle on crowded Taiwanese roads). It is therefore necessary to meet several conditions for this type of tourism to develop and grow in harmony with the other versions of practising tourism.

Within the academic literature, there is a consensus that recreational vehicle users (RVers) are a group of highly mobile travellers who are motivated by a desire to experience freedom and escape the constraints of routine home life (Counts & Counts 2004; Hardy & Gretzel 2011; Mings & McHugh 1995; Onyx & Leonard 2005). Pearce (1999) examined the self-drive market in particular and notes that this form of travel is ideal for older Australians for ease of access, as a purposeful, shared activity providing a reflective experience. Therefore, today the motorhome as a form of self-drive tourism is experiencing a boom due to two of its main characteristics: freedom and autonomy. The motorhomers who visit the Algarve during the winter season are not only mobile, but in some ways are really avant-garde – they represent new ways of living in a global world with increasing opportunities for mobility (Blaakilde & Nilsson 2013). A motorhome is a vehicle constructed for recreation, merging accommodation and transportation together, thereby enhancing the possibility for people to go wherever they want, whenever they want. The motorhome is a hybrid phenomenon that embodies conflicting ideals: total freedom of movement and the reinvention of the self at the other extreme. It is both individualistic and community-based, and its urban forms are highly adaptable to societal changes, mirroring society's development as well as the changing landscape it inhabits. Motorhome users therefore cover a range of different market segments.

The three key segments identified are full-timers, short- and long-term users (Figure 29.1) (Brooker & Joope 2013). The full-timers cover travellers who live permanently in their motorhome (Hartwigsen & Null 1991; Brooker & Joppe 2013) or permanent residents who decide to live year-round in a motorhome (Counts & Counts 1992). Indeed, due to economic and/or political stress resulting, these types of vehicles are increasingly being used as a form of budget accommodation for the homeless and poor (Lashley 2015), particularly in countries where RVs are most present. Long-term occupancy includes the movers that follow the warm and sunny weather. This occurs in Australia, namely the *grey nomads* (Mings 1997; Holloway et al. 2011; Onyx & Leonard 2005; Cridland 2008; Mahadevan 2014), in the

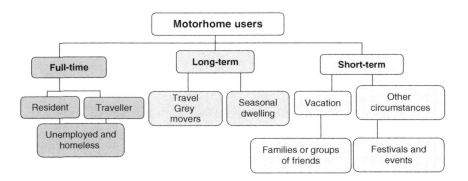

Figure 29.1   A typology of motorhome users.

United States, where they are usually called *snowbirds* (Patterson et al. 2011; Hardy et al. 2012), and in Western Europe (Bruner 2005; Prideaux et al. 2001; O'Reilly 2000; Viallon 2012), South Africa and Canada (Patterson et al. 2011). Long-term motorhoming also occurs during the summer months, but with less intensity, where individuals park their motorhome on a particular site and return to that site annually for vacations and weekends (Brooker & Joppe 2013; MacTavish, Eley & Salamon 2006; Sheng, Simpson & Siguaw 2014). The last segment that was identified was the short-term segment which corresponds to short periods of time, resulting in periodic travel on vacations or weekends. This can include specific holidays such as Christmas, New Year's Eve, Carnival and Easter as well as sports events (Van Heerden & Van Heerden 2008; Wu & Pearce 2016).

Grey movers

Retirees as tourists is an area which has been carefully examined over the last twenty years in either case-studies or as a general phenomenon by North American and European experts (Viallon 2012). Demographic changes in the EU are likely to be of considerable importance in the coming decades as the vast majority of models concerning future population trends suggest that the EU's population will continue to age, due to consistently low fertility levels and extended longevity. Grey nomads are different, because they are generally time rich, are free to choose whether to work or not, and generally do not have many of the burdens that limit the holidays and journeys of others in society (Onyx & Leonard 2005). Mcleish (1976) coined the term "*Ulyssean* adult" to identify individuals who continue to seek new adventures and opportunities in their later years. The individuals who participated in our study enter the *Ulyssean* world. The term "grey movers" is not a strict characterisation and has a narrow definition. However, tourism researchers have generally defined senior travellers as those who are 55 and older, and older adults have also been defined according to the retirement age of 65 or older (Patterson 2006). Retiree travellers are becoming one of the largest travel segments globally (Hsu & Kang 2009; Ye 2015). Examples of studies on senior tourism can be found, among others, in Patterson et al. (2011), Hillman (2013), Wu and Pearce (2014, 2016) and Chen and Shoemaker (2014). Nevertheless, even though seniors move less than any other age group according to statistics, there has been a gradual increase of both national and international retirement migration, especially among recent retirees (Abramsson & Andersson 2012; Blaakilde & Nilsson 2013). Nevertheless, understanding mobility holistically means paying attention to the sum of movements, meanings and practices, in the context of the *Ulyssean* lifestyle.

The Algarve

The Algarve region, located in the extreme southwest of Europe and along the south of Portugal, enjoys a pleasant climate with warm winters and mild summers, and has year-round light and sunshine. Algarve has, on average, 259 days with sunshine per year, a warm temperature and has excellent quality of light (Turismo de Portugal: Algarve 2016). In 2015, Faro Airport had its busiest year since it opened in 1965, with 6.4 million passengers passing through the airport (ANA Portugal Airports (ANA) 2016). Tourists who come to the Algarve are from various international markets, particularly those located in Europe, especially the UK, Germany, Spain, France and the Netherlands and others, which together accounted in 2015 for over 70% of the total tourists visiting the region (ANA 2016). These nationality profiles are also similar to those for motorhome tourism in the Algarve

Method

This study was situated within an interpretive theoretical approach, in which experiences and meanings were viewed as personally and socially constructed, and uses a grounded theory methodology, including qualitative procedures such as interviews (Charmaz 2000). The analysis is based on a convenience sample of 160 motorhome users from five countries which regularly visit the Algarve (France, UK, Germany, the Netherlands and Sweden). The empirical material is based on a semi-structured survey, which was undertaken during January and February 2016. The surveys were conducted and carried out by four interviewers and were applied along the Castro Marim border accompanied by the Republican National Guard (Guarda Nacional Republicana (GNR)). Whenever any motorhome passed on the border, it was stopped with the support of the GNR and the interviewers applied the survey. The sample collected totalled 160 valid anonymous questionnaires; the sample was determined by the funding of the Comissão de Coordenação e desenvolvimento regional do Algarve (CCDRA) (Algarve Regional Development and Coordination Commission). Since our target audience was seniors with available time and due to the qualitative nature of some of the research questions and that little is known about the phenomenon under consideration, we used the in-depth interview as a method of data collection. The interviewers were often invited into the motorhome, while a few German motorhomers refused to answer the questionnaire, mostly referring to their ignorance of the English language. The questionnaire consisted of 52 questions, 30 closed and 22 open questions. The results were entered into an SPSS database. In-depth interviewing of key informants identified through the screening process also occurred as the opportunity arose. From this instrument reasons for travelling by motorhomes, why they chose the Algarve and information related with the motorhomes network were analysed, such as material resources, future plans and understanding interactions with others (host communities and other motorhome users). Altogether, 15 motorhome users were interviewed (mostly represented by couples but single informants were also invited to participate). The interviews were conducted with the help of a written interview guide. All interviews were transcribed, analysed and examined recursively by the researchers, and patterns were noted.

During their stay, the respondents are also responsible for the performance and behaviour of their peers, such that the length period of stay (three months is the average) gives an opportunity for the motorhomers to influence others motorhomers through their suggestions, actions and behaviours. The investigation focused mainly on who the tourists are and how they project their Algarve trip and what they did as motorhome users in the Algarve on their last visit. It explores how tourists perform in a vehicle built for home comfort, trying to understand motorhome tourism as a phenomenon. Therefore, this study functions as an entry point in order to understand what these motorhomers are describing and making salient in their Algarve experience.

Results

Table 29.2 provides a profile of survey respondents. It was found that the majority of motorhomers who visit the Algarve during the winter season were mostly foreign. France was the most represented country and also the largest contributor to the share of new visitors to the Algarve, with the UK and Germany following well behind France. The majority of travellers are *Ulyssean adults*, individuals who continue to seek new adventures and opportunities in their later years, and the vast majority are married or travelling as a couple. Sixty-four percent of respondents also suggest that both partners drive. Of those surveyed, only 7% reported being employed, with 93% having retired, an expected result considering the average age of the population interviewed. For these reasons we name them "grey movers" and since they choose to drive to follow the sun during winter months they are classified as long-term tourists (average length of stay of 39 days). The Algarve is a relatively new destination choice (first visited in the previous five years) for 74%, and 33% of respondents were visiting the Algarve for the first time.

How do motorhome grey movers reach the Algarve during the winter season?

All movements are dynamic: the motorhomers depart from their home city/country and they all intend to reach the Algarve (Table 29.3). Constant movement does not favour the development of normal relationships between citizens and community (Cresswell 2006), so we characterise the trip from departure to the Algarve based on the assumption that this information would help to construct the movement in a deep way. The large majority (65%) of French motorhome users drive directly to the Algarve. The French motorhome users mentioned the

Table 29.2 Profile of survey respondents

Country of origin	France	40%
	United Kingdom	19%
	Germany	15%
	The Netherlands	10%
	Sweden	4%
	Spain	2%
	Portugal	1%
Age	>61 Years	80%
Marital status	Couple/married	88%
Highest education level	Primary school	12%
	High school	58%
	Higher education	30%
Frequency of visit	First visit	33%
	Return visit	66%
Period since first visit	1–5 years	74%
	6–15 years	17%
	>15 years	9%
Length of stay	Average length of stay	39 days

Table 29.3 Travel strategies for motorhome drivers travelling to the Algarve

Country of origin	Travel straight to the Algarve	Tour before arriving at the Algarve
France	35%	65%
United Kingdom	58%	42%
Germany	83%	17%
The Netherlands	80%	20%
Sweden	84%	16%

abandonment of Morocco as a tourist destination several times; for many years, the French used to drive to Morocco (Viallon 2012). Comments included:

> We no longer felt safe in Morocco, the nights were "too long" and the feeling of insecurity was always present. The Moroccan community ceased to be hospitable, even to be rude in some specific situations.
>
> *(Informant, France)*

> Morocco as a destination is no longer a safe place for the French.
>
> *(Informant, France)*

Drivers from Germany, the Netherlands or Sweden seem to prefer touring around spending several nights in different places. However, they opt for the Algarve when they decide to make a long stay. The average stay in the Algarve by nationality of motorhome users changes depending on the proximity of the country. The Spanish have the shortest length of stay in the Algarve (<10 days), just as the Swedes (>50 days), Norwegians (45 days) and Dutch (34 days), from more distant countries, stay longer than average in the Algarve.

Meanings ascribed to motorhome tourism in the Algarve during the winter season

The most common meanings related to travelling by motorhome were: experiencing nature, self-esteem, freedom, relaxation, social interaction, adventure/challenge, escape and culture/knowledge seeking.

Experiencing nature

In addition to natural features being a relevant topic of motorhome practices, experiencing nature was also a considerable meaning. This idea was symbolised by natural aesthetic beauty. A few motorhome users expressed this:

> If we stay the winter period at home, we don't have the opportunity to have contact with nature so often, to see such beautiful scenery, and go for walks. (informant France; informant, the Netherlands) This is our sanctuary ....
>
> *(Informant, Germany)*

> The sea view, the rocks, the mountains .... I used to live near the sea. (Informant, France) Because it is beautiful, just quiet with the silence of nature.
>
> *(Informant, UK)*

I love flowers, birds and it is fantastic to walk with William (dog).

(Informant, UK)

The amazing Algarve light, and the unforgettable sunsets, the winter feels like spring.

(Informant, Sweden)

It is fabulous to benefit from the calm of quieter winter months and at the same time enjoy the walks on the golden sand.

(Informant, the Netherlands)

Freedom/escape

Most motorhome users describe their motorhome option as a lifestyle, much more than a vehicle to reach destination(s). We could not compare it with a plane, bus or even a car, but as technological change has impacted the world, bringing access to many options for travel, the extent of current motorhome or other Recreational Vehicle (RV) availability continues to be viewed as a "key to escape" or a symbol of gaining independent freedom:

When I am in my motorhome, I feel free, relaxed, on the open road.

(Informant, France)

I decide when and where we go after, there is flexibility, you can move to wherever you want.

(Informant, Sweden)

I am able to choose silence or not, more freedom, plus choices.

(Informant, Germany)

As long as I can, I will be in my motorhome till I die.

(Informant, France)

It's a way to escape …. the harsh environment where I live, many refugees are being hosted in my city, I'm still getting used to the idea.

(Informant, Germany)

The retirement is paradise, before my day to day executive, I was always in stress, with schedules for everything, many trips, airports, always with dead line … traveling by motorhome is tranquility, there are no scheduling requirements, we can enjoy the day.

(Informant, France)

The mobile motorhome users' fluid lifestyle is reflected by 56% of respondents deciding to travel and visit other places before reaching the Algarve, while the remainder preferred to drive directly to the Algarve. The majority of respondents were long-term tourists who drive for two or three months once or twice a year. The freedom or escape can be understood as a way of being young again (Patterson et al. 2011), with no obligations, no rules and no dates. Home represents security, tradition and stagnation, quite the opposite of courage, mobility and freedom (Blaakilde & Nilsson 2013). However, there are many motorhome users who behave as if they were at home, so being a motorhome user is not necessarily a synonym for freedom. We will return to this question later.

Relaxation

Multiple references to the terms relax and rest were made by participants in surveys and interviews. Relaxing and resting appears to be the main activity that is most often mentioned by the grey movers. Enjoying retirement is also tied to the ability to rest and relax. There is no obligation to perform tasks or work but the desire for rest and relaxation could not be the intrinsic motivation as the possibility of rest and relaxation is guaranteed; however, at this age they require days of peace and tranquillity. One participant explained the importance of relaxing and resting among grey movers. Driving for months in a motorhome with one's partner could be difficult, so sleep and rest is crucial to avoid bad moods.

> We just drive during the daylight, never at night, because we have got plenty of time, so things could be done in a slow and relaxed way.
>
> *(Informant, France)*

> Now it's possible to enjoy the day – we have spare time during the day.
>
> *(Informant, Germany)*

Social interaction

Interaction with others seems to often be mentioned by the motorhome users that we interviewed. It is part of the travel experience, although contact with the local community is briefly referred to, and most of the contact described is related with practical episodes (shopping, the vet, the police, petrol stations, repair cars). It appeared that the majority of interactions occur at motorhome ASAs, line-ups and diverse stops. It also appeared that much of the conversation shared by motorhome users is an exchange of tips or suggestions.

> It is an opportunity to meet people. I tend to look at their license plate – usually when we decide to park it is important to see the nationality of our neighbour, if I want silence I never park near by a Spanish or Italian couple – they usually to talk loud.
>
> *(Informant, Germany)*

> Although we have a habit of travelling with a small group of friends, we are happy to meet new people, one of the pleasures of travelling around Europe was meeting new people with similar interests and lifestyle.
>
> *(Informant, France)*

> I do not aim to know anyone else, just me, my wife and our dog.
>
> *(Informant, UK)*

Drive challenge/adventure

Travelling by motorhome is an adventure – it can be different every day and motorhome users may have a trip planning strategy or a vague idea of where to stay overnight. The challenge of driving the motorhome and being independent is regarded as good for the grey movers' self-esteem. The majority of respondent couples both drive. Only 41% stay only in the Algarve region and the remaining 59% visit other regions with Lisbon, Porto and Alentejo being the places that received most interest for a visit.

> We like to drive/travel in the off season when in south of Europe it's cooler, the accommodation rates are cheaper, where roads and highways are quieter and [there is] less traffic.
>
> *(Informant, Sweden)*

> I want to drive my motorhome until my last days.
>
> *(Informant, UK)*

Rather than being organised or structured, the grey movers prefer instead to do their own thing and seek out experiences that serve to offer a sense of freedom and adventure in their retirement years (Mings 1997; Onyx & Leonard 2005).

Exploring the Algarve experience

Travelling with a motorhome allows more direct and easier contact with nature, even when motorhome users opt for ASAs (motorhome parking) or campgrounds. Walking and biking were the activities most quoted (40% and 37% respectively), 36% of the participants have a dog and 56% own a bicycle. Social interaction (such as storytelling, playing cards and bingo) are good examples of what they describe as typical days for motorhomers, and sending emails or Skyping, either to contact home or other friends (on the road or not) are practices that many motorhome users perform in their regular day when they are away from home. New communication technologies make the virtual co-presence of family and friends possible, allowing everyday relationships to continue while touring. The use of a caravan or motorhome also facilitates the establishment and continuance of many domestic routines (Holloway 2009). Not surprising therefore, informants mentioned that low-cost airlines provide an easy and inexpensive means to fly home and return to the Algarve in a few days. They do not miss any family birthdays, medical appointments or other commitments.

Traveller networks are regarded as the best source of information regarding the best places to stay, and in particular the location of good, free camping places, that are usually not advertised, although only 10% of respondents claim to only overnight in informal locations. From the survey, it appears that 45% of people learned about their current campsite from other travellers, 49% learned from brochures or private maps, while only 11% learned of it through an information centre (allowing for multiple information sources).

Conclusions

This chapter gives a good illustration of how movements, meanings and practices (Cresswell 2006) can be applied to point out and give more visibility to the motorhome phenomenon in the Algarve during the winter season. Figure 29.2 identifies the main tourism factors (push and pull) for motorhome practices. Other elements are interlinked with motivation to influence motorhome users, such as the personal insights like personality characteristics and lifestyles, as well as emotional states.

There is an almost absolute dominance of foreign nationals during the winter season. They are almost all European retirees, driving from north of Portugal and following the sun, which is

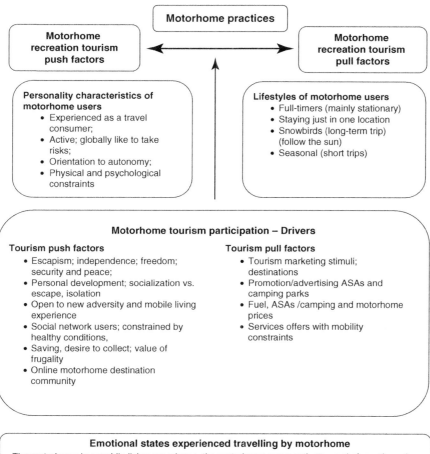

Figure 29.2 Drivers of motorhome tourism participation, practices and emotional states.

the main motivation of their trip. They drive mostly on secondary roads or toll-free highways. Some prefer to drive direct from home to the Algarve destination and others like to visit other countries (especially along the coast of the Mediterranean) on the way. The majority of expenditure is on fuel, accommodation and meals (restaurants or local markets and supermarkets). Previous word of mouth from friends or others motorhomers is one of the most used vehicles for information in this community and they also search for specific information on blogs and web pages focused on this theme.

Doing tourism with a motorhome it is not synonymous with a desire to be alone, independent or with no links to homeland (Lorentzen 2015). You are "home" but you are also "tourists". Based on the grey movers that we analysed, freedom and independence were stressed but in a sense that gave security, self-esteem, life extension and above all freedom of choice. The motorhome users who visit the Algarve during the winter season neither park nor drive alone. The results suggest that grey movers do not travel to escape life, but so that life does not escape them. Cresswell (2008) outlines a notion of constellations of mobility that entails considering the historical existence of fragile senses of movement, meaning and practice, with each entailing forms of mobility politics and regulation. However, further research is needed to fully understand why people choose to take holidays of this type, how they choose their destinations and how they behave and interact while on holiday. Moreover, the socio-cultural, economic and environmental impacts of this rapidly growing sector are yet to be fully studied. Nevertheless, as this chapter has demonstrated when considering mobility, we need to deal with contextual as well as spatial and temporal and more specifically, *mobilized situatedness of interaction* in particular contexts and relations.

Acknowledgements

This research was the result of a collaborative relationship between the following partners: Regional Commission for Coordination and Development of the Algarve, Comissão de Coordenação e Desenvolvimento Regional do Algarve (CCDRA), The National Republican Guard, Guarda Nacional Republicana (GNR), the City Council of Castro Marin and the Camara Municipal de Castro Marim (CMCM). Special thanks also to Raquel Costa and Marília Poeira for the professionalism and willingness demonstrated during fieldwork. To José Brito for his knowledge and Catarina Cruz's support. To the City Council of Castro Marim; and a special thanks to Tenente Coronel J. A. Palhau (GNR) and the members of this force during the fieldwork.

References

Abramsson, M. and Andersson, E. K. (2012) 'Residential mobility patterns of elderly –Leaving the house for an apartment', *Housing Studies*, 27 (5): 582–604.

Adey, P. (2004) 'Secured and sorted mobilities: Examples from the airport', *Surveillance & Society*, 1 (4): 500–519.

Adey, P. (2006) 'If mobility is everything then it is nothing: Towards a relational politics of (im) mobilities', *Mobilities*, 1 (1): 75–94.

ANA Portugal Airports (ANA) (2016) Os nossos Aeroportos. [online] Available at: https://www.ana.pt/pt/negocios/aviacao/os-nossos-aeroportos

Blaakilde, A. L. and Nilsson, G. (2013) 'Nordic seniors on the move: Mobility and migration in later life', *Lund Studies in Arts and Cultural Sciences*, 4.

Bourdieu, P. (1990) *The Logic of Practice*. Stanford, CA: Stanford University Press.

Brooker, E. and Joppe, M. (2013) 'Trends in camping and outdoor hospitality – An international review', *Journal of Outdoor Recreation and Tourism*, 3–4: 1–6.

Bruner, E. (2005) *Culture on Tour*. Chicago: University of Chicago Press.

Büscher, M. and Urry, J. (2009) 'Mobile methods and the empirical', *European Journal of Social Theory*, 12 (1): 99–116.

Büscher, M., Urry, J. and Witchger, K. (eds) (2010) *Mobile Methods*. London and New York: Routledge.

Caravanning Industry Association (CIVD) (2016) Market analysis: Overview, CIVD. [online] Available at: https://www.civd.de/en/market-figures/market-analysis.html

Charmaz, K. (2000) 'Grounded theory: Objectivist and constructivist methods'. In N. Denzin and Y. S. Lincoln (eds) *Handbook of Qualitative Research*, 2nd ed. Thousand Oaks, CA: Sage, 509–535.

Chen, S. C. and Shoemaker, S. (2014) 'Age and cohort effects: The American senior tourism market', *Annals of Tourism Research*, 48: 58–75.

Cheng, J.-C. and Chen, B. T. (2006) 'Growing a house on wheels: Understanding and promoting RV as a tourism activity and industry in Taiwan'. In *International Society of Travel and Tourism Educators. Imagining the Future of Travel and Tourism Education. Annual Conference Proceedings of Research and Academic Papers Vol. XVIII*, October 12–14. Las Vegas, U.S., 315–328.

Cook, S., Shaw, J. and Simpson, P. (2015) 'Jography: Exploring meanings, experiences and spatialities of recreational road-running', *Mobilities*, 11 (5): 744–769.

Counts, D. A. and Counts, D. R. (1992) 'They're my family now: The creation of community among RVers', *Anthropologica*, 34 (2): 153–182.

Counts, D. A. and Counts, D. R. (2004) *Over the Next Hill: Ethnography of RVing Seniors in North America*, 2nd ed. Peterborough, Canada: Broadview Press.

Cresswell, T. (2006) *On the Move: Mobility in the Modern Western World*. New York: Routledge.

Cresswell, T. (2008) *Constellations of Mobility*. Department of Geography, Royal Holoway, University of London. Available at: http://www.dtesis.univr.it/documenti/Avviso/all/all181066.pdf

Cresswell, T. (2010) 'Towards a politics of mobility', *Environment and Planning D: Society and Space*, 28 (1): 17–31.

Cridland, S. (2008). An Analysis of the Winter Movement of Grey Nomads to Northern Australia: Planning for Increase Senior Visitation. PhD. James Cook University, Cairns, Australia.

Dias, J. A. and Domingues, A. (2016) Apresentação CCDRA, Perfil do Autocaravanista que visita o Algarve durante o Inverno, RAARA – Rede de Acolhimento das Autocaravanas Região Algarve, 31 de maio 2016 DL 39/2008. [online] Available at: http://www.oasrn.org/upload/apoio/legislacao/pdf/tur392008.pdf

European Caravan Federation (ECF). (2016) Caravans and Motor Caravans Indicators. [online] Retrieved from: http://www.e-c-f.com/index.php?id=25 (accessed 12 May 2016).

Eurostat European Commission (2012) *Methodological Manual for Tourism Statistics. Version 1.2, European Union (EU)*. Luxembourg: Publications Office of the EU.

Hall, C. M. (2005) *Tourism: Rethinking the Social Science of Mobility*. Harlow, UK: Pearson.

Hannam, K., Sheller, M. and Urry, J. (2006) 'Editorial: Mobilities, immobilities and moorings', *Mobilities*, 1 (1): 1–22.

Hardy, A. and Gretzel, U. (2011) 'Why we travel this way: An exploration into the motivations of recreational vehicle users'. In D. Carson and B. Prideaux (eds) *Drive Tourism: Trends and Emerging Markets*. London: Routledge, 194–223.

Hardy, A., Hanson, D. and Gretzel, U. (2012) 'Online representations of RVing neo-tribes in the USA and Australia', *Journal of Tourism and Cultural Change*, 10 (3): 219–232.

Hardy, A., Gretzel, U. and Hanson, D. (2013) 'Travelling neo-tribes: Conceptualising recreational vehicle users', *Journal of Tourism and Cultural Change*, 11 (1–2): 48–60.

Hartwigsen, G. and Null, R. (1991) 'Full-timers: Who are these older people who are living in their RVs?', *Journal of Housing for the Elderly*, 7 (1): 133–148.

Hillman, W. (2013) 'Grey nomads travelling in Queensland, Australia: Social and health needs', *Ageing and Society*, 33 (4): 579–597.

Holloway, D., Green, L. and Holloway, D. (2011) 'The intratourist gaze: Grey nomads and "other tourists"', *Tourist Studies*, 11 (3): 235–252.

Holloway, D. J. (2009) Grey Nomads: Retirement, Leisure and Travel in the Australian Context. PhD. Edith Cowan University, Joondalup, Australia.

Hsu, C. and Kang, S. (2009) 'Chinese urban mature travellers' motivation and constraints by decision autonomy', *Journal of Travel & Tourism Marketing*, 26 (7): 703–721.

International Trade Administration (ITA) (2016) *2016 Top Markets Report. Recreational Tansportation: Sector Snapshot*. Washington, DC: ITA, Department of Commerce, United States of America.

Landin, K. (2015) Nomad Cities. Investigating Spatial Practices within the Fluid Network Societies of the American RV Community. Master's Thesis. The Swedish School of Planning, Blekinge Institute of Technology, Karlskrona, Sweden. [online] Available at: http://www.diva-portal.org/smash/get/diva2:818023/FULLTEXT03

Lashley, C. (2015) 'Researching snails on holiday: An agenda for caravanning and caravanners?', *Research in Hospitality Management*, 5 (2): 115–122.

Laurier, E. (2004) 'Doing office work on the motorway', *Theory, Culture Society*, 21 (4–5): 261–277.

Lorentzen, R. (2015) Home or on the Road. A study of Motor-Home Tourism as a Norwegian Phenomenon. Master's Thesis. Finnmark Faculty, Department of Tourism and Northern Studies, The Arctic University of Norway, Tromsø, Norway.

Lue, C., Crompton, J. and Fesenmairer, D. (1993) 'Conceptualisations of multi-destination pleasure trips', *Annals of Tourism Research*, 20 (2): 289–301.

McLeish, J. A. B. (1976) *The Ulyssean Adult: Creativity in the Middle & Later Years*. Toronto and New York: McGraw-Hill Ryerson Ltd.

MacTavish, K., Eley, M. and Salamon, S. (2006) 'Housing vulnerability among rural trailer-park households', *Georgetown Journal on Poverty Law & Policy*, 13 (1): 95–118.

Mahadevan, R. (2014) 'Understanding senior self-drive tourism in Australia using a contingency behavior model', *Journal of Travel Research*, 53 (2): 252–259.

Middleton, J. (2009) '"Stepping in time": Walking, time, and space in the city', *Environment and Planning A*, 41 (8): 1943–1961.

Mings, R. and McHugh, K. (1995) 'Wintering in American sunbelt: Linking place and behavior', *Journal of Tourism Studies*, 6 (2): 56–61.

Mings, R. (1997) 'Tracking "snowbirds" in Australia: Winter sun seekers in far north Queensland', *Australian Geographical Studies*, 35 (2): 168–182.

Olsen, M. (2003) 'Tourism themed routes: A Queensland perspective', *Journal of Vacation Marketing*, 8 (4): 331–341.

Onyx, J. and Leonard, R. (2005) 'Australian grey nomads and American snowbirds: Similarities and differences', *The Journal of Tourism Studies*, 16 (1): 61– 68.

Patterson, I. R. (2006) *Growing Older: Tourism and Leisure Behaviour of Older Adults*. Cambridge, MA: CABI International.

Patterson, I., Pegg, S. and Litster, J. (2011) 'Grey nomads on tour: A revolution in travel and tourism for older adults', *Tourism Analysis*, 16 (3): 283–294.

Pearce, P. (1999) 'Touring for pleasure: Studies of the self drive travel market', *Tourism Recreation Research*, 24 (1): 35–42.

Prideaux, B. and Carson, D. (eds) (2010) *Drive Tourism: Trends and Emerging Markets*. London and New York: Routledge.

Prideaux, B., Wei, S. and Ruys, H. (2001) 'The senior drive market in Australia', *Journal of Vacation Marketing*, 7 (3): 209–219.

Recreation Vehicle Industry Association (RVIA) (2015) RV Business Indicators. [online] Available at: http://www.rvia.org/?ESID=indicators

Scott, N. (2002) 'Product market perspective of self-drive tourism', In D. Carson, I. Waller and N. Scott (eds) *Drive Tourism: Up the Wall and Around the Bend*. Melbourne: Common Ground, 81–90.

Sheller, M. (2014) 'The new mobilities paradigm for a live sociology', *Current Sociology*, 62 (6): 789–811.

Sheller, M. and Urry, J. (2006) 'The new mobilities paradigm', *Environment and Planning A*, 38 (2): 207–226.

Sheng, X., Simpson, P. M. and Siguaw, J. A. (2014) 'U.S. winter migrants' park community attributes: An importance–performance analysis', *Tourism Management*, 43: 55–67.

Shih, H. Y. (2006) 'Network characteristics of drive tourism destinations: An application of network analysis in tourism', *Tourism Management*, 27 (5): 1029–1039.

Spinney, J. (2009) 'Cycling the city: Movement, meaning and method', *Geography Compass*, 3 (2): 817–835.

Turismo de Portugal: Algarve (2016) Plano de Marketing Estratégico para o Turismo do Algarve, 2015–2018. [online] Available at: http://estrategia.turismodeportugal.pt/sites/default/files/Plano%20Mkt%20Turismo%20Algarve%202015_2018.pdf

Urry, J. (2007) *Mobilities*. Cambridge, UK: Polity.

Uteng, T. P. and Cresswell, T. (eds) (2016) *Gendered Mobilities*. London and New York: Routledge.

Van Heerden, N. and Van Heerden, C. H. (2008) 'Leisure motorhoming: The case of the motorhome club of South Africa', *South African Journal for Research in Sport, Physical Education and Recreation*, 30 (1): 125–136.

Viallon, P. (2012) 'Retired snowbirds', *Annals of Tourism Research*, 39 (4): 2073–2091.

Wu, M. Y. and Pearce, P. L. (2014) 'Chinese recreational vehicle users in Australia: A netnographic study of tourist motivation', *Tourism Management*, 43: 22–35.

Wu, M. Y. and Pearce, P. L. (2016) 'The rally experience: Exploring motivation patterns of Australian Grey Nomads', *Journal of Destination Marketing & Management*, 6 (4): 407–415.

Ye, X. (2015) A Netnography of Goal Pursuit in Retirement Travel. PhD. University of Ottawa, Ontario, Canada.

PART VI

The future of second homes

30

THE FUTURE OF SECOND HOMES

C. Michael Hall and Dieter K. Müller

Introduction

Second homes have become an increasingly important component of both tourism and housing studies. They directly and indirectly contribute a significant number of domestic and international visitors to destinations but, importantly with respect to long-term destination development, often contribute to longer-term retirement, lifestyle and amenity migration that can have significant economic and social effects on communities. They also contribute substantially to regional economies in their own right, whether from construction and maintenance, or the expenditure of occupants. In a number of countries, second homes have also become a significant part of household investment strategies, particularly given the potential for short-term letting and holiday rentals, including via companies such as Airbnb. Second homes are therefore deeply embedded in notions and understandings of circulation, home, mobilities and multiple dwelling as well as their wider impacts, planning and governance. Importantly, and as Müller and Hall (2004) pointed out, although second homes have often been positioned in relation to counter-urbanisation and "sea change" movements, second homes indicate the development of fluid patterns of mobility and place relationships. 'These, rather than setting the "rural" and the "urban" as opposing categories, as often traditionally envisaged, position them as part of an interrelated and networked whole' (Müller & Hall, 2004: 273). The second home therefore cannot really be understood outside of the relationship to the first home, and vice versa. They are, after all, homes.

There is no internationally accepted definition of a second home. The term acts as an umbrella expression for a variety of cognate terms including the "cabin", "cottage", "crib", "holiday home", "hut", "leisure home", "recreational home", "summer home", "summer house", "vacation home" and "weekend home" as well as "dacha" in Russia, and "bach" in New Zealand. The common element of these terms is that the primary use of the second home is leisure and recreation oriented. Originally, the second home concept was geared towards non-commercial residences but increasingly the term is being applied to second residences that are also available for short-term holiday accommodation. Caravans, mobile homes and houseboats are also sometimes included as categories of second homes in some jurisdictions, although most research attention is given to non-mobile second homes. However, the differences between mobile and non-mobile second homes is often quite fluid because of the growth of "permanent" caravan parks and mobile home sites that are used for second homes and retirement migration. This mobile second home trend is also being reinforced by the growth of interest in "tiny houses" – small, often mobile, self-contained houses occupying limited space and having a low environmental imprint. The analysis of second homes is further complicated because the different approaches to defining second homes means that although their extent can usually be recognised at a national level, such figures are not readily comparable at an international scale. It is unlikely that these issues of definition will be solved in the foreseeable future.

The field of second homes has seen substantial growth since the seminal work of Coppock (1977) and the more recent volume by Hall and Müller (2004) (see Chapter 1, this volume). Tourism and leisure researchers and geographers are the major sources of publications on second homes, a situation that reflects the dominance by geographers of research on second homes until the late 1990s and early 2000s. More recently, research in anthropology, ethnology, sociology, housing studies and planning journals have become significant. The work of Paris (2009, 2010) from a housing studies perspective is particularly important because of the emphasis on the improved understanding of the relationship between second homes and owner investment strategies. A broader appreciation of the housing stock context of second homes also provides for a much-improved understanding of often simplistic criticism of second homes serving to displace permanent populations, an issue that will be returned to briefly below. Major approaches include surveys, interviews and regional case studies. Ethnography has become increasingly used as a research method since the late 1990s. Statistical and spatial analysis has often been limited by the difficulties attached to identifying second homes in official databases but has been growing in strength, especially in the European context. Regardless of approach it appears likely that second homes will continue to be an important research topic for years to come. However, a number of significant themes and issues can be identified that may provide some new directions for research on second homes.

Sustainability

Sustainability is emerging as a new challenge for second homes. Many second home owners appear to perceive themselves as environmentally friendly (Long & Hoogendoorn 2013; Hiltunen et al. 2016). However, there is growing recognition of the pressures that second homes can place on environments, especially with respect to sewage and nutrient loads, and water quality. These can be managed, but the growth of new second homes presents substantial environmental and aesthetic challenges, especially in amenity landscapes. Permanent homes, of course, can have the same impacts, but because second homes serve a different housing function they are often framed differently as an environmental issue, while their fluid populations may place stress on public services, such as water, waste treatment, health services at periods of peak demand for which such services usually have not been designed for (Gunko & Medvedev 2016).

Another area of environmental research is the extent to which second homes contribute to wider emissions arising from travel and lifestyle consumption. It has been argued that if people would not travel to their domestic second homes, they would potentially travel abroad which would be even worse for the environment. Gallent, Mace, and Tewdwr-Jones (2005) speculate that although second homes are a "luxury good", 'if we take a practical view, that people with surplus income will spend that income in one way or another, then it could be argued that discouraging second home ownership in Britain could lead to alternatives that are even more detrimental to the environment' (p. 62). Nevertheless, there is limited knowledge of the extent of greenhouse emissions arising from second home travel and its relative contributions to tourism emissions, and the extent to which domestic second home tourism may substitute for international and long-haul travel.

In the case of Finland, Adamiak et al. (2016) found that owners and users of domestic second homes travel for leisure purposes less frequently than others. But this can potentially be explained by the limited time budgets that people have for travel, and time taken for second home visits therefore excludes its use for other travel (Hall 2005). Significantly, this replacement effect mostly affects domestic trips, and not long-haul international trips, which cause the largest share of travel-related emissions. In other words, second home ownership and access may potentially reduce the number of trips people take but not reduce the distance travelled. As a result, when looking at the amount of CO_2 emissions, Adamiak et al. (2016) found that second home owners produce significantly more CO_2 by their overall leisure mobility than others (users or non-users). This finding reflected that of Gössling et al. (2009) who suggested that hypermobile travellers own more second homes than the French population on average (+25%). 'Rather than be a substitute for high emission travel, for the majority of second home owners the second home is instead part of an overall highly mobile leisure lifestyle' (Adamiak et al. 2016). Nevertheless, further research may shed light on the potential for future substitution of long-haul holiday travel by domestic second homes.

Future demand

Another significant issue in a number of countries in which second homes are a significant part of the culture and cultural heritage is the future prospects for younger generations to take on family second homes. In the Swedish case, Strandin Pers et al. (Chapter 23, this volume) note that the strength of bonds to properties are stronger among owners who inherited the property as compared to owners who had bought it. Although the average age of second home users appears to be increasing (Müller et al. 2010), demand for second home access remains. In a national survey of users of Finnish second homes, Pitkänen et al. (2014) asked those already using second homes how they would estimate their annual use to develop in the next five years. Youth respondents estimated their use of second homes would remain the same more often than other respondents; 14% said they would increase their use of the second home in the future; 81% reported their use would remain the same; and only 6% estimated that their stays at the second home would decrease.

In the Finnish survey, regardless of current use of second homes, all respondents (n = 1189) were asked if they planned to acquire a second home in the future. Altogether, 44% of Generation Y planned to own a second home in the future, 7% during the next 10 years, and 37% after that. Forty-one percent estimated that it is likely that they or a member of their household will inherit a second home at some stage in the future. Interestingly, given concerns over the future of second homes in Finland, Generation Y respondents were even more eager to acquire a second home in the future than the rest of the respondents (Pitkänen et al. 2014). However, there was also some suggestion that such second home use may be in addition to other mobility rather than a substitute.

Outside of family and inherited second homes, future demand appears to remain strong. However, arguably, such demand also needs to be understood in the context of housing and investment regimes and the financial advantage that they may offer for the purchase of second homes as real estate properties rather than as a lifestyle choice (Paris 2009, 2010) and as an example of place attachment. One of the longer-term studies required, therefore, is to examine how purchasing decisions affect longer-term use of a second home, including inter-generational use and relationships to place.

Future use

As noted above, significant differences may exist in the use of a property and relationships to place depending on whether the second home was inherited or purchased. To this we can also add previous access. The adoption of life course approaches to second homes may help provide further information as to how the nature of a property and its role and meaning in the lives of owners and users changes over time. There is substantial evidence that in many locations the occasionally used second home may gain increasing use and become a de facto primary residence, or even the solo residence, once owners retire (Osbaldiston & Picken 2014). In such cases, owners may become lifestyle migrants (Osbaldiston et al. 2015). However, this process can place significant pressures onto community social and health services unless there are support measures in place. In some jurisdictions, this may require transfers of public funds to help provide relevant infrastructure and services. Indeed, in the drive by some regions to attract second home developments, the longer-term implications of potential retirement migration may not have been fully considered in the evaluation of the costs and benefits of second homes.

Despite potential longer-term implications for infrastructure, second homes can potentially help maintain the availability of cheap domestic tourism to high amenity areas and the visitation rates of "others" (friends and family) to second homes may help counter narratives of the "emptiness" of second home destinations (Osbaldiston & Picken 2014). It also demonstrates the role these places have in providing for tourism, in evening out seasonality and injecting money into destination economies beyond that immediately provided by the second home owner (Müller & Hoogendoorn 2013; Osbaldiston & Picken 2014). Nevertheless, a major emerging issue for second home development is the extent to which properties become holiday rentals and how such properties not only are accepted by the local community but also the formal accommodation sector. The commercialisation of the second home may therefore also rekindle the debate over displacement effects in some locations. Although, perhaps of even greater value, is the need to develop an improved understanding of second homes in the context of housing policy, and house affordability issues, as well as the investment rationales of individuals for the second home over time (Hall 2015; Stergiou et al. 2017).

The future of the (second) home

As a number of the chapters in this volume have made clear, the second home cannot be understood in isolation, either from the primary home or from the wider social and environmental forces in which it is embedded. Despite the re-emergence of nationalisation as a political force and opposition to migrants in many communities, the further internationalisation of second homes can be expected given their role in regional development and the desire to attract international capital (Paris 2010; Hall 2015). Although, it is possible that more effort will be taken by governments to encourage the second home to be used for residential tourism or become a springboard for high-end economic migration, rather than allowing them to stay empty given public concerns over housing access and affordability (Osbourne 2017; Pawson 2017). In Australia, for example, as of January 2018, anyone who owns a home in Melbourne and leaves it empty for more than six months will face an annual tax equal to 1% of its value. The 2017 Australian federal government budget also brought in an annual charge for foreign investors who buy-to-leave. Any new purchasers who leave a property unused for six months face an annual charge of at least AU$5,500 (Osbourne 2017).

Most second home owners appear content with their second home lives (Lundmark & Marjavaara 2013; Adamiak et al. 2015), even when faced with generalised local discontent

(Lipkina & Hall 2014). Except when purchased purely as a real estate investment, the second home *is* a home. It is an important setting for place and social attachments in a highly mobile and changing world (Kaltenborn 1997a, 1997b; Kelly & Hosking 2008). Second home owners and users are engaged in multiple communities and in multiple homes. Increasing multiple dwelling implies that second home communities can be seen as nodes and anchors for bundles of individuals' time-space trajectories. As a result, second home communities and the second home itself may be even more important to individuals and families than the so-called primary home, especially when they are framed as something which is more permanent in a changing world and as somewhere to "escape". Over time, second homes are important places of transition that contribute to individual and collective identities (White & White 2004), while potentially providing a place to call home at all stages of the life course. They are places where significant events occur and, in many cases, they will become the residence to retire to, or at least spend much of the latter periods of one's life when there is time for more play and less work. Second homes, like any home, therefore reflect something important about us, the way we live our lives, and how we would prefer to live them both now and in the future. Accordingly, we should regard them not only as potential common ground or elite space, but as significant places for research on the lives and lived experiences of individuals and the society in which they live.

References

Adamiak, C., Hall, C. M., Hiltunen, M. J. and Pitkänen, K. (2016) 'Substitute or addition to hypermobile lifestyles? Second home mobility and Finnish CO_2 emissions', *Tourism Geographies*, 8 (2), 129–151.

Adamiak, C., Vepsäläinen, M., Strandell, A., Hiltunen, M. J., Pitkänen, K., Hall, C. M., Rinne, J., Hannonen, O., Paloniemi, R. and Åkerlund, U. (2015) *Second Home Tourism in Finland: Perceptions of Citizens and Municipalities on the State and Development of Second Home Tourism*. Reports of the Finnish Environment Institute 22, Helsinki, Finland: SYKE.

Coppock, J. T. (ed.) (1977) *Second Homes: Curse or Blessing?* Oxford: Pergamon.

Gallent, N., Mace, N. and Tewdwr-Jones, M. (2005) *Second Homes. European Perspectives and UK policies*. Aldershot, UK: Ashgate.

Gössling, S., Ceron, J. P., Dubios, G. and Hall, C. M. (2009) 'Hypermobile travellers', In S. Gössling and P. Upham (eds) *Climate Change and Aviation*. London: Earthscan, 131–149.

Gunko, M. and Medvedev, A. (2016) '"Seasonal suburbanization" in Moscow oblast: Challenges of household waste management', *Geographia Polonica*, 89 (4), 473–484.

Hall, C. M. (2005) *Tourism: Rethinking the Social Science of Mobility*. Harlow, UK: Prentice-Hall.

Hall, C. M. (2015) 'Second homes: Planning, policy and governance', *Journal of Policy Research in Tourism, Leisure & Events*, 7 (1): 1–14.

Hall, C. M. and Müller, D. K. (2004) *Tourism, Mobility and Second Homes: Between Elite Landscape and Common Ground*. Clevedon: Channel View.

Hiltunen, M. J., Pitkänen, K. and Halseth, G. (2016) 'Environmental perceptions of second home tourism impacts in Finland', *Local Environment*, 21 (10), 1198–1214.

Kaltenborn, B. P. (1997a) 'Nature of place attachment: A study among recreation homeowners in Southern Norway', *Leisure Sciences*, 19 (3): 175–189.

Kaltenborn, B. P. (1997b) 'Recreation homes in natural settings: Factors affecting place attachment', *Norsk Geografisk Tidsskrift*, 51 (4): 187–198.

Kelly, G. and Hosking, K. (2008) 'Nonpermanent residents, place attachment, and "sea change" communities', *Environment and Behavior*, 40 (4): 575–594.

Lipkina, O. and Hall, C. M. (2014) 'Russian second home owners in Eastern Finland: Involvement in the local community'. In M. Janoschka and H. Haas (eds) *Contested Spatialities of Lifestyle Migration*, London: Routledge, 158–173.

Long, D. P. and Hoogendoorn, G. (2013) 'Second home owners' perceptions of polluted environment: The case of Hartbeespoort'. *South African Geographical Journal*, 95 (1): 91–104.

Lundmark, L. and Marjavaara, R. (2013) 'Second home ownership: A blessing for all?', *Scandinavian Journal of Hospitality and Tourism*, 13 (4): 281–298.

Müller, D. and Hall, C. M. (2004) 'The future of second homes'. In C. M. Hall and D. Müller (eds) *Tourism, Mobility and Second Homes: Between Elite Landscape and Common Ground*, Clevedon: Channel View, 273–278.

Müller, D. K. and Hoogendoorn, G. (2013) 'Second homes: Curse or blessing? A review 36 years later', *Scandinavian Journal of Hospitality and Tourism*, 13 (4): 353–369.

Müller, D. K., Nordin, U. and Marjavaara, R. (2010) *Fritidsboendes relationer till den svenska landsbygden.* Umeå: Kulturgeografiska institutionen, Umeå universitet.

Osbaldiston, N. and Picken, F. (2014) 'Ongoing and future relationships of second home owners with places in coastal Australia: An empirical case study from Eastern Victoria', *Tourism Review International*, 18 (3): 137–152.

Osbaldiston, N., Picken, F. and Duffy, M. (2015) 'Characteristics and future intentions of second homeowners: A case study from Eastern Victoria, Australia', *Journal of Policy Research in Tourism, Leisure and Events*, 7 (1): 62–76.

Osbourne, H. (2017) 'Location, location, location: How the world is tackling issue of empty homes', *The Guardian*, 2 August.

Paris, C. (2009) 'Re-positioning second homes within housing studies: Household investment, gentrification, multiple residence, mobility and hyper-consumption', *Housing, Theory and Society*, 26 (4), 292–310.

Paris, C. (2010) *Affluence, Mobility and Second Home Ownership.* London: Routledge.

Pawson, H. (2017) 'Taxing empty homes: A step towards affordable housing, but much more can be done', *The Conversation*, 17 July.

Pitkänen, K., Puhakka, R., Semi, J. and Hall, C. M. (2014) 'Generation Y and Second Homes: Continuity and change in Finnish outdoor recreation', *Tourism Review International*, 18 (3): 207–221.

Stergiou, D. P., Papatheodorou, A. and Tsartas, P. (2017) 'Second home conversion during the economic crisis: The case of Artemida, Greece', *Social & Cultural Geography*, 18 (8), 1129–1151.

White, N. R. and White, P. B. (2004) 'Travel as transition: Identity and place', *Annals of Tourism Research*, 31 (1): 200–218.

INDEX

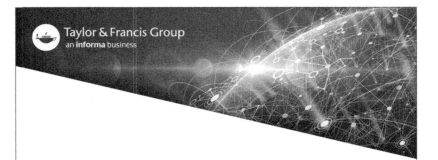

Printed in Great Britain
by Amazon

29365482R00216